RED ARMY TANK COMMANDERS
★ ★ ★ ★ ★ ★
THE ARMORED GUARDS

RED ARMY TANK COMMANDERS

COMMANDERS

★ ★ ★ ★ ★ ★

THE ARMORED GUARDS

COLONEL RICHARD N. ARMSTRONG

Schiffer Military/Aviation History
Atglen, PA

To Bonn, my Home Guard

Book Design by Robert Biondi

Copyright © 1994 by Richard N. Armstrong.
Library of Congress Catalog Number: 93-87474

Printed in the United States of America.
ISBN: 0-88740-581-9

We are interested in hearing from authors with book ideas on related topics.

Published by Schiffer Publishing Ltd.
77 Lower Valley Road
Atglen, PA 19310
Please write for a free catalog.
This book may be purchased from the publisher.
Please include $2.95 postage.
Try your bookstore first.

Contents

PREFACE

The eastern front decided the Second World War. The Soviet-German fighting involved staggering totals of soldiers and equipment, dwarfing the scale of combat on the western front. Even after the Allies landed at Normandy in 1944, the Germans retained over 235 divisions in the east, with only 85 divisions deployed in the west. The Red Army, as Winston Churchill observed, "tore the guts out of the German Army."

Despite the magnitude of the war on the eastern front, many in the west know little about its course beyond major battles for Moscow, Leningrad, Stalingrad and Kursk. Even less is known about the Red Army leadership. While Soviet Marshals Zhukov, Konev and Rokossovskii may be half-familiar names, operational and tactical commanders remain virtually unknown. Yet, the heart of every major Red Army victory pulsed with brilliant tank force commanders. These were the men who propelled Soviet operations forward; yet, they have received little western recognition or serious study.

This *terra incognita* in military history exists because few of the western allies fought on this front. The common western understanding and perceptions on the course of fighting in the east is filtered through translated memoirs of German generals or histories built upon their recollections. Names and actions of numerous German commanders, such as Guderian, von Mellenthin, von Manstein, Balck, are familiar to the general military history reader. Through their experiences and interpretations, the men against whom they fought are judged. For the Germans, a cultural bias reduced the Russian foe to an "untermensch," or subhuman. Consequently, in German military writings, the Soviet unit commanders are left largely nameless: opponents unworthy of individual recognition. The collective foe was acknowledged only to enhance the fighting prowess of the Germanic warrior. Memoirs by German military leaders convey an undertone of alibi to explain their lost war at the hands of Russians. For the invasion into Soviet Russia and their failure to reach Moscow, the German commanders universally blame weather rather than flawed logistical and operational planning. For the excessive losses incurred when fighting a withdrawal from Russia, they blame Hitler's interference rather than acknowledging the increasingly honed skills of the Red Army's operational commanders.

From this tainted body of German recollections, we have drawn a collection of war vignettes that conspicuously shape our perception of the Red Army. In the initial months of the German invasion, Guderian's panzer group, for example, pocketed tens of thousands of defeated Russian soldiers. The Germans' heroic winter defenses held against desperate Soviet human wave attacks. General Balck's astonishing panzer fight at the Chir River overcame seemingly incredible odds, killing Soviets at a ratio of 12 to 1. Field Marshal von Manstein deftly dealt a swift and deadly blow to a blundering Soviet armor force in the Donbas. The extraordinary German accounts from the eastern front have been the influential impetus in forming our current attitudes and judgments about Red Army commanders.

Western accounts of the Soviet-German fighting occasionally name Red Army operational-level commanders, but, for the most part, these men remain faceless, devoid of personality or character. Cold war estrangement, combined with German military partisanship, characterized a Soviet military leadership within a "monolithic" Red Army war machine, led by unthinking automatons, driven forward by pistol-wielding commissars. This faceless and colorless portrayal of Red Army commanders gives little recognition to individual military prowess, and, in the end, erroneously extends oversimplified German descriptions. Consequently, the history of the eastern front has been narrowly shaped by a small number of participants whose works have fed most of the existing accounts in western military literature on the Soviet German fighting. The results are a grossly stereotyped image of Red Army commanders, with little understanding for those who fought "on the other side of the hill."

The Red Army victories and defeats were fundamentally the accomplishments and failures of a specific group of men. Consequently, the men in battle rather than isolated operations on the eastern front must be developed for a more balanced assessment of the Soviet-German fighting during World War II. A more accurate representation of Red Army commanders as personalities and combat leaders simply has not been available. Many of these unknown Soviet commanders fought at the operational level from 1941 to 1945, while the better known German commanders who wrote and published memoirs did not fight the entire war on the eastern front.

Interestingly, few German military memoirs cover those grim final years when Red Army offensive operations, spearheaded by tank forces, advanced hundreds of kilometers at a stretch, pocketing tens of thousands of German prisoners.

The Soviets have published a vast number of memoirs, unit histories, and operational accounts from the "Great Patriotic War" – their name for the fighting on the eastern front. These remarkable accounts have been read and studied by few in the west, partly because of their relatively scarce availability and our own skeptical mistrust of them as sources. Professor Seweryn Bialer noted in the late 1960's, the neglect of Soviet sources is more attributable to our "anti-Soviet bias" than a sheer void of information. More recently, Colonel David Glantz, a United States military expert on the Soviet Army, wrote, "The dominant role of German source materials in shaping American perceptions of the war on the Eastern Front and the negative perception of Soviet source materials have had an indelible impact on the American image of war on the Eastern Front."

Through limited access to the archives and tight controls in censorship, Soviet officialdom undeniably managed their war literature, thus a researcher's concern for Soviet sources run the double guantlet of hazards common to memoirs and what Professor Bialer called the "politics of Soviet war literature." Yet, the diligent effort is ultimately rewarded.

Red Army generals, like most memoirists, succumb to embellishments, justifications, and inventions in describing their roles in battles and operations. In their memoirs, they usually do not openly discuss other generals' personality flaws or major battlefield blunders. But, within the official facts, they will hint at the difficulties of a comrade, allude to an operational error, or show a personable moment with a fellow officer or superior. Culling a large body of memoirs yields insights, hints, and clues that challenge generally accepted notions of a cold, unfeeling, and unthinking leadership in the Red Army. In this capacity, the memoirist does make a significant contribution to history in conveying atmosphere and detail while offering motives and thoughts – especially considering a smoldering desire in any veteran to tell his side of the story.

Political demands imposed on Soviet writers a conventional approach to major events in the war. One can always read that Soviet soldiers had a higher morale than their capitalist counterparts, that the Soviet system mobilized its economic power and out produced the German war machine – and the Soviets seldom acknowledged the worth of Allied Lend-Lease support. More importantly for our purpose is the frequent change in the treatment of military figures by civilian authority. For example, the rise, fall and restoration of Marshal Zhukov's accomplishments under Stalin and Khrushchev yields points for comparison and contrast that offer insightful clues to personalities. Conflicts between Soviet marshals and generals over honors due, as in the case of Zhukov and Konev for Berlin, or Eremenko and Malinovskii at Stalingrad, must be kept in mind. In an account closely resembling a western memoir, Nikolai Popel, a tank army political officer, put his own view to events in contravention of official policy at the time. He faced official condemnation, yet his outspoken work provides useful color on a usually drab landscape.

In the early post-war years, Stalin's role as the sole architect for Red Army victories dominated Soviet accounts. Upon Stalin's death in 1953, Soviet war literature improved in veracity with Nikita Khrushchev's assault on Stalin's wartime role, highlighting Red Army administrative inadequacies and operational failures as part of the destalinization campaign. Soviet war literature, as historian Michael Gallagher observed, was driven to a "marriage between utility and truth." For a realistic appraisal of the Red Army's competence, it required rigorous analysis and study of their main source of knowledge concerning warfare – combat experience. For a brief period, Nikita Khrushchev's bold reforms included stark anti-Stalinism. Khrushchev's denigration of the "cult of the individual," the attribution of individual accomplishments in Soviet society, as well as in the army, have been shared in the context of the common effort. The results of this selfless portrayal is a shallow picture of the individual at the expense of personality development and individual credit for major victories and accomplishments.

The degree of assistance the marshals and generals received in writing their memoirs and articles is at best relative to their writing abilities and publishing criterias. Marshal Zhukov's memoirs, for example, were prepared at a time when he was very ill. An appointed group of writers pieced official histories with his tape-recorded recollections with bedside interviews reconciling the text. Other memoirists with strong academic credentials appear to have written their own accounts, while still other works suggest heavy ghost-writing assistance. Disparities, no doubt, exist, but the various writings indicate distinctive personalities and characters that are representative of the commanders. The reader's concern is often for what is not said, in the Soviet art of reading between the lines. The blemishes on the Soviet military man are not trumpeted, only hinted in a veiled passing remark. In fast, superficial reading, one may feel as the Soviet historian, Adam B. Ulam, that "most Soviet military memoirs exude an air of amiable unrealism." But, there are parts, particularly in a remark about a contemporary, that Soviet memoirists suggest a tough reality. For example, the memoirists acknowledge pressure from higher command, however, the consequences were not as dire as westerners believe. On the personable side, during the war, Stalin and other members of the Soviet High Command referred to fronts, armies, tank and mechanized corps by the names of their commanders, such a Katukov's or Rybalko's army. There are examples of Soviet generals who argued and disagreed with Stalin and won his consent.

Each publication must be read from several planes at the same time. On one level, one must understand the party line on major events and policies concerning the war; on another one must identify the distortions from ideological dogmas; and, yet another, one must read between the lines for what has not been said rather than the bold Soviet version. Also at work is the Marxist notion that man is shaped by his environment. So often the biographies, memoirs, and histories must exhibit the proper Soviet man in battle. So, even within Soviet military writings, the researcher's task is to pierce "socialist realism" in biographical sketches. This can be done by combining the glimpses of personality offered in the available military literature with unit battlefield performance to determine the measure of commanders.

These hazards have been reduced by shifts in Soviet governments policies or leadership. When the Soviets alter the past to conform to present policies by a more recent leadership, they create disjunctions allowing researchers to extract a considerable body of factual information and insight to the Red Army effort on the eastern front. If the reader of Soviet war memoirs considers the biases and deletions that can taint their reliability, such literature can provide invaluable sources for ferreting information about Red Army operations and commanders. The researcher, like a detective, must piece together uncoordinated fragments, such as, memoirs, comments in memoirs, official histories, German records, and other seemingly unpromising material for valuable insights in constructing the character and personality of Red Army tank commanders.

Recently, with the demise of the Soviet regime, access to Soviet military archives has been possible. While the flow of information out of the archives is a trickle now, it may grow to a flood in the future as Russian histories work to fill in "blank spaces."

The pursuit of a totally objective history is impossible. The hope is to approach the historical truth to the greatest degree. In this small measure, I hope the book takes a step toward a more knowledgeable representation of Red Army tank commanders who previously have been nameless or faceless. Let us pull them from the shadow of a monolithic system, into a light where their tragedies and triumphs can begin to show.

I have gathered the available materials, to make a "stab at sorting them" and determining what is possible to know about the character of the Red Army tank commanders from existing sources. The primary intent is to humanize and make credible the tank commanders as men in battle, to break through the stereotype and understand their style of command and leadership for its strengths and weaknesses.

The venture into historical research can rarely be a one man effort. In fact one of the very enjoyable aspects of putting together a book is the number of people willing to help an author. In that regard, I must recognize a number of people who provided invaluable assistance. The moral support and good pen of Ralph Peters made the book possible. David Glantz who pulled me out of the sandlot introduced me to Soviet sources. Roger Spiller instilled the desire to convert pursuits of an avid reader into writing military history.

A number of good people helped in the all-important information gathering, running the hundreds of little clues to ground and contributing in other important ways: Kira Ciafa, Lyle Minter, David Beachley, Lance Elderidge, Joe Welsh, Graham Turberville, and Jacob Kipp. A special thanks to Carl Silber who moved me into the computer age. One can tell good friends by how rough a draft they will endure reading; I must thank Sam Carroll, Allen McKee, and Randy Weikle. Despite all the help, any errors are mine.

INTRODUCTION

T he tank army as a permanent operational formation appeared in the Red Army in May 1942. The six tank armies were commanded at various times throughout the remainder of the war by eleven generals. This study profiles six of the commanders who either finished the war or commanded their respective tank armies the longest. The commanders and tank armies are as follows: Mikhail E. Katukov, 1st Guards Tank Army; Semen I. Bogdanov, 2nd Guards Tank Army; Pavel S. Rybalko, 3rd Guards Tank Army; Dmitri D. Lelyushenko, 4th Guards Tank Army; Pavel A. Rotmistrov, 5th Guards Tank Army; and, Andrei G. Kravchenko, 6th Guards Tank Army.

The profiled tank commanders represent successful commanders, with demonstrated abilities on the battlefield, who rose to the highest level of tank commands. These tank commanders opposed the famed German panzer units, handing German armor formations their first and final defeats. And, as conquerors, the commanders of the Red Army's armored guards occupied the German capital, Berlin.

The careers of these tank commanders moved in parallel with development of the Red Army armored force – both grew and hardened with experience and trial by ordeal with the German army. Before examining the tank commanders within the armored guards, a general understanding of the development of the Soviet tank force prior to and during the Second World War is appropriate.

The "avtobronie" (armored car) section of the Tsar's Army interested the Bolsheviks as they rose to power. Thanks to intensive communist inducements, the Petrograd armored troops defected early in the October Revolution. And, as the Bosheviks established power, the new Red Army appreciated the value of tanks and armored cars as it forged a revolutionary military doctrine, and made great efforts to construct armored vehicles by its own industry.

In January 1918, the People's Commissar for Military Affairs directed the creation of armored detachments. Beginning with eight such detachments, the Red Army put together 37 armored detachments in the course of the first desperate year of the Russian Civil War. By 1920, they had 52.[1] And, in May 1920, the Military Revolutionary Soviet ordered the creation of the army's first tank detachment. The first operational use of Red Army tanks supported an infantry attack.

In the 1920's and 1930's, the revolutionary Red Army continued to embrace the potential of new technologies, especially the combustible engine, for warfare. The Soviet military leadership was interested not only in the motorization and mechanization of ground forces but also the implications of airplanes and airborne troops. Contrary to the small professional mechanized forces advocated by western military theorists, Soviet military thinkers endorsed mass mechanization and motorization. In pioneering large mechanized forces, the Red Army, by 1933, formed two mechanized corps, five mechanized brigades, two separate tank regiments, 12 mechanized regiments, and 15 separate tank battalions.[2] This expansive effort by the Soviet led to large scale maneuvers. The Kiev Military District maneuvers in 1935 proved to the Soviet's mind, if not to all foreign observers, that large-scale operations composed of mechanized units radically altered the nature of combat.[3]

With the building of large armored formations, Soviet military theorists, such as Vladimir Triandafillov, Gusev and Isserson, working in concert with Marshal Mikhail Tukhachevskii, developed a unique concept of deep operations employing airplanes, airborne forces, and mechanized forces to simultaneously strike throughout the entire depth of an enemy's disposition. Such an ambitious application of varied forces and weapons was beyond immediate achievement by available technical means and force capabilities. But this theoretical goal, with its major role for tank forces, shaped the direction of the army's development.

The Red Army's bold, early commitment to massed armored forces waned in the late 1930's, as Stalin's purges eliminated many of the major advocates. Additionally, a woeful misinterpretation of the Spanish Civil War experience cast doubt on the feasibility in independent use of tank forces.[4] Influential Red Army advisers, returning from the Spanish Civil War, saw tanks as infantry support weapons, with no utility as large mechanized formations.

The Red Army's first combat actions seemed to confirm these conclusions about mechanized corps. During the Polish campaign of 1939, Red Army tank units experienced logistical problems on long road marches. The large, cumbersome corps – with too few wireless signal communications sets – proved woefully complicated for novice commanders to control.[5] Then, in the Finnish War of 1940, large armored units seemed of little value in the extremely rugged and broken terrain. [6] Consequently, the Soviet leadership decided to dismantle their carefully-built large mechanized forces in order to place smaller tank units in direct infantry support.

However, the victory of General Georgi Zhukov at Khalkin-Gol and the Soviet observations on German armor successes against France in May 1940 prompted a nervous reconsideration of the utility of large mechanized forces operating independently. In a major military conference in December 1940, the Soviet military leadership decided to reinstate the mechanized corps organization. The corps' hasty reconstruction in spring 1941 ensured an immature mechanized force at the time of the German invasion of the Soviet Union in June. The quickly cobbled equipment and personnel had little time to establish necessary operating procedures and hone their fighting capabilities.

These huge unpolished corps consisted of two tank and one motorized divisions each, for a corps total of 1030 tanks. Given too few radios, command and control remained difficult, at best, and this was particularly so at the tactical level. The mechanized corps' subsequent performance revealed a number of problems that had been masked by overly-managed peacetime exercises, widening the inevitable disparity between ideal doctrine and practical application.

On the eve of the Second World War, the Red Army continued its efforts to educate and train a large portion of its leadership. In the Frunze Academy and the Armored Force Academy were many of the future tank commanders who would later demonstrate a remarkable leadership talent against the Germans. Other tank commanders such as Rybalko, Lelyushenko, Kravchenko had been through the Frunze Military Academy previously. By 22 June 1941, the Soviet border military districts had deployed more than a dozen mechanized corps. However, these corps had neither a full complement of personnel nor of combat equipment.[7] The Soviet five-year plans, because of the impact of Stalin's purges in the economic sector, failed to produce the planned numbers of new tanks. While the Red Army possessed an impressive number of armored vehicles, many of these were outdated, poorly maintained light tanks. In spite of the fact that by early 1940 new models of all types of tanks had begun to replace these outdated, lighter tanks, derisively referred to as "sparrow shooters" or "knights in plywood," the new heavy KV and medium T-34 tanks made up only a small percentage of the total tank inventory.

The T-34 and KV tanks only began to arrive in the western military districts in April-May of 1941, but, by the beginning of the German-Soviet war, they were in all the frontier districts, totaling 508 KV and 967 T-34 tanks. The fleet of old style tanks sat in poor mechanical repair, since industry had not filled orders for spare parts; 29% needed major overhaul and 44%, medium repair. The remaining 27% of the old model tanks rusted and were simply inoperable.[8]

Mechanized units suffered other shortcomings. The organizational artillery possessed an inadequate allotment of ammunition. Incomplete staffs existed in some of the mechanized corps. Untrained junior officers led platoons and companies. In the frank words of one Soviet military historian, "the cumbersome mechanized corps in conditions of under strength staffs with untrained personnel, along with their poor cohesiveness and insufficient number of radios, proved difficult to control on the battlefield."[9] The Red Army had moved full circle by re-building the identical structure that gave them problems in Poland.

In a pre-war deployment, the majority of the mechanized corps were assigned to rifle armies. When the fighting began, decentralized employment of these mobile forces precluded focusing combat power. Very early in the military district's frontier battles against the German army's invasion, the confusing situation moved beyond any individual effort by brave Red Army soldiers or cowards, good commands or bad, planning or lack of it – all were in the grip of the raging battles.

Most of the tank army commanders-to-be fought in these early mechanized corps battles. Katukov and Bogdanov commanded tank divisions. Rotmistrov and Kravchenko were chiefs of staff for mechanized corps. Lelyushenko commanded a corps. But, the mechanized corps battles were short-lived. Following their first counterstrikes, mechanized corps defended operationally and tactically important lines and objectives, ensuring more favorable conditions for withdrawal of rifle formations to new lines. [10]

The mechanized corps' performance, or rather lack of performance, became an important catalytic impetus for change. The Red Army realized that early lessons must be acted upon if they wanted to survive the onslaught of German panzer forces. In the fall of 1941, mechanized corps were replaced by smaller, more manageable separate tank brigades and battalions. These compact armored units could be controlled more easily and fought more effectively in tactical defensive missions.

Because the Soviets were losing the battlefields, their tanks losses were only fractionally recovered. The army that owns the battlefield after a fight can recover its damaged tanks, while the defeated loses all combat equipment it cannot carry away. Combined with the hasty displacement of many of their war plants to the east, the tank industry was not able to promptly replenish these losses. The sharp decrease of the Soviet Army's tank inventory and the rapidly changing situation required changes both in the organization of the tank forces and in the methods of their combat use. The formation of tank brigades, regiments and separate tank battalions allowed their attachment to the armies in a number of sectors.

In early October 1941, separate tank brigades and separate tank battalions began to support rifle armies, while mechanized corps and tank divisions became disbanded. Considering the losses in tanks and personnel in the early months of the war, the Red Army had little choice but to form tank brigades composed of battalions with new T-34 and KV tanks.

A combination of tactical and technical characteristics made the Soviet T-34 medium tank the best tank of World War II. The T-34 was relatively simple in construction and could be produced quickly in large numbers by unskilled labor. The tank performed well in the basic functions of firepower, armor protection, mobility, speed, and reliability. The T-34 tank's salient strength was its suitability for service and repair. Maintainability had a considerable effect on the time a tank remained forward in the troop combat formation. The high degree of maintainability made it possible for mobile repair facilities to do all types of repairs in the field, immediately behind combat troop formations.[11]

The T-34 tank was not a decisive weapon in the summer of 1941 for two reasons. One, Soviet tank tactics fought the T-34 piecemeal with light, more vulnerable tank units or as infantry support. Instead of using them in mass for speed and surprise at the enemy's front or flank and driving deep into the enemy's rear area, the Soviets violated their concept of massed use of tanks. The second mistake was a serious shortcoming in tank crews. The T-34's crew of four – driver, gunner, gun-loader, and radio operator – lacked the fifth man, the commander. In a T-34, the gunner commanded the tank while working the gun. His distraction in directing the tank interfered with efficient and rapid fire in tank battles, restraining a T-34 main gun fire of one shell to a German Mark IV's three.

Three of the tank commanders, Katukov, Rotmistrov, and Kravchenko, assumed command of brigades equipped with the new T-34 tanks. The headquarters of a tank brigade consisted of a chief of staff, military commissar, deputy chief of staff for operations, assistant chiefs of staff for intelligence, personnel reporting and cipher work, signals officers and technical workers. The headquarters provided command and control of brigade subunits through a limited number of radio sets. A Red Army shortage of radio crystals reduced the number of available radios, and it was not until the end of the war that radios were installed in tanks other then the commanders.[12] Radios, which had revolutionized warfare, were essential to mobile armored warfare.

In the fall of 1941, the Germans rapidly approaching Moscow possessed more tanks than the Soviets. The majority of Soviet tanks, 80 per cent, were still light tanks.[13] Five of this study's tank commanders, Katukov, Bogdanov, Lelyushenko, Rotmistrov, and Kravchenko, fought many key armor engagements in the intense defensive battles for Moscow. In these formative battles, increasingly capable commanders trained their tankers to stand in ambush at safe distances and wait for the German tanks to expose themselves upon their exit from a village.

During the winter counteroffensive of 1941-42, around Moscow, the Red Army's attacking Western Front units could not outrace the withdrawing Germans, allowing the Germans to escape entrapment and establish new defensive lines.[14] The use of cavalry corps and small tank units possessing insufficient striking power failed to achieve success by turning tactical gains into an operational advance, nor could they maintain a fast pace attack.[15] The Front operations essentially remained unfinished. The use of cavalry corps and temporarily improvised mobile groups to exploit the success of the rifle armies raised the rate of advance of the Red Army forces, but it did not solve the overall problem of their rapid advance throughout the entire depth of an operation. The weak mobile groups did not have sufficient combat power. The tank force experience in attacks demonstrated the need for armored units designated for independent actions at greater depth and faster advance, requiring a larger force to reach around encircled enemy groupings.

Large operations confirmed that deep strikes, encirclement, the division of enemy groupings, and successful conduct of an offensive to considerable depths and at a rapid pace required not only the presence of separate tank units for direct infantry support, but also the availability of large tank formations and large strategic units operating as breakthrough exploitation forces for the advancing armies and fronts. In essence Red Army troops were unable to surround large enemy groupings and press home the deep attack. Combat experience demanded a return to large tank and mechanized formations.[16]

Soviet tank plants started their relocation in July 1941. In order to accelerate the production of armored vehicles, the evacuated plants were merged with existing facilities. The Leningrad, Kirov and Kharkov diesel engine plants were consolidated with the Chelyabinsk Tractor Plant. These three high capacity plants made up the Soviet's largest tank producing factory, which was affectionately named "Tankograd"(Tank City) during the war. Another group of plants centered on the Stalingrad Tractor Plant.[17] The number of available tanks grew steadily for the Red Army. The counteroffensive around Moscow involved only 774 tanks. In the battle around Stalingrad, 1463 tanks and self-propelled assault guns fought. In Belorussia, 1944, 5200 tanks and self-propelled assault guns were present. Beginning in January 1945, 1st Belorussian and 1st Ukrainian fronts fielded more than 7000 such systems. By the end of the Great Patriotic War the Red Army possessed six tank armies, 23 separate tank and mechanized corps, 59 separate tank brigades, and 55 separate tank regiments.[18]

In 1942, the displaced factories resumed regular tank production, allowing the formation of tank corps by spring and mechanized corps by fall.[19] The new corps were created with a brigade instead of a divisional organization. This structure held down the required quantity of tanks and other combat vehicles. While making them more mobile and easier to control. Tank corps consisted of three tank brigades and one motorized brigade: 168 tanks total. Mechanized corps had three mechanized brigades and one tank brigade, totaling 175 tanks. A shortage of trucks restricted the number of mechanized corps formed by the Red Army.

Katukov, Bogdanov, Rotmistrov, and Kravchenko, as experienced tank commanders of smaller units, were called to build and fight these larger tank formations. The headquarters of a tank corps consisted of a chief of staff, military commissar, deputy chief of staff for logistics, senior signal officer, assistants for special communications, communications officer, technical personnel and also two branches: operations (branch chief, two senior assistants, an assistant and chief clerk) and intelligence (branch chief, two assistants and a translator). There were a total of 24 men in a tank corps headquarters, as first organized.[20] By the end of 1943, the strength of a corps headquarters had grown to 35 officers.[21]

The first four tank corps formed in April 1942, did not possess their own combat support and rear services units. They depended entirely upon rifle armies and fronts for all their support requirements. This dependency limited their tactical and operational autonomy. First use of these corps in offensive combat came in May 1942 at Kharkov. The operation showed that the new formations did not have the necessary operational-tactical independence in conducting combat operations. The key problem lay in how to organize and fight large, highly mobile tank formations which possessed such great hitting power.

These new armored formations evolved under fire. The disastrous Kharkov operation squandered three of these new tank corps through inept operational handling, precluding any real test of their tactical mettle. Subsequent mobile armored warfare in the southern sector of the Soviet-German front for the remainder of the year were also actions characterized by mistakes – and lessons that would not be forgotten.

A total of 28 tank corps were created in 1942. They did not all possess the same organizational structure. From April to the end of the year, "the following (modifications) were introduced into the corps table of organization: in June – a fuel and lubricant supply company, in July – a rocket launcher (8 M-13, nicknamed Katyushas) battalion, a reconnaissance battalion and a motorcycle battalion, in December – two mobile repair bases."[22]

The formation of mechanized corps began in September 1942. They differed from tank corps in possessing a larger quantity of motorized infantry. This increased their independence in combat in both offensive and defensive missions requiring close infantry support to secure flanks, lines, and other objectives. Six mechanized corps were created by the end of the year. They were organized in three ways. In the first variant, the mechanized corps possessed 175 tanks, in the second 224, and in the third, 204.[23]

Analysis of armored warfare experience from the first part of the war allowed the Soviet leadership to refine tactical and operational use of tank and mechanized formations. Principles for their employment were specified in the People's Defense Commissar (NKO) Order No. 325, dated 16 October 1942. The order summarized all of the experience in the combat use of tank units and formations in the initial period of the war, and it spelled out the principles of their subsequent use in offense and defense. It defined the purpose of tank and mechanized corps, the principles of their use, and the methods of their combat activities in offensive and defensive operations in clear terms.

The order directed that tank and mechanized corps were to be a resource of the front or army commander and that they were to be used in the main sector as a breakthrough exploitation force to pursue and rout the enemy. Breaking a corps down into smaller units was prohibited. Using one to exploit a breakthrough was permitted only after rifle units penetrated the main defensive zone in sufficient depth to capture the enemy's artillery positions.

In an offensive operation, the mission of a tank corps was to make a massed attack to isolate and encircle the enemy's main troop grouping, destroying them in joint actions with rifle formations and frontal aviation. The corps was not to engage in tank battles with enemy tanks if superiority over the enemy was not clearly evident. Its main mission was to annihilate enemy infantry since most forces in all armies in World War II were infantry. In all forms of combat, surprise was considered the decisive element in applying the tank corps.[24]

The order spelled out procedures for preparing and committing corps to a breakthrough in detail. For instance, a corps had to be given 2-3 days to carry out all of the measures of preparing for its commitment to a breakthrough.

These generalized experiences passed in the form of directives from the NKO were not meant to prop up an unthinking leadership but to quickly incorporate vital lessons and experience. Tank commanders, like Katukov, Rotmistrov and Kravchenko, who led the corps in 1942, and had commanded tank brigades in 1941, provided a core of hard, battled seasoned armored combat veterans.

The directives of NKO Order 325 were applied directly to the

Red Army's devastating counteroffensive at Stalingrad in late 1942. Nine tank and six mechanized corps were used in the course of the counteroffensive. These armored formations were massed on the main strike axes, and were employed as army breakthrough exploitation forces. Because of a shortage of tanks, tank and mechanized corps were committed in the first day of the operation in order to complete the breakthrough of the enemy defenses, in coordination with rifle divisions.[25]

The first two tank armies were created in May-June 1942. Rybalko, initially a deputy commander in one of the tank armies, was designated commander of the 5th Tank Army in July 1942, and of the 3rd Tank Army in September of the same year. Originally, the fighting strength and organization of the tank armies was determined by the directives initiating their formation and was not uniform.[26]

The experience of using tank armies in defensive and offensive operations in the summer of 1942 on the Voronezh axis (5th Tank Army), near Kozel'sk (3rd Tank Army), and especially in the counteroffensive below Stalingrad (5th Tank Army) made possible a number of important conclusions concerning their combat capabilities and organizational structure. Major contributors to shaping the future tank armies were Rybalko and Rotmistrov whose experiences in these operations identified shortcomings and practical approaches.

The armored corps played a major role in the course of the general offensive of the Red Army in the winter of 1942-43. In the battle on the Volga river, 11 tank and mechanized corps fought around Stalingrad in December 1942. Three commanders of concern to us, Rotmistrov, Bogdanov and Kravchenko, led corps in these operations. They provided the decisive element in breakthrough and transferring tactical into operational success. They led many of the offensive drives to push the Germans back from Stalingrad, breaking the German grip on southern Russia.

Relying upon growing production of armored vehicles and the combat experience of commanders, the Soviet Supreme High Command began forming tank armies in parallel with deployed tank and mechanized corps. There were two sharply differing stages in the history of their creation.

In the initial stage, in April-May 1942, the first tank armies, 3rd and 5th, were mixed structures, including tank corps, rifle divisions, cavalry divisions or corps, artillery and mortar units; and various support elements. Soviet theorists, at the time, believed tank armies could independently break through a prepared tactical defense and develop the tactical success into the operational depth. However, experience quickly revealed such a structure to be too slow and awkward for agile maneuver. Tank army commanders were unable to manage their forces or organize continuous cooperation among units of differing mobility and maneuverability. The difference in troop mobility, combined with a lack of effective communications, seriously hampered troop control during the development of an offensive into the operational depth. With combat power weakened from tank losses and the depth of tank strikes limited, operational successes rapidly stalled. These differentials had become evident during the Stalingrad operations. But the Red Army leadership was already learning the connection between force structure and unit agility by the summer of 1942.

By July 1942, German units reached the Don river, crossed it and began the battle for Voronezh. The Soviet's 5th Tank Army, which had been transferred to the Bryansk Front, was ordered on 5 July, by the Supreme High Command General Headquarters, to carry out counterattacks from 6 to 12 July. The first experience in the combat use of a tank army in the war provided insignificant results, and by mid-July, the 5th Tank Army, which had suffered heavy losses in men and tanks, was disbanded.

But, in August 1942, the 5th Tank Army was already being re-activated. Beginning on 19 November, the tank army participated in the Red Army counteroffensive at Stalingrad. In January and February 1943, the 5th Tank Army fought in the Donets Basin operations, reaching the Mius river. However, in mid-April 1943, the army was disbanded a second time.

In January 1943, the 3rd Tank Army subordinated to the Voronezh Front participated in the Ostrogozhsk-Rossosh operation and the Kharkov offensive. In March, the tank army transferred to the beleaguered Southwestern Front where in bitter defensive fighting it was virtually eliminated, leading to disbandment.

These circumstances shaped fundamental re-examination of the principles in the combat use of tank armies and of their organizational structure.[27] Combat experiences dictated transformation of the tank armies into highly mobile major formations possessing speed and firepower so that they could serve as the principal means of exploiting breakthroughs in front and strategic offensive operations.[28]

Red Army experiences in offensive operations from the winter campaign of 1942-43 revealed that a breakthrough exploitation force must have operational independence and that mobile formations must be coordinated by the Front for actions in the operational depth.

The previously mixed composition of the Red Army's tank armies did not satisfy these highly important requirements; they were not yet mobile formations. There was little difference between the tank army of 1942 and the rifle army operating in the direction of a Front's main strike. Attacking within strictly indicated unit boundaries, mixed tank armies were deprived of the potential for fast maneuver within the frontal zone, and they could not use their full combat capabilities of their tank formations. Operational experience showed the possibility of creating uniform, highly mobile tank armies which possessed great strike and fire power. For tank armies to obtain decisive results required freedom from the slower, less agile non-motorized infantry formations, greater mobility for artillery and rear services support, and provisioning the army with engineer support.[29]

On 28 January 1943, the State Defense Committee (GKO) adopted Decree No. 2791 creating tank armies of homogeneous composition.[30] The development of a totally mechanized and motorized force structure supported more agile armored formations.

On 30 January, the Supreme High Command General Headquarters created the lst Tank Army under the command of Katukov in the Northwestern Front in the vicinity of Ostashkovo. The lst Tank Army was to be used in offensive operations to eliminate the German's Leningrad blockade. Considering the terrain, winter conditions, and the intended mission of the tank army, airborne and ski formations were specially included. The planned operation was rescinded owing to the major thaw that began in February. By April, the lst Tank Army, without its airborne and ski troops, was transferred to the Voronezh Front for the impending operations around Kursk.

The 4th and 5th Guards Tank Armies were formed in February and June 1943, respectively. Rotmistrov commanded the 5th Guards Tank Army. The 2nd and 3rd Tank Armies appeared in April and May 1943. Rybalko commanded the 3rd Guards Tank Army. Bogdanov and Lelyushenko would receive their commands of the 2nd and 4th Tank Armies later in the war.

These armies consisted from one to two tank corps and one mechanized corps, separate tank and self-propelled artillery brigades, artillery formations, reconnaissance, engineering, chemical and other support units. The selected force structure for brigades and corps introduced for mobile forces a greater flexibility and agility. The brigade and corps structure allowed a richer variation in numbers and types of battalions. This presented the opportunity to continually tailor forces such as the forward detachment, based on a specific mission. The planned combat strength of the tank armies numbered 600-700 tanks and self-propelled assault guns, 500-600 guns and mortars, and 30-35,000 men.

The tank and mechanized corps remained the backbone of all tank armies for the remainder of the war. In practice, the composition of every tank army was distinct. The structure was tailored for the combat operation depending on a series of factors, situation, mission, and availability of forces.

Beginning in the summer and fall of 1943, the tank army was the formation used predominately to develop the operational success of front offensive operations. Experiences at Kursk would show that their use in defense was not excluded, either. The new tank armies received their "baptism of fire" in defensive operations on the flanks of the Kursk salient. Katukov and Rotmistrov fought their tank armies on the southern face. After completion of the defensive operations on the northern face of the salient, the 4th Tank Army and Rybalko's 3rd Guards Tank Army advanced in the offensive on 12 July. The most effective use of the new tank armies in the attack was in the Belgorod-Kharkov operation in August by Katukov and Rotmistrov's tank armies.

The tactical tank battles had become difficult. The technical superiority of the Soviet T-34 tanks waned temporarily with the new German Panther and Tiger tanks. The 88mm armor piercing shells of Tiger tanks had such a terrific impact that they ripped off the turrets of many T-34's and hurled them several yards. The German soldiers immediate reaction was the quip, "The T-34 raises its hat whenever it meets a Tiger."[31]

By the summer of 1943, the Soviet High Command had created five tank armies as mobile groups to operate on the Fronts' main axes of advance. In the front, tank armies were used for developing success in the offensive and as a powerful means for inflicting a counterstrike in defense. In January 1944, the Red Army formed its last tank army of the Great Patriotic War: 6th Tank Army.

In March 1944, the Red Army campaigns to recapture the Western Ukraine began with offensives by the 1st and 2nd Ukrainian

Fronts. Each received three tank armies. The 1st Ukrainian Front gained Katukov's 1st Tank Army, Rybalko's 3rd, and Lelyushenko's 4th. The 2nd Ukrainian front was reinforced by Bogdanov's 2nd Tank Army, Rotmistrov's 5th Guards and Kravchenko's 6th Tank Army.

The experience of offensive operations in the summer and fall of 1943 and in the campaigns of 1944 showed that tank armies were committed mainly for accomplishing the breakthrough of the enemy's tactical zone because of insufficient tanks for direct infantry support in the front's first echelon rifle armies.

In the summer and fall campaigns of 1944 and 1945 in Europe, when the structure and capability of the Front grew significantly, tank armies committed after the rifle armies broke through the tactical defense. The best examples are the 1st Guards Tank Army at Lvov-Sandomierz, 2nd Guards Tank Army at Lublin-Brest and Vistula-Oder, 5th Guards Tank Army in Vitebsk-Orsha and East Prussia, and 6th Tank Army at Yassy-Kishinev. In 64 Front offensive operations during the war, tank armies contained two corps in half the operations. As their war experience showed, tank armies possessing only two corps were very often limited in capabilities. The possibilities for carrying out a maneuver required by a given situation and the required disposition in depth and the needed depth could not be achieved by formations designed for operational missions.[32]

By the end of the war, the two corps organization of tank armies practically disappeared. Almost all tank armies began to maintain three corps. This became possible after the breadth of the Soviet-German Front was reduced by almost half.

In a number of offensive operations, the tank armies had to be reinforced by rifle formations. This usually occurred when large urban population centers required capture, when actions were carried out in mountain forests, when defensive lines required penetration in the course of an offensive apart from rifle armies, when strong enemy counterstrikes had to be repelled, during pursuit of the enemy or at the end of an operation when it became necessary to consolidate captured lines.[33]

Separate tank brigades usually comprised the tank army's reserve used during the course of the operation to exploit a breakthrough, to reinforce corps, to buttress flanks, for action as the army's forward detachment, or to parry enemy surprise attacks.

Within the existing force structure for tank armies, tank corps, and mechanized corps, agile forward detachments (often a reinforced brigade) were created. The designated forward detachment usually consisted of the most combat effective unit, commanded by the most experienced, innovative, aggressive officer.[34] The forward detachment was assigned missions disrupting enemy command and control and destroying the coherence of their operations. These detachments swiftly separated themselves from the main forces and seized road junctions, bridges, crossing sites and bridgeheads in river crossings, and held them until the approach of the main forces. The detachments ensured an unimpeded advance by the main force, creating favorable conditions for their offensive.

Tank armies generally formed the exploitation force, or echelon for developing success. In a few cases when enemy defenses were not well fortified and prepared in depth, tank armies operated in the first echelon. Kravchenko's tank army fought most often in the first echelon. After penetration of the tactical zone, tank armies had a variety of important missions they could perform: destruction of operational reserves, seizure of subsequent lines of defense, forcing water obstacles, and pursuing a withdrawing enemy.

Highly mobile, tank armies increased the offensive pace of the operation. Success resulted mainly from effective reconnaissance, surprise and determined operations. The reconnaissance effort focused on revealing the disposition and the outline of the German's forward defensive positions, weak spots in their defense, and the approach for reserves. After reconnaissance, the forward detachment with air support suddenly attacked unprepared German intermediate lines. Taking advantage of the success achieved by these detachments wedged into the German defense, the army's main efforts concentrated on narrow sectors of 3-4 kilometers, penetrating the German defense with a swift attack from the march. With the support of artillery fire and air strikes, the offensive developed in the depth, reaching the flank and the rear area of the Germans' defense.

The quality of the tank armies's operational employment matured as aggressive and experienced commanders and staffs became more confident. By late 1943, the tank armies began to show their potential for greater mobility and agile commitment in support of front-level operations.

Qualitative improvement of the organizational structure of tank and mechanized brigades and corps was achieved by increasing their striking power and mobility and making them more independent in combat operations. The main and decisive factor determining the organizational structure of tank armies was the requirement for ensuring their independent capability of fulfilling operational-level missions. Tank corps possessed three tank and one motorized rifle brigade, its own artillery and antiaircraft resources, units of special branches of troops, and rear subunits and services. This composition allowed the corps to carry out combat missions independently and successfully in extremely complex tactical and operational situations. With their combat strength, the tank army could create a powerful first and second echelon, maintain different types of strong reserves, be streamlined, and easily controlled.

The Soviet efforts to fix tank armies was not without limited resources. Even by 1944, the tank armies had not received all of their authorized artillery, except in the case of the Guards rocket launcher regiments. In early 1944, a light self-propelled gun brigade (60 SU-76s and 5 T-70 tanks) and a light artillery brigade (48 76mm and 20 100mm guns) was introduced into their composition. Although, by the end of September, all six tank armies had such artillery brigades, problems in sufficient artillery support were not solved.

Prior to mid-June 1944, artillery commanders of tank armies and corps possessed neither signals equipment, nor the means of moving and controlling artillery in battle. Consequently, artillery was used sporadically; it remained almost without leadership during critical parts of battle and could not help tank army formations. This situation made it necessary to subordinate organic and attached artillery to the corps. But the corps could not provide much better command and control and usually subordinated the artillery to the brigades. The brigades, however, were often entirely helpless in using attached artillery.[35]

All tank armies experienced a shortage of engineer forces in the course of offensive operations, especially when carrying out assault crossings of large rivers and when operating in complex geographic and climatic conditions. Fronts could not always reinforce tank armies with the needed number of engineer units. A single pontoon bridge battalion of a motorized engineer brigade was not enough for a successful river crossing by tank army formations. Often heavy crossing equipment was delivered too late.[36]

Tank army units did not possess organic armored recovery vehicles during the war. This compelled armored units to use tanks with faulty armament and tanks from the line to evacuate tanks and self-propelled guns from the battlefield.

In most of their offensive operations, tank armies did not possess the quantity of personnel, combat equipment and armament to which their formations and units were entitled by their table of organization.

In the winter-spring campaigns of 1943-44, Front offensive operations with tank armies followed one another with short or no operational pauses for refitting or resupply. The availability of combat equipment to tank armies was the lowest in the Krivoy Rog, Zhitomir-Berdichev, Korsun-Shevchenkovskii, Proskurov-Chernovitsy and Uman-Botoshansk operations. In contrast, the 1st Belorussian Front's Vistula-Oder operation and the 1st Ukrainian Front's Sandomierz-Silesian operation, when the time allocated to the preparatory period was significant, the armies were at full strength.[37]

The tank armies, as the principal resource of the Supreme High Command, could transfer between Fronts and quickly shift the focus of Front combat actions to develop an offensive into operational depths. The capabilities of the tank armies allowed them to make deep independent strikes in conjunction with air. Their deep penetrations fragmented enemy forces into small groupings that could be quickly and easily encircled in coordination with other types of units. The power of tank armies allowed them to successfully destroy the enemy's operational reserves, creating advantageous conditions for Fronts to maintain continuous, deep operations.

The effectiveness of tank armies grew when two or more tank armies operated on parallel or converging axes. Several tank armies advancing in the same direction brought powerful results in the shortest time and at a dramatic pace. By the end of the war the Red Army tank armies became the means for developing operational and strategic success.

The contributions of the tank forces during the war were recognized by the "guards" honorific given to units and individuals. The Soviet "Guards" concept, building on a tradition within past Russian armies, was created in September 1941. The Guards designation recognized valiant and heroic fighting units in the desperate defense of Moscow with the first fall and winter campaigns of the war. No doubt in an effort to boost morale and instill a sense of fighting pride, Stalin had the Russian honorific reinstated to inspire and exemplify the defense of the motherland.

To be a Guardsman had its compensations. They received extra pay and rations. But, they were also expected to take on the toughest missions. The tank forces of the Red Army were often in a position to perform feats that would be rewarded with the Guards title. The best of the Red Army tank commanders led the armored Guards.

NOTES

1. P.A. Rotmistrov, *Vremya i tanki*, Moscow: Voenizdat, 1972, p. 23.

2. A.I. Radzievskii, *Tankovyi udar*, Moscow: Voenizdat, 1977, p. 9.

3. A. Eremenko, *The Arduous Beginning*, Moscow: Progress, 1966, pp. 9-10.

4. Rotmistrov, p. 63.

5. Eremenko, pp. 15-17.

6. Rotmistrov, p. 71.

7. M. Dorofeev, "O nekotorykh prichinakh neudachnykh deistrii mekhanizirovannykh korpusov v nachal'nom periode Velikoi Otechestvennoi Voiny," *Voenno Istoricheskii Zhurnal* (hereafter *Vizh*) Vol. 3-1964, p. 34.

8. O.A. Losik, *Stroitel'stvo i boevoe primenemie sovetskikh tankovykh voisk v gody velikoi otechesvennoi voiny*, Moscow: Voenizdat, 1979, p. 10.

9. Dorofeev, pp. 35-6.

10. I.M. Anan'ev, *Tankovye armii v nastuplenii*, Moscow: Voenizdat, 1988, p. 38.

11. Losik, p. 18.

12. Ibid., p. 38.

13. Ibid., p. 25.

14. A.I. Radzievskii, *Proryv*, Moscow: Voenizdat, 1979, p. 21.

15. P.A. Rotmistrov, "Boevoe primenenie bronetankovykh i mekhanizirovannykh voisk," *Vizh* Vol. 12-1967, p. 39.

16. Anan'ev, p. 43.

17. Ibid., p. 44.

18. I. Krupchenko, "Kharakternye cherty razvitiya i primeneniya tankovykh voisk," *Vizh* Vol. 9-1979, p. 25.

19. Rotmistrov, Vizh 12-1967, p. 40.

20. Losik, p. 277.

21. Ibid., p. 278.

22. Anan'ev, p. 51.

23. Ibid., p. 52.

24. Ibid.

25. Ibid., p. 55.

26. Losik, p. 54.

27. Anan'ev, p. 61.

28. Ibid., p. 61.

29. Radzievskii, *Udar*, p. 25.

30. Anan'ev, p. 64.

31. "German Defense Tactics Against Russian Breakthroughs," Department of the Army Pamphlet No. 20-233, October 1951, p. 7.

32. Anan'ev, p. 71.

33. Ibid., p. 74.

34. F.D. Sverdlov, *Peredovye otryadu v boyu*, Moscow: Voenizdat, 1986, pp. 21-22.

35. Anan'ev, p. 88.

36. Ibid.

37. Ibid., p. 84.

CHAPTER I

KATUKOV

On 22 June 1941, the day the Germans invaded the Soviet Union, Colonel Mikhail Efimov Katukov lay recovering from surgery in a Kiev military hospital. The utterly unexpected shattering of hospital windows from a sudden midday German air raid told Katukov the dreadful news – war had begun. Despite unhealed sutures and a high temperature, he discharged himself from the hospital in order to join his unit. A professional soldier knew where he should be in wartime.

Tall, slender in build, Katukov's oblong face had large hazel eyes under thick eyebrows. Although stern in expression, he was good-natured and liked to joke. Born 1900, in a small village about sixty miles from Moscow, he grew up in a large peasant family. As a child, he worked as a day laborer. Later, his father took the boy to work in a Petersburg factory. At the age of 17, Katukov joined the revolutionary movement in Petrograd, and enlisted in the Red Army during March 1919. He fought in the ranks with the 54th Cavalry Division against the Whites during the Civil War, and participated in the Russo-Polish War, 1920.

After the Civil War, Katukov, attracted to the profession of arms, decided to remain in the military. In 1925, he was chief of the regimental school for the 81st Rifle Regiment, 27th Rifle Division in Vitebsk. A student in Katukov's unit course recalled his manner, "My lesson is simple," Katukov often repeated, "do as I say, and everything will be in order."[1] He always had expectations for his subordinates, but, mainly, he wanted them to fulfill their responsibilities. By 1932, he became a tanker when the Red Army first experimented with organizing large tank units. He took the officer's

Mikhail Efimov Katukov

course and worked himself up the command ranks from company to battalion commander. By the beginning of the Second World War, Katukov, a colonel, commanded the 20th Tank Division in the 9th Mechanized Corps.

With his unit stationed near the frontier borders in the Ukraine, Katukov, leaving his sickbed, caught a ride in a passing vehicle on the road to war. He was anxious to return to his tank division, which, in a state of reorganization and reequipment, was woefully unprepared for battle. Insufficient tank production in the Soviet's latest Five-year Plan by the summer of 1941 left Katukov's unit, like many of the other armored units, without the new T-34 and KV tanks. In his motorpool stood 33 second-hand and broken down BT-2 and BT-5 light tanks. Other parts of the division were also understrength: the artillery regiment was armed only with howitzers and the motorized rifle regiments received no artillery. Even the engineers were without their pontoon bridges.[2]

Reaching his headquarters on the evening of the 23rd, he discovered from his staff that the deputy commander, Colonel V.M. Chernyaev, had two of the tank regiments already in combat with the Germans forward in the vicinity of Lutsk. After repeated attempts over the telephone to get through to the corps commander, General Konstantin Konstantinovich Rokossovskii, Katukov finally made contact and reported his arrival to the corps staff. Katukov asked the corps staff for a quick update on the combat situation.

Meanwhile, the corps commander and Katukov's deputy saw within the 20th Tank Division's sector a seemingly endless column of German trucks and artillery moving from Dubno in the direction of Rovno. The corps' mission, despite confusion at the army level, was to get into position to attack the advancing German's flanks. Organizing resistance against the German onslaught, General Rokossovskii directed placement of the tank division's artillery regiment with its 85mm guns on the road. Colonel Chernyaev quickly and enterprisingly executed the maneuver. The guns were set up in road ditches, on heights overlooking the road, and in the middle of the road for direct fire. Letting the German formation close on the waiting artillery, the unit guns opened at the last minute, inflicting a horrific fire. Rokossovskii remembered vividly the wreckage of motorcycles, armored cars, and dead bodies piled up on the highway.[3] With severe losses to their lead elements, the Germans sought other ways to break the resisting Soviet line. The stubborn defenders drew attacks from German dive bombers.

Moving to the forward area, Katukov's first battle as division commander occurred 24 June in the vicinity of Klevan against the German's 13th Panzer Division. Attacking directly from the march, Katukov lost all 33 of his "Betushkas," – BT light tanks. The BT's, which were undergunned and flamed like torches when hit, were derisively referred to by Red Army tankers as "sparrow shooters" and "knights in plywood." The fighting around Klevan exacted a toll in friends and acquaintances of peacetime service: Katukov's tank regiment commander was killed, and Chernyaev received a serious leg wound. Although evacuated to the Kharkov hospital, Chernyaev died later from gangrene.

Hampered by lack of information, the forward units fought as best they could, but were pushed behind Klevan. In the early engagements, the mechanized corps proved difficult to manage for commanders. Most of these large, cumbersome formations exhibited identical problems in combat. Equipped with outdated light tanks and only a handful of radios per corps, the corps were too hard for inexperienced commanders and staffs to effectively control and logistically support in their trials by fire. Rokossovskii managed to keep his defending corps in front of the advancing Germans.

In the course of three days, Katukov's division suffered startling losses, but still remained on the battlefield, contesting the Germans for every kilometer in the Dubno area. Soviet forces fighting on the Southwest Front offered the German stiff resistance, prompting German Army Chief of Staff, General Franz Halder to note in his diary on 26 June, "Army Group South is advancing slowly, unfortunately with considerable losses. The enemy on this front has energetic leadership."[4] And, on 27 June, Halder again entered, "...the Russian command in the Ukraine...is doing a pretty good job...."[5]

Katukov called these early battles in and around the woods and marshes of the western Ukraine, the "real combat school." He observed and noted German unit tactics, and he began thinking about countering German advantages in tanks and aviation.[6] Fighting from the defense and stabilizing the situation, creating order out of chaos, appealed to Katukov.

He conceived a counter-technique that disposed his motorized riflemen within trenches and false fighting positions while placing his tanks in defensive ambushes. The dummy positions would be occupied with a few troops with real guns to be "actors."[7] The actual positions would be arrayed in depth, with a tank reserve held back to cover key approaches. For camouflage, the tankers used natural terrain, such as bushes, trees, corn stacks, haystacks, and reverse slopes. Each crew made two to three positions between which they could shift undetected. Beforehand the crews determined the bearing and distance to them. The tank positions had to have good fields of vision and fire, integrated with the other positions, and the tanks were required to be prepared to come to one another's aid.

The dummy positions would draw the air attacks and artillery preparations. The "actors" would withdraw to the real line of defense. Tanks would remain silent and hidden. Only when the German tanks had advanced to within 200-300 meters would the tank in ambush fire at point blank range. The tankers identified targets, fired two or three shots, then moved back under cover changing positions. Katukov's pragmatic and utilitarian determination to learn from his initial experiences would serve him well later. A clear and constant aspect of Katukov's command style began to emerge in these early fights. He studied his enemy so he could take them apart based on their actions – an inclination particularly suitable for defensive fighting.

By mid-August, 1941, the Red Army was still painfully giving ground. Outside of Malin, however, there was a pause in the fighting for the mechanized corps. While bathing in a river, Katukov was informed by his excited adjutant of a corps telegram. The telegram ordered Katukov to hand over his division command and report to corps. Arriving at corps headquarters, he received notification from the Chief of Staff that he had been awarded the Order of the Red Banner. More importantly, Katukov had orders to report to Moscow immediately. He had been selected to lead a new unit with the latest, most capable tanks.

Upon arrival in Moscow, Katukov met with Lieutenant General Yakov Nikolaevich Fedorenko, Commander of the Armored Tank and Mechanized Forces of the Red Army. He informed Katukov that his command was a new tank brigade. After division command, the lesser command of a brigade disappointed Katukov. Taking time with the capable, but dejected, tank leader, General Fedorenko explained the evacuation of factories to the east and the inadequate industrial capacity simply made it impossible at that time to field tank units larger than brigade.

The representative of the State Defense Committee at the Stalingrad factory recalled the medium height colonel who entered his office in early September. His lean weather-beaten face and faded uniform blouse revealed the colonel's recent arrival from the front lines. After identifying himself, Katukov solicited the representative's help, "I ask your cooperation in the acceleration of the assembly and transfer of the allocated 50 T-34's assigned to my brigade, and also to receive additional spare parts for them." Lowering his voice, Katukov unofficially confided, "You understand, the situation at the front will not allow us to remain here too long."[8] Katukov's immediate enemy was time.

The war created an urgency in the brigade's training unlike normal peacetime exercises. Katukov's new brigade with combat vehicles and equipment from the Stalingrad Tractor Factory organized itself as the 4th Tank Brigade in the vicinity of Stalingrad. Receiving the first battalion of T-34's, Katukov began training his new unit for combat.

Katukov understood from his early fights the importance of individual and crew training for future tank battles. He tailored training to achieve the necessary skill level, concentrating the brigade's training on defensive fighting. Uncompromising on principle points, he firmly, and at times severely, instilled his lessons. In one of his first speeches to the brigade, Katukov told his men, "We are insufficiently prepared in tactical terms. We are especially poor in the conduct of the defensive battle...."[9] He taught such techniques as using favorable terrain, maneuvering, use of reserves, and deception. In earnest Katukov applied his lessons learned from the Ukraine battles. He tolerated no easy, nor routine solutions, everything had to be just as it would be in combat. He operated on the dictum of the famed Russian General, A.V. Suvorov: "Hard in training, easy in battle."

In training, as in combat later, Katukov possessed a couple of talented brigade staff officers who would remain with him for the remainder of the war. The young captain, Pavel Grigorevich Dyner, Chief of Technical Support, organized and maintained the new tanks. Captain Matvei Timofeevich Nikitin became the brigades operations officer. "Nikitin always perfectly understood the situation and possessed perfectly the art of staff work," Katukov wrote after the war.[10]

But time for training worked against Katukov and his staff. Defeats at the front allowed no luxury of a long, thorough build-up. And, despite the promise of a new brigade fully equipped with T-34's and KV's, Katukov's hurriedly formed second battalion substituted BT-7 light tanks.

His brigade moved to their railroad loading platforms on 23 September, a mere three weeks after his arrival. Traveling northwest towards Moscow, the rail trip took five days under sporadic strikes from marauding German warplanes. The brigade off-loaded at Kubinka station, 60 kilometers west of Moscow, along the Minsk highway, and the staff established a brigade field headquarters in the nearby woods.

Concurrent with Katukov's move, German General Heinz Guderian's Panzer Group launched an offensive against the Bryansk Front on 30 September. With priority air support, his Panzer Group quickly penetrated the Bryansk Front's defenses, smashing open a gap. The 24th Panzer Corps rapidly advanced into the unprotected breach, heading towards the town of Orel on the southern major highway to Moscow.

Responding to Guderian's serious threat, the Soviet Stavka Supreme High Command designated General Dmitri Danilovich Lelyushenko to command "reserve units," forming the lst Guards Rifle Corps. His corps, ordered to strike from Mtsensk in the direction of Orel, had to buy time for the Bryansk Front to withdraw, reorganize, and form a new defense along the Zusha river at Mtsensk.

The hastily formed corps consisted of an assortment of units: 4th and 6th Guards Rifle Divisions, 4th and 11th Tank Brigades and two artillery regiments, and, later, received reinforcement with the 5th Airborne Corps, three guards mortar battalions, a Tula Military School detachment, and an attack aviation unit. For reconnaissance, the corps also received the 36th Motorcycle Regiment.

General Lelyushenko immediately dispatched his motorcycle riders on reconnaissance, and on 2 October, began moving his staff to Mtsensk. On 3 October, the corps staff set up in Mtsensk. The same day German armored units arrived in nearby Orel, making contact 10 kilometers northeast of the town with a withdrawing NKVD border guard regiment.

Meanwhile, on 2 October, Katukov's 4th Tank Brigade, despite its recent off loading at Kubina, reloaded on rail cars and moved to the Mtsensk rail station. Orders, counterorders, then a hasty march resulted in a shuffling of tactical units not unusual for such conditions in any army.

By early morning 4 October, Katukov's first battalion arrived at Mtsensk and immediately dispatched two strong reconnaissance groups. The first group under Captain V. Gusev, the battalion commander, had 11 T-34's and 2 KV's. His group assumed the mission of advancing to Orel, and would attempt to capture prisoners. The second group, with 8 T-34's under the command of Senior Lieutenant Aleksandr Fedorovich Burda, advanced toward Orel on another route intending to capture prisoners for information.

On the morning of 5 October, the Germans attacked northeast out of Orel along the Orel-Mtsensk highway. After a 15 minute artillery preparation, some 40 German tanks with infantry struck against the remnants of an NKVD border guard regiment in the vicinity of Ivanovsky, Optukha. Although having reconnoitered the outskirts of Orel, CPT Gusev's tank group pulled back and assumed defensive positions on the flanks of the NKVD unit. These lead tanks defended against an attacking German fighting group while the remainder of the 4th Tank Brigade arrived in Mtsensk.

Unable to dislodge the makeshift defense by ground attack, the Germans during the evening conducted strong airstrikes against Mtsensk rail station and town, hoping to disrupt any further reinforcement in the path of Guderian's panzer group. Katukov assuming command of the forward defense directed the NKVD regiment and Gusev's battalion to withdraw to more defensible terrain in the vicinity of Naryshkino, Voin. At this point in the fight, they were joined by the remainder of the 4th Tank Brigade and a student detachment from the Tula Military School.

As the defense began to coalesce, the lst Airborne Brigade, which airlanded nearby, assumed the center sector. On the left flank was the NKVD regiment, with the 4th Tank Brigade assuming positions on both flanks 2-2.5 km in front of the line. Applying his hard-learned tactical solutions, Katukov formed the brigade in a false defensive line to deceive the Germans as to the real location of the main defensive line.

At 1000 hours on 6 October, Soviet air reconnaissance reported 100 German tanks with motorized infantry and artillery moving towards Katukov's position. German bombers hit the false defensive positions with two flights for 15-20 minutes. At 1130 hours, strong German artillery fire was followed by 50-60 attacking tanks which were subsequently reinforced by another 40 tanks. The weight of the attack wedged German tanks some 2-3 kilometers into Katukov's defense. A tank battalion from the newly arrived 11th Tank Brigade which formed the corps' reserve moved to the trouble spot on the right flank, helping to hold the situation.

Katukov's command post of two staff tanks was located in a low draw. Sappers dug long narrow slit trenches in which the communicators and staff officers worked, headed by the deputy commander. Katukov threw a sheepskin over his arms and listened to reports. He forbade his officers wearing sheepskin coats on the frontline, since they made too good a target for German snipers. He asked them to wear more inconspicuous jerseys and greatcoats. But, in the safety of his command post, he could partake of this simple pleasure in warmth.

Armed with a light machinegun on his back and a mauser pistol in his belt, he went on foot at night to visit various points in the defensive position. Katukov had a good eye for the tactically significant terrain, and he could see where it would be necessary to dominate the fight. He had to ensure that his young commanders placed their tanks and other weapons properly so the Germans on the most likely avenue of approach did not drive by them too quickly. He checked the location of the battalion command posts and made sure the tank commanders had thought out the impending battle.

He outwardly exhibited a calm and self-controlled manner. His leadership style was to motivate and inspire using jokes and encouragement in the preparation stage. But, under pressure, his criticisms could be direct and biting. Subordinates never forgot admonishments from Katukov.

Late evenings in his command post, Katukov called the young battalion and company commanders for summary reviews of the day's fighting. He would note what was good and what was bad. "Each battle for us is a school," the colonel would say, "analyze, weigh, compare, dissect shortcomings, not just the positive...."[11] As his light tank battalion commander observed, "We knew Katukov did not throw words to the wind."[12] Katukov needed facts and details in advance. He always wanted his subordinates to get to the point and stick to the facts. In a world of facts, Katukov could reduce the fog of war and risk. His courses of action and decisions became more apparent, information reduced uncertainty.

During the early morning hours on the 7th, General Lelyushenko, concerned for the flanks of the corps, withdrew Katukov's force 4-6 kilometers north of Voin and assumed a defensive line at Golovlevo, Sheino. That evening, two guards mortar battalions, a cover name for the famed Katyusha multiple rocket launcher units, fired several devastating volleys to suppress the Germans and cover the withdrawal.

On the right next to the railroad the NKVD regiment with a tank battalion of the 11th Tank Brigade held the defense. On the left flank stood Katukov's tank brigade. The remainder of the corps' 6th Guards Rifle Division and 5th Airborne Corps with two brigades continued building a defense northeast of Mtsensk behind the Zusha river. On a larger scale, the Red Army scraped together enough forces to close the breach and defend the southern approach to Tula and Moscow.

The Germans did not attempt to advance in the morning, and afternoon activity consisted of airstrikes and reconnaissance. On 8 October, the Germans remained inactive. Katukov's strong resistance on the Orel-Tula highway had snapped the German's overstrained logistical tether. Guderian's panzer units had to stop for two days resupplying tanks with fuel and ammunition before resuming the attack. The surprisingly aggressive and unusually effective defense by Katukov's brigade forced the Germans to a standstill two days before the first snow fell. The tank battles before Mtsensk harbingered more ominous signs for the Germans than the gathering winter storm clouds.

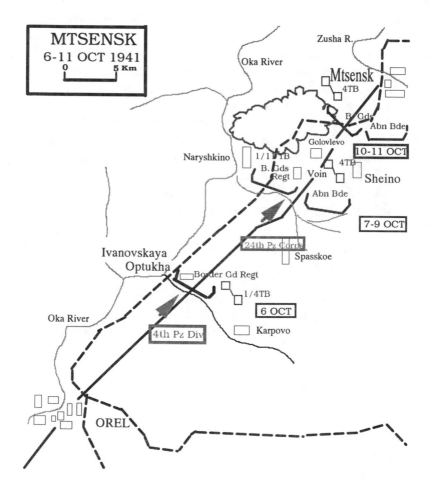

MTSENSK
6-11 OCT 1941
0   5 Km

Zusha R.

Oka River

Mtsensk
4TB

B. Gds
Abn Bde

Golovlevo

10-11 OCT

Naryshkino   1/11 TB
B. Gds   4TB
Regt   Voin   Sheino

Abn Bde

7-9 OCT

Ivanovskaya   24th Pz Corps
Optukha   Spasskoe
Border Gd Regt

Oka River   1/4TB

6 OCT

4th Pz Div   Karpovo

OREL

On the morning of 9 October, after a powerful German artillery and air strike preparation, 100 German tanks with motorized infantry attacked. An intensive four-hour battle ensued in which the Germans moved around Katukov's left flank, broke his defensive line, and threatened to cut off withdrawal routes. Katukov's brigade fought from ambush positions, claiming 41 German tanks and 13 guns destroyed. During the evening, German airstrikes resumed, and the German panzer units attempted to move around both flanks.

Early the following morning, Katukov, recognizing the threat to his flank, moved his force to a new defensive line 3-4 kilometers southwest of Mtsensk. Withdrawing under pressure required a close organization of defensive tank fires. At daylight the attacking Germans with some 130 tanks penetrated into Mtsensk and captured the highway bridge over the Zusha river. A damaged railroad bridge, near the edge of town, remained intact and uncaptured as Katukov's brigade's only escape route.

In an extraordinary scene of confusion and heroics, the brigade's night crossing on this bridge had all the potential for disaster. To ease the movement of people, animals, and vehicles over the rails, the soldiers laid wood planking which became slippery under the horses' hooves, breaking the horses' legs or causing them to fall off the bridge. The rise of moonlight brought German artillery and machinegun fire on the tired, withdrawing force. Katukov's calm, confident presence on the bridge controlled a situation that could otherwise have swiftly slipped to panic and rout.

Katukov's tank battles before Mtsensk exemplified good defensive armor tactics. Fighting with open flanks, Katukov fought a mobile defense from successive positions. Playing on German contempt for previous Russian defenses and their penchant to stay near major roadways, Katukov slowed their advance by energetic, aggressive tactical surprise and tenacious fighting. Katukov's efforts held up Guderian's advance and ultimately foiled his panzer group's rush to Moscow on the southern approach. While never acknowledging by name the Red Army tank commander who fought his panzer group, Guderian noted in his memoirs that the "quality and, above all, the new tactical handling of the Russian tanks were very worrying."[13] Guderian's panzers advanced only 30 kilometers in eight days. "The damage," he continued, "suffered by the Russians was considerably less than that to our own tanks."[14] Katukov's tank brigade's heroic fight won national recognition and was officially credited with destroying 133 tanks, 49 guns, 6 airplanes, 15 tractors with ammunition, and approximately a regiment of infantry, six mortars and other combat equipment. Guderian's encounter with Katukov evoked his first doubts about the German Army's ability to capture Moscow before winter, if at all.

After successfully pulling back across the Zusha river with all its surviving combat vehicles, Katukov's brigade moved into the recently placed and defending 5th Army's second echelon. The 5th Army's extensive defense was prepared with time bought by the 4th Tank Brigade.

On 16 October Katukov received telephonic orders from the Supreme High Commander, Stalin, himself, to load personnel and equipment on trains with a new combat mission: the defense of Moscow. Katukov reported that it was too dark to load, and he feared exposure to German air raids while loading and traveling on the trains. He urgently asked to move by road in order to arrive without losses. Stalin asked about the mileage remaining on tanks to the next routine maintenance overhaul.[15] Katukov replied that his unit had sufficient mileage for conducting the road march.

Avoiding use of railroads and certain risk of German airstrikes, Katukov moved his brigade 360 kilometers to the north. Without a single accident or breakage, Katukov's brigade arrived on the northern approach to Moscow to help staunch the German army's advance.

An incident during the march north almost brought Katukov before a military tribunal. An unidentified General from the Front staff met the brigade on the outskirts of Kubinki to assist in rapidly moving the brigade to its frontline position. Arriving in Katukov's command post, he drew a line on the map indicating the route along which the brigade must travel. Katukov, noting unimproved field roads along the route, objected that not only trucks but also his T-34's could not travel in that direction. Colonel Katukov pointed out a route less direct, but faster because of better roads near Moscow.[16]

Intolerant of the challenge to his judgment, the General ordered the Colonel to fulfill his orders and ended the conversation. Katukov nevertheless, at personal risk, disobeyed the directive and sent part of his unit the roundabout way across Moscow. His trucks arrived earlier than the tanks and his staff which had moved along the broken field road. The T-34's, despite their cross-country mobility, had difficulty negotiating the designated route. The next day the General was still located with the armored column, but by midnight his whereabouts were unknown.[17] Katukov's actions saved time for the brigade in spite of the general's assistance. By the evening of 19 October, 4th Tank Brigade finally reached its destination – Chismena – 105 kilometers from Moscow along the Volokolamsk highway.

On 11 November 1941, the 4th Tank Brigade became the 1st Guards Tank Brigade, the first tank unit to earn the honorific "Guards" title. Katukov received promotion to Major General of Tank Forces, as well as being awarded, the Order of Lenin. Unable under the strained supply conditions at the front to get his new rank insignias, Katukov had stars drawn on the lapels of his rough army greatcoat in indelible ink.

The following day the 1st Guards Tank Brigade attacked Skirmanovo, a village which the Germans had exploited as a springboard for an assault on the 16th Army's flank. Katukov situated his command post in a well-camouflaged dugout by the woods a kilometer from the village.

Katukov organized his brigade in three echelons to give the attack depth and focus. In heavy fighting, his brigade claimed 21 German tanks destroyed and captured one battle trophy, a famed 88mm antiaircraft gun which the Germans used as an antitank gun against heavy tanks. On 13 November, after routing the Germans at Skirmanovo, the tank brigade along with other units continued its attack towards Kozlovo. Katukov, with dark circles under his eyes from forty-eight hours without sleep, directed the fight from his command post. At 2000 hours 14 November, the town was liberated. The same night infantry relieved the tank brigade which pulled back to its former position. The tank brigade's operation attempted to foil not only the German flank attack but also the German's greater designs to resume a major offensive towards Moscow.

Less than twenty-four hours later, the 1st Guards Tank Brigade received a mission to cover the withdrawal of rifle and cavalry units. On the morning of 18 November, the Germans moved to the Istra river in two tank wedge formations of approximately 30 combat vehicles each. Katukov's brigade was operating with only 20 tanks. Delaying ambushes failed to stem the German progress. Only the reinforcement of a KV heavy tank battalion helped stabilize the situation. For five days, 16-21 November, against a strong renewed German offensive, the brigade fought rearguard battles claiming 33 German tanks, seven antitank guns, enemy personnel and other equipment destroyed. The retreat along forest paths had been difficult. The tanks skidded in the soft slushy snow. Snow hid muddy, swampy ground, which bogged down the heavy vehicles. The withdrawing soldiers had to find detours, recover stuck tanks, and keep the Germans at bay.

During the course of this operation, Katukov did not sleep. Despite growing thinner and more stooped in posture from a chronic illness, Katukov gave up his vehicle to carry his wounded soldiers. He walked with his unit, knowing its powerful effect of personal example on soldiers' morale. Again, Katukov's handling of his tank brigade gained the notice of his immediate superiors who placed more forces under his command. He showed courage and initiative in organizing tank combat against larger enemy forces.

On 21 November, the 27th and 28th Tank Brigades were united under Katukov's command for defense along the line, Nazarovo and Yadromino, to support a cavalry corps withdrawal from battle.[18] Katukov decided to defend with a single string of tank ambush positions at intervals of 1.5-2 kilometers. Altogether, seven such ambush positions, with 3-4 tanks each were established, allowing German tanks to approach closely before engaging and wearing down the strength and momentum of the German attack.

On the night of 23rd, the tanks of this group took up a new defensive line – Zorino, Kholshchevnik – with the mission of covering rifle divisions withdrawing to the Istra river's east bank. To confuse the Germans, ambush positions were situated not on a single line but in a chess board pattern this time. With two additional tank brigades, 23rd and 33rd, from the rifle army defending in sector, Katukov created a reserve and prepared them for counterattacks in several directions. The rifle divisions successfully withdrew to assume new defensive positions behind the river, followed by the tank brigades, which reinforced their struggle to hold the German advance.

At night on 29 November, Katukov's brigade received further instructions to withdraw to Kamenka and Barantsevo, and form a defensive line. For five days, the Germans attempted to break through to Moscow, but failed.

On 3 December, General Rokossovskii, now commander of the 16th Army, ordered Katukov to attack towards Istra and continue northwest to reduce the German bridgehead at Kryukov. The 1st Guards Tank Brigade, already reinforced with a battalion of border guards, also received a separate tank battalion armed with the slow British Matilda tanks.[19] In difficult going on 4-6 December, the tank brigade's effort proved unsuccessful. Katukov's tankers found themselves stuck in minefields. A debate among the army's senior commanders who argued whether to attack with the tanks strung out or in a 'fist' did not help the effort. The Red Army was going back to school on basic tactics. And, Katukov, a new master of the defense, still had much to learn about attacking with tanks, such as, coordinating engineers, artillery, and logistical support and synchronizing actions.

Combat operations on the Istrin began 7 December. Attacking only after a thorough reconnaissance of the German positions was axiomatic for Katukov. "I always gave reconnaissance paramount importance. Any forces spent in clarification of the enemy unit's actions always justified itself."[20] Katukov's demands in reconnaissance actions or demands for information on the situation from his staff revealed his cautious nature in the attack. Nonetheless, Katukov recalls, "The offensive battle in Kryukov bridgehead enriched our combat experience."[21] Tank attacks, in these early months of the war, provided valuable lessons for him.

The 16th Army's tank brigades attacked in close cooperation with the infantry and broke into the German's defense. 1st Guard Tank Brigade with 8th Guards Rifle Division captured the key road junction and town, Kryuvoi, forcing the 4th Panzer Group to withdraw. With two hastily formed mobile groups under Generals Katukov and Rezimov, the commander of the 16th Army continued attacking toward Istrin. On 14 December, the tank groups forced the German line in the vicinity of Istrin reservoir and pushed the Germans to the west. Five days later, the Army commander gave Katukov the mission to seize Volokolamsk. General Rezimov's tank group became subordinate to Katukov for the operation. Aggressively pursuing the Germans, Generals Katukov and Rezimov spearheaded the army's operation for Volokolamsk. Katukov's group attacked from the southeast and south while Rezimov's attacked from the northeast and north.

With the 16th Army attacking on the heels of the withdrawing Germans, the army's Chief of Staff reported, "Katukov's group, joining with another tank group on the morning of 19 December, pursued withdrawing enemy in the direction of Volokolamsk. Katukov's group stormed Volokolamsk from the east and southeast, taking the town at 0600 hours. Nearly 1200 Germans killed or captured in the area of Volokolamsk and a number of destroyed combat vehicles and equipment. On 20 December, his group moved in the attack against a fortified line on the Lamoi river. This was his part in the major Red Army counteroffensive in December 1941."[22] The arduous and tenacious fighting by Katukov's brigade represented the Red Army's armored capabilities in the early winter battles.

In January 1942, General Katukov greeted a group of arriving officer replacements. Eying the group of new, young officers, he gave them his welcoming speech. Then he gave them his more pointed lesson, "There's a lot to tell you, and I'll never manage to cover everything at one go. So just remember the main thing. Fighting requires skill. We have plenty of people we can learn from. In the brigade we have real professors of tank warfare, who have been fighting since the first hour of the war. Professor Burda has destroyed over thirty enemy tanks. So has Professor Samokhin, and we've plenty of others in that class...there's no counting them all. Some have won two or three medals, some have even earned the title of Hero of the Soviet Union. Learn from these professors."[23]

Katukov always enjoyed talking about his young fighting officers who he called his "professors of tank warfare," and readily praised their accomplishments on the battlefield. Katukov stated that, "combat experience is what decides everything." And he fully expected his professors to be commanding regiments and even divisions in the near future.

The winter fighting of 1941 was bitter. Especially hard on armored units, the daily temperatures averaging 25-28 degrees below zero with much lower windchill factors required great expenditure of fuel to warm engines for movement. By the beginning of the counteroffensive near Moscow, there were 18 separate tank brigades and 19 separate tank battalions operating in the Kalinin, Western and Southwestern Fronts.[24] With armored units no larger than these brigades, in the counteroffensive, tank units could carry out only tactical missions and then in close cooperation with the rifle troops. To fully use tank units, some rifle armies created an improvised mobile group which included tank, rifle, and cavalry units in their formation.

Tank brigade operations in the first winter offensive showed that they did not possess enough combat power to extend the tactical victories into the operational depth well behind German lines and that they were not large enough to encircle the German forces for destruction. These shortcomings would drive the Red Army to reorganize its armored forces under the seasoned hands of its successful tank brigade commanders.

In April 1942, Katukov and his political officer were called to the Commander of Armored Tank and Mechanized Forces in Moscow. General Lieutenant Fedorenko announced Katukov's designation as commander of the 1st Tank Corps. Boiko would remain as his commissar. The tank corps consisted of three tank brigades, one motorized rifle brigade, a katyusha battalion, reconnaissance battalion and other support units. The corps contained nearly 170 tanks.

General Fedorenko asked Katukov for his personal considerations in chief of staff and commanders. Katukov tended to be formal and impersonal until well acquainted with colleagues who he sought to keep with him. He asked to take with him from the 1st Guards Tank Brigade Nikitin, the operations officer, and Dyner, the technical service deputy. Of Dyner, Katukov believed, "a better specialist for repairing equipment I could not get."[25] General Fedorenko recommended General Andrei Grigorevich Kravchenko as Katukov's Chief of Staff.

By the summer of 1942, the Bryansk Front covered the sector from Tula and Moscow on the right to Voronezh on the left. Soviet High Command fears of a German summer offensive against Moscow ensured a large number of tank units assigned to the Front. In addition to four tank corps, the Front also had a number of separate tank brigades giving the Front a total of nearly 1500 tanks.

The German Army Group "Weisch," consisting of the 2nd and 4th Panzer Armies and 2nd Hungarian Army, opposed the Bryansk Front. The German command planned to launch a powerful strike that would destroy Red Army forces west of the Don river and breakthrough to the Volga river.

In May-June 1942, Katukov's 1st Tank Corps placed under the control of the Bryansk Front deployed northwest of Voronezh. General Filipp Ivanovich Golikov, the Front commander, assigned the 1st Tank Corps the mission to be fully prepared to inflict a counterstrike against a German offensive. On 28 June, following German successes against the Southwest Front around Kharkov to the south of General Golikov's Front, Army Group Weisch began its offensive by breaking through at the junction between the Soviet 13th and 40th Rifle Armies. Control of the two armies immediately broke down. That evening, Katukov's corps received orders to strike from the north into the flank and rear of the penetrating German units. Meanwhile, the 16th Tank Corps, also attacking from the north, was assigned to destroy the Germans between adjacent, nearby villages. General Golikov and his staff, however, did not realize the newly formed tank corps' unpreparedness for decisive combat.[26]

On 29 June, the German ground units continued advancing 30-35 kilometers in the center sector. The attack approached the Front's second defensive line along the Kshen river raising the alarm of a possible breakthrough. Golikov reported his concerns to Stalin, and remarked that Katukov's corps "did not have any serious force."[27] Despite concerns, the Bryansk Front commander quickly committed his tank reserves against the Germans in an uncoordinated effort. By the 30th, Golikov's Front had a major ground wedge driving into his lines. Katukov's corps on the German's northern flank was unable to reach the bulk of German armor moving south of the Kursk-Voronezh rail line away from Katukov.

During these defensive operations, the Front commander believed he was not getting the most effect from the tank corps, so he directed creation of a composite tank group from brigades of the two tank corps. He placed this ad hoc armored force under Katukov's command. Fighting from 28 June to 7 July 1942, the lst Tank Corps and other tank elements counterattacked into the flank of the German penetration without success.[28] With little aviation support, the lst Tank Corps was repelled by German ground and air forces. Holding along the Kshen river, the corps with the 13th Rifle Army fought to keep the German advance from expanding north.

The Stavka was clearly displeased with the Front commander's use of his tank corps. The Front commander's and staff's actions had been conducted without consideration for tank corps requirements, which indicated weak cohesion and low tactical training. Fearing for their flanks and rear, the tank corps did not break away from the rifle units despite the fact there were no large German tank forces present.[29] After the operation, General Nikolai Fedorovich Vatutin replaced General Golikov. Katukov's first significant attempts at fighting offensively with his corps fell far short of his mastery of the defense. But, as always, Katukov observed and learned. Of this period, he noted, "Across a few months we learned to employ not only tank corps but also tank armies simultaneously."[30] But, operating armored forces on the edge of chaos was still beyond mastery by Red Army tactical and operational level commanders.

In the course of this fighting, Katukov thought about offensive warfare and came to conclusions for future operations, and in 1942 penned a short book, *Tank Combat Actions*, in which he described the employment of the tank "desant," "...infantry mounted on tanks and using them as a means of advance for closing with the enemy...."[31]

By the middle of August, the lst Tank Corps went into the Stavka reserve and concentrated in an assembly area south of Tula. The Soviet's High Command conclusions on the fighting and handling of tank corps from the late summer resulted in Peoples Defense Commissar Special Order No. 325, dated 16 October 1942. The directive prescribed for Red Army commanders how to use their tank units. Generally, separate tank brigades and regiments were to be used in direct support of the infantry. Tank and mechanized corps were to be used by the Front and army commanders on main axes of attack for the development of success. The order also gave procedures and measures for the planning and execution of breakthroughs with tank and mechanized corps.

On 17 September, Katukov received orders to report to the Kremlin for a visit with the Supreme High Commander, Stalin. Katukov, a man who had braved the trials of combat, grew very nervous. Stalin ushered Katukov into his office inviting him to sit and smoke. Katukov, a chain-smoker, did not dare light up a cigarette. He sat on the edge of his chair. As was Stalin's habit, he preferred to pace about the room while he talked. Stalin reached into his pocket, pulled out two cigarettes of coarse Georgian tobacco, broke them open and poured their contents into his pipe. He lit up, producing a dense, pungent cloud of smoke.

Looking at Katukov, Stalin continued, "You don't want to smoke? Then tell me, one after the other, how are you and your corps at the front? How are the motorized infantry? And, how are our tanks?"

Katukov told him about the combat operations on the Bryansk Front and about the operations of his riflemen and tankers.

Still pacing, Stalin asked Katukov further questions, "How do you consider our tanks, fine or not? Tell me straight, without mincing any words."

Katukov, who knew his trade well, answered that "the T-34 fully acquitted itself in battle, and the tankers put great trust in it. But the heavy KV and the combat vehicles T-60 and T-70 were not liked."

Stalin stopped a minute, questionably raised an eyebrow. "For what reason?"

"The KV, comrade Stalin, is very heavy, slow-moving, and, as you know, unmaneuverable. They overcome obstacles with great difficulty while the T-34's do it with ease. KV's break bridges and generally cause unnecessary troubles. And, the armament of the 76mm gun is the same as that on the T-34. So what's the combat advantage of the heavy tank?"

"I criticized the light tank, T-60," Katukov continued. "It has only a 20mm gun. In serious combat with armored forces it just does not have it. Its under clearance is too low. To attack in the snow or mud is a deadly affair. In the battles around Moscow, we continually had to drag them in tow. The light T-70 has more armor protection, and a 45mm gun, but it has only begun to enter service, and it has not shown us anything special."[32]

Stalin, open to the technical advice of his professionals, listened attentively not interrupting. He continued to question Katukov on the strengths and weaknesses of the tanks. Katukov also reported the shortage of radios. Again, Stalin, educating himself with one of his top armor fighters, turned the conversation to combat techniques.

As the meeting came to an end, Stalin informed Katukov that he had been designated commander of a mechanized corps to be formed in the Kalinin district. Stalin offered Katukov brigades from his lst Tank Corps to form the base maneuver units in the new mechanized corps. Katukov accepted the brigades. The Red Army built fewer mechanized, than tank, corps throughout the war because of their requirement for trucks to move the motorized infantry. For Katukov, to have commanded both a tank and mechanized corps, was a rare opportunity and a strong measure of the high command's confidence in his abilities.

After Stalin made arrangements by telephone for the units to be transferred, Katukov asked a favor of Stalin. To form the mechanized corps, Katukov wanted to keep P.G. Dyner on his staff as his technical deputy and M.T. Nikitin for chief of operations. To Katukov's relief, Stalin approved.

His new corps was located in an assembly area between the town of Belyi and the railroad station, Nelidovo. The 3rd Mechanized Corps reinforced the 22nd Rifle Army. The 22nd Army's chief of staff, M.A. Shalin, would become another of Katukov's key staff officers for the remainder of the war, and Nikolai K. Popel became Katukov's political officer for the duration of the war.

Nikolai Popel, a political officer with armored units since the beginning of the war, led an armored task force from encirclement in the vicinity of Dubno during the summer months of July and August 1941. Gregarious, dedicated to the party ideals, he genuinely liked and supported his tactical commanders. He turned down opportunities for softer party positions to remain with fighting units. He accepted proudly his position with the newly formed 3rd Mechanized Corps, and he remembered his first meeting with the corps commander. In the vicinity of Klin, at the edge of Kalinin Misha, Popel arrived in a half lit barracks, and fumbled by the door for the light switch.

"It doesn't work," some voice announced, "there's no light and don't expect any."

"Not only were there no lights," Popel recalled, "but not even chairs and tables. The commanders sat on log blocks and they worked from macaroni crates. The next day I was leaving the barracks by the door when, suddenly, splashing mud, up pulls a Willy jeep. from it leaps a man in a soldicr's greatcoat, on the green tabs were general's stars."

The general, striding towards him, asked, "Popel?"

"Yes."

"Katukov. We will become acquainted."[33]

At one end of the barracks was Katukov's room; at the other end, Popel's. This sharing of full responsibility in Soviet combat units often made strange bedfellows within a system of high paranoia. Many of the successful "teams" of political officers and military commanders made a lasting and trustful bond. Popel and Katukov had such a relationship, and stayed together for the remainder of the war. But, in the first meeting, in ageless warrior tradition, Popel would have to prove his worth before receiving acceptance by the fighting corps commander. The power of a party representative made little difference in the struggle for survival on the battlefield. Dual command on the battlefield has been historically catastrophic. However, Popel seems to have ensured a good working relationship with Katukov – he sought to truly help his combat commander.

As the commander of the 3rd Mechanized Corps, Katukov interviewed his new brigade commanders. He went straight to the point on past tank experience. He demanded technical experience and questioned commanders on the technical aspects of their equipment and unit. He continued to insist that his tank commanders be "Professors on Tank Warfare."[34]

Combining his command of the trade and his intuitiveness about human nature, Katukov easily understood his officers.[35] In an initial interview with a lieutenant colonel who was to be his chief of intelligence, Katukov made the following admonition, "All right, I understand you myself, because keep in mind, in the past, I, too, was an intelligence officer. The wisdoms of this profession are familiar to me. Therefore, do not try to lead me. About the enemy you are obliged to report the truth and only the truth. I like accuracy, and I do not tolerate approximations. Consequently, in no way must your vocabulary have "obviously," "presumably," "requires more accuracy." Throw out these words once and for all."[36] Katukov knew what he wanted from his intelligence officer, and he wanted it to be totally reliable information.

In late November 1942, the 3rd Mechanized Corps received orders to go over to the offensive in coordination with rifle units in the Rzhev-Sychev offensive operation of the Kalinin and Western Fronts. On 5 December 1942, the eve of Katukov's corps commitment to the attack, the rifle division commander through whose unit the corps was to be committed arrived in Katukov's command post. The colonel complained that his unit had insufficient ammunition, little artillery and that not all his soldiers had their felt boots.

Katukov patiently listened to the colonel's lamentations, but when he heard the colonel admit that he did not know were the German fields of fire were located, he perked up. The first truth, which Katukov adopted while still a brigade commander, was "without intelligence, to wage war is impossible." Katukov dumbfounded by the colonel's admissions, clearly saw not only the rifle division unprepared but also its commander professionally and psychologically unfit for the attack.

The mechanized corps found it difficult to attack with the infantry unit. The marshy terrain with snow combined with the German defenses covered by minefields and the poor preparation by the forward rifle units all contributed to an operational standstill. By 20 December, the grueling Rzhev-Sychev operation concluded indecisively.

During operations Katukov paced along the dug-out bantering with the radioman and cracking jokes, a sign of his good humor and high spirits. A chain-smoker, Katukov usually held a lit cigarette. Often, his pockets bulged with packs of captured cigarettes that he would occasionally hand out to personnel in the command post.

When he suddenly discovered that he was low on cigarettes, he would jump up and rush to a stowage cabinet ,and begin filling his pockets again.

At other times, the corps commander quietly sat at the window smoking one cigarette after another. His favorite pose was sitting with his left leg tucked under is body smoking a series of cigarettes. He would say, "Smoking, good for the breath. Smoking is good entertainment." Then, he would at that exact moment take the pleasure of prolonging a drag of his coarse tobacco smoke.[37] He would often be in this pose when he took reports from subordinate commanders. Or, he would stare gloomily at the radio, waiting for situation reports. When he spoke to take action, he would spit out the unfinished cigarette.

Other times while working, he would sit with the staff at a table in a low dugout with a large working bench. Finishing one cigarette, he threw the butt in a flat tin can, lit another and inhaled again.[38] Sweet cigarette smoke always layered close to his command post ceiling. To his staff, cigarettes seemed to fuel Katukov's energy.

Katukov, an active commander, constantly moved; he could not relax for long. He would sit down with soldiers and talk, present them awards, firmly shake their hands. Like many successful commanders in combat, Katukov could instantly go to sleep when time permitted – a talent that his political officer, Popel, admired, because, while he struggled to keep the same pace as his commander, he could not sleep so readily.

Much of the time was spent in preparing the new corps for combat. In the lull after battle, Katukov and Popel went forward to visit one of the battalions. They sat down with the soldiers while they ate. Soldiers were used to seeing their platoon leader, company commander, and sometimes battalion commander. But, two generals, the corps commander and his deputy, in their midst was rare. Understandably, conversation in the beginning was slow, but Katukov in a relaxed manner with cigarette in hand and friendly questions, prompted soldiers to start talking. The soldiers typically asked the commander about frontline concerns: "When would their battalion get more wheat millet?" "Why is our artillery so stingy with its artillery shells?" For the wise commander, the soldier perspectives were additional sources of information and insights into how well subordinate units were operating and identified problem areas.

Katukov handled their questions, then he called for his adjutant, who brought a portfolio containing awards. With the soldiers informally gathered around standing and sitting under the trees, Katukov presented awards as Popel read loudly the order, "In the name of the Supreme Soviet Presidium (of the) USSR...", the text continued in the stylized form of military award citations.[39]

In January 1943, Katukov received a telegram that he was again to fly to Moscow and see Stalin. He entered Stalin's office, in which a number of other staff officers were present. After the usual gracious greeting, Stalin suddenly asked, "So, comrade Katukov, can you manage, if we place you in command of a tank army?"[40]

Surprised and speechless for a few moments, Katukov managed to thank the Supreme commander for his confidence and expressed a hope that he could manage. Katukov retained Popel as his political officer and, again, Katukov asked for his key staff officers, Dyner and Nikitin to accompany him. As before, his request was granted.

A 30 January 1943 directive from the Stavka Supreme High Command created the lst Tank Army, in the Northwestern Front in the vicinity of Ostashkovo, south of Lake Ilmen. In forming the lst Tank Army, the Stavka planned to use it in an offensive operation to eliminate the German blockade around Leningrad. Within the composition of the army were included a tank and mechanized corps, separate tank regiments and brigades, two airborne divisions, and ski-rifle brigades.[41]

With success in bringing his staff, Katukov asked General Georgi Zhukov, commander of the Northwest Front, to replace the assigned chief of staff who Katukov considered "too far removed from tank affairs." He asked for General Mikhail Alekseevich Shalin, the man Katukov had seen when his 3rd Mechanized Corps supported the 22nd Rifle Army. On 18 February, Shalin became Katukov's chief of staff and a valued adviser for the remainder of the war.

In an interesting relief operation for Leningrad, the army planned to drop a parachute force in the vicinity of Dno rail station junction along the axis of attack towards Pskov. Developing the offensive, the airborne troops, skiers and other troops had to reach lakes Pskovskoye and Chudskoye and dig in on the shores. After completing their mission they formed a screen facing west blocking the German possibility of transferring reinforcements to their isolated Leningrad grouping.[42]

However, the planned operation was rescinded because of a

major thaw in February and major actions elsewhere on the front. A new Stavka directive on 7 March moved the tank army, less its airborne and ski units, to the Voronezh Front in anticipation of a major German spring offensive in the Kursk area. The 1st Tank Army consisted of the 3rd Mechanized Corps, 6th Tank Corps, 100th Separate Tank Brigade and four separate tank regiments for a total of 631 tanks.

By 28 March, with the 6th Tank Corps leading the army's deployment, Katukov's army began to concentrate in the area of Oboyan where the army's medical teams found typhus. Typhus, a disease found in the dirt of besieged cities and on campaign trails, is liable to occur in conditions where soldiers are crowded, wearing the same uniform for prolonged periods, and not routinely bathing. This disease, which had for centuries made and broke Kings' fortunes in war, was a serious concern for Katukov. The infested area had to be cleared up before the remainder of the tank army moved in. After the medical problems had been resolved, the army paid particular attention to camouflaging the units as they moved in, in order to hide them from German aerial reconnaissance.

Katukov studied his army's organization and believed the tank regiments were too understrength for independent action. He decided to combine the four tank regiments and tank brigade into an additional tank corps. The Voronezh Front staff would not help. Katukov got General Zhukov, now the Stavka representative for the Kursk operation, to support the reorganization and, with final approval from Stalin, created the 31st Tank Corps giving the 1st Tank Army two tank and one mechanized corps.

On the eve of the great Kursk battle, the Voronezh Front commander, General Nikolai Fedorovich Vatutin, called his army commanders to a late night meeting on 4 July. After the meeting, Katukov, with prompting from Popel, decided to watch an English comedy film in an improvised field theater. Over the whirl of the projector, a distant thunder was barely audible in the smoke-filled theater. Then Katukov's enjoyment of the movie was interrupted by a rustling at the back of the tent.

"What have you brought?" Katukov asked discontentedly.

A low voice told the projector operator to cut the machine and turn on the lights.

"Part of the German forces are advancing to the attack," Katukov's intelligence officer reported. "A few have reached the first defense sector."

"It has begun, comrades," Katukov summed up. "Everyone to his place."[43]

Katukov, with Popel, drove to the command post of the 6th Guards Army which formed the first line of defense on the southern face of the Kursk salient. They found the commander, Lieutenant General Ivan Mikhailovich Chistyakov finishing his breakfast and sipping tea while giving out instructions. "One could see from the spread on the table," Popel wrote in his memoirs, "that the portly Chistyakov loved to eat, and despite the situation the army commander did not change his habit."[44]

General Chistyakov, distressed that Katukov and Popel had missed breakfast, summoned the orderlies to cover the table again, "Must feed brother tankers," remarked the army commander. But their meeting was interrupted by artillery fire and by the appearance of Chistyakov's chief of staff who announced the penetration of a large German force.

Katukov and Popel exchanged glances and departed for their units on the front line. In the 6th Guards Army sector, Katukov had placed a forward brigade in order to cover approaches into his second line of defense. The tank brigade battle lines were dug in. As the Germans advanced, Katukov took a position well forward in the tank brigade company nicknamed, the "Iron Company," since every crew was a veteran. Satisfied with the action, he moved to his headquarters.

Mikhail Alekseevich Shalin, Katukov's chief of staff, received an order by telegraph from the Front. By 2400 hours, 5 July, the tank army was to send two corps to the 6th Guards Army's second line and assume the defense. And, the army was to be prepared to counterattack at dawn on 6 July.

Reading the order, Katukov for a long time did not release it from his hand.

"What do you make of the order for execution, Mikhail Alekseevich?"

"Corps commanders have a warning about the relief part."

"When do you plan to advance?"

"At twenty-two zero zero."

Katukov nodded. In the stifling heat, he got up, took off his tunic and threw it on the back of his chair. With his undershirt still on, he moved up to the situation map and stared at it.

"Counterattack – this is a meeting engagement. We to them and they to us. They have larger units, they have heavier tanks.... Let us think this out. So what do you think, Mikhail Alekseevich?" What concerned Katukov was the German Tiger tank's 88mm gun that ranged approximately two kilometers, a distance greater than the 76.2mm of his T-34's.

Shalin, wiping perspiration from his clean shaven head, replied, "Of course, it would be expedient to fight from this place, and not on the move, however, the order. Front must have its reasons."

Katukov made a face, then addressed Popel, "Concerning the order, your opinion, Kirillovich."

"I would inform the Front military soviet of our considerations – to fight from present place, with fine positions, in these conditions, of course, it's more advantageous," Popel replied.

Katukov again sat down on the chair and then moved beside the map, turned to the telephone operator. "Front commander!"

General Vatutin, not interrupting, listened to Katukov's consideration.

Katukov sighed in relief, replacing the receiver. He had been ordered to wait. The Front commander would consult with Nikita Khrushchev, the Front political officer, and his chief of staff.[45]

Accounts at this point begin to vary. Katukov claims that he received no answer from the Front commander by the end of the night.[46] While Katukov waited for Vatutin's answer, Stalin called

Katukov (center) with N.K. Popel (left) and M.A. Shalin.

Katukov in the tank army command post. Katukov explained his concerns to Stalin and recommended holding in place. Stalin agreed and told him to contact Vatutin and inform him that there would be no counterstrike.[47]

Another version is the phone rang, with Vatutin announcing the Front military soviet confirmation of Katukov's suggestion. The Front forces were to wear down the German attack with defensive battles on their main direction, stop, them, and then inflict a counterstrike.[48] Like many good tactical decisions in combat, they have many fathers; the poor ones are orphans. In either case, the decision for Katukov's tank army in the initial stages of the Kursk battles was to wait and fight defensively, allowing the German tanks to come within range of the T-34's – a solution that fully satisfied Katukov's cautious fighting style and ability to effectively use his tanks technical capabilities.

On the morning of 6 July, after accomplishing a night march, the lst Tank Army assumed defense along its assigned line. The tank army had moved from Oboyan area 30-40 kilometers south taking defensive positions along the northern bank of the Peny river. In the first echelon of the defense were the 6th Tank and 3rd Mechanized Corps. The newly formed 31st Tank Corps was in the second echelon. Katukov pulled the 112th Tank Brigade from the 6th Tank Corps for his army's reserve.

In Soviet military post-war writings, Katukov received criticism for taking the tank brigade from the mechanized corps to create an additional tank corps. The loss of the tank brigade and the placement of the mechanized corps in the first echelon of the defense to Vatutin's mind and other tank commanders weakened a strong armored formation that should have been held for a powerful counterstrike against the advancing German panzer formations.[49] Only after the difficulty of the fight did the merits of Katukov's organization become challenged.

Ever mindful of reconnaissance, Katukov had his corps send their reconnaissance units forward with the 6th Guards Army's defensive position to begin reporting on the situation. Katukov wanted no surprises either from the enemy or lapses in friendly reporting.

On the morning of 6 July, the Germans resumed their offensive on two main axes. One German axis drove directly into the 6th Tank Corps sector, and the other against the 3rd Mechanized Corps, wedging forces into the junction between Katukov's corps. The Germans used their enormous Ferdinand assault guns to bend back the defending Red Army tankers. While the 1st Tank Army held against a breakthrough, the Front using two separate tank corps hit the advancing German units' right flank. In hot, tenacious fighting, the German forces gained a 10-18 kilometer penetration by the end of the day.

The next morning, German armored units attempted to widen the penetration in the 3rd Mechanized Corps sector, continuing the drive to the northwest. Katukov moved his reserve, the 112th Tank Brigade, behind the mechanized corps. Also, on Katukov's orders, the 6th Tank Corps commander sent two of his Katyusha rocket regiments there. Katukov managed deftly a quick response to the German thrust.

Directing his units over the radio, Katukov waved his hands in the air, calling the brigade commanders simply by their first names. "Hold Volodya. Alexsandr attack, Armo assist." During the fierce struggle against the German advance, the Front fed reinforcements into the tank army. By the day's end, Katukov's intelligence officer provided him an intercept of a German aerial reconnaissance report. The text read, "The Russians are not falling back. They stand there on line. Our tanks are stopped. They are burning."[50] This report allowed Katukov to make the assessment that "...the Germans did not achieve on the Oboyan direction an appreciable success, they began to be nervous."[51]

All night on the 7th, Katukov escorted by a group of staff officers visited the forward units. Like many good commanders in history, he went forward to assess the situation for himself, inspecting the battle damage, the reconstitution efforts, the morale of the men and his subordinate leaders. Listening to their after-action reports from the day's battle, he drew his conclusions for the next day's fight.

"The day 8 July," Katukov recalled, "was a decisive day for our army. Clearly, this time the German command, despairing, decided to stake everything."[52] The situation became especially critical by midday, with genuine alarm in the 3rd Mechanized Corps. Katukov waited impatiently for reports from the flank. The first troubling reports, indicated that the desired effects from the employment of reserves had not been achieved. Fortunately, the Voronezh Front, reinforced from the Stavka reserve with four tank corps, sent the 10th Tank Corps to the 1st Tank Army.

The situation also became worrisome in the 6th Tank Corps sector. The 1st Tank Army lay on the path of a major German armor approach. The Voronezh Front estimated approximately 300 tanks attacking against Katukov's sector.[53] Despite all the Soviet's efforts, the Germans still wedged into their defense another 4-6 kilometers, forcing Katukov to withdraw the 3rd Mechanized Corps to a new line. This worried Katukov because now his army fought from a single echelon. Vatutin, who shared Katukov's concern, sent more forces, allowing Katukov to rebuild his defense in depth.

On 9 July, the German SS divisions, *Adolf Hitler* (LAH) and *Death's Head* (Totenkopf), hit part of the 1st Tank Army along the Solotinka river, driving the Soviets northwest. With a potential breakthrough in his sector, Katukov ordered part of the 10th Tank Corps from the vicinity of Orlovka, to conduct a counterstrike against the penetrating SS units and restore the situation.[54] The counterthrust saved the line.

While stubbornly resisting the German advance, the 6th Tank Corps sustained heavy losses. Considering the losses sustained by the tank corps, Katukov reinforced the corps with everything he could get his hands on – a tank regiment, a katyusha rocket regiment, and two assault gun regiments.

On 10 July, the Germans wedged against the 112th Tank Brigade in the vicinity of Tostoye and Noven'koye. Katukov used the 10th Tank Corps to easily restore the situation by 1900 hours. By late evening, hearing the reports of the deputies and staff chiefs, Katukov felt so tired that he was not able to stand. He staggered to his hut and collapsed on his bed with his boots still on. For the past several days he had forgotten to sleep, getting no more than two hours a day in the course of traveling in a combat vehicle. Now he slept so soundly he looked dead. His adjutant had to shake him hard to wake him after seven hours.

The weight of the 5th Guards Tank Army, under the command of General Pavel Rotmistrov, slammed into the German penetration on 12 July deciding the course of the Kursk operation. Rotmistrov's big five armored corps tank army combined with counterattacks by Katukov's 1st Tank Army and Kravchenko's 5th Guards Tank Corps to decisively turn both the tide of the German advance and the fight on the southern face of the Kursk salient. By the end of the day the Germans pulled back from the largest tank battle in history, leaving the Red Army's tankers in possession of the battlefield.

On 13 July, the 1st Tank Army began its reconstitution for upcoming offensive operations. The Front commander, General Vatutin, arrived at the tank army command post, and he announced that the tank army and its corps deserved a "guards" designation. He informed the gathered officers that the request had been sent to the Defense Commissar.

However, there was bad news. "In front of Vatutin was a notebook," Popel remembered. "On the first page a column of figures written in violet." In twenty days of battle, the army lost nearly half its tanks, and a significant loss in personnel. In Vatutin's figures was an accurate listing of the army's status.

"You hope for reinforcements," remarked Vatutin, reading the thoughts of the commanders and staff. "There will be no reinforcements," he continued. "Not one vehicle, not one man. Such is the Stavka's decision."

"I think," Vatutin spoke, "the Stavka cannot, and does not, have the means to do otherwise."[55]

If the Front had no extra tanks to give the tank army, then Katukov would have to rely on what Dyner could fix from the battlefield casualties. Fortunately, unlike the early battles in 1941 and 1942, the Red Army owned the battlefield and could recover battle losses in combat vehicles and tanks. Lightly wounded soldiers would have to be returned to the rifle units, and piecing together wrecked tanks was apparently the only way the tank army would get its reinforcements in time for an August offensive. By the beginning of the later summer operation, the 1st Tank Army repaired 1215 vehicles.[56]

For the Belgorod-Kharkov offensive operation, the Voronezh Front arrayed in a single echelon to generate maximum punch with the initial blow. Two tank armies, 1st and 5th Guards Tank Armies, were, to develop the offensive as an exploitation echelon, moving rapidly through the forward rifle formations. The operation required close coordination.

On 31 July, General Vatutin with Marshal Zhukov held a meeting to finalize the plans for the operation. After the Front mission had been briefed, the various army commanders were given a few minutes to report on their decisions. When the meeting was over, General Rotmistrov, commander of the 5th Guards Tank Army, contacted Generals Zhadov, commander of the 5th Guards Army, and Katukov. They made an appointment to meet in the 5th Guards Army command post, so that together with their chiefs of staff and chiefs of operations sections might coordinate every phase of the operation and most importantly to plot lines of advance for the tank corps in the sector of the offensive with the 5th Guards Army.

Upon arrival at General Zhadov's command post in the evening the two tank army commanders were briefed thoroughly by the rifle army commander on his decisions for the operation. He planned to break through the German defense in-depth by a strike of five reinforced infantry divisions to secure the commitment of the tank armies. He was certain of success because his army had been heavily reinforced with artillery. This made it possible to plan a massive artillery preparation of about three hours with a density of 230 guns and mortars per kilometer at the breakthrough point.

"This is all very well," Rotmistrov said in response. "But will not your troops, fighting deep in the enemy defenses, find themselves cut off from our tanks?"

"Why do you think so?" the rifle commander's thick eyebrows went up in puzzlement.

"Because you will breakthrough in a sector just 10 kilometers wide. As soon as your assault units penetrate the first line of the enemy defenses, second echelon troops and rear units will pour into the corridor after them, blocking lines of advance for our tanks."

"It is indeed a problem," Zhadov agreed.

"Let us together see what can be done about it," Katukov put in an anxious concern to get the issue resolved.[57]

Both tank army commanders were worried about two questions: the absolute specification of march routes for the tank corps to the line of commitment for the breakthrough and reliable fire support for the tankers at the time they deploy on the line.[58]

"Actually," General Zhadov recalled,, "the question about march routes was very complicated."[59] In a relatively narrow sector, approximately 10 kilometers wide, was to move simultaneously four tank corps, the first echelons of the tank armies, which required a minimum of four but normally eight march routes. When the rifle army forces were located in the jumping off positions, a strict control of movement on the march routes was enforced. While it was necessary for the lead elements of the rifle army to use the roads initially, the first echelon brigades of the tank corps were to locate near the attacking infantry at a distance of 2-3 kilometers. And the march routes belonged to these tankers."

Supporting fires for the tank corps was assigned to the rifle army's artillery group and four regiments of guards mortars. Their fires were for counterbattery against German artillery and especially antitank positions on the path of the attacking tank units.

On the morning of 3 August, after three hours of artillery and air preparation saturating the German positions, the Voronezh and Steppe Fronts advanced in the offense. The Belgorod-Kharkov operation was Katukov's first offensive operation as an army commander. He put his 6th Tank and 3rd Mechanized Corps in the first echelon, and the 31st Tank Corps in the second.

In the early morning hours, Katukov and his operational group consisting of his political officer, artillery commander, chiefs of operations and intelligence, signal officer and three liaison officers arrived in the forward observation post of the 5th Guards Army commander. The 1st Tank Army on two major routes would attack on a three kilometer sector through the 5th Guards Army into the attack. Between the columns visual signals were used. The convergence of the two tank armies behind the 5th Guards Army impressed Katukov, "In all the war not one of us had seen such an accumulation of Soviet tanks in so narrow a front sector."[60]

By midday, the rifle units penetrated the German defense. General Vatutin decided to commit the lead tank elements of the two tank armies. Each of Katukov's corps led with a tank brigade configured as a forward detachment. The 200th Tank Brigade, the forward detachment for the 6th Tank Corps, was committed at 1200 hours, but was unable to push through and break away from the infantry for the entire day.[61] The 49th Tank Brigade, forward detachment for the 3rd Mechanized Corps, was committed at 1300 hours and also experienced difficulty pushing through the German defense. Its slow advance failed to penetrate a second line of defense. Not until mid-afternoon had Katukov's tank brigades cleared the main defensive belt and by evening advanced 25-30 kilometers in depth.

The slow rate of advance by both forward detachments allowed the Germans to bring up the 19th Panzer Division and occupy a defense in the vicinity of Tomarovka. The 6th Tank Corps engaged the German tanks on the northern outskirts of Tomarovka late in the day. The 3rd Mechanized Corps halted by German tanks and antitank fires reached the vicinity of Domnin.

The 6th Guards Army was also attacking in the vicinity of Tomarovka. Marshal Zhukov arriving in the rifle army command

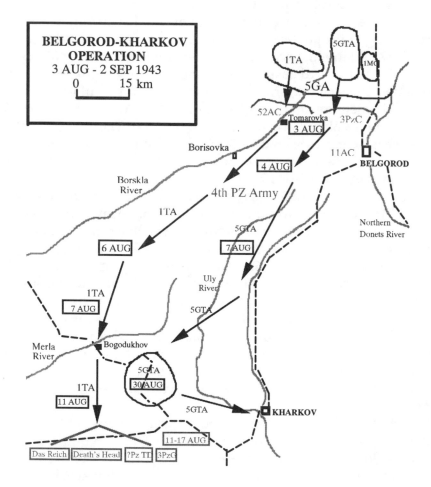

BELGOROD-KHARKOV OPERATION
3 AUG - 2 SEP 1943
0   15 km

post wanted the commander, General I.M. Chistyakov, to commit immediately Kravchenko's 5th Guards Tank Corps. Zhukov asked upon arrival, "Have you committed the tank corps?"

"Not yet."

Not waiting to hear Chistyakov's explanation, Zhukov said, "Such an experienced army commander, and you are unable to commit the corps. It's not necessary to give the tank corps to you. Commit the corps in the 1st Tank Army sector!"

Chistyakov knew from experience that in such situations it was not worth objecting to the Marshal, and he called Katukov. He told Katukov that Marshal Zhukov ordered the commitment of Kravchenko's tank corps in his sector. Katukov responded imploringly, "Don't you break into my combat formations." Katukov's agitation was his concern for the tempo of his operation which could be slowed by the introduction of additional forces on the already crowded roads. It could break down traffic management. Katukov asked Chistyakov, "Bargain for anything."

"What's to bargain," Chistyakov replied. "Anyway, Kravchenko will now drive towards you."

Later, Zhukov returned to ensure the lesson, "So, comrade commander, sometimes you can and must use a neighbor's terrain."[62] At the operational level of warfare, Soviet commanders learned to ignore unit boundaries when pushing armored units into the depth of an enemy defense.

On the morning of 4 August, the 6th Tank Corps and Kravchenko's 5th Guards Tank Corps with four rifle divisions resumed the attack on Tomarovka. The fiercely resisting German panzer unit held the tank army at bay until midday. General Vatutin ordered the tank corps withdrawn and sent after the 3rd Mechanized Corps which had found a weak point in the German's second defensive line. That night, the mechanized corps penetrating the defense rushed southwards towards Bogodukhov. The 6th Tank Corps followed. These corps advanced some 50 kilometers by midday on 6 August.

Meanwhile, the 31st Tank Corps together with Kravcehnko's 5th Guards Tank Corps which now was assigned to the tank army, encircled Tomarovka on 5 August, and proceeded to destroy the 19th Panzer Division.

The victory was so complete, the German division commander preferred suicide to captivity.

Marshaling the 1st Tank Army's two corps, a 5th Guards Rifle Army corps, and portions of the 5th Guards Tank Army, the Red Army massed enough force to resume the momentum of its advance. For developing the offensive after the Belgorod-Kharkov operation, Katukov improvised in his army's structure. The three corps of the army numbered only 141 tanks.[63] For example, the 242nd Tank Brigade, 31st Tank Corps lost approximately 80% of its tanks and 65% of its personnel. Losses in the command cadre of the 3rd Mechanized Corps were nearly 90%. Consequently, to support the advance of the rifle units, Katukov created composite detachments. In the 3rd Mechanized Corps, five brigades reformed as two brigades: tank and motorized rifle. Staffs from the other brigades led the composite battalions in combat.[64]

On the fourth day of the operation, the 5th Guards Army and 1st Tank Army, with part of the strike force, temporarily fended off threatening enemy forces on their flank from the Tomarovka and Borisovka areas. When Stalin heard of the situation, he instructed the Voronezh Front commander. General S. M. Shtemenko, Chief of Operations for the Red Army Staff, recalled Stalin's words, "From the position of Zhadov's 5th Guards Army it was evident that the army's strike focus had become scattered and the army's divisions were operating in divergent directions. Comrade Ivanov(Stalin's code name at the time) ordered that the strike focus of Zhadov's Army be led compactly, without dissipating its forces in several directions. This applied equally to Katukov's 1st Tank Army."[65]

By 6 August, Katukov's corps were heading for the major rail junction at Bogodukhov. Katukov led his army with forward detachments assigned to cut the railroad southwest of Kharkov. They moved ahead of the tank army some 30-40 kilometers. 1st Tank Army struck into the German's defense and attempted to cut-off the Kharkov-Poltava railroad. By evening 7 August, Katukov's lead elements reached Bogodukhov. The 3rd Mechanized Corps ran into heavy fighting on the 7th and 8th of August, against the German SS unit, "Das Reich."

The Germans, understanding the serious threat to its troops, inflicted a powerful counterstrike by three SS divisions (Das Reich, Death's Head, and Viking) against the tank army. The fluid front line began to stabilize as additional German reinforcements arrived in the area. Katukov consolidated his army's position just south of Bogodukhov awaiting the arrival of his trailing tank corps before continuing the offensive.

On 11 August, Katukov began committing his corps in the attack, southwards towards the Merchik river. The forward detachments had moved south of the Kharkov-Poltava rail line. By 1100 hours, the Death's Head and Das Reich SS Divisions encircled these forward detachments and destroyed them, reducing Katukov's tank army strength by some 30%. Fighting forward detachments and attacking with the large tank armies presented problems that required experience not only for Katukov, but also for other Red Army tank commanders. How do you hold together the various forces, keep up the tempo, and yet balance forward detachments' freedom of movement with survival? In blood, Soviet commanders paid for their lessons, but such lessons were learned well and not easily forgotten.

Simultaneously, a motorized regiment from the SS Death's Head Division reinforced with 25 tanks from the area of Konstantinov attacked the flank of the 6th Tank Corps. After serious fighting in the area of Sharovki, the right portion of the 6th Tank Corps withdrew to the Merchik river.

A no less tense situation unfolded in the 3rd Mechanized Corps sector. The corps had been unable to push through the resistance in the vicinity of Krysino while only a small part of the corps had pushed on towards the railroad.

Uncharacteristically, at this stage of the war, the Soviets followed the German counterattack with a rapid response. On 13 August, the 6th Guards Rifle Army struck back against the SS Totenkopf (Death's Head) Division, while the 1st Tank Army fought off continued attacks by the SS Viking and elements of the Das Reich south of Bogodukhov. Three days later, the 1st Tank Army stalled, sapped of any significant offensive striking power.

From large losses in personnel and equipment, Katukov's army on 22 August withdrew six tank brigades to the rear. The tank army's sector was immediately assumed by the 4th Guards Army. With this relief, the 1st Tank Army's participation in the Belgorod-Kharkov operation was completed.

The 1st Tank Army received orders to concentrate in the area of Sumy and enter the Stavka reserve. The respite would allow the tank army to be restored for future combat operations. However, the tank army was transferred from Sumy to the west bank of the Dnepr river west of Kiev in the area of Svyatoshino-Sofievka between 29 November and 20 December prior to receiving replacements in tanks and self-propelled assault guns. Only a few days before the beginning of the Zhitomir-Berdichev offensive operation did the tanks and guns arrive from the factories.[66]

At the end of November 1943, 1st Tank Army was subordinated to the 1st Ukrainian Front(formerly the Voronezh Front, redesignated on 20 October). Because of their fighting at Kursk, the army's corps won the honorific title "Guards." The 6th Tank Corps became the 11th Guards Tank Corps; the 3rd Mechanized Corps, the 8th Guards Mechanized Corps.

At the end of December 1943, and through the first half of January 1944, the 1st Tank Army participated in the Zhitomir-Berdichev operation as part of the 1st Ukrainian Front. The operation recaptured the right bank Ukraine. In this operation, the 1st Tank Army consisted of the 11th Guards Tank and 8th Guards Mechanized Corps, 64th Guards Tank Brigade, 8th Air Defense and 79th Guards Mortar battalions. The army numbered over 42,000 men, 546 tanks and self-propelled assault guns, 585 artillery guns and mortars.

In the period from 29 November to 20 December 1943, the tank army was transferred to the west side of the Dnepr river on 70 trains. For the impending operation, the 1st Tank Army was to advance in the fighting southeast of Brusilov after the 38th Rifle Army broke through the tactical defense zone.

Katukov decided to commit the army to the fight along four march routes with the 11th Guards Tank Corps advancing on the right flank and 8th Guards Mechanized Corps on the left. The reserve consisted of the 64th Guards Tank Brigade which was still unorganized for combat. The 31st Tank Corps had been withdrawn from the tank army.

Soviet commanders, rather their staffs, five unit orders to their subordinate commanders. The Soviet command and control system required a personal meeting between commanders so the higher commander could ensure a complete understanding of missions and taskings by the subordinate leaders. This allowed the commander to receive the non-verbal communications from the subordinate's eyes, gestures, and body language. Katukov often laced his instructions to subordinates with "You understand?"

After a powerful artillery and airstrike preparation on the morning of 24 December, the 1st Tank Army was committed to the attack in the 38th Rifle Army sector. In short winter days, the lead brigades cleared the jumping-off areas about midday and advanced rapidly in daylight to a depth of 20 kilometers. Rains washed out the roads.

Maneuver became difficult, and the tempo of the offensive was less than what Katukov wanted.

In preparation for the Zhitomir-Berdichev operation, Katukov had wargamed on a map possible German actions with his Chief of Staff, Chiefs of Intelligence and Operations. This wargaming session typified Katukov's leadership style in which he worked closely with his staff. He held war councils soliciting their opinions and comments. He was not a commander to charge around the battlefield without the benefit of his staff's wisdom.

Katukov approached operations and their execution with a clear concept of the operation and the possible actions of the enemy. "The Army moves out on this line. What will "your" forces do?" Katukov asked his chief of intelligence, Colonel Aleksei Mikhailovich Sobolev, who was bending over the map.

"I can move "my" force from here to here," Sobolev responded while outlining a circle with a blue pencil (Soviet military use blue for enemy and red for friendly), marking the area of German force concentration. He continued, "True, for this I would require three to four days. But, for this period, you are able to move toward Karatin."

"Where would you inflict a strike on our flank?" Katukov asked.

"Right here." Sobolev's pencil set on the town Klin.

"They know the forward detachments are advancing here. Here, I would put the covering detachments. What do you think, Mikhail Alekseevich?" Katukov addressed the Chief of Staff, Shalin, whose opinion he valued and always included. Shalin agreed with Katukov's decision. The Chief of Operations quickly marked notation on the map.[67]

In the initial stages of the offensive, Vatutin, unsatisfied with Katukov's advance told him, "The army has superiority in forces over the enemy, but instead of developing success it has not moved out from the infantry and has remained on line with them."[68]

Katukov went forward to check the delays. At the 8th Guards Mechanized Corps, he entered a low hut with a hot stove and in the corner with 'rosy cheeks' sat the corps chief of staff, Colonel V.G. Aleksandrov, getting a haircut. On the table before him was a pile of papers, maps and schematics. In his hand was a sharpened pencil. With Katukov's appearance, he jumped up, stood erect and reported that the corps commander was forward in the sector.

"And what is your job?" Katukov asked.

"I am preparing materials for the commander's decision."

"What decision?"

"Connected with the capture of the Popelnya station."

Katukov's gaze fell on the neatly drawn diagrams and schematics.

"Beautifully drawn, but doesn't say anything! And you know," Katukov said attempting to suppress a sudden fury in himself, "while you are engaged there drawing, the Germans ship off people to Germany? It continues, you know, and all the while you calmly keep on drawing!"

The colonel offered excuses but Katukov did not listen. "I never liked a chief of staff whiner," Katukov recalled in his memoirs.[69] Katukov responded abrasively to people when he became over-tired and under pressure. He got the corps commander on the radio and designated objectives for immediate capture.

By the second day of the operation, the tank army became significantly active. Katukov could motivate his commanders to action. Developing the offensive to the southwest with the 11th Guards Tank Corps, the army's main force, the 8th Guards Mechanized Corps, together with rifle forces participated in the battle for Kornin.

On the night of 27 December, after regrouping, the 1st Tank Army received reinforcement from the 68th Guards Rifle Division. Katukov's plan had the 8th Guards Mechanized Corps, along with the rifle division move in the area of Kazatin the following day. The 11th Guards Tank Corps in view of the vague situation at Zhitomir remained on guard in the area of Volitsa to repel a possible German counterattack against the army's flank.

By the morning of 30 December, commander of the 11th Guards Tank Corps received a new order, "The corps' main force must shift its sector to the south and southeast edge of Berdichev, with part of the 38th Army and advance in the direction of Kazatin."[70] Shifting the 11th Guards Tank Corps to Kazatin, an important railroad center, Katukov took into consideration the northern approach towards Berdichev covered by the 18th Army, operating on the right flank of the 38th Army.

From 1 to 5 January 1944, two battalions of the 44th Guards Tank Brigade became encircled in Berdichev by the 1st SS Panzer and 20th Motorized Divisions. Despite capturing Berdichev and encirclement, the tank brigade continued to operate with the 18th Army until mid-January when it was relieved.

On 6 January, when the 1st Tank Army was ordered to turn toward Vinnitsu, Katukov arrived in the 8th Guards Mechanized Corps with the new corps commander, General Ivan Fedorovich Dremov. In conversation, Katukov, in his usual half-joking manner, referred to a group of colonels as generals, and proceeded to tell them about a change in mission based on discovery of a large German grouping. When one of the colonels challenged the discovery, Katukov reminded them it was found by reconnaissance and reconnaissance should always be in their repetoire.[71]

Moving about the battlefield, Katukov with his chief of staff personally delivered the missions to the corps for turning the tank army at Vinnitsu.[72] Regardless how much Katukov relied upon his staff for situation assessments, he never let it substitute for his going forward to see for himself. The Soviet command system demands a commander to know and to be constantly informed on his unit's most forward elements. One cannot lead when totally insulated and isolated in a command post – a commander's presence must be shared on the battlefield.

The decision to turn the 38th and 1st Tank Armies toward Vinnitsu was made late in response to German actions. On 10 January, the German command managed in the area of Vinnitsu to create a large force which struck into the flank of the 38th Army creating a significant threat to Katukov's army and the Front offensive operation. The German tank force cut across the rear of the 8th Guards Mechanized Corps. Katukov called General Dremov, the corps commander, "What do you say brand-new Major General," Katukov asked over the radio.

"Poor affair, comrade army commander," Dremov answered.

"I know," Katukov voice changed growing warmer. "But you hold, grind down the approaching enemy reserves there, show great skill and stubbornness, I don't want to learn that you were not bold in this battle. The mission, I hope is clear, corps commander? I wish you success."[73]

With the German attack, Katukov instructed his corps to fortify their positions on the line of advance and be prepared to repel a German assault. Additionally, to cover the right flank in the area of Lipovtsa, he moved his reserved force, the 64th Guards Tank Brigade.

The potential for operations around Cherkassy and Krovograd excited Katukov. The situation to him seemed like another opportunity for a repeat of the Stalingrad encirclement. Katukov, discussing the situation with Shalin, fidgeted with a stubby pencil in his hand. Interestingly, Popel, in his memoir, felt the need to justify Katukov's holding of a pencil: he "had not become a bureaucrat, but rather used it for his approving signature on the plan." Apparently, in terms of status and roles, the commander was not suppose to require the use of a pencil, except for signatures. During the conversation Katukov, disgusted with the turn of events in the operation, threw the pencil. Throughout the meeting, as he always did, Katukov mechanically lit cigarettes with his capture lighter.

Katukov's tank army carried out a number of complicated maneuvers on new axes and decisively dealt with the German's counterattacking operational reserves. After the operation, the German command had no hope for restoring the front of their defense along the Dnepr river in the vicinity of Kiev.

In the recapture of the western portions of the Ukraine in March 1944, the 1st Tank Army had the mission as the 1st Ukrainian Front reserve to develop the offensive in the direction of the Carpathian mountains, encircling the German Army Group South. On 4 March, the Front began the offensive operation named, Proskurov-Chernovitsy.

Assigning the mission and giving instructions to the 1st Tank Army, Marshal Georgii K. Zhukov said, "You have the chance to distinguish yourself, Katukov. Is everything clear to you? Fine...you will cross the Nedelky here with the army," he showed on a map the place in the area of Ternopol, "and then hurrah, and all will be fine...."[74] Such general guidance left plenty of room for initiative by the tank army commander.

Once committed to the engagement, the 1st Tank Army operated independent of the forward rifle armies. Katukov created a forward detachment from his reserve with the 64th Guards Tank Brigade commanded by Lieutenant Colonel I.N. Boiko. The detachment had the mission to capture Chernovitsy. In seven hours Boiko's forward detachment advanced nearly 80 kilometers, forcing the Dnestr river, and conducted a surprise night attack seizing the Moshi railroad station, north of Chernovitsy.

During the Prokurov-Chernovitsy operation, nearly 200 tanks of the 1st Tank Army crossed the Dnestr by deep fording. Having breeched the German defenses east of Ternopol, the 1st Tank Army mounted a swift offensive to the south and on 24 March struck the Dnestr river on a 35 kilometers front (from Ustechko to Kolobrodka).

No bridge over the river remained intact. The railroad and vehicular bridges at Zaleschika and Ustechko were blown during the 1st Guards Tank Brigade approach. The tank brigade operated as the 8th Guards Mechanized Corps' forward detachment. The army possessed no organic pontoon-crossing equipment, and the attached 3rd Pontoon Bridge Brigade lagged behind due to the bad spring roads. The engineer-sapper battalions of the corps and army were not in shape to repair or build bridges quickly. The motorized infantry made hasty crossings on local crossing equipment and improvised materials, and captured a bridgehead. The situation demanded the immediate crossing of tanks into the bridgehead since the German command began to bring fresh forces to the river, intending to dislodge the infantry from the bridgehead and stabilize the front line.

The width of the Dnestr in this sector was between 100 and 200 meters and the water was over 2.5 meters deep. Only at Ustechko, where the river's depth diminished to 2.2 meters, was it possible for the tanks to wade across. With techniques mastered earlier in the war, Katukov's tankers sealed all the cracks and hatches of the tanks and their exhaust pipes extended upward with the aid of canvas hoses. Then, the tanks were driven across the bottom of the river.

First across the river were the tanks of the 1st Guards and 64th Separate Guards Tank Brigades, followed by the tank regiments of the 8th Guards Mechanized Corps. In the 11th Guards Tank Corps crossing area the river was over 2.5 meters deep. The tank corps' delay in crossing prompted Katukov to have all tanks regrouped in the offensive zone of the 8th Guards Mechanized Corps for a river crossing by the Ustechko fords. As the tanks crossed, they entered the battle, reinforcing the motorized infantry.

Katukov liked to use witty words that he made-up himself. For example, on one occasion he described a German rifle unit as having "crutched" forward. The unit was composed of wounded, and the Russian language has no word for crutch in verb form. This was Katukov's favorite form of humor – a cross between a pun and fabricated words.

While Katukov loved plays on words for humor, he was also quick in using his command of words for a sarcastic reproach to disappointing commanders. General Andrei Lavrentevich Getman, commander of the 11th Guards Tank Corps, drew Katukov's sniping remarks for his delay in crossing the Dnestr river. Upon meeting

Getman, Katukov caustically offered such barbs as "sunburned on the bank," "don't like to force crossings and get our boots wet," "attack with caution.'[75] This kind of sarcasm cost Katukov close personal relationships with his subordinate commanders – a distance evident in their post war writings. A commander must use humor judiciously, and he must reprimand without humiliating sarcasm. Katukov, at times, went too far.

The Dnestr river crossing bothered Katukov. Towards the end of the crossing he reflected on the operation and confided in Popel his concerns about how the army failed to support the corps. The candor of Katukov's reflection reveals the degree of trust Popel had established with his commander. Popel and Katukov were laying on their backs on the damp sandy bank of the Dnestr river. "It was clear to use," Popel recalled, "that even if the crossing went successfully, it was no credit to the army command."

The army staff had insufficiently prepared the subordinate corps in planning nor the allocation of equipment for the dash across the Dnestr. While some actions and requirements became blatantly obvious in retrospect, Katukov was not comfortable with the well-known aphorism, "you cannot foresee everything."

"Brigade commanders must think at the corps scale," Popel said, "and corps commanders at the army. And in reality, did we think before the Dnestr at the Front scale?"

Katukov lay silently on the cold sand. He closed his eyes and bit his lip. "We easily lecture the others, but don't always adhere ourselves to our advice. As if advice is good only for subordinates. The pontoon brigade battalion was stuck at the other end of the world – this, agreed, wasn't our fault. But, here the units advanced towards the Dnestr poking around as blind kittens. We owed them the location of the crossing points, and the enemy."

Katukov turned on his side to look at Popel. His half-length sheepskin coat had grown dark from laying on the damp sand. "How long will you live to still regret our actions?" Katukov asked.

"It will be no less for me than for you," Popel replied soothingly.

"I am not the better for it."

"I firmly believe that Gorelov and Boiko are able to fulfill the mission without our instructions." Popel changed direction of thinking, hoping to ease the commander's mind. "We forced the Dnestr, higher command gratefully sent decorations to be given. And we ought...."

"Well, strictly speaking, we ought to do what? Do we take away the awards? Your food for thought is not very creative. Give it some work this self-criticism of yours. Do you like it?"

"Who likes it?" Popel sighed.

"That's enough," Katukov rose, shaking off his coat. "In a principle of reciprocity, we forgive each other's sins and we go our way, so talk with your brother political workers, study it by group."

"In spite of Katukov's playful tone," as Popel characterized a dangerous remark by his commander, "I saw, he keenly endured everything about which we had spoken. He suffered the losses, for the kind which he wished he was not responsible, blunders, which nearly no one notices in the general background of success."[76] Katukov tended to exaggerate the possibilities for things to go wrong. He usually compensated for this tendency with prior planning. On this occasion he failed to anticipate, and he felt guilty in his failure of responsibility.

After the battle for Chernovitsy, the tank army aggressively advanced on Kolomyyu and Stanislava. Katukov's army carried out a number of hasty river crossings, cut off the routes of withdrawing German units to the south and west, and then captured Chernovitsy, reaching the foothills of the Carpathian mountains. As a result of the tank army's actions in the whole operation, it received on 25 April its honorific title, "Guards" unit.

In the lull after the operation, Katukov suffered a sudden appendicitis attack. Marshal Zhukov, the Front commander, suggested that Katukov go to Moscow's Kremlin hospital for the operation. But, Katukov preferred to receive his operation in his army hospital. He did not believe an appendectomy was serious enough to merit a 1000 kilometer journey.

On 26 June, as the tank army regrouped in a new area, Katukov, recovered from surgery, Popel and Shalin visited the Front staff. The new Front commander, the hard, aggressive Marshal Ivan Stepanovich Konev, announced the Front's concept for the upcoming operation and assigned the 1st Guards Tank Army's mission. Konev ordered the commanders to have their units prepared for an offensive operation by 12 July.

In regrouping for the Lvov-Sandomierz operation which was to recapture the remainder of the Ukraine and reach into Poland, the 1st Guards Tank Army had to move nearly 300 kilometers from the left flank to the right flank of the 1st Ukrainian Front. This relocation of the tank army was undetected by German reconnaissance. The tank army's location would not be discovered by the Germans until three days into the operation when the tank army was already moving through a large gap in their defense.

The lst Tank Army had been assigned the mission to attack in the direction of Rava-Russkaya. The plan committed the tank army in the breakthrough sector of the 3rd Guards and 13th Rifle Armies after they had penetrated the tactical defense. According to the plan by the fourth day of the operation the tank army was to capture Rava-Russkaya.

Naturally, the attention of the command and staff were riveted on the actions of the forces in the breakthrough sector. However, the dynamics of the situation quickly moved events in a direction not quite intended or assumed. Timely commitment of German reserves in the area of Gorokhov created strong resistance on the planned axis of the lst Guards Tank Army's commitment. The 3rd Guards Rifle Army's bogged attack did not manage to seize the German's second defense zone until 17 July. The commitment of the tank army along the planned axis of attack would not be the most effective nor the quickest way into the German's rear area.

As the situation unfolded, Katukov, in agreement with the Front commander's decision, committed his forward detachment, lst Guards Tank Brigade reinforced, in the direction of the 3rd Guards Army. Katukov reasoned that, if the brigade's operation turned out successful, favorable conditions for committing the tank army would be created. And, if the brigade's operation was not successful, its commitment would still disorient the German command concerning the time and place of the tank army's commitment.

On the afternoon of 14 July, the forward detachment began carrying out the assignment and rapidly approached the Western Bug river in the early morning hours of 15 July. The Germans over-estimated the tank brigade's strength and failed to recognize its parent unit, the lst Guards Tank Army. Katukov received reports that the Germans were shifting forces from other sectors to the zone of the lst Brigade penetration. He ordered the brigade commander to hold the ground to the last round in order to pin down as many German troops as possible.

Meanwhile, the 13th Army attack, further south, turned out more favorably. There, the German 291st Infantry Division unsuccessfully withdrew its main force to the second line of defense and faced a very destructive attack, creating a 12 kilometer wide gap in the sector.

Immediately, the Front commander committed a cavalry-mechanized group into the breach. Konev, studying the situation, received Katukov's suggestion for a possible commitment of the tank army after the cavalry-mechanized group in the 13th Army's gap.[77] Despite the deteriorating weather, Konev decided to commit the tank army in the new direction, and lead elements of the 11th Guards Tank Corps began moving on the morning of 17 July.

At 1000 hours, the 8th Guards Mechanized Corps received the signal to begin moving its units forward. The infantry rode on the tanks. The corps brushed of light attacks by the 17th Panzer and 291st Infantry Divisions as they began to withdraw to the Western Bug river, attempting to stop the lst Guards Tank Army.

Meeting unorganized resistance, Katukov's corps achieved the line of commitment without deploying into combat formation and advanced forward rapidly. By 1200 hours, the tank army was moving into the operational depth behind the German lines.

But, later in the day, German Tiger tanks with other hastily thrown together forces counterattacked against the 44th Guards Tank Brigade, the forward detachment for the 11th Guards Tank Corps, on the west side of the Western Bug river. Heavy fighting for the bridgehead over the Western Bug lasted for two days before German resistance broke. Katukov typically organized bold decisive actions by his reconnaissance group against withdrawing German columns. In the fight to widen the Western Bug bridgehead, in the vicinity of Sokol, a separate reconnaissance patrol of the 8th Guards Mechanized Corps circumvented the German defensive positions and organized an ambush. A column of withdrawing German combat vehicles was destroyed and prisoners were taken for identification of German units.[78] At midday on 18 July, Katukov instructed the commander of the 8th Guards Mechanized Corps to maneuver to the southwest, cross the Western Bug behind the 11th Guards Tank Corps and continue the offensive in the direction of the San river and the old city of Yaroslav. The tank army began an unimpeded advance into the German rear.

Katukov's armored spearhead breached the German defenses along the Soviet-Polish border. Penetrating westwards, the tank army's forward detachments reached the San river to the north and south of Yaroslav on 22 July. Two days later, the tank army's main body crossed the river encircling the strong German force in Yaroslav. On 27 July, after four days of close, bitter fighting, the troops of the lst Guards Tank and 13th Armies cleared Yaroslav of the enemy.

On the early morning of 28 July, Katukov after the capture of Yaroslav and Peremyshl, received over the telephone a new mission for the Front commander. The tank army was to hand over its position to the 13th Army and complete concentrating the tank army by the morning of 29 July. Without delay, Katukov's army was to continue the offensive crossing the Vistula river from the march south of Sandomierz, and, by the morning of 1 August, secure a bridgehead on the western bank.

Rains delayed the army's regrouping and continuation of the offensive. The corps' forward detachments started the offensive between 1000-1200 hours, and the main forces between 1600-1800 hours on 29 July. Katukov rushed his army toward the Vistula river without encountering serious resistance on the way. By 1530 hours, 29 July, the lst Guards Tank Brigade, the 8th Guards Mechanized Corps' forward detachment, reached the Vistula in the Baranov area. A few hours later, the 44th Guards Tank Brigade, 11th Guards Tank Corps reached the river south of Tarnobrzeg. The army's reconnaissance detachments had reached the river several hours earlier. Since Katukov's tankers had arrived earlier than the German's main retreating units, no prepared defenses awaited them. Only small German units occupied the opposite river bank.

However, the forward detachments could not cross the 4-5 meter deep, 600-800 meter wide river. Again, the tank army's lead elements outran assigned pontoon bridging units. These units were tied up at the San river. Nonetheless, in the early morning hours of 30 July, the motorized infantry of the brigades crossed the Vistula on local river crossing equipment and rafts made from available materials. The tanks and self-propelled assault guns remained on the east bank. With daylight, the corps main forces reached the Vistula and, by midday, their motorized infantry also began crossing on improvised equipment. The 15th and 1134th Pontoon Bridge Battalions arrived late on 30 July, and the tanks and assault guns began crossing at dawn on 31 July. The crossing was easy and successful because the army arrived at the Vistula well ahead of the enemy troops.

Once Red tankers were across the river, the Germans responded quickly attempting to eliminate the bridgehead. In the course of the battle for the bridgehead, Katukov and his chief of operations,

Guards Colonel Matvei Timofeevich Nikitin, more than once visited the corps. They calmly and adroitly moving in bounds advanced around artillery fires and bomb explosions to visit the forward battalions in dug outs, trenches and artillery positions. Arriving in General I.F. Dremov's command post, Katukov commented on their tour of the front lines.

"You wouldn't believe it, Ivan Fedorovich," began Katukov. "Today comrade Nikitin was born again. A series of shells fell and didn't explode." And he joked, "Matvei Timofeevich didn't escape from death, he ran from it."

"As you know, not only today we ran from death," Dremov joined the joke, "but around Moscow, and around Kursk, and on the fields of the Ukraine. The poet Aleksei Surkov was right: The brave are afraid of the bullet."[79]

The battle for the Sandomierz bridgehead shifted to the western bank. The German command hurled all available reserves and fresh troops against Katukov's hold on the western bank. In the bridgehead, Katukov saw the German's King Tiger tank for the first time. The Soviet T-34 now carrying an 85mm gun was capable of piercing its thicker armor.

Both sides fought tenaciously for the bridgehead, bleeding their forces until exhaustion set in by mid-August. The 1st Ukrainian Front managed to extend the bridgehead to a frontage of 75 kilometers with a depth of 50 kilometers. The 1st Guards Tank Army had suffered serious losses, requiring time to reconstitute. The seizure of the Sandomierz bridgehead held tremendous strategic importance for the Red Army as the launch point for a future 1st Ukrainian Front's offensive into Silesia and a southerly approach to Berlin.

In the Lvov-Sandomierz operation, Katukov's tank army conducted bold decisive actions. His forward detachments crossed and secured bridgeheads over the Western Bug river. The tank army moved rapidly into the operational depth of the German defense. After crossing the Western Bug and beating attempts to cut off the advance, his army crossed the San river and raced towards the Polish border, securing crossing over the Vistula river. Katukov's tank army was demonstrating a battlefield agility that it was not capable of performing earlier in the war.

Katukov received the country's highest award, "Hero of the Soviet Union." In the crucible of heroic fighting on the eastern front, Katukov displayed personal courage and great skill as an operational commander in combat actions with his tank army. For his cunning, quick wit, and use of deception, his soldiers affectionately called him "General Sly."

The operation kept Katukov and members of the command constantly on the move. Upon returning to the army staff, Katukov sat down with his head leaning to the side, instantly asleep. "I was always astonished at his fortunate capacity for this. I never learned to sleep sitting up," Popel recalled.[80]

After the Sandomierz bridgehead fight, lst Guards Tank Army moved into the Stavka reserve, and then re-subordinated to the lst Belorussian Front for the Vistula-Oder offensive operation in that began on 14 January 1945. The dark night before the attack, no one slept. The tank army was to be committed to the fight through the 8th Guards Rifle Army. Katukov recalled, "As a tanker, I am not concerned with the first sector, it is for the rifle units to penetrate. Mainly for me, I want to know what can the enemy do in the depth, there, where the forward detachments will operate."[81]

Katukov went forward. The forward detachment commanders were always hand-picked for their boldness and decisiveness. Katukov asked the corps commander Amazasp Khachaturovien Babadzhanyan, "How is the corps?"

"It's prepared for battle, comrade commander."

"Who goes first?"

"Karabanov's battalion. It moves with the third infantry echelon."

Katukov sought out the battalion commander. "Is the mission clear, comrade Karabonov?"

"Exactly so, comrade army commander. To force the river Pilitsa and to capture a bridgehead on the opposite bank."

"Good Luck!" Katukov strongly embraced the battalion commander. In his memoirs, Katukov remarked, "What is never said, to be first in battle is a hard role. They catch the first antitank gun and panzerfaust, the first mines."[82]

On 14 January, the lst Belorussian Front attacked. At 0800 hours the Front artillery announced the offensive. By afternoon, the 8th Guards Army penetrated the German's main defensive sector. Marshal Zhukov telephoned Katukov, "Play your hand." The lst Guards Tank Army began moving into the breach. General Dremov watching his combat formations passing by pressed the telephone receiver closer to his ear and heard the army commander's voice.

"Ivan Fedorovich, can you hear me?" Katukov had a send off

message, "You operate according to plan."

The corps attacked aggressively, and German units were unable to organize a defense on intermediate lines. By 2000 hours, the corps' forward detachments were in Moisk, Dombrov and Murshaty. The next day, the tank army completely committed through the 8th Guards Army, forced the Pilitsa river. A pontoon bridge across the river at Nowe Miasto was laid in a channel cleared by demolitions. Katukov noted only combat engineers guards the bridge. The tank army's lead units bypassed Warsaw on the southeast.

Katukov always looked for and found workable forms and methods of combat against the Germans and aspired to achieve victories with less forces. He lost patience with subordinate commanders who always asked for more troops and weapons.

Shattered remnants of German units smashed by the 1st and 2nd Guards Tank Armies were withdrawing on both banks of the Pilitsa river. One of the "roaming pockets" was fighting its way to Nowe Miasto. Katukov sent Colonel Nikitin across the river to assess the situation on the west bank. Colonel Nikitin soon returned reporting a German assault on Nowe Miasto. Only a reconnaissance company with six tanks was fending off a much larger German force. Katukov gathered up his operational command group with its security element and headed for the critical bridge. En route his radio operator contacted the tank army's reserve tank brigade. Katukov briefed the brigade commander on the situation. "I won't be long," the brigade commander replied.

With artillery shells bursting close to his command post, Katukov formed a skirmish line. As the line was thinning out the reserve tank brigade arrived along the highway. Without stopping, they deployed into combat formation with their guns ready. The Germans failed to escape.

Advancing 240 kilometers, the lst Guards Tank Army went around Lodz, advancing towards the Warta river in the vicinity of Poznan. Coming up against the German's fortified region around Poznan, reconnaissance reported the preparations and the availability of German reserves to make it a difficult battle ahead for the tank army. Katukov looked for a way that a raid might ease the situation. He summed his conclusion, "Sometimes a sledgehammer is required for opening the enemy defense. But now it can be achieved by a skillful locksmith...."[83]

Katukov's tank army forced the Warta on 22 January, and his

forces engaged German units on the southern side of Poznan. Despite Katukov's considerations for alternatives to avoid Poznan's defense, his tankers had difficulty taking the city. "Poznan was a typical tank 'gas chamber,'" Katukov recalled in his usual play on words. He used an encircling maneuver to blockade the city with its garrison of 62,000 German soldiers until the approach of the 8th Guards Army riflemen. He found part of his unit tied up until 29 January before lead elements continued to move west, crossing the Obra into Germany.

Having smashed a large German grouping and captured a major town, Katukov's tank army went over to the pursuit. Maneuvering in the German rear area, the tank army reached the Oder river by the 16th day of the operation. In a fast-paced operation as the Vistula-Oder offensive, the ability to control the formations is strained. All aspects of the operation are in constant change; commanders and staffs must adjust to its rhythm and tempo. They cannot comfortably stay in one place. Katukov's main command post moved 13 times from 14-31 January 1945.

For his dynamic, aggressive role in leading the 1st Guards Tank Army, Katukov received his second Hero of the Soviet Union Gold Star. As twice winner of the Gold Star, he moved into a select and honored group of war heroes.

By 1 February, the 1st Guards Tank Army advanced on a wide front north and south of Frankfurt am Oder. Katukov drove his combat weary units forward. When his forward detachments closed on the Oder river, Katukov and his staff had the next 1st Belorussian Front's order. Marshal Zhukov, the Front commander, viewed the situation favorably in that the Germans were ill-disposed, with no concentration of force for any powerful counterattack. The German forces were covering only separate axes of advance, but they had been able to transfer four tank and five infantry divisions from the west.

Katukov and his staff sat around the map and discussed the situation. At first impression, the operation looked good, in a week's time they could be in Berlin. Katukov measured the distance, "70 kilometers in a straight line – ah, that's nothing! Babadzhanyan's corps has covered more than that in a 24 hour period before now. But the flanks of the Front are open!"[84]

General A.L. Getman, one of the corps commanders, moving his had as a fist into a position behind the tank army's depicted positions on the map, remarked, "If I were in Guderian's position I would strike here. Rokossovskii is taken up with the business of destroying the East Prussian concentration of enemy. He has turned his Front to the north and thus the right flank of our Front stretches for about 300 kilometers. Konev has turned his Front to the southwest and left his left flank run for some 120 kilometers. What could be a more favorable position for the Germans for mounting a blow!"[85]

The tank army's chief of staff, General Shalin, putting on his dark rimmed glasses leaned over the map, 'that little balcony is full of danger." He traced with a pencil a huge salient on the map from the north of the Oder river to Konigsberg. "Here, there are more than nine German infantry divisions, some tank divisions, and a mass of combat groups. And the main thing is this – they are continuously gathering together new forces. In such a situation as this an immediate offensive on Berlin would be extremely risky."

Katukov asked, "Well, possibly political information demands an immediate seizure of Berlin?"

"I know only what the others know," Popel shrugged his shoulders.

A strong sense of concern began to grow in the staff and commanders as they worked more thoroughly the operational concept of the new order. General Getman spoke again, "The alphabet of war (teaches) that victory does not depend on taking towns but on the destruction of enemy forces. Napoleon in 1812 thought otherwise, he lost Moscow and we all know how that turned out. And he was no small leader of men in war. Tell me frankly," addressing Katukov, "can we go forward?"

"Why, yes, we can."

"Can we take Berlin?"

"Well that would depend..." Katukov attempted to remain realistic about the order.

"Well, what doubts have you got?" Getman continued, "it is necessary to expand our bridgehead, to bring up the rifle armies, and the main thing is to liquidate the "Pomeranian Balcony." Getman, caught up in making his case addressed the group, "The army's tanks require a technical inspection: by direct route they have covered 570 kilometers but according to what is registered on the odometers they have covered 1200, in fact. A man has no odometer and nobody knows what wear and tear has taken place there in the last 18 days. Those 18 days without rest and now without any kind of preparation then rush into the attack shouting "hurrah," and into the most difficult new operation where the enemy will fight to the last SS man, and where on our flanks there remain three intact enemy armies. And, so Hitler has one hope that we are going to lay our head into his noose and then from the north, from Pomerania one blow, and then from the south, from Glogow, two blows! He strikes and then he destroys!"

The war council stood silent for some time. The telephone rang. The Front's member of the Military Council, General Konstantin Fedorovich Telegin, asked, "Comrade Popel? Have you received the order and the instructions?"

"Exactly so," Popel responded.

"Have you gone down to the troops?"

"Well, no not yet," Popel replied. "We have just been sitting; we have been turning things over in our minds."

"Then hold on a while," Telegin directed, "that is the personal instruction from Zhukov. They are deciding things now in Moscow. So wait for a new order."

All eyes of the group were on Popel. "We have been ordered to hang on," he announced. "We are not the only clever ones to be found. Andrei Lavrentevich (Getman) rather lost his nerve for nothing."

"Don't waste your sympathy," Getman replied.[86]

In the beginning of February 1945, a serious threat to the Red Army's advance did, indeed, develop from the East Pomeranian German forces. Against this threat, General Rokossovskii's 2nd Belorussian Front conducted an operation which began on 1 March. The offensive quickly ran into trouble not only from undeveloped roads but also a lack of tanks.

On 8 March, Stalin telephoned General Katukov. Stalin was especially interested in the condition of the 1st Guards Tank Army's tank inventory. Katukov reported that he had nearly 400 tanks operating, but nearly all had used up their motor hours, many greater than 1000 kilometers. In conclusion, Stalin gave his purpose for the inquiry.

"Even so, help Rokossovskii. You consider and do everything you can."[87]

Katukov's tank army turned 90 degrees to the north to help Marshal Rokossovskii. By afternoon on 8 March, Katukov was at the staff of the 2nd Belorussian Front to help in the operation. In a short diversion from the drive on Berlin, the 1st Guards Tank Army supported the Front's elimination of the German resistance in Eastern Pomerania. The tank army finished their support in the operation by the 28-29 March, and reverted back to First Belorussian Front's control.

In the course of the offensive during January-February, Katukov centralized the army's maintenance support with a hierarchy of maintenance responsibilities from the brigade and corps maintenance facilities back to the army. As a result, on 1 February, of the 758 authorized tanks and self-propelled assault guns, 577 (76%) were fighting.[88]

In the first part of April 1945, Katukov paid a visit to the Army Tank Repair and Maintenance Battalion. This unit operated under the direction of Major General Pavel Grigorevich Dyner, known as the "Tank Doctor." Dyner had risen right along with Katukov from the brigade, corps and then the tank army. There were times at the end of an operation when the tank army had few tanks left for action. Right under enemy fire, crews belonging to the Dyner repaired damaged combat vehicles. His mechanics saved enough tanks to equip more than one tank army.

Over the past months, Katukov had visited the combat units and had neglected the rear service support units, such as Dyner's. Dyner wanted the commander to notice the work being done, "For the past three months, from January our tanks have covered a combat course of more than 2,000 kilometers, and they have surpassed the guarantee norms of the life of the machine by two and half times, which is to say the Army repair units, in fact, have presented the army with a whole tank corps," observed Popel.

Walking through the repair shops, Katukov addressed the men briefly. "We came with a member of the Military Soviet to see with our own eyes whether it would be possible for the army to receive in this very short time, the combat machines for the blow against Berlin. By your labors you are freeing masses of transport which are coming to and from the front, and you are enabling the rear factories to supply the army reserves with new tanks. The main thing is this: you are saving valuable time for the preparations of our blow against Berlin. Can we rely on you so that at the beginning of the offensive units of our army will be able to move forward and the tanks will be able to move right up to Berlin?"[89] The speech brought a shout of affirmation from the workers.

After the East Pomeranian operation, the 1st Guards Tank Army returned to the 1st Belorussian Front and began movement towards

Berlin. Marshal Zhukov, commander of the 1st Belorussian Front, briefed his senior army commanders on the Berlin operation. Zhukov anxious to lead the Red Army into Berlin, identified specific buildings for capture on a detailed relief map of Berlin copied from reconnaissance, photographs, captured documents and interrogation of prisoners.[90] The nearly 1000 square kilometers of the city had been prepared for determined resistance, using tank turrets sunk in concrete, firing positions in brick buildings, road blocks made from streetcars filled with rubble. The terrain around Berlin, dense with forest, marsh, rivers and canals, was difficult maneuvering for tanks. In the operation, the 1st Guards Tank Army would be committed through the 8th Guards Army.

Katukov gave his combat briefing for the Berlin operation on 6 April. On the walls were maps of the forthcoming offensive. The attention of the commanders of all formations and the chiefs of the political sections was drawn to them. Three red bunches of arrows streaked across the center of the broad expanse. To the north the arrows split the front and pierced the depths of German territory. The Stavka had ordered Marshal Rokossovskii to destroy everything in the way of resistance which would be encountered between the sea and Berlin. Marshal Konev's Front was to cover Berlin from the south illustrated by a bunch of smaller arrows pointing forward towards the Elbe. But, the main blow was to be mounted from the center where Zhukov's 1st Belorussian Front operated. This was the Kustrin bridgehead, where five powerful arrows concentrated. The whole area was covered with red. The arrows then moved forward for a short distance into the German headquarters and then they were absorbed into solid black geometrics of the city itself. In the spaces between the main attacks by the 1st Belorussian and 1st Ukrainian Fronts remained a small area which was surrounded by red arrows. This encirclement trapped the 3rd Field and 4th Panzer Armies of the Germans.

Standing by the map Katukov reported, "There is no great depth, but do not forget about raids. Raids have become the history of the 1st Tank Army. But now we have got to learn to fight a new way. The time for the preparation of the operation is short, events are heating up. We won't have the blessings of former days when we had 40 to 60 days to prepare for the operations. Nine days to prepare and that's all! Our assignment will be to secure the 8th Guards Army of Vasilii Chuikov – you know them...."

Katukov continued, "Our formations will go into the offensive after the breakthrough by Chuikov's (army) of the main enemy defense zone. His army will tear a sector which will be 8 or 9 kilometers wide. We know that Chuikov's army will have up to 42 tanks for each kilometers of breakthrough sector. The main thing is that we should, as quickly as possible, sew up the Berlin garrison and not give them any possibility of organizing a defense in their last defensive line. And then on the second day we will move forward." Katukov checked himself and then he thought and said, "No, not move forward – we will break into Berlin!"

"Let us now prepare the breakthrough," he began assigning the corps their tasks. The corps commanders had questions, the usual for a raiding army, such as organization of forward detachments. Who would lead the tank army into Berlin was a question of honor earned.

In conclusion, Katukov sketched out a general map of preparations for the operation, "In the Berlin operation three of our fronts will be taking part, that is, for example, half a million men, forty thousand guns and mortars, six thousand tanks, seven thousand aircraft...." each figure was greeted with cheers from the group.

Eager for the offensive to begin, Katukov was still grateful for the slight delay. His men needed the rest, and his maintenance crews needed a chance to repair the armored vehicles.

At 0500 hours, Moscow time, and 0300 hours, Berlin time, the 1st Belorussian Front offensive began on 16 April. The 11th Tank Corps which had been assigned to the 1st Guards Tank Army was deployed in the Kustrin bridgehead. The corps was to be sent in earlier to support and secure the general movement of the tank army. Katukov went forward into the Oder bridgehead to look over the routes his army would take to pass through the 8th Guards Army. All the roads were congested and blocked. "Damned roads," Katukov swore. "Snow today, rain tomorrow, and so for all week. Muddy, as in the Carpathians... No driving, only slipping..."

Katukov went to see General V.I. Chuikov, hero of the defense of Stalingrad and commander of the 8th Guards Army.

"Chuikov paced up and down the dug-out. He was clearly nervous," Katukov recalled.

"Well, how's the penetration? You will make it in time?" Katukov asked.

"Penetration, penetration..." the army commander bit his lower lip. "It's unlikely form the march you'll go around these four hills. You can see, what the Germans have built there."[91]

General returned to his table and showed Katukov aerial photographs of the German entrenchments on the Seelow Heights. The heights were a sandy escarpment varying from 100 to 200 feet above the Oder river valley floor. An in-depth German defense incorporated interlocking strongpoints with deadly crossfires, natural terrain obstacles combined with tank ditches and minefields. Accurate German artillery fire pinned down Chuikov's guardsmen.

What Chuikov recalled of Katukov's visit to his command post was Katukov's medals and awards displayed on his tunic. Chuikov wondered if he was on parade or in combat.[92]

Katukov's tanks failed to improve the situation, they milled around in the swampy lowlands becoming road bound and creating great traffic jams. Delays in positioning the forces caused confusion in the tactical units preparing for the assault.

On instructions from Marshal Zhukov the storming of the heights must begin that night. The tank army's forward detachments on 16 April, crossed the Oder river in the Kustrin bridgehead. Katukov and Popel watched the tanks of the army moving up to the front. As the lead tank passed, on its side was written names of its advance: Bridgehead Zero, Muenchenberg, Berlin and Reichstag. Although some of the tanks had two words, Moscow-Berlin, Katukov observed, "that's not a combat vehicle, that's more like a moving advertisement platform."

Later in the evening of 16 April, General Shalin, chief of staff, reported that in spite of the continuous attacks of the infantry and tanks, the army had simply not succeeded in taking the Seelow Heights. A report from the officer leading the 65th Guards Tank Brigade on the Seelow Heights indicated the Russians were getting nowhere. "we are standing on the heels of the infantry," General Ivan Yushchuk, commander 11th Tank Corps, had told Katukov. "We are stuck on our noses!"[93] The Front commander's mission for the day had not been fulfilled. The 8th Guards Army had control of only part of the Seelow Heights, and the tank army was bogged down.

Katukov, tunic collar unbuttoned, drew in his breath. "I have never seen such resistance in the whole course of the war. These Hitlerite devils are standing and fighting! We have been ordered to press on with the offensive day and night, to drive forward, tanking no account of anything! We have to go and take a look at the troops."[94]

Pressure rolled down the chain of command.

Early morning, 17 April, Chuikov and Katukov appeared in the command post of the forward rifle corps of the 8th Guards Army. Also in the command post was Babadzhanyan, commander of the llth Guards Tank Corps. While Chuikov screamed at his corps commander, Katukov merely said to his corps commander, "You are doing nothing here, speed up the force – orders must be fulfilled on time!"

Babadzhanyan thought, "Yes, orders are orders. In operational-tactical matters tactical commanders apparently are not to contradict him. Such is the nature of military art." Babadzhanyan's remark in his post-war memoir about this incident indicates his estrangement with Katukov.[95] Katukov's personal handling of corps commanders had been apparently too harsh on more than one occasion. Judging people as good and bad, Katukov corrected individuals in front of others creating tension in relationships caused by his being, at times, unnecessarily critical and denigrating.

On the 17th, the tank corps' forward brigades were fighting with the infantry units to push through the Seelow Heights. The following day, the battle reached a high pitch, with the tank army advancing no more than four kilometers each day. Under terrific pressure to advance, the Front commander, Zhukov, demanded immediate reports on the situation from the forward tank units.

The fight on 18 April resulted in heavy casualties. The bulk of the 1st Guards Tank Army crawled behind infantry. Strong resistance held up the tankers advance on the northern edge of the heights for two days. Katukov relied heavily on his supporting aviation corps. When he received reports from corps and brigade commanders on German strongpoints, he passed them to the air corps commander so his air crews could quickly fly to the "hot point." "This was very effective support," Katukov recalled.[96]

The 1st Guards Tank Army staff was located in a small dark home in the northern suburbs of Sellow itself. Around a table sat General Shalin; on the side, Katukov held a telephone receiver in his hand. His head seemed to be resting on his chest, and from time to time he would make remarks like, "Yes I received your message – understood."

One of the signals which came through was from Marshal Zhukov, "Where is Popel?"

"Out with the troops," Katukov replied.

Shalin turned to Popel as he arrived in the command post, "Kirillovich, the Marshal is calling for you." It took Popel nearly twenty minutes to get back through to Zhukov.[97]

According to Zhukov's information at this point the 11th Tank Corps was about 20 kilometers west of Seelow. At the end of the conversation, Zhukov gave Popel a personal order. He was to go at once to Yushchuk's (11th Tank) corps and there organize the redeployment of the entire army. Zhukov was putting pressure on Katukov by working through his political officer.

First, Popel had to find Yushchuk's actual location. General Popel did not want to ring Marshal Zhukov once again and ask him where to find the corps. So, he contacted the corps' forward brigade commander, who connected Popel with the corps commander by radio. That night Popel was able to report that he had fulfilled his assignment, after which he returned to the army headquarters.

Late evening on the 20th of April, the army staff received a message from Zhukov: "Katukov, Popel

1st Guards Tank Army is entrusted with the historic mission to be the first to break into Berlin and raise the victory banner. We entrust you personally to organize the execution. You are to dispatch from each corps its best brigade to Berlin and assign them the mission at any cost to penetrate the outskirts of Berlin not later than 0400 hours the morning of 21 April. Zhukov, Telegin."[98]

A similar message was sent to the 2nd Guards Tank Army. In response to the Front's instructions, the 1st and 44th Tank Brigades were dispatched to aggressively move toward Berlin. In turn the pressure was passed to subordinate commanders. Lead units of the 8th Guards Mechanized Corps reached the outlying town of Marzhan, and late on 22 April began to battle for Berlin. With anti-tank fire from doors, streets, alleys, and barricades and mines, the city fight was slow.

"You have a call from "Top", comrade General, reported the radio operator. General Dremov took the receiver and heard the displeased voice of the army commander,

"Report your situation."

General Dremov's excuses angered Katukov who did not want to hear them. Only when Dremov asserted that the assigned mission would be fulfilled, Katukov seemed soothed and directed, "You execute and don't lose your combat reputation, Major General."[99] The command pressures in combat can be psychologically brutal.

At 2300 hours on 24 April, the commander of the tank army's motorcycle regiment sent the following message, "have reached suburbs of Teltov. On canal have met tank unit of Rybalko." Shalin had received this report from units of the tank army. He said, "Excellent, the 1st Ukrainian Front has reached Berlin." This information was immediately transmitted to the Front commander.

With a certain amount of disbelief, Marshal Zhukov asked, "Is this report reliable?"

"We are reporting on the basis of the combat report of the regimental commander," General Shalin replied.

Marshal Zhukov sent the following message: "Members of the Military Council will personally go to the forward detachments and ascertain who, in fact, actually reached the line of the Teltov Canal."[100] In compliance with Zhukov's directive, Generals Popel, Getman and Colonel Sobolev went to the front line and met a tank commander who took them to Colonel General Pavel Semenovich Rybalko.

General Rybalko took them to his observation post which was situated on the roof of a six-story building, and there he showed them the layout of the Teltov Canal. Rybalko added, "And this is only one piece of good news for you. I have been talking with General Lelyushenko. He has just reached Potsdam. There he has managed to link up with the forward units of the 61st Army and the Polish Army."

"Well, how long have you been here?' Popel asked, remembering his mission from Marshal Zhukov.

"We got to the Teltov Canal yesterday evening," Rybalko replied.[101]

Popel made his report to Marshal Zhukov.

"I gave a personal order that you were to take the airfield. Have you done this?" Zhukov asked.

"Certainly."

"And you've taken the pilots prisoner?"

"Certainly, they've been taken prisoner Comrade Marshal. Operations are proceeding," Popel answered.

"Then, this means that we were the first there?!" Zhukov concluded.

"Comrade Marshal," Popel did not want to shade the truth of the report, "in truth, those were only small detachments, but Rybalko had been there since the 23rd of April. He had broken through on a broad front of some ten kilometers and had seized the bridgehead on the northern bank of the Teltov Canal."[102]

The delay in fighting through the Seelow Heights precluded Katukov's tank army being the first in Berlin. General Rybalko's 3rd Guards Tank Army, lst Ukrainian Front, penetrated Berlin from the south, much to Marshal Zhukov's dismay.

Still, Katukov's tankers encountered serious fighting in Berlin. Their tactic was to have three tanks moving in a line, the first tank moved to the left, the second moved to the right and the third tank drove straight forward. The tank that had moved to the left directed its fire to the right, the tank that had moved right directed its fire to the left, and the tank that moved forward covered for both. Using a reserve of up to ten tanks behind the lead three tanks, the small unit commander could replace one of the three tanks if they were knocked out. The heaviest fighting encountered was by the railway station and the Brandenburg Gate near the Reichstag.

As the lst Guards Tank Army moved into Berlin, the tank army had the objective to capture the Reich's Chancellery. On the morning of 1 May, Popel called Telegin, and reported that the army had captured the Zoological Gardens. The tank army was within 200 meters of the Chancellery. On the radio Moscow held its May Day parade in Red Square, Popel recalled, "And, we were located in the enemy's capital, 1000 kilometers from the Motherland."[103] Katukov's army, on 2 May, took nearly 15,000 prisoners. Berlin capitulated.

Katukov developed a very specific command style during the war years. Working often from his main command post, he constantly directed his staff. He always listened with great attention to the staff officers, assessing their work and not discounting their practical opinions, used his staff in a war council fashion. While he could be decisive when the occasion called for it, Katukov preferred to allow his staff to make their studies and provide their recommended courses of action.

A conservative risk-taker, Katukov earned the reputation of being a careful, cautious commander who always worked out plans, weighing the consequence of an operation trying to see the practical results before committing a single tank from his reserve. This cautiousness was particularly true in the early days, as he developed his skills in combat. He preferred the enemy coming after him on his terms and known ground. Katukov liked controlling events, and enjoyed stabilizing situations. He quickly grasped that Soviet tanks were able to concentrate for a tactical advantage due to the superior mobility of their tanks. Later, as a corps and army commander, he sought ways to avoid the massed and mindless direct approach to tactical and operational problems. He would rather pick the lock than wield the sledgehammer. Katukov liked the use of forward detachments in raid to predetermine situations and preempt enemy actions.

Katukov's leadership style and the use of his staff makes him a good example for the collective approach encouraged by the Soviet military's ideal for command. In the war from the first to the last days, Katukov often at the spearpoint of an operation expertly led the armored guards against the masters of armored warfare and won.

NOTES

1. I.F. Dremov, *Nastupala groznaya bronya*, Kiev, Politicheskoi Literatury, 1981, p. 13.

2. M.E. Katukov, *Na ostrie glavnogo udara*, Moscow, Voenizdat, 1976, p. 11.

3. K.K. Rokossovskii, *A Soldier's Duty*, Moscow, Progress, 1985, p. 19.

4. Franz Halder, *The Halder Diaries: The Private War Journals of Colonel General Franz Halder*, Boulder, Colorado, Westview, 1976, p. 173.

5. Ibid., pp. 175-76.

6. Katukov, p. 22.

7. Ibid., p. 23.

8. A.A. Vetrov, *Tak i bylo*, Moscow, Voenizdat, 1982, p. 51.

9. A. Raftopullo, *V atake "tridtsat'chtverki,"* Saratov, Privolzhskoe Knizhnoe Izdatel'stvo, 1973, p. 14.

10. Katukov, p. 20.

11. Raftopullo, p. 39.

12. Ibid., p. 42.

13. Heinz Guderian, *Panzer Leader*, London, Futura, 1974, p. 234.

14. Ibid., p. 235.

15. M.V. Zakharov, editor, *Proval: Gitlerovskogo nastupleniya na Moskvu*, Moscow, Nauka, 1966, p. 179.

16. Katukov, pp. 58-59.

17. Ibid., p. 58.

18. F. Tamonov, "Primenenie bronetankovykh voisk v bitve pod Moskvoi," *Voenno istoricheskii zhurnal* (hereafter *Vizh*), 1-1967, p. 18.

19. Katukov, pp. 100-101.

20. Ibid., p. 30.

21. Ibid., pp. 106-107.

22. L.M. Sandalov, *Na Moskovskom napravlenii*, Msocow, Nauka, 1970, p. 264.

23. Yuri Zhukov, "The Birth of the Tank Guards," *Moscow-Stalingrad: Recollections, Stories, Reports*, Moscow, Progress, 1974, p. 252.

24. O.A. Losik, *Stroitel'stvo i boevoe primenenie sovetskikh tankovykh voisk v gody Velikoi Otechestvennoi*, Moscow, Voenizdat, 1979, p. 114.

25. Katukov, p. 144.

26. M. Kazakov, "Na voronezhskom napravlenii letom 1942 goda," *Vizh*, 10-1964, p. 34. General Kazakov, at the time, was Chief of Staff of the Bryansk Front.

27. Ibid., pp. 34-35.

28. M.I. Kazakov, *Nad Kartoi bylykh srazhenii*, Moscow, Voenizdat, 1971, p. 104.

29. M. Kazakov, p. 38.

30. Katukov, p. 160.

31. Raymond L. Garthoff, *Soviet Military Doctrine*, Glencoe, Illinois, 1953, p. 310.

32. Katukov, pp. 172-73.

33. N.K. Popel, *V tryazhkuyu poru*, Moscow, Voenizdat, 1959, p. 334.

34. A.Kh. Babadzhanyan, *Dorogi Pobedy*, Moscow, Voenizdat, 1981, p. 96.

35. D.A. Dragunskii, *Gody v brone*, Moscow, Voenizdat, 1975, p. 87.

36. Ibid., p. 85.

37. N.K. Popel, *V peredi Berlin!*, Moscow, DOSAAF, 1970, pp. 17-18.

38. Ibid., p. 189.

39. N.K. Popel, *Tank povernuli na zapad*, Moscow, Voenizdat, 1960, p. 37.

40. Katukov, p. 189.

41. I.M. Anan'ev, *Tankovye armii v nastuplenii*, Moscow, Voenizdat, 1988, p. 65.

42. Katukov, p. 193.

43. Popel, *Tanki...zapad*, p. 108.

44. Ibid., p. 109.

45. Ibid., pp. 116-117.

46. Katukov, p. 219.

47. Ibid., p. 220.

48. Popel, *Tanki...zapad*, pp. 116-117.

49. P.A. Rotmistrov, *Stal'naya gvardiya*, Moscow, Voenizdat, 1984, pp. 204-5.

50. Katukov, p. 226.

51. Ibid.

52. Ibid., p. 232.

53. A.L. Getman, *Tanki idut na Berlin*, Moscow, Nauka, 1973, p. 99.

54. I.M. Kravchenko, V.V. Burkov, *Desyatyi tankovyi Dneprovskii*, Moscow, Voenizdat, 1986, p. 80.

55. Popel, *Tanki...zapad*, p. 156.

56. A.I. Radzievskii, *Tankoyi udar*, Moscow, Voenizdat, 1977, p. 221.

57. Rotmistrov, pp. 209-210.

58. A.S. Zhadov, *Chetyre goda voiny*, Moscow, Voenizdat, 1978, p. 103.

59. Ibid.

60. Katukov, p. 244.

61. Anan'ev, p. 275.

62. I.M. Chistyakov, *Sluzhim otchizne*, Moscow, Voenizdat, 1985, p. 163.

63. Radzievskii, p. 213.

64. Ibid.

65. S.M. Shtemenko, *The Soviet General Staff at War*, Book 1, Moscow, Progress, 1985, p. 248.

66. Anan'ev, p. 127.

67. Katukov, p. 273.

68. I.I. Yakubovskii, *Zemlya v ogne*, Moscow, Voenizdat, 1975, p. 299.

69. Katukov, p. 275.

70. Getman, p. 146.

71. Babadzhanyan, p. 162.

72. R. Portugal'skii, "Postanovka(dovedenie) zadach voiskom v nastupatel'noi operatsii obshchevoiskovoi (tankovoi) armii," *Vizh,* 12-1975, p. 14.

73. Dremov, p. 63.

74. A.Kh. Babadzhanyan, et al, *Lyuki otkryli v Berline,* Moscow, Voenizdat, 1973, p. 133.

75. Popel, Tanki...zapad, p. 314.

76. Ibid., pp. 296-297.

77. A. Dement'ev, S. Petrov, "Izmenenie obstanovki i novoe reshenie," *Vizh* 7-1978, p. 32.

78. Anan'ev, p. 203.

79. Dremov, p. 97.

80. Popel, Berlin, p. 42.

81. Katukov, p. 344.

82. Ibid., p. 345.

83. Popel, Berlin, p. 240.

84. Ibid., p. 269.

85 Ibid.

86. Ibid., p. 270.

87. Babadzhanyan, et al, p. 280.

88. P.P. Tovstukha, R.M. *Portugal'skii, Upravlenie voiskami v nastuplenii,* Moscow, Voenizdat, 1981, p. 169.

89. Popel, Berlin, pp. 288-89.

90. Cornelius Ryan, *The Last Battle,* New York, Simon and Shuster, 1966, p. 302.

91. Katukov, p. 394.

92. V.I. Chuikov, *Ot Stalingrada do Berlino,* Moscow, Sovetskaya Rossiya, 1985, p. 528.

93. Ryan, p. 368.

94. Popel, Berlin, p. 301.

95. Babadzhanyan, p. 285.

96. Katukov, p. 399.

97. Popel, Berlin, p. 305.

98. Katukov, p. 401; Popel, Berlin, p. 315.

99. Dremov, p. 149.

100. Popel, Berlin, p. 325.

101. Ibid., p. 326.

102. Ibid., p. 328.

103. Ibid., p. 359.

CHAPTER II

BOGDANOV

O
ne of the first Red Army tank commanders to fight the Germans, Colonel Semen Il'ich Bogdanov led his 30th Tank Division into unequal armored battles on 22 June 1941. On the war's first day located well forward near the Soviet border in Belorussia, Bogdanov's unit lay astride the main invasion path for the strong, mailed striking fist of the German Army, Panzer Group Guderian. Within a kaleidoscope of fast moving events, the wargames of his unit's field training exercises turned into deadly serious combat duels. Bogdanov would survive his initial catastrophic encounters with Germany's leading tank commander, the famed German General Heinz Guderian, to eventually lead a tank army on German soil for the capture of Berlin in the last days of the war.

Semen Il'ich was born 29 August 1894, in Petersburg, to a worker's family – a fact of circumstance that may have saved his life in later years during Stalin's purges. At the age of 12, he went to work in the legendary Putilov Works, Russia's largest and most important military and industrial enterprise. In these gigantic works where approximately 30,000 men and women labored in arms production and shipbuilding, he began as an apprentice metal worker, and later worked as a fitter. The Putilov workers rebelling against working conditions and the First World War became a source of revolutionary manpower for Tsarist Russia's revolutions.

In 1915, Bogdanov caught in the large conscriptive net for the Great War served in the Tsar's Russian Army, performing its hardest service in the infantry. He first entered as a private, and, in 1917, became an officer in the first platoon, first company of the elite Life

Semen Il'ich Bogdanov

Guards Semenovskii Regiment.[1] The Semenovskii Guards, which had crushed an armed workers' uprising in 1905, marched in July 1917 in support of the revolution against the Tsar, carrying young Bogdanov toward the Bolshevik regime. He would realize the old Tsarist Army saying, "He's a bad private who doesn't see himself a general." After the revolution, this adage became a real possibility in the Red Army, not a soldier's dream.

In 1918, during the Russian Civil War that followed on the heels of the First World War, Bogdanov joined the Red Army. Commanding a platoon, company, and finally battalion, he fought against the White Guards and the Bolshevik labeled bandit, Antonov. For his courage and bravery while commanding a company in the Western Front against the Polish Army, he received the Order of the Red Banner in 1920, solidifying his loyalty and position in the Workers-Peasants Red Army. In July 1920, he received a serious wound in battle, and he had to be hospitalized.

After the Civil War, Bogdanov commanded the 134th Rifle Regiment in the 45th Rifle Division, then a newly formed mechanized training regiment. His early association with mechanized and light tank brigades moved into the Red Army's new branch of armored and mechanized troops. In 1930, he completed the "Vystrel"(the Shot), a school with course in tactics and gunnery, designed for tactical leadership at the battalion and regimental levels, and in 1936, he graduated from a commander's course for mechanized and motorized forces. Schools bored Bogdanov, he was impatient with theory and attended fewer courses than his contemporaries. Very early the calm, deliberate young officer thrived on action. Among the first in the new, and somewhat experimental, armor branch, Bogdanov commanded a tank regiment and then a tank brigade.

In January 1937, Bogdanov received orders that designated him commander of the 9th Mechanized Brigade, which was located in the Leningrad military district.

Later in 1937, his successful career became interrupted by a gruesome wave of terror. Stalin turned from his purging of political opposition to the military leadership. In a crippling sweep more devastating than any defeat in a national war, the mass repression from 1937-39 befell a staggering number of promising Soviet officers who succumbed in the purges. The following tally represents those imprisoned or executed: 231 brigade commanders out of 397, 136 divisional commanders out of 199, 60 corps commanders out of 67, 14 army commanders out of 16, and 3 marshals out of 5 (M.N. Tukhachevskii, V.K. Blyukher, and A.I. Yegorov).[2]

The greatest numerical loss was borne in the Red Army officer corps from the rank of colonel and below, extending in some cases to company commanders. An estimated 30,000-35,000 officers were caught in the tragedy. The bulk of these were imprisoned rather than executed. While there is no discernible pattern, the accused were charged as "fascist spies," ex-tsarist officers and noncommissioned officers, or implicated for vouching for a senior or fellow officer already accused. The accused officers were summoned for a review of their case by the State Security organs. Bogdanov's plight was no different for the rest who were dragged off after interrogation, tortured and sent to rot in a Siberian forced labor camp.

After a poor military performance in Poland and an operational fiasco in Finland, the Red Army required immediate measures to restore and strengthened command, discipline and combat readiness. Many of the new commanders was too young and too inexperienced for the rigors of command in high positions. The Communist leadership was forced to return to the Siberian labor camps for experienced military leaders. More than one-quarter of the total number of repressed commanders and political workers were considered "rehabilitated" and released prior to the German invasion.[3]

On the eve of the Great Patriotic War, Bogdanov, who survived the labor camp, returned and endured a final review and assessment of his case.[4] He rested and gained his health back as commander of the 30th Tank Division in the 14th Mechanized Corps, assigned to the 4th Army on the frontier borders in Belorussia. From February to April 1941, the 14th Mechanized Corps, as part of the Red Army's decision to rebuild the large armored forces for independent border operations, began to reorganize its units, receiving new equipment, combat vehicles, and personnel. The 30th Tank Division was organized around the nucleus of the 32nd Separate Tank Brigade near the town of Pruzhany.[5] The 14th Mechanized Corps had only old model light tank, T-26, and the obsolete T-38 tank. The field and antitank guns, as well as tanks, had only a small amount of armor piercing shells in their basic ammunition loads.

In early spring 1941, the 4th Army Staff summoned division commanders, chiefs of staffs, and chiefs of operations and signals to its headquarters in Kobrin for an important, secret conference. For several days the gathering worked alert plans for the divisions, including orders for assembly areas, communication networks, and instructions for divisional duty officers in the event of a combat alert. The secrecy of the planning was so tightly controlled that even regimental and battalion commanders were prohibited from studying the contents of the plan. The pre-positioning of command posts, of particular concern for the signal chiefs, was also not permitted.

The German invasion on 22 June 1941, caught the Red Army's mechanized corps in the midst of a major reorganization effort, with tragic consequences for these armored formations. A major miscalculation on war with Germany by the Soviet leadership is evident in the mistake of constituting and reconstituting these powerful units in the frontier districts. With the German invasion, these ill-equipped and untrained formations were incapable of sustained fighting.

Bogdanov's division more fortunate than other units had its fuel supplies stored in Slobodka, six kilometers from his assembly area. His food supplies were nearby in Pruzhany. The division's ammunition load consisted of one unit of fire per combat vehicle while two more were in dumps at Slobodka. This was a logistical disposition better than most tank units on the frontier borders. Many units within a week of the invasion had been ordered to place their on-board basic loads in nearby storage dumps.

Despite reports from 4th Army and other forward border units on German ground force movements and aircraft intrusions, the Red

Army higher command failed to place its units in a higher state of readiness. On 21 June, Bogdanov's division conducted field training exercises southwest of Pruzhany. The 4th Army Chief of Staff, General Leonid Mikhailovich Sandalov, viewing the unit training observed, "Even with a superficial acquaintance with the regiment, I was at once struck by the weakness of its preparedness. The battalions and companies operated with no coordination, tanks became confused on the course and often stopped to determine their location."[6]

Tank crews composed mostly of new recruits explained the poor performance. The few experienced tankers occupied key leadership positions: tank commanders became platoon leaders, driver-mechanics became assistant company commanders for maintenance. Regimental staffs were in fact glorified battalion staffs. In the highly technical and complicated business of armored warfare, too few soldiers and leaders had mastered their individually required skills or basic job tasks. Standard operating procedures for the tactical units was haphazard. The army in addition to enduring catastrophic purges suffered years of theoretical, organizational and personnel turbulence. And, the effect of the long series of misjudgments were obvious to a casual observer.

Colonel Bogadnov, accompanying the Chief of Staff, complained that the division possessed obsolete and worn-out tanks. Half the tanks were only good for training. The majority were armed with 45mm guns, but a few still had only the 38mm gun or a machinegun. Bogdanov's unit like most in the hastily formed new mechanized corps, had light tanks, and the supply system held few repair parts to fix the old, broken vehicles. Motor pools held tanks rusting from neglect.

"By your report I can conclude that the tank division, which began as a weak tank brigade, still remains as such," General Sandalov noted.

"Between us, it is so," Bogdanov said confidingly. "If a bottle of wine is diluted with three bottles of water, this will also not be wine."[7]

At approximately 0200 hours during the early morning of 22 June, telephone lines were broken between the military district, army staff and combat units. With communications restored at 0330 hours, the 4th Army commander, Major General A.A. Korobkov, issued orders to the 14th Mechanized Corps. The orders alerting the troops were too late.

At 0400 hours, at first light, German artillery opened fire on the Soviet state's frontiers. At 0430 hours, 60 German bombers struck the airfield near Bogdanov's field exercise area. Nearly 75 per cent of the fighter regiment's aircraft were burned out, along with all the airfield equipment at Pruzhany.

Bogdanov's tank regiments spent the night after training in the woods southwest of Pruzhany, just 60 kilometers from the border. Despite the early spring planning by the army, the instructed actions failed to occur because the plan lacked reality and was never tested. Finally sounding the alarm at 0600 hours, Bogdanov's first tank regiment, acting as a forward detachment, moved an hour later. The mechanized corps liaison officer reported the division had one unit of fire and one load of fuel.[8] These "officers on wheels", as messengers, were the only reliable communications in the first days of the war. Bogdanov's tankers moved along deep, sandy tracks in the direction of Podubno arriving at 1100 hours. Russia's undeveloped roads determined not only the pace and advance of tank units but also the places for armored battles. Between 1200-1300 hours, Bogdanov's forward detachment engaged the advancing German 18th Panzer Division moving along the road near Pilishchi.

The Guderian's Panzer Group led by the famed Panzer leader, Heinz Guderian, tore into the Soviet frontier. Totaling 850 tanks, Guderian's Panzer Group consisted of the 24th Panzer Corps on the right wing, 12th Army Corps in the center, the 47th Panzer Corps on the left, and the 46th Panzer Corps in reserve. The 47th Panzer Corps, with the 17th and 18th Panzer, 29th Motorized, and 167th Infantry Divisions, opposed Bogdanov's unit. At 0415 hours 22 June 1941, the 17th and 18th Panzer Divisions, with specially-waterproofed diving tanks, led the German Army attack by fording the Western Bug river.[9] Eighty tanks necessary for the protection of the bridgehead crossed the frontier river under water.[10] Guderian noted their initial contact at Pruzhany in his memoirs, "...the 18th Panzer Division became involved in the first tank battle of the campaign."[11] Facing the German invaders in a seemingly solitary fight, Bogdanov had no technical communications with his higher headquarters. In fact, he had few of the modern invention, the radio, necessary to control his armored force's movement through the expanse of western Belorussia or to fight a rapid combat action. His division entered the fight with one basic load of ammunition and one supply of fuel. These were conditions under which no military leaders believes he will go to war. Bogdanov did not like the unfamiliar situation that he himself had not wrought.

Behind Bogdanov's forward elements, his second tank regiment and motorized rifle regiment with supporting units formed a smoking, rattling line of vehicles hastening down country tracks to war. Before the march, the division totaled 120-130 light tanks. But, after the march, the number of surviving tanks was significantly less, due to German air strikes.

Arriving by 1230 hours in Pilishchi after a 55 kilometer march, the division deployed and advanced with both tank regiments spearheading the attack. Ill-coordinated and without an artillery preparation, the attack lacked a synchronization of combat force which might have helped the light tanks. The Germans, sidestepping this aggressive counterattack, deflected Bogdanov's units, bypassing to the south. The first day's advance pleased General Guderian who wrote, "we had managed to take the enemy by surprise along the entire Panzer Group front."[12]

Although Bogdanov's division fought courageously on the Baranovichsk-Slutskiy axis, his unit barely slowed the onslaught of the superior forces of Guderian's tankers. The panzer group's tanks pressed on rapidly into the Soviet rear areas aiming for the capital of Belorussia, Minsk. From his observation post, Bogdanov viewed his tank regiments' battle against the German tanks and their accompanying artillery. His two tank regiments opposed two German panzer divisions. The battlefield strewn with charred and destroyed armored remnants were mostly Soviet light tanks. In those chaotic early days, tank commanders everywhere in the Red Army lamented the lack of new, more powerful Soviet tanks. Instead, they fought with older 45mm guns and the light tank's 15mm frontal armor against the German's 75mm guns and 40mm armor protection.[13] Even, the well controlled German fires from 37mm and 50mm anti-tank guns had little trouble penetrating the old, lightly armored Soviet tanks. In armored warfare, a decisive advantage in firepower and armor protection allows one to fight with greater impunity. The situation was virtually hopeless.

Offering dogged resistance, Bogdanov's unit conducting the most difficult of military operations, a withdrawal, fought to the east. By 0800 hours the next day, Bogdanov organized a defense at Pruzhany. Again, the slow, lightly armored tanks were little match against battle-proven German tanks and crews. Opposition from isolated groups of Red Army tanks manned by confused crews were easily put out of action by the German Mark III and IV tanks. The Soviet tankers now fought to slow the enemy advance and to breakout of potential encirclements. Bogdanov's division fought strongly and heroically to hold together a rapidly fragmenting front. The 17th Panzer Division began outflanking from the north near Kamenets. Bogdanov's division caught between two panzer divisions took the full brunt of their assault. Two hours later, Bogdanov's mismatched division was reduced to only 70 vehicles.[14] A half hour later, the 18th Panzer Division captured Pruzhany.

With the corps reserves, a motorized rifle unit, Bogdanov organized a desperate defense on the eastern edge of Pruzhany. Ineffective, dispersed tactics continued to frustrate a coherent defense. The army and corps commanders were unable to influence the fighting since they had no reserves. At midday, Bogdanov counterattacked unsuccessfully attempting to dislodge the Germans from the city. The day's fighting cost Bogdanov half his remaining tanks.

By 2000 hours, the flanks of the tank division were under attack. Unable to hold the Germans in Pruzhany, Bogdanov's division was pushed back from the Pruzhany-Slonim highway to the southeast. Before withdrawing, units of the 30th Tank Division refueled the vehicles and tanks at the district fuel dump in Orchanchitsy, then Colonel Bogdanov ordered the dump blown. His division, unable to stem the advance of the oncoming German forces, fell back to the east. Very low on ammunition, his tankers continued conducting the tough tactical maneuvers of a fighting withdrawal. Bogdanov read through the riddle of confusion on the battlefield and moved his units effectively. His ability to mentally match the pace of speeding German panzer units demonstrated a mind elastic enough to accept the new form of combat, armored warfare. In a war of rapid movement, combat leaders have little time to learn the lessons of their initial mistakes. Colonel Bogdanov demonstrated flexible command traits in these early tank battles. Not laden with rules of war, he was expedient, willing to troubleshoot. Despite the confusion, he was like a wolf in the woods, ready to be the predator, not the prey.

Bogdanov's unit waged a defensive fight from a succession of improvised positions. As the 4th Army's mobile group, the 14 Mechanized Corps stopped in vain to form another defensive line.

On 24 June, General Guderian had a close encounter with two of Bogdanov's tanks. Red tankers attempting to force their way into

Slonin spotted a group of German officers, which included Guderian, standing by a road junction. The tanks immediately fired at close range. The group of officers, deafened and blinded by the close firing hit the ground, and the tanks sped off towards Slonin, where they were eventually put out of action.[15] All Soviet armor was lost, reducing surviving tankers to fighting infantry.

On the morning of 26 June, Bogdanov's motorized regiment, after withdrawing 70 kilometers over four days, miraculously managed to hold the Germans on the approaches to Slutsk. His unit's heroic fight allowed the Army staff to withdraw out of the path of the German 24th Panzer Corps attack. But, Bogdanov's defense only slowed the Germans, and, by nightfall, his shrinking detachment fell back to another defensive line.

The following day, the German panzer group's leading tanks pressed forward, capturing Minsk. Many of the Soviet's armored formations across the front had been badly led and senselessly sacrificed, and by this time had ceased to exist. The remnants of Bogdanov's unit, only the cremated ashes of its former self, were combined with other parts of the 14th Mechanized Corps under its chief of staff. But, on 28 June, Bogdanov took command of the 14th Mechanized "detachment" from the fatally wounded chief of staff. He, again, withdrew, attempting to form a defense along the Berezina river.

Maintaining a pressure to break the Soviet forces, General Walther Model's 3rd Panzer Division, 24th Panzer Corps drove through Slutsk to cross the Berezina river on the way to Bobruisk. General Andrie Ivanovich Eremenko, who had assumed temporary command of the Red Army's Western Front, issued his first order, "...hold the line along the Berezina river...."[16] The stand along the Berezina was to gain time – the Soviets were fighting for time to regain their balance. But, the new Front commander failed to grasp fully the extent of the Red Army's disaster in the frontier battles.

With elements of General Model's 3rd Panzer Division reaching the river on the same day, Guderian believed "the foundation had been laid for the first great victory of the campaign," and ordered the 24th Panzer Corps to continue east towards Bobruisk.[17]

During the course of these early battles, outmanned, outgunned, and outequipped, Bogdanov demonstrated qualities necessary for a command of large tank units: firmness, decisiveness and persistence in accomplishing assigned missions. He rapidly and correctly assessed complex and often dramatically changing situations. Thorough and comprehensive in his analysis, he made the most appropriate decisions and effectively commanded his troops. Bogdanov's strongest trait was his ability to organize his thoughts with maximum brevity and clarity, and then precisely assign missions to his subordinates. A commander's ability to reduce battlefield confusion to simple prescriptive instructions has long been a hallmark of successful battle captains. Succinct timely orders are a prerequisite for the armored battlefield.

Bogdanov was a tall, trim, and impressively handsome man at the age of 47. In all of his actions, conversations and commands, one felt fierce demandingness, strong-will and self-discipline. After he made his decision and issued his orders, as a rule, he moved among the forces and commanded the battle with calm and confident authority. As a commander, he had everything – talent, energy, and confidence in his own powers.[18]

At this juncture in the war's maelstrom, Colonel Bogdanov temporarily fades from recorded Soviet military history in his country's chaotic struggle to survive. He works behind-the-scene positions, first on the staff of the Southwestern Front through August, then on an unknown assignment in the Moscow area. He briefly steps back into the foreground in the fall of 1941.

By the end of September, the German High Command and Army Group Center were prepared to resume their drive on Moscow with Operation Typhoon. The force at the disposal of Army Group Center consisted of 44 infantry divisions, 14 panzer divisions and one cavalry division. The general offensive opened on 2 October according to plan with a tactical surprise inflicted on the Soviets, cracking open the front in several places. The battle for Moscow had begun.

In early October, the danger of German tanks breaking into Moscow existed. The situation deteriorated to such an extent that Stalin recalled General Georgi Zhukov from Leningrad where the military situation was also bad. General Zhukov assumed command of the Western Front where his experience and infamous iron will would stabilize the disastrous military situation. Zhukov immediately undertook decisive measures for establishing firm control of the Front. Talented and experienced officers were placed in critical sectors.

On 5 October, the Mozhaisk defensive line, extending from Volokolamsk through Mozhaisk, had been selected by the Defense

Commissar as the place for a Red Army stand against the German Army advance on Moscow. The line was to be held by gathered forces transformed into the Moscow Reserve Front. Colonel Bogdanov, who commanded the Moscow district armor, assumed a special command, the Mozhaisk Fortified Region. The Mozhaisk defensive line was constructed by civilians without technical assistance or heavy equipment. The keystone to the defensive line was a makeshift strongpoint across the major highway to Moscow near Borodino, less than 120 kilometers from the Soviet capital. This was the historical battlefield for Russia's celebrated stance against Napoleon in 1812. Now, 132 years later, the Soviet High Command sought another battle on an invader's path to Moscow.

Late night on 5 October, Marshal Zhukov, as the Western Front commander, drove to the Mozhaisk sector to inspect the main defensive line for Moscow. He met the sector commandant, Colonel Bogdanov. He gave Bogdanov instructions to place artillery on all the road junctions on the west side of town. Bogdanov was to select brave artillery officers to command the positions and their mission was not to allow enemy tanks towards Moscow. In stern measures to stiffen the resolve of the defense, they were also not to allow the withdrawal of friendly forces.[19]

By 11 October, the troops on the Mozhaisk line had been combined into the 5th Army under the command of General Dmitri Danilovich Lelyushenko. Colonel Bogdanov, now deputy commander for the 5th Army, reported to his newly appointed commander. In accordance with Stavka orders forces redeployed urgently from the right wing of the Western Front, Northwestern Front, Southwestern Front, divisions arriving from the Far East and the Urals, and tank and artillery units from the Stavka reserve began to be funneled into the Mozhaisk line. Many of the units were marginally trained, no fully equipped. Bogdanov, who until recently had been the commander of the Mozhaisk line, grimly reported that the defenses were still unprepared. Evidently, the decision for constructing the fortified line had come late. A growing sense of alarm pervaded the defensive line efforts. While refugees moved east, a large number of women dug trenches for the defensive positions and antitank ditches. The Red Army employing its new Katyusha rockets batteries and T-34's in new tank brigades hoped to halt the German advance.

On 16 October, a cold fall day, Colonel Bogdanov beside General Lelyushenko in the army's observation post near the 32nd Rifle Division watched the battle unfold on the Borodino battlefield. German bombers continuously tossed their bomb loads along the defensive positions, and German tanks followed the bombardments. Towards evening, the German's 10th Panzer and SS "Das Reich" Motorized Infantry Divisions advanced in coordination with the attacking dive bombers. Approximately 30 tanks with supporting infantry broke through, heading straight for the Army observation post.

Occupants in the observation post quickly took up rifles and bottles of a gasoline mixture, the famous Molotov cocktails, and assumed fighting positions in the trenches. Bogdanov lay beside the Army commander. The German tanks approached them. At the moment of attack, while engaging the German infantry and tanks, General Lelyushenko received a serious wound that required his evacuation. Colonel Bogdanov assumed command of the battle.

General Zhukov and his political officer, Bulganin, arrived at the headquarters of the Mozhaisk Fortified Region. Bogdanov greeted them. Artillery fire and bomb explosions could be heard distinctly as the men conferred. Bogdanov reported that the 32nd Rifle Division, reinforced by artillery and a tank brigade, was locked in combat with advancing German mechanized and armor units on the approaches to Borodino. As part of the necessary instructions given to Bogdanov, General Zhukov ordered to hold his defensive sector at all cost. Bogdanov's handling of this grave situation gave him not only a huge responsibility but also the opportunity to come to the attention of the high command. Bogdanov understood glory, and he would communicate through actions – lead the charge with sword in hand.

Fortunately, the Mozhaisk Fortified Region offered a number of advantages to the Red Army units that held it. The defensive line was protected in front by the Lama, Moscow, Kolocha, Luzha, and Sukhodrev rivers, all of which had steep banks and offered natural obstacles to German armor movement. The line connected with a road and rail system that permitted quick and easy troop movements in all directions, maximizing interior lines of the defense. But a lack of troops to occupy the 136 mile long line plagued the desperate Red Army command. Again, Bogdanov, with poise and a strength of will, fought to hold a fragile line when the onslaught came.

While Bogdanov's forces bought time, General Zhukov formed

an antitank defense behind the Mozhaisk line to cover the near approaches to Moscow, a mere 60 miles away. The Red Army's last bit of reserves were expended to defend the capital. A pause ensued.

Despite the pause in the German Army's operations before Moscow, the Soviet's remained in a difficult position. The pause allowed the Soviet High Command to introduce troops reinforced with tank brigades, rocket launchers, and artillery. In mid-November the second stage of the fighting for Moscow began with German forces conducting major thrusts on the northwest and southern approaches to Moscow. By late November a major German attack at the central sector of the Western Front against the junction between the 5th and 33rd Armies. In the course of several days' fiery battle, the defenders managed to liquidate a breakthrough by German units.

On 5-6 December, the Red Army conducted a counteroffensive. The 5th Army, as with other attacking Soviet units, managed to achieve their immediate objectives and recover some of the occupied Soviet territory. During these operations in October through December, the 5th Army's commander for armored forces remarked on Bogdanov's manner under pressure. Even in the most critical minutes, he never saw on Bogdanov's face neither confusion nor dejection. He operated clearly and efficiently, and he was daring and decisive. Bogdanov, again, fades from visibility in history during the terribly strained winter fighting to surface in the spring.

The People's Defense Commissar Order, dated 9 May 1942, created the 12th Tank Corps. General Bogdanov, as the designated commander, formed and organized one of the Red Army's new tank corps. While the brigades had a large number of light tanks, T-60's and T-70's, the medium and heavy tanks, T-34's and KV's respectively, provided the unit's basic combat power. On 2 June, the corps was assigned to the 3rd Tank Army under the command of General Prokofii Logvinovich Romanenko and deputy commander General Pavel Semonovich Rybalko. By the end of June, the brigades with their full complement of tanks averaged between 35-40 T-34's and 5-10 KV' per brigade.

On the evening of 12 August 1942, Bogdanov was called to the army commander, who advised him that the army had been assigned to the Western Front. He was to assemble his corps in the area of Kozelsk in preparation for commitment to battle. Bogdanov returned to his unit in a heavy rain and told his chief of staff, "Finish our training, we're going to the front. Prepare orders...."[20] General

Bogdanov for the first time in the war was about to enter combat on somewhat favorable terms and on the offense.

The Soviets were reacting quickly to an offensive initiated by the German Army Group Center on 11 August. While the main effort for the German Army during the summer was the drive on Stalingrad, a strategy of slicing off a Soviet salient in the vicinity of Kozelsk and Kaluga would reopen the southwestern approach to Moscow. Such an approach concerned Stalin and Red Army High Command, since they believed that Moscow was the primary objective for the German Army.

The 3rd Tank Army moved rapidly from Tula to Kozelsk by a combination of transportation means. The total transfer made by the railroads during the period of 15-19 August was 75 echelons, primarily tanks brigades. Motorized and motorcycle units covered a distance of 120 kilometers in march formations in four days.

Bogdanov's tank corps participated in the Western Front's counterstrike against the German Second Panzer Army. On the evening of 19 August, General Bogdanov's 12th Tank Corps assembled in the area of Kozelsk. The 19th of August had been the original date for the offensive, but the late arrival of other 3rd Tank Army units delayed the attack 48 hours. During the night of 21 August, the tank corps moved to its attack positions on the line northeast of Gryn. Bogdanov commanded a mobile group consisting of one rifle division, one motorized rifle brigade, three tank brigades, three artillery regiments, and one Katyusha rocket unit.[22]

Bogdanov's mobile group was directed to attack on the axis of Ozerna, Gos'kovo, Sorokino, Obukhovo, and Staritsa. His immediate mission was to destroy the opposing German units, force the Vytebet river and seize a bridgehead on its western bank. In his sector were two German infantry regiments of the 26th Infantry Division and an artillery regiment. Bogdanov decided to strike the Germans along a narrow three kilometer sector in the assigned direction, having in the first echelon a rifle division and a motorized rifle brigade. In accordance with Bogdanov's plan the rifle unit would create a breach in the German defense. The tank brigades would be committed to the battle after the infantry achieved crossings over the Vytebet river. The tank brigades had the mission to develop the infantry's success, destroying German forces in the area of the objective towns.

The offensive began in the gray dawn light on 22 August, preceded by a very powerful 90 minute artillery preparation. At 0615 hours, the corps attacked. Within five hours the lead tank brigades quickly outdistanced the attacking rifle divisions, reaching the eastern portion of Gos'kovo. The next day, German reinforcements attempted to cut off the attacking forces, and a strong battle ensued. The first echelon rifle division of Bogdanov's group penetrated the German's defense to a depth of 4-5 kilometers. However, upon contact with the German's second defensive line, the slower rifle units, with no tank support of their own, came to a halt. The rifle division lacked the strength to drive the penetration any deeper.

The tank corps offered no support to the stalled infantry, since the previous day, the tankers received the assignment to prevent the German's withdrawal. In order to cut off the shattered German units pulling back from their front line of defense, the 12th Tank Corps moved in the new direction of Mizin and Durnovo. Reacting to their new assignment, the tank brigades moved hurriedly forward without any preliminary organization of route reconnaissance, and, as a result, stumbled into minefields and swampy sectors along the front. The attack had been "smooth on paper, but they forgot about the gullies", as a Russian military saying has it. The tankers soon lagged behind their supporting infantry.

Other problems in the hasty commitment of the tank brigades resulted from insufficient artillery support and a lack of the necessary air cover. The tank units suffered heavy losses from German airstrikes and artillery fire. By the end of 22 August, the tank brigades came out of the battle line without contact with German ground forces. Subsequently, the tanks executed a series of local security missions of both an independent nature and in support of the infantry, but gave no substantial results to the expansion of the operation, wasting a great deal of time and fuel in regrouping.[23]

On the night of 23-24 August, units of the 3rd Tank Army conducted a night attack. A sketchy plan that lacked detailed coordination and support doomed the effort. By dawn the next morning, the units, having suffered great losses, were pounded to a halt by German aircraft and artillery fire after a meager 1-2 kilometer advance.

Towards evening, Bogdanov's lead tanks stopped. In the course of the day's fighting, the 12th Tank Corps advanced a depth of 18-20 kilometers, but the tank corps' attack slowed with each hour. Heavy German air attacks and violent counterattacks by ground units forced part of Bogdanov's corps onto the defensive. The tank brigades attempted to continue the offensive in the direction of Sorokino but failed to gain ground. The army commander instructed the corps to hold its limit of advance and fortify its position. In the defense, the corps continuously suffered from intense German airstrikes.

The concept of the operation called for the commitment of the 12th Tank Corps to battle after the infantry divisions had breached the enemy front, destroy opposing German units and the nearest reserves, and cross the Vytebet river. Red Army after-action studies determined that this mission proved too much for the strength of the rifle division. Critical of the 3rd Tank Army command group, the study concluded that they completely overestimated the penetrating capabilities of the rifle division, especially in view of the established correlation of forces. The delayed commitment of Bogdanov's tank corps permitted the Germans to delay the rifle division and to organize a new defensive line.[24]

In most situations the tanks operated without any engineer support. Often the tankers bogged down at fords or in swamps, and suffered considerable losses in minefields. The operational employment of the tank corps was flawed. Soviet tank formations still needed air defense placed around the formation and coordinated support of air armies to break up the systematic air attacks by the German air force. Red Army tank commanders had much to learn about supporting mobile armored warfare. The agility of armored forces depends on their ability to move through the environment, hence the importance of reconnaissance, engineers, and air defense.

Much like the early disastrous battles against the German invasion in the previous summer, commanders and staffs at all levels needed to improve their command and control of forces. They lacked the ability to maneuver existing resources quickly, and husband some units in an economy of force while simultaneously exhausting the enemy. Despite the poor showing, Bogdanov, as a commander, acquired combat experience though at a high price in difficult battles. His lack of attention to detail cost him in early operations with large armored forces. He needed the support of a strong staff and chief of staff.

Once in combat, the observation posts of the 12th and 15 Tank Corps turned out to be side by side. A 15th Tank Corps political officer recalled his first meeting with Bogdanov under combat conditions. Tall and slender, Bogdanov gave the impression of an energetic, determined commander. Under German artillery fire, he behaved courageously, calmly, authoritatively giving out the necessary instructions, and firmly controlling his corps units.[25] A political officer within the 12th Tank Corps thought Bogdanov in battle was decisive and brave, even seemed excessive. Bogdanov believed his presence had a positive effect on the battlefield; he could reinforce the situation by inspiring and motivating his soldiers to acts of bravery. He possessed a charisma that led by example.

By the end of the month, Army Group Center and the Western Front were stalemated with the German forces holding their own, while Hitler drew off panzer units for other sectors. By mid-September, the 12th Tank Corps pulled back to Kaluga as a reserve to be repaired and refitted. Despite a later hard critique by the Red Army General Staff, the corps' actions received the praise of the high command, and a number of the officers and soldiers received awards and decorations for their brave fighting. In the same month, Bogdanov was recalled to the Main Armor Directorate in Moscow. Since the Stavka often used the experienced tank corps commanders to handle the formation of the more complex mechanized corps, General Bogdanov received reassignment to another command after the operation.

In November 1942, the Stavka directed the formation of the 6th Mechanized Corps from units of the 14th Tank Corps. The Red Army built fewer mechanized than tank corps because the mechanized corps required more of the precious few trucks – many of which were being provided by the United States under Lend-Lease while Soviet factories continued to produce tanks. Bogdanov was the designated commander.

In December 1942, the Germans began their operation "Winter Thunder" with the aim of breaking through the Red Army ring around the German 6th Army trapped in Stalingrad. On the morning of 12 December, German Hermann Hoth launched his relief force from Kotelnikovo on a 150 kilometer strike northeast towards the trapped 6th Army. General Hoth's force had the 6th Panzer Division fresh from France and the 23rd Panzer Division which possessed a battalion of new Tiger tanks, a 69-ton behemoth with an 88mm gun.

By 19 December, lead tank crews of the 6th Panzer Division could see flares fired on the Stalingrad perimeter. But they could not continue their advance across the steppe. Pressure from the Red Army was collapsing German units on all sides of the relief force. By Christmas day, Hoth's command was in full withdrawal.

In vicious and grueling combat for Stalingrad, Bogdanov continued to command the 6th Mechanized Corps and, in the month of December, took an active part in the destruction of the German Kotelnikovo grouping. During the Soviet counteroffensive around Stalingrad, the Southwestern Front establishing another encirclement ring sent Bogdanov's mechanized corps to the vicinity of Kotelnikovo.

At 0340 hours, 22 December 1942, Bogdanov received orders from General Rodion Yakovlevich Malinovskii, commander 2nd Guards Army, to move his corps to the Zety area on the night of the 24th. This move significantly reinforced the left flank of the 2nd Guards Army which was to attack in coordination with the 5th Shock and 51st Armies to eliminate the German Kotelnikovo grouping.

General Friedrich Wilhelm von Mellenthin, who fought in the sector, remembered, "On Christmas eve the Russians attacked in great force along the whole line."[26] While some of the German units held, others suffered heavy casualties and had to withdraw.

The 6th Mechanized Corps began the operation in the second echelon of the 2nd Guards Army. Assessing the situation, Bogdanov concluded that the corps' commitment to the fight had the best chance of success in the 13th Guards Rifle Corps sector. In plans to develop the attack, Bogdanov's corps could inflict a strike from the line Kapkinskii-Vasil'evka-Stalingrad railroad-Kotelnikov in the general direction of Gremyachaya. However, the German forces in the 13th Guards Rifle and 7th Tank Corps sectors put up a surprising resistance and repulsed the attack. The 2nd Guards Army Staff quickly found another sector within the army that permitted a successful advance. To capitalize on the favorable situation, the army commander decided to send Bogdanov's corps along the flank of the enemy Kotelnikovo grouping. Bogdanov received his mission: "6th Mechanized Corps at 2000 hours, 25 December, concentrate in the area of Aksai(40 km south of Zety), Peregruznyi, and on the morning of 26 December be prepared to attack in the direction of Gremyachaya, Zhutov. Forward of the river Aksai-Esaulovskii operates 13th Rifle Corps and along Rossosh' river, 126th Rifle Division, 51st Army."[27]

The course of the fighting rapidly changed the situation. On the morning of 26 December, Bogdanov received an adjusted order from General Malinovskii:

"Enemy forces 7th and 8th Cavalry Regiments, 5th Rumanian Cavalry Division and parts of the 8th Cavalry Division(Rumanian, reinforce with German units), approximately 15-20 antitank guns, one artillery regiment defend a well-prepared defense line Samohin-Zhutov.

The defense is echeloned in depth to 18-20 kilometers and has intermediate line along river Aksai-Kurmoryaskii.

6th Mechanized Corps operating in the general direction of Darganov, Kotelnikovo, inflict strike along Kotelnikovo grouping on flank from the east, cut off its withdrawal route to the southwest and by the end of 26 December seize Darganov. On the right attacks 13th Guards Rifle Corps, on the left, part of 51st Army."28

General von Mellenthin recalled in his memoirs that the Russians exploited every success. "The main effort of the attacking Russian armor was speedily switched from one point to another as the situation demanded. ...the tactical conduct of the battle by the Russians was on a high level."29

In minus 25 degree centigrade temperatures, Bogdanov's corps, in its first battle as a unit, overcame the right flank of the German forces, inflicting a strong flank attack. The combat situation, however, forced a change in the mechanized corps' direction of attack. This redirection increased the distance to the corps objective, Kotelnikovo, from 30-40 kilometers to 120 kilometers.

At 1100 hours on 26 December, the corps' brigades deployed for battle. In spite of the strong German fires from the forward edge and from the depth, they penetrated the German line, taking Samokhin by the end of the day, and continued pursuing German units toward the Aksai-Kurmoyskii river.

The next day, a quick skirmish flared with new German forces on the line Darganov-Sharnutovskii. Feeling threatened, the German command brought two infantry regiments up to the defensive line. At 0700 hours, all three mechanized brigades of Bogdanov's corps attacked. The Germans resisted strongly, but neither the strong fire, nor tenacious fighting by their soldiers, could stop the attack. In a few hours, the defense was breached, and Bogdanov's 55th Mechanized Brigade seized Darganov.

After finishing the battle for Darganov and Sharnutovskii, the 6th Mechanized Corps received the mission to seize Pimen-Cherin, Nizhne-Cherin, and Karaichevom.30 The momentum of the Soviet advance recaptured numerous Russian villages, a major measure for success in the Red Army. Over a period of two days, under conditions of frost and a heavy snow cover with the temperature at 20 degrees below zero, the corps successfully carried out its missions in accordance with the 2nd Guards Army commander's concept.

Through 28 December, Bogdanov's corps continued attacking in the direction of Karaichev and Kotelnikovo on basic combat instructions from the army commander. In coordination with General Pavel Rotmistrov's 7th Tank Corps, Bogdanov's corps worked to capture Kotelnikovo. Rotmistrov's tank corps attacked the Germans from the west and southwest, while Bogdanov's corps assaulted from the east and southeast.

Bogdanov's mechanized brigades seized the eastern part of Kotelnikovo by 1200 hours, 29 December. And, towards evening the western half was taken by 7th Tank Corps. In the fight, the mechanized corps captured large stores of German equipment and weapons.[31] The opposing German 57th Panzer Corps, as von Mellenthin described, "...was almost nonexistent; it had literally died on its feet."[32] The capture of Kotelnikovo opened the south bank of the Don river to Rostov, exposing the vulnerable right flank of the German forces. Bogdanov's corps continued advancing and seizing villages and towns on the north side of the Don. Field Marshal von Manstein reported to Hitler that the 4th Panzer Army was no longer capable of holding the broad front south of the Don. By 2 January 1943, Bogdanov's lead battalions crossed the Don river.

Based on the Stavka High Command intentions, forces of the Southern Front (2nd Guards, 51st, 28th Armies), after destroying the German's Kotelnikovo grouping, concentrated their main forces in the direction of Rostov, attempting to capture the great bridge over the Don river leading to the south, towards the Caucasus. Simultaneously, parts of the force seized Tikhoretskom, cutting off the German path of withdrawal from northern Caucasus to Rostov.

On 6 January, General Malinovskii gave the corps the following combat mission: "6th Mechanized Corps seize the line farmstead Atamaskii, Stoyanovskii, Novyii Gashun and advance towards Krasnyi Oktyabr. And further cross the railroad in the area of Grushevka, Amta (7km southwest of Zimovnikov)."[33] The order pushed Bogdnaov's corps to the southwest towards Rostov.

The 6th Mechanized Corps advanced against the German defense of prepared trenches and coordinated artillery and gun fires. All the villages and towns had prepared antitank positions. At dawn on 7 January, after a short artillery preparation, the corps doggedly attacked the German defenses. By the end of the day the brigades had fulfilled their immediate missions advancing to the line Kranyi Oktyabr-Novyii Gashun. And by noon the following day, the corps seized the line Grushevka-Amta railroad station – Gorobtsev – western edge of Zimovnikov, fulfilling its assigned mission. As a result of these actions the corps won the honorific Guards designation and redesignated the 5th Guards Mechanized Corps on 9 January 1943. Bogdanov's skillful handling of his corps through multiple missions captured the attention of senior Red Army commanders. His reputation clearly marked him for higher command when the opportunity arose.

From 10 January to the middle of February, the 5th Guards Mechanized Corps continued in heavy fighting. During the operation, on 12 January, seeking better control of his dwindling mechanized and tank corps, General Malinovskii created a mechanized group under Lieutenant General Pavel Rotmistrov. The mobile group consisted of the 3rd Guards Tank, 2nd, 3rd and 5th Guards Mechanized Corps. Forward detachments of this group moved along the lower Don river.

General Rotmistrov assigned the 5th Guards Mechanized Corps a mission to continue pursuing the forces of the 17th Panzer and 16th Panzer Grenadier Divisions, to force the Manych river, and to develop the attack in the direction of the cities of Kranogo and Bataisk. Fulfilling this mission, the corps force marched and seized the villages of Samodurov and Krasnyi.

On 26 January, General Malinovskii ordered Bogdanov to seize the line Pustoshkin-Usman and conduct aggressive reconnaissance in the direction of Zelenoi Roshchi, Poltvask. In the process of the offensive the corps combat losses were not replenished, therefore, after continuous battle in the course of the month the tank and motorized battalions became significantly understrength. In addition to the need for replacements, a majority of the tanks required maintenance work. Bogdanov decided to reduce the number of brigades, organizing composite tank regiments, motorized battalions and artillery groups.[34] Demonstrating initiative to continue the mission despite losses, Bogdanov showed an innovativeness and determination that kills on the battlefield and wins victories. In situations of constrained resources, he repeatedly organized scarce resources and found a solution, allowing him to maintain the attack.

On the Pustoshkin-Chernshev-Usman line, the corps ran into strong German resistance. Here, a sharp battle arose against superior forces consisting of the 17th Panzer and 16th Panzer Grenadier Divisions. In the ensuing battles, the corps held, but suffered heavy losses in personnel and a significant loss in commanders from the brigades and battalions.

On 7 February, the corps was placed in the Front reserve near Limanskogo (90km east of Rostov). At the end of the month, the 5th Guards Mechanized Corps, on Stavka instructions, moved from the Southern Front reserve to become part of the newly formed 5th Guards Tank Army along with the 3rd Guards Tank Corps, under the command of General Rotmistrov. General Bogdanov received the award, Suvorov 2nd Degree.

In March 1943, Bogdanov received a new command, the 9th Separate Tank Corps. In July, the 9th Tank Corps became the Central Front reserve, concentrating on the northern face of the Kursk salient. General Konstantin Konstantinovich Rokossovskii commanded the Front. Rokossovskii, an experienced veteran, had been implicated in the 'anti-Soviet conspiracy' during Stalin's purging of the military, just as Bogdanov. A mishandling of evidence against Rokossovskii held his case back for "investigation" and bought him time in a labor camp. Because of pressures on the eve of World War II to replace officer losses, he survived, to become in June 1940 one of the newly appointed major generals of the Red Army. He took command of the 9th Mechanized Corps. He had built a reputation before his internment as a specialist in modern, mobile warfare.

The Central Front, consisting of five rifle armies, one tank army and one air army, prepared to meet the great German summer onslaught, called "Operation Citadel," in the greater battle of Kursk. General Rokossovskii's Central Front bore the brunt of the German General Walther Model's northern pincer attacking from the Orel salient. By the end of the first day, 5 July, during the evening General Rokossovskii decided to lose no time in launching a counterattack and ordered the 2nd Tank Army to move up to support the left wing to the 13th Army. General Aleksei Grigorevich Rodin, commander 2nd Tank Army, was slow in getting his tanks on the move. With the short summer nights helping the German's aerial reconnaissance, the tank army was unable to launch a surprise attack, and was reduced to supporting the 13th Army along its second defense line.

As a reserve for the Central Front, Bogdanov's tank corps prepared to operate on the morning of 6 July in the direction of Verkh. Smorodnoe, Ponyri and Stanovoe, Samodurovka. The next night, the 9th Tank Corps deployed for action. "By the end of the third day almost all of the Front reserve had been committed to action, yet the enemy continued to bring in new forces on the main line of attack," Rokossovskii recalled. "What could we do to hold out against him? I decided on a calculated risk and sent my last reserve – General S.I. Bogdanov's 9th Tank Corps which was protecting Kursk from the south – against the main attack."[35] After two hours of hard fighting, the Soviets managed to press the enemy back one to two kilometers, depleting the German force and checking its main blow. While General Model's attack failed to breach any part of the Soviet defensive line, General Rokossovskii used his force totally to hold the line.

The German offensive began to weaken perceptibly. By 11 July, their troops, having suffered heavy losses and achieved none of their objectives, discontinued their attacks. In six days of continuous fighting, the German forces had succeeded in penetrating Rokossovskii's defenses by only 6 to 12 kilometers. The initiative passed to the Soviets who followed with a counteroffensive beginning in mid-July.

In the Central Front's Orel operation beginning in mid-July, the 2nd Tank Army conducted attacks against prepared defensive positions. On 22 July, in an advance of four to six kilometers, the tank army lost 119 tanks, a third of its original complement. The tank army's attack lasted until 29 July. In six days fighting, the tank army lost 207 tanks, nearly 60 per cent of its force. In the losses were 79 burned out tanks that could not be retrieved and put back into service. General Rodin had moved the tank army too late supporting the Central Front's counterattack in the defense. His unit was slow getting tanks on the move from the assembly areas. General Rokossovskii, generally unimpressed by tankers, was upset with the tank army's performance. General Rodin's tardiness in the defense and subsequent high casualties in the offense may have led to his replacement by Bogdanov. General Rodin was, at least officially, described as very ill and being sent to the rear for treatment.[36] He never received another unit command, relegated to the position of deputy commander for tanks and mechanized forces for the Western and 3rd Belorussian Fronts for the remainder of the war.

On 3 August 1943, Bogdanov assumed command of the 2nd Tank Army after its intense battles the first two days of the month. The

Germans brought up continuously fresh reserves and both sides suffered heavy losses. Arriving at the army staff, Bogdanov attentively studied the situation in front of the army and the adjacent sectors. With a chance to threaten the German position with an encirclement, Bogdanov played upon the circumstances and regrouped the tank army during the night to conduct a concentrated strike on a narrow part of the front. But, Bogdanov's chief of staff did not agree and recommended transfer of the tank army into the 70th Army sector, where the Germans offered only weak resistance. "Otherwise, we risk fighting head on instead of maneuvering," declared the tank army Chief of Staff in his final report.[37]

While tank armies were used generally for developing success in the rifle armies sectors, this complicated situation required immediate action, in order not to give the Germans the chance to organize a solid defense. Bogdanov believed transferring the tank army to another axis with the objective to develop success would not achieve desirable results.[38] "With the present situation, we do not have the experience for a worthwhile independent tank army action," Bogdanov concluded. Addressing the chief of staff, he continued, "You say, that it is fighting head-on – this is a risk. But to be able to risk reasonably is the necessary quality of every commander. In battle, the commander's will manifests itself in risk. And in order not to be a gamble, risk must have under it a solid basis. We put the whole effort in a strike on the head. Now, the Germans lose any hope in victory. And, what's more, they now are afraid of us, afraid of the least threatening sign of encirclement. Initiative is in our hands. The enemy can only react. Everything will depend on the forces' initial strike and decisive action by the tank corps. Our success deprives the enemy of the will to resist."[39] Bogdanov's exchange with his chief of staff indicated trouble in a key relationship within any army, but particularly the Soviet command system. A conflict between a commander and his chief of staff often leads to poor performance in all staff sections because the vital coordination of information and perceptions are crucial to harmonious staff coordination and functions. Additionally, subordinate commanders will be reluctant or confused in accepting chief of staff recommendations in achieving missions and other informal, but necessary, communications between chiefs of staff and commanders.

In his memoirs, Marshal of the Soviet Union Sergei Emenovich Biryuzov, who served as a chief of staff from division through Front, wrote about the chief of staff position: "The commander must believe in his chief of staff as he would himself. It is impossible to work otherwise. The chief of staff is not simply an executive agent. His is one of the commander's closest assistant and must have a creative mind and disposition. The chief of staff, on the basis of the general concepts of the commander, considers all the details of the situation with his staff and prepares motivated proposals. It is through him that the execution of orders is monitored and command and control is provided."[40]

After working out the plan, Bogdanov went to the 3rd Tank Corps observation post on the right flank. On his orders the main forces of the army ceased the offensive in the direction of Kromy and sharply turned, while two brigades of the 3rd Tank Corps continued the attack in the Kromy direction, masking the tank army's redirection. The tank corps forced the Nezhivka river from the march. The dynamic maneuver caught the Germans by surprise. Tank units advanced rapidly, creating a threat of encirclement for German forces operating in the Orel area, as Bogdanov had anticipated.

In the August counteroffensive after Kursk, General Bogdanov demanded maximum performance from his new unit. If subordinate commanders allowed themselves to be halted by German resistance, he would call them back in the evening to the army command post and sharply, though impartially, reproach them on their inability to fulfill assigned missions. These upbraided commanders would go back on the short summer nights, regroup, and personally lead their units, often receiving serious wounds.[41] Bogdanov equally demanded a high standard of performance from his staff. He had little tolerance for slow, unthinking staff officers.

By 26 August, the Central Front began an offensive in the Sevsk direction. The 65th Army captured a bridgehead on the west bank of the Sevsk river, and its further advance met stiff resistance. In order to maintain the momentum of the advance by completing the breakthrough of the German defenses, General Rokossovskii committed the 2nd Tank Army on the following morning. Bogdanov's 3rd Tank and 7th Guards Mechanized Corps seized Sevsk, but could not develop the advance into the operational depth, the German rear area. Bogdanov found himself in a situation similar to Rodin's in the Orel operation a month earlier. The tank army penetrated the enemy defenses, but within one day it suffered irretrievable losses – 97 tanks. The Germans pulling available reserves into the sector counterattacked fiercely, grinding down the Russians. The tank army successfully repelled the counterattacks, but, by 1 September, only one tank corps managed to move slowly forward, paying an exacting toll in men and equipment. The 2nd Tank Army had to be withdrawn into the reserve. In five days, Bogdanov's army lost 195 out of 236 tanks.[42] In these early battles of the newly created Red Army tank armies, the Front commanders used them prematurely against prepared defenses resulting in high casualties, and the tank army commanders could not advise differently nor handle the difficult assignments.

After these battles north of Kursk in the Orel salient, the tank army concentrated in the area of L'gov. Bogdanov's army needed refitting, rearming, and replenishing. From September through December 1943, the tank army received new combat equipment and personnel.

Described as a "man of astonishing audacity," Bogdanov from the beginning of January 1944 onwards fought his army in nearly all the decisive battles of the war.[43] Concentrating west of Kiev in the area of Svyatoshino, the 2nd Tank Army became part of the 1st Ukrainian Front.

After Kursk, the Red Army triumphantly developed a general strategic offensive along a two thousand kilometer front from Velikie Luki to the Black Sea. The German Army faced the problem of withdrawing behind the wide, formidable Dnepr river. With only five crossings over the river, the situation could only be managed if the Red Army advance was delayed with a 'scorched earth.' However, by the end of September 1943, Soviet forces in the Ukraine captured twenty-three bridgeheads along the Dnepr river. The 1st Ukrainian Front from mid-October to the end of December carried out offensive operations across the river and captured the Ukrainian capital Kiev.

During the 1st Ukrainian Front's Zhitomir-Berdichev offensive operation, 24 December 1943 to 14 January 1944, the Germans quickly transferred their reserves to the Vinnitsy and Uman area, delivering a major counterstrike led by Tiger and Panther tanks into the Front's flank. The German command wanted to restore their defensive line along the Dnepr river. With the 1st Ukrainian Front advance stalled, General Nikolai Vatutin, the Front commander, drew the 2nd Tank Army from the Stavka reserve located in the area of Beloi Tserki. On 16 January, Bogdanov's army in cooperation with the 38th Rifle Army repelled a major German counterattack. Bogdanov personally led on the meeting engagements in which both sides suffered losses. The tank army finally stopped advancing Germans in the area of Ocheretin and Oratov.

The 2nd Tank Army along with the 38th Rifle and lst Tank Armies fortified a line at Konstantivnovka, Ocheretin, Oratov, Shulyaki. By mid-January the lst Ukrainian Front had advanced to the line Sarny, Kazatin, Prokorovka. The 2nd Ukrainian Front conducted an offensive from the south, defeating Germans in the area of Kirovograd, forming a salient in the area of Korsun-Shevchenkovskii. From the salient, the Germans hoped to launch counterattacks into the flanks and rear of both the Fronts, restoring a defense along the Dnepr river.

On 24 January, forces of the 2nd Ukrainian Front probed the German defense with a strong reconnaissance-in-force, and followed the next morning with the main offensive in a northwesterly direction. Two days later, the lst Ukrainian Front launched its offensive to the southeast. By the 28th, tank units from both Fronts linked in the vicinity of Zvenigorodka, encircling a sizable German force.

Bogdanov's tanks and German tanks maneuvered against each other at distances of 600 to 800 meters in savage fighting. Standing silent, Bogdanov watched the battle. He became impatient with the results, and turned to his chief of artillery.

"Drive to the corps commander," he decided. "Together think about what to do. And you have a rough idea here of what can help the tankers."

The artillery chief brought up Katyusha rockets and regrouped the corps artillery to stop the German's advance.

The Front commanders worked rapidly to complete a continuous inner front of encirclement, and by 3 February the Soviet command had also created a stable line of troops along an outer ring of the encirclement.

On 4 February, in fighting around Korsun-Shevchenkovskii, the First German Panzer Army sought to penetrate the Red Army's large encirclement of German forces. The lst Ukrainian Front commander again used his reserve, the 2nd Tank Army. As a consequence of the crisis situation and due to the fact that the tank army's units were arriving successively by rail in the concentration area, several detachments were organized by Bogdanov by putting the unloaded battalions, brigades and corps under a unified command.[44] Attacking from the march, Bogdanov's tankers struck the penetrating German forces and, with tanks from the 6th Tank Army, pushed the Germans south, ensuring a tight Soviet grip on the Korsun encirclement.

A week later, German panzer divisions delivered another powerful strike, attempting to breakthrough to their encircled forces. Bogdanov sent from his army the 3rd Tank Corps to attack the flanks of the German relief force. The German tank force, bled white from costly fighting, could not hold.

On 22 February, the infested relationship between Bogdanov and his chief of staff was resolved. General Aleksei Ivanovich Radzievskii was designated the new Chief of Staff for the 2nd Tank Army. At the start of the war, Radzievskii served as Chief of Staff for the 53rd Cossack Cavalry Division from Central Asia. As chief of staff, he organized combat operations behind the German lines that were characterized by surprise and bold, highly mobile maneuvers. He later rose to become chief of staff for the 1st and 2nd Guards Cavalry Corps. In November 1943, Radzievskii participated in his last major cavalry operation with the 1st Guards Cavalry Corps in the 1st Ukrainian Front's Kiev operation. This operation with a deep thrust into the German operational depth provided the necessary experience Radzievskii would need for mobile group operations with a tank army.

Upon arrival at the 2nd Tank Army headquarters, Radzievskii immediately began to plan the army's combat actions for the Uman-Botoshansk operation. In a short time, he was completely versed in the situation, understood the army's mission and thoroughly studied the enemy. Radzievskii quickly put his imprint on the staff; he demanded from his staff chiefs exactness and objectivity, constantly reminding them that in war the severe cost for small staff errors or misrepresentations is soldiers' blood. The staff officer's operational lines on a map set daily life and death objectives for the fighter. Radzievskii knew that, and soon his staff learned.

Radzievskii's strong control and theoretical understanding as chief of staff provided the requisite support for Bogdanov's style of command. Bogdanov needed a thoroughly organized staff that could give him reminders, schedule the unpleasant and detailed tasks, consider long term issues, make the required reports. Bogdanov seemed uninterested with the mundane aspects of controlling a tank army.

On the day of Radzievskii's arrival, the tank army's staff received notification from the 1st Ukrainian Front of its transfer to Marshal I.S. Konev's 2nd Ukrainian Front.

After a few short combat actions and fully in command of the 2nd Tank Army, Bogdanov showed his qualification for command in the Uman-Botoshansk operation, 5 March to 17 April 1944. The operation began two weeks after the completion of the Korsun-Shevchenkovskii operation. Preparation of the tank army relied on Bogdanov's keen organization ability. All the tank armies had significant shortages, the 2nd Tank Army had only 231 tanks and self-propelled assault guns.[45] Radzievskii paid great attention to the development of the artillery plan and considered, weather permitting, the use of aviation in the main sector attack.

Acting as the mobile armored fist for the 2nd Ukrainian Front, the 2nd Tank Army advanced in the sector of the 27th Army on 5 March 1944, into a penetration achieving a breakthrough of the German defense north of Uman. In the advance, the tank army's reconnaissance identified the presence of bridges over the Gornyi Tikich river in the vicinities of Buka and Berezovka. Forward detachments from the two tank corps were tasked to seize and hold the bridges before the Germans could destroy them. The forward detachments reinforced with combat engineers and motorized riflemen reached the river on the night of 7 March, on the heels of retreating German units. They hastily crossed the river, capturing the bridges and establishing a small bridgehead. The bridge captured by the 16th Tank Corps's detachment at Buka suffered little damage, while the other captured bridge near Berezovka was in poor shape. With the Buka bridge easily restored, the entire 16th Tank Corps crossed through the night. Bogdanov ordered the 3rd Tank Corps to abandon its damaged bridge and to maneuver along the river to the restored bridge. After crossing the 3rd Tank Corps resumed its pursuit in their assigned sector. In the course of three days, 5-7 March, the rifle and tank armies with air and artillery support penetrated the German tactical defense, forcing the Gornyi Tikich river. After a concentration in the bridgehead, three tank armies, 2nd, 5th Guards, and 6th, advanced in the attack with the 6th on the right, 2nd in the center, and on the left flank the 5th Guards. Overcoming German resistance on the southern bank of the river, the 2nd Tank Army fought its way towards the Potash area along the railroad lines south and southwest of Zhelud'kov. Bogdanov's tank army in coordination with the

29th Tank Corps, 5th Guards Tank Army and 73rd Rifle Corps, 52th Army, captured Uman on 10 March, seizing a windfall booty of 500 operating German tanks and more than 350 guns.[46]

During the course of the offensive, Aleksei Radzievskii used any occasion to drive to forward units. From there he could see and feel the general character of the fighting.[47] He was educating himself on armored operations. He taught his staff and subordinates how operationally to choose in the flow of communications and reporting that which was necessary and valuable. As a result the staff prepared exact, well-grounded and timely information, allowing General Bogdanov to make correct decisions. Such a reliable staff complemented Bogdanov's forward leadership, allowing him to be with the lead units.

Marshal Konev remarked in his memoirs, "It must be said, that the leadership of the 2nd Tank Army's combat operations, taking into consideration complicated terrain and weather conditions, was accomplished personally by the Army commander General Lieutenant S. I. Bogdanov, all the time finding him directly in the combat formations. He firmly and confidently led his subordinate forces and staff organizing control and receiving information, checked the fulfillment of his orders. It must be said, that in developing the situation the army commander's personal presence in combat formations had great significance and promoted the high tempo of the 2nd Tank offensive."[48] The Front commander's praise was passed to the Soviet High Command which ordered on 11 March the awarding of the Hero of the Soviet Union and its coveted "Gold Star" medal to Bogdanov.

As the fighting continued, forward detachments of the 2nd Tank Army with riflemen and sappers riding on the tanks received the mission to capture bridges across the Southern Bug river southwest of Dzhulinki. At 2300 hours 11 March, the tankers pressed the attack towards the river. The river was 90 meters wide and up to two meters deep. The Germans, using scorched earth tactics, had blown the bridges. Lacking usable bridges and crossing equipment, the tank army was unable to cross the river from the march. Stalled for nearly twenty-four hours, the tankers gathered local crossing equipment, improvised materials, and built rafts. At night the motorized infantry of the tank corps crossed the river and secured a bridgehead. Engagements flared up around the bridgehead.

The Germans attempted at all cost to drive back the motorized infantry from the bridgehead and to reestablish a defense on the Southern Bug. Tanks were needed to repel the German counterattacks. However, the army did not have sufficient number of engineer sapper units to restore the bridge that the Germans had blown over the river. The tank army solution sent a unit of T-34 tanks by deep wading across the river.

A fording site was established with markers and prepared approaches. The tanks' exhaust pipes were extended and moved upward using canvas hoses. The hatches and slits were battened down, plugged and caulked with grease. Air intake was through the hatches on top of the turret. This improvised technique for crossing was first used by General Kravchenko's 5th Guard Tank Corps at the Desna river in October 1943.

Late on the afternoon of 12 March, seven tanks forded the river and attacked the Germans unexpectedly at the bridgehead. The rest of the army's tanks and self-propelled assault guns crossed over the restored bridge.[49]

The 2nd Tank Army continued the attack. On 14 March, aggressively pursuing the Germans, the tank army after forcing the Southern Bug moved towards the Dnestr river. Again, General Bogdanov decided to cross the river from the march. The corps commanders dispatched reinforced forward detachments to capture crossings over the river. Bogdanov with his operational group drove forward to the lead elements of the 16th Tank Corps. In the corps commander's command post, Bogdanov received the report that his units were experiencing a shortage of ammunition and fuel.

"What are you going to do, in order to forestall the enemy's withdrawal towards the crossings on the Dnestr?" Bogdanov asked.

"I have in the rear area a reserve brigade with 20 repaired tanks," the corps commander answered. "I am sending an officer in a PO-2 (biplane used for liaison) with instructions there, in order to load these tanks with fuel and ammunition, and quickly send them to the 15th Motorized Rifle Brigade. This brigade we plan to use as a forward detachment. The repaired tanks will reinforce the brigade."

"Fine," Bogdanov said, "and how long will this take?"

"By morning the brigade will prepare to transfer to pursuing the enemy," the corps commander replied.[50]

The next morning was too late for Bogdanov. He ordered the 15th Motorized Brigade to immediately begin pursuit. And, by morning the brigade had advanced to the east bank of the Dnestr river.

By the end of 18 March, the brigade had secured a bridgehead on the west bank of the Dnestr for the rest of the tank army to begin crossing.

Again, Marshal Konev used words of praise in his post-war writings, "S.I. Bogdanov, who I first met in the Uman-Botoshansk operation, made a great impression on me beginning with his outward appearance and then his business like quality. This was a tall, impressively handsome man. In all his actions, conversations, in command, it was evident of high demanding standards, strong will and organization. After making a decision and giving out instructions he, as a rule, personally drove to the units and operated calmly and without fussiness. The 2nd Tank Army staff headed by general A.I. Radzievskii, made the impression of a very well organized organism, on which the army commander could fully place him anywhere. In the staff operation they did not make mistakes or allow failures."[51] A salient characteristic of Bogdanov's command was organization. Radzievskii's "staff culture" and attention to detail perfectly complemented his commander's capabilities and style. Radzievskii personified the ideal German staff officer in his ability to organize and run tank army operations.

The distance of 160 kilometers between the Southern Bug and Dnestr rivers was covered by the tank army in four days. Advancing in combat 240 kilometers, Bogdanov's tank units forced the rivers, Southern Bug, Dnestr, and Prut, and towards the end of the operation the 2nd Tank Army along with General A. G. Kravchenko's 6th Tank Army advanced towards the town of Yassy.

On orders from the Front commander, Bogdanov, on 29 March, began regrouping his army in the sector of the 27th Army which was crossing the Prut river. After the rifle units secured the river crossing, the 2nd Tank Army was to assume the offensive toward the town of Yassy and seize it.

Operations during April met with sporadic success, but no major penetration of the enemy lines. The Fourth Rumanian and Sixth German Armies resisted tenaciously on the approaches to Yassy and Kishinev. Despite renewed offensive efforts in May, the 2nd Tank Army only probed the enemy defense unable to reach Yassy.

In April, 2nd Tank Army operated with a drastic shortage of tanks. Bogdanov, with only 20 tanks left in the army, attempted to take Kishinev but could not manage it against determined resistance offered by the Germans and Rumanians. The terrain conditions around the town were also very difficult. Attacking Kishinev from the northwest, the tank army encountered great difficulties in overcoming hills, streams, and ravines. Konev observed that Bogdanov exploited the full potential of the 2nd Tank Army.[52]

After its skirmishing battles along the Romanian border in May and early June, Bogdanov's tank army was pulled from its defensive positions on the front line for regrouping, and, on 12 June, the tank army transferred to Stavka reserve. From 15 June to 3 July, it moved 650 kilometers from the Romanian border to assembly areas near Manevishi (50 kilometers north of Lutsk) to reinforce the 1st Belorussian Front under Bogdanov's old commander Marshal Konstantin K. Rokossovskii.

In preparation for the upcoming operation, Bogdanov managed a major restoration effort of the 2nd Tank Army. The tank army's brigade command post staffs dwindled to ineffectiveness. Brigade staffs had to be strengthened by officers from the army and corps command posts. The army's self-propelled assault gun regiment and a number of other units were shifted to the command of the 11th Tank Brigade.[53] In a relatively short time, Bogdanov possessed an operational tank army.

By the summer of 1944, the Red Army sought to destroy the German Army Group Center in the Belorussian operation. The Belorussian offensive, code-named Operation Bagration, involved the 1st Baltic, the 3rd, 2nd, and 1st Belorussian Fronts. With converging assaults by the Fronts, the Red Army aimed to dismember the German Army Group Center by encircling and destroying major elements, creating a huge gap for armored formations. Operation Bagration planned to liberate the whole of Belorussia, part of Lithuania and Latvia, and eastern Poland. The 2nd Tank Army became part of the 1st Belorussian Front on the southern, or left, wing of this strategic offensive operation. The general concept of the 1st Belorussian operation was a strike by its left wing around the Brest fortified area from the north and south to destroy German forces at Lublin and Brest, and then develop the offensive to the west towards the Vistula river.

Bogdanov with Radzievskii bent over a map of the operational area considering the impending operation. They chose the direction of the main strike. Weighing all the factors, Bogdanov decided to advance the tank army in the breakthrough in two echelons. "This," he announced, "allows the army to operate compactly in a 12 kilometer breakthrough sector, intensifying the force of the strike not only at the line of commitment, but also during the course of the whole operation."

In accordance with this concept, Bogdanov's staff under Radzievskii performed an enormous planning effort for the tank corps attacks, working out their coordination and actions with the rifle armies in the first echelon and with cavalry corps that would operate on the flanks of the tank army.

Radzievskii's cavalry experience became evident in planning to achieve the ultimate penetration, a clean (chistya) breakthrough. A clean breakthrough penetrated the enemy's tactical zone with the forward rifle units so the tank army passed through without deploying and fighting until in the enemy rear area. "Our basic attention was given to securing the tank army's commitment to the fight," Radzievskii wrote. "In order not to suffer unnecessary losses in tanks, we organized an aggressive and reliable artillery cover."[54]

In typical Radzievskii attention to detail, he explained, "supporting the commitment of the tank army to the engagement planned to be accomplished by the method of a series of artillery fire concentrations to a depth of 15 kilometers. For this, across the 1.5-2 kilometers a designated fire line, a total of eight, on which all potential strongpoints and enemy centers of resistance were marked sectors of concentrated fires. Availability of fire scheme to artillerists and tankers permitted easy calls for artillery fire along any sector."[55]

In the 2nd Tank Army, additional means were sought to increase the number of repair and evacuation units. Evacuation platoons were set up using severely damaged tanks and captured tractors under the corps's mobile tank repair bases. The technical training of the personnel improved with each passing day, 425 drivers were awarded various skill specialties.[56] Bogdanov used riflemen to maintain the equipment for the evacuation units.[57] Soviet recovery and repair of damaged tanks became an instrumental aspect in sustaining tank forces in longer operations. Their remarkable capability drew the respect of German commanders. General Hasso von Manteuffel, a panzer commander on the eastern front, remarked after the war, "Their(Red Army) salvage and repair services...were very good. They performed extraordinary feats.... I therefore issued orders that on principle, tanks were to be set on fire."[58] Captain von Senger, who commanded a German tank unit in Russia, paid a similar compliment, "...their normal maintenance service was very efficient, and they had plenty of well-trained mechanics. Indeed, we came increasingly to employ Russian mechanics in our own tank maintenance companies."[59]

On 11 July 1944, the second stage of the Belorussian offensive began with a great advance by the first echelon rifle armies of the lst Belorussian Front. By the third day they had advanced nearly 70 kilometers and a wide gap existed in the German line. Cavalry and tank corps captured three bridgeheads over the Western Bug river. On 16 July, the Front's armies reached the Svisloch-Pruzhany, recapturing the area Bogdanov lost in fighting three years earlier when he commanded the 30th Tank Division. By midday 20 July, two corps of the 8th Guards Army forced the Western Bug on a 15 kilometer wide front. Developing their drive westward, the remainder of the 8th Guards Army organized ferry crossings on the river. On 21 July, the 2nd Tank Army began moving towards the Western Bug.

The 2nd Tank Army, the principle strike force for the lst Belorussian Front, remained inactive, although originally it was to have been committed on the second day of the operation. The tank army was late in deploying behind the rifle armies and gaining the Western Bug. So far, 8th Guards Army was making do with the llth Tank Corps.

With calm, deliberateness, Bogdanov waited. One learned patience in the Soviet penal system. Patience in a commander allows time for reconnaissance and other necessary but time-consuming actions. But, now, his sense of timing and expediency told him to seize the moment. He was ready to fully exploit the situation with available resources.

Bogdanov went forward to see General Vasilii Ivanovich Chuikov, commander 8th Guards Army. General Chuikov remembered Bogdanov's mood, "His impatience was understandable and so was his sense of self-restraint. His army was poised for action like a raised sledgehammer over the anvil. Every step had to be taken to ensure that the blow delivered by such a powerful army would fall on exposed lines."[60]

On 21 July, Marshal Rokossovskii, who could wait no longer, decided to immediately throw the 2nd Tank Army into the breach. The tank army received orders to head for Lublin, Deblin, Praga(a Warsaw suburb). Late night on the 21st and early the next morning, all the corps of the tank army crossed into the bridgehead over the Western Bug. Receiving the mission to commit to the fight through

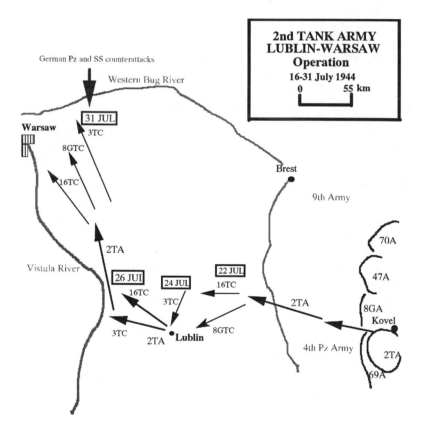

German Pz and SS counterattacks

Western Bug River

2nd TANK ARMY
LUBLIN-WARSAW
Operation
16-31 July 1944
0   55 km

31 JUL
3TC

Warsaw

8GTC

16TC

Brest

9th Army

2TA

70A

47A

Vistula River

26 JUL
16TC

24 JUL
3TC

22 JUL
16TC

2TA

8GA
Kovel

3TC

2TA Lublin

8GTC

4th Pz Army

2TA

69A

the 8th Guards Army sector, and by the end of 23 July seize Lublin. Bogdanov's concept was at dawn on 22 July to pass through the 8th Guards, and advance aggressively towards the Vepsh river. In typical fashion, Bogdanov wanted to force the river from the march. To avoid possible German defensive preparations, the tank army commander planned to go around Lublin and in coordination with the 7th Guards Cavalry Corps simultaneously strike Lublin from the north, west and east.

The northwest part of Lublin and the highway from Lublin to Warsaw were captured by units of the 3rd Tank Corps toward evening on 23 July. In the outskirts of Lublin, troops of the tank army discovered the Majdanek death camp. Majdanek, in place since August 1941, was an extermination camp where one and a half million people were put to death. Captured in tact, the Soviets were shocked and the smell of the camp stayed with Bogdanov's tankers on their way to Berlin.

In the southeastern part of the city, the Germans continued to offer stubborn resistance against the 8th Tank Corps. The tank corps commander understanding Bogdanov's emphasis on the advance informed the army staff of the slow going.

The 3rd Tank Corps commander reported that a tank brigade had captured the highway on the western side of Lublin, leading to Warsaw. Bogdanov arrived at the corps' command post, which had settled in the northwest suburb of the city. The corps commander told the army commander that the city had been penetrated with tanks since the motorized rifle brigade had lagged behind. With the arrival of the riflemen, the corps commander planned to begin clearing the city in the northwest from house to house.

Bogdanov decided the corps commander was simply too slow and exaggerated the German forces in the city. He suggested to the corps commander that he drive across town with him. Bogdanov shrugged off the corps commander's warning of danger. For security only one tank accompanied the two command groups.

The security tank moved out ahead, the army and corps commanders with a few staff officers in two jeeps following. The tank moved quickly forward and disappeared around a street corner. The jeeps continued to follow the tank. They drove past a burning tank, broken German vehicles and wagons.

Everything was quiet. No one could hear a shot; no signs of life appeared in the stone houses. Driving further, they heard shots similar to a panzerfaust. Before their eyes they saw the tank which had moved out before them jolt from a direct hit.

Bogdanov ordered a lieutenant to look around the tank. There turned out to be no one around the tank. Then, Bogdanov ordered their return to the command post. When the vehicles drove off from the tank a few meters, they heard shooting from a machinegun. The army commander's jeep stopped, and Bogdanov got out of his jeep, and suddenly, but slowly, lowered himself in pain to the pavement. The rest of the party ran up, and picked up the commander. The small group returned fire, withdrew from the machinegun fire, abandoning the jeeps.

The Germans attempted a few times to cut off their escape route. The situation became easier, in that Bogdanov who possessed a robust health and strong will was not a hindrance. Although seriously wounded, he walked more than three kilometers to get back to the 3rd Tank Corps command post.[61]

Upon hearing that General Bogdanov had been wounded, Stalin ordered the tank commander's immediate evacuation to Moscow for treatment.[62] Command of the 2nd Tank Army passed temporarily to the able chief of staff, General Radzievskii.

On 22 July, in the command post, Radzievskii received the member of the Front's Military Soviet, Nikolai A. Bulganin, who announced that Stalin requested that Lublin be taken by 25 July. Radzievskii reported that Lublin would be captured no later than 23 July. "Our promise we fulfilled. On the night of 23 July, Lublin was taken," Radzievskii remembered proudly.[63]

General Chuikov, well forward on 24 July, heard the news of Bogdanov's wounding, "It was just like him to be in the thick of battle. He always wanted to see everything with his own eyes and guide his troops directly on the battlefield, rather than from a command post in the rear."[64]

General Chuikov visited Bogdanov in an army hospital north of Lublin. He was about to be evacuated.

"How are you feeling, Seyon,?" Chuikov asked.

"Not too bad, Vassya," he replied cheerfully enough, though he was in great pain. "I will be back soon and we'll definitely enter Berlin together."[65]

With the fall of Lublin, the way opened towards the Vistula river. The 2nd Tank Army sliced deep into the rear area. The German forces resisting stubbornly in the Belostok-Brest area began to withdraw, managing to destroy crossings over the Vistula river in the vicinity of Demblin and Pulav. "Unfortunately,, we did not have the crossing means and could not manage to force the river from the march because of strong German fires," Radzievskii recalled.[66]

On the morning of 27 July, in accordance with Marshal Rokossovskii's decision, the 2nd Tank Army under Radzievskii began moving north along the Vistula toward Warsaw to seize the suburb, Praga. Radzievskii with his staff had only 15 hours to prepare for the attack in a new direction. He had to regroup within the army. Using the 16th Tank Corps in a defense along the east bank of the Vistula in the area of Demblin, he covered the army during its regrouping. Radzievskii immediately dispatched reconnaissance along the new axis. Forward detachments also moved ahead of the corps to capture roads in Tsegluv and Sennitsa. Reconnaissance reports of German engineer preparations on the Warsaw, Praga approach influenced Radzievskii to push the army and operate at night in order to arrive there before the Germans completed their build up. The 2nd Tank Army's northwesterly advance threatened to complete encirclement of German units in the Brest-Litovsk area. The tank army's advance was conducted under increasingly heavy air attacks, and the corps ran low on fuel and ammunition. Supply trucks lagged seriously behind the units. The frictions of war were working against Radzievskii's tank army.

After an artillery preparation on the morning of 29 July, the 2nd Tank Army resumed the offensive north cutting roads and railroads between Warsaw and Bialystok. Radzievskii began receiving reports on the extent of fortifications in the Warsaw suburb of Praga. The famed Russian General Aleksandr Vasil'evich Suvorov stormed a fortified Praga in 1794, forcing the capitulation of Warsaw early in a Polish rebellion against Russia. Suvorov's brilliant victory was not so easily repeated.

By evening 31 July, Radzievskii knew his army had run into a significant concentration of German armor. Believing the strength of the German panzer units with their latest heavy "King Tiger" tanks to be considerable and the tank army at the long end of their Lublin-Brest operation, Radzievskii issued orders for the tank units not to attack the fortified area of Praga.

"By the morning of 31 July," Radzievskii later wrote in a memoir article, "the tank corps, fighting hard, seized a few points around Praga's fortified area. But attempts to penetrate it from the march were not crowned with success. I was forced to give the orders to the army's weakened march units, operating on a front of more than 60 kilometers to transition to defense. Our decision was confirmed by the Front commander."[67]

By 1 August, the tank army had transitioned to defense. On 2 August, the Front commander, Marshal K.K. Rokossovskii, arrived at the army's observation post. He climbed the high factory smoke stack on which the observation post was based. Through stereoscopic telescope, he could see Warsaw through a smoke screen of fires and explosions. The Warsaw Polish partisans uprising struggled without Soviet relief. While some accusations believe the Soviets deliberately stopped and allowed the Germans to crush the pro-western Allies' underground, the Soviets contend they did not have the combat power to move into Warsaw.

An unexpectedly serious situation arouse on 3 August when the Germans executed a strong counterstrike against the tank army's right flank. Strong resistance by the tank units and with friendly air support, "we stood and repelled all their attempts to throw our army from its position," Radzievskii recounted.[68]

The 2nd Tank Army suffered heavy losses: 284 tanks and self-propelled assault guns, 40 per cent of which were irretrievable. The army was put in Front reserve for reconstitution on 7 August. During the ten days of the Lublin-Brest operation, the tank army had advanced nearly 250 kilometers to the outskirts of Warsaw. For its brave and decisive actions, the tank army on 21 November 1944, officially received its "Guards" designation.

The Belorussian operation had been a colossal success for the Red Army. The destruction of the German Army Group Center was the greatest defeat suffered on the eastern front, beyond Stalingrad and Kursk. Nearly 30 divisions had been destroyed costing the German Army 350,000 men lost. Virtually the whole 4th Army and most of the 4th and 3rd Panzer Armies were destroyed. The German Army lost 10 generals killed and 21 captured. The German remnants consisted of eight scattered divisions along a 350 kilometer front.

The newly assigned political officer to the 2nd Guards Tank Army, Colonel Mikhail Moiseyevich Litvyak visited Bogdanov in the Moscow military hospital. Litvyak had met Bogdanov while he commanded the 12th Tank Corps, but on his visit to the ward, he did not recognize him. "His face had grown lean, his appearance unathletic," he recalled.[69]

They discussed key personalities in the command, and it was evident to the new political officer that Bogdanov respected and treasured his staff. Later, reporting to the tank army, Colonel Litvyak recalled his first meeting with Radzievskii. He was stately in presence, medium height, brunet with an intelligent face. His athletic build gave him a good appearance in a well-fitted and pressed uniform.

Radzievskii organized and fully used his time. He kept himself on a tight schedule, cutting off dinner discussion to attend lessons with an interrogator who was teaching him German. He was noted for the breadth of his knowledge and high staff culture (shtabnaya cultura). Before the war he had studied in the Frunze and General Staff Military Academies. His operational work was considered by many without equal in the army. He was highly valued by the Front command. In general, he was considered affectionately as a genuine military "nit-picker."

In the middle of October 1944, Radzievskii conducted a review on the Lublin-Brest operation with the corps and brigade staffs. He presented a lecture. The political officer who listened to his presentation was carried away by the breadth of his operation-tactical understanding, conclusions in thought and words, ability to carefully analyze the course of the operation, extracting everything new and instructions that could be useful for subsequent combat operations.[70]

Radzievskii spoke easily, did not make use of analytical notes or summaries. He used a staff scheme, showing the concept of developing and executing the operation. Deep in content, brilliant in reporting format, his minute by minute outline testified to his diligence and creative treatment of the staff process.

In the course of an offensive operation because of the volume of material Radzievskii had to review and work, he did not have time for current newspapers. He, at times, asked the political officer to send him current lectures so he could see, "what is happening in the wide world."[71]

Returning from his convalescence, Bogdanov greeted people with his left hand since the right was in a sling. His mood was cheery. Word of his return to command spread rapidly through the army by the soldiers' "telegraph." The 2nd Guards Tank Army political affairs officer, Litvyak noted, "the tankers liked their commander. Semen Il'ich Bogdanov as a general, as a communist, was extremely close to the soldiers and officers."[72]

As a result of the devastating rout of the German Army Group Center in Belorussia and in the Western Ukraine, Red Army units seized three major bridgeheads over the Vistula river. For the impending Vistula-Oder offensive operation, the lst Belorussian Front's main effort was to be unleashed from the Magnushev bridgehead by forces of four rifle and two tank armies with the addition of one cavalry corps in the general direction of Poznan.

In the preparation of the 2nd Guards Tank Army for the operation, thirty days were assigned for the training of the troops and staffs. On 25 November 1944, Bogdanov issued an order which set the dates, tasks, and forms for instruction as well as the subjects for the troops and command staff exercises. The commanders of the specific supporting branches, such as engineers and artillery, had to work out detailed instructions for the combat training of their subordinate units. Bogdanov's corps commanders had to submit a combat training plan for December by 30 November. Even the army staff together with the political section and the staffs of the commanders of the branches of special troops worked out a summary schedule for training. Then a master training plan and calendar were developed. This provided Bogdanov with a listing of subjects and types of training so he could centrally control and evaluate the progress and direction of his army's training and preparations for the impending offensive in the winter of 1945.[73]

Approximately 70 percent of the time was allocated for improving the individual soldier's field skills and marksmanship. The remaining training hours were allocated in subjects, such as, political, drill, engineer chemical, technical training and topography. Two or three days assemblies were set for the specialist.

Radzievskii ensured the command staff exercised using communications equipment, and half of these drills were conducted at night. Each day a two hour staff training session taught and drilled officers in their specific section's activities, responsibilities, and procedures.[74]

The lst Belorussian Front staff conducted wargames with its subordinate army chiefs of staff, operations sections, chiefs of rear services, and special branches such as engineers. Conferences hammered out the issues of close coordination between ground units, particularly tank armies and aviation units.

At the end of December, the lst Belorussian Front held a meeting of army commanders and staffs on the final preparations for the impending operation. At the table next to Bogdanov sat an old friend from before the war, Nicholai Kirillovich Popel, first member of the military Soviet for the lst Guards Tank Army. Popel teasingly remembered Bogdnanov's prior service in the Tsarist Army with the Life Guards.[75] Bogdanov found little humor in the political officer's jibe on a bit of personal history that had cost him three years in a labor camp. Bogdanov who lived fully in the immediate moment could forget ties to the past – yesterday was gone and forgotten.

On the night of 26 December, with instructions from General Bogdanov, the tank army's engineers, supported by one battalion from each tank, motorized, and mechanized brigades, deployed to a wooded area on the east side of the Vistula river. These units had the mission of preparing assembly area shelters, dugouts and ramps for the units and to repair roads and bridges across the Vistula.

At the beginning of the Vistula-Oder operation 2nd Guards Tank Army numbered 840 tanks and self-propelled artillery pieces.[76] The tank armies for this large operation were all handsomely augmented with tanks and assault guns. The tank army consisted of two full corps and a mechanized corps. With the eastern front considerably shortened in width as the Red Army advanced in the western Europe, more armored units were available to make the tank armies full three corps units.

Managing and balancing the staff actions, Radzievskii examined the different variants for projected actions during the course of the upcoming offensive operation. In case of last ditch resistance by the Germans in Warsaw, he wanted to turn part of the force – the lst Mechanized Corps, and he would have them go on the defensive, not allowing the Germans to slip back to the east to establish a new defensive line. The variants ultimately selected would depend on German actions and perceived intentions.[77]

On 10 January, Radzievskii and his staff completed a fully worked out plan for each variant of the impending operation. Issues and questions of coordination with the rifle and air armies in a multitude of combat situations, such as reconnoitering march routes, crossings in the bridgehead, organizing service regulators and road guides for crossings, and conducting preparation of forces for the march from their concentration area to the assembly areas were carried out. The staff had planned and developed deception and security measures to protect the force and ensure success.

Looking ahead at the area of operation, Radzievskii's staff re-

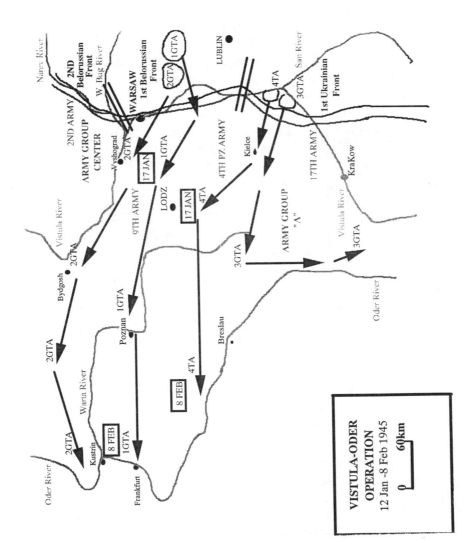

VISTULA-ODER
OPERATION
12 Jan -8 Feb 1945

0   60km

mained very busy. A primary consideration, as pointed out by Radzievskii, was the territory between the Vistula and Oder in which flowed a large number of small rivers and canals, such as the Bzura, Pilitsa and Warta. All the rivers flowed from south to north crossing and blocking the tank army's movement from east to west.[78]

On 14 January 1945, the 1st Belorussian Front attacked from the Manushev bridgehead. In the course of the offensive operation, night operations were widely conducted by forward detachments of the tank and mechanized corps and also by army level forward detachments. As a rule, night operations of forward detachments proved successful. For example, the 47th Guards Tank Brigade, which comprised the forward detachment of the 9th Guards Tank Corps of the 2nd Guard Tank Army in the operation, was committed to the breakthrough at 1700 hours on 15 January. At 2000 hours that night, they took the city of Grojec with a surprise night attack. In the evening of the following night the forward detachment cleared the Germans from the city of Zyrardow, and by 2300 hours had joined battle for the city of Sochaczew, after cutting off the German path of retreat from Warsaw to the west. Operating predominately at night, the 9th Guards Tank Corps' forward detachment covered 90 kilometers in 24 hours, with serious fighting along the way.[79]

On 15 January, a bridge was constructed over the Pilits river two hours earlier than the designated time. In the morning Bogdanov went there. For exemplary fulfillment of the combat order he announced his gratitude to the sappers and directed that the most outstanding receive awards.[80]

Bogdanov always could reward good as quickly as he could reproach poor performance. Awards for Bogdanov showed his appreciation to encourage others. Just the reward of a brightly colored ribbon at the right time achieved extraordinary results. And, he also knew soldiers do well what the commander checks.

By evening of 15 January, reports filtered back from the forward units of street battles for the towns of Gruets and Mshchonov. The Germans used a new gun, called a panzerfaust, against their tanks. This was a bazooka-type weapon. The antitank gun could punch holes at any point in the armor of tanks and self-propelled assault guns. The Soviet inspection team sent to investigate was impressed with the simplicity of construction and use, and with the effectiveness of the new weapon.

General Bogdanov determined that draft combat instructions on how the gun operated and how the Germans tactically employed it need to be sent down to the units. An ad hoc group under Radzievskii's staff, the chief of technical services and political workers, inspected the scenes of street battles and interrogated a captured German panzerfaust instructor. Radzievskii quickly coordinated the publication of practical combat instructions. The document contained requirements to raise the awareness of soldiers, to improve organization of the reconnaissance, quickly notify forces about the appearance of the new gun, and, in the course of the battle, to immediately take under fire likely panzerfaust positions. The 2nd Guards Tank Army's combat instructions gave concrete recommendations for dealing with the new gun, and more importantly, the information was passed to the soldiers who had to deal with the new gun without delay.[81]

In a typical example of its ability to improvise on the battlefield throughout the war, the Red Army showed a quick, pragmatic ability to adjust to new weapon systems with complementary tactical techniques. The Red Army had set up a impressive system using their best officers to collect and study their war experiences for immediate conversion into directives and combat instructions. This is how an army collectively improves, learns, and adapts itself under fire. As for the danger of the panzerfaust at the soldier level, innovative tank crews took wire mattress springs from beds and attached them to their combat vehicles to break the impact of the German's antitank weapon. By the time of street fighting for Berlin, Soviet tankers had developed several defensive methods, utilizing sandbags and sheet metal in countering the growing number of hand held antitank weapons encountered in close combat.

On 16 January, Bogdanov's tank army pushed through a gap and rapidly exploited operations toward the key objective of Sochaczew, a major city on the main road and rail line to Warsaw. Bogdanov hoped to seize the important bridges there before the German's Warsaw garrison broke out to the west.

The next day lead elements of the 2nd Guards Tank Army seized Sochaczew, 80 kilometers northwest of Warsaw, blocking the German 56th Panzer Corps. Controlling the city and bridges, Bogdanov's army forced the German corps to withdraw across the Vistula river. Unhesitatingly, Bogdanov continued his army's advance west, covering the 80 kilometers in 24 hours. In the first three days of the operation, the tank army advanced 170 kilometers at a mean rate of 57 kilometers per day.

In the sector of the 9th Guards Tank Corps lay the important town of Vlotslavek, through which seven highways passed. The Germans were prepared to strongly defend this key piece of real estate. By midday, the corps' lead brigade attempted unsuccessfully to take the town. Bogdanov arrived in the command post. He was clearly not in good spirits.[82]

"Where is Plotnikov and his political affairs officer? What are they doing?" he demanded.

"Colonel Plotnikov is now with the corps' forward detachment. And the political affairs officer is located in the corps command post," the corps staff officer replied.

"They are operating poorly. According to our order, General Vedeneev must take Vlotslavek today. And the 65th(Rifle Army) by midday tramples by it.... What, they forgot to take the town from the march? Well then, you must quickly go to Vedeneev and pass to him and Lieutenant Colonel Efimov, the we," the commander nodded to General Major Latyshev's side, "are dissatisfied with such a course of events. We need to speed up taking the town. The offensive is not to cease at night. By 0800 hours the town must be in our hands."

The main command phone rang. Bogdanov quickly picked up the telephone receiver. The Front commander had tracked the tank army commander to the forward corps command post.

"Now, comrade commander, I report," Bogdanov said, his left hand energetically came to his map and he began to report on the situation of the army's units, as usual, enumerating the location of its corps from right to left.

Those in the room remained silent while he reported. Bogdanov's voice resounded firmly and cogently. Finally, he came to the 9th Tank Corps.

"9th Tank Corps, its right flank commands the battle for Vlotslavek."

And, then followed an untimely pause indicating the Front commander's dominance in the conversation, after which General Bogdanov uttered only a few phrases – "...will make it....", "I will take measures....", "I follow...."

With that the conversation ended. Slowly lowering the receiver, Bogdanov took a breath. "We must get ourselves into Vlotslavek on our right flank." Bogdanov began to pace the room.[83]

During the tense hours of the operation, Colonel Litvyak visited

Radzievskii. A discontinuous line for friendly forces was marked on his work map while there were a large number of blue arrows representing attempts by the Germans to breakthrough to the west. Aleksei Ivanovich was calculating intensely. "The telephone rang non-stop," Litvyak recalled. "The army commander and staff asked about the situation. The army units sent in their combat reports." Radzievskii remained collected, calm, business-like – never an unnecessary word, nor an unnecessary gesture.[84] Radzievskii was the personification of the Red Army's adoption of the Napoleonic epigram, "There are no trifles in battle."

Marshal Konev, closely observing the operation of the tank army remarked, "The staff, headed by General Radzievskii, made the impression of a very well coordinated organism, in which the commander can fully place his reliance. In the staff's operation was not allowed failures and mistakes." He added, "this was a finely organized army, in combat terms preparation, organization, and in operations notably courageous, forcefully and great activeness."[86]

Approximately at midday on 21 January, Litvyak, the political affairs officer was called to General Bogdanov. As soon as Litvyak appeared in the room, Bogdanov spread out a map and immediately got down to business.

"The town of Bydgoshch (Bromberg) disturbs us. And not only us, but also the Front command, " Bogdanov announced as his pencil stopped on the town name. Then, he cursed, "again on the right flank." He no doubt mentally noted the commander, General Vedeneev, who had gotten Bogdanov into trouble with the Front commander for slow progress previously in the campaign.

Litvyak recalled, "I touched his map, added it is so, because the Bydgoshch area was beyond."

"You must drive quickly to the 9th Tank Corps command post and to give Vedeneev – to him, unfortunately, the radio does not reach – an order. He must immediately take all measures for quickly forcing the Notetsi from the march. At night, the offensive action will cease. By morning, I will bring up to him army refueling transports with diesel fuel. Bydgoshch must be taken tomorrow morning. Here is the mission. Clear?"

After Litvyak's satisfactory answer, Bogdanov continued,

"And still one more detail. I sent Vedeneev a pontoon-bridge regiment, in truth I'm not very sure that he has sufficient fuel in order to reach there...."[87] During the operation, fuel became a serious consideration, requiring ad hoc arrangements for the army to continue operating.

With his forces in march column, Bogdanov attempted a strike on Bydgoshch from the south, but it failed. He had to withdraw his forces, pass around the town, and attack from the west. The town was taken on 23 January.

The busy army staff had its furious flow of information jolted by a report that caused alarm: a German infantry battalion was moving around the open right flank of the 6th Heavy Tank regiment and approaching the army's command post along the highway. Also located in the immediate vicinity was a standing truck convoy with a precious cargo of ammunition, fuel, and food. Radzievskii decided to throw into battle the army's specially attached 274th Separate Motorized Battalion, a wheeled amphibian unit. Radzievskii had been in command posts under attack before, and remained remarkably cool. Later that evening the situation cleared up with additional forces.[88]

Fuel shortages continued to plague the tank army's efforts. On 23 January, General Bogdanov notified the Front on the chronic fuel problem. In post war writings, Radzievskii noted, "...in the Vistula-Oder operation the 2nd Tank Army for 16 days of the offensive waited for fuel in general some 5 days (30% of the time)."[89]

On 23 January, when the army forces advanced towards the German border, based on the decision of the Front commander, they received a short breathing space. Bogdanov's army had to regroup south of Speidemuhl for a couple of days.

Bogdanov sent a message to the Front commander, "I report that the forward detachments of the lst Mechanized Corps fulfilled the assigned missions as of 1500 hours, 23 January. The main forces could not because they lacked petrol, oil, lubricant. After receiving your order on the morning of 23 January I sent messages for transports with POL, and by all calculations they returned only the morning of 24 January. Bogdanov."[90]

Misinformation by radio was successfully employed during the Vistula-Oder operation. On 23 January, at the instructions of Marshal Zhukov,, commander of the lst Belorussian Front, the commanders of the 9th and 12th Tank Corps sent false radio messages to General Bogdanov, "Danzig mission received. We have adequate fuel."[91]

The purpose of those messages was to deceive the German command with respect to future operations by the Front's right wing and to conceal the lack of fuel in the tank army. The operation of the 9th Guards Tank Corps in the direction of Bydgoshch and the intercepted messages by the command element of the German 2nd Army were indicators of the beginning of an offensive on a new axis. In order to cover the rear area of their Pomeranian grouping, the German command deployed three newly arrived divisions to cover the Danzig sector, leaving the area of Charnkov with practically no cover. The Front's offensive toward the Oder surprised the Germans, whose main forces were in the area of Speidemuhl.

After serious fighting, the forward detachments of the 1st Mechanized Corps seized Oborniki, located on the northern banks of the Warta river. But, because of German resistance they had not managed to force the river from the march. A shortage of artillery and fuel stopped the effort.

General Bogdanov unexpectedly appeared in the corps' command post. He wanted the latest news. Listening to the corps commander's short report on the situation, he informed him about the recent conversation with Zhukov. Marshal Zhukov remained dissatisfied that the corps had not been able to force the Warta river from the march. Learning from Bogdanov's report that a weak spot in the German defense was located in the area of Charnkov, Zhukov gave the order, "Where you choose to force the Notecs river is your affair, but it is necessary without fail to penetrate the fortified region."[92]

On 25 January, Bogdanov personally gave a new mission to the commander of the 1st Mechanized Corps to change direction of its operations to the area of Charnkov. He ordered the corps commander to quickly redeploy the corps from the Warta river, march to the northwest seizing Charnkov, force the river Notecs, and capture a bridgehead on the west bank.[93]

The corps commander assessed the situation, made his decision and gave out the necessary instructions to his chief of staff.

"When are the forward detachments departing here?" Bogdanov asked looking at his watch.

"I believe in a half hour," the corps commander answered.

"Fine, we will verify, since Red Guards are able to turn," Bogdanov smiled.[94]

Then, Bogdanov worked with the corps commander to see what assistance and reinforcements were needed. To help the forward detachment, the army commander promised sappers, artillery and a pontoon-bridge battalion. Bogdanov was already working to solve the fuel problem for the corps.

The corps sent advance elements to Kustrin on the Oder river. Two brigades on 26 January crossed the former German-Polish border, entering the territory of Germany at Charnkov. Bogdanov with the corps commander drove to the town, while street battles continued. Bogdanov was immeasurably glad that he could be present with the first Red Army troops on German soil. While the lead elements accomplished the mission, the remainder of the corps ran into fuel problems.

Despite disruptions in the fuel supply, the 2nd Guards Tank Army poured across the Notes river heading toward Kustrin on the Oder river, by 28 January. The feinting actions and false information transmitted by the radio had confused the German command, and made it possible to achieve surprise in offensive operation.[95]

The 2nd Guards Tank Army operated in conjunction with General Katukov's lst Guards Tank Army. Bogdanov and Katukov had served together in the 134th Tank Brigade in the summer of 1935. Bogdanov commanded the brigade while Katukov served as the brigade's chief of the operations section. Nearly ten years later, they both commanded tank army's driving on Berlin.

The 2nd Tank Army, along with the 5th Shock Army, reached the Oder river near Kustrin establishing a bridgehead on the western bank. The Front political officer, Konstantin Telegin, used their success to prod other army commanders. On 1 February, Telegin called the lst Guards Tank Army command post and announced that Bogdanov's tank army and Berezin's shock army had crossed the Oder. He asked, "Why not lst Tank?"[96] Zhukov's command remained constantly competitive.

Bogdanov demonstrated a talent for leading deep tank strikes. In the Vistula-Oder operation as a mobile group for the lst Belorussian Front, his tank army advanced nearly 700 kilometers in 15 days of combat. The pace and duration of the operation that Bogdanov's army maintained indicated the outstanding condition of the unit's equipment and their ability to maintain and sustain their combat activities. On 6 April 1945, Colonel General of the tank forces, Semen Il'ich Bogdanov received in recognition for the tank army's feat his second Gold Star, Hero of the Soviet Union.

Major General F.W. von Mellenthin in his post war memoir, describing the Vistula-Oder operation, wrote, "...the Russian offensive was delivered with a weight and fury never yet seen in war. It was clear that their High Command had completely mastered the technique of maintaining the advance of huge mechanized armies.... What happened between the Vistula and the Oder in the first months of 1945 is beyond description; nothing like it has been seen in Europe since the collapse of the Roman Empire."[97]

On 1 February, the 2nd Guards Tank Army, and on the following day the 1st Guards Tank Army, changed their route of advance to participate in the East Pomeranian operation. While the 1st Belorussian Front had pushed forward to the Oder, the 2nd Belorussian Front on the northern flank ran into strong resistance. The large number of German forces represented a major threat to the flank of the 1st Belorussian Front's continued advance, so the Front's tank armies were diverted to assist in clearing up the resisting German units. Committed to the fight on 2 March, by 5 March the 9th Guards Tank Corps advanced to the shores of the Baltic Sea, seizing the towns of Kamminan and Tessinan. The 12th Guards Tank Corps fought for Gollnov. The tank army's participation was short, but decisive. With the 2nd Belorussian Front brought on line for the final assault on Berlin, Bogdanov's tank army returned to the 1st Belorussian Front.

In preparation for the Berlin offensive operation, Bogdanov used the occasion for awarding a Guards banner to a brigade and talking to his tankers. He had the officers, sergeants and soldiers circle around him. "Comrade guards. Now your brigade goes to Berlin with a Guards Banner. In the old Russian Army there was a guards motto: 'Old Guards don't surrender, but die.' For us this doesn't fit. Our motto must become, 'Soviet Guards don't surrender, don't die, but conquer.' I wish you to win a victory, and under the guards banner, be the first to enter Berlin."[98]

In accordance with assigned missions, Marshal Zhukov decided to deal his main blow from the Kustrin bridgehead with the 1st and 2nd Guards Tank Armies exploiting success. The tank armies were to be committed to action on the first day of the operation after the Seelow Heights had been seized. Marshal Zhukov narrowly focused the Front, unleashing a blow on Berlin from the east.

On 5 April, Bogdanov, during a planning meeting with Marshal Zhukov, argued for more freedom of movement and depth for his army in going around Berlin from the north. Despite Bogdanov's past performances and demonstrated abilities, Zhukov in his characteristically abrupt manner with commanders checked the tank army commander with a barbed comment, "Are you going to wage combat for Berlin, comrade Bogdanov, or will you the whole time pass to the north?"[99] The basic mission for the 2nd Guards Tank Army was to outflank Berlin to the northeast and north, capturing the city's northwestern part.

In preparation for the impending operation, Radzievskii conducted summaries of the winter offensives. With an analysis similar to previous operations, the leadership of the army, corps, and brigades gathered with Radzievskii. He reviewed the well known positive examples, and ensured an understanding in combat actions that had failures, in order to not repeat them in the future. Preparation for the upcoming operation required different tactics. A great deal of time was spent preparing the battalions to operate in larger populated cities.

In mid-April 1945, on the eve of the Berlin operation Marshal Zhukov, commander of the lst Belorussian Front, making the last minute checks on the actions of his subordinate commanders wanted to ensure the close cooperation between his tank armies and the forward rifle armies in making the penetration of the German defenses and the commitment of the tank armies through the defenses. He had contacted the lst Tank Army and found that General Katukov had already been forward to check with the 8th Guards Army in order to finalize the coordination.

From the command post of the lst Guards Tank Army, Marshal Zhukov phoned the headquarters of the 2nd Guards Tank Army and asked for Bogdanov. He was not present in the headquarters at the time. He, too, had gone to the command post of the 5th Shock Army, in the sector through which his tank army would be committed. The call was taken by Radzievskii. Answering Zhukov's questions as to the whereabouts of the commanders of the corps which had been designated for action in the assault, Radzievskii replied, "They are up front in the units of Vasilii Ivanovich Kuznetsov (5th Shock Army Commander) in connection with the forthcoming job."[100]

Starting out from the Kustrin bridgehead, 2d Guards Tank Army began the operation concentrated on the eastern bank of the Oder river in the woods north of Kustrin, having one tank corps in the bridgehead. The overflowing spring waters of the Oder river flooded many cellars in Kustrin. The old Frederician fortifications had not been able to stand up to the bombardments. This eliminated the fortifications being used by the Germans for defense. With Kustrin in Soviet hands, their chances of mounting an offensive against Berlin improved dramatically. Between the Oder and Berlin no further natural obstacles had to be overcome. The Germans had made a mistake in their hopes that the swollen Oder and other terrain would check the Russian advance.

Fulfilling the front commander's order, the 2nd Guards Tank Army, consisting of the 9th and 12th Guards Tank and 1st Mechanized Corps, at 1630 hours, 16 April, began moving. The forward detachments crossed the Oder river into the Kustrin bridgehead with the mission to develop the strike in the general direction of Reikhenberg, Bernau. The rifle armies failed to breach the German defense on Seelow Heights the first day of their offensive, as had been planned. Marshal Zhukov decided to commit both of his tank armies. However, by 1900 hours, the tankers ran into strong German resistance and were stopped, too. The tank armies fought beside the rifle armies.

In an attempt to push his corps as far forward as possible and to get them moving, Bogdanov worked his tank corps in close support of the forward armies. The 12th Guards Tank Corps fought with the 5th Shock, 1st Mechanized assisted 3rd Shock, and 9th Guards Tank Corps moved with the 47th Army. Bogdanov, like most Soviet commanders, considered giving forces to someone else like lending your wife, so he maintained control of his corps despite their being spread through three armies. The corps maintained steady communications with the tank army commander and the chief of staff. Having completed the penetration of the German Oder river defensive line jointly with the rifle armies, Bogdanov's tankers broke through to the northeastern outskirts of Berlin on the sixth day of the operation. By 20-21 April, Bogdanov's tanks began penetrating the German defense and moving towards the northwest in the direction of success by the 47th Army. The 9th Guards Tank Corps bypassed to the north.

The 12th Guards Tank Corps upon reaching Alt-Landsberg on 21 April, turned southwest towards Berlin. In the wake of the tank corps' advance followed the 5th Shock Army.

Bogdanov's army maneuvering around Berlin to the north captured the city of Nanen on 24 April. Bogdanov reinforced the 9th Guards Tank Corps and turned it south making contact with lead 4th Guards Tank Army units on 25 April, fully encircling Berlin.

Parts of the 12th Guards Tank Corps forced the Spree river, successfully developing the attack to the southwest. Studying the movement, General Lieutenant Bogdanov on the morning of 27 April ordered the forces of the 1st Mechanized Corps across the Spree on the tank corps crossings, to seize the southeast part of Vestenda and southwest part of Charlottenburg, after that to attack along the main avenue in the direction of the Teirgarden in the center of Berlin. In the street fighting for Berlin, the 2nd Guards Tank Army lost 50% of its tanks to panzerfaust fire.[101] All the tank armies deprived of their maneuverability and striking power suffered high losses in the street battles. Forces of the 9th Guards Tank Corps together with units of the 47th Army at the same time advanced in battle in the area of Spandau and Potsdam.

General Bogdanov, as a good organizer and personally brave, was respected by German commanders as one of the best Red Army tank commanders. It is a mark of a great military leader who can first choose and then trust his subordinates. The combination of Bogdanov and Radzievskii is reminiscent of the famed German military duo of Hindenburg and Ludendorf. Bogdanov, as a military commander in the field with a great many things to do, offered the bold command image, while Radzievskii provided a superb analytical and military mind. Freed from constant supervision of his staff and the minute details of his operations, Bogdanov, a very paladin of courage and efficiency when fighting began, moved forward on the battlefield to ensure the subordinate commanders understood their tasks and missions. Using his physical presence to motivate and inspire, he could correct problems on the spot with his ability to clearly and precisely set the mission. His presence on the battlefield from the first to the last days added an unwearied tenacity and vigor. Bogdanov exemplified the universal, great combat leader who must be up front with sword in hand. Capitalizing on enemy mistakes, Bogdanov looked for an opponent backing up on the battlefield and that is where he poured his armored force.

NOTES

1. N.K. Popel, *Vperedi Berlin!*, Moscow: DOSAAF, 1970, p. 141.

2. O.F. Suvenirov, "Vsearmeiskaya tragediya," *Voenno-istoricheskii zhurnal* (hereafter *Vizh*), 3-1989, p. 41.

3. Ibid., p. 44.

4. Dmitrii Volkogonov, *Triumf i tragediya*, Book l, Part l, Moscow: Novosti, 1989, p. 284.

5. L.M. Sandalov, "Stoyali Nasmert," *Vizh.* 11-1988, p. 6.

6. L.M. Sandalov, *Perezhite*, Moscow: Voenizdat, 1966, p. 83.

7. Ibid., p. 84.

8. L.M. Sandalov, "Stoyali Nasmert," *Vizh* 2-89, p. 35.

9. Heinz Guderian, *Panzer Leader*, London: Futura, 1952, p. 153.

10. Paul Carell, *Hitler Moves East*, New York: Ballantine, 1971, p. 16.

11. Guderian, p. 153.

12. Ibid., p. 154.

13. Sandalov, *Pereshite*, p. 108.

14. L.M. Sandalov, "Oboronitel'naya operatsiya 4-i armii v nachal'nyi period voiny," *Vizh* 7-1971, p. 26.

15. Guderian, p. 156.

16. A. Eremenko, *The Arduous Beginning*, Moscow: Progress, 1966, p. 67.

17. Guderian, p. 158.

18. A.M. Zvartsev, *3-ya gvardeiskaya tankovaya*, Moscow: Voenizdat, 1982, p. 10.

19. *Marshal Zhukov: Polkovodets i chelovek*, Vol l, Moscow: Novosti, 1988, p.15.

20. N.G. Nersesyan, *Kievsko-Berlinskii*, Moscow: Voenizdat, 1974, p. 11.

21. *Sbornik materialov po izucheniyu opyta voiny*, No. 5, March 1943, Moscow: Voenizdat, 1943, p. 69.

22. Ibid., p. 70.

23. Ibid., p. 73.

24. Ibid., p. 74.

25. M.M. Litvyak, *Porodnennye bronei*, Moscow: Voenizdat, 1985, p. 8.

26. F.W. von Mellenthin, *Panzer Battles*, New York: Ballantine, 1980, p. 236.

27. A.P. Ryanzanskii, *V ogne tankovykh srazhenii*, Moscow: Nauka, 1975, p. 20.

28. Ibid., p. 21.

29. Mellenthin, pp. 237-8.

30. Ryanzanskii, pp. 26-7.

31. Ibid., p. 29.

32. Mellenthin, p. 238.

33. Ryanzanskii, pp. 35-6.

34. Ibid., p. 45.

35. K.K. Rokossovskii, *A Soldier's Duty*, Moscow: Progress, 1985, pp. 200-201.

36. Malcolm Mackintosh, *Juggernaut*, New York: MacMillan, 1967, p. 210; F.I. Vysotskii, et al, *Gvardeiskaya Tankovaya*, Moscow: Voenizdat, 1963, p. 50.

37. Vysotskii, p. 51.

38. Ibid.

39. Ibid., pp. 51-2.

40. D.A. Ivanov, V.P. Sabel'ev, P.V. Shemanskii, *Osnovy upravleniya voiskami v boyu*, Moscow: Voenizdat, 1977, p. 82.

41. P.D. Kazakov, *Glubokii sled*, Moscow: Voenizdat, 1982, pp. 97-8.

42. I.M. Anan'ev, *Tankovye armii v nastuplenii*, Moscow: Voenizdat, 1988, p. 270.

43. S.M. Shtemenko, *The Soviet General Staff at War*, Book One, Moscow: Progress, 1985, p. 480.

44. P.P. Tovstukha; R.M., Portugal'skii, *Upravlenie voiskami v nastuplenie*, Moscow: Voenizdat, 1981, p. 166.

45. "Otvety na Pis'ma Chitatelei," *Vizh* 9-1973, p. 123.

46. I.E. Krupchenko, et al, *Sovietskie Tankovye Voiska*, 1941-1945, Moscow: Voenizdat, 1973, p. 177.

47. V. Kasatokov, "General Armii A.I. Radzievskii," *Vizh* 7-1981, p. 92.

48. I.S. Konev, *Zapiski Komanduyushchego frontom*, Moscow: Voenizdat, 1981, p. 162.

49. O.A. Losik, *Stroitel'stvo i boevoe primenenie sovetskikh tankovykh voisk v gody velikoi otechestvennoi voiny*, Moscow: Voenizdat, 1979, pp. 195-6.

50. Vysotskii, p. 96.

51. Konev, pp. 170-71.

52. Ibid., p. 197.

53. Tovstukha, p. 167.

54. A.I. Radzievskii, "Na puti k varshave," *Vizh* 10-1971, p. 71.

55. Ibid.

56. Tovstukha, p. 169.

57. Ibid.

58. B.H. Liddell Hart, *The Other Side of the Hill*, London: Cassell, 1973, p. 333.

59. Ibid.

60. V.I. Chuikov, *The End of the Third Reich*, Moscow: Progress, 1978, p. 34.

61. Vysotskii, pp. 121-22.

62. Shtemenko, Book Two, p. 78.

63. Radzievskii, p. 74.

64. Chuikov, p. 40.

65. Ibid., p. 41.

66. Radzievskii, p. 74.

67. Ibid., p. 75.

68. Ibid.

69. Litvyak, p. 8.

70. Ibid., p. 13.

71. Ibid.

72. Ibid., p. 47.

73. Tovstukha, p. 110.

74. Ibid.

75. N.K. Popel, p. 142.

76. "Otvety na Pis'ma Chitatelet," *Vizh* 9-1973, p. 123.

77. Litvyak, p. 70.

78. A. Radzievskii, "Stremitel'nye deistviye tankovykh armii," *Vizh* 1-1965, p. 11.

79. Losik, p. 147.

80. Litvyak, p. 67.

81. Ibid., pp 68-9.

82. Ibid., pp. 112.

83. Ibid., p. 113.

84. Ibid., p. 73.

85. G.G. Semenov, *Nastupaet Udarnaya*, Moscow: Voenizdat, 1970, p. 268.

86. Konev, p. 171.

87. Litvyak, pp. 129-30.

88. Ibid., p. 74.

89. Ibid., p. 141; A.I. Radzievskii, *Tankovyi Udar*, Msocow: Voenizdat, 1977, p. 236.

90. Litvyak, p. 141.

91. M.M. Kir'yan, *Vnezapnost' v nastuplatel'nykh operatsiya Velikoi Otechestvennoi Voiny*, Moscow: Nauka, 1986, p. 177.

92. Litvyak, p. 144.

93. Ibid.

94. Ibid.

95. Kir'yan, p. 177.

96. Popel, p. 265.

97. Mellenthin, pp. 411-12.

98. Vysotskii, p. 191.

99. A.Kh. Babadzhanyan, *Dorogi Pobedy*, Moscow: Voenizdat, 1981, p. 281; Zhukov Pokovodets, p. 341.

100. G. Zhukov, *The Memoirs of Marshal Zhukov*, New York: Delacorte, 1971, p. 602.

101. Radzievskii, *Tankovyi Udar*, p. 177.

CHAPTER III

★ ★ ★

RYBALKO

War came abruptly. From the first days after the German invasion, General Pavel Semenovich Rybalko, instructing at a military school, struggled against army bureaucracy to get into battle. He finally received his assignment to the front lines, commanding a tank army. His first operations proved costly learning experiences, thrusting him to the verge of destruction as a tank commander. Despite losing an entire tank army in combat, Rybalko survived not only to command a tank army longer than anyone else, but also to emerge at the end of the war as his country's premier tank commander. His career during the Second World War belies the notion that Red Army commanders who lost in battle were eliminated by pistol toting commissars.

Born on the fourth of November, 1894, in a small Ukrainian village near Lebedin, Rybalko shared a small dwelling with seven brothers and a sister. His father worked in a sugar refinery, and every family member worked. If a Russian childhood was not fatal, it was short. At the age of 13, Pavel apprenticed as a lathe operator. Conscripted into the Tsar's army in 1914 for the First World War, Pavel Rybalko, the young soldier, was decorated with the St. George's Cross for personal bravery. He stayed at the front until the October 1917 revolution, when he joined the Red Guard, the Bolshevik's fighting arm. In the early struggle for political and physical survival in the following Russian Civil War, Rybalko led a Red partisan detachment against both invading German forces and rebelling Ukrainian nationalists.

In 1919, as the Russian Civil War continued, Rybalko joined the Communist Party serving as a commissar at regimental and brigade

Pavel Semenovich Rybalko

levels in the famed First Cavalry Army of General Semyon Budyenny. With the Cavalry Army, he fought against White Guards around Rostov, the anarchist guerrilla leader, Nestor I. Makhno, and other white Russian regiments in the Crimea. He received the Order of the Red Banner for personal bravery in combat around the towns of Dublyany and Berestechko in 1920. In five years of the Russian Civil War, Rybalko received 14 combat wounds, sustaining severe injuries which would stay with him for life.

Like many new commissars, Rybalko shifted from political affairs to military actions, commanding the 80th Cavalry Regiment, 1st Brigade, 14th Cavalry Division. Participating in a major offensive operation against Polish forces in the Russo-Polish War, on 20 June 1920, he led his unit in overcoming a stubborn Polish defense in a savage engagement for Novograd-Volynsk. The victorious battle, however, became lost in the greater Red Army defeat in war.

Between 1926 and 1931, Rybalko received military schooling in the Red Army Military Academy, a course for improving higher command staffs. In a short interlude to his military education he served as commander and commissar for a cavalry regiment and brigade. In 1931, he studied at the Frunze Military Academy, graduating three years later. After brief service as the assistant commander in a mountain-cavalry division, Rybalko worked a year in China advising Chinese cavalry units active against the Japanese Kwantung Army in Manchuria. From 1937 to 1939, he continued diplomatic service as a military attaché to Poland. As the Soviet military attaché in Warsaw at the time of the German invasion of Poland, September 1939, Rybalko sent reports on German air raids and the capture of Polish cities. Later in the year, he returned to the Soviet Union. Rybalko's foreign service and lack of a major unit command may have saved him from Stalin's catastrophic purging of the military in 1937-38. In 1940, Rybalko, at a time when the loss of senior leaders to the purges had to be replaced, benefited by rapid promotion to Major General.

The German Army invaded the Soviet Union on 22 June 1941, while Rybalko instructed at the Kazan Armored School. The Kazan courses, a result of the German-Soviet cooperation between the wars, offered advanced training to military technical personnel in special-ties, such as, assistant commanders of a tank company, battalion and brigade officer for technical affairs, petroleum, oil and lubricant tech-nician. Serving on the tank school faculty for the technical aspects of armored warfare, Rybalko developed an in-depth understanding of the tank as an instrument of war, and he mastered its mechanical as well as fighting capabilities. However, he continually sought relief from his uneventful instructor position in order to serve in combat. By May 1942, through the intervention of friends in higher places, mainly General Andrei Ivanovich Eremenko, Rybalko succeeded fi-nally in obtaining reassignment to a fighting unit, and, in June, he arrived as the deputy commander for infantry in the 3rd Tank Army. The corps and brigades of the 3rd Tank Army had assembled in the wooded areas south of Tula. Since the Soviet High Command planned to commit the tank army to battle any day, the newly formed units had little time to prepare for combat.

Upon joining the tank army, Rybalko realized his unfamiliarity with the Red Army's latest tanks, particularly the T-34, and imme-diately acted to remedy his shortcoming. The new deputy com-mander, in freshly pressed overalls, appeared at a subordinate tank brigade's motor park. He received instruction on the T-34 systems, components and instruments. After a few days of technical instruc-tion and talks, Rybalko wanted to observe the tank in operation. After talking with drivers and mechanics, he assumed the role of a driver-mechanic and spent more than 15 driving hours in the tank, putting it through different and difficult terrain. Rybalko was unafraid to put his hands on the controls nor too proud to learn the basics of his trade. He wished to know every aspect of the tank thoroughly and firmly established his reputation for his knowledge of tank forces in detail.[1] Rybalko's mastery of the technical aspects of armored warfare is indicative of all great battle captains who commanded effectively their engines of war.

In a short time, in July 1942, Rybalko became commander of the 5th Tank Army after the loss of its commander, General Aleksandar Il'ich Lizyukov. But, in September, he was again reassigned – as commander of the 3rd Tank Army, the position he would hold until war's end.

Rybalko, a short, squat man, built like a fireplug, had a scarred face with a long, saber-like cut down the right cheek. He shaved his head in the fashionable style of the inter-war period, giving him a forceful, resolute appearance. Extremely strong-willed as a commander, he was direct and blunt in his speech. Yet, he was also very intelligent, knowledgeable and competent, and fellow commanders looked forward to working with him.[2]

Upon assumption of command, Rybalko organized an analysis of the tank army's poor performance in the difficult Kozel'sk operation. The tank army had been placed on the southern approach to Moscow since the Soviet High Command feared the Germans would resume their offensive in the summer of 1942 with Moscow as the strategic objective. As it turned out, the area was of secondary importance in German plans. Instead, they struck toward Stalingrad and the Caucasus mountains. The tank army had performed poorly in relatively minor engagements. Rybalko studied the operation and concluded the main cause of tank losses was poorly trained drivers.[3] His critique focused on individual skills of drivers, tank commanders, and small unit leaders. "We are a tank army, an attacking army," Rybalko stressed in a straight forward manner. "Therefore, in preparation of the force, the basic job must be the conduct of the attack."[4] He also directed that fifty percent of the time be spent in night training. Rybalko immediately brought to bear his previous combat experience – experience which taught the need to ensure proper execution of individual soldier skills and tactics before attempting larger unit operations.

Rybalko, who paid close attention to training his tankers, checked the army units' compliance with his instructions. A ruthless pragmatist, he demanded everything in training and quickly chastised for omissions. Simple and direct in his rebukes with subordinates, he was considered fair and respected by his soldiers.

By late October 1942, after three months of refitting and training, the 3rd Tank Army stood prepared for combat. The Soviet High Command shifted the tank army within the Tula district, southwest of Moscow. On 21 December 1942, the Stavka ordered the Voronezh Front commander, General-Lieutenant Filipp Ivanovich Golikov, to prepare for offensive operations with the objective of destroying German forces on the Don River between Voronezh and Kantemirov. In order to achieve surprise in the impending operation, the 3rd Tank Army preparations required deceptive efforts and a secret repositioning of the army, in Soviet military parlance, a regrouping. These quick and secretive measures altering the orientation of the force through regrouping the tank army became Rybalko's hallmark. His first experience at regrouping the large, cumbersome tank force, however, was accomplished under difficult winter conditions constantly threatened by German aerial reconnaissance and air strikes.

In January 1943, the 3rd Tank Army, still assigned to the Voronezh Front, distinguished itself in the Ostrogozhsk-Rossosh offensive operation, and Rybalko came to the attention of the Supreme High Commander, Joseph Stalin. In a dispatch from Stalin's personal representatives at the front, Generals Georgi Zhukov and Aleksandr Vasilevskii reported, "On Rybalko, personally, we might say the following: he is an experienced general and his appraisal of the situation is accurate."[5]

For the operation, in early January, Rybalko, with his subordinate commanders, technical branch chiefs, and army staff officers carried out terrain reconnaissance for the tank army's actions in the direction of Rossosh. He planned to use the tank army operationally, as its force structure had been designed. With three rifle divisions and a rifle brigade, reinforced with tanks and artillery, his army would use the rifle formations to breakthrough the German's prepared defensive positions, followed by the tank and cavalry corps to develop success by exploiting the gap. His reconnaissance determined that the German defensive depth did not exceed four kilometers, so Rybalko planned to commit his tank corps to battle after the rifle divisions had advanced to a depth of three kilometers.

The difficult winter of 1943 stymied the fighting armies. Severe freezes, combined with frequent snowfalls and strong snowstorms, often created snow depths greater than a meter. The tank army's 130-170 kilometers march from a remote debarkation rail station to Kantemirovka in mid-January, proved especially difficult for the rifle troops and motorized infantry. Since all the army's combat vehicles were required to deliver ammunition, fuel, and food, the infantry marched on foot.[6]

Combat vehicle repair problems took its toll on the approach march. From the debarkation rail station, the tank army departed with 493 tanks, but upon arrival in the Kantemirovka area only 371 remained operable.[7] The lessons learned in practical measures to be taken on the approach march to minimize mechanical attrition were lessons all tank army commanders learned in the early war years through trial and error. Some aspects of peacetime training never match the rigors of wartime actions. After a 9 to 15 days travel by rail, the 3rd Tank Army concentrated at Kantemirovka on 4 January, completing assembly on 13 January, which delayed the attack by one day.

Responding resourcefully, Rybalko ordered all functioning tanks of the 12th Tank Corps transferred to the corps' 88th Tank Brigade, and the hollow brigades were placed in the army's reserve with the mission to organize the collection and repair of the tanks left behind from mechanical breakdowns.[8] Rybalko improvised on the move, setting a fast-paced style of operations for his headquarters. The 3rd Tank Army's newly assigned deputy commander, General Evtikhii Emel'yanovich Belov, recalled his attempts to catch up with Rybalko's command post. General Belov drove to the village of Bobrov to be told by the garrison commandant that the army staff had left a few hours earlier for Kozlov. At Kozlov, he was informed, the army headquarters had just left for Losev. "I took three days to catch up with the army staff," General Belov wrote.[9]

In preparation for the attack, Rybalko instructed his staff to issue specific tasks. The corps were directed to conduct detailed reconnaissance of the German's forward defense, in order to determine their system of fire and unit displacements. He wanted his commanders to conduct terrain reconnaissance and to coordinate the actions of their infantry, armor and artillery. Secrecy in regrouping was maintained during the preparation by categorically forbidding units to use their radios until the attack began.[10] The Red Army, throughout the war, had trouble with poor radio discipline, and their tendency for uncontrolled radio transmissions often compromised impending operations. Commanders imposed the easiest remedy, a strictly enforced prohibition on all radio transmissions. In this case, Rybalko was successful. The German intelligence assessment dated 13 January 1943, failed to identify the 3rd Tank Army in the Red Army deployment.[11]

On 14 January, the morning of the army's offensive, snowfall with dense fog significantly reduced visibility northwest of Kantemirovka. The artillery preparation scheduled for 0800 hours was delayed until late morning after the snow. With grey-white geysers suddenly exploding upward along the German front defense line, the artillery preparation lasted an intense half hour. After the infantry units advanced forward slowly, the anxious Rybalko committed his tank corps into the penetration.

By evening, Major General Vasilii Alekseevich Koptsov's 15th Tank Corps seized Zhilin from the march, destroying in the process the headquarters of the German 24th Panzer Corps and the 385th and 387th Infantry Divisions. Continuing the offensive the next morning, the corps seized Aleksandrovka and, by evening, cut the road between Rossosh and Roven'ki. Also that morning, Rybalko's 12th Tank Corps operating on the right flank, began successfully to develop the offensive, reaching Rossosh by the end of the day. Rybalko's tankers captured the town from the march destroying the headquarters of the 156th Italian Infantry Division west of the city. In the fighting, an Italian General with two of his staff officers were captured. Rybalko, who involved himself in every facet of the operation, ordered his intelligence officer to take them immediately to the Front staff.

From Rossosh, Rybalko's army continued advancing north to Podgornoye completing the encirclement of the Italian Alpine Corps. Rybalko stopped forces only to capture or to destroy enemy units. But, at Podgornoye, Rybalko admittedly erred. Carried away by the army's initial success, he allotted only a small force of one rifle division, to handle the encircled Italians. The Italian force broke out, crashing through the thinly spread Soviet rifle forces and withdrew west to Valuiki.[12]

On the left flank, 15th Tank Corps met serious resistance. On the morning of 16 January, Rybalko ordered the 15th Tank Corps to attack westerly and seize Ol'khovatka. By evening, after intense fighting the tankers captured the town.

During the night of 16 January, Rybalko's army resumed the offensive in a raging snowstorm, making the road over which the main body of the 12th Tank Corps traveled impassable from covering snow. Struggling forward, the corps commander by the morning of 19 January, counting only 44 operable tanks, shifted to the defensive with diminished combat strength.[13]

The 15th Tank Corps ran into strong German opposition forcing the tank corps to withdraw to the southern edge of a major road junction straddling the German's primary withdrawal route to Ostrogozhsk. Repelling the retreating German forces, the tank corps resumed its attack on 21 January, linking up with elements of the 40th Army encircling the German Ostrogozhsk grouping.

The Ostrogozhsk-Rossosh operation encircled and destroyed a large enemy force by 23 January. In 16 days, the 3rd Tank Army advanced nearly 300 kilometers under difficult conditions. Rybalko's tank army fought German, Hungarian, and Italian infantry units to recapture occupied territory, and the Soviet High Command greatly appreciated the tank army's feat. Rybalko received the Order of Suvorov lst Degree and promotion to Lieutenant General.

Despite the toll from heavy fighting on Red Army troops who had been in combat for a month, the Stavka planned to continue the offensive westward. The Voronezh Front, with five rifle armies, used Rybalko's tank army as its armored striking force. Consisting of the 12th and 15th Tank and 6th Guards Cavalry Corps, and four rifle divisions supported by a tank brigade and regiment, Rybalko's army still numbered only 165 tanks.[14]

With the capture of Kharkov as its objective, the Voronezh Front's main attack would converge on Kharkov from the northeast and east. Rybalko's tank army would advance through Veliki Burluk, cross the Northern Donets River, swing southwest through Chuguyev, and then turn westward and northwestward to Lyubotin, south of Kharkov, in a close enveloping maneuver designed to link up with 40th Army. General Golikov spread the Front into a single echelon, putting his combat power forward. He hoped for a rapid advance to preclude the Germans from erecting a strong defensive line.

On the eve of the operation, Rybalko called his staff together to give his operational decisions. The army's intelligence officer, Lieutenant Colonel Cheprakov, reported the latest reconnaissance information. The Front intelligence staff calculated nearly 300 tanks in the area.[15] "This is important, because these figures were unsubstantiated," Rybalko observed skeptically. "But in general, comrade Cheprakov, you know very well, intelligence must carry on during the whole operation. If there is any change discovered in the course of battle, you report to me without delay."[16]

Having established his primary intelligence concerns, Rybalko refined the offensive missions and tasks for each corps commander. His concept for seizing Kharkov sent the 15th Tank Corps with two rifle division from the east while the 12th Tank Corps with one rifle division attacked from the south. The 6th Guards Cavalry Corps was to link up with forces of the 40th Army, and together surround the Germans in Kharkov preventing their breakout to the south-west.

On the morning of 2 February, the 3rd Tank Army attacked under a strong covering artillery preparation, hammering German defenders. Rybalko's army rapidly advanced west toward the Northern Donets river, receiving losses and casualties primarily from German bombers. By the third day of the operation, German Stukas methodically struck the army's right flank. The 12th Tank Corps snagged capturing the town of Chuguyev. German resistance in the town allowed other German units reinforced by a powerful artillery grouping to fortify the west bank of the Northern Donets.

Returning from his forward units to the army command post, Rybalko was in a poor mood.

"Why so gloomy, Pavel Semenovich?" asked General Semen Ivanovich Melnikov, the tank army's member of the Military Council.

"I gave Kobzarya (chief of rear services) a dressing down, and I'm afraid I handled it badly."

"What was the problem with him?" Melnikov pursued.

"It was about the motorized rifle troops."

Smoking a cigarette in agitation, Rybalko began to explain. "During the day the sun comes out, the snow melts, and they plough through it on their bellies, and they get wet to the skin. Then, at night it's 10 degrees, and the clothing on the people is like a coarse coat of mail. Consequently, they never get a chance to dry themselves. To look at them is a heart ache."

"But what can Kobzarya do? He hardly manages to deliver the fuel and ammunition."

"What can be done?" Rybalko interrupted bitterly. "What Potopov's (Commander 97th Tank Brigade) deputy for rear did. For three nights running, he delivers his motorized riflemen dry under-clothes, clothes, and hot food in thermoses. And the people began to fight with higher spirits. This captain was probably a fine manager before the war."[17]

The protracted fight around Chuguyev with reports of the SS Panzer Division "Das Reich," 2nd SS Panzer Corps moving forward from Kharkov disturbed Rybalko.[18] As Rybalko learned later, the 2nd SS Panzer Corps had been hurriedly moved from France to the eastern front. Unless the German resistance was dealt with quickly, the arriving German forces could erect defenses along the Northern Donets, impeding severely 3rd Tank Army's progress. In an attempt to speed the advance, Rybalko committed his two tank corps the following day before they completed refitting. Shifting the direction of his army to the southwest, Rybalko ordered the 12th and 15th Tank Corps to attack as soon as possible toward the Pechenegi area for crossings over the Northern Donets. Rybalko used his 6th Guards Cavalry Corps reinforced with a tank brigade and the 111th Rifle Division to sweep southwest for the rail line from Kupyansk to Chuguyev cutting German withdrawal routes and covering the army's southern flank.

On 3 February, Rybalko's tank army attacked. Although the two tank corps and the cavalry corps made good progress initially, they met resistance after crossing the Burluk river in the Veliki Burluk area. The Germans slowed Rybalko's right flank, drawing off his armored strength to deal with the growing threat. Advanced elements of the 12th Tank and 6th Guards Cavalry Corps approached to within 10 kilometers of the Northern Donets River at Pechenegi. The SS Panzer Division "Adolf Hitler" from the 2nd SS Panzer Corps assumed positions along the river's west bank and began moving into bridgeheads along the east bank from Zmiyev northward to beyond Pechenegi.

The following day 15th Tank Corps with a supporting rifle division captured Veliki Burluk, and its lead tank brigade reached German positions on the Northern Donets at Pechenegi. Simultaneously, on the left flank, lead elements of the widely spread 12th Tank Corps kept advancing. And, by evening, the 6th Guards Cavalry Corps units, along with its rifle division, secured Shevchenkovo, cutting escape routes from Kupyansk toward Chuguyev for the retreating German 298th Infantry Division.

The German SS Panzer Division "Das Reich" with strong delaying action hampered the 3rd Tank Army's progress. Driven from Veliki Burluk by the 15th Tank Corps, "Das Reich" units established strong defenses north of the village holding a firm salient on the 3rd Tank Army's northern boundary. With the arrival of more German reinforcements, the salient became a potentially dangerous base for a counteroffensive against Rybalko's increasingly exposed flank and rear.

By 5 February, already two days behind schedule, Rybalko, watching his vulnerable right flank, sought ways to overcome the stubborn resistance. The initial rifle division bridgehead across the river had been driven back with heavy losses by the "Adolf Hitler" SS Panzer Division. Waiting for the arrival of lagging units from the 15th Tank Corps and its rifle division, Rybalko's lead units probed other German positions.

At first light on 6 February, the 15th Tank Corps' motorized riflemen and the 160th Rifle Division after a short artillery preparation, attempted a crossing, but were repulsed. The 12th Tank Corps with its rifle division eliminated the German's bridgehead east of the river at Malinovka, and attempted to force the Northern Donets near Chuguyev only to be denied a crossing.

Although time was on Rybalko's side in his battle with SS Panzer Division "Das Reich" counterattacks, he had to learn to guard against dissipating his armored force's power by spreading tank units across the front. The ensuing four-day contest distracted Rybalko from his main task which was to overcome German defense lines on the Northern Donets River and drive on Kharkov. Thwarted in his attempts to cross the Northern Donets river east of Kharkov, Rybalko decided to exploit the success of the neighboring 6th Army to the south. He sent the 6th Guards Cavalry Corps across the river at Andreyvka in a sweeping envelopment south of Kharkov to Lyubotin in a risky attempt by a relatively fragile force to redeem the tank army's partial failure.

But in the first week of the Voronezh Front offensive, the operation fell well behind schedule. Moreover, the Front now faced determined German resistance in prepared defenses outside Kharkov. Only the 40th Army's advance exceeded expectations, and its advance forced the Germans to give up positions east of the Northern Donets river, including "Das Reich" units in front of the 3rd Tank Army. On 9 February, Rybalko's right wing followed closely over the Northern Donets. Primarily, the 40th Army's success and advance to the north ultimately threatened to envelop German units and made possible the 3rd Tank Army advance.

The 3rd Tank Army's progress soon struck against the German defenses north and south of Rogan where the Soviets again came to a grinding halt. Rybalko planned an assault against the German defenses east of Kharkov by attacking from the southeast. From the start Rybalko's attack went awry. The 6th Guards Cavalry Corps ran into heavy resistance south of Merefa, and the German SS Panzer Division, "Das Reich," ultimately drove the horse corps down the Mzha river. The 12th Tank Corps tried to penetrate German defenses at Rogan but failed in all of its attempts. Other 3rd Tank Army units continued to regroup and failed to join the attack on 11 February. Command and control difficulties within 3rd Tank Army prevented a coordinated attack and permitted German forces time to erect even stronger defenses.

When Rybalko's renewed the attack on the morning of 12 February, tank army units repeatedly struck at German positions but made only meager gains in heavy fighting. For two days, Rybalko's forces advanced 6-12 kilometers. The 15th Tank Corps, with two rifle divisions drove SS "Adolf Hitler" from the outer to the inner Kharkov defense lines and battled for the factory district in the city's eastern suburbs. By 14 February, all attempts by Rybalko's army to envelop the city proved unsuccessful. Drawn in by inexperience, Rybalko's tank army spent its strength rapidly in costly fighting against prepared defensive positions.

Outside the city Rybalko's headquarters and staff received constant German air bombardments. Subsequent air strikes against the house where Rybalko was located resulted in serious casualties and a close call for the army commander.

When German indecision on defending or giving up Kharkov resulted in abandoned defensive positions, General Golikov ordered his armies to open a final assault on the city from the west, north and southeast. On 16 February, Rybalko's tankers met General Andrei Grigorovich Kravchenko's 5th Guards Tank Corps tankers in the Kharkov city square. The Front Chief of Staff, General Mikhail Il'ich Kazakov, also met Rybalko on a Kharkov street. He asked Rybalko why fresh columns of 3rd Tank Army continued to flow into the city when they ought to be attacking south from Kharkov to Lyubotin as ordered. Rybalko explained that he had only the rear elements of his tank corps in Kharkov to protect the local industrial base. "While that may be true," General Kazakov later wrote, "the town was already beginning to feel the results of overcrowding with troop units."19

After a brief occupation of positions covering Kharkov, Rybalko's tank army immediately resumed the offensive towards Poltava. Third Tank Army units, early on 17 February, struck the German Corps Raus ("Großdeutschland" Panzer Grenadier and 320th Infantry Divisions) defending south, southwest of Kharkov. The next day 15th Tank Corps secured Pseochnya and fought the "Großdeutschland" Division troops for Lyubotin while the 12th Tank Corps penetrated the German defense reaching Merefa.

As a result of serious losses in army personnel and equipment, the army offensive moved at a slow pace. German tactical unit commanders skillfully delayed in cooperation with SS Panzer Division "Adolf Hitler," defending south of Novyay Vodolaga, in order to buy necessary time for Field Marshal Erich von Manstein, commander of the German Army Group South, who planned an operational counterthrust. By 18 February, Rybalko's army fought with only 110 operable tanks. The tank army's extended supply lines failed to deliver enough fuel and ammunition, and the troops were exhausted from 40 days of constant battles.20 Rybalko requested a three day pause to restore the army's combat effectiveness, but the Front commander denied his request. Red Army commanders had much to learn about the pace of campaigns, sustainment of operations, and the endurance of men and machines.

The overextended Voronezh Front proved unguarded at the moment. Field Marshal von Manstein sought to crush the Southwestern Front with converging thrusts by the 4th Panzer Army. On 19 February, the German's 2nd SS Panzer and 48th Panzer Corps went on the offensive against the vulnerable flanks of the Southwestern Front.

Calls for assistance from General Nikolai Vatutin, commander Southwestern Front, grew urgent as the German units carved up the 6th Army and General Markian Mikhailovich Popov's armored group to the south of Rybalko's tank army. On 23 February, Rybalko received a new mission to turn his army south and deal with the advancing German counteroffensive which had advanced to Krasnograd. However, the 3rd Tank Army in conjunction with 69th Army could not muster the strength to break the German defenses in the vicinity of Krasnograd.

Five days later, the Soviet High Command transferred the 3rd Tank Army to the beleaguered Southwestern Front. Rybalko's army wheeled sharply southward to blunt the German advance and save 6th Army units. Unfortunately, possessing only 30 operable tanks in both corps, 3rd Tank Army lacked the power to shift into the attack.[21] With shortages in fuel, ammunition, and supplies, the tank army's offensive had to be postponed until the morning of 3 March.

Meanwhile, on 2 March, the German Fourth Panzer Army tore into the 3rd Tank Army from the south. The German Operations Group Kampf, with the SS "Adolf Hitler" Division, attacked Rybalko's right flank from Krasnograd. By the evening, German forces succeeded in surrounding the 12th and 15th Tank Corps near Kegichevka.

Almost as soon as the tank army attacked on the morning of 3 March its units went over to the defensive against an overwhelming German assault. In defensive actions, the 15th Tank Corps commander, Major General V.A. Koptsov, who had been awarded Hero of the Soviet Union for his actions as a tank battalion commander at Khalkin Gol, was killed. For a brief moment in the action, Rybalko, for whom relationships were usually conditional, lamented the death of such a popular and good fighting tank commander.[22] Fighting defensively, the tank army, for the next few days, gave ground. Rybalko's army mustered less than 50 tanks in various mechanical conditions.[23] By 5 March, 3rd Tank Army ceased to exist as a coherent unit with its two tank corps essentially destroyed. Rybalko tried in vain to construct a defensive line, while the Germans reduced the remainder of his trapped forces.

Through desperate resistance, Soviet forces held the Germans out of Kharkov until 7 March, then the German command changed direction of their main strike along the boundary between the 69th and 3rd Tank Armies covered by the 6th Guards Cavalry Corps. The German units began to drive north through the Voronezh Front forces retaking Lyubotin. By 12 March Germans fighting on the northeast approaches penetrated to Kharkov. Rybalko with a spent force could not counterstrike.

On the night of 12-13 March, SS Panzer Division "Death's Head" struck east and south from its positions north of Kharkov. By 1900 hours lead elements of the division reached Rogan, east of Kharkov, and cutting through the 3rd Tank Army's rear area and routes to the Northern Donets river. The following day SS Death's Head cut the remaining 3rd Tank Army lines of communications. The 3rd Tank Army was encircled. The Red Army tankers had no ammunition, fuel or food. Rybalko reported the bleak situation to the Voronezh Front commander, and then to the Soviet High Command. On the night of 14 March, Rybalko received permission from General Golikov to abandon Kharkov and withdraw his units across the Northern Donets river.

Rybalko with his staff cut off from the Northern Donets sent a message to the Deputy commander, General E.E. Belov, "Evtikhii Emel'yanovich, the army must save itself. It will be very difficult but fall back to Mokhachi."[24] It was very difficult indeed. With little to stop the German tanks, remnants had only artillery guns in direct fire.

Fighting off disaster, Rybalko decided to withdraw the encircled forces in a southeasterly direction through small villages on the night of 15 March. By the evening of the 16th, a large remaining portion of the army crossed the Northern Donets river. That night, Rybalko believed further resistance was futile and issued orders for his units to break out of the encirclement to the northeast and north. Disaster struck. The 15th Tank Corps and its supporting division were unable to organize a concerted breakout, but continued to struggle for several days after which only scattered groups made their way northward toward Soviet lines.

The 12th Tank Corps reacted in a more organized fashion, disengaging from German forces and moving in a northwest direction. On the following days, the corps ran into a series of hasty and heavy fights with German defensive positions, but on 16 March the corps's remnants reached Red Army lines .

For the next week the withdrawing Soviet forces attempted to hold along river lines while the Soviet High Command poured reinforcements into the Belgorod-Kharkov area to bolster the seriously weakened armies. The 3rd Tank Army unit history candidly summed the disastrous operation as, "due to underestimating the strength and capabilities of the enemy and not knowing his intentions, as well as over-assessing their own successes and giving the troops an impossible mission, the offensive by the 3rd Tank Army to Poltava failed."[25]

Unable to restore the lost tanks, on 26 April, the 3rd Tank Army ceased to exist. Remnants were redesignated the 57th Army. On 1 May, Rybalko departed for Moscow to argue restoration of his lost tank army. He proposed to General Yakov Nikolaevich Federenko, commander of the Red Army tank and mechanized forces, and to the General Staff, that the 3rd Tank Army should be reestablished as an operational tank formation. Rybalko showed the 3rd Tank Army had successfully carried out offensive operations over the course of nearly a year and had an experienced and well-trained cadre of tankers. General Federenko who backed the proposal conferred with Stalin. On 14 May 1943, the Supreme High Command issued a directive to form the 3rd Guards Tank Army by 5 June 1943.

May 1943 proved a tragic month for Rybalko in another way. In addition to his devastating combat loss and subsequent fight to regain his tank command, he received notification that his only son, 19 years old, was missing in action. Rybalko, visibly upset by the news, controlled himself well with only those close to him knowing the additional personal anguish he bore.[26] His vigorous involvement in the war distracted him from his personal loss and mourning.

In June, Rybalko, returning to his army command post after a three day visit to the newly reconstituted 15th Tank Corps, shared his impressions with the General Semen Ivanovich Melnikov, the tank army's member of the Military Council. It was late night, but no one was sleeping in the stuffy summer air of an approaching thunderstorm. "We were dripping with sweat, even after wiping our face and neck with a moist handkerchief," Melnikov recalled.

"It would be good to pour a little cold water over ourselves," Rybalko mused out loud.

"What stops you from doing it? I'll order it at once..." Melnikov was rising, but Rybalko interrupted.

"We have time. But first, lets talk about assigning Rudkin as the corps commander."

Sensing a serious conversation, Melnikov sat back down and prepared to listen attentively.

"You remember how he was as a brigade commander?" Rybalko began. "His brigade always fought successfully in the most difficult sectors. And how he defended Taranovku? And several times a day committed his force to counterattacks and withdrew only after orders. Then Rudkin was at his height."

"But now?"

"He's not on top of his corps," Rybalko shook his head despondently. "What's surprising, he finished the Armored Tank Academy, a competent combat commander, but now – he doesn't pull his weight." Rybalko paused, then added, "But, perhaps I am too critical?"

"Rudkin recently became corps commander," Melnikov reminded. "It's necessary to help him. You spent three days with him, what was your assistance?"

Rybalko shortly threw out, "I helped." Then he suggested, "Lets drive over to Rudkin tomorrow. You see if I'm not right."[27]

Rybalko visited training sites in General Filipp Nikitich Rudkin's corps area, and he corrected tank gunnery errors on the firing range. After spending more time looking at soldier training, Rybalko seemed mollified. The individual soldier training requirements were greater than he first believed, and the problems were not necessarily all Rudkin's fault. The tank army's personnel replacements were new, hastily drafted soldiers who needed extensive training in all aspects of fieldcraft and fighting techniques.

Rybalko spent the whole day with the corps staff giving the commander, his deputy and political officers advice. He let them know that in the near future, in all probability, he would order combat training in such a subject as, "Combat in the Depths of the Enemy Defense," and the exercise would show how much the corps commander learned about errors in organizing combat formations.[28]

Rybalko once observed that "the art of troop control included many very different components; all of them, a part of the whole, and have different significance in achieving success. But, only the military leader, who assesses the enemy and friendly forces not only decides the correct decision, but also knows the possibilities of ensuring combat actions by his force, has the right to say what is perfectly mastered in this art."[29]

On a report from the chief of rear services, Rybalko had written on the eve of the Kursk battle an extensive quote from M.V. Frunze on the requirements of material preparations for combat and the necessary organizations for combat operations. Many years later, Melnikov studying Frunze's writings ran across the quote which Rybalko often used. In Rybalko's personal belongings and books he possessed a large collection of extracts and notes which he turned to in his spare time. And when he quoted them, from memory or from his notes, depending on the situation, the quote was always appropriate for the place and time.[30] Rybalko appreciated the power of appropriate words in making a point clearly and motivating his subordinates.

In the summer of 1943, the buildup of Soviet and German forces focused on the Kursk salient. Early morning on 5 July, the German forces began their attack to regain the strategic initiative. With two major pincers formed by advancing panzer units, the Germans attempted to slice off the salient from the north and south. With dawn, the Soviet Voronezh and Central Fronts heavily shelled the German attack positions and command posts. In spite of the disruption from Soviet artillery, the German assault on the northern face concentrated on a 40 kilometer sector of the Central Front.

Rybalko watched closely the Kursk operation unfold. On 9 July, he drove to the 15th Tank Corps command post to receive reports of its preparedness for combat. The tank corps had a complete complement of units, three tank and one mechanized brigades, self-propelled artillery, multiple rocket launchers, assault guns and air defense regiments. The tank brigades each had approximately 65 tanks, T-34's and T-70's, with two basic loads of ammunition and two resupplies of fuel.

Rybalko listened attentively and nodded satisfactorily to the corps' reported readiness. He told the staff about German operations in the area of Orel and Belgorod. Believing the tank army would be called any day into battle, Rybalko announced, "Therefore, I call upon you to be prepared at any moment to move along assigned march routes." He then offered, "I think our guard tank army could be transferred right there, and it will have a primary role in the fighting. I'm telling you to be prepared at any moment to carry out instructions for march."[31] Rybalko liked to anticipate his missions.

He lightly tapped the palm of his hand on the table top and concluded, "your corps is basically ready for combat operations. In completing any unfinished business I will give you three days. That's all, comrades." Ending the meeting, the short, stocky army commander with the corps staff walked out of the dug out.[32] Rybalko moved to other business within his command.

By 8 July, the Germans expended their forces against the strongly prepared Soviet defensive positions. The German command halted the offensive on 9 July, regrouping its remaining units for a renewed blow. The offensive resumed but the German forces failed to penetrate the Central Front defenses. Meanwhile, the Soviet High Command ordered the final preparations for the Bryansk and left wing of the Western Fronts to assume the offensive. The waiting Red Army forces struck back with a counteroffensive, code-named Operation

Rybalko (center) listening to his tank commanders' report.

Kutuzov, towards Orel, aimed at the rear of the German units striving for Kursk from the north. The left wing of the Western and Bryansk Fronts assault on 12 July began the turning point in the Battle of Kursk. The Central Front offensive followed on 15 July. The Germans threw large reserves against the attackers and offered stiff resistance.

Since the Stavka's decision to reconstruct the 3rd Guard Tank Army, Rybalko's tank corps and other units were withdrawn from the Southwestern Front and placed in Stavka reserve to form the tank army. Rybalko's tank army remained in the Stavka reserve south of Plavsk a forested assembly area until 14 July 1943.

On 14 July the Bryansk Front Commander, Colonel General Markian Mikhailovich Popov and his chief of staff General Leonid Mikhailovich Sandalov attempted to more precisely define when the Front was to be reinforced with the 3rd Guards Tank Army. At midday Rybalko arrived in the Front's command post, and as Sandalov recalled, Rybalko reproached him, "You think the tank army is unlike a cavalry corps?" He gave a short, rapid tutorial to

General Sandalov on the necessities of a tank army's preparations for combat. Rybalko wanted instructions for movement from the area of Plavsk. He had to deliver subordinate units' their missions, and organize the coordination with rifle armies, aviation, artillery and air defense forces.

"As far as I know," General Rybalko continued in disgust, "you still don't have to commit the tank army to the fight. Which shows exactly how lightly you look at this."[33]

General Sandalov with some difficulty calmed Rybalko, and together they sought out the Front commander who again tried to get a decision about the subordination of the tank army. In a late night decision, the Stavka transferred the 3rd Guards Tank Army to the Bryansk Front.

After the demise of his army in early spring under the Southwestern Front's leadership, Rybalko became keenly aware of Front operations in order to anticipate the implications of the situation for his tank army. Rybalko after the war observed, "I knew everything, or almost everything, Front commander's concept and missions, which stood before the Front."[34] He always became acquainted in good time with the Front's commanders forces not only in the sector of impending operations but also with the whole front. Rybalko, in fact, had anticipated this operation when he visited his corps on 9 July, to get a status report on their preparations for combat.

On the rainy night of 14 July, Rybalko's tank army was alerted and moved to its assembly area in the direction of Orel highway. After two days march over an exhausting 130 kilometer route, the tank army's personnel and equipment hid in the woods along the road. Towards evening 16 July, Rybalko's units finished concentrating in the area of Novosil (60 kilometers east of Orel), 15-20 kilometers from the forward edge of the Bryansk Front. The addition of the 2nd Mechanized Corps made the 3rd Guards Tank Army, a three corps tank army. Rybalko's impending attack would be the first use in the offensive of the new tank army organization.

Despite changes in the tank army's force structure minimizing the earlier unwieldliness of an infantry, tank and cavalry mixture, the Kursk experience, in mid-1943, revealed other serious shortcomings. In committing the 3rd Guards Tank Army, as in other tank armies, during the breakthrough of strongly fortified enemy defenses, the major problem arose in which the army had insufficient supporting reinforcements, primarily heavy artillery. The necessary fire support failed to compensate fully for artillery fires from supporting rifle armies. As a result, tank armies suffered unnecessary casualties when breaking through a defense. Rybalko, in particular, consistently took heavy casualties in breakthrough operations. His high tank losses became a major point of contention in the post-war studies in which military analysts, primarily General A.I. Radzievskii as commandant of the Frunze Academy, were critical of Rybalko's premature commitment of tank forces without his waiting for the rifle armies to create the protected gap.[35] Rybalko impatient, as his Front commanders often were, involved his tankers in the penetration of the tactical defense with all its obstacles and coordinated fires to speed up the advance – which resulted in higher tank losses than those more cautious tank commanders, such as Katukov.

For the Bryansk Front counteroffensive, Rybalko decided to commit the tank army into the breakthrough along three routes, with the 12th and 15th Tank Corps in the first echelon, 2nd Mechanized Corps in the second, and the 91st Separate Tank Brigade and 50th Motorcycle Regiment in reserve. Each tank corps deployed forward detachments, consisting of a reinforced tank brigade.

On the night of 16-17 July, the corps moved to assembly areas located 8-10 kilometers from the Oleshen river. Throughout 17 July, preparation of soldiers and equipment continued. During the last hours of preparation, the tank army's mission changed. On the morning of 18 July, the Bryansk Front commander, on instructions from the Stavka, ordered the 3rd Guards Tank Army to shift to the second of several planned attack variants. The Front commander, General Popov, ordered Rybalko's army the attack through the 3rd Army sector the next morning. Attacking in the general direction of Spasskoe and Otrada, Rybalko's tank army was to cut off the railroad and highway between Orel and Mtsensk, cross the Oka river north of Orel, capture a bridgehead and continue advancing towards Naryshkino. This new mission gave Rybalko's units less than a day to prepare for the redirection.[36]

On 18 July, the 3rd Guards Tank Army strength was 475 T-34s, 224 T-70s, 492 guns and mortars and some 37, 266 personnel.[37] The tank army occupied its attack positions for commitment into the gap which was forming east of the Oleshen' River in the Strel'nikov, Zhabino sector. Without changing the army formation and basic actions, Rybalko wisely minimized disruption to the plan and assigned the corps missions as follows:

"The 12th Tank Corps is to attack in the direction of Sychi and Stanovoy Kolodez(northern); by evening of 19 July, it is to seize the Pugacheveka, Stanovoy Kolodez, Il'inkskii area, and its forward detachments are to capture the enemy airfield in the Grachevka area and crossings over the Rybnitsa river vicinity Lyubanovo and Stupino.

"The 15th Tank Corps is to attack in the direction of Bortnoye and Khotetovo; by evening on 19 July it is to seize the Kuleshovka, Khotetovo, Stanovoy Kolodez(southern) area, and its forward detachments are to seize crossings over the Rybnitsa river at Golokhvastovo as well as the Yeropkino station.

"The 2nd Mechanized Corps is to advance in the army's second echelon behind the tank corps; by evening on 19 July, it is to reach the Shlykovo, Nepyuyevo, Sobakinskiye Vyselki area, protecting the army from enemy strikes from the south; and its forward detachments are to seize Novopetrovka and Znobishino."[38]

At approximately 1030 hours, 19 July, after a brief but intensive and well-coordinated artillery and air preparation, Rybalko's first echelon tank corps launched their offensive in the Panama-Zabrody sector. The forward detachments of the 12th and 15th Tank Corps crossed the Oleshen river, deployed into combat formation and attacked the Germans. The Germans responded to the powerful armor avalanche with all available aircraft on the Orel area. In addition to intensive airstrikes, by midday, the Germans struck Rybalko's tank army with two panzer and one infantry divisions. The German armored units were equipped with a number of new heavy tanks and assault guns, Tigers and Ferdinands, ensuring deadly armor engagements.

Despite the German efforts, by evening 19 July, the tank corps advanced to a depth of 10-12 kilometers, pursuing withdrawing German units. During the night, the 12th Tank Corps advanced another 10-15 kilometers while the 15th Tank Corps was unable to advance against stiffening resistance. General Mikhail Il'ich Kazakov, deputy commander for the Bryansk Front, noted that the success in penetrating the German's tactical defense zone was achieved through Pavel Rybalko's perfectly organized fulfillment of the Front commander's decision.[39]

On the morning of 20 July, Bryansk Front commander, Colonel-General M.M. Popov, ordered Rybalko to attack in a northwesterly direction with the mission of reaching the Otrada area by day's end.

There the tank army was to cut across the Orel-Mtsensk road and railroad. By 21 July, Rybalko's tank army was to seize Mtsensk, and complete the destruction of the German forces in the surrounding area. Rybalko did not want his tank units to become involved in fighting in either Mtsensk nor Orel, and he cautioned, "In the narrow streets the Fascists will subject our tanks to heavy fire at point blank range."[40] Rybalko remembered his bitter lessons from Kharkov months before.

Rybalko hastened regrouping his force for the attack in the new direction. With the morning of 20 July, 3rd Guards Tank Army together with units of the 3rd Army began the attack in the assigned northwest direction. By early morning, parts of the tank army penetrated towards the Orel-Mtsensk highway, and later with elements of the 3rd Army advanced towards the Oka river. Attempts by lead forces of Rybalko's tank army to cross the river, however, were unsuccessful. Prior to forcing the Oka by the 3rd Guards Tank Army, Red Army tank armies possessed little practical experience in the forcing of major water obstacles.

The Bryansk Front's slowed advance drew a call from Stalin who asked the Front chief of staff, General Sandalov, "Why hasn't Rybalko taken Stanovoi Kolodez yet? Pass on to the Front commander that I am dissatisfied with the tank army's control."[41]

General Sandalov recalled, "While I searched for a telephone to call the Front commander, apparently Moscow had found him. He called me and dictated the following instructions for Rybalko, "Boss ordered 22 July to seize Stanovoi Kolodez. Still time demands to send I.P. Korchagina (commander 2nd Mechanized Corps) across Mokhovoe to Stanovoy Kolodez, in order to strike together with M.I. Zin'kovichem (commander 12th Tank Corps) to destroy resisting enemy. Popov. 1.20.22.7."[42]

In part, Rybalko's difficulties were blending operationally the variety of tanks in the tactical units. The Stavka representative, Artillery Marshal Nikolai Nikolaevich Voronov, reported that the English tanks, Matilda and Valentine, with which some of the Soviet armored units had been equipped did not measure up to the T-34 in performance. Soviet crews believed the tanks to be unreliable and called them, "field crematoriums."[43] Red Army tankers blamed some of their tactical problems on the inferior Allied Lend-Lease tanks.

In order to shift the offensive more quickly onto the new axis, Rybalko committed his second echelon, the 2nd Mechanized Corps, in the new direction while his forward tank corps prepared to shift their operations. The success of this operational technique for turning his formations by redirecting the trailing corps became a blueprint for quick attacks in new directions for the remainder of the war. Sharp changes in direction combined with aggressive action became another of Rybalko's trademarks in armored warfare.

At 0300 hours, 21 July, the Bryansk Front commander assigned Rybalko's army a new mission – to make a sharp turn to the southwest and attacking towards Zolotarevo and Stanovoy Kolodez, reach the Rybnitsa and seize the area of Stanovoy Kolodez.

Not waiting for the 2nd Mechanized and 15th Tank Corps to finish transferring their captured Oka river bridgeheads to relieving rifle units, Rybalko decided again to turn his second echelon, the 12th Tank Corps and the reserve, 91st Separate Tank Brigade.

By afternoon, the corps and brigade shifted their attack on a new axis under strong German air attacks. Their initial attempts to cross the Optukha river failed. By evening, the 15th Tank Corps reinforced the battle area. The next morning, both tank corps and the separate tank brigade fought along the river. The following day Rybalko's units, together with a strike group of the 63rd Army, attempted several times to penetrate the German defensive line on the Optukha in the direction to Stanovoy Kolodez. Despite the pressure by the Soviet forces, Rybalko's attempts failed to dislodge the defenders.

Concentrating on the new offensive axis, Rybalko's units renewed the advance southeast to Orel. Although the army's main forces would not be concentrated in the new direction until the end of the day, the 91st Separate Tank Brigade made strong, steady progress.

When first assigned to the 3rd Guards Tank Army, Colonel Ivan Ignatevich Yakubovskii, commander of the 91st Separate Tank Brigade, reported to Rybalko on the status of his unit. Rybalko remarked, "We will learn about each other in action – in hot action."[44] Yakubovskii recalled the first combat mission in his memoirs and Rybalko's conduct of a precombat inspection of his tank brigade. Rybalko "was extremely exacting and expressed a great many observations, it seemed insulting at first. But he operated exceptionally fair." [45]

After receiving a report of strong enemy resistance from his lead brigade, Rybalko immediately drove to the brigade. The trip to the frontline fighting nearly cost him his life. On the way German fighters spotted his command group and struck, destroying his vehicle, killing his driver, and seriously wounding his adjutant. Rybalko miraculously escaped harm. He arrived at the brigade command post on foot.[46] For a commander who habitually moved along and in the front lines, Rybalko's survival was remarkable.

Colonel Yakubovskii reported that his brigade captured the northern part of Sobakino, and movement towards the south was delayed by the river Optushka. The boggy bottom, covered with silt, was impassable for tanks. The tankers had to find crossings.

"Why don't you arrange it?" Rybalko asked.

"We are about to begin soon. The soldiers are dismantling houses in the nearby village and taking the crossing material to the river. And sappers..."

"Speed it up!" Rybalko cut off the brigade commander. "What else prevents your fulfilling the missions?"

"The enemy line is strongly fortified in engineer terms. They actively counterattack us. After conducting a crossing one brigade's force will be difficult to break the German's resistance."

Listening to the brigade commander, Rybalko went to the radio and returned in a few minutes.

"You will not be attacking alone, but in coordination with the 12th Tank Corps. I gave the corps commander an order. His forward detachment will capture a crossing to the west bank. I order you to seize Sobakino by 1200 hours."[47]

Rybalko (left foreground) with 3rd Gurds Tank Army T-34s in column.

At midday on 22 July, Yakubovskii radioed that, in cooperation with the 12th Tank Corps, they had forced the river capturing Sobakino, and they continued attacking into the depth of the German defense. Only after a tenacious effort, indicative of Rybalko's style, did the tank army on the evening of 23 July, cross the river in the area of Zolotarevo and Sobakino. Having cleared out the bridgehead at the bend of the Optukha and Optushka rivers, lead tank units pushed forward to Krasnaya Zvezda.

Taking into account that the tank army's combat actions were becoming drawn out, the Bryansk Front commander decided to change Rybalko's axis by striking towards Stanovoy Kolodez from the southeast. On Popov's command, Rybalko ordered a flanking march on the night of 23-24 July. At this early stage in Rybalko's command of the tank army, the army learned to routinely conduct regroupings under the cover of darkness. By morning, Rybalko's forces concentrated in the area of Novo-Petrovtsa with the mission of seizing Stanovoy Kolodez and reaching the Stish river line by evening. Mid-afternoon under a broiling July sun, the 12th Tank and 2nd Mechanized Corps led the tank army's assault. By evening of the following day, Rybalko's lead elements seized the Yeropkino area cutting the Orel-Kursk rail line, approaching Stanovoy Kolodez.

Developing the offensive west, Rybalko, like most Red Army commanders, moved around the battlefield in the ubiquitous Willy Jeep. The American Lend-Lease Willy Jeep, called "villises" in Russian, had been given to the Red Army by the tens of thousands. Rybalko reminded his staff of an important lesson, "When the enemy locates one vehicle on the road he considers that it is an insignificant rank driving. If it is two or three Willy and also accompanied by an armored vehicle, they conclude that this is some important chief and, of course, fire to destroy him."

Melnikov recalled the recent near miss Rybalko had in his trip to Yakubovskii's brigade in one jeep.

"Mere chance." Rybalko joked.[48]

Melnikov remarked on Rybalko's uncommon bravery and lack of concern for his personal safety. If the situation required, he drove without delay in a vehicle or tank to the forward units and personally influenced the course of the battle. Once forward he could personally assess the situation better, and if necessary take charge of the situation. He did not leave the forward edge of the battlefield until he was satisfied that the developing events were in his favor.

Rybalko with nerves of steel seemed exhilarated by working close to the edge of death. Red Army tankers, like soldiers in any army, wanted to see their commander on the battlefield instead of in a headquarters dugout.[49]

Rybalko also had the habit of arriving at corps or brigades without warning. It happened in the course of a march; he met a vehicle commander on a desolate crossroad and gave unsolicited instructions. Colonel Yakubovskii, commander of the separate tank brigade, recalled an encounter with the omnipresent tank army commander, "Your command post is located here. The brigade must force the river. You determine the place to cross. The means are at hand. With your instructions, there is little time. Take action!"[50] In short, direct sentences, Rybalko constantly pressed his commanders forward. Soviet officers and soldiers have a nickname for such a commander, a "hammer," describing a commander who is always pounding hard. Rybalko, the hammer, had the reputation throughout the Red Army as a hard, aggressive commander.

In recognition of the tank army's persistent and aggressive actions, the People's Commissar of Defense ordered, on 26 July, all of its corps and their brigades redesignated as "guards" units. The 12th and 15th Tank Corps became the 6th and 7th Guards Tank Corps, respectively, and the 2nd Mechanized Corps became the 7th Guards Mechanized Corps.

Suffering heavy losses, the tank army was pulled from the front-line by the Front commander and placed in the Front's second echelon. A few days later, the Stavka transferred the 3rd Guards Tank Army to the Central Front under the command of Army General Konstantin Konstantinovich Rokossovskii. Disturbed by the Central Front's slow rate of advance, the Stavka on 1 August, directed General Rokossovskii to complete the 3rd Guards Tank Army's concentration in the Koros'kovo area by 4-5 August. The tank army received the mission to develop the 13th Army's success by striking in the general direction of Kromy, breaking through the German's defense on the left bank of the Oka River. Such an offensive effort would facilitate the 48th Army advance on an adjacent sector.

By 4 August, the 3rd Guards Tank Army, short on tanks and personnel, was reinforced with 200 tanks, giving them a total of 417 tanks and self-propelled artillery pieces. The crews, however, came from poorly trained reserves or new recruits. A severe shortage of officers existed at battalion, company, and platoon levels. The army headquarters suffered shortages, too. The army had too few engineer troops and needed artillery reinforcements.[51] Rybalko knew these were important shortcomings that inhibit performance and cause high casualties.

On the afternoon of 4 August, 3rd Guards Tank Army attacked with all corps forward on line, the 91st Separate Tank Brigade and 50th Motorcycle Regiment in reserve. Approaching the Kromy river, the army received strong German artillery fires and air strikes, bringing the advance to a halt. The following day after resuming the attack, Rybalko's tankers successfully forced the river, capturing Kromy.

Despite the army's diminished striking power, the 3rd Guards Tank Army was again required to break through a prepared defense. To accomplish the combat mission, Rybalko reorganized his remaining forces on the main attack axis. He created an ad hoc tank group consisting of the 91st Tank Brigade, tank brigades of the 6th Guards Tank Corps, 57th Tank Brigade of the 7th Guards Tank Corps and the tank company of the 50th Motorcycle regiment totaling 110 tanks.[52]

General Rokossovkii recalled Rybalko's plight, "A quick review of the army revealed that it was in a sad state. It had suffered considerable losses and its setbacks had had an adverse effect on morale – which I quickly perceived on the very first day of fighting."[53] General Rokossovkii respected Rybalko as a "good", "firm and resolute" commander, but, in this instance, Rybalko's tank crews in spite of all their efforts were unable to overcome German resistance. "To prevent unnecessary losses," Rokossovskii remarked in post-war writings, "I requested the High command to withdraw Rybalko's tank army to the reserve."[54]

Fortunately for the tank army, its offensive actions in the Orel operation were concluded on 11 August. In accordance with a People's Commissar for Defense order, 3rd Guards Tank Army, minus the 7th Guards Mechanized Corps, became resubordinated to the Stavka reserve, and by the morning of 17 August, withdrew to a major assembly area south of Kursk.

A number of shortcomings in 3rd Guards Tank Army's employment during the Orel operation were evident. Mainly, the break through of a strongly prepared German defense with insufficient reinforcing support, primarily in heavy artillery, had a debilitating impact. Artillery support from the rifle armies proved inadequate.

As a result, the tank army suffered unnecessarily high casualties when breaking through the defense. Another important shortcoming was the absence of close air support, contributing further to the significant loss of men and military equipment.[55]

The frequent and sharp changes in the tank army's offensive directions repeatedly placed it in difficult situations. The insufficient time to prepare an offensive led to serious omissions in the organization of control, coordination, reconnaissance and other necessary aspects of operational and logistical support.[56] Later in the war, with more operational experience, Rybalko and his staff could be more responsive to short notice redirections. However, at this stage of the war and staff development, operations showed that a tank army required no less than two days of preparation for a breakthrough of a prepared enemy defense.

In an analysis of the 3rd Guards Tank Army's operation, a General Staff report concluded that Rybalko's tank army was aimed five different times for commitment in breakthroughs. On the first and second days, the army did not succeed in fulfilling its mission, penetrating only the tactical defense. The tank units did not have the opportunity to break away into the operational depth. The repeated changes in the direction of attacks compelled Rybalko's army to slide along the front, losing time in marches, limiting coordination, and exacerbating organization of the force. The area of operations, covered with ravines and under heavy rainfalls, made it difficult for wheeled vehicles with artillery and motorized infantry to keep up with the tanks. The report finally concluded that such operational use of the tank army did not give the necessary effect, and it suffered unjustified losses.[57] Rybalko's tank army had not achieved the results for which such a formation had been designed. However, a rigorous self critique by the Red Army General Staff helped improve the use of armored guards.

The early use of tank armies at Kursk demonstrated no quick solution for effective and efficient operational employment of large armored formations. Matching the dexterity of German armored forces required a seasoning of the Soviet commanders and staffs at all levels for wielding these potentially powerful units. Tank armies at Kursk, as in the Orel operation, were prematurely enlisted for the breakthrough of the German's tactical defensive zone. The Bryansk Front's 3rd Guards Tank Army attempted to penetrate the German defense and reach its operational depth seven times between 19 July and 8 August, but Rybalko's army was unable to gain freedom for maneuver. From 19 July, up to 1000 German aircraft pounced on the massed armored formation as they advanced into the battle. Operating slowly in the offensive, the tank force penetrated the defense "in an infantry manner." The army suffered large losses while achieving only limited operational results. During the Orel operation, it lost 60.3 percent of its T-34s and 72.9 percent of the T-70 tanks.[58] The army's considerably reduced fighting strength required removal to reserve status for reconstitution. Lack of experience in using tank armies for breaking through a prepared defense, the limited time available to prepare for the defensive, and the absence of surprise for committing the tank formations to the battle should be regarded as the main causes for Rybalko's tank army losses.[59]

Within the tank army, Rybalko imposed his centralized style of command and control. Yakubovskii praised Rybalko's staff for their preparations to get his orders to him in a timely manner. Instructions were sent by radio, and if that was not possible, by means of a staff officer with a map on which Rybalko had specified Colonel Yakubovskii's mission.[60]

Rybalko's dynamic style of operation became evident throughout the tank army. Operating under difficult conditions of repeated regroupings from one sector to another, the tank army maneuvered along the line of the front under constant attack from German air and, in the course of some 25 days, managed an advance of 500 kilometers. In the Orel operation, Rybalko showed his potential to respond quickly and handle calmly emergencies. The Stavka and the Front made him responsible for key and difficult missions. He constantly maintained a cohesive, unified focus with his force – a difficult task at the chaotic operational level. For this action, Rybalko won the Order of Suvorov lst Degree.

After the fighting around Orel, the 3rd Guards Tank Army received a short respite. The tank army transferred from the Central Front to the Stavka reserve. Rybalko knew his army would not be in the reserve for long and worked hard the replenishment effort. Rybalko gained valuable experience and knowledge in rebuilding a battle worn tank army. He concluded that a tank army should be withdrawn from combat prior to total exhaustion, in order to achieve a faster reconstitution.[61]

The Red Army counteroffensive around Orel lasted thirty-seven days. During that time the Soviet forces advanced 150 kilometers opening potentials for further offensive operations to the west, offensives requiring robust tank armies.

In mid-August, the 9th Mechanized Corps was assigned to the 3rd Guards Tank Army. Major General Konstantin Alekseevich Malygin, commander of the mechanized corps, recalled his first meeting with Rybalko, describing him as average height, stout, with knitted brow. Rybalko asked sharply, "You know that the corps came to my subordination?"

"We've received our directive," Malygin answered calling his staff to attention with Rybalko's arrival in the command post.

"I hope it's a satisfactory subordination? In our army," Rybalko spoke as he took a seat behind a table in the staff, "you will interact with tankers. I hope all will understand that. The corps plans are to be used in fixing the enemy direction."

"I, too, understand the role of mechanized corps in tank armies,' Malygin replied. "Not all my people have had a baptism of fire, nor have the combat organized staff and units been tested in battle. The corps was promised two echelons with vehicle transports, but they took them away, so one brigade is dismounted. Transports by authorization were only 70%, but it was reduced still more. In what are the motorized infantry and battle reserves to be transported?"

Rybalko frowned and thought. "You have many tanks that will carry the motorized infantry riding on top into battle," he responded.

"Non-organic transport battalions," Melnikov added, "will deliver supplies there, when sending echelons with vehicles."

"Motorized infantry riding on tanks cannot always be transferred," Malygin objected. "And our tanks are light, how many people on them can you seat? And 82mm mortars? There are 90 in the corps! And machineguns? 135 of them! They cannot be loaded on the tanks."[62]

The army commander listening attentively understood, that nonorganic battalions did not carry supplies for the army. Such tedious, managerial gruel compose the day-to-day decisions for all fighting commanders. Combat decisions are often easier and more obvious than logistical support considerations. Rybalko could do little to alleviate the transport problem.

On the night of 6 to 7 September, elements of Rybalko's tank army marched partly on foot to the Romny area in a move to reinforce the Voronezh Front. On 18 September, the Front commander, General Nikolai Fedorovich Vatutin, a hard, aggressive leader, shorter in height than Rybalko, drove forward to the 6th Guards Tank Corps' command post and asked Rybalko, who was also there, to report on the condition of his army.

"The tank brigades, " reported Rybalko, " are at 50 percent of their assigned new T-34's with the 85mm guns." Then, discussing the new T-34's with 85mm main guns and the Joseph Stalin (JS) heavy tanks with which Rybalko had already familiarized himself, he continued, praising the T-34. "It's capabilities to conduct combat are maneuvering at high speeds and covering great distances. I doubt they (Germans) will challenge the heavy tanks with 122mm gun regiments. Tracks and suspension are shabby, they cannot reach the Dnepr river. But this is a strong force – 40 machines."

"Does Moscow know about the condition of the heavy regiments?" General Vatutin asked.

"They know. The Military Council reported to General Fedorenko. He promised to help, to send forward rollers, tracks, wheels, but nothing at this time," Rybalko replied.

General Vatutin shook his head, then talked to Rybalko about the corps and brigade commanders. After getting a short report from Rybalko, Vatutin gave a brief summary on the situation in the Front's sector. His concern was the German attempt to fall back behind the Dnepr river, "Your tank army must move over a hundred or more kilometers a day, calculate being in the area of Pereyaslava not later than 22 September. Keep in mind, that the success of the whole operation will depend on your army's quick actions."

General Vatutin followed his remarks with specific instructions and missions for the 3rd Guards Tank Army.

"Everything is clear, comrade commander," Rybalko answered. "You must not have any doubts that the army can fulfill the order."[63]

Later in the day in Piryatin, the staff of the 6th Guards Tank Corps paused in the advance, and there appeared Rybalko. In a conference with commanders and staff he conveyed the Front commander's concern about the German army's attempt to hold the Donbas and not allow the Russians across the Dnepr. Following a short pause, the army commander continued, "From the Dnepr line Fascist leaders link further on-going plan, they hope for a protracted positional war. They want our prosperous region (Donbas). Not excluding the dragging out of the war in the east, Hitler will actively bargain with our allies in the west. Only we, with our powerful Red Army, can ruin the Fascist leaders' treacherous plan. This is why it is impossible to lose even a minute. A decisive attack to the Dnepr is our answer to Hitler, Manstein and all this Fascist gang."[64]

Going up to the map covered with red and blue arrows, Rybalko described the general situation in detail, paying special attention to the German's system of defense on the Dnepr's west bank and commanding hills and heights. The army commander indicated the line along which the 6th Guards Tank Corps would travel. This direction led to the Dnepr's Great Bukrin bend south of Kiev.

Rybalko's assessment on the preparedness of the German position behind the Dnepr river were overstated because in Hitler's reluctance to retreat he had not allowed the German army to prepare fortified positions along the Dnepr river. The difficulty experienced by Rybalko's units in crossing the river was the naturally higher western bank and the great expanse of the river which enhanced the defense by even a small unprepared force, and the Red Army's general unpreparedness to conduct rapid, engineer supported river crossings.

On 20 September, General Malygin received a summons to Rybalko's command post. Upon arrival, Malygin recalled, "Rybalko was in a fine mood, smiling. Beside him stood two generals and a colonel. I reported what was happening."

"And, 'angry' Malygin," the army commander shook hands with the new mechanized corps commander. "You know them," Rybalko pointed to the assembled group of officers. "These are the commanders of the tank corps." They were General Major Mitrofan Ivanovich Zinkevich, commander 6th Guards Tank Corps, Kirillon Filippovich Suleikov, commander 7th Guards Tank Corps, and Colonel Ivan Ignatevich Yakubovskii, commander of the 91st Separate Tank Brigade.

"Everyone assembled?" asked Rybalko looking around. "So let's begin, comrades."[65] Rybalko liked to talk directly with his commanders – it was not his leadership style to direct them solely through his staff. And, Rybalko preferred to go forward to visit his commanders, but the magnitude of the impending operation required a meeting with the commanders at his main headquarters.

Beginning at night on 20 September, the 3rd Guards Tank Army moved aggressively to pick up the offensive tempo, and, as the Voronezh Front's mobile group advanced rapidly towards the Dnepr river. Forward detachments raced two hundred kilometers ahead. However, the rapid advance created a problem for the tank army –

how to cross the formidably wide Dnepr from the march. With this concern, Rybalko went forward on 21 September to see General Malygin, 9th Mechanized Corps commander.

"What are we to do, comrade army commander, lst Battalion, 9th Mechanized Corps stands prepared to cross, but cross on what?" asked the corps commander.

"Why are you asking me this?" Rybalko responded angrily. "You have a corps objective! Really, can't you find people with ways to invent how to fulfill the mission?"

"But my people searched the riverside villages and found nothing."[66]

While Malygin did not raise this problem in his memoir about the crossing, the Germans had applied their scorched earth retreat, and the advancing Red Army found it difficult to find anything useful intact. The initial crossings by Rybalko's tank army relied upon personal initiative and any makeshift means. Red Army tank forces beginning with the Dnepr river began to learn how to force major rivers from the march.

Rybalko, remaining forward, also visited his new commander of the 7th Guards Tank Corps, General Major Sergei Alekseevich Ivanov. Addressing the corps commander, Rybalko said, "All military theory and practice confirms that for forcing such a wide expanse of river one must prepare well, must have crossing means, and, finally, must have artillery fire support. And, it must be timely. For example, in Italy our allies prepared ten days for the crossing of the Volturna. But we don't have time to prepare, comrade Major General. We must throw ourselves across the Dnepr from the march."[67]

The 56th Guards Tank Brigade, lead element of the 3rd Guards Tank Army, forced the Dnepr and captured a bridgehead in the Bukrin bend. Rybalko placed himself at the command post near the crossing. Together with his assistant, he searched and could not find a way out of the lack of crossing materials. When captured bridging trains were brought up, Rybalko decided to attempt loading the light British tanks, Valentines, on them.[68] Rybalko, resourceful, ingenious in problem-solving, worked relentlessly to resolve tactical problems that would stop a lesser commander. As often is the case, these problems were not directly about fighting tactics.

With dawn on 24 September, German Messerschmitts bombed the eastern bank and the tank army's crossing sites. General

Mitrofanov Ivanovich Zinkovich, commander of the 6th Guards Tank Corps, who stood with his staff at the crossing site directing operations was killed in the strafing air attack. Rybalko, in the midst of his difficult crossing operation, had to designate a new commander. He had no one in mind, so General Vatutin directed the new appointment. For all his bluntness and graceless confrontations under fire, Pavel Rybalko had a great respect and closeness. He exhibited a close bond with his subordinate commanders that comes from sharing hardships and dangers with them.

The Germans reacted quickly to the Red Army's Dnepr river crossing in the Bukrin bend area dispatching armored forces to seal the area. The fighting drew to a stalemate. Twice in October, the 3rd Guards Tank Army attempted unsuccessfully to renew the offensive from the bridgehead, suffering heavy losses.

Meanwhile in late September and early October 1943, the 38th Army, lst Ukrainian Front, operating north of Kiev, secured a bridgehead across the Dnepr river at Lyutezh. A second major bridgehead offered another opportunity to the lst Ukrainian Front for an offensive towards Kiev on the west side of the Dnepr. With the capture of the Lyutezh bridgehead, General Vatutin decided to shift the Front's main effort to the right flank. He requested Stavka approval and asked for a tank army as reinforcement for his plan. On 24 October, denying Vatutin's request for additional forces, the Stavka ordered the Front to regroup its forces for an offensive from the Lyutezh bridgehead and directed Vatutin to transfer Rybalko's army northward. The 3rd Guards Tank Army became a major participant in the Front's redirection of its main effort.

By 1830 hours on 25 October, the Front commander assigned the 3rd Guards Tank Army a three stage mission of withdrawing from the Bukrin bridgehead, marching north, and occupying jumping-off positions for an offensive north of Kiev. In passing the order to Rybalko, the Stavka representative, Marshal Georgi Zhukov, emphasized, "I direct your attention, comrade Rybalko, to the secret withdrawal from battle and organizing the crossing of the tank force over the Dnepr. The march and maneuver on the east bank of the river you are to execute with full maintenance of cover and concealment."[69]

In a short assembly with the tank army's commanders and staff, Rybalko announced the army's transfer to north of Kiev. The 27th Army would assume the tank army's defensive sector. Success of the impending offense was directly dependent on the army's managing to ensure secrecy in the regrouping of its forces and equipment as Rybalko emphasized in a commanders' meeting.

On the night of 26 October, a large regrouping of Front's forces began under the leadership of the Front deputy commander, General Andrei A. Grechko, a future Minister of Defense of the Soviet Union. For preparation of the impending operation only 7-8 days were allowed.

After receiving the order for the forced march to the Lyutezh bridgehead the staff of the 3rd Guards Tank Army held a conference for the corps and army staff. Rybalko, as usual, addressed personally the command group. Leaning on a long, black cane, he explained how little time was available to execute the difficult and unexpected maneuver by secretly withdrawing the tanks from battle, crossing them from the Dnepr right bank to the left, and completing a march along the line of the front to the northwest. In concluding remarks, he said, "There's no escaping, the army has a severe test ahead. You and I understand how great are the responsibilities entrusted on all of us. However," Rybalko smiled warmly, "guardsmen are not used to easy missions."[70]

General Rybalko, in a tight fitting uniform over his bloated body, was not the picture of a healthy man. The retention of body fluid put pressure on his joints, he needed the aid of a walking cane. He continued his briefing and emphasized that the march would be extremely hard, going in short time nearly 200 kilometers.

"You explain to each soldier and officer," he directed. "Movement will only be at night, without a single signal, tank and vehicles move with headlights turned off. At dawn, all movement stops, combat vehicles camouflaged and covered in roadside woods."[71]

In a post-war publication, Rybalko described his army's efforts to conceal the move:

"To conceal the withdrawal of tank formations from the Bukrin bridgehead and their transfer to the new concentration area, strict deception, camouflage and concealment measures were used. Command posts of formations and several radio stations were left in the bridgehead. All of these continued their usual work, while deceiving the enemy. In place of tanks withdrawn from positions we constructed mock-ups of wood and earth. Mock-up guns were placed in firing positions. The movement of tanks and trucks for the designated march was permitted only at night and under strict light discipline. Strict camouflage and concealment also occurred in the new concentration area. The inclement weather during the days of our movement facilitated maintaining secrecy of our preparations for the new offensive. By our efforts we deceived the enemy, having forced his aviation in the course of the week to bomb our abandoned positions."[72]

Over the Dnepr river were two pontoon bridges, one at Grigorovka and the other south of Zarubentsy for personnel, light vehicles and artillery. A wooden-pile low-level bridge at Kozintsov, with a 30 ton capacity, accommodated tanks. However, about 100 meters of the wooden bridge had been knocked out by German aerial bombings. Rybalko reviewed the situation. He raised concerns for the pontoon bridge at Grigorovka, located one and half kilometers from the front lines and under German artillery fire. He decided to replace the destroyed part of the wooden bridge at Kozintsov with pontoon spans from dismantling the Grigorovka pontoon bridge. The pontoon bridge's remaining spans were used for additional ferry crossings. The tank army's staff calculated it would take two nights to cross the entire army.

The corps began moving late at night on 25 October. With the help of road regulators carrying lanterns, lead elements reached the Kozintsov wooden bridge by 2200 hours. Eight tanks of the 50th Motorcycle Regiment and 28 tanks of Colonel Yakubovskii's 91st Separate Tank Brigade crossed in one and half hours when the 37th tank careened off the bridge, fell into the water, taking out part of the bridge. The accident knocked out five wooden pile supports, wrecking 25 meters of decking. Traffic stopped for bridge repairs.

The ferry action the first night managed to cross another 30 tanks. By dawn on 26 October, only tanks of the motorcycle regiment, separate tank brigade and some of the 9th Mechanized Corps were on the opposite bank.

No daylight movement during the day on the 26th ensured the army fell behind its planned movement schedule. During the night, the army operated up to nine ferries. Some 80 tanks and self-propelled artillery guns crossed. A thick fog moved in, enhancing concealment but also slowing the rate of the crossing, taking 30-40 minutes for each ferry to cross and anchor.

At 0800 hours, 27 October, repairs on the bridge were finished. The fog remained until 1100 hours allowing tanks and other equipment to continue moving across the river. After another 39 tanks crossed the bridge, it required additional repairs which were not finished until 0300 hours, the next morning. However, using pontoon ferries and the other bridges, the tank army completed concentration on the opposite bank, a day late, at 0600 hours 28 October.

The veteran tank army secretly slipped to the rear under a cover of fog and darkness. Some 400 tanks, 3500 vehicles with fuel, 500 tractors and nearly 300 guns moved away silently from the Germans undetected. The movements for units during the second stage up the east side of the river had to be adjusted to the unexpected delays. Red Army regulations specified tank forces accomplish daily road marches of 100 kilometers with an average speed of movement at 12-20 kilometers per hour – a standard normative. Rybalko, considering the poor conditions of the march routes, the fact that most of his infantry was on foot, and the roads were crowded with other Front units moving north, decided to organize the daily march distances to 21 to 50 kilometers with a movement rate of 8-12 kilometers per hour. Bringing to bear his judgment, he quickly altered normative standards to accommodate the situation. Rybalko exercised the kind of judgment expected in operational level commanders.

Crossing the Desna river was organized better than the Dnepr crossing since the Front had prepared beforehand wooden bridges in the area of Letki without delaying the tanks advance. However, some units, like the 6th Guards Tank Corps, had only one bridge on which to cross its entire corps.

By late night on 30 October, the 91st Separate Tank Brigade led units through the last assembly area and across the Dnepr into the Lyutezh bridgehead. Using one wooden bridge and ferries, approximately 110 tanks were put across the first night; the second, 185, and the rest of the tanks by 0800 hours 2 November.[73]

The German Eighth Army intelligence situation maps for 30 October still located the 3rd Guards Tank Army in the Bukrin bridgehead.[74] From 31 October to 6 November German intelligence situation maps depicted the 3rd Guards Tank Army outside the Bukrin Bend on the east side of the Dnepr river southwest of Borispol.[75] The German Fourth Panzer Army situation map for 3 November showed the 3rd Guards Tank Army on the east side of the Dnepr opposite the Lyutezh bridgehead, but German intelligence was four days behind in accurately tracking the 3rd Guards Tank Army.[76] The 1st Ukrainian Front commander could count on the German commanders not knowing the 3rd Guards Tank Army's presence in the Lyutezh bridgehead. Rybalko's attack completely surprised defending German forces, which were quickly overwhelmed.

In his memoirs, Lost Victories, Field Marshal Erich von Manstein, commander of Army Group South, in whose sector the Bukrin and Lyutezh bridgeheads were located, describes the battles for the Dnepr river. His account on the holding battles in October 1943 against the Bukrin bridgehead notes, "By the end of the month it had more than five armies (one of which was entirely armored) in there...."[77] After some description of the fighting farther south, he describes the Lyutezh bridgehead fight: "At the beginning of November, the enemy again attacked the northern wing of the Army Group, Fourth Panzer Army's Dneiper front, with strong forces. It was not clear whether this was an offensive with far reaching aims or whether the enemy first intended to win the necessary assembly space west of the river It soon becomes evident that the formations of the Fourth Panzer Army would be unable to hold the Dneiper against the far stronger Russians..."[78] In addition to confirming the confused view of the situation by Army Group South, Manstein leaves the impression – quite falsely – that the Red Army maintained strong forces all along the Dnepr, particularly in the bridgehead areas. And, for whatever reason, he fails to identify or acknowledge the 1st Ukrainian Front's major regrouping of the 3rd Guards Tank Army and other forces that made the breakout from the Lyutezh bridgehead possible.

On 4 November, the morning of the Kiev offensive operation, the weather turned for the worse. Drizzling rain limited visibility, and a thick fog hung over the ground. People a few steps apart could barely distinguish nor recognize each other. The Red Army had learned to use effectively adverse weather to advantage.

The 6th Guards Tank Corps commander ordered his corps to rest during the day since combat actions for the offensive would begin at night. For the 3rd Guards Tank Army launching its attack at night was a departure from the standard practice of fighting on the eastern front. But its direction from the army commander inspired confidence in the subordinate commanders.

General Vasilii Sergeevich Arkhipov, 53rd Guards Tank Brigade commander, recalled, "General Pavel Semenovich Rybalko was an extraordinarily interesting man. He attracted not only by appearance, but also by a skill to speak eloquently. But wherever he was, in a circle of soldiers or in an officer conference, he knew how to present a complicated problem very simply."[79] Arkhipov, who had won a Hero of the Soviet Union Gold Star in the Soviet-Finnish War, was impressed by Rybalko, and continued, "...Two main qualities of General Rybalko won me from our first meeting: mind and inquisitiveness. He intelligently sought the new in the already known." As an example of Rybalko's versatile thinking, the brigade commander recalled Rybalko's point, "Fascists don't like, don't understand and fear night combat. This is their weakness – that must become our strength."[80]

In a post war article, Rybalko described his units' actions in the Kiev operation, "We used the enemy's confusion, calling a night operation, in order not to give them the opportunity to come to their senses, and aggressively advanced into the operational depth, crossed the Berlin-Kiev railroad, one corps advanced to Vasilkov, the other to Fastov, covering us with the motorized corps.[81]

General Arkhipov's observation on Rybalko's quality of seeking 'new in the known' is at the heart of innovation and creativity on the battlefield. The successful warrior with weapons, soldiers, and formations adapts old and new things in new ways. Innovation on the battlefield does not require a totally original invention, just a variation on an existing method, technique, or weapon. It is the mark of a strong personality and will that has the confidence to act beyond the familiar range of ideas and actions, and possesses the strong leadership trait to overcome resistance to his innovation.

Churning through the dark morning hours of 5 November, the 9th Mechanized and 7th Guards Tank Corps liberated Svyatoshino, approached the important Kiev-Zhitomir highway. The 6th Guards Tank Corps in coordination with the 50th Rifle Corps and 167th Rifle division also made a short advance against the Germans. Rain slowed the offensive tempo. Attacking in pitch-dark woods became too difficult. The corps commander instructed his units to assume an all-round defensive position and told Rybalko, who reported the situation to the Front commander.

"Do you intend to stop the attack until morning or to operate in the night?" General Vatutin asked.

"The 6th Guards Tank Corps has gone over to the defense, but I think they must continue to attack," Rybalko replied.

"That's right," approved the Front commander.

"To attack," repeated Rybalko, adding, "with fully lit headlights. Give me two hours to prepare."

The Front commander agreed.[82]

General Rybalko immediately directed the 6th Guards Tank Corps to prepare for further actions. On the signal, "Lightning," the corps lunged forward by the illumination of searchlights, combat vehicle headlights, and thousands of launched flares, stunning the German defenders. After reaching the Kiev-Zhitomir highway, the tank corps rapidly turned towards Fastov.

Late evening on 5 November, General Rybalko called the corps commanders to his command post in a small house where he had stopped after capturing the town of Suyatoshino. Colonel Yakubovskii arrived first and was alone with Rybalko. The army commander discussed with the brigade commander on the importance in seizing Fastov on the German's line of communications. "A very important mission and is highly difficult," Rybalko observed. "But by the end of 6 November it must be fulfilled."

Rybalko, warming himself by a tile covered stove, asked, "Do you know who is from this house in which we are now located?"

Yakubovskii replied he did not know, but the place seemed like any ordinary town outskirts.

"If you want to know, for me it's not very ordinary," Rybalko resumed talking. "Before the war I lived here with my family." From his momentary lapse of reminiscence, Rybalko explained the importance of the battle for Fastov and the other towns in the area – his childhood home.

"Never before had I seen the army commander so agitated and excited," Yakubovskii remembered. [83]

In a rare revealing moment, Rybalko's mood about the war merged with personal motive baring a part of his unique personality, that few people grasped. Upon the arrival of the other corps commanders, Rybalko congratulated them on the 26th anniversary of the Great October Revolution and then announced, "We have information that the Hitlerite's tank corps are from the Great Bukrin. An enemy grouping in the area of Beloi Tserkvi threatens our army's left flank. In Kazatin, the SS Division "Liebstandarte" is disembarking."

After a short pause, the army commander continued, "Kravchenko's tankers just captured documents from the Panzer Division SS "Das Reich". In them, the point is stated how and when they will inflict a strike to Kiev. As you see, the situation is extraordinarily complicated. Manstein in every way will aggressively try to take Kiev, again."[84]

General Konstantin Vasilevich Krainyukov, member of the 1st Ukrainian Front military council, visited Rybalko in his headquarters. Krainyukov knew Rybalko as a cavalry regiment commander in 1929-30; Krainyukov had been the regimental party secretary.

"What's new, Pavel Semenovich?" General Krainyukov asked.

"A new German division," Rybalko jested joylessly, "and mainly tanks. Unfortunately this circumstance has not gained the attention of the Front's staff." Rybalko opened a folder with documents and, finding the necessary page, offered it to Krainyukov to read.

Krainyukov read a Front report on the dispositions of German forces in sector. Rybalko drew his attention to the line, "Other enemy units against you at this time not noted."

Then, Rybalko exclaimed, "How's this, other units not noted? Besides isn't the twenty-fifth German tank division, transferred in our sector from France, moving towards Fastov, as revealed by a prisoner." Rybalko knew this because he had personally interrogated the prisoner. "We also sent reports to the Front but we ask you, Konstantin Vasil'yevich, inform the Front commander that the enemy is concentrating a large force. The situation implies not increasing just for a counterattack, but a powerful and growing counterstrike with far-reaching objectives."[85]

As Krainyukov continued reading the report, he saw the Front staff assessed the situation more narrowly than Rybalko. Rybalko pressed his point that the Front needed to bring in the reinforced 38th Rifle Army and not leave the sector to his tank army. Krainyukov upon his return to Front headquarters discussed the situation with General Vatutin, who, with the chief of staff, agreed to reinforce the 38th Army and place it on the left flank of the Front.

That night General Vatutin called Rybalko to his command post. After Rybalko reported the situation, Vatutin directed Rybalko to turn over his sector to the 40th and 38th Armies and withdraw his tank army to an assembly area for a more focused attack.

Rybalko decided on the morning of 6 November to conduct two simultaneous strikes: first with the forces of the 6th Guards Tank Corps and 91st Separate Tank Brigade to Fastov, and the second with 7th Guards Tank Corps to Vasilkov.

Colonel Yakubovskii, commander 91st Separate Tank Brigade, remembered, late night on the eve of the attack, General Rybalko called the commanders together to organize directly the seizure of Fastov. It "... cuts the enemy's communications, along which he maneuvers reserves throughout the whole front," Rybalko reminded them.[86]

On 6 November, Field Marshal von Manstein decided to concentrate all available panzer divisions in the area of Fastov-Zhitomir, with the aim of thrusting towards Kiev. Manstein intended to build up a defensive line through Fastov covering the concentration of his panzer divisions, but General Vatutin's lst Ukrainian Front moved surprisingly and unexpectedly too fast. The 25th Panzer Division, which had just arrived from France, was prematurely involved in the fighting at Fastov and ran into Rybalko's tankers at noon on 7 November. "Unused to any fighting, the troops streamed back in great disorder," observed General von Mellenthin, 48th Panzer Corps Chief of Staff. "They had great difficulty in escaping from the Russians, who destroyed most of their transport."[87]

Rybalko's tank army, developing the offensive southwestward encountered the counterstriking German 48th Panzer Corps in the area of Fastov. The resulting meeting engagement involved the 54th Guards Tank Brigade, 7th Guards Tank Corps with the forward units of the German 25th Panzer Division. In the course the fight, the 54th Guards Tank Brigade held against the Germans but had insufficient fuel to continue a successful engagement.

On the night of 7 November, Rybalko arriving at the 6th Guards Tank Corps looked over the battlefield covered with German armored personnel carriers and told his adjutant, "Count, will you!"

After totaling the destroyed vehicles, the adjutant reported, "Seventy-two, comrade general!"

"Here's a lazy fellow," Rybalko remarked, looking at the nearby brigade commander.

"Who's lazy?" the commander did not understand.

"My brigade commander!" Rybalko replied seriously and added, "You reported what enemy loss figures to the staff?"

"Fifty armored vehicles. From a spy-hole, comrade general. Night, fires ...." the brigade commander began defensively.

Rybalko suddenly burst out laughing, "New times, new songs. For sure in the year forty-one, on such a dark night, the count in enemy losses were few. And some added a bit, for round figures, eh?"[88]

Rybalko and the officers laughed and joked about the tally. Rybalko possessed a developed sense of humor and sharp wit. He liked humor, when circumstances permitted. For a commander as severe and demanding as Rybalko, this ability to laugh balanced his personality in the eyes of his subordinates. However, his humor often had a sharp point. Colonel General David Dragunskii alluded to this in his memoirs. He had just returned after recovering from serious wounds and already a Hero of the Soviet Union when Rybalko introduced him to the commander of the Front artillery: "This is the commander of our 55th Tank Brigade. He has been in the hospital. But is back in time. He feared he would not make it to Berlin. Now, if he enters Berlin first, he'll get a second Gold Star, and if he doesn't, we'll take his first from him."[89]

But, on the night of 7 November, Rybalko was serious. He received a radio message from the General Staff in which the Supreme High Commander required Fastov to be held at all cost. "Stand to the death!" ordered Rybalko and he drove to the other brigades.[90] Rybalko passed from unit to unit with ceaseless energy, animating the troops and commanders; seeing and directing everything within the path of his tour. Rybalko organized his operational group to consist of half his army staff officers and half the communications means of the headquarters. The operational group as a personal command post allowed him to operate fairly effectively, however, its size risked discovery and being brought under hostile fire. Elimination of Rybalko's operational group would have brought the tank army to a standstill. Rybalko's very close, centralized style of command, reduced his chief of staff and main command post to a planning cell and message center to the Front command.

The following day Rybalko committed his 9th Mechanized Corps, striking the left flank of the German's counterattacking group. While Rybalko's attack began successfully, the Germans threw in the SS Division "Adolf Hitler," stopping further advance by the mechanized corps. Germans panzer units completed maneuvering their main force for a left flank attack on the 3rd Guards Tank Army, forcing the tank army onto the defense.

In the heat of the action, Rybalko arrived in the 55th Tank Brigade's headquarters to Colonel Dragunskii's surprise.

"Well," the army commander snapped without preliminaries, "is the brigade ready for more fighting tomorrow?"

"Yes, Comrade Army Commander. All we need is a short rest."

"Fine. Rest until morning. Tomorrow," Rybalko approached the map and pointed with his finger at a black spot, the town of Pavoloch. "Your brigade, acting as the forward detachment, must detour Fastov to the south, thrust far into the enemy rear, and take Pavoloch. Avoid any drawn out battles, and don't go any farther than Pavoloch until the main force catches up with yours. To the right of you, Colonel Lupov has an identical mission: he is to take railway junction Popelnia. Clear?"

The brigade commander hesitated, and delayed his reply as he tried to figure out the mission he had just been given.

"I have no contact with corps headquarters," he said. "I have no idea where it is, and how to report the mission you have just assigned us."

The army commander stared at Colonel David Dragunskii, one of the few successful Jewish officers in the Red Army, for a minute, then announced: "Don't worry. I'll let them know."

As they walked out into the night, "Move out of here at dawn or the enemy will catch you," Rybalko warned.[91]

By 8 November Colonel Dragunskii's brigade advanced to Pavoloch, and attacked the village in conjunction with partisans. Extending his units forward, Dragunskii's brigade became surrounded and cut off in the German rear, losing communications with the corps and the army. Later, Dragunskii received only a verbal reinforcement over the radio from Rybalko, "Destroy the enemy in the rear, we are moving to you..." Then the communications were cut off again.[92] Often in combat, the commander's voice, as the only reinforcement, is all that is offered to hold the situation.

Taking Kiev and Fastov opened an avenue for the 1st Ukrainian Front to attack the German Army Group South from the north, and created further potential for continuing the advance to the west and southwest. During these active days, Rybalko constantly appeared at the front with his forces. He personally organized tank operations, antitank defenses on the flanks, and other preparations to ensure the Germans did not cut off his tank army, as Field Marshal von Manstein had done to General M.M. Popov's armored group eight months earlier.

For the counterattack on the Kiev salient, the 48th Panzer Corps was given six panzer divisions and one infantry division. "Our plan," writes von Mellenthin, "was to use this powerful force to advance from Fastov directly towards Kiev."[93] On 11 and 12 November, the 48th Panzer Corps attempted to recapture Fastov, but the effort met with little success. Manstein decided to shift the attack towards Zhitomir and turn for Fastov.

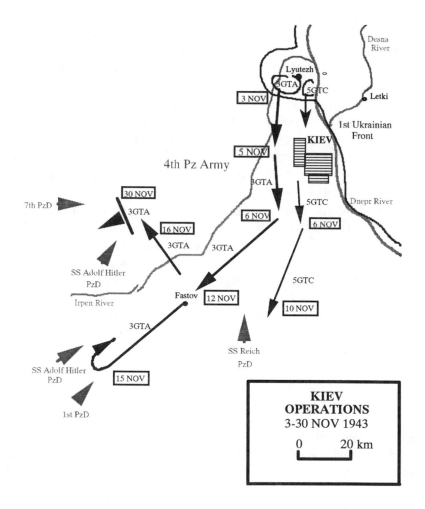

Desna River

Lyutezh
3GTA 5GTC
3 NOV
Letki

1st Ukrainian Front

4th Pz Army

5 NOV

KIEV

3GTA

30 NOV
7th PzD
3GTA
16 NOV
3GTA
3GTA

5GTC

6 NOV

6 NOV

Dnepr River

5GTC

SS Adolf Hitler PzD
Irpen River

Fastov   12 NOV

10 NOV

5GTC

3GTA

SS Reich PzD

SS Adolf Hitler PzD
15 NOV

1st PzD

**KIEV
OPERATIONS
3-30 NOV 1943**

0   20 km

On 14 November 1943, the 48th Panzer Corps attacked with better results. The Soviet's 38th Army which had assumed the 3rd Guards Tank Army sector lacked a coordinated defense. Although defending stubbornly, the rifle units gave way. Rybalko committed the 9th Mechanized and 6th Guards Tank Corps to the area. They attacked from the march. By 19 November the panzer corps captured Zhitomir, and, by 23 November, turned towards Fastov. But, several days of rain turned the roads to mud and Manstein called a temporary halt because of weather. From the Soviet side, the intensity of the fighting reminded the veterans of battles at Kursk. The 3rd Guards Tank Army had stubbornly resisted the German attack, grinding the panzer attack to a halt, stabilizing the front line by 30 November. The German counterstrike and capture of Zhitomir forced the 1st Ukrainian Front to transition to defense, wearing down the Germans while the Red Army brought up strategic reserves to initiate a counteroffensive.

The operation for the Dnepr river, the capture of Kiev and Fastov, collectively won Rybalko the country's highest award, Hero of the Soviet Union, on 17 November 1943. With the Kiev operation, Rybalko solidified his reputation in the Red Army and with the Soviet High Command by his ability to boldly maneuver and aggressively fight his tank army.

On 24 December 1943, The 1st Ukrainian Front resumed the offensive in the Zhitomir-Berdichev operation with the objective to destroy the 4th Panzer Army and preempt German attempts to retake Kiev. The Front had seven rifle, two tank and one air armies for the operation. Rybalko received the mission to commit his tank army in the 18th Army's breakthrough sector, developing the tactical success. On the main effort axis, German resistance proved very determined, and it became clear to the Front commander, that the rifle corps would not achieve their assigned lines of advance. General Vatutin committed the tank army to the fight completing the breakthrough. By 1500 hours, Rybalko's tankers broke through and successfully repelled several German counterattacks. The tank army advanced 20 kilometers with the 6th Guards Tank Corps cutting the Kiev-Zhitomir highway.

After multiple breakthroughs along the entire front, the Front commander anticipated the German's effort to withdraw behind the Teterev river and assigned a new mission to Rybalko's army. The 3rd Guards Tank Army, in coordination with the 1st Guards Army, was to strike in a westerly direction towards Zhitomir, and, by the evening of 25 December, achieve the area of Korostyshev, about half-way to Zhitomir. The new mission meant Rybalko had to turn his army on a new axis. Rybalko and his staff in the course of a single night made the necessary calculations, estimates and issued orders. The next morning, the tank army attacked under the new plan advancing under difficult weather conditions. Wet snow fell, frequent rains, reduced all roads in the sector to unusable ribbons of mud, and off-road movement by wheeled vehicles proved impossible.

Studying reconnaissance reports, Rybalko concluded that the attack to Zhitomir along the highway would be costly and changed the direction of the advance. He called lagging units forward to envelope German units. On 26 December, he regrouped his force attempting to force the Teterev river through night actions. The effort was unsuccessful. The next morning, his units launched a concentrated attack against the German defenders, forcing the Teterev river and seizing Korostyshev by 28 December.

In the village festivities celebrating their liberation from the Germans, the villagers filled tables with food, meats, cheeses and bakery items. Looking at the food, Rybalko sighed sadly since he observed a strict diet. He suffered from a severely injured kidney. No one, to include military doctors, was aware of this ailment. Rybalko bravely bore severe pains. He would lie down for hours with a hot water bottle, and before the pain completely subsided, he would be back at work. Only in moments of rare candidness after a serious bout with pain did he disclose to his political officer his condition.

In the Civil War Rybalko had commanded a cavalry regiment. Once at the height of a pursuit for counterrevolutionaries, his horse, stumbling on a railroad bed, threw Rybalko from his saddle onto the steel rail. The strike fell across his kidney, injuring him for life.

"I don't understand," asked Melnikov hearing the story, "Why you did not consult with doctors? They can help."

"That's not all!" Rybalko replied. "Then, there would be rumors that the army commander is ill. And you understand, what I wrote on the questionnaire when designated to command the army?" Rybalko had written on the form, "Healthy, I can fight."[94]

Rybalko was burdened by episodic pains. In many of his war photographs, one can see his bloated face and body, and he sought the aid of a cane to ease the discomfort in his swollen leg joints. His moods could often be attributed to his pain. If in pain, he wasn't to be bothered; he often smoked and remained silent looking off into space. He would act similarly when nervous, smoking and frowning with a faraway look. On the other hand, he would be cheerful if physically, albeit temporarily, well.

By 31 December, the tank army battled south of Zhitomir, leaving the city for capture by rifle armies. The next afternoon, Rybalko received the mission to attack south bypassing Berdichev on the west and cutting off possible German withdrawal routes westward. Continuing the offensive on New Year's day 1944, the tank army advanced 8-10 kilometers inflicting substantial losses on the Germans. Involved in heavy fighting, Rybalko countered stubborn resistance by the using several axes simultaneously to push the Germans back. After 16 days of combat, the protracted use of the tank army led to damaging losses and wearing down of its combat effectiveness. By 8 January, Rybalko's units possessed only 59 tanks and 26 self-propelled assault guns. [95]

Rybalko directed the consolidation of all 6th Guards Tank Corps tanks in the 53rd Guards Tank Brigade under Colonel V.S. Arkhipov and the 7th Guards Tank Corps tanks to Colonel I.I. Yakubovskii's 91st Separate Tank Brigade. These brigades fought with the rifle armies to continue the attack. The remaining tanks of the mechanized corps were placed in what the Soviets called, a composite detachment. Rybalko sent the composite detachment through a weak point in the German defense for a key road junction at Ulanov. The appearance of Soviet tanks in the rear hastened the collapse of the defense, despite the fact the detachment had to fight surrounded for three days.

On 14 January 1944, the 1st Ukrainian Front shifted to the defense. A week later, the 3rd Guards Tank Army was placed in Front reserves. The tank army stayed relatively close to the front line for reconstitution because it was repeatedly used for local counterattacks throughout February.

In the late winter and early spring, the 3rd Guards Tank Army resumed the Front's advance southeast of Proskurov. The army and corps commanders closely watched the lead brigade advance. The brigade commander, Colonel Zakhar Karpovich Slyusarenko, recalled the close command scrutiny.

"How are you there? Report." the brigade commander heard Rybalko's calm voice over the radio.

"Everything is in order, no incidents, we are progressing."

"Mud right up to the top?"

"Right up to the top."

"Why don't you go on the road? Are you afraid?"

"No, I am not afraid. Simply the distance between two points is not always the most straight nor the shortest."

Rybalko was silent for a minute. Obviously he was studying the terrain on the map.

"I agree, that is correct," he spoke in a deep voice. "Are you moving covered?"

The brigade commander understood the army commander was interested in his moving his tanks with closed hatches.

"And with everything in the formation covered," responded the brigade commander.[96]

Shortly after this call , the brigade commander's unit came under fire from a surprise ambush by German tanks. The action forced the unit temporarily onto the defensive. The commander reported the situation to Rybalko.

"Poor beginning, comrade brigade commander," Rybalko replied angrily leaving the brigade commander hanging onto the telephone receiver.

The same brigade later in the operation participated in the liberation of Proskurov. For the unit's decisive actions in the capture of the city and important railroad station, Rybalko announced the awarding of the Order of the Red Banner to Slyusarenko's brigade. The brigade commander thanked him and promised more from the unit.

Rybalko nodded, then again looked at the brigade commander, and unexpectedly frowned, "Now what, brigade commander? Standing before you is a new very urgent mission and you must make up for lost sleep. Twelve hours. Not a minute more, not a minute less. I am warning you, I am checking!"[97]

On 5 March, 6th Guards Tank Corps, advancing in the difficult spring conditions the Russians call, "rasputitsa (the thaw)," seized the railroad station Narkevichi, cutting the railroad Proskurov-Ternopal. However, the rains and mist quickly devoured the snow cover and roads dissolved. The fields became impassable. Russian mud is a thick, sticky black oily earth that clings to vehicles and will suck the heel off a soldier's boot. The soil becomes seemingly groundless when wet. Where the tanks could go, the transport vehicles could not pass. In the first days of the offensive, rear services fell visibly behind; tanks needed fuel and ammunition. Rybalko ordered the use of captured fuel and directed ammunition to be delivered by airplane.[98]

During this period, Colonel Vasilii Sergeevich Arkhipov, a brigade commander, recalled an encounter with Rybalko. Early on a mid-April morning, General Rybalko arrived at his location and asked, "Where's the enemy? What are they doing?"

The brigade commander replied, "At the present moment, I don't have any information available."

"Well, from all of that, what must you surmise?"

Colonel Arkhipov reported to him about the night artillery preparation and the counterpreparation, then began to theorize, but Rybalko, who became impatient with the theoretical or abstract, interrupted him.

"The enemy abandoned the Strypa(river). Everything moved out – 100th Infantry and 9th Tank Divisions. You don't rest if before us you have 10 kilometers of empty space! You let them slip away?!" Rybalko questioned in disbelief.

"Yes, we let the withdrawing enemy slip away from the Strypa (river line)," the embarrassed brigade commander admitted.[99]

In April in the vicinity of Ternopol the tank army transitioned to the defense, Rybalko went forward to see to the placement of the antitank guns. Rybalko demonstrated that quality of mind indicative of great battlefield captains, the ability to grasp infinite details of his craft and to hold suspended vast amounts of information until a decision required its use or indicated the course of action he should take. He met with a battalion commander and discussed the details of locating platoon positions. Rybalko understood such details as the siting of antitank weapons, how long it took to emplace them, what shape the fighting position should take.

After three months in Stavka reserve, the 3rd Guards Tank Army returned to the 1st Ukrainian Front for the Lvov-Sandomierz operation. The operation fought in the shadow of the Belorussian operation which destroyed the German Army Group Center contributed to a major Red Army offensive in the summer of 1944 when the Allies stormed the beaches of Normandy. Marshal Ivan Stepanovich Konev, commander of the 1st Ukrainian Front, decided to attack in two directions. The northern axis from the vicinity of Lutsk toward Rava-Russkaya consisted of the 3rd Guards and 13th Armies, 1st

Guards Tank Army, and General Baranov's Cavalry-Mechanized Group. On the southern axis from Ternopol toward Lvov, the strike force consisted of the 38th and 60th Armies followed by the 3rd Guards and 4th Tank Armies. The 1st Ukrainian Front offensive operation began 13 July, with the 3rd Guard and 13th Armies attacking on the northern axis in the direction of Rava-Russkaya. The Germans, surprised by the appearance of the 1st Guards Tank Army in sector, gave way to the Soviet advance, which gained momentum daily.

On the southern axis, where the 3rd Guards Tank Army fought, a more difficult situation existed in that the Germans prepared and held a better fortified position. On 14 July, the attack began with the 60th and 38th Armies. The situation became complicated by the end of 15 July when two German panzer divisions counterattacked. Soviet forces eked out a 3-5 kilometer advance in the General Pavel Alekseevich Kurochkin's 60th Army zone in the Koltov area. In efforts to frustrate the offensive, the Germans, true to form, counterattacked savagely with their tactical reserves, followed by a counterstrike with the 1st and 8th Panzer Divisions. The German panzer fist managed not only to stop the 38th Army attack, but to push it back 2-3 kilometers.

But, the 60th Army pushed ahead and cut a narrow gap, six kilometers wide and 18 kilometers deep, through the first and second defense zones. Continuous local counterattacks by the Germans threatened to eliminate the Soviet penetration. Although completing the breakthrough of the defense quickly was urgent to the Soviet command, the 60th and 38th Armies lacked sufficient combat power, particularly in tanks, to break open the German defense. Rybalko believed his tank army could help the forward rifle army complete the breakthrough, despite the use of the tank units against the tactical defense being expressly forbidden by the Stavka.

Rybalko called Marshal Konev and reported his decision.

"Risky, Pavel Semenovich," Konev replied. "It forms a maneuver corridor which deprives your tanks of maneuver. And from the flanks the enemy can cast artillery and mortar fire on us. Did you consider this?"

"I considered it. But I considered that for the army's advance into the operational depth it is necessary to use this narrow corridor, for the time being the enemy cannot reinforce his forces. Otherwise, we'll again have to create a breakthrough."

"I agree. I permit the commitment. Act!"[100]

Rybalko began feeding his army into the fight in the general direction of Krasnoe, not waiting for advancing infantry to capture the planned commitment line of Sasov, Zolochev. Rybalko described the moment, as one of 'iron necessity': "You want, or you don't want, to commit to the breakthrough, although the width of the breakthrough front by no means satisfied the army."[101]

"You can't imagine what was in this area?" Rybalko described to the Front's reserve army commander, General Aleksei Zhadov. "In the narrow, cross compartmented and swampy sector terrain, the enemy's machineguns, artillery, covers the route along with a continuous downpour of rain."[102]

With the higher command's approval to enter the breakthrough corridor, Rybalko drove forward to the brigades assigned as the forward detachments for the impending operation. Arriving in the 56th Tank Brigade, he playfully addressed the commander,

"Slyusarenko, are you bored?"

"We're bored."

"Well, we've found you some urgent work."[103]

Attempting to force the situation, Rybalko sent two forward detachments (the reinforced 69th Mechanized and 56th Tank Brigades) for commitment with the lead rifle units of the 60th Army against the German's second defensive belt. Continuing the offensive through the night of 15 July, the brigades, the next morning, reached the Sasov-Zolochev line – the line at which the tank army was to be committed into the breakthrough.

Early morning on 16 July, battalions of the tank brigade in coordination with units of the 15th Rifle Corps began to move along the narrow corridor south of Koltov. Attacking in the direction of Zolochev, 56th Tank Brigade continued to go around the main centers of enemy resistance. Moving to the north of Zolochev, the Germans managed to close the corridor. The tank army with infantry again had to punch the gap through the German defense.

The brigade commander contacted Rybalko by radio with difficulty.

Rybalko asked if the 56th could hold for a day without support. The brigade commander answered affirmatively.

"Excellent!" Rybalko responded enthusiastically, "Tomorrow we shall meet without fail."[104]

The tank army advanced through the narrow 6 kilometers wide

gap. At Koltov, the sector narrowed forcing the tank units onto a single road, called the "Koltov Corridor." Rains poured on 16 and 17 July, turning the single village road into a thick mush. Each meter of advance required tremendous effort by the soldiers. Staff officers splattered with mud pushed their staff cars. During the course of 16 July and the following morning, lead elements of the 9th Mechanized and 7th Guards Tank Corps broke through German resistance, crossing the Zolchuvka river and drove swiftly west. By evening on 17 July, both corps reached the Peltev river, shattering the German defense and moving well into their rear area.

By midday on 18 July, the tank army seized Busk, an important road junction, helping to seal an encirclement of eight German divisions to the north in Brody. As the 3rd Guards Tank Army pushed through the gap, Rybalko continually protected the army's exposed right flank by posting screens along the avenues of possible withdrawal of the encircled grouping until the 60th Army units approached. The 91st Separate Tank Brigade, Rybalko's reserve force, operated in the vicinity of Sasov, the 70th Mechanized Brigade, 9th Mechanized Corps, from the second echelon, operated at the Western Bug river, and the 50th Separate Motorcycle Regiment, also the army reserve, operated in the vicinity of Kamenka and Strumilov.

These brigades and regiment secured the tanks army's flank and closed the ring of encirclement around the German units at Brody preventing their escape. They took an active part in the reduction of the encircled forces jointly with the 60th Army. Forces following the 3rd Guards Tank Army through the corridor began expanding the gap and resisting German counterattacks. Their actions freed Rybalko's army to continue attacking toward Lvov.

By noon on 22 July, the encircled German Brody grouping was eliminated through the joint effort of the cavalry-mechanized group, 3rd Guards Tank Army, 13th and 60th Armies, 4th Guards and 31st Tank Corps. More than 30,000 soldiers and officers were killed and 1700 captured and more than 1,100 guns and mortars, 1500 vehicles and other military equipment were seized.[105]

The summer rains took their toll on the tempo of the offensive slowing the pace and losing the element of surprise. German reinforcements and forces withdrawn off the front line to Lvov formed defenses on the eastern approaches. While the 1st Ukrainian Front enjoyed overall success, attempts by the 3rd Guards and 4th Tank Armies to take Lvov from the east met with little success. The heavy rains continued dissolving the roads to tracks of mud. But, a major reason for failure was that the commander of the 3rd Guards Tank Army "... made a mistake in assessing the terrain before Lvov," noted Marshal Konev. "...General Rybalko moved his force to the city straight along the Krasno-Lvov road and brought it up short in peat bogs that were to the northeast of the city. This was such difficult terrain for a tank force...."[106]

Rybalko and his staff had obviously failed to organize reconnaissance and prepare the army's approach routes. The routes selected on the map for bypassing Lvov by the tank army consisted of peaty ground normally difficult for wheeled transport equipment to cross especially during the rainy season. The motorized infantry arrived at their new assembly area 7-10 hours behind the tanks. The ill-conceived maneuver did not achieve its objective.[107]

Marshal Konev decided to send the 3rd Guards Tank Army further north and west around Lvov, attacking the city from the northwest. Rybalko's army in a difficult position quickly regrouped, losing two days in the offensive. By 22 July, passing through a constrained area northwest of Lvov, the tank army by 24 July, from the vicinity of Yavorovi attacked in two directions – Lvov and Peremyshl. Rybalko's army was moving in opposite directions!

Melnikov, the member of the tank army's military council, contributed to the offensive effort by working logistical support for the army. When the routes became too congested on the southern breakthrough axis, he moved supplies from the northern axis behind the path cut by General Baranov's mechanized-cavalry group to the Yavorov area.[108]

Animated by the dynamic maneuver and confident with the course of his army's combat action, Rybalko met with the 6th Guards Tank Corps deputy commander, General Novikov. "My time, Vasilii Vasil'evich, is very short, and yours is weighed in gold," Rybalko announced, "that is why we must get to business at once. Go with the corps' main force to Peremyshl. Forward detachments must seize the railroad center from the march and disrupt the unloading of enemy reserves which have moved to Peremyshl. All German forces withdrawing from Lvov are covered by the 7th Guards Tank and 9th Mechanized Corps. And, from Colonel Yakubovskii's command a forward detachment is bypassing from the south."[109]

The 91st Tank Brigade and the 50th Motorcycle Regiment, which made up the army reserve, were advanced forward, where they positioned themselves as stationary screens and blocked the path of two infantry and one motorized German divisions to Peremyshl, forcing the German's Army Group of Northern Ukraine to withdraw towards the Carpathian mountains.

In combat for 18-19 days, the 1st Ukrainian Front's main forces attacked on a sector nearly 200 kilometers wide and advanced a depth of 400 kilometers. On 28 and 29 July, part of the 3rd Guards Tank Army destroyed remnants of the German forces from Lvov in the forested area near Sambor while the main forces continued towards the Vistula river and the Polish frontier.

After the battle for Peremyshl, the 6th Guards Tank Corps was pulled into the second echelon for refitting and restoration. "I understand your situation and sympathize," Rybalko told a conference of tank corps' officers. "At another time you would be given 2-3 days. Now, I can't let a minute escape, it's too expensive. You must immediately make ready to aggressively cross the Vistula."[110]

By 1100 hours 31 July, forward units of the 6th Guards Tank Corps were to cross the Vistula and secure a bridgehead. The army commander was notified that the multiple cross compartments and large number of swamps in the sector made maneuver difficult. The primary difficulty lay in the area between the Vistula and San rivers. In typical short, direct speech, Rybalko advised the 6th Guards Tank Corps commander, "Intensely manage reconnaissance, operate boldly, but cautiously."[111]

By the end of the operation, one brigade commander recalled the effect of fatiguing battles, sleepless nights, agonizing marches on the tankers. When withdrawn for rest to the evergreen pine woods east of the Vistula, the soldiers during all brief stops fell asleep instantly – in the tank, at the steering wheel, beside a gun, or standing upright at the roadside.[112]

By noon on 31 July, 6th and 7th Guards Tank Corps reached the Vistula river in the Baranov area. Using all available means, the tank army crossed the river from the 31st to 3 August, continuing the attack. Marshal Konev, considering the rapid German build-up on the western bank, decided not to strike for Krakow but to attack north along the river to seize Sandomierz and broaden the bridgehead. The remainder of August was spent expanding the bridgehead and defending it against German counterattacks. By 30 August, the Germans exhausted their capability to continue assaulting the bridgehead and shifted to defense. On the same day, the 3rd

Guards Tank Army transferred its sector to the 13th Army, withdrawing to the Stavka reserve.

With the first days of 1945, the 1st Belorussian and 1st Ukrainian Fronts prepared for the Red Army's largest strategic offensive of the war, the Vistula-Oder operation. The Soviets would conduct their offensive out of three major bridgeheads along the west bank of the Vistula river. In the largest bridgehead, the Sandomierz, the 1st Ukrainian Front concentrated approximately 90 percent of its forces which included the 6th Army, 3rd Guards Army, 13th Army, 52nd Army and 5th Guards Army, backed by Rybalko's 3rd Guards Tank Army and Lelyushenko's 4th Tank Army. Konev decided to use all his armor on the first day of the attack committing 3rd Guards Tank Army due west from the bridgehead.

Speaking at a gathering of party activists in the tank army, Rybalko said: "We must do what we can so our tanks can enter the lair of the Nazi beast and finish him off there. Our vehicles can make it to Berlin, but it is necessary to overcome all defensive lines while preserving our tanks. This is no easy matter. In order to do this, it is necessary to make known the best driver-mechanics and teach the rest by their example."[113] Rybalko, as earlier in his command, emphasized the importance of maintenance and the individual driver's skills and proficiency.

The best driver-mechanics spoke at party meetings in units and subunits about how they were successful in exceeding the guaranteed service life of the machines. In the formations and units there were meetings of officers, technical personnel, combat vehicle commanders and driver mechanics, and technical conferences devoted to the struggle for improving operation of the tanks and self propelled assault guns. In the subunits and crews there were discussions on "The Role of Crews in the Struggle for Extending the Life of a Tank", "The Best Driver-Mechanics and Experience", "Care for Equipment under Winter Conditions" and others.[114]

In other combat preparations Rybalko traveled to the lowest unit levels making contact with his veterans and recruits. Colonel Slyusarenko, commander of the 56th Tank Brigade, recalled the army commander's visit to his unit. Rybalko ordered all personnel to be called out. With the brigade commander he reviewed the ranks. Rybalko asked the tankers, "What complaints do you have?"

From the ranks: "Comrade Army commander, mother writes that the village soviet is not supporting her with firewood,' complained a sergeant.

"We will find out, we will help, comrade guards sergeant."

Staff officers, following in Rybalko's wake, wrote down the tanker's name, family, home address and his complaint.[115]

At times, tank armies were significantly reinforced beyond authorized strength. The Soviets clearly task-organized tank armies depending on the terrain, enemy, mission, and other factors. Rybalko's tank army often consisted of three corps and a large number of tanks. For the Vistula-Oder operation his tank army began with 925 tanks.[116]

Rybalko's operational group, which comprised his forward command post, consisted of the deputy chief of staff, the chiefs of operations and intelligence, the artillery commander with his staff, the chief of engineers with his staff, 50% of the officers in the operations, intelligence, and cipher sections, and the signal section. Also 50 per cent of the army command's communications means were with the operational group, i.e., 15 of 30 radios, 3 PO-2 aircraft.[117] With such a large forward command post, Rybalko maintained full control of the tank army. His main command post operated as a message center and conduit to higher command.

With basic Front directives and instructions, Rybalko studied Front intelligence and army reconnaissance reports. He directed his staff's work on a plan for the upcoming operation. He met with the commanders and political officers of the subordinate units for two days in planning sessions. Rybalko acquainted them with the peculiarities of the operation. For the Red Army, the Vistula-Oder operation would set up the final assault on Berlin and end the war. They expected a strong German resistance. Rybalko in his talk with his commanders sought to remind them that hard fighting still remained. "Our army has ahead to breakthrough and overcome in battle seven defensive sectors prepared by the enemy from the Vistula to the Oder. In engineer assessments, they are strongly fortified, saturated with pill-boxes, bunkers, minefields, antitank, and other."[118]

On 12 January 1945, the offensive began aggressively under the heavy artillery preparations. Rybalko required a high tempo attack. "Don't look back and don't be afraid of open flanks!" he prompted his corps commanders. "Pass the westward retreating Germans, destroy their rear, disrupt control. Forward, only forward!"[119] Rybalko's tank army by midafternoon exploded out of the bridgehead. His army swept past waiting reserve panzer divisions. These were engaged by separate tank corps and rifle units.

Increasingly, as the Red Army drove into western Europe, an exceptional amount of planning attention had to be given to crossing rivers encountered in the course of offensive operations. On the second day of the operation, the 3rd Guards Tank Army forced the Nida river; on the fourth, Pilitsa; on the sixth, Vartu. Rybalko's planning and preparation for the operation placed significance on the forced crossing of these rivers. With the quick, deep penetration, Rybalko's army organized itself for exploitation. The tank corps sent out in advance a forward detachment in the form of a reinforced tank brigade. These forward detachments from the first echelon corps (reinforced 51st Guards Tank Brigade from the 6th Guards Tank Corps and the reinforced 70th Mechanized Brigade from the 9th Mechanized Corps) were not only supposed to support the corps commitment to battle, but also make a hasty crossing of the Nida (the first river on the route of the offensive), capture its bridgehead and hold it until the main forces arrived. Powerful reconnaissance groups reinforced with sapper units were detailed from each corps to conduct not only reconnaissance but also capture crossings, mainly bridges.

The 6th Guards Tank Corps forward detachment quickly moved around Khmenik on the north and moved to Podlese. There, the lead battalion collided with the German 17th Panzer Division's advance guard and identified the German 24th Panzer Corps as moving in for a counterstrike. The forward detachment opened fire and continued advancing to the Nida river. On the morning of 13 January, the forward detachment was some 60-70 kilometers ahead of the tank army's main body.

Although communications with the forward detachment were lost, the 3rd Guards Tank Army was committed to the fight. The 6th Guards Tank Corps moved north of Khmenik and encountered units of the 24th Panzer Corps. The tank corps repelling continuous counterattacks worked in concert with the 10th Guards Tank Corps, 4th Tank Army. Both corps managed to inflict a serious loss on the 24th Panzer Corps, and by the end of the day Rybalko's tank army began moving into the operational depth, advancing 30-40 kilometers a day until crossing the Nida river.

Engineer support of the army's operation focused attention on the forced crossing of the Nida, Pilitsa, and Warta rivers. Corps sapper battalions made prefabricated constructions (single bent piers and decking) for 60-ton wooden bridges (one per corps). The army's

19th Bridge Engineering Brigade made constructions for building three such bridges. For reinforcement of the forward detachments, one corps sapper company and one army sapper company with pre-fabricated bridge components were attached to each. Their job was to lay four 60-ton bridges(two bridges per corps) across the Nida. The sapper companies attached to the 7th Guards Tank Corps forward detachment, located in the army's second echelon, were charged with laying two 60-ton bridges on the next river obstacle – the Pilitsa. The main forces of the 19th Bridge Engineer Brigade were located in Rybalko' s reserve. They included a full strength pontoon bridge battalion to be used for bridgelaying at other rivers. In preparation for the crossing of the Nida river operation while in the assembly area, the tank army staff selected a section of the Leng river, similar to the Nida, and sent all the brigades of the armys' corps across the Leng in a rehearsal. The forward detachments of the first echelon corps practiced twice.[120]

By the end of 14 January, Rybalko appeared in the most advanced element, the command post of the forward detachment, and assigned the mission to secure the town of Vloshova. By 15 January, Rybalko's tankers crossed the Pilitsa river. In the course of these operations, Rybalko assigned the 54th Guards Tank Brigade responsibility for the capture of the town, Chenstokhov. Driving to the brigade near midday, Rybalko found the brigade commander and his deputy having a meal.

"Sorry to disturb your meal," Rybalko said as he spread a map over the table.

Rybalko marked a point with his pencil. It was situated to the west of the brigade's current location.

"This is Chenstokhov – an important railroad center on the Silesia-Warsaw line. In addition, it is an important raw material base for the Polish metallurgical industry. ...The town must be saved." The pencil scarcely shifted and the army commander continued, "And this is the gate towards Chenstokhov. Population center, Mstuv. The approaches are covered with antitank ditches and minefields. The Hitlerites don't call it "Fortress Mstuv" by chance."[121]

A battlefield encounter on 16 January 1945, involving a subordinate commander, illustrates Rybalko's intuitive understanding of people. He received reports on the capture of Chenstokhov and ordered the tank corps commander to seize Petrovkov by the next morning.

"Petrovkov?" General V.V. Novikov asked. "But it's located in the 4th Tank Army's attack sector."

Rybalko explained the necessity of taking the town to prevent German attacks from that direction. He concluded, "Is it clear why we must quickly seize Petrovkov?"

"Exactly so, comrade army commander," the corps commander replied perfunctorily.

Rybalko, sensitive to the commander's understanding, caught uncertainty in the corps commander's answer and asked, "What remains unclear?"

"We have no information about the enemy forces in the area of Petrokov."

Taking time to ensure the corps commander had what he needed, Rybalko described the enemy situation, "Their forces are significant: large garrison, parts of the 97th Infantry Division, Division Brandenburg and the security regiment Ostland. All the territory around the city is mined. In the town are strong fortifications."[122] The telephone and the radio did not replace the personal meeting for Rybalko. He liked to be forward facing his commanders and ensuring his commanders fully understood his intent and their missions. Rybalko was uncanny in observing a person's motivation and sensitive to nonverbal clues.

Petrokov was taken on 18 January and seriously weakened the German operational defense. Its capture received a twenty volley salute in Moscow. In six days of continuous offense, the 1st Ukrainian Front on a 250 kilometer sector seriously defeated the German 4th Panzer and 17th Armies, advancing to a depth of 140-150 kilometers. The 3rd Guards Tank Army at the cutting edge of the advance made a significant contribution in this operational success.

Having achieved their objective, units of the 1st Ukrainian Front on 18 January attacked on all axes. The main forces moved at forced march pace advancing on average 30-40 kilometers a day, reaching 70 kilometers on some days.[123] By 20 January, Rybalko's tank army had reached the Germans fortified line 70 kilometers east of Breslau. As German resistance stiffened east of Breslau, Konev decided to change Rybalko's mission. Instead of advancing toward Breslau with the tank army, Konev directed Rybalko to turn south into the rear of German forces defending the Silesian area.

General Rybalko's 3rd Guards Tank Army operations in Silesia in January 1945 are an excellent example of redirecting a tank army

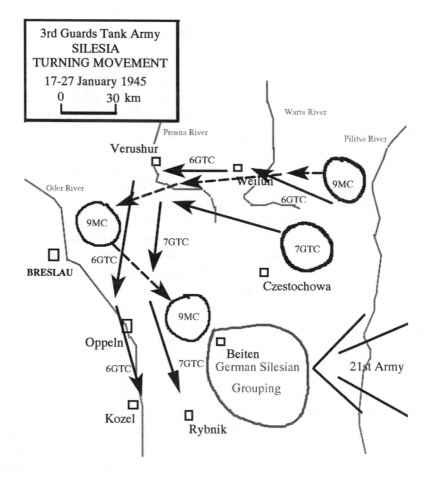

on the move. The operation exhibited the Red Army's tank force mature capability to accomplish agile maneuver, particularly in the hands of a capable commander such as Rybalko. While the 3rd Guards Tank Army successfully advanced on Breslau, the Front's left flank began to seriously lag in front of stubborn German resistance in the Silesian industrial region, which had tremendous economic importance to both sides. In order to disrupt the German plan to withdraw their forces behind the Oder and speed up the movement of the 5th Guards Army to the river, the Front commander, Marshal Konev, decided to turn 3rd Guards Tank Army to the south, striking the rear of the German's strong defense.

At 0300 hours, 21 January, Konev ordered the 3rd Guards Tank Army to strike southwesterly toward Namslau, and Oppeln instead of attacking toward Breslau; to seize the area of Oppeln by evening 22 January; to cut the railroads and highways leading to Oppeln from the east and southeast and to prepare to force the river behind the 5th Guards Army to attack further to the west.

Marshal Konev refined the army's mission and ordered it to force the Oder from the march, without awaiting the approach of the 5th Guards Army, and seize bridgeheads near Oppeln. Rybalko's tank army changed direction of its offensive 90 degrees and advanced by nightfall on the second day a depth of 70 kilometers. Owing to the rich experience acquired by Rybalko, his staff and subordinate commanders, the army accomplished the turn to the new axis in a very short time. By 0550 hours 21 January, army units received their missions, and at 1000 hours, they went on the offensive.

While the 3rd Guards Tank Army moved southward, three rifle armies (21st, 59th, and 60th) from the north, east and south reached the approaches of the Silesian industrial area where bitter fighting ensued. The Soviets calculated the German forces in the area consisted of nine infantry and two panzer divisions, approximately 100,000 officers and men.

Rybalko decided to attack toward Oppeln with two tank corps in first echelon and his mechanized corps in second echelon. The reinforced 55th Guards Tank Brigade, in the area of Landsberg, was designated as forward detachment for the 7th Guards Tank Corps, and the reinforced 51st Guards Tank Brigade, which had been previously in the corps second echelon, was assigned as forward detachment for 6th Guards Tank Corps. The army dispatched reconnaissance groups to lead the advance.

By evening 22 January the tank corps reached the Malapane River. In a heavily forested, mountain area, overcoming mined barriers and fierce German resistance, the tank units forced the Malapane river at night and drove swiftly toward the Oder. The next morning motorized elements of the 6th Guards Tank Corps seized Eyzenau and Groshovets. Later in the day, the 7th Guards Tank Corps reached the Oder south of Oppeln and cleared German troops from the eastern bank. In order to fulfill the Front commander's order, Rybalko had to move his army 70-80 kilometers and its forward detachments approximately 100 kilometers by mid-day on 24 January.

In the 1st Ukrainian Front's Sandomierz-Silesian offensive operation, the 3rd Guards Tank Army surprised the German commander by reaching the rear areas of the his Silesian grouping along the right bank of the Oder from the area of Oppeln on 24 January 1945. Rybalko's tank army fought its way more than 100 kilometers in three days, drastically altering the axes of its strikes and routing the enemy's reserves and rear service facilities. By moving into the rear area of the Silesian grouping, the tank army forced the enemy to abandon that important industrial region of Upper Silesia.

At 0310 hours 24 January Rybalko's tankers were assigned new missions, and by dawn shifted their offensive to a new axis. Rybalko decided to place the 9th Mechanized Corps in first echelon and move the 6th Guards Tank Corps to second echelon. The first echelon corps led with forward detachments. On 24 January, Marshal Konev directed the 3rd Guards Tank Army to turn southeast for the capture of the Silesian industrial region. The maneuver presented basic difficulties including diesel fuel supplies which were almost completely used up and stretched lines of communications that also precluded immediate resupply. Based on the situation, Rybalko decided to give the available fuel reserve to the forward elements of the 9th Mechanized Corps. The commander of the 9th Mechanized Corps created two forward detachments, the 69th and 71st Mechanized Brigades, reinforced with artillery assault guns.[124]

At the end of January, after the 3rd Guards Tank Army boldly turned behind the German Silesian grouping, Konev wrote in his memoirs about a meeting with Rybalko in which Konev identified a second 90 degree turn for the tank army. Marshal Konev decided to take the Silesian industrial area intact and let the German forces out of the trap. Letting the enemy go was not easy for the two war hardened professional soldiers. Konev recalled his encounter with Rybalko.

"It is difficult to recall a dialogue which is 20 years old, but the one with Rybalko was of the unforgettable kind and, if my memory does not fail me, it was as follows:

He: "Comrade Marshal, to carry out your order, I must turn the army again."

I: "It's all right, commander, this is nothing new to you. Your army has just made a brilliant turn. Let's make one more turn. Incidentally, one of your corps has not deployed yet and is marching in the second echelon. Let's send it at once in the direction of Ratibor(Raciborz) and stop the other two corps, especially since I know you have excellent radio communications with all your corps."

He:(making a wry face and, as I could see, still inwardly resisting) "Yes, I suppose that can be done."

I: "If I am not mistaken, you have good communications? Are they good with all your units?"

He: "Yes, with all of them. The radio is working faultlessly."

I: "Then at once send the order. 'Stop' to these two corps and the order 'Forward, to Rabitor' to the other corps."[125]

Marshal Konev thought very highly of Rybalko. He considered him "...a very competent and self-confident commander..." possessing "...exceptional self control, combined with energy and a strong will which were clearly manifested in all his actions."[126] Konev wrote in his memoirs, "In friendly chats he was witty and resourceful, as well as fond and capable of arguing. But his main positive quality, his great virtue was, I would say, his ability to rally those who surrounded him and whom he commanded."[127] He continued, "Rybalko's method was not one of concessions and patting on the back, cajoling or being all-forgiving. On the contrary – and in the army this was necessary – he was very exacting but at the same time just and considerate."[128]

Rybalko was quite physically fearless and morally courageous. He knew how to distinguish really decisive moments from the apparently decisive ones and knew exactly when and where he should be, which is extremely important for an operational level commander. The operational level commander who cannot rely on the sounds and immediate sights of battle must read intangible indicators of when and where the battle is taking a decisive character. Admittedly, in fashioning an offensive operation, the commander should know not only when and where he will create the decisive action, but also must be prepared for the unexpected. This is more art than science, and the tacit knowledge comes primarily from experience.

"I was often at his headquarters," wrote Konev, "when on a sand-table, a relief map or any large scale map he was taking his commanders through the operations to be carried out by corps or brigades and their variations. I was present when he prepared the Lvov operation on an army scale and when he prepared the Vistula-Oder operation. Thorough briefing of his commanders was one of his main concerns."[129]

Konev paid Rybalko the ultimate military professional compliment, "Rybalko was a man on whom I completely relied. I was sure that in any matter that concerned him he would never overlook anything, even if I somehow overlooked it."[130]

On 28 January, Konev assigned Rybalko a limited mission: to complete the destruction of isolated enemy groupings in the areas of Rybnik and Nikolai, destroy the enemy as it was escaping encirclement and attacking in the direction of Ratibor, reach the Oder river. This maneuver produced the desired result, allowing the Germans an escape route from the Silesian industrial area, saving it from the destruction of close combat. The tanks moved to clear the east branch of the Oder in the area of Rabitor. At noon on 30 January, 6th Guards Tank Corps withdrew from battle; the 7th Guards Tank Corps, the following night. The 9th Mechanized Corps continued fighting with the 60th Army to reach the Oder, stopping on the night of 31 January.

In 19 days of battle, Rybalko's army traversed approximately 600 kilometers crossing multiple rivers. They arrived at the Oder, seizing bridgeheads, concluding the Vistula-Oder operation – one of the largest operations in the Second World War. The German Army's defeat between the Vistula and Oder rivers foreshadowed the final collapse and surrender of Germany.

During the lst and 2nd of February, the 6th and 7th Guards Tank Corps repaired their equipment and replenished supplies. After which the corps moved 250 kilometers in three night marches, concentrating their units in the area of Volov. The 9th Mechanized Corps joined the army on the evening of 8 February. In the first week of February, the lst Ukrainian Front redeployed its forces to the bridgehead north of Breslau which the Germans still held.

On the morning of 8 February, Rybalko's army crossed the Oder river occupying attack positions. After breaking the German defense on the west side of the Oder river, fighting off counterattacks, the

3rd Guards Tank Army smashed its way out of the Steinau bridge-head and, by evening, began turning south behind Breslau. In three day's heavy fighting, the tank and mechanized corps with the 6th and 5th Guards Armies completed encirclement west of Breslau. By 9 and 10 February, the tank army's lead elements reached Gaynau and seized a bridgehead over the Bobr river. At this point the tank army's advance slowed from weather and German resistance. An unseasonable January thaw broke up the ice on the Oder river, making it more an obstacle than it might otherwise have been. The mud slowed Rybalko's tanks.

By 14 February, 3rd Guards Tank Army disengaged its corps from battle, concentrating in the areas of Mechku and Goldberg to receive supplies and repair their equipment. The 9th Mechanized Corps pulled off the battle line before the arrival of relieving 5th Guards Army. German reconnaissance detected the lapse in front line coverage. While the 9th Mechanized Corps' brigades formed into march columns, they were suddenly attacked from the south by the 8th Panzer Division. Rybalko handling the emergency well averted the disaster by rapid decisions.

While the corps was fighting, Rybalko having been ordered to reach the Neisse and capture Gorlitz decided to carry out a bold double encirclement of the entire Gorlitz enemy group with the two corps remaining at his disposal.

"This decision," Konev noted, "was not one of Rybalko's best. The point is that even before then the 6th Guards Tank Corps had already unsuccessfully fought intense battles in the same direction. Now, it had been given essentially the same mission, but with smaller forces to perform it, and of course, there was still less reason to expect success."[131]

Rybalko soon realized his mistake and redisposed his forces. However, the situation had sharply deteriorated. The forward units of the 7th Tank Corps engaged the newly arriving German panzer reserves from the march, while the rest of the corps tried to cross the Kwisa against strong enemy resistance and failed.

In the following two days, the Germans brought up their 8th Panzer, 408th Infantry and 10th Motorized Divisions, cutting into the rear and flank of the 7th and, to some extent, the 6th Guards Tank Corps. The German assault began to envelop Rybalko's army from the east. A very tense situation developed. Only by joint attacks by all three corps and with the support of Koroteyev's 52nd

Army did Rybalko finally manage to defeat the German threat that had broken through northeast of Luban.

"Finding myself in those days at General Koroteyev's advance command post," Konev recalled, "I was in a position to assess the complexity of the situation on Rybalko's sector personally. I knew, if anybody did, that by this time the strength of many brigades of the 3rd Guards Tank Army were down to 15-20 tanks each. And, yet the army commander came out of this unenviable situation with credit. We must give him his due, having somewhat overreached himself at first, overestimating his own forces and underestimating the enemy, he subsequently displayed sober calculation and enviable cool-headedness which, in the end, enabled him to frustrate the rather dangerous plans of the Germans."[132]

In the Vistula-Oder operation, 3rd Guards Tank Army lost 85% of its total tank and self-propelled assault guns.[133] The 3rd Guards Tank Army was about to be withdrawn into the reserves for reconstitution. The Red Army practice was to disengage tank armies from combat for replenishment, when an offensive operation bogged down. By that point in the operations the tank army was exhausted. Only a small portion of the tanks and assault guns remained functional. The engines and undercarriages of tanks were at the limit of their endurance. Rybalko after the war noted that a tank army should be withdrawn from combat for replenishment before it loses not more than 80-85 percent of its tanks. A tank army at 15-20 percent begins to take losses in hard to replace skills and equipment, such as army and corps staff officers, technical specialists, motor transportation, radio stations and other unique equipment. A tank army with few tanks suffers a considerable decrease in its combat capabilities, and it suffers losses that are not compensated by any brief replenishment. He believed that a tank army should be withdrawn from combat prior to total exhaustion, the latter being defined as 20 percent of the organic quantity of tanks remaining. In this case less time would be needed to restore the army on the basis of its surviving personnel.[134]

In the final assault for Berlin, a large number of the armored forces participated – four tank armies, nine separate tank and mechanized corps, nine separate tank brigades, nearly 30 separate tank and more than 60 assault gun regiments. The tank armies of the 1st Belorussian and 1st Ukrainian Fronts played an important role in the Supreme High Command's concept for the operation. They were to aggressively attack around Berlin from the north and southwest encircling the city and together with the rifle armies destroy German forces in and around Berlin.

The 1st Ukrainian Front commander, Marshal I.S. Konev, in his directive from 8 April 1945, established the mission for the 3rd and 4th Guards Tank Armies after the infantry forced the Spree river to advance into the penetration. In six days strong forward detachments were to seize the areas of Ratenau, Brandenburg, Dessau to create conditions for encircling the German forces in Berlin. One corps of Rybalko's army was to strike for Berlin from the south.

The Berlin operation began for the 1st Ukrainian Front on 16 April. The attack commenced at 0600 hours, and unlike the tactics of the 1st Belorussian Front to the north, Konev's Front attacked across the Neisse by laying down a massive smoke screen to hide his movements enabling his engineers to complete bridges. The power of Konev's offensive was like a sledgehammer, crumbling the German forces on the opposite bank.

"From the first day of the operation all our actions could be characterized in one word – aggressiveness," Rybalko wrote in a postwar recollection.[135] Marshal Konev instructed his tank army commanders to bypass cities and large population centers and not to get bogged down in protracted engagements taking full advantage of the armored force's mobility and speed.

The forward detachments were committed at 1400 hours. The commander of the 52nd Tank brigade as the forward detachment for the 6th Guards Tank Corps remembered the arrival of Rybalko at the banks of the Neisse river.

"The army commander was absolutely calm," recalled his political officer, "although the air everywhere literally hummed with bursting shells and mines."[136] His political officer believed him to be naturally fearless.

Marshal Konev's orders to the 3rd Guards Tank Army were to drive in the general direction of Luchenwalde and reach the line Treuenbristzen-Luckenwalde by the fifth day of the operation. With strong forward elements take Brandenburg and with a reinforced tank corps attack Berlin from the south.

On the evening of 16 April, the main forces of the tank army crossed the Neisse, and the next day penetrated the German's second defensive zone, to a depth of 20 kilometers. By the end of the day, Konev assigned the 3rd Guards Tank Army the mission to attack Berlin from the south, to operate according to the second variant of the Front's plan. The brigades pushed aggressively towards the Spree river on the path to Berlin.

On 18 April, Marshal Konev could see that Marshal Zhukov's armies had slowed down. Konev kept his tank armies on the northern flank poised and prepared for a decision to strike towards Berlin. That night, Rybalko received a telephonic directive from the Front commander: 3rd Guards Tank Army, in the course of the night from 17 to 18 April, must force the river Spree and develop the offensive in the general direction of Fetshau, Golsen, Barut, Teltov, southern edge of Berlin. The army mission at night from 20-21 April, is to penetrate Berlin from the south. On the 3rd's left was the 4th Tank Army under the command of General D.D. Lelyushenko.

"At 1310 hours 18 April when we were two kilometers from the Spree and rushing toward Brandenburg, I received directions from the Front Commander to force the Spree and develop the attack aggressively in the general direction...southern edge of Berlin. So – aggressively towards Berlin. How this order inspired us!" Rybalko recalled.[137]

By morning on 19 April, the two tank armies had captured a bridgehead over the Spree assuming a favorable position to strike for Berlin. Rybalko's army had considerable freedom of maneuver, operating by the end of the day 30-50 kilometers ahead of the rifle armies. At this point, Rybalko committed his second echelon, the 9th Mechanized Corps, to develop the attack on Berlin, moving in a single day 35-50 kilometers.

By 22 April, Rybalko's units swiftly overran Zossen and advanced toward Berlin, while other units were involved in stubborn battles with the German units at Cottbus. The next day his tankers approached the Berlin defensive ring at a point about 20 kilometers from the southern edge of the capital. Marshal Konev decided to reinforce Rybalko's attack. The 10th Artillery Breakthrough Corps, the 25th Breakthrough Division, and the 23rd AAA Division were assigned to the 3rd Guards Tank Army. Additionally, the 2nd Fighter Corps was also transferred to Rybalko.

At this point, Rybalko's tankers, advancing on Berlin from the south, were separated from lead riflemen of the 8th Guards Army, advancing on Berlin's southeastern edges by only 10 kilometers.

Rybalko's army ran into a major obstacle, the Teltov Canal which was 30-35 meters wide and 4-5 meters deep, and could not take it from the march. The Germans had prepared strong defenses on its northern bank. At the southern edge of Berlin Kurista's forward detachment from the 6th Guards Tank Corps took the town of Teltov and advanced towards the canal.

When the 3rd Guards Tank Army reached Berlin, Konev reinforced Rybalko's army with five heavy artillery divisions. The artillery, a powerful fist, cut a path for the attacking tankers through the German fortifications. Konev assigned Rybalko the mission: the morning of 24th force Teltov canal and penetrate to Berlin. Rybalko decided to cross the Teltov canal simultaneously with all corps. In the center operated the 6th Guards Tank Corps. Organizing the forced crossing continued in compressed time.[138]

Rybalko reported that to overcome from the march the Teltov canal with its granite facing could not be done by his tanks, that on the western edge of Berlin, he employed by-passing and capturing to prevent possible retreat to the west by the Berlin garrison. He asked for help in the form of one rifle division, in order to capture a bridgehead on the north bank of the Teltov canal, and an engineer sapper brigade for repairing bridges.[139]

Rybalko's command post was situated in the highest building in Teltov. Located on the seventh floor, Rybalko's command post gave him a commanding view. When forward with the units, Rybalko quietly sat in his Willy, leaning on his cane, tormented by back pains. The high perched command post eased the strain on him physically.

Marshal Konev arrived in his command post to assist and support the operation. Rybalko's tankers participated in the final assault on the city.

After the fall of Berlin, the 3rd Guards Tank Army along with other forces of the 1st Ukrainian Front immediately turned towards Prague to complete the encirclement of the German Army Group Center in Czechoslovakia. The operation began on 7 May. At 1400 hours a powerful artillery preparation introduced the offensive. The 3rd and 4th Guards Tank Armies penetrated the German defense with part of their force and with leading rifle units and broke swiftly for Prague. With air support, the tank armies on the morning of 19 May broke through to the capital of Czechoslovakia and joined forces with the 6th Guards Tank Army making an attack from the vicinity of Brno. This was the final combat action for Rybalko and his tank army.

At the end of the war for his personal reputation and the accomplishments of his tank army he was awarded his second Gold Star for Hero of the Soviet Union, awarded on 6 April 1945.

Hard driving, demanding Rybalko, the hammer, imposed his resourceful and direct style on all aspects of his command. Impatient, graceless, at times, in dealing with subordinates, he could be inspirational with a judicious, satiric humor. He was always fair. He operated a swift, surprising style of warfare that made him a kindred spirit of the American General George S. Patton. Rybalko understood the characteristics and potential of large tank units, appreciating the technical capabilities and limitations of tanks – his distinguishing mark as a tank commander. Adaptable, cunning, Rybalko's nerves of steel allowed him to fight close to the edge of disaster.

Rybalko's subordinates who became very successful in the post war years fondly recall him in their many writings. They cherished their encounters with the short, no nonsense commander. Rybalko's legacy was a school of officers who rose to the highest levels in the Soviet Army, with a few just relinquishing commands in the past few years. Rybalko finished the war as the premier tank commander eclipsing the other tank army commanders in the swift race across Poland and the bold capture of Berlin.

NOTES

1. A.A. Vetrov, *Tak i bylo*, Moscow: Voenizdat, 1982, pp. 79-80.

2. K.S. Moskalenko, *Na yugo-zapadnom napravlenii*, Vol 2, Moscow: Voenizdat, 1973, pp. 401-2.

3. S.I. Melnikov, *Marshal Rybalko*, Kiev: Izdatel'stvo Politicheskoi Literatury Ukrainy, 1980, p. 54.

4. Ibid., p. 55.

5. A.M. Vasilevsky, *A Lifelong Cause*, Moscow: Progress, 1981, pp. 237-8.

6. A.M. Zvartsev, *3-ya gvardeiskaya tankovaya*, Moscow: Voenizdat, 1982, p. 32.

7. Ibid.

8. Ibid.

9. E.E. Belov, *Syny otchizny*, Moscow: Izdatel'stvo Politicheskoi Literatury, 1966, pp. 129-30.

10. Melnikov, p. 65.

11. David M. Glantz, *Soviet Military Deception in the Second World War*, London: Frank Cass, 1989, p. 138.

12. M.I. Kazakov, *Nad kartoi bylykh srazhenii*, Moscow: Voenizdat, 1971, p. 150.

13. Zvartsev, p. 38.

14. David Glantz, p. 233.

15. Melnikov, p. 75.

16. Ibid., p. 76.

17. Ibid., pp. 76-7.

18. Ibid.

19. Kazakov, p. 168.

20. Zvartsev, p. 50.

21. Ibid., p. 52.

22. Melnikov, p. 88.

23. Kazakov, p. 175.

24. Belov, pp. 135-6.

25. Zvartsev, p. 52.

26. Melnikov, p. 94.

27. Ibid., p. 99.

28. Ibid., p. 102.

29. Ibid., p. 103.

30. Ibid., p. 105.

31. Vetrov, p. 134.

32. Ibid.

33. L.M. Sandalov, *Na Moskovskom napravlenii*, Moscow: Nauka, 1970, p. 349.

34. I.M. Anan'ev, *Tankovye armii v nastuplenii*, Moscow: Voenizdat, 1988, p. 128.

35. Radzievskii, , Vizh 2-76, p. 20.

36. G.A. Koltunov, B.G. Soloviev, *Kurskaya bitva*, Moscow: Voenizdat, 1970, p. 233.

37. Ibid.

38. Zvartsev, p. 68.

39. Koltunov, p. 236.

40. Melnikov, p. 112.

41. L. Sandalov, "Bryanskii front v Orlovskoi operatsii," *Vizh* 8-63, p. 71.

42. Ibid.

43. Koltunov, p. 236.

44. I.I. Yakubovskii, *Zemlya v ogne*, Moscow: Voenizdat, 1975, p. 125.

45. Ibid., p. 126.

46. Melnikov, p. 113.

47. Ibid.

48. Ibid., p. 117.

49. Ibid., p. 118.

50. Yakubovskii, p. 157.

51. Zvartsev, p. 81.

52. Ibid., p. 82.

53. K.K. Rokossovskii, *A Soldier's Duty*, Moscow: Progress, 1985, p. 205.

54. Ibid.

55. Zvartsev, pp. 84-5.

56. Ibid., p. 85.

57. Koltunov, p. 244.

58. A.I. Radzievskii, *Tankovyi udar*, Moscow: Voenizdat, *1977, p. 113;* A.I. Radzievskii, *Proryv*, Moscow: Voenizdat, 1979, p. 67.

59. M.M. Kir'yan, *Vnezapost' v nastupatel'nykh operatsiyakh Velikoi Otechestvennoi Voiny*, Moscow: Nauka, 1986, pp. 128-9.

60. Yakubovskii, p. 313.

61. Anan'ev, p. 125.

62. K.A. Malygin, *V tsentre boevogo poradka*, Moscow: Voenizdat, 1986, p. 77.

63. Melnikov, pp. 124-5.

64. N.G. Nersesyan, *Kievsko-Berlinskii*, Moscow: Voenizdat, 1974, pp. 64-5.

65. Malygin, p. 79.

66. Melnikov, p. 128.

67. Z.K. Slyusarenko, *Poslednii vystrel*, Moscow: Voenizdat, 1974, p. 90.

68. Melnikov, p. 133.

69. Ibid., p. 143.

70. Ibid., p. 144.

71. Nersesyan, p. 82.

72. V.A. Matsulenko, *Operativnaya maskirovka voisk*, Moscow: Voenizdat, 1975, pp. 78-79.

73. S. Alferov, "Peregruppirovka 3-i gvardeiskoi tankovyi armii v bitve za Dnepr," *Vizh* 3-80, p. 21.

74. Germany, Army, Eighth Army, Intelligence Records, Situation maps, microfilm series T-312, roll 58, frame 7573794, National Archives and Records Administration, Washington, DC.

75. Ibid., frames 7573801-4.

76. Lieutenant Colonel David M. Glantz, "The Kiev Operation, an Overview," 19, in 1985 Art of War Symposium – From the Dnepr to the Vistula: Soviet Offensive Operations, November 1943 - August 1944, Transcript of Proceedings 29 April - 3 May 1985, edited by Colonel David M. Glantz (Carlisle Barracks, PA: Center for Land Warfare, U.S. Army War College, August 1985).

77. Erich von Manstein, *Lost Victories*, Novato, CA: Presidio Press, 1982, 1982, p. 481.

78. Ibid., p. 486.

79. V.S. Arkhipov, *Vremya tankovykh atak*, Moscow: Voenizdat, 1981, p. 147.

80. Ibid.

81. Melnikov, pp. 148-49.

82. Nersesyan, p. 88.

83. Ibid., p. 230-231.

84. Nersesyan, pp. 91-2.

85. K.V. Krainyukov, *Oruzhie osobogo roda*, Moscow: Voenizdat, 1977, pp. 80-1.

86. Yakubovskii, p. 230.

87. F. W. von Mellenthin, *Panzer Battles*, New York: Ballantine, 1980, p. 303.

88. Arkhipov, pp. 158-9.

89. D.A. Dragunskii, *Gody v brone*, Moscow: Voenizdat, 1975, p. 271.

90. Arkhipov, p. 159.

91. Dragunskii, p. 125.

92. Melnikov, pp. 152-3.

93. Mellenthin, p. 305.

94. Melnikov, p. 161.

95. Zvartsev, p. 149.

96. Slyusarenko, pp. 98-9.

97. Ibid., p. 100.

98. Nersesyan, pp. 109-10.

99. Arkhipov, p. 192.

100. Melnikov, p. 184.

101. Yakubovskii, p. 454.

102. A.S. Zhadov, *Chetyre goda voiny*, Moscow: Voenizdat, 1978, p. 189.

103. Slyusarenko, p. 104.

104. Ibid., p. 100

105. Zvartsev, p. 172.

106. I.S. Konev, *Zapiski komanduyushchego frontom*, Moscow: Voenizdat, 1981, p. 246.

107. M.M. Kir'yan, p. 169.

108. Krainyukov, pp. 246-50.

109. Nersesyan, p. 131.

110. Ibid., p. 136.

111. Ibid., pp. 136-7.

112. Dragunskii, pp. 188-9.

113. Losik, p. 247.

114. Ibid., p. 109.

115. Slyusarenko, p. 151.

116. A. Novikov, *Otvety na pis'ma chitalelei, Voenno-istoricheskii zhurnal*, 9-1973, p. 123.

117. Anan'ev, pp. 267-8.

118. Melnikov, p. 199.

119. Ibid., p. 200.

120. Losik, pp. 131-32.

121. Melnikov, p. 200.

122. Ibid., p. 202-3.

123. I. Yakubovskii, "Udar nebyvaloi sily," *Vizh* 2-70, p. 69.

124. Radzievskii, *Tankovyi udar*, p. 238.

125. I.S. Konev, *Year of Victory*, Moscow: Progress, 1969, pp. 37-8.

126. Ibid., p. 40.

127. Ibid.

128. Ibid.

129. Ibid., p. 41.

130. Ibid., p. 42.

131. Konev, *Victory*, p. 63.

132. Ibid., p. 64.

133. A. Tsynkalov, "Iz opyta povysheniya zhivuchesti tankov v nastupatel'nykh operatsiyakh," *Vizh* 3-83, p. 29; Radzievskii, *Tankovyi udar*, p. 220.

134. Anan'ev, p. 125.

135. P. Rybalko, "Udar s yuga," *Shturm Berlina*, Moscow: Voenizdat, 1948, p. 186.

136. Melnikov, p. 214.

137. Rybalko, p. 187.

138. Radzievskii, *Tankovyi udar*, pp. 162-3.

139. A. Luchinskii, "Na Berlin," *Vizh* 5-65, pp. 84-5.

CHAPTER IV

★ ★ ★ ★

LELYUSHENKO

An energetic, aggressive fighting commander, Dmitri Danilovich Lelyushenko became Stalin's one-man fire brigade in the early months of the war. With experience in two wars, he had already won his country's highest decoration, Hero of the Soviet Union, before the German invasion. Lelyushenko, a rough and ready combat leader, fought against Germany's top commanders on three major approaches to Moscow in the fall and winter of 1941. Often, he salvaged a collapsing situation by force of will. General Georgi Zhukov, as Western Front commander, knew the measure of this tough fighter in late November 1941, when he directed Lelyushenko to move his command post into a gap in the Front defense. Lelyushenko placed his headquarters on the path of assaulting German panzer units, scraping together a thin band of mixed forces to resist the onslaught. His effort gave the Red Army time to launch a counteroffensive within a month, pushing back the German army from the outskirts of Moscow.

Dmitri Danilovich Lelyushenko was born in 1901. At the age of 17, Lelyushenko fought in the Russian Civil War as a rifle-toting infantryman and later rode with the famed Budyenny, in the First Cavalry Army. Always close to the action, he was severely wounded and twice a "shell-shock" casualty. After the Civil War, the Red Army needed literate commanders and political cadre. Lelyushenko called to advanced military studies, graduated from the Leningrad military-political school followed by two more years of military schooling, before he became a cavalry commander. After a brief duty with troops, he attended in 1933 the Frunze Military Academy. After completing his military education, Lelyushenko made the transition from

Dmitri Danilovich Lelyushenko (right).

cavalry to an armored unit. Initially, he was assigned as the deputy chief of the operations section for a mechanized brigade. Later he became a tank company commander and continued a successful rise in command.

Major Lelyushenko commanded a tank regiment in the Moscow Military District. Stocky, athletic with the militarily fashionable shaved head, he was restless with boundless energy, and, at times, could be abrupt and quick tempered. He loved all aspects of sports, stressing the necessities of combative and physical preparation. In the winter, he required his lieutenants after dawn to sponge bathe with snow.[1] Through lengthy, often intensive, questions and answers, he developed a constant dialogue in his training lessons with junior officers. His questions and answers covered equipment, arms and army regulations. Lelyushenko could be found invariably on firing ranges in the tank training area. Appearing suddenly, he gave young tank commanders lessons on firing and driving their combat vehicles. The talkative Lelyushenko always checked their knowledge and forced his young officers to constantly think about working through various conditions.[2] He enjoyed coaching and teaching, focusing on the usefulness of people.

Totally dedicated to military service and his duties as commander, Lelyushenko hung on his office wall large sheets of paper listing all his officers, noting their level of training and their personal preparedness. After each name would be an appraisal – an open, running efficiency report. Lelyushenko characteristically gave concise, incisive assessments on individuals. "Captain so-and-so, he is boiling hot in his work." Or, "This lieutenant is not going to live..."[3]

In September 1939, Lieutenant Colonel Lelyushenko became the commander of the 39th Separate Light Tank Brigade. His unit, primarily armed with the T-26, light tank, received orders unexpectedly to load on rail cars for an unknown destination. Lelyushenko's brigade moved west through Belorussia, eastern Poland, as part of the Soviet response to the German invasion of Poland. Although the tank brigade fought no actual engagements in the Soviet occupation of eastern Poland, its maneuvers provided valuable experience in controlling and sustaining an armored force on a long march. As one Red Army General noted, "Our logistics...were not up to the mark. Fuel had not been brought up quickly enough for our rapidly advancing troops."[4] The Polish campaign gave the Red Army its first hard look at the difficulties of operating large armored forces.

Three months later in the first weeks of December 1939, Lelyushenko's tank brigade again received transfer notification. This time his unit moved to the Karelian isthmus, adjacent to Finland. Assigned to the 13th Rifle Army in the Finnish War against the Mannerheim line, the tank brigade fought in a major Red Army operation during February-March 1940. The brigade's area of operation was located on the lower Vuoksinksoi water system which had been the scene for a previously unsuccessful Red Army attack. After an unsuccessful first venture against the Finnish Army, the Red Army wisely focused its main effort against the isthmus.

Colonel Lelyushenko's brigade operated directly against the Mannerheim line. While he moved his unit to an assembly area and prepared for combat, his brigade staff along with the 13th Army's rifle corps planned an assault crossing of the Taipolen-Ioki river to capture a small bridgehead. With a dawn artillery preparation, lasting some three hours, the offensive operation began. Rocket flares fired in the frigid air signaled the tanks advance. With difficulty, the tanks overcame the deep snow in low gear, advancing 300-400 meters. The accompanying infantry fell behind the tanks and went to ground in the snow. Without infantry protection, the tanks returned, collected the infantry, and advanced again – a scene repeating itself several times. These blundering actions proved costly, causing several tanks to be damaged from Finnish antitank fires. One tank burst into flames. While the battle continued, the tanks returned to their initial assault positions without results.

Success in combat often builds fighting morale, the opposite is equally true. Lelyushenko with a major task to turn his routed brigade around physically and psychologically prepared for another attack. He sent out reconnaissance to observe the Finnish positions, determining minefields and their system of antitank fires. With a better understanding of the enemy's positions, Lelyushenko's brigade advanced in a new direction with the 23rd Rifle Corps. After an artillery and air preparation, the tanks rushed forward in the attack and succeeded in breaching the Finnish defensive positions. In difficult fighting for the heights around Kirkha Muola, Lelyushenko demonstrated his ability to adopt quickly improvised fighting techniques. The dug-in Finnish positions presented a particularly tough tactical problem for the Soviet soldiers to overcome. Lelyushenko decided to coordinate better action between tanks and flamethrowers. As the attack began with the usual artillery preparation, the tanks moved forward followed by attacking infantry. This time, however, flame-throwers moved behind the tanks. As the Finnish soldiers in their trenches fired on the tanks, the flame-throwers "smoked out" the Finns who were cut down by tank machinegunners.[5] In close, gruesome fighting, Lelyushenko's tankers succeeded where other armored forces had failed against the tenacious Finnish defenders.

By the last days of February, the Red Army had pushed the western portion of the Finnish line back. At night on 1 March, the 50th Rifle Corps attacking around Vyborg from the north, took the rail station Syainie and on 2 March advanced toward the Finnish defensive sector on the approaches to Vyborg. At the same time, parts of the 34th Rifle Corps gained the southern edge of Vyborg. By 5 March, forces of the 7th and 13th Army fully advanced towards the rear line of the Finnish fortifications covering Vyborg. Favorable weather helped the Soviet operations, permitting the movement of tanks and artillery over frozen lakes. As one of nine tank brigades participating in the successful penetration of the Mannerheim line, Lelyushenko's tank brigade won the Order of Lenin. Lelyushenko, for personal bravery, received his country's highest honor, Hero of the Soviet Union.[6]

Finland was unfavorable tank country, presenting many difficult problems for tank units and their commanders. Successful operations against an active and resourceful Finnish Army demanded innovation and improvisation by Red Army tactical commanders, and winter warfare had its own particular requirements. The extreme cold conditions required Soviet tank forces to develop specially prepared oil and fuel and maintain a good supply of anti-freeze for the engine radiators. The Red Army tankers learned to keep a lamp in the engine compartment and dig pits for small fires underneath tanks to keep vehicle engine blocks warm. The Red Army tankers learned when moving through snow to steer clear of each other's tracks in order not to dig themselves in too far and become embedded in a morass. Hill crests and ridgelines, that tankers normally avoided because of exposure, were the best going in snowy conditions. To have successfully commanded tanks in Finland was a major professional accomplishment, and brought great credit to Lelyushenko.

Stalin's purges in the Red Army military leadership left a major gap in the senior ranks. In late 1939, Stalin reviewing the command personnel in the army and navy discovered that 85 percent of army and navy commanders were under the age of 35.[7] Rapid promotion had placed youth, not experience in higher positions of authority. The average age of the regimental commander was 29-33 years, division commanders were 35-38 years, corps and army commanders, 40-43 years.[8]

By the end of 1940, Major General Lelyushenko, reaping the benefits of the post-purge promotions and his reputation from the Finnish war, became commander of the prestigious lst Moscow Workers Motorized Rifle Division in the Moscow Military District. With the re-formation of the Red Army's mechanized corps, Lelyushenko, a decorated and experienced tank commander, in the spring of 1941, was designated as commander of the 21st Mechanized Corps formed in the Moscow Military District. The corps consisted of two tank divisions and one motorized rifle division. In fighting armored vehicles, the corps had 98 light, outdated BT-7's and T-26's. The new T-34 and KV tanks had not been distributed to his corps.

On 21 June, Lelyushenko received a call to report to the Red Army General Staff. Late that night in Moscow, Lelyushenko telephoned the duty officer who informed Lelyushenko that his appointment would be the next morning with the Chief of the Operations Directorate of the General Staff, Lieutenant General Nikolai Fedorovich Vatutin.

The next morning, 22 June 1941, when Lelyushenko arrived in the Operations Directorate, he learned of the German invasion. General Vatutin busily received status reports on the mechanized corps locations and actions. Turning to Lelyushenko, he directed, "Return quickly to your corps. All your instructions will be sent in message directives."[9]

In the early morning hours of 23 June, Lelyushenko arrived at his corps and prepared for war. His partially formed corps required a solution outside of regulations and instructions for fighting its 98 light tanks and 129 guns.[10] To compensate for insufficient equipment, Lelyushenko reorganized his understrength corps to create a tank "fist" of 60-70 combat vehicles. With preparations complete, he waited for combat orders. That afternoon, German bombers found his corps, inflicting losses in personnel and equipment. The long grim war began in bloody earnest for Lelyushenko and his corps.

On 25 June, he received orders from Marshal Semen Konstantinovich Timoshenko, the Defense Commissar, to move immediately towards Daugavpils in the Baltic region and prevent the Germans from capturing the town. The corps was to assume a defense along the Western Dvina river. By 1600 hours, Lelyushenko's corps moving forward in the direction of Daugavpils met an endless refugees column heading east from the invaders. Marauding German warplanes continually bombed his corps, but, by the afternoon of 27 June, his divisions, despite significant losses from air attacks, advanced to the west of the Western Dvina river 20-30 kilometers northeast of Daugavpils.

The Northwest Front Deputy commander arriving in the mechanized corps command post informed Lelyushenko that the lead units of the German General Erich Hoepner's Fourth Panzer Group had already crossed the Western Dvina and penetrated to Daugavpils. Daugavpils, with its two bridges over the wide Western Dvina, was the first objective of the Panzer Group, and its capture was entrusted to 56th Panzer Corps. Attempts by a partially formed Soviet 5th Airborne Corps to clear the Germans from the east side of the river failed. Major General Nikolai Erastovich Berzarin's 27th Army assumed the sector, and the 21st Mechanized corps would be subordinated to the rifle army.

Believing his corps could attack the next morning, Lelyushenko informed the Deputy Front commander who approved the decision. Lelyushenko's staff prepared the order in two hours. Restless with the staff process he drove forward to the divisions to see his unit commanders and soldiers who would fight their first combat in a few hours.

At 0500 hours, 28 June, Lelyushenko's corps attacked. Within two hours, Lelyushenko received reports of contact with the advancing Germans forces in the vicinity of Malinov, a village 12 kilometers northeast of Daugavpils. Lelyushenko drove forward to the area of contact where the 46th Tank Division engaged General Erich von Manstein's 56th Panzer Corps. "What are you considering?" Lelyushenko asked General Vasilii Alekseevich Koptsov, the division commander.

"Going around Malinov on the right and striking towards Daugavpils," the commander quickly responded.

"Fine. You act."[11]

During the next two hours, the division in coordination with the 5th Airborne Corps penetrated towards Daugavpils. In heavy fighting near the town, the division suffered more serious casualties,

notably the artillery regiment commander and the division commander. Additionally, the division began experiencing shortages in
fuel and ammunition, many tanks held only two or three rounds.

The situation required Lelyushenko to commit his other divisions, the 42nd Tank and 185th Motorized Rifle. The other divisions'
movement was hampered by German air strikes. While he left instructions for the 46th Tank Division not to allow the Germans out
of the town, Lelyushenko drove to his 42nd Tank Division in order
to speed up its movement. En route Lelyushenko learned the 42nd
Tank Division's advance guard engaged the German's 121st Infantry Division. Immediately, Lelyushenko began to head for the advance guard's contact and over the radio gave the instructions to
the advance guard commander, "Goryainov. Speed up movement.
Strike to Daugavpilsa. Lelyushenko." The radio message was not
sent in the clear, but in a five word brevity code, "Grach (Goryainov).
Wind (speed up movement). Thunder (Strike). Dar (Daugavplis).
Lom (Lelyushenko)."[12]

Lelyushenko coordinated a short ten minute artillery strike for
the force's attack along the northern bank of the Western Dvina to
cut off the German river crossing. The 42nd Tank Division reached
Sargelishti, where it stopped since further advance against the Germans was impossible. The 185th Motorized Rifle Division battled
strong German resistance 20 kilometers from Daugavpils. However,
Lelyushenko's corps could not restore the river defense.

In the fighting around Daugavpils on 28 June, the 21st Mechanized Corps inflicted a serious strike on the 56th Panzer Corps. General von Manstein recalled, "...we were having our work cut out to
beat off attacks he(Soviets) launched on the northern bank of the
Dvina with an armored division in support, and at a number of points
the position became quite critical."[13]

On the night of 29 June, Lelyushenko left forward detachments
on the Western Dvina and withdrew the remainder of his corps to a
new line 40 kilometers northeast of Daugavpils. In the new position, the corps' right flank joined the 5th Airborne Corps; on the left,
112th Rifle Division of the 22nd Rifle Army.

The Stavka ordered the Northwestern Front commander, Colonel General Fedor Isidorovich Kuznetsov, to prepare a defensive line
along the Velikaya river, relying on previously created fortified areas in Pskov and Ostrov. On 30 June, General Kuznetsov ordered
his defending forces on the Western Dvina to withdraw to the an-

cient city of Pskov and Ostrov. During the withdrawal, General Kuznetsov rescinded his previous orders and directed a shift to the offensive by the morning of 2 July to restore the defense. The order caught the forces in motion; they were expected to redirect quickly under contradictory orders. Confusion in command added to the chaos in the situation.

Before resuming its advance to the northeast, Manstein's panzer corps held crossings over the Western Dvina waiting for the arrival of the SS "Death's Head"Division and the 41st Panzer Corps. This delay in German operations prevented Manstein's corps from moving beyond the river until 2 July.

At 0200 hours 2 July, Lelyushenko received orders from the 27th Army commander to withdraw to another line and not allow the German forces to penetrate, destroying the 27th Army.[14] But, six hours later, the army commander countermanded his order for defense and directed the army to attack by 0900 hours and eliminate German forces north of the Western Dvina, and then recapture Daugavpils. Lelyushenko received the order at 1000 hours. Lelyushenko recalled, "Unfortunately, at the beginning of the war cases happened when orders were given out without taking stock of the real situation."[15] The Army commander's second order was forced by the Northwestern Front commander who erred grossly in assessing the situation and his decision. The army commander, despite his distance from the fighting, demonstrated a confusion equal to his tank crews in the armored melee; he failed to grasp clearly the situation. The 27th Army's insufficient force lacked ammunition and fuel. Lelyushenko's corps fought with only seven tanks and 74 out of its original 129 guns. The 21st Mechanized Corps units missed taking their jumping-off positions for the attack. By midday, the Germans attacked with units of the 3rd and 8th Panzer, SS "Death's head", and two infantry divisions against Lelyushenko's corps. Resuming the offensive, Manstein noted, "The enemy's resistance proved tougher and more methodical than in the first few days of the campaign, but he was still being outfought over and over again."[16]

During the morning, Lelyushenko set off for his 42nd Tank Division to watch its fierce defense 12 kilometers southwest of Dagda, opposing lead elements of the SS "Death's Head" Division. SS "Death's Head" performance in this operation caused Manstein concern, "...I repeatedly had to come to the division's assistance, without even then being able to prevent a sharp rise in casualties. After a matter of ten days the three regiments of the division had to be re-grouped into two new ones."[17] In stubborn battle, Lelyushenko's corps resisted succumbing to panic and defeat in the face of the German's overwhelming assault. Suffering heavy casualties, the corps lost nearly half its personnel and equipment. Lelyushenko had little choice but to withdraw.

On 3 July, to the right of Lelyushenko's corps, the Germans penetrated the 27th Army, seizing Rezekne 100 kilometers northeast of Daugavpils. Lelyushenko received written orders that evening directing his corps to withdraw to a new line and hold it through the next day. The 27th Army commander, General Berzarin, characterized Lelyushenko's performance throughout the chaotic combat as "...strong, persistent, and exacting."[18]

On 4 July, however, German attacks drove Lelyushenko's mechanized corps further back into Russia despite the corps's counterattacks and resistance. The 27th Army commander tried to move the corps into reserve, but German pressure disrupted the army's relieving rifle units. With the situation rapidly disintegrating and unable to close with neighboring units, Lelyushenko's corps fought with unprotected flanks.

General Manstein's 56th Panzer Corps had little hope in outflanking Lelyushenko's corps to the east because, as Manstein described, "... the marshiness of the ground and the strength of the enemy's resistance."[19] Lelyushenko's corps fought better and with greater cohesion than most mechanized corps in the first days of the war. His corps truly performed as one Soviet historian generously summed for other Red Army mechanized corps, "Following the first counterstrike, the mechanized corps defended operationally and tactically important lines and objectives, ensuring more favorable conditions for withdrawal of rifle formations to new lines."[20]

By the time German Panzer elements arrived in Ostrov, Manstein believed, "...the enemy, though pushed back to the east, was still not destroyed...."[21] The German general's perception was correct. Although Lelyushenko's corps was a shadow of its former self, the unit and its commander remained poised and balanced within the withdrawing fight. The defensive operation by the Northwestern Front failed to stop the German advance. In the first 18 days of the war, Red Army forces on the Leningrad approach withdrew to a depth of 450 kilometers. Counterstrikes by two mechanized corps did little to blunt the lightning attack by German panzer units. Despite the Front's confusion and disaster in the northwest sector which belied any individual heroics, Lelyushenko's tenacious defensive actions earned him the Order of the Red Star.

The disastrously poor performance and eventual elimination of the mechanized corps across the Red Army front drove the Stavka's decision to abolish them in the second half of July. The few remaining tanks were to be reformed into smaller units, primarily separate tank brigades and regiments.

At the end of August, Lelyushenko, recalled to Moscow, remembered, "I went to the Kremlin with great nervousness."[22] Having trouble finding the waiting room for his meeting with Stalin, he looked up a friend in the Stavka. Unable to find his friend, Lelyushenko met another staff officer who showed him a model of the new T-34 tanks for Red Army tank units while guiding him to the waiting room outside Stalin's office.

After an hour's wait, Lelyushenko was led to his meeting with the Supreme High Commander, Stalin. Upon entering the private study, Lelyushenko saw Stalin and Marshal Boris Mikhailovich Shaposhnikov, Chief of Staff for the General Staff. Stalin, in reflective thought, stood over a sprawling operational map. Lelyushenko introduced himself. Stalin attentively looked at him and asked, "When do you form the tank brigades?"

Apparently, Stalin thought Lelyushenko knew about a new assignment.

"What?" Lelyushenko responded awkwardly. "I don't know what brigades you're talking about."

"Really?"

"I only returned from the front last night."

"Well, fine." Stalin, a master at keeping people off balance in his presence, continued, "They are bestowing on you a responsible mission. Comrade Shaposhnikov, you will explain in detail to Lelyushenko the purpose of our summons."

Marshal Shaposhnikov began, "You are designated the Deputy Chief of the Main Armor Directorate of the Red Army and Chief of the Main Control for Formation and Completion of the Armored Force. You have the responsibility to form 22 tank brigades in a short time. Materiel parts will be received from the country's factories and repair shops. The Main Armor Directorate has the unit completion plan. Along with preparation measures, you report to us through Comrade Fedorenko, or directly to the Stavka, when we require."[23]

Stalin, never missing a chance to gain first-hand accounts from commanders, asked about the front. After Lelyushenko responded, the meeting concluded.

The decision to abandon the unwieldy mechanized corps and to build the tank brigades resulted, in part, from the large number of tank losses on the battlefield from which the Red Army could not recover and repair damaged tanks. The iron law for successfully sustained armored warfare is hold the battlefield long enough to recover casualties and losses. Additionally, the Red Army tank losses were not being replaced because, in the late summer months, many of the war plants displaced further east. Dwindling tank production could not replenish the losses. Available tanks were used best in close, coordinated defensive fighting with rifle units.

Through September, Lelyushenko worked on the formation of tank brigades armed with the new T-34 and KV tanks. These tank brigades formed around Moscow and other places were manned by combat experienced personnel and commanded by successful tank colonels and generals. Lelyushenko's new brigades were given to promising and rising stars in the armor force, such as, M.E. Katukov, M.D. Solomatin, P.A. Rotmistrov, A.G. Kravchenko, and others.

After midnight on 1 October, Lelyushenko, who like most General Staff officers, worked and lived 24 hours a day in his office, received a summons to the Stavka. Puzzled at being called since he had given recently several status reports on forming the brigades, he grabbed his papers and traveled through the dark deserted Moscow streets to the Kremlin.

In a few minutes Lelyushenko stood in the reception room outside of Stalin's office. He remembered not waiting long, and upon entering, Stalin greeted him, "You have asked many times to go to the front. Now, I have an opportunity to comply with your request."

"I will be glad."

"Well, fine. Quickly give up your affairs in the directorate and take the lst Guards Rifle Corps. In truth, this corps, as such, does not exist yet, but you will form it in a short time. Your mission: to stop Guderian's tank group penetrating the Bryansk Front and attacking toward Orel. All the rest will be more precisely defined by comrade Shaposhnikov."[24]

Lelyushenko thanked Stalin for his trust and departed with Marshal Shaposhnikov. The Marshal informed Lelyushenko that the decision to create the corps had been made on 27 September, and it would be necessary to form the corps in four or five days. The corps, when hastily collected, would consist of the 5th, 6th Guards Rifle and 41st Cavalry Divisions, 4th and 11th Tank Brigades, and two artillery regiments.

The remainder of the day, Lelyushenko called friends and acquaintances, putting together his corps staff. That night his phone rang, and again, he was called to the Stavka. Entering a small room, he found Stalin untypically sitting, and he was surrounded by his close advisers Voroshilov, Mikoyan, and Marshal Shaposhnikov. Turning his head from the map, Stalin said, "We called you again, since the situation has changed sharply. Guderian is already too close to Orel. Forming the corps cannot take five days, but two. You with General Zhigarevym (commander Soviet Air Force) must immediately fly to Orel and get to know the situation on the ground."

"I ask permission to report my considerations," Lelyushenko responded quickly.

"Report."

"There is no sense in flying to Orel now. Neither our ground nor air forces are there. I ask that the 36th Motorcycle Regiment be subordinated to me. It is located in your reserve, and also give me the Tula Artillery School. With them we'll move to meet Guderian. Along the way I will pick up units retreating from encirclement. With these units I can organize a defense until the arrival of the corps' main force. I will locate the corps staff in Mtsensk," Lelyushenko announced.

"I think, that we must take Lelyushenko's suggestion," Voroshilov responded after a short hesitation. Kliment Efremovich Voroshilov, a Stalin crony from the Civil War, in desperate times, would latch on to any man of action. Marshal Shaposhnikov recommended giving Lelyushenko the motorcycle regiment and artillery school, and act quickly.

" Alright," said Stalin. And he added, "Comrade Lelyushenko, do not allow the enemy any further than Mtsensk!" With a red pencil, he drew for Lelyushenko on the map the final defensive line along the Zusha river.[25]

Lelyushenko walked from the meeting and without delay called the commander of the 36th Motorcycle Regiment, Lieutenant Colonel T.I. Tanaschishinu. The newly appointed corps commander directed the regiment to prepare immediately for movement. He also prescribed for the regimental commander his unit's combat loads in ammunition, mines, and other supplies. The motorcycle regiment had to be on the move within two hours along the route Moscow-Serpukhov-Tula. From Tula, the regiment spread reconnaissance groups on a wide front in the direction of Tula-Mtsensk-Orel. Quite prepared to orchestrate the operation on the move while still gathering his force, Lelyushenko decisively set his unit in motion. With the nearly impossible task of creating a unit in the face of battle, Lelyushenko, the veteran, seemed to relish the staggering challenge. Late night on 1 October, Lelyushenko and his operational group drove out of Moscow, heading southwest for Mtsensk.

Penetrating into the operational depth of the defending Red Army Fronts, the famed Panzer Group Guderian attempted to develop the attack through Orel to Moscow, the ultimate objective. The situation reminded Lelyushenko of his June encounter with General Manstein's corps which rushed forward taking Daugavpils with the further objective of Leningrad. In both cases German air dominated the skies. With a similar operational situation, Lelyushenko organized his unit on the move attacking with open flanks and no neighboring units for support.

At dawn on 2 October, Lelyushenko overtook the motorcycle regiment commander on the road just south of Moscow. Later in the day, he reached the Tula Artillery School. On the school parade ground stood artillery guns, but no transports to move them. While the students fell out for combat, city buses were mobilized to pull the guns. Lelyushenko used every expedient to propel his force into place.

The next morning, the corps staff located its headquarters in Mtsensk. German air attacks struck the town's major buildings and railroad station. By afternoon, Lelyushenko received his first report from the commander of the 36th Motorcycle Regiment. At 1200 hours, a reconnaissance group, 8-10 kilometers north of Orel, reported an encounter with Germans moving from the city in the direction of Mtsensk. This report slightly cleared the situation for Lelyushenko. Never content to wait for reports over the radio, he decided to drive to the point of contact and determine how much force the Germans had in Orel. After talking with a tanker in the fight and receiving word that the Germans withdrew to Orel, Lelyushenko ordered Lieutenant Colonel Tanaschinshin to reconnoiter Orel.

The following morning, Lelyushenko while conducting a personal reconnaissance was approached by four motorcycles. On one of the motor bikes was the commander of the 34th Frontier Guards, an NKVD (People's Commissariat for Internal Affairs) Regiment, Lieutenant Colonel I. I. Piryashev. Lelyushenko asked the commander his mission and his unit's location. The lieutenant colonel indicated his unit was in a grove about two kilometers ahead, and they were suppose to go to Orel.

Lelyushenko nodded knowingly and said, "From this moment, you are subordinate to me. We will fight the enemy together."[26] He instructed the commander to place his regiment astride the Orel-Mtsensk highway and hold the line until Lelyushenko arrived with the corps' main force.

Early morning on 4 October, the first train load with the 4th Tank Brigade arrived in Mtsensk. As the tank battalion unloaded, Lelyushenko created two reconnaissance groups dispatching them forward towards Orel. By late afternoon, the second trainload of the tank brigade arrived with its commander, Colonel Mikhail Efimovich Katukov. Lelyushenko found Colonel Katukov by his staff car. In their first conference, they shared their concerns for the total vagueness in the situation. Upon hearing the situation from Lelyushenko, Katukov, a native of the Moscow district, remarked, "I didn't think that we would have to fight for our own field."[27] The two commanders worked out their course of actions to send reconnaissance to Orel and organize a defense.

Marshal Shaposhnikov, sent by Stalin to assist in the emergency, informed Lelyushenko that he would receive the next day two battalions of new secret rocket artillery. Shaposhnikov cautioned Lelyushenko that he must not let the rocket launchers fall into the enemy's hands, no matter the circumstance. Lelyushenko asked how to employ these new rocket weapons, and Shaposnikov assured him a technical expert would accompany the secret weapon.

On the morning of 5 October, Lelyushenko was forward in Colonel Katukov's brigade command post. They discussed how to fight the upcoming battle. After their consultation, Lelyushenko hurried off, placing the rest of his corps. Later that day, the 6th Guards Rifle Division detrained in Mtsensk, followed by the 11th Tank Brigade. The forming 1st Guards Rifle Corps had enough activity even for the tireless, industrious Lelyushenko. The 6th Guards Rifle Division began preparing a defensive line along the northern bank of the Zusha river which Stalin designated as the place for the corps' final, decisive battle.

Landing at an airfield northwest of Orel, the 201st Airborne Brigade, 5th Airborne Corps arrived providing additional troops for Lelyushenko's command. The paratroopers were placed immediately on an intermediate defensive line astride the Orel-Mtsensk highway.

Meanwhile, on the morning of 6 October, the corps' covering force under Colonel Katukov withdrew to the line Pervii Voin, Naryshkino. By 1100 hours, Soviet aerial reconnaissance spotted approximately 80 German tanks with motorized infantry moving parallel to the highway three kilometers from Pervii Voin. Katukov, coordinating the defense with the NKVD regiment, an airborne brigade, and his tank brigade, had his hands full fighting a force no less than a division in Lelyushenko's estimate.[28] In fact, the German force was the 4th Panzer Division organized into a fighting group.

After heavy fighting all day and through the night, Colonel Katukov's force withdrew assuming a new defensive line at Sheino-Golovlev. The withdrawal was covered by the awesome fires of the new rocket weapons, which the Russians affectionately called, Katyusha (Katie). The firepower delivered by these simple trucks with rails and rockets impressed all on-lookers. Unsurprisingly, the Germans regarded the weapons with less affection. With the front-line soldier's macabre humor, they called the rockets "Stalin's Organ" – apparently a reference to the rocket's high-pitched shriek as it approached impact.

With the pewter dawn of 7 October, the airborne brigade straddled the highway, on its left flank stood the NKVD regiment and one battalion of the 11th Tank Brigade. Katukov's tank brigade held the right flank. The first snow fell that day. The Germans whose stretched supply line finally snapped paused for two days with their ground forces. However, the German air force remained active, striking Lelyushenko's forces throughout the sector.

On 9 October, a powerful artillery preparation announced the German's resumption of the offensive. Artillery shells gouged the earth around defending Soviet units, immediately followed by close air attacks. During the next two days, Guderian's forces pushed back the Soviets to Mtsensk on the Zusha river. Late night on the 10th and early morning 11 October, Katukov's covering force began withdrawing over a railroad bridge to the corps defensive line behind the Zusha river. Lelyshenko's corps held Guderian's panzer group assault on the southern approach to Moscow for nine days, providing time for the Bryansk Front to hastily reorganize and regroup, allowing the Front to move the 50th Army into the Tula area. In his memoirs, Guderian wrote despairingly about this point in his campaign, "The prospect of rapid, decisive victories was fading in consequence."[29] With control of the sector passed to the Front, specifically, the 50th Army, Lelyushenko received a summon to the Stavka.

Upon entering Stalin's office, Lelyushenko reported the position along the Zusha river stabilized. Stalin, his usual self, paced about the room, stuffing tobacco into his pipe. Marshal Shaposhnikov was bent over a map. Molotov, eyeing Lelyushenko, unexpectedly asked, "Why didn't you dislodge the enemy from Orel?"

"There was nothing to dislodge!" Lelyushenko responded angrily. "Our flanks were completely open for a hundred kilometers. The enemy could easily go around the corps and rush to Tula, and then further...."

Stalin instantly stopped and looked at Lelyushenko, silently waving off Molotov. "Thanks for Mtsensk," Stalin said. "And in another moment, army commander, another mission stands before you. Comrade Shaposhnikov will explain everything to you."[30]

With Guderian's panzer army neutralized, the central approach to Moscow contained the ominous threat of the 3rd and 4th Panzer Armies. The German panzer armies had advanced to the vicinity of Vyazma where they encircled a significant part of the Western and Reserve Fronts. The situation grew as bad as the Bryansk Front where Lelyushenko had been dispatched to plug the gap. In the direction of Borodino-Mozhaisk, the 4th Panzer Group under the command of General Erich Hoepner whose panzer force Lelyushenko faced before in battles around Daugavpils, rapidly advanced.

Lelyushenko was assigned to command the newly formed 5th Army and the Mozhaisk defensive line. His deputy commander, Colonel Semen Il'ich Bogdanov, was already at Mozhaisk attempting to fortify the defense. On 11 October, Lelyushenko with his operational group drove from Moscow towards his new command, arriving late that evening. Colonel Bogdanov gave him a full report, and, in a personally conducted tour, he pointed out the unpreparedness of the defensive line. While his army staff worked out a defensive plan, Lelyushenko, again, put together a motley collection of units to hold the line on a critical approach to Moscow.

The following night, Lelyushenko received instructions from the Stavka making the 5th Army part of the Western Front. The army's mission remained unchanged – prevent German penetration of Mozhaisk defense. The next morning, the Front commander, General Georgi K. Zhukov, confirmed the Stavka mission and reviewed the progress of defensive preparations. By noon, German fighter-bombers struck the fields around Borodino. Clearly, the German ground forces were not far behind.

Early the next morning, German panzer units pressed the Mozhaisk defensive line, driving back two tank brigades operating as forward detachments in a security zone. Once through the security zone, the German tank assault began in earnest against the Red Army riflemen in defensive positions.

By dawn 15 October, after a short 15 minute artillery preparation, the Germans attacked along the major Minsk-Moscow highway. Lelyushenko's defense with coordinated fires and reinforced by four battalions of the new rocket launchers resisted the German assault. With his staff and Colonel Bogdanov, Lelyushenko occupied his army observation post well forward. He remembered it was the coldest fall day in all his life.[31] His army formed a defense on the well-known Napoleonic battlefield, Borodino, where, in 1812, the famed Russian General Kutuzov fought the French invaders. Nearly one hundred and thirty years later, Lelyushenko was defending the approaches to Moscow from another invader.

Rifle regiments of the 32nd Rifle Division held against repeated German assaults. The Germans, the following day, moved around the flanks of Lelyushenko's infantry, advancing to the rear of the division. Towards evening, the Germans renewed their attack in coordination with air strikes. Nearly 30 German tanks with infantry successfully broke through and aggressively advanced towards the army observation post. Lelyushenko signaled his reserve, 20th Tank Brigade, to attack the Germans in the direction of the army observation post.

All the post staff personnel, officers and soldiers, collected Molotov cocktails, bottles with a fuel mixture, carrying armfuls to the nearby trenches. The reserve tank brigade arrived as the German tanks bore down on the army commander and staff. In close, fierce fighting between the staff and the Germans, Lelyushenko received a serious wound and lost consciousness. Remaining on the hectic battlefield until a lull in the fighting, he waited for evacuation.

Late night on 18 October, the wounded General Lelyushenko was transferred rearward to a hospital in Gorkii, 400 kilometers east of Moscow. While recovering, Lelyushenko sought an appointment with the Stavka. Impatient to return to the front lines, he wanted to get his assignment cleared and settled.

On 14 November, Marshal Shaposhnikov finally received Lelyushenko. Lelyushenko requested to be sent to a front unit. Shaposhnikov replied, "But we want to send you to Gorkii to inspect English tanks. It is necessary that you familiarize yourself with them and find out for us their technical and tactical capabilities. And, then we will decide where to send you."

"I am prepared. But I really request to be sent quickly to the front," Lelyushenko implored.[32]

With a group of engineers from the Main Armored Directorate, Lelyushenko examined the British tanks, Valentine and Matilda. For two days the inspection team studied the motor system, armament, and armor protection. Lelyushenko concluded, their "...gearbox puzzled us, it was not similar to ours. These machines were a low class. However, we were forced to take them. Our tank industry still could not full satisfy front needs."[33] Criticism of Lend-Lease equipment from the allies is a common theme in Soviet military memoirs.

On 17 November, Lelyushenko received an early morning call to return to Moscow from Gorkii. Stalin announced Lelyushenko's assignment as commander of the 30th Army. The 30th Army, as part of the Kalinin Front, fought strong, violent engagements on the northern approach to Moscow. The Front commander, General Colonel Ivan Stepanovich Konev, recently pulled the army into the reserves for reconstitution. On 16 November, the Germans began an offensive against General Konstantin Konstantinovich Rokossovskii's 16th Army and advanced forward. The recommitted 30th Army's right flank came under heavy pressure from the attacking force and withdrew. However, German attempts to cross the Volga river were unsuccessful, until a major effort late on the 16th succeeded in the 30th Army sector.

The 30th Army the next day fought with its forces split by the Germans. On 18 November, the Stavka transferred the 30th Army from the Kalinin Front to the Western Front, reinforcing the beleaguered army with additional forces. With another difficult situation on his hands, Lelyushenko arrived at the staff of the Western Front on 18 November 1941. The Front commander, General Zhukov, was amid the forward fighting units, not in the command post. The Front chief of staff, General Vasilii Danilovich Sokolovskii, familiarized Lelyushenko with the situation. The 30th Army's mission was straight forward – stop the German attack. Upon Zhukov's return, Lelyushenko received a very specific mission from the aggressive Front commander, "Your mission is not to allow the enemy east of the Leningrad-Moscow highway in the sector of Zavidovo-Reshetnikovo-10 kilometers north of Klin."[34]

Lelyushenko inheriting an unbelievably critical situation had to understand quickly the situation, establish communications with all his forces, determine their combat capabilities, and organize a repulse of the advancing Germans. He took command of these actions while his army's left flank received the German's main attack. With no radio communications to his army staff nor his neighboring units, Lelyushenko faced a horrible dilemma: to fight either against encirclement or to breakout of an encirclement.

With dawn the next day, a thunderous German artillery cannonade with air strikes began. All along the front German units advanced five to six kilometers, severely testing Lelyushenko's new command. The Germans pressed towards Klin. But Lelyushenko's army managed to delay the German tanks, fighting from encirclement

Using desperate measures to stem advancing German armor, the Red Army used anti-tank dogs. Dogs and handlers would wait in trenches along probable routes of approaching German tanks. As the tanks neared to within 50 meters, the dogs were released. They ran, as trained, between the tracks and underbellies of the tanks. Strapped onto the dogs' back were explosive packs with a vertical rod, which when tilted by the dog crawling under the tanks would detonate the explosives. The 30th Army employed a dog detachment. Lieutenant Colonel Hasso von Manteuffel, a regimental commander in the 7th Panzer Division, fighting on the northern approach, considered reports on the anti-tank dogs "latrine rumors." However, taking no chances, he directed, "Safety first – you never can tell or know what beastliness the Russians can cook up."[35] He ordered all dogs shot on sight. The radio operator in von Manteuffel's armored personnel carrier counted 42 dead dogs on the forward drive with no reports of blown tanks.[36] Lelyushenko believed that the use of the dogs helped the army to disrupt the German tank attacks, concluding "...the antitank dogs were necessary to the army and it is necessary to train them well."[37]

Early morning on 20 November, the Germans renewed the battle in the Zavidovo area, 25 kilometers northwest of Klin. Lelyushenko with his political officer drove to the troubled spot. His vehicle moved slowly down a battle torn and littered forest road. The crack of shells and weapons in the normally peaceful woods unmistakably marked the front line. While forward, Lelyushenko received first hand reports and made his personal observations. His staff informed him that the rifle army's 107th Motorized Rifle Division had withdrawn from encirclement. Lelyushenko rushed off to personally assess the shape of the division. After hearing the division commander's report, Lelyushenko believed the division was prepared to assume another mission.

At dawn next day, Germans tanks surprised the army staff located in the village of Zaitsevo. Lelyushenko, once again in the war, joined his staff and soldiers in defending his command post. These early months of defensive fighting found danger everywhere on the battlefield, even army headquarters were often engulfed in the fury of battle. The Germans were repulsed, and a short respite in the battle followed. However, to the south, the 16th Army retreated from Klin, creating a gap between the 16th and 30th Armies.

In the latter part of November, the 30th Army was reinforced by the 8th Tank Brigade under the command of Colonel Pavel Rotmistrov. Upon Lelyushenko's assumption of command, Rotmistrov was impressed by the new army commander's ability to quickly understand the situation and the capabilities of the rifle army. Lelyushenko was able to absorb, remember, manipulate and manage a great amount of detailed information. Rotmistrov described Lelyushenko as "...stocky...shaved head, restless, indomitable energy, at times abrupt and quick tempered...."[38] Colonel Rotmistrov's unit, very low in tanks fought heroically under Lelyushenko's command and later won designation as the 3rd Guards Tank Brigade. Lelyushenko at this point in the war had commanded three of the Red Army's future tank army commanders, Katukov, Bogdanov, Rotmistrov.

On 25 November, despite the minus 7-10 degrees temperature, the Germans advanced a major attack force against the left flank of the 30th Army. Lelyushenko needed additional units to handle the situation. In hours of violent, desperate battle, General Zhukov managed only to send an understrength antitank battalion, but, at the time, Lelyushenko took any reinforcement and used it well. The

16th Army retreated from Solnechnogorsk, exposing the 30th Army's left flank. That evening, Lelyushenko received a call from General Sokolovskii, the Front chief of staff, who instructed Lelyushenko to move his command post to Dmitrov by the morning of 28 November. When Lelyushenko looked at the map, he was disconcertingly surprised. Dmitrov was located in the gap between the 16th and 30th Armies. And, how one got from his sector to Dmitrov without forces was beyond Lelyushenko. It was not by chance that Zhukov had sent the army command post to Dmitrov. The demanding General Zhukov obviously believed an army commander could scrape together a battalion and close the penetration if his headquarters was at stake.[39]

It was a critical situation. The Germans were about to burst into Dmitrov, covered by Lelyushenko's staff and no other forces. When the situation seemed like it would collapse around the army commander, reinforcements began to arrive in a trickle. An armored train appeared on the railroad tracks in Dmitrov, providing additional artillery support. With a battalion of eight tanks, KVs and T-34s, arriving in the town square, Lelyushenko placed them on the edge of town. When the attack came, the defending force consisted of the 58th Tank Division and 8th Tank Brigade, 29th and 50th Student Brigades, the armored train and the 30th Army staff and lightly wounded from a nearby hospital. The motley grouping managed to repel the Germans. General Zhukov had managed to collect an odd sort of units for the gap, the resourceful Lelyushenko pieced them together for the fight.

On 1 December, Lelyushenko and his political officer were called to the Western Front staff where they received the Front's plan for a counteroffensive. With the attack to begin on 5 December, Lelyushenko had little time to develop and pass his plan to subordinate commanders and staffs. Additionally, his army was to be reinforced by some fresh Siberian and Ural divisions. Lelyushenko believed his forces clearly insufficient for the assigned task. Remembering a battle in the Civil War in 1919, around Voronezh in Budyenny's cavalry corps, he experienced a fight in which the Red forces had only two divisions while the white guards had six divisions.[40] Lelyushenko, fortified by his past experience, conceived a plan to attack at night to minimize the German strengths in tanks and airplanes. He planned his main strike in the direction of Klin with a single group consisting of three rifle divisions and two tank brigades. The army's 52 kilometers attack sector presented a problem; it was far too wide for his forces. Lelyushenko gave the tank brigades separate directions of attack, reinforcing each with a rifle battalion.[41]

Using a tactic, from the 1930's, which the Red Army ceased in training, Lelyushenko taught his rifle companies and battalion night formations and operations. "In battle, especially at night," Lelyushenko believed, "it is important for soldiers to feel their neighbor's shoulder....a sense of elbow to elbow...."[42] Current Red Army infantry regulations excluded the combat formation called, a 'chain', for platoon, company, and battalion. This close, interlocking formation permitted the commander to see his unit in the attack and the soldiers to have a sense of closeness. Rifle units advanced more vigorously in the attack. The "chain" was replaced by various combat formations called, "pack", "serpentine", "wedge", spreading units and soldiers into isolated groups. Lelyushenko's fellow officers explained that with the new formations fewer soldiers would be hit from enemy fire and soldiers would become creative. The dispersed concept rejected also continuous trenches and emplacements, communications routes which was replaced by separate cells, scattered in chess board fashion. Theoretically, everything was correct, but Lelyushenko, the old warhorse, remembered intuitively that it was ultimately men in battle and their psychological considerations. In practical terms, the new formations did not permit commanders of detachments, platoons, companies to watch and control their units in the defense or on the attack.[43] In his infantry tactics, Lelyushenko demonstrated a conservative and traditional reliance on war experience as he restored the old combat formation. The lethality of the modern battlefield actually forces greater dispersion in tactical formations and tactics. Modern armies continue to grapple with Lelyushenko's dilemma.

During the winter of 1941, the Red Army drew together reinforcing divisions that came from the Urals and Siberia. Although the "Siberian" divisions brought fresh manpower to the battle, they did not have all their authorized strength, nor possessed sufficient guns and mortars. Lelyushenko with his army staff worked to alleviate problems with the new "Siberian" units. Instead of using the new units as separate entities, they integrated the "Siberians" into the existing formations while the larger guns and weapons were spread throughout all the formations.

As the time for the operation drew near, Lelyushenko believed a night attack might go better without an artillery preparation. In his command post, he met with his subordinate commanders who reported everything ready. Towards midnight on 5 December, the forces moved to their initial assault positions. At 0600 hours, with dawn more than three hours away this time of the year, Lelyushenko's army attacked without artillery or air preparation. Initial combat reports from the divisions indicated a successful advance.

Later, an army staff officer informed Lelyushenko that the 371st Rifle Division, having begun the attack successfully, was stalled by a German counterattack. Quick to intervene if events were not to his liking, Lelyushenko drove to the stymied unit. He directed reinforcement of the rifle unit with tanks, and a half hour later the attack resumed with the unit moving forward. After three hours, Lelyushenko returned to the army command post.

Meanwhile, General Zhukov arrived in Lelyushenko's command post to thank the army for its success. Simultaneously, with the pat on the back, he directed an increase in the tempo of the advance. Additionally, while Lelyushenko drove forward to lead units, Zhukov had tried unsuccessfully to call Lelyushenko. He admonished Lelyushenko for spending too much time in the forward units. Lelyushenko acknowledged the admonishment, "Zhukov was right. For him, it was necessary to maintain continuous communication with army commanders, and it was possible then by the mode of telephone and telegraph. Unfortunately, radio communications still were not a sufficiently reliable means at that time. But the situation was complicated and my presence in the force was also extremely necessary."[44] The German's stiffening defense before his forces was such a moment when Lelyushenko believed he must see the actual course of the battle. He considered that it was no time to be writing dispatches to the division staff. "Only in this condition," he continued, "was it possible to determine the enemy's intentions and forces, and correspondingly, to define precisely your decision, in good time assign additional missions to the forces."[45] In an aphorism worthy of the great Russian general, Aleksandr Vasil'evich Suvorov, Lelyushenko summed, "Delay in such a case is likely death."[46]

As a battlefield command philosophy, Lelyushenko believed, when the situation became dangerous with serious consequences, "...it is very important that soldiers see senior leaders whose order they carry out in battle. ...It raises the steadfastness of soldiers and commanders."[47]

Lelyushenko recalled from his Civil War days an "... attack by Budenny's cavalry division against the White guards in the direction of Tsaritsyn when the 10th Army commander, Aleksandr Ilich Egorov, accompanied us in battle. An enemy bullet wounded the army commander in the shoulder, but he did not abandon the battlefield."[48] This example of heroism served as a role model for Lelyushenko's leadership style in combat.

By evening on 6 December, Lelyushenko's tank brigades penetrated the German defense 18 kilometers, opening a 22 kilometers wide gap. By the next nightfall, the army continued to advance widening the breach to 35 kilometers and to a depth of 25 kilometers. During fighting the next two days, the Germans brought reinforcements into the sector. On the night of 9 December, Lelyushenko's forces stormed and seized Rogachev. The ultimate and important objective was Klin, a key road junction necessary for the Germans to withdraw their forces from Dmitrov. The 30th Army continued fighting in the Klin direction. However, on 12 December, the army's attack became checked temporarily. The Germans resolutely brought to bear a force supported by a large number of tanks. Inflicting terrific losses on the Germans, Lelyushenko's forces resisted the counterattacks and resumed the advance. By 0200 hours on 15 December, Lelyushenko's forces cleared Klin. Ending the year, Lelyushenko had fought German panzer pincers on three major approaches to the Soviet capital. For the Germans, the capture of Moscow became too great a feat. The Battle for Moscow was the first major German Army defeat on land in the Second World War. For the German command, Moscow was the objective to end the war, but actually, only the beginning.

For the most part in 1942, Lelyushenko's 30th Army held on the approaches to Moscow. From 30 July - 23 August, his army participated in an offensive to Rzhev primarily to hold down German forces so they could not be transferred to the Stalingrad area.

In early November 1942, Lelyushenko received a call from the Western Front commander, General Ivan S. Konev, who informed him that he was to be at the Stavka at 0800 hours 13 November. At the appointed time, Lelyshenko arrived in the Kremlin where he was informed of his designation as the commander of the 1st Guards Army, which had been effective since 1 November. In addition to his command assignment, Lelyushenko received the Order of Lenin for his actions with the 30th Army and promotion to Lieutenant General.

The next day, Lelyushenko flew from Moscow to the Southwestern Front command post. There the Front commander, General Nikolai Fedorovich Vatutin, and chief of staff familiarized him with the general situation. The Southwestern Front, formed only in late October, was to participate in a major counteroffensive by three Fronts around Stalingrad. The Southwestern Front played a key role in the initial phase of the counteroffensive. Striking from its bridgeheads on the west side of the Don river, the Front's armies were to dash south and link up with the Stalingrad Front, completing the encirclement of the main German forces in Stalingrad.

After the briefing, Lelyushenko drove to the 1st Guards Army command post, immediately setting to work. The strength of his army was 75-85% of authorized strength; his divisions averaged 7,000 soldiers which was good for this period of the war. Materiel and equipment were 80-90%, and the supply of ammunitions was one to one and a half the basic load, fuel was sufficient for five days.[49] In 1942, the Red Army was at its lowest point for equipment in the war.

The Southwestern Front commander, General Vatutin, arrived in the 1st Guards Army command post, and discussed the impending operation with Lelyushenko. General Vatutin personally assigned Lelyushenko his army's mission.

At 0850 hours 19 November, after an hour and twenty minute artillery preparation, the 1st Guards Army attacked beside the 5th Tank Army. Fighting against strong enemy resistance, the army advanced only 1-3 kilometers. After three days of combat, Lelyushenko reported to the Front commander that his slow progress was due to insufficient artillery. General Vatutin, a decisive commander, quickly reinforced the left flank of the army with five artillery regiments and ten battalions of the multiple rocket launchers. As a result, the army smashed through the enemy's tactical defense the next day, inflicting significant losses and advancing 30 kilometers to the west. By 23 November, Red Army forces with 1st Guards Army participation closed the ring around the Germans in Stalingrad. Through continuous and demanding combat, from 19 November to 16 December, the 1st Guards Army (redesignated 3rd Guards on 5 December 1942) fulfilled its assigned missions. Lelyushenko's army penetrated the German's defense, advancing 55 kilometers to the west and capturing important lines of communication.

Lelyushenko's army quickly prepared for a subsequent Red Army offensive code-named, "Saturn." Released on 14 December, the plan assigned the main strike to the Southwestern Front in the direction of Kamensk-Rostov. Two days later, Lelyushenko from his army observation post launched his army in the "Saturn" offensive. Under limited visibility, the artillery fire began the attack, working the forward edge of the enemy positions. Although the artillery preparation failed to suppress the reserve forces in depth, Lelyushenko had little concern for its impact on his offensive exploitation force, the 1st Guards Mechanized corps. Aggressively employing his armored force, Lelyushenko ordered the mechanized corps not to wait for the breakthrough of the enemy's tactical defense by the rifle units, and committed the corps to the close battle. The corps attacked to the northwest capturing the small town of Astakhov and the western bank of the Krivaya river the next day. Early the following morning, the corps captured the Bokovsk station continuing the attack toward Kruzhilin. The army's quick advance in the wake of the mechanized corps followed the plan, surpassing Lelyushenko's expectations.[50] A week later, the 1st Guards Mechanized Corps seized the station Selivanosk more than 100 kilometers into the operation.

Southwestern Front commander directed the 3rd Guards Army to destroy enemy forces in the area of Skoryrsk, Tatsinskii, and by 31 December, advance to the Vystra river to cut off withdrawing German forces from the Northern Donets River. But Lelyushenko's army had lost too many men and combat vehicles for such an extended mission. "The army's forces," Lelyushenko recalled, "had significant losses, especially in tanks. Although for reinforcements the 3rd Guards Army was given Badanov's 24th Tank Corps and the 25th Tank Corps we totaled only 50 tanks."[51] These tank corps also had been consumed in previous phases of the operation. Nonetheless, the 3rd Guards Army continued attacking in January. By mid-month, the offensive encircled a large German force west of Tatsinskii, and, a week later, the 3rd Guards Army forced the Northern Donets river. The Front fed units into Lelyushenko's army to keep it going. In the first part of January 1943, he received the 2nd Tank Corps; on 2 February, the 8th Cavalry Corps.

Nicknamed, "General Forward," by contemporaries, Lelyushenko continued a style of command in which he rarely stayed in his army headquarters. At all hours of the day, he would be forward near the front. He was difficult to find once his unit became engaged in battle. "I remember," wrote General Sergei Matveevich Shtemenko, Chief of Operations Red Army General Staff, "the time, during the fighting in the Donbas, when the Supreme commander (Stalin) wanted to speak personally with Lelyushenko and the General Staff had to spend a whole day searching for him, even though there was good communications with his army headquarters. The result was a special directive forbidding army commanders to leave their command posts for any length of time."[52]

On 4 February 1943, 3rd Guards Army advanced towards Voroshilograd, meeting strong resistance. The Germans successfully drew in strong armored formations, 6th, 7th, SS "Das Reich" Panzer Divisions, 335 Infantry Division, and other units. After a 45 minute artillery preparation and air strikes at 0800 hours the next morning, the 3rd Guards Army attacked. Lelyushenko's units managed to cut through two lines of German defense, advancing to a subsequent line around Voroshilograd where German units stopped the attack.

Lelyushenko held council with his subordinate commanders for a decision on the army's best course of action. "The assault came to a vote," Lelyushenko recalled, "for those for and against a course of action that brought part of the force against the flank of the defending German forces in Voroshilograd."[53] At night on 13 February, 3rd Guards Army units took their jump-off positions for the attack. Each first echelon division designated a battalion for a reconnaissance-in-force. Following the reconnaissance-in-force, the 3rd Guards Army charted its course for the capture of Voroshilograd and Krasnodon. Lelyushenko struck for the rear, deeply around the southwest of Voroshilograd; his army with the 8th Cavalry Corps moved in the direction of Debaltsevo, an important railroad junction in the Donbas. As Lelyushenko noted, "Our raid really alarmed the Germans...."[54]

Field Marshal von Manstein, already concerned about supplies for the battle front, was faced with the threat of the lst Panzer Army being out flanked from the west. "In particular, one enemy cavalry corps had managed to penetrate as far as the important rail junction of Debaltsevo.... As a result 17th Panzer Division, which was urgently required on the army's western wing, remained tied down here for the time being," wrote Manstein after the war.[55]

On 19 February, Field Marshal von Manstein ordered the 4th

Panzer Army to begin a strong counterstrike in three directions against the forces of the Southwestern Front, encircling the main forces of General Markian M. Popov's mobile group. The German panzer divisions crashing through Popov's overextended combat formation and the 6th Army, breaking into the operational depth on a wide front. By the evening on 22 February, an alarmed Stavka shifted the 3rd Tank and 69th Armies from Voronezh Front southward, against German forces in the Krasnograd area. On 24 February, the Southwestern Front's forces received the order to transition to the defense. "But this was too late," Lelyushenko believed.[56] German forces after heavy battles drove back the Southwestern Front's right wing and center from the Northern Donets river. On the Front's left wing, the 3rd Guards Army repelled German attacks along the Northern Donets. The 4th Panzer Army achieved its objective in defeating the Soviet armor threat. As Manstein summed the operation, "With that the initiative in this campaign at last passed back to the German side."[57]

Anchored on the 3rd Guards Army defense, the Southwestern Front held in place and on the defense until the German's Operation Citadel five months later. After a successful stand by the Red Army at Kursk, Lelyushenko's army participated in the strategic offensives of August and September 1943, resulting in the capture of the Donbas region. The 3rd Guards Army quickly crossed the Northern Donets moving aggressively forward, beating German rear guard actions and bypassing strong resistance. By evening on 2 September, his army advanced 30 kilometers recapturing a number of towns, followed by two more days of rapid advance.

Field Marshal von Manstein requests for additional forces and permission to withdraw behind the Dnepr river immediately drew Hitler to the Army Group South headquarters in Zaporozhe on 8 September. Manstein and Hitler disagreed on how to stop the Red Army advance on the Dnepr. While Hitler disapproved of shortening the front line, he promised to strengthen Army Group South.[58] But, the promised forces would not arrive in time to stop Soviet forces east of the Dnepr.

The 1st Guards Mechanized and 23rd Tank Corps struck ahead of the Lelyushenko's rifle army 100 kilometers, advancing well into the operational depth. Lelyushenko's forces attempted to cut off elements of von Manstein's Army Group South from withdrawing behind the Dnepr river. Reaching the Dnepr river by 21 September,

Lelyushenko's army participated in the battles for Zaporozhe, Dnepropetrovsk and Nikopol from October 1943 to February 1944. In the latter part of October, the 3rd Guards Army transferred to 4th Ukrainian Front (Southern Front redesignated on 20 October 1943) under the command of General Fedor Ivanovich Tolbukhin.

On 7 March 1944, Lelyushenko was called to the Front headquarters where General Tolbukhin informed him that he was to return to the Stavka for a new assignment. That evening, Lelyushenko was in the Stavka where Stalin told him to take command of the 4th Tank Army. Lelyushenko had the established reputation as a capable field army commander. General Shtemenko noted, "...probably for his energy, optimism and mobility that he was put in charge of the 4th Tank Army...."[59] Stalin no doubt remembered how much he relied upon Lelyushenko in the terrible early months of the war – and Lelyshenko had not disappointed him.

Happy to receive command of a tank army, Lelyushenko knew the important role the tank army played in operations. His penchant for dynamic action suited the maneuverability, fire power and independence of tank army operations. His new command, at the time, was conducting an attack with the 1st Ukrainian Front in the western Ukraine.

On 8 March, Lelyushenko with his signal officer and an operations officer of the 3rd Guards Army set out for the 1st Ukrainian Front. Marshal Zhukov, the Front commander, met him and familiarized him with the situation and general missions, followed by the 4th Tank Army's specific mission. In the short orientation, Lelyushenko learned what he needed for the 4th Tank Army in the operation. The operational concept committed the tank army into a breakthrough in the 60th Army sector on the Vyazovets-Skop line, developing the offensive in the direction of Proskurov and Svyatets by the conclusion of the first day of operation. By the end of the third day, the tank army was to be in the Volochisk area, and by the fourth and fifth to seize Proskurov (Khmel'nitskii).

The 4th Tank Army by 5 March 1944, reached the Ternopol-Proskurov rail line. Although the tank army received the mission to attack towards Volochisk, a shortage of fuel forced a short pause. During the two day lull, the ailing 4th Tank Army commander, Lieutenant General Vasilii Mikhailovich Badanov, was replaced by Lelyushenko. The new tank army commander did not get a chance to meet with General Badanov who had been flown immediately to

Moscow. General Badanov had commanded the 24th Tank Corps in the Tatsinskii raid in December 1942, capturing the key German airfield used to resupply the German 6th Army at Stalingrad during encirclement. The action won the 24th Tank Corps the designation 2nd Guards, and Badanov was the first commander to be awarded the order of the Suvorov, 2nd Degree. The promising tank commander rose to command the newly created 4th Tank Army in the summer of 1943.

On 10 March, Lelyushenko left the Front headquarters for his army. Light rain limited visibility, so his plane flew low. During the flight, he saw many vehicles, even tanks, stuck in mud. Everywhere was a miserable morass; weather and terrain seemed the greater enemy. On the ground, in the improvised army observation post 500-600 meters from the front line, General Evtikhii Emelyanovich Belov, who had been the deputy commander and now the newly appointed commander of the 10th Guards Tank Corps, gave Lelyushenko a situation report. Belov told Lelyushenko about a number of subordinate units under the control of other armies. Lelyushenko called Marshal Zhukov and asked him to return all 4th Tank Army units. The Front staff directed the action the following day. One unit, the 62nd Tank Brigade from the 3rd Guards Tank Army, came back with only staff and rear elements, and not one tank.[60] Red Army commanders did not like giving out their troops to other commanders.

The army headquarters moved to a new location, a good precaution against attacks, and Lelyushenko continued to study the tank army's combat operation. The army had received an order from the Front to replenish itself and prepare for further offensive action. Lelyushenko had inherited a difficult situation. Operating poorly the first three days of the operation from lack of thorough preparation, the tank army had insufficient fuel, and its ammunition supply was interrupted.[61] Lelyushenko visited the corps and brigades.

On 13 March, he arrived at a brigade headquarters in the 10th Guards Tank Corps. Shaking hands with the tank brigade commander, Colonel Mikhail Georgievich Fomichev, Lelyushenko directly asked, "Your fighting is not bad, but how well are your people eating?"[62]

The brigade commander walked Lelyushenko over to a group of tankers sitting down by a spread raincoat covered with American food tins. "It is clear, what the people feed on is not bad," the new tank army commander observed.[63] Using a Russian recipe for stewed meats, called Tushyonka, American meat packers shipped more than 700,000 tons of canned meats to the Red Army. Soviet soldiers before the Allies' Normandy invasion called the tins of meat the "Second Front."

Colonel Fomichev saw the deputy Army commander, General Evtikhii E. Belov, arrive. Lelyushenko introduced him as "your new corps commander" to the brigade commander and his staff.[64] The group then returned to the brigade command post. Once inside, Lelyushenko announced a new combat mission for the tank brigade. The brigade was to move down the highway towards the west to the village of Romanuvka 18 kilometers east of Ternopol, and cover the assembly of the tank corps.

Fomichev listened to the army commander's order and when he stopped, asked: "And what about fuel? Our fuel tanks are dry. And, no ammunition."

"We'll give you fuel and ammunition," Lelyushenko responded. "We'll drop them by air."

Soon after Lelyushenko left, the skies over the tank brigade were filled with small transport bi-planes dropping the necessary supplies with parachutes. The brigade commander remembered, "The odor of gasoline and diesel" permeated the air everywhere.[65] Lelyushenko had demonstrated his ability to get things done.

The tank army attacked towards the Dnestr river, seizing Gusyatinu, advancing to within 20 kilometers of Kamenets-Podolskogo. The army captured 55 German tanks, of which 15 were Tigers; and 10, Panthers.[66] The offensive operation soon took on the character of an artillery duel without any further advance not only in the 4th Tank Army sector but also in the other armies. However, the Stavka ordered the lst and 2nd Ukrainian Fronts to encircle and destroy the German lst Panzer Army which had found itself extended and separated from the 4th Panzer Army.

A renewed offensive began on 21 March. After a short artillery and air preparation, the 4th Tank Army attacked, penetrating the German defense, repelling three counterattacks. The 4th Tank Army poured southward through a gap between the lst and 4th Panzer Armies. The 10th Guards Tank Corps by late afternoon seized the village of Gzhimaluv; the 6th Guards Mechanized Corps, Okno. However, the spring "thaw"(rasputitsa) and resulting mud slowed considerably the offensive tempo. The tank army's sector contained only one fairly good road with cobble stone surface that went south to Chertkov. Supporting simultaneously transport of fuel and ammunition became a basic problem. The failure to get shells to the tanks jeopardized completing the operation. Straining all means to get fuel and ammunition to the tanks, the support units used tracked transports, oxen, and horses. To reach the lead units at the greatest distances from the supply base, the PO-2 biplane dropped containers of fuel in designated places.[67]

General Katukov's 1st Guards Tank Army had forced the 4th Panzer Army back southwest of Ternopol. On 23 March, Field Marshal von Manstein directed the 1st Panzer Army to "...halt the Russian forces moving south along the Zbruch River, regain control of the Chertkov-Yarnobintsy railroad, and extend the army's line of defense to the Seret river at Trembolya."[68] General Hans Hube, commander 1st Panzer Army, could not begin to execute Manstein's order. Surprising the Germans, Lelyushenko's army had advanced too rapidly toward Kamenets-Podolsky, overcoming Marshal von Manstein's solution to the impending encirclement of the 1st Panzer Army.

During the course of operation, Lelyushenko strengthened his control over the operations of his radio communications with a tactical innovation. Through a number of passive measures, such as the use of directional antennas, radio net discipline, transmitter capacity, radio operators countered German communications jamming. Lelyushenko, never satisfied with passive measures, sent out sabotage and reconnaissance groups to destroy German radio jammers.[69]

On 24 March in the area of Chertkov, the tank army received instructions from the Front commander to aggressively develop the attack and by the 25th capture the area of Kamenets-Podolsky. "The offensive spirit did not slacken" Lelyushenko later wrote.[70] Bypassing the main forces of the German 1st Panzer Army on the west, Lelyushenko's tank army, on 26 March, seized Kamenets-Podolsky at a depth of 150 kilometers from the original front line. The capture of Kamenets-Podolsky cut-off the withdrawal routes of the Germans 1st Panzer Army to the west and southwest. The 4th Tank Army together with the troops of the 38th Army closed an inner perimeter around the trapped panzer army. In recognition of the 4th Tank Army's seizure of Kamenets-Podolsky, on 27 March, Moscow gave a 20 volley salute from 224 guns.[71] In the area of Kamenets-Podolsky the Germans continuously counterattacked as the 1st Panzer Army in a magnificent breakout cut Lelyushenko's lines of communications from 28 March to 2 April. The German panzer army slipped the Soviet death trap.

For two weeks, Lelyushenko's army along a solidly defended Strypa river line repelled German counterattacks. On 19 April, the tank army gave up its sector, assembling 60 kilometers southeast of Ternopol, for preparations in a summer offensive. Marshal Ivan S. Konev, an austere man who enjoyed quoting Livy and Pushkin, assumed command of the 1st Ukrainian Front and set in motion plans for a Front offensive operation to liberate the remainder of the Ukraine and to advance to the Carpathian mountains and eastern Poland.

The 1st Ukrainian Front Lvov-Sandomierz offensive operation against the German Army Group Northern Ukraine began on the right wing of the Front on the morning of 13 July, with an attack in the direction of Rava-Russkaya. By the end of the day, the forces managed to advance 8-15 kilometers. In the Lvov direction, the 60th Army, fighting with the 69th Mechanized Brigade of the 3rd Guards Tank Army, drove into the German defense 3-8 kilometers by the evening of 14 July.

In the 38th Army sector, to ensure the successful commitment of the 4th Tank Army, Lelyushenko committed two forward detachments. General Kiril Semenovich Moskalenko, commander 38th Army, complained that he received only 10 tanks from the tank brigade and only a company from the other forward detachment.[72] "I had no doubts that a greater number of tanks would speed up the penetration...," he wrote after the war.[73] The Germans, quick to use their tactical reserves, on the first day began to gather their reserves. On 15 July, the Germans, with two panzer divisions and parts of an infantry division, counterattacked with results that not only stopped the advance of the 38th Army but also pushed it back some 2-4 kilometers. The German assault cut across the planned path for commitment of the 4th Tank Army. That evening, Lelyushenko received a call from the Front headquarters directing the 4th Tank Army to expediously commit behind the 3rd Guards Tank Army through a small gap in the 60th Army sector.

At 1400 hours 16 July, Lelyushenko received the order from the Front commander to leave the 63rd Guards Tank and 17th Guards Mechanized Brigades in the 38th Army sector and move the tank army's main forces north to the 60th Army sector. With dawn 17

July, Lelyushenko's lead elements followed the 3rd Guards Tank Army in the penetration.

The redirection of an army in the course of the battle is no simple task. "It was necessary to coordinate all the questions of coordination and support over again, in this case with the 3rd Guards Tank and 60th Armies," Lelyushenko recalled.[74] Making everything move ahead without delay in a difficult night march, Lelyushenko, over the radio, ordered the corps commanders north towards the new sector of commitment in the vicinity of Koltov. Convinced his commanders had their orders and the army staff had control of the movement, Lelyushenko with his operational group drove to the command posts of the 60th and 3rd Guards Tank Armies. By moving forward, Lelyushenko sought a clearer understanding of the situation and to begin what he enjoyed – getting things settled and wrapped up. The march routes for the brigades and corps crossed the paths of the neighboring units and their lines of communications. At the crossroad, arguments flared up over who had right of way; often, the timetables of the traffic regulators were disturbed. "The night was very dark, and rain came pouring down," Lelyushenko remembered. With great difficulty, at 0200 hours on the 17th, Lelyushenko found the command post for the 3rd Guards Tank Army, and then the 60th Army. The two command posts were located near one another, in the woods outside of Nushche.

Lelyushenko gained a clear grasp of the situation. The attack corridor for the 3rd Guards Tank Army was 4-6 kilometers wide covered by enemy artillery and machinegun fires. General Pavel Rybalko was located with his operational group well forward in the village of Monastyrek. In an update over the radio, Lelyushenko knew that his corps were approaching their designated assembly areas, and he assigned 10th Guards Tank Corps the mission to enter the penetration in the area of Koltov, attacking behind the 3rd Guards Tank Army in the general direction of the village Trostyanets Maly.

On the night of 17 July, the 10th Guards Tank Corps's forward detachment, the 61st Guards Tank Brigade, under the command of Colonel Fomichev, passing the combat elements of the 15th Rifle corps, repelled three counterattacks south of Trostyanets-Maly, and crossed the Strypa river under the cover of darkness. At 0800 hours the next morning, the forward detachment seized a strongpoint near Zolochev, which turned out to be in the hands of the Germans although the 3rd Guards Tank Army had passed through to the northwest. Following the forward detachment, the 10th Guards Tank Corps moved into the narrow gap.

While fighting southeast of Lvov, Colonel Fomichev remembered the drizzling rain on the 17th, and his constant radio transmissions to the corps commander.[75] Often, in the heat of combat, the obligation to report higher seems a nuisance. The forward detachment continuously met fire from ambushes by heavy tanks or dug-in antitank guns. The brigade became held up for two days at Slovita.

From the vicinity of Zolochev, the tank corps turned southwest moving south of Lvov, seeking to destroy German reserve forces. After the tank corps, the 6th Guards Mechanized Corps followed. At this point in the operation, Lelyushenko recalled, "... there awaited new troubles for us."[76] As his army advanced 5-8 kilometers into the gap German reserves conducted a counterattack on both flanks of the mechanized corps with a force of more than 100 tanks from the 1st and 8th Panzer Divisions from the south and part of the German 13th Army Corps from the north. Lelyushenko overstates the strength of the counterattacks. In reality, the panzer divisions were low in tanks and assault guns. However, the corridor would collapse at times, concerning Lelyushenko and the Front commander. Lieutenant General A.I. Akimov, commander of the 6th Guards Mechanized Corps, directed the repulse of the German counterattacks but could not manage to widen the corridor.

On 18 July, from the Front, Lelyushenko received the following instructions: 10th Guards Tank Corps to continue to attack around Lvov from the south and 6th Guards Mechanized Corps together with units of the 60th Army remain in the Koltov corridor until further instructions. The complicated situation separated the 4th Tank Army in two parts. One corps attacked into the depth while the other held with no coordination between the two units. The separate actions precluded a focused objective for Lelyushenko's tank army.

The 10th Guards Tank Corps on 18 July captured the village of Olshantsy 40 kilometers east of Lvov, and the 6th Guards Mechanized Corps continued to hold the Koltov corridor. The distance between the corps reached 70 kilometers. "The situation for the 4th Tank Army grew extremely disadvantageous," Lelyushenko remarked.[77] He requested the Front commander release his 6th Mechanized Corps in order to join the rest of the army's attack in depth. But, Marshal Konev fearing the corridor could still be closed held the corps in place. However, after a visit by the Front chief of staff who appraised the situation later that evening, Konev gave his consent to free the mechanized corps. The 4th Tank Corps under General Pavel Pavlovich Poluboryarov assumed defense of the corridor.

Early morning on 19 July, the 6th Guards Mechanized Corps moved into the breakthrough with the mission to capture Peremyshlyan. Lelyushenko overtook the corps' lead elements and asked the commander how he intended to fulfill his assigned mission. Lelyushenko recommended to the commander that he put out an advance guard under the command of his "bravest, quickest officer".

The 6th Guards Mechanized Corps followed in the attack behind the 10th Guards Tank Corps. From the area of Zolochev, the mechanized corps turned southwest capturing the town of Peremyshlyan. Leaving one brigade in the town, the corps' main force attacked German reserves in the area of Svizh, southeast of Lvov, and advanced on line south of Gorodok.

Lelyushenko and his operational group went forward to Olshantsy at 2200 hours on 19 July. Out in a dark, rainy night, Lelyushenko's group, finding it hard to orient, arrived at the 10th Guards Tank Corps headquarters with difficulty. With the sudden appearance of the tank army commander, Belov reported the corps' attack around Lvov from the southeast in the general direction to Gorodok.

Meanwhile, the 3rd Guards Tank Army maneuvered around Lvov to the northeast with elements advancing towards Peremyshlyan. Both tank armies moved cutting off withdrawal routes and encircling German forces in Lvov. The tank armies' actions also prevented the arrival of German reinforcements. Late that night, Konev sent a directive to the tank army commanders:

"The situation from aggressive action by our tank armies turned out favorably. In the area of Lvov, the enemy has no reserve. I order:

1. Commander 3rd Guards Tank Army not later than 20.7.44 in a circumventing maneuver from the north and northwest seize Lvov.

2. Commander 4th Tank Army aggressively strike around the city of Lvov from the south in cooperation with 3rd Guards Tank Army to seize Lvov."[78]

Marshal Konev's directive changed the mission. Lelyushenko's army was not to outflank, but to take Lvov. Lelyushenko immediately turned his army 90 degrees to the north in order to strike the city from the south.

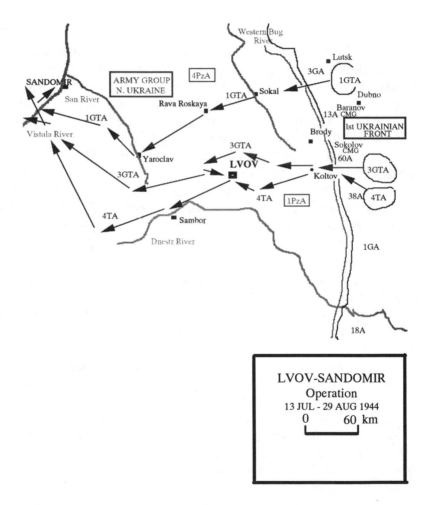

LVOV-SANDOMIR
Operation
13 JUL - 29 AUG 1944
0   60 km

General Belov recalled Lelyushenko with a pencil confidently moving along the map to Lvov giving him the mission to attack. "The Front commander worked out an interesting Lvov liberation plan," Lelyushenko commented. "Look Belov, General Rybalko's army is going around Lvov on the right, to the north, and left, to the south, our tank army is moving around the city. Our armies must capture Lvov in pincers and close further to the west. And before they know it, Lvov will find itself in the rear of Soviet forces. But, here you must break into the city from the southern outskirts with our tank army. Mainly your brigades will go, you understand, Belov? And, as you know the Germans are afraid of your guardsmen with the short daggers, the devil running away from incense (avoiding someone like the plague). They call your corps "the black dagger division."

Belov noted in Lelyushenko's remark, "The General is a stern man, he did not like jokes, but now laughed merrily."[79]

Lelyushenko accompanied by General Belov arrived in Fomichev's brigade command post. Lelyushenko congratulated the brigade on a successful mission. "I'm giving you a new assignment, Fomichev," Lelyushenko announced. "First penetrate the southwest edge of Lvov. This is very important. You will receive the mission specifics from the corps commander."[80]

General Belov drew an arrow on the map. He identified for the brigade an area of the German defense to penetrate and to conduct a raid into the enemy rear area. Colonel Fomichev was not impressed with the assignment. Following the arrow, his brigade was to move along a highway directly into the German defense – he "thought it absurd."[81] His reconnaissance would have to find him a way through the German positions.

At dawn on 20 July, while the tank army's main force attacked Lvov, eight German divisions encircled in the area of Brody began to breakout to the south and southwest. The Germans units encircled to the north by the Front operation concentrated their breakout effort to the south across the 4th Tank Army's lines of communications. In a densely packed formation, the Germans pushed across the area of Knyazhe (10-12 kilometers west of Zolochev) in the location of Lelyushenko's main army headquarters. All the staff personnel – officers, sergeants, soldiers and the security element dropped their staff actions in the command post and fell out to fight. For the next three days, scattered German groups drifted through the area, destroying vehicles, killing horses and men, knocking out mortar positions, and cutting telephone lines. The draws and ravines in the Zolochev area in the direction of Lvov were covered with German soldiers and officers. Lelyushenko sent his 93rd Separate Tank Brigade, the Army's reserve force, along with self-propelled artillery and rocket launcher units to help clear up the situation. Simultaneously, the tank army also fought off German counterattacks against its left flank at Peremyshlyan.

General Belov had an experienced corps cartographer who knew the area around Lvov. Slogging through the marshy approaches, the cartographer knew the marsh was not deep in certain areas, and as he suspected – a submerged, paved road crossing the marsh was not on the map.[82]

General Belov, hoping to meet fewer Germans, decided to advance into Lvov across the marshlands. He needed sappers to make an additional corduroy road through the swampy sector. Corps reconnaissance destroyed a few barns and warehouses for road material and a passable throughway was prepared in a short time.

At 1800 hours 21 July, Colonel Fomichev's brigade was in the outskirts of Lvov. He reported with the codeword, "Roses," indicating Lvov as his location. General Belov came back over the radio, "Quickly, quickly, take Rose!" Entry into Lvov was a personal triumph for Fomichev. In the disastrous summer of 1941, he withdrew from this area with a tank regiment.[83] Now, he spearheaded the city's recapture.

That night, 4th Tank Army began its assault on Lvov. Using surprise, Colonel Fomichev's forward detachment of the 10th Guards Tank Corps wedged into the outskirts of Lvov. While the 10th Guards Tank Corps was heavily committed to battle in Lvov, the 6th Guards Mechanized Corps moved around to the southwest side of Lvov cutting off German withdrawal routes. In the small town of Svizh, southeast of Lvov, during the tank army's offensive, 72 severely wound soldiers and commander of 6th Guards Mechanized Corps were kept by the local citizens. When tank armies or corps operated in the operational depth, this was the main means for handling friendly casualties. At selected collection sites for casualties, the wounded tankers would wait for advancing rifle armies to link up for medical evacuation. This freed the large tank units to continue moving in the enemy rear without being tied to a semimobile hospital facility.

On 27 July, Lvov fell to the 1st Ukrainian Front. In order not to give Army Group Northern Ukraine time to assume a defense behind the Vistula river, the 4th Tank in coordination with the 38th Rifle Army resumed immediately the advance west toward Sambor, capturing the city on 28 July. By mid-August, Lelyushenko's army covering 200 kilometers marched into the Vistula bridgehead, assisting in the bridgehead defense for the remainder of the month.

"The Lvov-Sandomierz operation," Lelyushenko wrote after the war, "increased our arsenal of combat and operational-tactical experience. We acquired the skill to quickly replan the commitment of the tank to penetrations in new directions in dynamic operations. And, the so-called Koltov corridor is highly memorable to us, tankers, for there occurred a critical and complicated situation, the army was forced to conduct battle simultaneously in four directions. The forces and commanders accumulated practical aggressive actions from the flanks and in the depth of the enemy's operational rear."[84]

In the Lvov-Sandomierz operation, the 4th Tank Army lost 91.8% of its tanks and self-propelled assault guns.[85] In November and December 1944, the 4th Tank Army reequipped and rigorously trained for the upcoming Vistula-Oder operation. Lelyushenko created firing ranges with a variety of captured tanks and assault guns as targets for his troops. The firing range commented the chief of armored forces in the 1st Ukrainian Front "looked like a zoo park" with the panthers, tigers and King tigers, referring to the German jungle cat names for tanks.[86]

On 23 December 1944, the 1st Ukrainian Front's directive for the Vistula-Oder operation assigned the 4th Tank Army to the breakthrough in the 13th Army sector, developing the offensive in a northwest direction towards Lodz. Lelyushenko's army at Petrokov would coordinate its actions with the 1st Belorussian Front.

For the operation, Lelyushenko located his operational group with the 13th Rifle Army command post two kilometers from the forward edge of the battlefield. Although each commander exercised a personal choice in composition, Lelyushenko's operational group had a fairly standard configuration. He was accompanied by the commander of the army artillery, chiefs of operation and intelligence sections, or their deputies, chief of engineer forces, representatives for supporting air, a group of officers from the basic staff sections. The trim, agile operational group allowed Lelyushenko to move rapidly forward. In his familiar tanker's overalls with goggles perched on his service cap and a leather map case hanging at his side, Lelyushenko often appeared in corps and brigade command posts or at critical combat actions.

On the night of 11-12 January 1945, the tank army's corps moved to their jump-off positions at 6-10 kilometers from the forward edge of the battle field. Early in the morning, Lelyushenko with a group of his officers took up their position in the forward observation post. At 1000 hours, the artillery preparation for the offensive began lasting one hour and 47 minutes. At 1235 hours, General Nikolai Pavlovich Pukhov, commander of the 13th Army, notified Lelyushenko that the lead infantry units of the rifle army had seized the first German positions and penetrated farther in several areas. Lelyushenko ordered the tank army's forward detachment to begin following with the infantry.

After checking the preparation of his corps for movement into the penetration, Lelyushenko reported his readiness to Marshal Konev. At 1350 hours, he requested commitment of his army into action. Marshal Konev gave Lelyushenko last minute instructions before committing the tank army to the fight. Marshal Konev, having received reports of German reserves at Keltse, directed Lelyushenko to move his army around the town to the southwest.[87] The assigned direction of attack would cut the withdrawal routes of the Germans at Keltse and assist the 3rd Guards and 13th Armies in seizing the town.

At 1400 hours, Lelyushenko ordered the 10th Guards Tank and 6th Guards Mechanized Corps to begin movement. The corps's forward detachments attacked with the lead infantry, paving the way for the corps' main forces thrusting into the penetration. In less than an hour, the tankers, passing through the lead infantrymen, took over the battle. With little staff work requiring his presence, Lelyushenko and his operational group drove forward to help the forward detachment and corps commanders. Forward, he expedited artillery fires in the army sector. In spite of the short winter days, the 10th Guards Tank Corps' advance achieved nearly 50 kilometers.[88] Shrugging off German tactical reserves, the tank army slipped into the German's operational depth.

The 10th Guards Tank Corps numbered 233 tanks and 62 self-propelled assault guns, and had nearly 98 percent of its personnel. The corps' forward detachment, the 63rd Guards Tank Brigade reinforced, entered the breakthrough gap in the German's main defensive sector at 1700 hours, 12 January. By the next morning, the detachment cut two kilometers into the Germans second defensive zone south of Maleshov, essentially defeating the German's main defensive belt.

At 0530 hours the next morning, the brigade's reconnaissance group received a counterattack from German tanks in Maleshov. "We expected without fail a meeting engagement with a large enemy tank reserve moving from the area of Keltse and Pinchuv," Lelyushenko recalled.[89] While the Germans withdrew their infantry divisions to the second defensive belt, the 24th Panzer Corps was brought up during the night, planning a counterstrike against the 4th Tank Army. The 24th Panzer Corps, made up of the 16th, 17th Panzer and 20th Panzer Grenadier Divisions about 360 tanks altogether, was in the reserve of the "A" Group of Armies and had the task of eliminating the 1st Ukrainian Front troops that had broken through, preventing them from mounting an offensive deeper in the defenses. Later in the morning, the forward detachments, separated 15-20 kilometers from the corps main bodies, forced the Charna Nida river and began battling German tank units. "This meant we were meeting the enemy's operational reserve," noted Lelyushenko.[90] Encountering the operational reserve told the Soviets how far they were inside the German defense.

At 1000 hours from aerial reconnaissance, Lelyushenko received information that two German tank groups were moving towards him. According to Soviet estimates, one group with approximately 200 tanks headed from the area southeast of Keltse for the small town of Lesuv. These were the 16th Panzer and 20th Panzer Grenadier Divisions. The second group, the 17th Panzer Division, with about 100 tanks moved from the town of Pinchuv going also in the direction of Lesuv.

A second forward detachment, the 61st Guards Mechanized Brigade, joined the 63rd Tank in actively operating against the German groups. At 0600 hours, 13 January, both tank brigades attacked seizing the grove southwest of Maleshov, then the villages of Lisuvom and Petrkovitse.

The powerful, converging attacks by the two German armored groups cut off Lelyushenko's forward detachments at the Charna Nida river. Anticipating the situation, Lelyushenko decided to attack the German tank reserve. Not losing any time, Lelyushenko radioed General Belov to stop the attack by the forward detachments

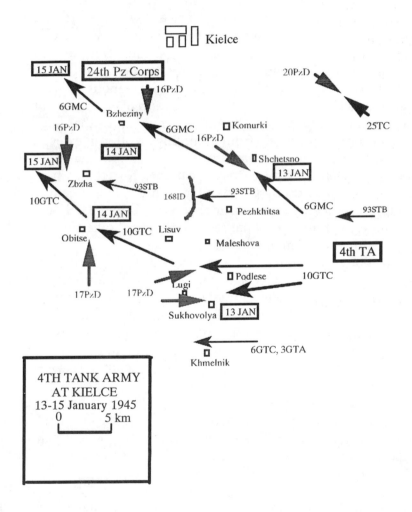

Kielce

15 JAN   24th Pz Corps   20PzD

                    16PzD
6GMC
                                                          25TC
16PzD   Bzheziny   6GMC   Komurki
                              16PzD
                                        Shchetsno
        14 JAN   13 JAN
15 JAN
        Zbzha   93STB
10GTC   168ID   93STB   6GMC   93STB
                          Pezhkhitsa
        14 JAN
        10GTC   Lisuv
Obitse   Maleshova
                                              4th TA
                    Podlese   10GTC
17PzD   17PzD   Lugi
        Sukhovolya   13 JAN

                          6GTC, 3GTA
                    Khmelnik

4TH TANK ARMY
AT KIELCE
13-15 January 1945
0   5 km

to the west and establish a shield on the army's left flank with his 10th Guards Tank Corps. By noon, after exacting and stubborn battles, General Belov committed his second echelon stopping the German 17th Panzer Division advance. The battle had cost the German panzer unit nearly a quarter of its tanks.

To complement the forward detachments attack, Leyushenko ordered all elements of the army to start driving aggressively westward, enveloping the Germans in the area of Lesuv from the north and south. Combat actions developed differently on the tank army's right flank.

The 6th Guards Mechanized Corps' forward detachment engaged the German 16th Panzer Division at the Bzhona river, costing the German panzer unit precious time. By 1300 hours, the mechanized corps main force, operating energetically and decisively, slammed into the 16th Panzer Division. By evening, the Soviet forces pushed the German tank unit out of the area. Lelyushenko's reserve, the 93rd Separate Tank Brigade, sliced through the gap between the 6th Guards Mechanized Corps and 10th Guards Tank Corps, adding Soviet tanks and control to the situation.

With the 6th Guards Mechanized Corps threatening the flanks of the weakened 17th Panzer Division, the 10th Guards Tank Corps went onto the offensive. The tank army's artillery delivered direct fire. In a series of meeting engagements, Lelyushensko's tank army defeated a major German counterstrike force and cut withdrawal routes of the German Keltse grouping, achieving its assigned mission. "The enemy, generally speaking, appeared between our artillery anvil and tank hammer," Lelyushenko remarked on the operation.[91] The bloody meeting engagement lasted for almost two days in which nearly 1000 tanks participated. According to Soviet estimates, the Germans lost over 180 tanks and a large number in other fighting equipment.[92] For the 4th Tank Army's aggressive action in destroying the large German armored reserve and subsequent crossing of the Oder river, Lelyushenko won his second Hero of the Soviet Union.

After the defeat of the German's 24th Panzer Corps in the Keltse area, the 4th Tank Army pressed the offensive westward, crossing the Oder river northwest of Breslau. At 0300 hours, 18 January, the tank army's main forces crossed the Pilitsa river achieving the first stage of the 1st Ukrainian Front's operation. For six days of battle, the 1st Ukrainian Front forces broke through the German defense on a 250 kilometers front, moving to a depth of 140 kilometers.

After crossing the Pilitsa river, Lelyushenko needed all his forces to maintain pressure on the Germans, but his fuel ran out. Faced with little fuel for his army's advance towards the Oder, Lelyushenko configured his separate tank brigade, 93rd Tank Brigade, as a forward detachment for the army.[93] He had enough fuel for the one tank brigade. Lelyushenko's plight exemplified the want of fuel on the modern battlefield and its potential to arrest the tempo of an armored force's advance or sharply limit its combat power. Lelyushenko also exemplified the extraordinary boldness, tenacity and initiative mobile armored warfare demands by reconfiguring units and by risking operations with a small tactical force.

Fulfilling its assigned mission, Major A. A. Dementev's 93rd Tank Brigade on 19 January, accomplished a 70 kilometer march, capturing an intact bridge over the Warta river near Osyakuv. Simultaneously, the 10th Guards Tank Corps, on 19 January, captured the town of Vershuv, and on 20 January, continued advancing across Polish territory toward the Warta river. In a fast paced attack, the tank corps' forward detachment, by the end of 21 January, surprised German forces in the towns of Brandu and Milich, capturing the towns and destroying the German garrisons.

The forward detachments, 63rd Guards Tank Brigade, 10th Guards Tank Corps, and 93rd Separate Tank Brigade aggressively attacked pulling ahead of the tank army's main body approximately 90 kilometers and more than 120 kilometers ahead of the trailing rifle units. With the German's defense shattered like a broken clay jar, the 4th Tank Army like red wine ran out across Poland.

Lelyushenko's mechanized corps captured the town of Grabuv by the Prosna river and continued attacking to the west. On the night of 22 January, lead elements of the corps raced towards the Oder river in the vicinity of Keben. With the army's bridging assets, Lelyushenko's 6th Guards Mechanized Corps prepared a hasty crossing of the river. By the next nightfall, they began crossing the river.

German observation posts discovered the assault crossing boats in the middle of the river and called in heavily concentrated artillery fires on the crossing force. "These were painfully severe minutes," Lelyushenko remembered.[94] Once ashore, lead elements of the 17th Guards Mechanized Brigade engaged a special German commando unit, Brandenburgers, in a seriously contested battle east of Keben and succeeded in establishing a bridgehead. German air continually bombed the tank army's bridgehead and tankers on the river crossings.

The events unfolded differently in the 10th Guards Tank Corps offensive zone. Early afternoon on 24 January the tank corps's forward detachment, eight tanks with submachine gunners and sappers, captured the 60-ton reinforced concrete bridge over the Oder at Steinau on the move. However, instead of holding the bridge, the detachment broke for the city and engaged in street battles. Only a small group of combat engineers remained behind to clear the bridge of mines and hold it. The Germans sent a small force to the bridge. After a short, violent fight, the Germans killed the detachment and blew up the bridge before the tank corps main forces reached it. Unable to hold the captured bridge at Steinau, on 24 January, the corps, using forces of the 29th Guards Motorized Rifle Brigade, crossed the Oder south of Steinau, capturing a bridgehead. The 23rd Engineer-Sapper Brigade attached to the corps began construction of a 60-ton bridge for passage of tanks and self-propelled assault guns. However, because of a dangerously shifting ice flow, the engineers were unable to build the bridge crossing. The German command took advantage of the gained time and moved fresh forces into the threatened crossing sector and attacked, pressing the 29th Motorized Rifle Brigade against the banks of the Oder river. With difficulty, the besieged brigade held tenaciously a bridgehead up to 3 kilometers wide and 500-700 meters deep.

On 26 January, Lelyushenko crossed into the bridgehead. Not losing time, Leyushenko with his operational group drove to Keben, where the Germans continued to offer stiff resistance. The 10th Guards Tank Corps secretly concentrated in an assembly area moved to Keben. Under pressure, Lelyushenko decided to regroup the tank brigades of the 10th Guards Tank Corps in the Keben area and to send them through the 6th Mechanized Corps bridgehead on the Oder. After crossing, on 30 January, the tank brigades struck the Germans defending in the area of Steinau from the rear. Their advance linked up with the beleaguered 29th Guards Motorized Rifle Brigade.

Lelyushenko's regrouping of the tank corps' main forces on a new axis and their decisive actions, by the evening of 31 January, combined the bridgeheads of the 6th Guards Mechanized Corps in the Keben area and the 29th Guards Motorized Rifle Brigade south of Steinau into a single operational bridgehead, 30 kilometers wide and 15 kilometers deep. The large bridgehead ensured a launch point for the 1st Ukrainian Front for further offensive operations in Lower Silesian. Close, hard combat for the strained soldiers and lagging rear support forced the tank army to pause in order to replenish the army with personnel, equipment, ammunition, fuel and rations.

At this point in the fighting on the eastern front, the Germans had an advantage in logistical support, their retreating brought them closer to their logistical bases while the Red Army became extended. To sustain the fast paced drive, fuel and ammunition had been air dropped to the tank army in containers on parachutes. The captured forward airfields were unequipped to service Soviet airplanes. In a five days respite, the Soviet High Command decided to get units quickly refitted, and secure the proper equipment to open the forward airfields for air cargo.

On 31 January 1945, Lelyushenko received notification that the 1st Ukrainian Front would resume the offensive against the German's Breslau grouping. His specific orders and instructions for his tank army indicated the offensive would begin on 8 February.

At 0800 hours 8 February, Lelyushenko with key members of his operational group assumed his position in the army's observation post within one kilometer of the battle front near the 13th Army commander's observation post. After an hour of artillery preparation, the 1st Ukrainian Front attacked out of the Steinau bridgehead between Glogau and Breslau. In spite of strong German resistance, the Red Army's 13th Rifle Army penetrated the German defense north and south of Raudtena. The 4th Tank Army launching out of the bridgehead north, took Primkenow, 12 kilometers east of Bobr river.

The offensive slowed with flooded roads, as well as by wooded and partly marshy country. The retreating Germans resisted stubbornly, using the terrain to advantage. All these factors took a toll in the physical fatigue of the soldiers. The average daily advance of the riflemen stretched to 8-12 kilometers which seemed to be the limits of the Red Army infantry forces. Nonetheless, the Red Army troops reached the Bobr river, forced it in a number of places, and began to expand the captured bridgeheads. Meanwhile, Lelyushenko's lead elements succeeded in breaking through to the Kwisa, allowing the army's main force across.

The Front operations, as a whole, seemed to proceed successfully with armored units aggressively driving ahead, while the rifle units, at their own rate, continued the offensive by themselves. The results became unfavorable for the advancing Front. The 6th Guards Mechanized Corps advanced towards the Neisse river on 14 February. By the following midday, units of the mechanized corps seized small villages on the west bank of the Neisse. On the same day, the 10th Guards Tank Corps advanced to the Neisse in the area of Forst and prepared for a hasty river crossing. However, the German 4th Panzer Army counterattacked cutting behind Lelyushenko's army. Marshal Konev turned General Rybalko's 3rd Guards Tank Army to restore the situation. After three days, the 4th Tank Army secured its flanks and closed on the Niesse river.

"Regrettably," recalled Marshal Konev, the Front commander, "our 13th Army failed to take advantage of the opportunities which had presented themselves and did not follow the tankers. Lacking vigor in this case, which can really be explained by extreme fatigue, the army did not reach the Neisse, and the Germans managed to plug the gap behind Lelyushenko's army. The fighting of the infantry assumed a protracted character and the communications to the tankers were cut for several days."[95]

Marshal Konev decided to visit the 13th and 4th Tank Armies, however, he could not reach the encircled tank army. He talked with Lelyushenko only by radio, coordinating a counterattack plan. By midday, Marshal Konev with the 13th Army commander managed a frontal attack, and Lelyushenko turned his army in the direction of the attack. This reaction checked the German attempt to cut off and destroy Lelyushenko's armored forces.

About the turn in events, Marshal Konev later observed, "It was a good thing that neither of the commanders – Plukhov or Lelyushenko – played the hypocrite and tried to act on the sly in order to avoid reproof from above. Unpleasant though it was for them, they reported everything, as it had actually happened, to the command of the Front, and this enabled us to do immediately all we could, including extensive use of the air force."[96]

The 4th Tank Army resuming the advance reached the eastern bank of the Neisse, although only in a narrow sector. Following Lelyushenko's tank army, the troops of the 3rd Guards and 52nd Armies also broke through to the river. After securing the advance and the crossing, the 4th Tank Army withdrew to the Front reserve for reconstitution. By 20 February, the 1st Ukrainian Front completed the capture of lower Silesia.

The campaign for Upper Silesia began on 15 March 1945, with the 21st Army and 4th Tank Army advancing simultaneously in the offense after a 40 minute artillery preparation. On 17 March, the 6th Guards Mechanized Corps, penetrating into the operational depth of the German defense. The 10th Guards Tank Corps crossed the Neisse river by Rothaus, developing the advance towards Noistadt. In the operation, one kilometer north of Rothaus, the tank corps commander, Colonel Nil Danilovich Chupov, was killed in combat. "This was for us a serious loss," Lelyushenko later wrote.[97] The command of the corps was again given to General Major E. E. Belov, who was serving as Deputy commander for the tank army since giving up his corps command.

On the 4th Tank Army's flank, the 21st Army commander believed he only needed a minimum amount of the artillery support to drive the Germans out of their defensive position. In order to save ammunition, which was still in short supply, the rifle army commander intended to use it for greater effect later in the attack. The rifle army advanced slowly, and its artillery support failed to eliminate many of the dug-in German troops and antitank positions. Many of them ended up surprising the advancing Soviet tanks, particularly Germans tanks dug into the ground and assault guns hidden in built up areas. Lelyushenko's tankers suffered serious losses. Marshal Konev, disappointed with the conduct of the current operation, believed the 4th Guards Tank Army had "needless losses in equipment" in working with the 21st Army – a comment indicative of Konev's critical standards.

With the morning of 18 March, 6th Guards Mechanized Corps attacked German reserves in the area. In these bloody, costly battle, the 6th Guards Mechanized Corps commander, Colonel Vasilii Fedorovich Orlov, severely wounded left the battlefield and the chief of staff took command of the battling unit forces. Lelyushenko's skilled and experienced leader eroded with the mounting battle casualties, complicating his command and control. Despite these difficulties and the Front commander's criticism, Lelyushenko's tank army drove west.

By evening, at the height of the Upper Silesia campaign, Konev and Lelyushenko received a telegram from Stalin:

"In the battle for our Soviet homeland against the German invaders the 4th Tank Army demonstrated exemplary valor and steadfastness, courage and boldness, discipline and organization.

Recent fighting on the front in the Patriotic war with the German invaders the 4th Tank Army in its destructive strikes, destroying enemy personnel and equipment, inflicted great losses on the enemy forces."[98] Further in Stalin's message, Lelyushenko's tank army was redesignated 4th Guards Tank Army and received the special banner which bore Lenin's portrait. On 24 March, the 4th Guards Tank Army received a third corps, the 5th Guards Mechanized Corps under the command of Major General Ivan Prokorovich Ermakov.

At the conclusion of the second stage of the Upper Silesia operation, the 4th Guards Tank Army in coordination with the 21st, 59th and 60th Armies captured the western portion of Upper Silesia. For the period of the operation from the Vistula river, 12 January to 15 February 1945, the 4th Guards Tank Army advanced more than 600 kilometers. In Soviet military history the forces on the left flank of the 1st Ukrainian Front which included the 4th Guards Tank army were credited with the destruction of nearly 40,000 Germans soldiers, capturing 14,000 prisoners, destroying or capturing 100 tanks, a thousand guns and mortars.

Planning for the Berlin operation commenced on 1 April, the day after the 1st Ukrainian Front completed the Upper Silesia operation. To meet the planned assaults for the final operation on Berlin, extensive regrouping of the Front forces were necessary. Marshal Konev made slight shifts with the rifle armies. Rybalko's 3rd Guards Tank Army moved from the Goerlitz area 80 kilometers north. The 4th Guards Tank Army traveled a longer distance, from the Neustadt area on the Front's left wing 250 kilometers northward to the right wing. In a remarkably fast march, Lelyushenko's army, recuperating from intense operations in Upper Silesia, made the trek in five days and nights. The rapid regroupment was designed to keep German intelligence off-balance. The German leadership knew the offensive on Berlin was coming, but when, where, and how much the Soviet command kept hidden.

In the middle of April 1945, the 1st Ukrainian Front forces were deployed along the western Neisse river from Rapdorf to Pentsikha, 145 kilometers from the German capital, Berlin. Twice during preparations for the Berlin operation, Lelyushenko and his staff met with General P.S. Rybalko, commander of the 3rd Guards Tank Army, working out the coordination between the two tank armies for the operation.

Two days before the start of the operation, Lelyushenko received instructions from the Front commander to use forward detachments for hastening the penetration of the German tactical defense to help the 5th Guards Army capture the opposite bank of the Neisse and develop the offensive westward. Marshal Konev became known and criticized for his early use of tank units in the breakthrough. Tank forces assisting in the breakthrough of the tactical defense zone suffered high tank losses detracting from a sustained performance later in the operational depth. This became accented in this operation since much of the replacement for 4th Tank Army battle losses were not made, leaving the army at 50-60% strength, 390 tanks and self-propelled assault guns.[99]

On the night before the attack, the army's corps took up their final assault positions for commitment to the breakthrough. At 0615 hours 16 April, a powerful artillery preparation began blowing chunks out of the German defensive positions. With the trailing shells of the preparatory fires, the 5th Guards Army advanced to cross the river. Smoke covered the rifle unit movement to the river. The rifle units' attack began successfully, crossing the river on rafts and boats. By 1200 hours, a 60-ton bridge spanned the water, and an hour later Lelyushenko's forward detachments, one reinforced brigade from each of the corps, rumbled forward.

Lelyushenko that evening told General Belov to commit his corps. Then, Lelyushneko drove to the corps commander's location to watch the operation unfold. Satisfied with the action, Lelyushenko soon returned to his command post where he reviewed the 6th Guards Mechanized Corps operation developing on the army's left flank.

The operation contained unique tactical features worth recapping, such as, forcing of the Neisse, the capture of bridgeheads on its western bank, the penetration of the first line of the enemy's defenses, the attack against the second line and its penetration, the further advance towards the Spree, its forcing and the penetration of the third line of German defenses were all carried out as a single and continuous action. "As far as I am concerned," Marshal Konev observed after the war, "it was the first time in the Great Patriotic War, that I had had to force a river, then, without any interruptions, immediately breakthrough the enemy's defenses, which had a well-developed fire system, obstacles, fortifications and minefields, and then breakthrough the second and third lines of defense, involving the forcing of another river. I think that this single, continuous process of developing an operation deserves some attention from the point of view of operational skill."[100]

At 2330 hours, 16 April, General Belov reported contact with German tank units. Lelyushenko's 4th Guards Tank Army, which had reached the Spree south of the Front Commander's observation post, encountered strong German resistance. The tank corps turned towards Konev's position, and, finding yet another ford, began to cross the river.

Lelyushenko and Rybalko stood with the Front commander on a hill beside an old baronical castle, watching the Spree river crossing. "The army commanders were worried about the burning woods ahead of us," Konev remembered. "Fires are very troublesome to tanks. They limit visibility which, under combat conditions, is poor anyway; moreover, movement through a zone of fires is continuously fought with the danger of explosion. The tanks entering a deep gap carry a good deal of their armor, including crossing equipment; the more far-sighted crews even carry a fuel reserve, in cans or special barrels."[101]

"But, of course, the fires were not their main worry," continued Marshal Konev. "The principle problem, which both the army commanders and I understood, was that we had to advance while fierce fighting nearby was still proceeding on our flanks."[102] The 3rd Guards Army repelled continuous, violent German counterattacks on the right flank and 5th Guards Army beat them back on the left.

That night, Marshal Konev in his command post received the directions from Stalin to turn his tank armies towards Berlin. As soon as Stalin hung up, Konev called the tank army commanders on the High Frequency ("V Ch" Vysoko Chastotny) telephone and gave them the warning order to turn towards Berlin. In the order, "Commander of the 4th Guards Tank Army: on the night of April 17, 1945, the army will force the Spree north of Spremberg and advance rapidly in the general direction of Drepkau, Kalau, Dane, and Luckenwalde. By the end of April 20, 1945, the army will capture the area of Beelitz, Treuenbritzen and Luckenwalde, and on the night of April 20, 1945 – Potsdam and the southwestern part of Berlin. When turning towards Potsdam the army will secure the Treuenbritzen area with the 5th Mechanized Corps. Reconnaissance will be made in the direction of Senftenberg, Finsterwalde and Herzberg."[103] Lelyushenko's command post received the instructions at 0300 hours 18 April. The Front commanders directive gave Lelyushenko's tank army the new mission to attack towards Berlin. The army staff with little loss in time wrote the corps orders.

Marshal Konev wanted the following point impressed on the minds of the corps and brigade commanders, "The tanks will advance daringly and resolutely in the main direction. They will bypass towns and large communities and not engage in protracted, frontal fighting. I demand a firm understanding that the success of the tank armies depends on the boldness of the maneuver and swiftness of the operation."[104]

By 18 April, Lelyushenko's army encountering little German resistance broke through into the operational depth and advanced 45 kilometers with the 10th Tank and 5th Mechanized Guards Corps. The next day, both corps advanced still more rapidly, gaining another 50 kilometers by evening. The forward detachments advanced 70-90 kilometers. Lelyushenko, moving about the army sector and well forward, visited Colonel Fomichev's forward detachment.

"Prepared to assault Berlin?" Lelyushenko asked a brigade tanker.

"Exactly so, comrade General."

"We'll see. Which battalion will you commit Fomichev?"

"The sub-machinegunners. They just now seized the Enikendorf woods," Fomichev replied.[105]

Lelyushenko went further forward to the battalion position. He awarded the Red Star for bravery on the spot to a tanker. Turning to a Senior Lieutenant who was the 1st Battalion commander, Lelyushenko asked, "Are your troops prepared to assault Berlin?"

"It will take at least a second," the young officer responded enthusiastically.[106]

Commanders by moving forward to the fighting positions and asking a simple question can gain a full sense of the morale and preparedness of a force. Lelyushenko stayed forward constantly for such an understanding of his soldiers and units.

On 20 April, Lelyushenko received new instructions from the Front commander, "Only for comrades Rybalko and Lelyushenko. Marshal Zhukov's forces are 10 kilometers from the eastern edge of Berlin. I order you without fail by tonight to penetrate to Berlin. ... Report execution. Konev."[107] The 1st Ukrainian Front had advanced swiftly due to a less developed enemy defense and density of troops than in Marshal Zhukov's 1st Belorussian Front sector. When

Rybalko's and Lelyushenko's tank armies turned north, they faced an unobstructed approach to Berlin. The German defensive positions faced eastward, and the tank units slipped past or between them.

In the latter stages of the Berlin operation, the tank armies of the lst Ukrainian Front, without encountering serious German resistance after crossing the Neisse defensive line, broke out into the operational depth, and began developing the offensive successfully toward Berlin. Lelyushenko's tank army which was fighting to the left of Rybalko's tank army, by the end of 22 April, had broken through the outer defensive perimeter to Berlin linked-up with the lst Belorussian Front troops, completing the encirclement of the entire Berlin area.

Lelysuhenko's tank army pursued the Germans on 22 April in the general direction of Potsdam without getting involved in combat, outflanked the town of Luckenwalde and advanced 20 kilometers, capturing Saarmund on the southwestern approach to Berlin. Lelyushenko's corps were approaching Berlin on a tangent, aiming ever farther northwest and moving to encircle Berlin on the west side.

At the same time, covering the left flank of its army and enabling it to turn north, Lelyushenko's 5th Guards Mechanized Corps guarded against the enemy by establishing a strong barrier facing west on the Jutterbog-Luckenwalde front. The mechanized corps soon had to repulse attacks by German General Wenck's 12th Army which, on Hitler's order, tried to breakthrough to Berlin. With the beginning of the German attack, Lelyushenko drove to the 5th Guards Mechanized Corps command post to assist the commander. Accompanied by his air army liaison officer who coordinated supporting ground attack aircraft, the army commander helped repulse the attack. After capturing Luckenwalde and the Beelitz-Treuenbritzen-Kropstedt line, the 5th Guards Mechanized Corps held firmly, protecting the tank army.

The following day, Lelyushenko's army continued successfully to advance in the Potsdam direction. Towards evening, his army already outflanked Berlin from the southwest. Lelyushenko's lead units were separated from the troops of the lst Belorussian Front whose lead elements were the 9th Tank Corps of Bogdanov's tank army by only 25 kilometers.

Lelyushenko's tank army reached the Teltov Canal west of

Rybalko's tank army, trying to cross, but encountered strong resistance. Marshal Konev told Lelyushenko that Rybalko's troops were successfully negotiating the canal, and that it would not be a bad idea if he redisposed his troops laterally, crossed the Teltov Canal in Rybalko's tracks, and then returned his troops west to his own zone, but now on the northern side of the canal. "Lelyushenko did not ignore my suggestion," Konev remarked, "and, following my good advice, redisposed his troops that very night and thereby avoided many unnecessary casualties."[108] Forcing the Teltov canal began late night on 23 April. Lelyushenko with General Belov observed the crossing through binoculars as the 10th Guards Tank Corps reinforced with the 350th Rifle Division continued storming the southwest edge of Berlin.

Thriving on the action, Lelyushenko drove to the 6th Guards Mechanized Corps to study the situation and render help to the young corps commander in quickly encircling Berlin. The 4th Guards Tank Army had to keep moving without involvement in protracted fighting on the outskirts of Berlin.

On the night of 25 April, 35th Guards Mechanized Brigade seized the town of Kettsin, 22 kilometers west of Berlin. Towards evening, the army reached the Havel river, which divides Potsdam in half, and that day succeeded in seizing only its southeastern part because the Germans had blown up all the bridges across the river. Preparations were made to force the river. Lelyushenko's 6th Guards Mechanized Corps had advanced 18 kilometers north and northwest, in the direction of Brandenburg and also reached Havel. By afternoon one brigade had broken into the eastern outskirts of Brandenburg. Lelyushenko's army continued fighting on 25 April for the crossing over the Havel southeast of Potsdam. Finally, the 6th Guards Mechanized corps made crossing in the afternoon, linking up with units of General Bogdanov's 2nd Guards Tank Army and sealing off the Berlin area.

On 27 April, Lelyushenko's tank army having liquidated the Potsdam enemy group in cooperation with the 47th Army fought Germans defending the Wansee island. A large German force of about 20,000 men, was established after their defeat and concentrated on the small island. "That day I was extremely dissatisfied with Lelyushenko for taking so long to smash this enemy group and allowing his troops to be diverted from Berlin," Konev later revealed. "But he was right in his own way. One could not overlook a group

20,000 strong, even if it diverted one from the main objective."[109]

Lelyushenko was preparing to force the channel south of the Wansee Island with the 10th Guards Tank Corps reinforced with pontoon units and a battalion of amphibian tanks, two assault engineer battalions and reinforcement artillery. At 2300 hours 28 April, after a brief artillery attack, Lelyushenko's tankers and Pukhov's infantrymen began to force the channel and by midnight captured the first bridgehead on the northern bank. They immediately launched a pontoon bridge.

"Frankly speaking, I was not particularly happy about that crossing," Konev recalled. "Tanks operating in that area of islands and intervening channels were at a great disadvantage. But since the corps was already involved in the fighting for the Wansee and the crossing was prepared for it, there was nothing I could do but agree to this plan, it was too late to change it."[110]

Fighting continued on Wansee Island until 30 April. On 1 May, Leyushenko's 10th Guards Tank Corps and Pukhov's 350th Rifle Division wiped out the German group on Wansee Island. The 6,000 German soldiers and officers who had crossed from the island to the mainland on the night of 30 April were annihilated in groups or taken prisoner within the lines of Lelyushenko's units. On the morning of 2 May, one of these groups, the largest one, about 2,000 strong reached the forest northwest of Schankensdorf, where Lelyushenko's headquarters was located at the time. Upon the alert, all the officers of the field headquarters took up arms. Lelyushenko with his chief of staff, General Karl Ivanovich Upman, directed the defense. The arrival of the army reserve, the 7th Guards Motorcycle Regiment, and other units broke up the German assault. In the last days of the war, Lelyushenko's command post experienced another close call with attacking enemy.[111]

In the course of the Berlin operation, the forces of the 4th Guards Tank Army was noted six times in Supreme High Command orders:

23 April-for penetrating the enemy defense on the Neisse river and taking the towns of Beelitts, Lukkenvalde, Treienbritsen;

25 April-for seizing the town of Kettsin and completing encirclement of Berlin in cooperation with forces of the 1st Belorussian Front;

27 April-for part in the capture of Vittenberg;

1 May-for finishing destruction of the Cottbus enemy grouping and for capturing Brandenburg;

2 May-for part in capturing Berlin;

2 May-for liquidation of German groups encircled in southeast Berlin.[112]

On 2 May Lelyushenko's army received a directive from the 1st Ukrainian Front to give his sector to the 1st Belorussian Front forces and to concentrate in the woods 35-50 kilometers south of Berlin for preparation for a strike on Prague. The 4th Guards Tank Army gave up its sector to the 69th Army, 1st Belorussian Front.

Lelyushenko received the regrouping mission at 1630 hours on 2 May 1945. Having made his decision in 30-40 minutes through the army staff, primarily his chief of staff and chief of operations, he issued preliminary instructions to the subordinate units. By 2200 hours, the combat order for the regrouping the tank army had been sent out to the lower formations, and by 0200 hours, 3 May, Lelyushenko's tank army began to march.[113]

Lelyushenko received orders to attack on the morning of 5 May. The combat instructions for the units to arrive in their jump off positions was issued by 1100 hours, and the missions to attack had been staffed by 1600 hours on 5 May. The order to attack reached the corps by 0400 hours 6 May.[114] The tank units took their attack positions. At 0830 hours, after a short artillery preparation, Lelyushenko's forward detachments began the attack. Two hours later, Lelyushenko reported the success of the forward detachment battles. Marshal Konev arrived in Lelyushenko's command post and gave instructions for the commitment of the tank army's main body. Forces of the 1st Ukrainian Front attacked from the north and northwest. From the east advanced units of the 4th Ukrainian Front and from the southeast 2nd Ukrainian Front.

Towards evening, Lelyushenko's tank army traveled 50 kilometers, advanced to the line Valdgeim-Zibelen. Forward detachments advanced approximately 65 kilometers and seized the railroad junction at Freiberg. German resistance held up the 3rd Guards Tank Army forward detachments along the Dresden-Chemnitz highway.

The following day, the 61st Guards Tank Brigade, which was operating as the forward detachment of the 10th Guards Tank Corps, was replaced by the 63rd Guards Tank Brigade to preclude a similar slow up of the 4th Guards Tank Army. By afternoon, because the pace of the pursuit was slowing down, Lelyushenko moved forward making things happen through improvisation in his last campaign of the war. He reinforced the existing corps forward detachment with an army forward detachment consisting of the 70th Guards Self-propelled Artillery Brigade, which was in the army reserve prior to this time.[115] The 4th Guards Tank Army advanced another 50-60 kilometers.

At night on 8 May, 5th Guards Mechanized Corps, which had been assigned to the 4th Guards Tank Army, reached the small village of Zhatets some 60 kilometers northwest of Prague. In the course of two and half days, Lelyushenko's tank army advanced 110-120 kilometers, crossed the Rudnye mountains, and, poised for a final rush on Prague.

In the early morning hours, 4th Guards Tank Army in a decisive drive entered the northwest part of Prague with the forward units of the 63rd Guards Tank Brigade. By 0400 hours, the main body of the 10th Guards Tank Corps closed with the Czechoslovakian capital. Lelyushenko with his operational group moved with the 10th Guards Tank Corps, locating his operational group in the western edge of Prague. Lelyushenko's army was in position for the final assault. He could quickly intervene if necessary. Prague fell easily, ending the long hard war for Lelyushenko and his guards.

Dmitrii Danilovich Lelyushenko, twice a Hero of the Soviet Union, becomes a Janus to western stereotypic notions of Red Army commanders. On the one face, Lelyushenko was quick to take the direct approach to impose his will on his opponent and suffer the casualties. While on the other face, he often showed a tremendous capacity to improvise combat operations on the move, not needing a complete plan to fight. He owed much of his success to a boundless energy that thrived on dynamic situations. Lelyushenko enjoyed decision making. Moving to trouble spots, he was authoritative in his command with little time for a collective or democratic approach to command, demonstrating an ability to absorb, remember and manage a great amount of detail. His desire to be well forward earned him a nickname and reputation, but considering the number of wounds and near misses, he was a lucky man. After four decades of fighting with the Red Army, Lelyushenko finished his biggest and most difficult test commanding an elite guards tank army. He has won a place in the pantheon of Red Armored Guards.

NOTES

1. E.F. Ivanovskii, *Ataku nachinali tankisty*, Moscow: Voenizdat, 1984, p. 7.

2. Ibid., pp. 6-7.

3. Ibid.

4. A. Eremenko, *The Arduous Beginning*, Moscow: Progress, 1966, p. 15.

5. Ivanovskii, p. 15.

6. I. Tyulenev, "General armii D.D. Lelyushenko," *Voenno-istoricheskii zhurnal* (hereafter *Vizh*), 11-1971, p. 124.

7. Dmitrii Volkogonov, "Triumf i tragediya," *Pravda* excerpt 20 Jun 88, p. 3.

8. O. F. Suvenirov, "Vsearmeiskaya tragediya," *Vizh* 3-89, pp. 39-47.

9. D.D. Lelyushenko, *Moskva-Stalingrad-Berlin-Praga*, Moscow: Nauka, 1973, p. 10.

10. V.A. Anfilov, *Nachalo Velikoi Otechestvennoi Voiny*, Moscow: Voenizdat, 1962, p. 77.

11. Lelyushenko, p. 13.

12. Ibid., p. 15.

13. Erich von Manstein, *Lost Victories*, Novato, California: Presidio, 1982, p. 186.

14. Lelyushenko, p. 18.

15. Ibid.

16. Manstein, p. 187.

17. Ibid., p. 188.

18. Tyulenev, p. 124.

19. Manstein, p. 192.

20. I.M. Anan'ev, *Tankovye armii v nastuplenii*, Moscow; Voenizdat, 1988, p. 36.

21. Manstein, p. 193.

22. Lelyushenko, p. 25.

23. Ibid., pp. 26-7.

24. Ibid., p. 31.

25. Ibid., p. 33.

26. Ibid., p. 37.

27. Ibid., p. 40.

28. Ibid., p. 42.

29. Heinz Guderian, *Panzer Leader*, London: Futura, 1974, p. 237.

30. Lelyushenko, p. 52.

31. Ibid., p. 64.

32. Ibid., p. 74.

33. Ibid.; Identifying shortcomings in Lend-Lease equipment sent to the Red Army is a conventional practice in Soviet writings. In this particular case, the British tanks when compared to the T-34 would not fare as well in performance and capability.

34. Ibid., p. 79.

35. Donald Grey Brownlow, *Panzer Baron: The Military Exploits of General Hasso von Manteuffel*, North Quincy, Massachusetts: Christopher, 1975, p. 78.

36. Ibid., pp. 78-9.

37. I. Sukhomlin, "Sluzhebnye sobaki na voine," *Vizh* 8-1971, p. 93.

38. P.A. Rotmistrov, *Stalnaya gvardiya*, Moscow: Voenizdat, 1984, p. 91.

39. Lelyushenko, pp. 85-6.

40. Ibid., p. 100.

41. P.A. Rotmistrov, *Vremya i Tanki*, Moscow: Voenizdat, 1972, p. 114.

42. Lelyushenko, p. 100.

43. Ibid., p. 101.

44. Ibid., pp. 108-9.

45. Ibid., p. 109.

46. Ibid.

47. Ibid.

48. Ibid.

49. Ibid., p. 135.

50. Ibid., p. 153.

51. Ibid., p. 159.

52. S.M. Shtemenko, *The Soviet General Staff at War*, Book One, Moscow: Progress, 1985, pp. 479-80.

53. Lelyushenko, p. 169.

54. Ibid., p. 172.

55. Manstein, p. 417.

56. Lelyushenko, p. 177.

57. Manstein, p. 431.

58. Ibid., pp. 462-3.

59. Shtemenko, pp. 479-80.

60. Lelyushenko, p. 221.

61. K.S. Moskalenko, *Na Yugo-zapadnom Napravlenii*, Book 2, Moscow: Nauka, 1973, p. 307.

62. M.G. Fomichev, *Put' nachinalya s urala*, Moscow: Voenizdat, 1976, p. 99.

63. Ibid.

64. Ibid.

65. Ibid., p. 100.

66. Moskalenko, p. 307.

67. Lelyushenko, p. 231.

68. "Encirclement and Breakout of the First Panzer Army (March - April 1944), MS #F-143a - VII, Carlisle Barracks, Pennsylvania: Military History Institute, p. 408.

69. P.P. Tovstukha, R.M. Portugal'skii, *Upravlenie voiskami v nastuplenii*, Moscow: Voenizdat, 1981, p. 175.

70. Lelyushenko, p. 231.

71. Ibid., p. 236.

72. Moskalenko, p. 398.

73. Ibid.

74. Lelyushenko, p. 255.

75. Fomichev, p. 148.

76. Lelyushenko, p. 257.

77. Ibid., p. 257.

78. I.S. Konev, *Zapiski komanduyushchego frontom*, Moscow: Voenizdat, 1981, pp. 245-6.

79. E.E. Belov, *Syny otchizny*, Moscow: Politicheskoi literatury, 1966, pp. 169-70.

80. Fomichev, pp. 148-9.

81. Ibid., p. 149.

82. Ibid., p. 181.

83. Fomichev, p. 152.

84. Lelyushenko, p. 274.

85. A.I. Radzievskii, *Tankovyi udar*, Moscow: Voenizdat, 1977, p. 220.

86. K.V. Krainyukov, *Oruzhie osobogo roda*, Moscow: Voenizdat, 1977, p. 325.

87. Konev, p. 347.

88. V. Smirnov, "Vstrechnyi boi tankovogo korpusa," *Vizh* 8-60, p. 57.

89. Lelyushenko, p. 288.

90. Ibid.

91. Ibid., p. 289.

92. O.A. Losik, *Stroitel'stvo i boevoe primenenie sovetskikh tankovykh voisk v gody velikoi otechestvennoi voiny*, Moscow: Voenizdat, 1979, p. 181.

93. Lelyushenko, p. 293.

94. Ibid., p. 298.

95. I.S. Konev, *Year of Victory*, Moscow: Progress, 1969, p. 54.

96. Ibid., pp. 53-4.

97. Lelyushenko, p. 317.

98. Ibid., p. 319; Krainyukov, p. 497.

99. I. Krupchenko, "Tankovye armii v Berlinskoi operatsii," *Vizh* 7-1960, p. 21.

100. Konev, Victory, p. 95.

101. Ibid., p. 102.

102. Ibid., p. 103.

103. Ibid., p. 107; Lelyushenko,p. 339.

104. Konev, *Victory*, pp. 107-8.

105. Fomichev, p. 201.

106. Ibid., p. 202.

107. Lelyushenko, p. 339.

108. Konev, Victory, p. 157.

109. Ibid., pp. 179-80.

110. Ibid., p. 186.

111. Ibid., pp. 190-1.

112. Lelyushenko, p. 354.

113. Radzievskii, p. 61.

114. Ibid.

115. Anan'ev, p. 304.

CHAPTER V

★ ★ ★ ★ ★

ROTMISTROV

rom a dugout in a half burnt apple orchard on a hilltop, General Pavel Alekseevich Rotmistrov looked over the wide open fields, intently inspecting the battlefield. He signaled for the attack to begin. Waves of the famous Soviet T-34 tanks rushed forward from the wood lines on his right and left. Through his binoculars, Rotmistrov looked back down the field and saw a host of advancing German tanks. In the course of the horrific collision of two armored forces, the battle for Prokhorovka became a tank slaughter. The resolute, soldier-scholar, General Rotmistrov led his 5th Guards Tank Army to victory over the German elite 2nd SS Panzer Corps. With a direct, aggressive fighting style he won the greatest tank battle of the Second World War. His victory propelled him to the pinnacle of Red Army tank forces only to be removed from command a year later. But, the intelligent and talented Rotmistrov proved to be a survivor, whether in the chaos of the battlefield or in the bureaucratic labyrinths of the Red Army.

Rotmistrov joined the Red Army at the early age of 17 years. In April 1919, participating in the Eastern Front counteroffensive against the White forces of the Russian Civil War, he fought his first battle. "For all my life, I remembered the first battle in which although inexperienced, I, frankly speaking, suffered through with great fear."[1] A month latter at the end of May, he became a student in the Samarsk Military Engineer School. After military schooling, Rotmistrov again marched to the sound of cannons in the Russo-Polish War, August 1920. Assigned to the 16th Army, his actions and experience gave no portent of his later rapid rise within the Red Army during the war's darkest hours.

Pavel Alekseevich Rotmistrov (right) on the eve of the battle of Kursk, July 1943.

The new Bolshevik government's enemies were not always White forces and Allied intervention. As a student in the Smolensk Infantry School, Rotmistrov was called to action in March 1921, to put down the Kronstadt sailors' rebellion. In the bitter, bloody suppression of the sailors' revolt, he, as a rifleman, assaulted the sailors' island redoubt over an open, frozen waterway against a withering machinegun and artillery fire. Rotmistrov received a leg wound and subsequently awarded the Order of the Red Banner.

By fall 1922, Rotmistrov returned to military school, graduating in 1924. His first assignment as an officer was as platoon leader in the 31st Rifle Regiment, 11th Rifle Division near Leningrad, serving an uneventful tour of duty.

Dark-haired, with a large mustache, Rotmistrov wore a well-fitted uniform on his lean, medium height body. His dark, bushy eyebrows and broad forehead from a receding hairline suggested a brooding intellect. Often adjusting his black, rimmed glasses, Rotmistrov's appearance conveyed the look of a college professor. He spoke deliberately, ensuring his listener understood fully what was being said. From the beginning of his career, Rotmistrov demonstrated a strong inclination for study, receiving an appointment to the Frunze Military Academy. After graduating in May 1931, he became the chief of staff for the 36th Transbaikal Rifle Division, becoming involved in the small armed border clashes with the Japanese Kwantung Army along the Manchurian frontiers.

In the spring of 1933, his assignment to reconnoiter the Soviet and Manchurian border took him along the Argun river. The clarity and incisiveness of his reports greatly impressed his superiors and in a short time he was pulled from the division and given the position of deputy chief of operations for the Osobaya Krasnoznamennaya Dal'nevostochnaya Armiya (OKDVA) (Special Red Banner Far East Army). In 1935, his more responsible assignment as the chief of the armored forces at OKDVA made an indelible impression on Rotmistrov. "Perhaps, it was then I first truly became interested in tanks, not knowing, that not much longer in time, when I would be in the tankers' camp," Rotmistrov recalled.[2] He found excitement in the massed use of tanks and the concept of deep operations.

With promotion to Colonel in June 1937, Rotmistrov became commander of the 63rd Rifle Regiment, 21st Rifle Division. But, by October 1937, he returned to Moscow to attend the Workers and Peasants Red Army (RKKA) Motorized and Mechanized Military Academy (forerunner of the Malinovskii Armored Force Academy). As a perceptive thinker, Rotmistrov's intellectual prowess and academic nature showed in his armor studies. After completion of his studies at the Motorized and Mechanization Academy, he transferred to the Frunze Academy faculty to teach armored forces operations, and began his candidacy for a Military Science Doctorate, a candidacy drawn out by two wars.

The first war, the Russo-Finnish War, in November and December 1939, proved difficult for the Red Army, particularly Soviet tank forces. Catastrophic Russian defeats at the hands of a small Finnish Army sharply illustrated major Red Army shortcomings in preparations and capabilities for winter combat operations. Winter conditions in wooded, lake country combined with little experience in breakthrough operations over minefields, obstacles, and dug-in infantry positions offered just the crucible Rotmistrov sought to refine his understanding of tank warfare. A natural brainstormer, Rotmistrov welcomed the challenge.

Colonel Rotmistrov, requesting a command to gain practical experience and a chance to study tank operations, received a position in the operations section of the 7th Army. Upon arrival in the army, he asked to be sent forward to any kind of tank unit in the Karelian isthmus. Although he was sent to the 35th Light Tank Brigade, Rotmistrov asked for permission from the brigade chief of staff to observe tank combat action at one of the tank battalions. As it turned out, the tank battalion commander was killed in action prior to Rotmistrov's arrival, and Rotmistrov took command of the unit. He found himself leading an attack slated to begin the next morning.

Rotmistrov's tank battalion attacked with infantry. Advancing slowly, in order not to leave the infantry, the combined force approached Finnish defensive positions. Suddenly, a "squall" of artillery and machinegun fire stripped away the infantry, leaving tanks to maneuver unprotected through the obstacles. Antitank fire knocked out the exposed tanks. Rotmistrov's command tank, a T-26 light tank, received a direct hit instantly killing the gunner. Rotmistrov and his driver miraculously survived unharmed, and Rotmistrov's tank was evacuated from the battlefield.

At the command post, soldiers removed the dead gunner from the tank. Rotmistrov found a replacement and rejoined the fight with his tank. The subsequent battle, however, proved unsuccessful not only for Rotmistrov's tanks but also for the entire Red Army attack. Rotmistrov believed Soviet forces "required a different method of combat action."[3]

Tank operations in the Finnish War presented a number of problems. Red Army tankers lacked experience against fortified positions. The Finnish systematic defense combined with difficult terrain prevented decisive tank attacks. Tank use in northern regions suffered climatic difficulties in low temperatures which were especially hard on the T-26, light tanks, with air cooled engines. If the vehicles stopped for a few hours, the crews were not confident that they could get them moving again and took special measures to keep tanks warm. At dusk, the tankers dug a pit underneath the tanks for a small campfire that they kept going all night.

On 7 January 1940, the Red Army created the Northwestern Front under the command of Marshal Semen Konstantinovich Timoshenko. After a month of regrouping and preparation, a powerful strike group consisting of the 7th and 13th Armies renewed the offensive against Finland. The Red Army offensive achieved success. In the battle for the Karelian isthmus the 7th Army's 12 rifle divisions and five tank brigades which included Rotmistrov's tank unit received unit awards. Rotmistrov received personally the Order of the Red Star.

From the tank operations in the war, Rotmistrov began to realize the combat potential of tank units, as mobile groups, when used to penetrate the enemy defense. These mobile groups were created from a tank brigade, reinforced with an infantry battalion and sappers.[4] Experience in battle also demonstrated the advances in antitank fire and the requirement for stronger armor on tanks and more powerful main guns.

Publishing a series of articles in Red Star from August to December 1940, Rotmistrov, as a doctorate candidate in military science, discussed tank operations against the "White Finns." His articles covered topics on tank operations in winter conditions, security zones, mountains and against fortified defenses.[5] These early writings launched Rotmistrov's reputation as a tank operations expert that subsequently led the young colonel to the country's highest levels as a trusted adviser. Rotmistrov's articles advocated the use of massed tanks at a time when senior military leaders favored tanks only in direct infantry support.

In late 1940, the Red Army High Command, after much debate, concluded that it was necessary to create large armored formations in the form of mechanized corps. Each corps included two tank and one motorized divisions. The tank divisions consisted of two tank regiments, a motorized rifle regiment, and artillery regiment, air defense battalion and support units. Formation of the corps came in two stages: the first step in late 1940 created nine mechanized corps; and the second, February-March 1941, twenty.

In December 1940, Rotmistrov's assignment as deputy commander of the 5th Tank Division, 3rd Mechanized Corps in the Baltic Military District gave him first-hand knowledge that the hasty formation of the large armored units proved too ambitious. The corps was authorized a total of 1011 tanks of various types to include 126 KV heavy and 420 T-34 medium tanks. However, the 3rd Mechanized Corps totaled 640 tanks, one of the most equipped of all the corps, but, most of the corps' tanks were light with only 52 KV and 50 T-34 tanks. The 5th Tank Division, located in Alitus, had insufficient parts and equipment on-hand for repairs and no communications equipment. With these shortcomings, Rotmistrov began the task of training and preparing the division for combat.

Five months later, Rotmistrov became chief of staff for the 3rd Mechanized Corps. The corps' subordinate divisions were spread throughout Latvia: the 2nd Tank Division northwest of Kaunus in Raseinyai, the 84th Motorized Rifle Division east of Kaunus in Kaishyadoras, and the 5th Tank Division south of the city of Alitus.

On 21 June 1941, hours before the German invasion through Latvia, Colonel General Fedor Isidorovich Kuznetsov, Baltic Military District commander, arrived in the 3rd Mechanized Corps headquarters. Rotmistrov, in the middle of a report to his corps commander, joined in greeting the senior commander. General Kuznetsov, acknowledging the greeting and without any preface, informed them of a potential surprise attack by Germany within two days. He directed the corps to deploy on the pretext of a field training exercise and move its units from the towns to wooded areas. The corps was to begin preparations for combat action. The corps headquarters established communications with 2nd Tank and 84th Motorized Divisions and with the 11th Army to which the 5th Tank Division would reinforce.

The Baltic Military District became redesignated the Northwestern Front. In June 1941, the Northwestern Front consisted of the 8th and 11th Rifle Armies and the 3rd and 12th Mechanized Corps.

At 0400 hours, 22 June 1941, German warplanes struck airfields, key railroad centers, ports, and major towns throughout the Baltic region. Simultaneously, heavy artillery fired along the German-Latvian border. Rotmistrov, in the corps headquarters, heard the rumble of the artillery preparation announcing the German invasion.

Between 0530 and 0600 hours, German troops crossed the border in the attack. Three hours later, the German 4th Panzer Group in a hard-driving assault overwhelmed a thinly spread Soviet frontier rifle forces, advancing quickly and deeply in the direction of Rotmistrov's corps. The 4th Panzer Group by evening achieved the Dubissa river, 35 kilometers northwest of Kaunus. Meanwhile, the German 3rd Panzer Group crossed the Neman river in the vicinity of Alitus.

Attempting to impede the invading Germans, and particularly the 3rd Panzer Group, the 11th Army commander threw the 5th Tank Division into battle. The tank division succeeded only in moving the artillery of its motorized rifle regiment, a tank battalion, and the air defense artillery to the bridge at Alitus. Despite a courageous defensive effort, they only delayed the German 39th Panzer Corps for one hour.

The next day Northwestern Front prepared a counterstrike, using two divisions, one rifle and a motorized rifle, to cover the areas of Shyaulya, Kaunus, Vilnius while parts of three tank divisions conducted an attack. Two tank divisions of the 12th Mechanized Corps were to attack from the area of Shyaulya in a southerly direction, and the 2nd Tank Division from Rotmistrov's 3rd Mechanized Corps would attack across Raseinyai to the west. However, by midday, the two corps failed to attack. The 12th Mechanized Corps had been struck four times by German dive-bombers and suffered heavy losses. The 3rd Mechanized Corps attempted to attack with no success.

Meanwhile, 11th Army reports informed Rotmistrov that the 5th Tank Division suffered heavy losses near Alitus and withdrew to Vilnius. On 24 June, the 2nd Tank Division, 3rd Mechanized Corps resisted German attacks, but, by the end of the day, it was out of fuel and ammunition. The German's parallel attacks towards Daugavpils and Shyaulya engulfed both flanks of the tank division, encircling it.

Hour by hour the situation grew worse. The 3rd Mechanized Corps lost communications with the 11th Army, and Rotmistrov's staff knew little of what was happening in their sector. Only after the fact did Rotmistrov learn that the Germans had captured Kaunus, and General Erich von Manstein's 56th Panzer Corps advanced to the area of Ionvary, 30 kilometers north of Kaunus. The German thrust separated the forward defending 11th and 8th Armies. Attempts to restore the situation by the 11th Army proved useless. German forces penetrated to the 2nd Tank Division and 3rd Mechanized Corps headquarters inflicting serious losses on the staffs. The battle continued until sunset when Rotmistrov's commander withdrew the 3rd Mechanized Corps deep into nearby woods. The 2nd Tank Division had no more than 10 tanks remaining. The division and corps were encircled by the relentless advance of German units, forcing the corps commander to attempt a breakout eastward. The corps commander ordered the consolidation of fuel and ammunition from unservicable tanks, preparing the few ready combat vehicles.

For nearly two months, remnants of the 3rd Mechanized Corps moved through the woods of Belorussia north of Bryansk. Moving at night around towns, villages, the group attacked small German targets in the rear area. With their personal weapons, documents and importantly their party cards, they reentered the Soviet lines. After fighting out of the encirclement, Rotmistrov was ordered to Moscow.

In Moscow, Rotmistrov met with the Chief of Red Army Armored Forces, Lieutenant General Yakov Nikolaevich Fedorenko.

"You're alive!" General Fedorenko squeezed Rotmistrov's shoulder and offered him, in a familiar tone, rather than as a subordinate, a seat on the couch. They talked about the Red Army's unpreparedness for war. Then, General Fedorenko familiarized Rotmistrov with the situation along the front from the Karelian isthmus to the Black Sea. Rotmistrov could not believe how much territory the Germans had seized in two months while he escaped from behind German lines.

"But now more immediate matters," General Fedorenko announced opening a folder with documents located in front of him. The papers were Rotmistrov's service records. General Fedorenko continued, "In connection with the great losses in armored equipment and the inability to replace them in near future the Supreme High Command decided to reform the mechanized corps."

"And what's next?" Rotmistrov asked.

"We collect everything that is remaining, including repaired and training tanks, hurry industry with fulfilling our orders, form separate tank battalions, regiments, and brigades, " Fedorenko replied. He explained the evacuation of the factories to the east, and the wait for their output. Until then no large units could be created, and they would have to change the tactics of the current units to husband resources for later. After eyeing the service records, General Fedorenko looked at Rotmistrov, and unexpectedly informed him, "It has been suggested to designate you, Pavel Alekseevich, Chief of Staff of the Red Army Armored Forces."

Noting the dissatisfied look on Rotmistrov's face, General Fedorenko quickly added, "You have experience on a large staff, theoretical studies, and after all, you taught at the academy, a candidate...."

"So, I find myself already beaten on this," Rotmistrov smiled ironically.

"But, you know, for one battle, two supporting actions are taken. It's not your fault. To fight as best you can."

"I still must prove...."

"Here's a funny man," interrupted an irritated Fedorenko. "Him, a colonel, they suggest the position of a Lieutenant General, but he, you see, is pig headed! Even above pride in yourself that the choice fell just to you!"

"Thanks for the confidence." Rotmistrov rose from the couch. "Only it is better duty at the front, I don't mind commanding a regiment or a battalion. I must fight, not write paper...."

The General's eyes flashed angrily, "You turn up a hero! And I, according to you, waste paper here? I shirk from the front?!" raged Fedorenko waving his hands.

"Go, and you still think over well my suggestion," said the General in a cold and formal manner.[6]

General Fedorenko wanted this brilliant man beside him working the very difficult problems in organizing Red Army tank forces. However, he used the wrong appeal to entice Rotmistrov to his staff. Authority based on position, rank or title did not impress Rotmistrov. General Fedorenko should have emphasized the greater opportunity and contribution to build a Red Army tank force from ashes.

Rotmistrov, determined to resist the staff position, decided to write a letter to Stalin, and delivered it to the Kremlin. In a few days, Rotmistrov received a summons to General Fedorenko's office.

"So, the petitioner appears! Who suggested to you to personally appeal to Comrade Stalin?" General Fedorenko uttered in a threateningly deep voice. But, Rotmistrov detected that the general had used the familiar "you" which he guessed meant his request had been granted.

"It came to me, myself, comrade lieutenant general."[7]

General Fedorenko informed Rotmistrov that he would receive remnants of the 2nd Tank Division, survivors from the border battles, to be reformed into the 8th Tank Brigade. As Rotmistrov would later write, "At that time all of us Soviet commanders understood the Motherland was in danger."[8] The imperative to command at the front was compelling.

In the village of Kostyrevo, 120 kilometers southeast of Moscow, Rotmistrov met old acquaintances from the early days of the war. His brigade commissar was the division commissar, Nikolai Vasilevich Shatalov, and chief of staff was Major Mikhail Antonovich Lyubetskii.

The formation of the 8th Tank Brigade had to be done quickly. It consisted of the 8th Tank Regiment with 61 tanks, 7 heavy KV, 22 T-34's, and 32 light T-40's.[9] Completing the refit task, Rotmistrov personally informed General Fedorenko of the brigade's readiness for combat. Orders soon followed that transferred Rotmistrov's brigade to the Northwestern Front.

Lieutenant General Pavel Alekseevich Kurochkin, a well-known and respected military leader who had served with the Red Guard in the storming of the Winter Palace, commanded the Northwestern Front. He directed the fight against German Army Group North that had penetrated to the southern edge of Lake Ladoga by Petrokreposti (Shlisselburg), blockading the land routes to Leningrad. The Northerwestern Front forces crossed the Lovat river in the area of Staroi Russi striking the southern wing of the German 16th Army. The German command responded by transferring additional forces from the Northern and Central Army Groups. However, by 20 September 1941, the German attacks on Leningrad had been worn to a stop.

The Front commander briefed Rotmistrov that his brigade would be assigned to the 11th Army, and with the 26th Rifle Division, make an attack in the direction of Luzhno. Rotmistrov arrived at the 11th Army command post on 23 September to receive his attack orders for the following morning. Rotmistrov with his chief of staff, Major Lyubetskii, posted the situation on the map and received a status report from the subordinate units. The tank regiment commander, Major Aleksandr Vasilevich Egorov, was also called to the command post. Familiarizing the tank commander with the army order, Rotmistrov directed him to prepare for offensive action by the next morning. Rotmistrov looked at the major – he did not respond quickly with answers.

"Something you don't understand?" Rotmistrov finally asked the major.

"Time is short, comrade colonel. I must carry out a personal reconnaissance, study the enemy defensive position, organize coordination with the infantry and artillery. Besides, diesel fuel for the heavy tanks has not been brought up. We still don't have maps for the area of the upcoming operation."

Rotmistrov knew that he should not attack his arriving tank unit straight from the railroad platform, but the situation required an immediate strike against the Germans. "In the developing situation,"

Rotmistrov explained, "your regiment must make do tomorrow or it won't be successful. Your maps you'll get from the brigade chief of staff, the heavy tank company remains as my reserve, and by 1700 hours report your decision."

"Everything clear," saluted Major Egorov. "Allow me to carry on."[10]

In the quiet woods, the brigade's combat preparations began. Using tractors without mufflers to simulate large tank movements, Rotmistrov demonstrated an inventiveness and extra effort in tactical deception that was not widely practiced by his contemporaries in the first months of the war.[11]

Major Aleksandr Egorov returned from his reconnaissance with a plan of attack. To better coordinate the combat actions between the medium and light tanks, Rotmistrov suggested the medium tanks with their firepower and thicker armor protection pave the way, destroying artillery positions and German tanks. He wanted the light tanks to concentrate on destroying enemy machinegun nests, infantry, armored transports and vehicles.[12]

As darkness fell, Rotmistrov returned to the brigade command post, spending an anxious night worrying about the Germans who might have decided to attack. Apprehensive how his first battle would turn out for his recently formed and untested brigade, he did not fall asleep, but relentlessly tossed through the remainder of the night.

Early the next morning, Rotmistrov from his observation post watched through binoculars as his lead tank battalion attacked along the Demyansk highway. His second tank battalion followed on the right. Behind the tanks, infantry rose up and advanced. "Youngsters," Rotmistrov thought, "correctly going in together."[13]

The tank battalions breaking through strong resistance pushed aggressively into the German defense. When the advance slowed, Rotmistrov called for a report over the radio. Major Egorov informed him that the Germans counterattacked with about 20 tanks supported by self-propelled assault guns from the grove to the right of the road in Demyansk. Another 15 German tanks attacked from another direction, prompting Major Egorov to call for artillery and heavy tank support.

Rotmistrov directed him to immediately throw an engineer mobile obstacle detachment across the highway. Turning to the heavy tank company commander beside him in the command post,

Rotmistrov ordered the heavy tanks to move quickly along the highway, assisting the lead battalion.

The rapid response repelled the German tank attack, but fighting continued for the remainder of the day with the Germans strongly fortifying the village of Luzhno. Rotmistrov's brigade was unable to dislodge them. With his tanks holding on the present line of advance, he ordered the resupply of ammunition and fuel, intending to resume the attack the next morning.

After a good first day showing followed by complete preparations for the attack, the next morning the brigade chief of staff, Major Lyubetskii, informed Rotmistrov that the Germans captured the tank regiment's chief of staff. "In war, joy is always accompanied by grief," Rotmistrov quipped.[14] Fortunately, the captured regimental chief of staff gave no advantage to the Germans.

After a short artillery preparation, the attack began against the German occupied village, and by mid morning Major Egorov reported success. Rotmistrov drove to the regimental commander's observation post on the southwest side of the village, directing him to move his forces to cut off the German withdrawal. As the tank battalions moved forward, they reported the roads to Demyansk mined. Belatedly discovered after the loss of three tanks. Rotmistrov along with the regimental commander drove forward to the tank battalions. Standing in the battalion's observation post beside the road, the battalion's chief of staff met them and reported that the battalion commander was forward personally in charge of the battalion.

Extricating themselves from the minefield, the tanks deployed in a line, all within a few hundred meters of each other. But, they floundered in marshy ground, sinking up to the tank bottoms. One after another the tanks became stuck. If the tanks managed to free themselves, they skidded, became stuck again, straining the tank engines. Soviet tanks were not immune to the Russian mud. Rotmistrov hoped they would remain undetected from German warplanes while his brigade recovered itself.

For seven days, the 8th Tank Brigade fought in the direction of Demyansk. The brigade's 10 kilometer advance was hailed in Pravda.[15] The Soviet press was desperate to publish any good news from the fighting front.

In the beginning of October, General Kurochkin decided to conduct another attack, to preempt German efforts against Leningrad with the 8th Tank Brigade, fighting as part of the 84th Rifle Division. Available intelligence on the Germans indicated they occupied strongly prepared positions. In wargaming the situation with his staff and commanders, Rotmistrov decided the operation required deceptive actions in order to achieve success. He noted woods on the right flank near the German position and the ravine on the left. Throughout the night, Rotmistrov moved a tank imitating a large number of tanks through the woods, drawing the Germans' attention in the wrong direction. The brigade's main force using the ravine quietly drew up on the left flank and waited for the attack signal in the morning.

The false brigade location in the woods drew German artillery fire. With three green rocket flares, the brigade attacked at 0800 hours on the opposite side of the sector, surprising the Germans. Moving forward, Major Egorov reported no losses in tanks, but asked for artillery support. Rotmistrov directed him to use his heavy tanks against the German artillery and increase the speed of the advance.

Advancing into the German position, Rotmistrov's tanks encountered antitank fire, slowing the Soviet attack under the weight of German defensive fires and counterattacks. As the battle dragged out, Rotmistrov drove forward to the regimental tank commander's command post for a closer look at the action. The heavy tanks advanced into the German defensive line, but the light and medium tanks with motorized infantry were unable to widen the penetration. The Germans paid heavily for their stand against Rotmistrov's relentless attack and the resulting exchange of fires.

Rotmistrov returned to his command post and found General Fedorenko who was visiting the Northwestern Front to study the use of tanks. Rotmistrov summarized his problems, explaining that he would have better success with more artillery and air support. He told the General how the tank brigade went into the attack from the march with little preparation and brigade commanders had no time for reconnaissance of the terrain nor to study the German defenses.

On 13 October 1941, Rotmistrov received a summons from General Pavel Kurochkin. As Rotmistrov walked into the commander's room, he easily guessed there was trouble. Motioning to a map on a nearby table, General Kurochkin paused and contemplated how he would address the situation. The Germans had just launched "Operation Typhoon" with the intention to drive for Moscow. German forces struck against Bryansk and Orel, initiating terrible battles around Vyazma. As General Kurochkin recounted the situation he was interrupted by the appearance of Lieutenant General Nikolai Fedorovich Vatutin, Front Chief of Staff, and Colonel Pavel Pavlovich Poluboyarov, the chief of armored forces. Rotmistrov knew them both.

"Well, what do you have new for us?" General Kurochkin asked Vatutin.

General Vatutin bent over the map and explained the situation along the Western Front. The Germans were poring troops into an 80 kilometer wide gap. He believed the Germans were ready to attempt a strike for Kalinin in the Northwestern Front sector, driving for Yaroslavl and Rybinsk, due north of Moscow.

The Soviet High Command had ordered General Kurochkin to move part of his forces to the Kalinin area. General Kurochkin believed there was a possibility that Germans would deploy along the Moscow-Leningrad highway. He created a mobile group consisting of two rifle and two cavalry divisions and Rotmistrov's tank brigade as a powerful strike force. General Vatutin would command the mobile group.

General Vatutin, not moving from the map, assigned Rotmistrov his mission. "In a short time the infantry and cavalry will concentrate here," General Vatutin indicated with a pencil the town, Vyshnii Volochek. "Your brigade reinforced with a motorcycle regiment will operate as the group's forward detachment. You are to force march not later than the morning of 15 October from the area of Valdaya to Vyshnii Volochek, and then towards Kalinin with the mission to prevent enemy tanks penetrating to Torzhok and Kalinin."

"What can we do to help comrade Rotmistrov?" General Kurochkin addressed Colonel Poluboyarov, the Front's chief of armored forces.

"In Valdaya are the Front's maintenance shops. But, unfortunately, we don't have tanks," Colonel Poluboyarov replied.

Looking at the map, Rotmistrov noted his birth place, the village of Skovorovo. Rotmistrov was now defending his childhood home from the German invaders. General Kurochkin touched Rotmistrov's shoulder, "Pavel Alekseevich, it seems you are a native to this area? We hope that this in some way makes it easier to fulfill your assigned missions."[16]

By evening, Rotmistrov returning to his brigade command post instructed the staff to concentrate the tank brigade and the motor-cycle regiment in Valdaya. After setting the plan in motion, he laid on his cot for a rest, but could not sleep. This fight was too close to home.

The 8th Tank Brigade had 49 operational tanks: 7 heavy KV's, 10 medium T-34's, and 32 light T-60's.[17] Launching the attack at the designated time, Rotmistrov's force moved in three echelons. He led with the motorcycle regiment along the Leningrad highway re-inforced by the fast, light tanks. Behind them moved the medium tanks, followed by the heavy. With each tank column, Rotmistrov assigned a maintenance section and a refueling vehicle, allowing repairs during rest stops.

Rotmistrov liked the weather, cool and dry, but cloudy. The cloudy weather held the German air force at bay. By midday, mov-ing at maximum speed his force advanced to Vyshnii Volochek. Cal-culating the Germans would already be on the move, Rotmistrov warned his tank regiment commander to be prepared for a meeting engagement.

By the regulations, tank forces moved 60 kilometers in a day, and force marched 80 kilometers, Rotmistrov had moved his main force nearly 200 kilometers; his forward detachment, 240 kilome-ters. Time is often an enemy in war, but Rotmistrov moved his force quickly in the tradition of the famed Russian Generalissimo Aleksandr Suvorov who was obsessed with the idea of speed. Suvorov believed, "One day decides the fate of empires, one hour the success of a campaign, one minute the outcome of a battle...I operate not by hours but by minutes."[18]

The brigade arrived in its jump-off positions at 1400 hours, and launched its attack at 1630 hours, 15 October.[19] The objective of Kalinin was within grasp. The commander of the forward detach-ment reported that he had the Gorbatov Bridge, over the Volga river, on the northern approach to Kalinin, after pushing off a German reconnaissance unit. With no time for a post-march rest, Rotmistrov decided to penetrate the city. He asked for and received the 934th Rifle Regiment, operating northwest of Kalinin. But, German panzer and panzer grenadier units forestalled the tank brigade by attack-ing the rifle regiment. Rotmistrov responded, sending a tank unit to assist the infantry in repelling the German attack. The Germans with-drew to Kalinin. Rotmistrov ordered the tank regiment commander to reorganize his reconnaissance and exploit the success. Major

Egorov, within an hour, reported German tanks in the village of Malitsa and south, but he did not know how many and was unable to stop them.

Rotmistrov approved Major Egorov's decision to deploy the first tank battalion toward the north, by the village of Staroye Kalikino. The second tank battalion would strike in the direction of Malitsa and be prepared to move to the Gorbatov Bridge. Rotmistrov informed Major Egorov that the attack would be without artillery support since it had not yet arrived. Additionally, Rotmistrov had the 934th Rifle Regiment attack on the southern edge of Malitsa and the 46th Motorcycle Regiment attack on the northwest approach to Kalinin.

Coordinating the assault, three red rockets signaled the attack. As the tank brigade attacked, Rotmistrov moved between the first and second echelon to quickly respond to actions on the battlefield. The heavy tanks advanced firing from short stops. German fighter-bombers appeared, but primarily struck the motorcycle regiment. When the first tank battalion reported encountering 30 German tanks with motorized infantry, Rotmistrov ordered Major Egorov to delay the German tanks with 3-4 tanks fighting from ambush while the main force attacked the flank. Rotmistrov wanted to crowd the German force into low ground for destruction by artillery in direct fire and antitank weapons. When the German tanks were within 400 meters, part of the first tank battalion opened a withering fire, while the remainder of the battalion, directed to move at maximum speed, simultaneously struck the Germans in the flank. The second tank battalion facing to the northwest interdicted the German's withdrawal routes, firing from halted positions on the trapped German tanks. Rotmistrov's brigade pursued the withdrawing Germans, moving across the Gorbatov Bridge. The 8th Tank Brigade penetrated the western edge of Kalinin while the motorcycle regiment encountered a German counterattack, forcing the motorcyclists onto the defense.

For two days the battle for Kalinin raged. Rotmistrov learned from captured documents that his units were fighting the 36th Panzer Grenadier and 6th Panzer Divisions. By midafternoon on 16 October, the large German armored force began maneuvering against Rotmistrov's flank. Despite the strong resistance, Rotmistrov's losses became evident, more than half of his tanks. The 46th Motorcycle Regiment also sustained significant losses.

The following day, the Germans violently attacked and penetrated to Rotmistrov's brigade headquarters in Malitsa, killing the brigade chief of staff, Major M.A. Lyubetskii. "We all endured this very terrible loss," Rotmistrov recalled.[20] The brigade also suffered serious losses in many of the company and battalion commanders. Major Egorov survived, reporting a total of 10 tanks remaining in good repair.

With the reprieve of dusk, Rotmistrov decided to withdraw his depleted force behind the Tvertsa river, then transition to the defense. To conceal the tank brigade's withdrawal from the Germans, he directed a few tanks and tractors to move along the front line during the night to imitate regrouping a large number of tanks. The deception worked well and the Germans did not attempt to pursue. In fact, Rotmistrov heard of his demise over the German radio net. The Germans reported that the 8th Tank Brigade had been defeated, and its commander, Colonel Rotmistrov, had been killed on the battlefield.[21]

On the morning of 18 October, Rotmistrov met with all his regimental and battalion commanders for reassigning leadership positions due to the losses in commanders. He also took the opportunity to review the situation and impressed upon them their mission not to allow the Germans towards Torzhok.

One commander, noting the number of German tanks present expressed his doubts on the brigade's ability to accomplish the mission. Rotmistrov responded, "Here now, as never before, we must fight not with numbers but with skill." As he looked at the grim young faces of his commanders, Rotmistrov gave a practical course of action. "In counterattacks against large enemy tank groups on open terrain, don't turn, exposing your flank. To fight them fire your tank and antitank guns from ambush."[22] All available guns were needed, even tanks with damaged motors. They were to be dug in along the roadside.

Fortunately for the beleaguered tank brigade, the Germans did not continue to attack in the tank brigade's sector. General Vatutin removed Rotmistrov's brigade from the defensive line in order to reconstitute itself and prepare for further combat operations.

The importance of the Kalinin sector prompted the Soviet High Command to create the Kalinin Front under the command of Colonel Ivan Stepanovich Konev on 17 October. The Kalinin Front included the 22nd, 29th, 30th, 31st Armies and General Vatutin's operational group. Immediately, the Front commander ordered General Vatutin's operational group to conduct a counterstrike destroying Germans to the west of Kalinin. The 8th Tank Brigade's mission was to attack from the south and in cooperation with the 185th Rifle Division, eliminating Germans in the assigned area. After launching the attack, the operational group was placed under the 31st Army on 19 October, and remained with the army until the end of the month when operations stabilized around Kalinin.

In the beginning of November, Rotmistrov received a mission for his tank brigade from the 31st Army. The 8th Tank Brigade, without the 46th Motorcycle Regiment, but with the 243rd Rifle Division, was to penetrate to Izbrizhe, 25 kilometers southwest of Kalinin, destroying German units across the Volga river. Then, Rotmistrov's brigade was to operate on both sides of the Volga in the direction of Staritsy, 65 kilometers southwest of Kalinin, destroying from ambush German supply columns. Rotmistrov's mission to operate on both sides of a river that could only be crossed by bridges was very ambitious under any circumstances. His tank brigade was in no shape for the task, as the 8th Tank Brigade had not had time to quickly repair tanks from the previous battles.

"Comrade brigade commander, you know we are caught in some kind of hell!" Major Egorov exclaimed when he saw the situation marked on the map.

"It's nothing, Aleksandr Vasilevich. We're just in a different scrape. You and your eagle courage for daring are not interested?" Rotmistrov prodded.[23]

Under darkness and low visibility, the brigade moved through the mixed snow and rain. At dawn the next morning, lead tanks brushed aside a German infantry unit and captured Zaborovem. As the falling snow became worse, Rotmistrov's brigade continued moving forward. At distances of 200-300 meters, the Soviet tanks were invisible to the Germans. By midday, the brigade unexpectedly came upon a large German supply column, destroying it. By night fall, Rotmistrov forward in the tank regiment command post planned the attack to take Isbrizhe and push the Germans across the Volga river.

"How many combat ready vehicles are in the regiment, carrying ammunition and fuel?" Rotmistrov queried.

"Twenty six in good repair, comrade brigade commander," Major Egorov replied. "The tankers with fuel and the vehicles with ammunition will within the hour replenish them."

"This is fine," Rotmistrov, beginning to assign the mission, acknowledged.[24]

After the tank regiment rested, at approximately 2300 hours, it moved into position for a dawn attack against Isbrizhe from two sides. Within an hour of the attack, the regiment secured the town. The decisive actions of the 8th Tank Brigade gave the Germans the impression of a large force operating west of Kalinin. Fearing encirclement, the German command committed reinforcements against Rotmistrov's unit.

At an operational level, the Germans were making a major drive for Moscow, on a northern approach, in mid-November 1941. At the tactical level, Rotmistrov and other commanders were not aware of the German plans. But each Soviet commander saw the manifestation of the German effort in increased air activity and a relentless drive to bypass Soviet forces.

On 13 November, a large German force attempting to go around the 243rd Rifle Division threatened the division with encirclement. At this critical time, Rotmistrov was in the division commander's observation post and advised him to immediately withdraw his rifle units while Rotmistrov's tank brigade covered them. But, the division commander did not agree, citing his orders to attack.

"What's to attack? You are ruining the division," Rotmistrov said challenging the division commander.

"You wait, don't get emotional. We must wait for reports from the units and pass them to the army staff," the division commander replied trying to remain inwardly calm.

At that moment they heard machinegun shots. In the next few minutes, Rotmistrov's driver appeared in the house shouting, "Comrade Colonel, Fascist tanks! Quickly to the vehicle."[25]

The division commander handed his map to his adjutant and left with Rotmistrov. In the street, the two commanders saw as they escaped the zone of fire by 15 German tanks, firing on the move and bearing down on the village.

Rotmistrov returned to his command post. His chief of staff, Captain Krasnov, reported that he had received information about a large German tank force moving east of the 243rd Rifle Division which was covering their left flank. Rotmistrov coordinated with the division commander a plan for withdrawing to a new line of defense.

The next morning Rotmistrov worked tying in defensive lines on the Lama river. His units did not have contact with 16th Army on the left flank. And, on the right, the 46th Motorcycle Regiment assumed the defense while Rotmistrov used his tank and motorized rifle battalions to cover the center of the sector.

On 15 November, the Germans going around Rotmistrov's sector, struck the 30th Army with a large force, penetrating to the Volga river. The Kalinin Front commander moved reinforcing rifle and cavalry divisions from his reserves to the east bank of the Volga. The following day the German's 3rd Panzer Group attacked in the direction of Klin-Solnechenogorsk, south of the Moscow sea, bringing to bear two panzer divisions in an attempt to force the Lama river in the 8th Tank Brigade's sector. Rotmistrov's brigade, along with the 107th Motorized Rifle Division, held against these attacks. However, the weight of the German offensive eventually secured crossings over the Lama on the left flank of the 107th Motorized Rifle Division. By late afternoon, on 16 November, the 30th Army was in a difficult situation.

At this critical juncture, Major General Dmitri Danilovich Lelyushenko assumed command of the 30th Army. Rotmistrov did not envy General Lelyushenko's predicament. In a difficult position, General Lelyushenko required time to understand the situation, establish communications with his units and determine the combat capabilities of his force and continue to repulse the Germans. General Lelyushenko's subsequent actions and perseverance earned Rotmistrov's respect.[26]

The situation worsened each day as the 8th Tank Brigade and the 107th Division fought as separate groups, half encircled. Despite the stubborn stand, Rotmistrov had to withdraw his unit to Klin. Ground was given grudgingly and always traded for time. The Soviet forces' strong resistance on the northwest approach to Moscow had important operational significance in allowing the Soviet High Command to muster reinforcements for the sector. By the latter half of November, additional Red Army forces from the Far East began arriving to resist the German advance. On 17 November, two cavalry division and a tank brigade were sent to the 30th Army.

General Georgi K. Zhukov, Western Front commander, ordered the formation of an operational group for the defense of Klin. The group consisted of a rifle and cavalry division and the 8th and 25th Tank Brigades. The group was commanded by the deputy commander of the 16th Army, Major General Fedor Dmitrievich Zakharov.

Ordered to attack immediately, Rotmistrov's brigade, on 24 November, executed a successful surprise attack on the advancing Germans. "The mission was not an easy one," Rotmistrov remembered. "In my instructions at this time was a significantly low number of tanks. I understood that I could not make the usual tank attack against such a superior force. I had to find a way quickly out of the unfolding situation."[27] Rotmistrov decided to mass machinegun fire with artillery and tank fire by forming a small motorized detachment of two medium tanks, two armored vehicles and 34 machineguns in other vehicles. The improvised method allowed the tank brigade to hold its position.

By 30 November, the 8th Tank Brigade was pulled to the relative safety of the 30th Army's second echelon. The next day, the 30th Army temporarily assumed a defensive sector around Dmitrov along the Volga river. Two days later, a directive from the Western Front ordered the 30th Army, on 5 December, in coordination with the 1st Shock Army to capture Klin from the north. Called to General Lelyushenko's command post, Rotmistrov received a update on the situation and his orders for the offensive. The 8th Tank Brigade was to attack in coordination with the 365th Rifle Division. General Lelyushenko had decided to begin the attack without an artillery preparation. Rotmistrov was in complete agreement with the decision.[28] The Germans had not had time to build a strong defensive position and the army's wide sector could not be covered by the artillery. The sudden attack with Rotmistrov's tanks could achieve surprise.

The attack had been delayed from 5 to 6 December. The cold weather produced temperatures dropping 20 degrees below zero. The extra day allowed more preparation for battle and more coordination with the rifle units. The signal for the attack came at 0600 hours, two hours before the winter dawn. Rotmistrov was in the observation post of the rifle division as riflemen captured a couple of villages and conducted a surprise attack from the north for Zabolote.

In the approach to Zabolote, Rotmistrov's brigade forward detachment encountered a mined portion of the road. The tank regiment stopped.

"What's happening? Why are you not moving?" Rotmistrov asked the regimental commander.

"The road is mined and the regiment has no sappers with mine detectors," the tank commander answered.

Alarmed by the obstacle's impact on the operation, Rotmistrov drove immediately to the mined road. He checked the situation and with a group of machinegunners turned over the snow beside the road in a small wooded area. They found no mines. He ordered the brigade's main force to attack towards Zabolote not in a straight line along the road but along the woods.[29]

Across the next few days the Soviet's offensive continued to roll through a number of small villages widening a gap of 20 kilometers or more in the German line. The 8th Tank Brigade moving along the Klin-Kalinin highway and attacking Yamuga, by 9 December, occupied a sector southwest of Klin. The 30th Army moved into a position to retake Klin. On 12 December, assessing the situation, General Lelyushenko decided to attack the nearly encircled German forces in Klin. He created an army mobile group consisting of the 8th and 21st Tank Brigades, 145th Separate Tank Battalion, and 2nd Motorized and 46th Motorcycle Regiments under the command of Colonel Rotmistrov.

On 13 December, Rotmistrov's mobile group attacked. After a good start, the group engaged in heavy combat as it advanced on Klin. By the morning of 15 December, the Germans reacted strongly against Rotmistrov's group. Under heavy artillery and mortar support, the Germans counterattacked with tanks and aircraft. However, by midday, the 30th and 1st Shock Armies recaptured Klin, defeating the defending Germans.

The successful Soviet operations by the Kalinin and Western Fronts held the Germans out of Moscow. Rewards were forthcoming. The 8th Tank Brigade for its efforts was redesignated the 3rd Guards Tank Brigade, and Colonel Rotmistrov won the Order of Lenin, concluding three months of continuous combat action for the brigade.

The operational-tactical maneuvering of Rotmistrov's brigade from October to February 1942, was conducted on three Fronts – Northwestern, Kalinin, and Western – and in seven armies. Rotmistrov found it hard to recall "how many times I went to coordinate combat actions with different rifle divisions and regiments."[30]

The use of tank brigades in the counteroffensive around Moscow showed that larger tank formations were necessary for conducting deep operations at a high tempo. Tank brigades expended themselves in support of rifle army's tactical battles and could not carry the Front offensive into the operational depths.

With the heavy industry relocated in the east and out of harm's way combined with the valuable lessons of the 1941-42 winter counteroffensive, the Stavka Supreme High Command decided in spring 1942, to form twenty tank corps and two tank armies. Rotmistrov was assigned to form the 7th Tank Corps in the area of Kalinin and to prepare it for upcoming operations. The corps consisted of the 3rd Guards, 62nd and 87th Tank Brigades, the 7th Motorized Rifle Brigade, a reconnaissance battalion, air defense artillery battalion, a separate guards mortar (Katyusha rocket) battalion, and rear support units. The size and strength of the tank corps created a powerful fighting unit, numbering 5600 men, 168 tanks, 32 field and antitank guns, 20 antiaircraft guns, 44 mortars and 8 Katyusha rocket launchers.[31] With the new operational capabilities came new missions. The independent tactical-operational missions for which a tank corps could be employed brought many unanticipated, demanding problems for its commanders.

Because of the close relationship with infantry units and small tank units in the defensive battles, the concept of operating tank units separate from the infantry seemed inconceivable for many tank corps commanders. The corps did not have staff experience in controlling tanks in such free flowing actions. Rotmistrov believed the time had come for commanders to quickly reorient their thinking and master new, more complicated methods and forms of armored warfare. The new large tank formation commanders needed to study bold commitments to penetrations, aggressive maneuvers, daring and forceful attacks and counterattacks on the enemy, forcing one's will upon him.[32] Commanders and staff had to master a flexible and operational control of tank formations in battles and operations, ensuring continuous, close coordination among tanks, infantry, artillery and aviation.

Rotmistrov, as with other successful tank commanders, emphasized the importance of the tank drivers' training. The success of the maneuver and effective firing of the tank depended on a good driver. If the driver was weak in his skills the effective potential of the tank in battle would not be realized. A driver, too slow to stop or move, risked the tank. Poor maneuvering along the terrain spoiled quick shots and offered a silhouetted tank as a target. Consequently, Rotmistrov strongly demanded special care "for the selection of this central figure in tank crews."[33]

Field training on a broader scope had its concerns also. The massing of the tanks into larger units was more difficult. Rotmistrov trained his junior commanders about the implications of employing different types of tanks with different tactical missions. For example, a tank company moving from its attack position in the offense, especially without roads, inherently had the difficult problem of the different types of tanks moving at different speeds and arriving at the attack line at different times. Control and coordination was further complicated by different tanks with different radios.

As the Germans successfully renewed the offensive in the Voronezh area towards Stalingrad in the summer of 1942, the Soviet High Command transferred two rifle armies and the 5th Tank Army which included the 2nd, 7th, and 11th Tank Corps, one rifle division and a separate tank brigade to the Bryansk Front. The 7th Tank Corps finished its formation at the end of July as part of the 5th Tank Army and moved to the town of Elets. From the train station, the corps moved to an assembly area 20-25 kilometers southwest of Elets. Upon arrival, Rotmistrov was met by Colonel General Aleksandr Mikhailovich Vasilevskii, chief of the Red Army General Staff. He gave Rotmistrov the mission to immediately move west and protect the arrival and deployment of the remainder of the 5th Tank Army. General Vasilevskii was not sure where the German forward elements were located, so he advised Rotmistrov to be prepared for a meeting engagement.

Rotmistrov called his commanders together and ordered them to be prepared immediately for marching. Leading with a reconnaissance group, Rotmistrov's tank corps by afternoon began moving on two parallel routes. Reconnaissance reported Germans in a nearby small village. "From experience we knew that they generally rested at night and actively operated only with full dawn," Rotmistrov noted.[34] He rested his corps.

July nights are short at the Russian latitudes, and the Germans were still asleep when Rotmistrov emptied a volley of Katyusha rockets on them. His tankers rushed forward at high speed aggressively firing from short stops, panicking the surprised Germans. The tank corps destroyed a number of combat vehicles and captured approximately 200 prisoners. From the prisoners, Rotmistrov learned that his unit had fought elements of the 11th Panzer Division, 24th Panzer Corps, one of Germany's veteran armored units.[35]

On the night of 4 July, the 5th Tank Army under the protective cover of Rotmistrov's 7th Tank Corps concentrated south of Elets. Rotmistrov visited the army staff and met the tank army commander, Major General Aleksandr Il'ich Lizyukov. The tank army was to attack not later than 6 July with its whole force to the Western Don river and intercept the approaching German forces penetrating towards the river. The attack would assist the withdrawing 40th Army. General Lizyukov and his staff had too little time to prepare the two arriving tank corps for the attack. Nonetheless, the army commander attempted to familiarize Rotmistrov with the 7th Tank Corps mission in the impending operation.

Rotmistrov was surprised at his assigned mission. His corps was not to attack in the direction of the main strike, but like a rifle army with an assigned sector with boundary lines, command post locations, and displacements, all instructions carried out on order by the army staff. "This obviously ran in violation of the principle for massed use of tanks, it stretched the corps along the front and complicated organizing its coordination," Rotmistrov complained.[36]

Rotmistrov attempted to tell the commander that such a mission was unsuitable for a large tank unit. The inexperienced tank army commander said the order had been worked out with the Front staff and was not subject to discussion or change. The military minds that often fail on the battlefield are closed minds that do not want qualification nor challenge in the face of the enemy, just blind compliance – only direct, supportive action and thought. The great battle captains have shown the ability to accept improvisation and suspend decisions until unfolding events suggest the appropriate course. Rotmistrov with a better mental grasp of armored warfare showed his willingness to challenge his commander's orders. But, his complaint was in vain.

The 7th Tank Corps, moving at midday on 5 July, did not wait for the full concentration of the tank army. The next morning the tank corps attacked towards Zemlyansk, seizing the town. With no further information on the enemy from the army staff, Rotmistrov formed a reconnaissance group to operate in front of the corps precluding any surprise encounters with the Germans. Towards evening, reconnaissance reported approximately 200 German tanks in the area of Krasnoi Polyany. Although the terrain proved difficult to traverse, Rotmistrov decided to attack.

At dawn the next morning, Rotmistrov formed the corps in two echelons and attacked. The rapid assault surprised the Germans who were still preparing for combat operations. At Krasnoi Polyany, a large meeting engagement ensued involving nearly 170 tanks.[37] Rotmistrov's units closed with the German formations to inhibit German use of air. By the end of the day, the Germans withdrew behind the Kobylya Snova river and organized a strong defense.

The next day Rotmistrov ordered an attack against the river position and continuation of the advance. But, stiff German resistance halted the tank corps. Again, on 8 July, the corps attacked for two continuous days with Rotmistrov's corps managing only a limited advance. Although unable to fulfill its assigned task, Rotmistrov's corps and the tank army's efforts forced the Germans to commit the entire 24th Panzer Corps and other units against them, weakening the German forces for their assault on Voronezh. General Lizyukov in frustration over the defeat rode his tank into the advancing Germans, ensuring his battle death.

Rotmistrov, in his memoirs still critical of the tank army commander, noted "if the commander had better used the large mass of tanks, organized information in the army, effective combat use would have shown a more significant success."[38] Without proper artillery and air support, the tank army was committed piecemeal: the 7th Tank Corps, on 6 July; the 11th, 8 July; and the 2nd, 10 July. The Voronezh Front preoccupied with its overall fight gave little attention to the 5th Tank Army which was left to organize the counterstrike itself. The hastily committed tank army did little for its corps. While the Soviets continued learning armored warfare at the operational level, the large operations would exhibit amateurism in coordination and execution.

On 25 August, Rotmistrov's corps received instructions for movement to the Stalingrad area. After unloading at a remote rail station, the corps road marched an exhausting 200 kilometers, and, on 2 September, concentrated in an area northwest of Stalingrad. The 7th Tank Corps reinforced the 1st Guards Army under the command of Lieutenant General Kirill Semenovich Moskalenko. General Moskalenko arriving in Rotmistrov's command post was interested in the composition and condition of the 7th Tank Corps. Rotmistrov told him the primary concern was fuel for his vehicles. General Moskalenko promised to look into the matter, and gave Rotmistrov a brief summary of the situation around Stalingrad.

The 1st Guards Army was to conduct an attack the next day in a southerly direction linking up with the 62nd Army in Stalingrad.

After the departure of the army commander, Rotmistrov called his commanders together and gave them a warning order to be prepared for combat operations the next day. Rotmistrov welcomed his new chief of staff, Colonel Vladimir Nikolaevich Baskakov and immediately set him to work, preparing the combat orders and papers.

At 0500 hours, 3 September 1942, while still dark, the lst Guards Army attacked after an artillery preparation of short duration. The army's advance encountered German aerial bombing attacks and counterattacks by German tanks and motorized infantry stopping the army after 5-6 kilometers. Regrouping the 4th and 7th Tank Corps, the lst Guards Army resumed the attack, but advanced slowly with a gain of no more than 6 kilometers.

For the following seven days, Rotmistrov's corps near the state farm Kotluban slugged forward four fiercely contested kilometers. The tank corps suffered high casualties, losing 156 of 191 tanks.[39] However, the tank corps effort brought praise from General Moskalenko who thought, "all the corps personnel fought selflessly, not sparing themselves."[40]

On 11 September, General Moskalenko put the 7th Tank Corps in the second echelon, noting the corps from 3 to 10 September had nearly 400 killed and wounded.[41] The corps had less than a week to repair and reorganize itself when Rotmistrov received instructions to prepare for a new offensive operation. For the operation the corps managed to field 87 tanks which were mostly light tank. The army objective remained a link up with the 62nd Army in Stalingrad.

Rotmistrov's put two tank brigades in the first echelon and the third brigade with heavy tanks in the second. In the early morning hours of 17 September, the corps moved closer in the direction of its line of commitment with a reinforced reconnaissance group out front. Moving forward Rotmistrov conducted a personal reconnaissance of the area and coordinated with the rifle division commander.

At 0500 hours, 18 September, after a powerful half hour artillery preparation, the 7th Tank Corps with the 308th and 316th Rifle Divisions advanced in the attack. Although the tank corps penetrated the first and second lines of defense, it attracted heavy German air attacks. For a time the 7th Tank Corps was the only committed armored force in the fight. The army commander attempting to help sent in the 4th Tank Corps on the right and the 16th Tank Corps on the left. They failed to achieve any success in the stalemated fighting that grinds down tank units. The German forces proved too strong. The lst Guards Army with its tank reinforcements could not punch through to the struggling 62nd Army in Stalingrad.

On 6 October, the 7th Tank Corps was withdrawn to the Stavka reserve and transferred to Saratov for reconstituting its equipment and personnel. Reserve status gave Rotmistrov time to think and analyze his tank corps operations. He noted the corps attacked from the march not knowing the location of the German's forward defense, let alone the placement of its antitank weapons, resulting in unnecessary losses. In the subsequent attack, even with knowledge about the German disposition, the corps suffered losses not during the penetration of the defense but in the depths when coordination with infantry, artillery and air support ceased.[42] With a focused attention to these aspects of an armored operation, Rotmistrov dramatically improved the performance of his tank corps.

In the first part of November 1942, Rotmistrov was summoned to the Red Army General Staff, for a purpose unknown to him. He flew to Moscow and met the deputy chief of staff for the General Staff, Lieutenant General Fedor Efimovich Bokov. Rotmistrov with General Bokov drove to the Kremlin where they were met by Aleksandr Poskrebyshev, head of Stalin's personal secretariat. The chief secretary told General Bokov to return to the General Staff, and he would drive Rotmistrov in his automobile. As the evening grew dark, the staff car carrying Rotmistrov sped through the streets of Moscow, crossed the Borodino bridge, leaving the outskirts of the capital. In a short time, they arrived at a private, two-story residence in a densely wooded lot. This was Stalin's private retreat called, the "near" dachi.

Rotmistrov trembling from nervousness stepped into the small entrance hall. Poskrebyshev directed him to take off his coat and step into a nearby room. Rotmistrov took off his military great coat, checked his dress in a standing mirror, and gently opened the door. Thinking the door led to a reception room, Rotmistrov was surprised to see Stalin already in the room. Stalin greeted him and asked him to sit down.

Stalin immediately asked questions about the tank corps while pacing up and down the room. Rotmistrov answered that everything was normal, and the corps was prepared for new combat. He added the staff was a little short of personnel, and there were insufficient radios that complicated command and control of the brigades in battle.

"And you told somebody about this?"

"Yes, I reported to comrade Fedorenko."

Stalin silent for a moment again spoke, measuring each phrase. "I read your articles in Pravda and Red Star. This is good that you share battles and express your views about principles in using large tank formations." Stalin moving closer to Rotmistrov, intently looked at him and suddenly changed the subject. "Russian soldiers are always famous for extraordinary endurance, courage and bravery. Suvorov called his soldiers "miracle-heroes." He also said 'Russians and Prussians always kill.' Our Red Armymen are still strong old Russian soldiers so far as they defend their national authority, our Soviet Motherland. Of this I was convinced in the years of the Civil War."

Stalin lowered himself into an armchair and continued, "It is known to me that you taught in the academy. It's known you are a literate man in military terms. So tell me, comrade Rotmistrov, honestly and candidly, as a communist to a communist, why we have so much failure? Why are we retreating?"[43]

The question was tough – the kind that does not lend itself to a short, quick answer. And, coming from the man who had purged the military leadership in 1937-38, the question could elicit a politically unacceptable response with unknown consequence. Rotmistrov's apprehension may have been justified.

Rotmistrov thought for a bit. "Comrade Stalin," he finally began after collecting his thoughts, "I can give you only a personal opinion, based on combat with the Fascists. Of course, our Red Armymen in their morale and combative spirit are above the soldiers of the Tsar's army and even more than the Germans. But, in this matter, it is that in this war collide two armies equipped technically different."[44]

Stalin was interested and motioned Rotmistrov to continue. Rotmistrov contrasted the opposing infantry divisions. The Germans had moved quickly to use various vehicles and transports, and motorcycles all with a potential for maneuver. The Russian rifle divisions had horse drawn carts, and in winter, sleds. The Germans using the disparity in mobility moved around the flanks, penetrating to the rear, and created psychologically, if not in fact, encirclements. Secondly, the Germans possessed a superiority in tanks, heavy artillery and airplanes. "For example," Rotmistrov explained, "we could not make our way through toward Stalingrad from the north, because the Germans organized an antitank defense and literally suppressed us with fire from heavy artillery and air strikes."[45]

Rotmistrov provided Stalin the kind of insider detail the Supreme High Commander needed. Stalin who went near the front only once during the entire war sought these informative sessions with commanders from the battlefields. Rotmistrov became a credible and valued advisor to Stalin.

Upon returning to his corps, Rotmistrov completed the refitting of his units with new combat vehicles. Anticipating employment in the elimination of the encircled Germans at Stalingrad, Rotmistrov had his units study fighting against encircled forces. The Stavka ordered the corps departure by train to a rail station northwest of Stalingrad, and by the end of November, loading the corps on the train was completed. On 3 December, the corps off-loaded the train marching more than 100 kilometers to its assembly area in the vicinity of Gorin and Novo-Petrovskii, southwest of Stalingrad. Halfway to the assembly area, an adjutant for the Stavka representative, Colonel General Aleksandr Mikhailovich Vasilevskii, overtook the column and reported that Rotmistrov was to immediately call General Vasilevskii. Rotmistrov ordered the corps to stop, refuel the vehicles, feed the troops, and continue moving to the designated assembly area.

General Vasilevskii was located in the Don Front command post filled with busy staff officers in the village of Zavarykin. He was clearly upset about something when Rotmistrov found him. Vasilevskii, sitting behind a table, greeted Rotmistrov, but did not offer him a seat. He began speaking, "The Supreme High Commander called and expressed indignantly his extreme dissatisfaction that we in the course of two weeks could not liquidate the German bridgehead in the area of the Rychkovskii farm. Two corps, rifle and cavalry, attempted to seize it, but were unsuccessful. Comrade Stalin entrusted this decisive mission with your corps. Therefore, I called you. How much time will you require for preparing a strike on Rychkovskii?"

"Not less than two days."

"Too much. The enemy can forestall your strike."

"But, comrade general, the corps has still not completed the march, and the situation around Rychkovskii is absolutely unknown to me."

Rotmistrov's sharp answer angered General Vasilevskii, a normally self-restrained and polite soldier.

"Your orders are to immediately liquidate the bridgehead personally outlined by Comrade Stalin! Do you understand this?" Vasilevskii raised his voice and stood beside the table.

"I am going to report to Comrade Stalin that I must have two days in order to prepare ourselves for the operation," Rotmistrov stood his ground.

General Vasilevskii looked at Rotmistrov, thought a moment and then in a quiet tone said, "Fine, return to your corps and get in contact with the commander of the Fifth Shock Army, General Popov, whom you are to reinforce in operational terms."[46] General Vasilevskii would not forget being drawn out in front of subordinates.

On the evening of 9 December, Rotmistrov was located in his corps headquarters at the farmstead Malay Luchaya when General Markian M. Popov, 5th Shock Army commander, arrived. Rotmistrov having previously known General Popov told him about the conversation with General Vasilevskii and the corps mission. General Popov explained in detail the Front's attempt to eliminate German units in the lower Chir river which included the Rychkovskii bridgehead. But the Germans had repelled all attempts. General Popov told Rotmistrov to make a reconnaissance of the area and report his decision the next day.

Rotmistrov with the commander of the 4th Guards Rifle Division who had previously attacked in the Rychkovskii area scanned the German defense through binoculars. The German positions covered a triangle formed by the Chir and Don rivers. From the north the German position was guarded by a small, but well fortified height. On the height the Germans placed a significant portion of their artillery and mortars which tore apart the previous infantry assaults.

Rotmistrov asked the division commander, "Where's your artillery?"

The commander understood the point of Rotmistrov's question. "We have enough artillery," he answered. "In truth, all of it is light, not capable of destroying firmly fortified Germans. We don't have air support. They say that all our air was taken for destroying the enemy encircling Stalingrad and liquidating nearby German airfields. But mainly, its insufficient ammunition, nearly all the large caliber shells. They brought them up, as they say, one teaspoon every hour (in driblets), totally on sleds. We had to accumulate shells and then strike against the German position. But authorities above required attacks every day."[47]

The two fighting commanders shared the unadulterated facts. Rotmistrov gathered all the details necessary for use in a planned approach to change the situation. The rifle division commander drew in his breath deeply, "Here we attacked. We are scared of the German artillery fires, they sit in deep cover and then they beat off our attacks with a hurricane of fire from all types of guns."[48]

Rotmistrov understood why the previous forces had been unable to dislodge the Germans. While returning to his corps staff, he formed a clear concept for his operation – a main strike aimed at the heights along the shortest route. The attack would be supported on the right flank around the heights, in order to cut off the enemy withdrawal towards the crossing and to paralyze their fires from the heights. The strike must be a surprise attack begun at dawn, when his tankers could orient on the terrain.

The plan was typical Rotmistrov. In these battles, Rotmistrov began to cultivate his style of combat for armored forces. Using a high degree of agility and powerful, direct, active maneuver, he would strike a devastating blow against the enemy. "Powerful strikes to upset the enemy, and the, utilizing in full measure of his unit's agility, broke up the enemy's main forces, encircled them, and destroyed them in detail – such was the favorite tactical conduct in battle of Rotmistrov," wrote his early commander, General Pavel Alekseevich Kurochkin.[49] The skillful combination of fire, maneuver and shock marked Rotmistrov's fighting style. "The success of Rotmistrov's corps resulted from his always carefully studying the enemy," observed Kurochkin, "weighing their strengths and weaknesses, he knew how to find the point for striking the main effort."[50] Rotmistrov possessed an uncanny ability to quickly assess a situation and devise a creative approach for a decisive result.

Rotmistrov reported his concept to Generals Popov and Vasilevskii. General Vasilevskii, friendly this time, informed Rotmistrov that his need for more time had Stalin's permission. Rotmistrov briefed his plan holding everyone's attention. When he announced that he would not use an artillery preparation for the attack, General Vasilevskii asked, "You are what, not recognizing the necessity of artillery?"

"I do recognize it," Rotmistrov answered, "But, as shown in the battles for the bridgehead, the Germans are so used to it that after our artillery preparation we attack without fail, and they are prepared to successfully repel it."

"Perhaps, there is room for agreement with Pavel Alekseevich. Operationally, the artillery preparation is still weak and only warns the enemy about the beginning of our attacks," General Popov added supporting Rotmistrov.

"Artillery is not completely without a role," Rotmistrov continued. "As the tanks move in the attack from the attack position, artillery will begin to work. The corps Katyusha rocket battalion will begin volley fires as a signal for covering artillery fire."[51]

"You are confident in success?" General Vasilevskii asked.

"Yes, confident!"[52]

Still unconvinced, General Vasilevskii asked Rotmistrov's brigade commanders their opinions, and each confirmed his agreement with their commander's plan.[53] General Vasilevskii, with no dissenting votes, agreed with the plan, and the other issues of coordinating the operation were worked out. By midday 12 December, the tank corps was prepared for combat operations.

Early the next morning, Rotmistrov moved to his observation point, a trench covered and camouflaged with snow. General Popov and Nikita Khrushchev, Front deputy commander for political affairs, joined the corps commander. At 0400 hours, the brigades were located in their attack positions. Lieutenant Colonel A.V. Egorov, a brigade commander, remembered "the gloomy morning and the raw wind that pierced one to the bone."

Rotmistrov called the brigade commander, "Move at the designated time. What do you see out front?"

"Over the enemy positions soar colored rockets. Probably for some reason or other they got wind," Lieutenant Colonel Egorov replied pessimistically.

"It's nothing, we long ago got used to this. Everything remains according to plan. There will be no artillery preparation. We will attempt surprise. Is it clear? Check the time. What do you have?" Rotmistrov asked.

"Six fifty."

"Exactly. You know its another forty-five minutes? Everything prepared?"

"Everything prepared, we wait the signal," Egorov replied.[54]

The artillery took their firing positions. Everything was in order. "Soon you will hear tanks," Rotmistrov announced confidently. "He was not mistaken," General Popov recalled.[55] They soon heard the noise of many engines as the heavy tank brigade passed the observation post. Daybreak began at 0700 hours. With first light, Rotmistrov quickly checked the German position as his lead brigade moved forward. The Germans were clearly caught by surprise. Rotmistrov radioed for the Katyusha rockets covering fire.

Within 50 minutes the lead brigade commander reported his tanks' penetration to Rychokovskii and continuation of the battle. Reconnaissance has established that the defenders were the tank corps' old friends, the German 11th Panzer Division. The remainder of the 5th Shock Army's offensive went well. That evening, General Popov arriving in Rotmistrov's command post informed him that the Front commander was pleased with the results of the battle. After fulfilling the assigned mission of seizing Verkhne-Chirskii, Rotmistrov was to prepare the corps for maneuver in the Kotelnikovo direction. But, Verkhne-Chirskii proved a strong German center of resistance with a large number of antitank guns, requiring a reorganization of the corps and a coordinated attack.

At 0730 hours, 14 December, after an artillery preparation, the tank and motorized infantry of the corps in coordination with other rifle units advanced in the attack. The difficult battle continued all day with heavy losses in fighting tanks to antitank fire and mines. Rotmistrov renewed the offensive effort at 0200 hours the following morning, the fighting continued to meet stubborn resistance. At midday, General Vasilevskii arrived in Rotmistrov's command post. More lively than his previous self-restrained, quiet manner, General Vasilevskii's good mood reflected the success of the 2nd Guards Army in the direction of Kotelnikovo and the encirclement battle around Stalingrad. He directed Rotmistrov to assemble the corps for refueling and refitting.

On 12 December, the Germans had opened a counteroffensive to relieve Stalingrad. General Hoth, operating as part of Field Marshal von Manstein's newly created Army Group Don, fought with a formidable concentration of 35,000 soldiers and 300 tanks. On the first two days of the offensive, the Germans thrust a powerful armored spearhead toward the Myshkova river in what von Manstein called, "a race with death."[56] A week later, the 57th Panzer Corps reached the Myshkova river crossing within 40 kilometers of the southern edge of the encircled German forces, but Hitler would not allow the German 6th Army to breakout from Stalingrad toward the relief force. The German relief effort from a single direction allowed the Soviets time to respond.

On 19 December, General Vasilevskii instructed the 7th Tank Corps to reinforce the 2nd Guards Army and concentrate further south to defend against the strong German relief effort for Stalingrad. At the time, Rotmistrov's corps possessed 92 tanks, 20 KV's and 41 T-34's. Although his unit was under authorized tank strength, he had sufficient ammunition and personnel to fight. The first echelon of the 2nd Guards Army reached the front line and succeeded in checking the German's advance. Rotmistrov's corps counterattacked causing the Germans heavy losses. With Soviet forces holding the lead panzer unit to the northern bank of the Myshkova river, Soviet tank corps cut into the German army group's left flank and took the airfield at Tatsinkii, turning the whole situation sour for Army Group Don.

Shifting forces from his group to stem the Red Army counterstrike, General Hoth, on the night of 23 December, ordered a retreat from the Myshkova river. Field Marshal von Manstein's counteroffensive failed, and he faced the undeniable fact that he would have to abandon the encircled 6th Army in Stalingrad. The battle's death rattle became an echo as the German Army shrank back from their deepest penetration into the Soviet Union.

On the evening of 23 December, Rotmistrov was called to the 2nd Guards Army command post for a meeting to outline the plans for a new operation. The counterattack by the 2nd Guards Army and 7th Tank Corps created favorable conditions for transitioning to a counteroffensive. Their objective was the destruction of the German's Kotelnikovo grouping. The 2nd Guards Army's main attack was reinforced by the 7th Tank and General Bogdanov's 6th Mechanized Corps. The 51st Army on the left flank and General Popov's 5th Shock Army on the right flank supported the operation. The counteroffensive began on Christmas eve 1942.

At 0800 hours, the lead divisions of the 2nd Guards Army after a short artillery preparation attacked the Germans across the Myshkova river. The attack slammed into Field Marshal von Manstein's 17th and 23rd Panzer Divisions. Thirty minutes into the attack, Rotmistrov's lead tanks encountered strong German artillery fire along the river crossing. While the brigade commander, Lieutenant Colonel Egorov, worked a solution to the tactical problem, he heard his codeword called by Rotmistrov.

"Violet! Violet! Where are you lost? Why are you silent?"

Lieutenant Colonel Egorov who recalled Rotmistrov's irritation was at a loss what to answer. "What the corps commander could see from the army observation post could be no worse than what he could see," Egorov thought.

"Why are you silent?" Rotmistrov asked, transitioning to the familiar 'you'.

"I can honestly say, comrade general, there is nothing comforting. Only reports about losses. Movement came to a standstill."

"I see it's at a standstill. In only one night the Germans cannot create a deeply echeloned defense here. Find a way out and quickly."

"Understood! I ask for the support of dive-bombers to strike the enemy's artillery positions."

"We are trying," Rotmistrov answered.[57]

One of Egorov's battalions found a ford across the river, piercing the German defense, allowing the tanks to move forward on the opposite bank. By 1300 hours the following day, the 3rd Guards Tank Brigade entered Nizhne-Kumskii, preempting further German attempts to counterattack.

At daybreak 26 December, Rotmistrov's tank brigades under the cover of antitank artillery began crossing the Aksai river. Aggressively maneuvering and seizing villages, the corps knifed into the operational depth more than 20 kilometers, distancing itself from the 2nd Guards Army's rifle divisions. The tank corps' advance put Rotmistrov's tanks on the approaches to Kotelnikovo, a large railroad center. The freedom of Rotmistrov's corps in the operational depth raised the question: how to act further – wait for the advance of the rifle units or to attack the city independently? [58] Rotmistrov's success raised new questions of employment for the fledgling armor force as the tank corps flexed its powerful new capability.

Reports from the army staff indicated that the army's rifle units were locked in combat with the German's Kotelnikovo grouping. General S.I. Bogdanov's 6th Mechanized Corps supported them in these battles. Reconnaissance reports indicated the Germans were not occupying prepared positions. Evaluating the situation, Rotmistrov decided to go for the city. On the morning of 28 December his corps attacked the city from the north.

Rotmistrov's tanks ran into heavy antitank fire as they approached the town. He ordered the beleaguered lead unit to back off from the German's killing zone. Although the tank corps' units found a small gap in the defense, it was quickly closed by artillery and mortar fire. At this point, the Germans began to bring air attacks to bear on Rotmistrov's exposed tanks. Both sides exchanged fires into the night.

Rotmistrov, again, found himself facing the question: what to do? Consulting with his command group, he received divided responses. One group of officers thought the corps should assume the defense securing crossings over the Aksai-Kurmoyarskii river and wait for the rifle units. The others urged reinforcing the attack from the north by committing the corps second echelon. After considering all the "pros" and "cons," Rotmistrov decided to concentrate artillery fire along the northern edge of the city with all the corps artillery while continuing the attack head-on with the 3rd Guards and 62nd Tank Brigades. Simultaneously, the 87th Tank and 7th Motorized Rifle Brigades went around Kotelnikovo from the west and southwest. Rotmistrov reasoned, "if these brigades did not manage a surprise penetration on the west and southwest edge of the city, their active operations inevitably contributed towards weakening the resistance of the enemy defending to the northern edge of Kotelnikovo."[59] Rotmistrov did not believe the German commanders could transfer a large force to the north since they were heavily committed in the fight against the 2nd Guards Army in other sectors.

Over the radio Rotmistrov reached the chief of staff of the 2nd Guards Army and reported his decision to strike Kotelnikovo. The chief's answer was short, "Act!"[60]

The next morning after a short artillery fire, Rotmistrov's brigades attacked in accordance with the plan. The brigades attacking from the west and southwest failed to achieve surprise but steadily advanced despite strong resistance. The 7th Tank Corps' swift approach to Kotelnikovo created a grave situation for the Germans, threatening the entire enemy grouping with encirclement. By 2000 hours, 29 December, Rotmistrov's corps after fierce and protracted street battles completely cleared the Germans from Kotelnikovo. Although the Germans succeeded in escaping encirclement, the capture of the town proved to be a big triumph, not only had it served as a major rail center but also a large logistical dump for the Germans. Rotmistrov reported his successful operation to General

Rodion Yakolevich Malinovskii, 2nd Guards Army commander. In the course of the offensive, the 7th Tank Corps in four days advanced 80 kilometers, destroying nearly 2000 soldiers, 25 tanks, 65 guns and taking 300 prisoners.

General A.M. Vasilevskii visited the corps. He informed Rotmistrov and his staff that Stalin had called him and had given his personal gratitude for the corps combat performance. General Vasilevskii also announced the 7th Tank Corps was redesignated the 3rd Guards Tank Corps. Personal rewards came to Rotmistrov: he received promotion to Lieutenant General and won the order of Suvorov 2nd degree – the second recipient of the newly created award.

In these battles Rotmistrov revealed his mastery in armored warfare. Using dynamic maneuver and heavy firepower, his operations inflicted destructive strikes on the enemy. His skillful combination of fire, maneuver and shock showed a decisiveness with initiative and a willingness to take risks. His exceptional ability to quickly assess the situation and devise an innovative approach for tactical missions, marked Rotmistrov's style of command with diversity and novelty.

The Stalingrad Front offensive routed the German forces around Stalingrad. The German operations, "Winter Storm," for the German relief attack from outside the encirclement, and, "Thunder Blow," a simultaneous attack from within the encirclement, were unfulfilled. The demise of the German 6th Army was close at hand.

On 1 January 1943, a Stavka Supreme High Command directive renamed the Stalingrad Front as the Southern Front. With the redesignation, the Southern Front received the important mission of striking towards Rostov to cut off the German forces withdrawing from the Northern Caucasus. The operation was a chance to encircle yet another large German grouping.

Within the Front's operational plan, Rotmistrov's 3rd Guards Tank Corps received the mission to force march to the area of Semikarakorskaya, at the junction of the Don and Sal rivers, and capture a crossing on the Don river. The corps' mission supported the 2nd Guards Army's offensive to Rostov. The 3rd Guards Tank Corps consisted of the 3rd Guards, 18th Guards (formerly 62nd), 19th Guards (formerly 87th) Tank Brigades and 2nd Guards (formerly 7th) Motorized Rifle Brigade.

By 1400 hours, 5 January 1943, forward reconnaissance detachments of the 3rd Guards Tank Brigade entered Semikarakorskaya,

east of Novocherkassk, capturing a small bridgehead on the southern bank of the Don river. The following day the corps' main body
engaged a large German force in Konstantinovsk and crossed the
Don, developing the attack towards Manychsk canal. Crossing the
canal, Rotmistrov's corps was immediately counterattacked by German tanks and panzer grenadier units, making a fierce and difficult
battle for the 3rd Guards Tank Corps.

Rotmistrov instructed his chief of staff to inform the 2nd Guards
Army about the corps' "miserable" situation with supplies – there
were none. The alarming report brought Lieutenant General Andrei
Ivanovich Eremenko, Front Commander, his political officer Nikita
Sergeevich Khrushchev, and Lieutenant General Rodion Yakovlevich
Malinovskii, commander 2nd Guards Army to Rotmistrov's com-
mand post. Rotmistrov reported the stiffening enemy resistance and
the corps' paucity of supplies in all areas.

Leaning on his walking stick, necessary for old war wounds,
General Eremenko became extremely upset, and walked excitedly
around the room in irritation, lamenting, "I have nothing, but the
mission has to be fulfilled. You must take Rostov – the Germans
have everything there."

"But how will we...."

"Listen," General Eremenko interrupted Rotmistrov. "You head
a mechanized group. I am transferring to your control the 2nd and
5th Guards Mechanized Corps. Unite your tanks, merge fuel from
out of action and unserviceable vehicles. Do anything you want,
but you seize Bataisk and Rostov. More than that, I am transferring
to you an 'aerosani' battalion. They scared the Germans stiff...."[61]

"And what are these?" Rotmistrov asked in puzzlement. He had
never hear of these machines or units.

"Plywood boxes with propellers on skis," smiled General
Malinovskii.

When Rotmistrov saw the machines, they were propeller driven
sleds. Inside the box, or small cabin, was a mounted machinegun
with several sitting machinegunners. The 'aerosani' proved very
effective in winter conditions. The "wonders," as Rotmistrov referred
to them, were suited not only as combat vehicles but also a means
for movement on the often tricky Don river which frequently
changed due to rain and slush. The 'aerosani' often suffered acci-
dents and were a main prey for enemy aircraft. Rotmistrov believed
them useful, "especially in a morale connection."[62]

For the quick liberation of Rostov, the Front commander subordinated the 2nd and 5th Mechanized Corps to Rotmistrov's mechanized group. As it turned out, these mechanized corps had few tanks and because of their recent combat were also in need of ammunition and fuel. Rotmistrov decided to create as best as possible a strong advance guard and a forward detachment based on his 3rd Guards Tank Brigade.

On the morning of 15 January, after a short battle for Manych-Balabinky, the commanders received orders to wait for General Rotmistrov. Upon his arrival new maps were distributed. "I invite you to listen attentively," Rotmistrov began the commanders briefing.[63] He directed the combining of the 18th and 19th Guards Tank Brigades reinforced by a motorized rifle battalion and a pontoon battalion under Colonel Egorov into a powerful forward detachment. By 1800 hours, 18 January, the forward detachment was to cross the Manych canal moving to cut off the key road junction south of Bataisk.[64]

The next morning Rotmistrov's group attacked in the direction of Bataisk, and the forward detachment captured its road junction. In Rotmistrov's strike for Bataisk, he found it heavily fortified. After three days of battle, his forward detachment had to fight out of encirclement, since Rotmistrov's group could not reach them. When the strength of the German positions were reported, the Front commander directed Rotmistrov to withdraw to the northern bank of the Manych canal and assume the defense.

Rotmistrov's group remained in position the first part of February when the Front commander ordered Rotmistrov to pass the command of the tank corps to General I.A. Vovchenko and depart for Moscow for a meeting with General Fedorenko.

Upon his arrival in Moscow, Rotmistrov met with General Fedorenko and General Fedor Efimovich Bokov, Chief of Staff for the General Staff. The Generals had arranged a meeting with Stalin. The question of reorganizing the tank army had become a major issue. General Bokov wanted Rotmistrov's opinion to counter Stalin's other advisers.

Rotmistrov arrived at the Kremlin in the evening. Stalin's work habit during the war was to work late night and early morning, sleeping the morning and rising early afternoon. The schedule made sense, since the daily reports in the evening could not be collected from the Fronts and collated by the General Staff until late evening.

As Rotmistrov sat in the outer office, he mentally rehearsed a more short and clear report. He knew Stalin disliked extensive reasoning or verbose responses.[65] After some time, Stalin's secretary motioned Rotmistrov to enter the office. Stalin was standing well back in the room with his pipe in hand and moved to meet Rotmistrov. Rotmistrov drew up, perfunctorily reported his presence as ordered.

"I didn't order you, I invited you, comrade Rotmistrov," Stalin extended his hand to Rotmistrov. "Tell us how you destroyed Manstein."[66]

The question caught Rotmistrov off-guard. He assumed everyone knew quite well the details of the operation. But, Rotmistrov immediately recounted the 3rd Guards Tank Corps operation in the offensive to Rychkovskii and Kotelnikovo with his analysis of the battles.

Stalin listened attentively, interjecting short questions. However, Stalin subtly turned the conversation to tank armies. "Our tank force," he said, "learned how to successfully destroy the enemy, to inflict on them deep, destructive strikes. However, why do you consider it inexpedient to have infantry formations in tank armies?" Stalin stopped pacing and stared intently at the tank corps commander.

"During the offensive rifle divisions lag behind tank corps. With this breaks the interaction between tank and infantry units, it complicates command and control of tanks running forward and infantry lagging behind."[67]

Stalin countered with opposing examples to get Rotmistrov's opinions and considerations. The discussions continued for two hours, during which Stalin noted Rotmistrov's views on the role of the tank armies in offensive operations as a means for Front commanders or even the Supreme High Command. It became evident to Rotmistrov that Stalin understood well the significance on the massed employment of tank forces.[68]

Several days after the meeting with Rotmistrov, Stalin approved the formation of the 5th Guards Tank Army leaving the requirement to work out its structure with General Fedorenko's office. Simultaneously with the signing of the order for the formation of the tank army, Stalin designated General Rotmistrov as commander.

"So, you slip away from me, again," General Fedorenko commented on the appointment.[69] He had asked Stalin to designate

Rotmistrov as his deputy, but the Red Army still needed its proven fighters at the front.

Rotmistrov's command group was first deputy commander, Major General Issa Aleksandrovich Pliev, second deputy, Major General Kuzman Grigorevich Trufanov, first member of the Military Council Major General Petr Griforevich Grishin, and the chief of staff, Colonel Vladimir Nikolaevich Baskakov. Colonel Baskakov from the 3rd Guards Tank Corps, Rotmistrov considered an "educated officer, fine understanding of staff work, and possessing an enviable, persistence in work."[70]

Initially, the 5th Guards Tank Army consisted of the 3rd Guards and 29th Tank Corps, 5th Guards Mechanized Corps, 6th Air Defense Artillery Division, a motorcycle, artillery, Katyusha rocket and two assault gun regiments. The elimination of the walking infantry made a more homogeneous structure of all motorized and mechanized units, overcoming the previous unwieldy tank army design.

In mid-March 1943, the army staff and some units, mainly the 29th Tank and 5th Guards Mechanized Corps, concentrated in Millerovo, 400 kilometers southeast of Kursk. With assignment to the Steppe Front, Rotmistrov's tank army relocated closer to the fighting front in the vicinity of Ostrogozhsk, 250 kilometers southeast of Kursk. In the new location Rotmistrov continued planning and preparing the staffs. He emphasized training on controlling the tank army, organizing reliable communications, maintaining continuous coordination between tank, infantry, artillery and air units under different conditions and situations. Special attention was given to commitment of the tank force into a penetration. By the end of June, Rotmistrov had trained his staff to a level he believed could handle most situations.

In the spring and early summer of 1943, the German and Soviet armies concentrated a large number of strong forces along the Kursk salient. With the summer campaigning, the Germans sought to regain their strategic initiative, as they had each previous summer recovering the winter's territorial losses through offensive campaigns. In addition to committing as many as 50 German divisions, recent German deployments in the latest fighting vehicles and other weapons offered a hope of victory. The Germans fielded the Panther and Tiger tanks, the self-propelled assault gun, Ferdinand, and new planes with powerful cannons and machineguns.

On the Soviet side, the strategic decision was whether to assume the offensive themselves or receive the impending German attack. The Soviet High Command decided to allow the Germans to beat themselves against the powerful defense, then assume the offensive. The Central and Voronezh Fronts were backed by the Steppe Front under the command of General Ivan Stepanovich Konev. The Steppe Front as a blocking Front guarded against a German breakthrough, and once the Soviet Army transferred to the offense, it could be used for the attack in depth.

On 5 July 1943, General Matrei Vasilevich Zakharov, chief of staff for the Steppe Front, informed Rotmistrov by telephone that fierce fighting had broken out at the Central and Voronezh Fronts. He told Rotmistrov that General Bakhorov's 18th Tank Corps had been attached as reinforcements to the 5th Guards Tank Army. "Contact them. Bring all your units to full alert, and wait for orders," the chief of staff finally instructed.[71]

The next day General Konev visited Rotmistrov, giving him more details on the situation in the Kursk salient. The Soviet High Command assessment expected the stronger German attacks against the salient's southern face occupied by the Voronezh Front. General Konev told Rotmistrov that the Stavka adopted the decision to attach his army and the 5th Guards Army to the Voronezh Front. "You must concentrate here in a very short time," Konev marked on the map with a red pencil an area southwest of Stary Oskol.[72]

About an hour after General Konev departed, Stalin telephoned Rotmistrov, "Have you received the directive on the army's deployment to the Voronezh Front?"

"No, Comrade Ivanov (code name for Stalin), but I have been told as much by Comrade Stepin (code name for Konev)."

"How do you think you will execute the redeployment?"

"We will do it on our own."

"Comrade Fedorenko, here says that the tanks will not survive movement over such a great distance, and it would be better to take them by rail."

"That cannot be done, Comrade Ivanov. The enemy air force may bomb the trains and railroad bridges, and it will take too long to reassemble the army. Besides, it would be impractical to transport the infantry along to the assembly area in case they meet enemy tanks and find themselves in a difficult situation."

"Do you intend to move only at night?"

"No, there are only seven hours of darkness and we would have to hide the tanks in the woods by day and bring them out by night, and there are too few woods along the way."

"What do you suggest?"

"I ask permission to move the army day and night."

"But they will bomb you during the daylight hours," Stalin interrupted.

"That is possible. Therefore I ask you to give orders to the air force to protect me from the air."

"Fine," agreed Stalin, "your request for air cover over the march will be fulfilled. You inform the Steppe and Voronezh Front commanders when you begin your march."[73]

Rotmistrov with his staff immediately began plotting the tank army on three march routes in a sector 30-35 kilometers wide. A tank corps on a single route would be strung out nearly 60 kilometers in depth. On two or three routes, the tank corps would be 20-30 kilometers in length.

Rotmistrov's birthday was 6 July. He wanted to celebrate the occasion with friends and had previously sent out dinner party invitations to the corps commanders, field officers and generals. But, as the situation changed, he decided to call off the dinner and use the gathering to give advance marching orders. "My guest were greatly surprised to see not a birthday dinner table but only me standing next to a map," Rotmistrov recalled.[74] He briefed the assembled officers on the forthcoming redeployment and formulated assignments for everyone. After discussing all the problems involved in the march, Rotmistrov served captured German champagne in a short celebration.

At 0130 hours, 7 July, the tank army began its long, hot, arduous trek in two echelons. The first echelon comprised of two tank corps; the second, motorized corps. In radio contact with his corps commanders, Rotmistrov received reports – everything was going well. General Konev in a plane followed the advance of Rotmistrov's columns.

Despite the heat, lack of sleep, and long hours on the march, the lead tank crews reached the assigned area southwest of Stary Oskol, with the remainder of the army following later in the day. Within 48 hours the tank army had covered 230-280 kilometers. The number of tanks which had fallen behind because of mechanical breakdowns were insignificant, and they were promptly repaired and returned to their units. These were impressive results for the first time a tank army moved under its own power over such an extended distance.

In the early hours of 9 July, Rotmistrov received orders to move towards Prokhorovka and by the end of the day be in full combat readiness. The tank army marched another 100 kilometers.

The next day, with the tank army attached to the Voronezh Front, Rotmistrov was summoned to the Front command post near Oboyan where he found Marshal Aleksandr Vasilevskii, representative of the Soviet High Command, who coordinated the operation of the Voronezh and Southwest Fronts, General Nikolai Vatutin, commander of the Voronezh Front, and General Semyon Ivanov, the Front's Chief of Staff. Rotmistrov received a briefing on the Front's current situation. The Voronezh Front had been fighting six straight days against the 4th Panzer Army commanded by Colonel General Hermann Hoth, an "old friend". In the fierce fighting both sides had suffered heavy losses, but the Germans had advanced 35 kilometers toward Oboyan.

General Vatutin called Rotmistrov to the map and pointed with his pencil to Prokhorovka. "Having failed to breakthrough to Kursk and Oboyan, the Nazis have apparently decided to shift the thrust of their main attack a little to the east, along the railroad to Prokhorovka." General Vatutin continued, "The 2nd SS Panzer Corps is being redeployed here, and will attack Prokhorovka with the 48th Panzer Corps and the panzer units of the fighting group 'Kempf'."

Casting a glance at Marshal Vasilevskii, General Vatutin turned to Rotmistrov, and continued, "So, Pavel Alekseevich, we have decided to put up our Guards tanks against the SS Panzer divisions and to deliver a counterstrike with our 5th Guards Tank Army, reinforced with two tank corps."

"By the way, the panzer divisions have new heavy Tiger tanks and Ferdinand self-propelled guns which inflicted heavy losses on Katukov's 1st Tank Army. Do know anything about such a force, and how do you plan to fight it?" Marshal Vasilevskii asked.

"We know about them, comrade marshal. We received tactical-technical information about them from the Steppe Front staff. We have thought about how to fight them."

"Interesting," General Vatutin interjected nodding to Rotmistrov to continue.

"The Tigers and Ferdinands have not only strong frontal armor but powerful 88mm guns with a long distance direct fire which gives them a superiority over our 76mm tank guns. They can only be fought successfully in close combat, where the T-34 tanks can use their greater maneuverability and direct their fire at the sides of the heavy German tanks."

"Figuratively speaking, we should fight them in hand-to-hand combat and overwhelm them," General Vatutin summarized. He turned the discussion back to the upcoming counteroffensive, in which the 1st Tank Army and the 6th, 7th and 5th Guards Rifle Armies would also take part. The 5th Guards Tank Army reinforced with the 2nd Guards and 2nd Tank Corps, numbered 850 tanks and self-propelled guns.[75]

In the afternoon Rotmistrov returned with his combat orders. On the morning of 12 July, the tank army together with the 1st Tank And 5th Guards Armies was to launch a decisive attack to destroy the Germans to the southwest of Prokhorovka and to reach Krasnaya Dubrva and Yakolevo by night. With no time to waste, Rotmistrov with his corps commanders conducted a reconnaissance of the area of operation and formulated the corps combat missions. Rotmistrov concluded that since they were to engage a strong German tank group which, according to Soviet intelligence, had nearly 700 tanks, he decided to deploy all four tank corps in the first echelon. The second echelon was made up of the 5th Guards Mechanized Corps, and a reserve brigade configured as a forward detachment and a self propelled assault gun regiment under the deputy commander, General Trufanov.

At 0400 hours, 12 July, General Vatutin ordered Rotmistrov to send his reserves immediately to assist the 69th Army. The 3rd Panzer Corps of Army Group 'Kempf' attacked the rifle army pushing back two rifle divisions and capturing three villages. If the German tank units continued advancing north, the 5th Guards Tank Army's left flank and rear would be jeopardized as well as the entire left flank of the Voronezh Front. Rotmistrov contacted General Trufanov by radio and ordered him to dispatch troops immediately against the Germans who had broken through in the 69th sector. General Trufanov's reserve with the 69th Army arrested the German tanks advancing northwards.

At 0600 hours, Rotmistrov arrived with a group of officers at the 29th Tank Corps command post. He chose a hilltop observation post because of its location southwest of Prokhorovka, affording a good view of the open approaches. From a solid dug-out in an apple orchard with half burnt and half cut down trees, he examined a panorama of the undulating plain with small groves and ravines on which an awesome tank battle was to be fought. The battlefield was Rotmistrov's choice and the battle would be on his terms.

German aircraft appeared overhead, bombing a path for the advancing panzer formations. Soviet aircraft appeared, and an air battle ensued overhead. At the same time, Rotmistrov's artillery opened fire. They had little time to locate precisely German artillery positions and tank concentrations, but Rotmistrov's artillery preparation put into action regiments of Katyusha rockets. The rocket fires signaled the attack, which was also repeated over Rotmistrov's command radio. "Steel, Steel, Steel,..." the radio station commander, a young lieutenant, kept repeating the codeword, and the commanding officers of the tank corps, brigades and battalions, and below took up the call immediately.

Rotmistrov through his binoculars watched his tanks pull from cover and rush forward, gathering speed. "At the same time, I caught sight of a host of enemy tanks," Rotmistrov recalled.[76] Apparently both sides launched their attacks simultaneously. The tank army commander was surprised to see how close the opposing tank forces were to each other. The German and Soviet "tank armadas were set for a head-on collision."[77]

The sun clearly outlined the German tanks for Soviet gunners. In a few minutes, the first echelon tanks of the 29th and 18th Tank Corps were firing on the move, crashing and breaking into the German armored formations. The Germans seemed surprised encountering such a large number of Soviet tanks. The resolute dash by Rotmistrov's tankers disrupted the German's control of the battlefield with their long range firing Tiger and Panther tanks which the Soviets denied by close combat. Attacking at close range the Soviet tanks intermingled with German in swirling tank engagements in which attack plane pilots could not distinguish friend from foe. The tank battle became enveloped in smoke and the earth was shook from strong blasts.[78]

Prokhorovka, the largest tank battle in history, hurled tanks against tanks, locking 1200 tanks in a bitter struggle. The SS Death's Head Division's daily report for 12 July with its "terse urgency eloquently underscores the awesome magnitude of the armored duel."[79] Fierce air battles were going on at the same time.

General Kirichenko's 29th Tank Corps advanced along the railroad and the highway engaging in heavy, savage fighting against

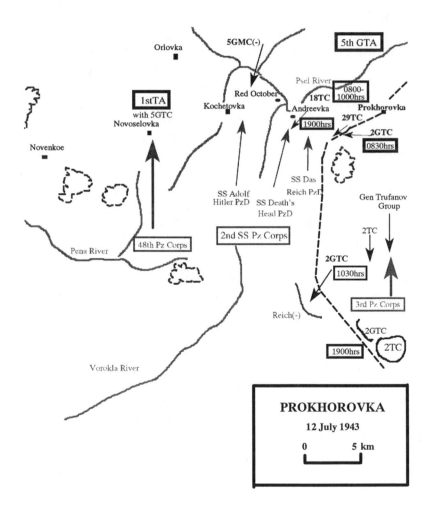

Orlovka

5GMC(-)

5th GTA

Psel River

1stTA
with 5GTC
Novoselovka

Red October

Kochetovka

18TC

0800-
1000hrs

Andreevka

Prokhorovka

29TC

1900hrs

2GTC

0830hrs

Novenkoe

SS Das
Reich PzD

SS Adolf
Hitler PzD   SS Death's
Head PzD

Gen Trufanov
Group

2TC

Pena River

48th Pz Corps

2nd SS Pz Corps

2GTC

1030hrs

3rd Pz Corps

Reich(-)

2GTC

Vorokla River

1900hrs

2TC

PROKHOROVKA

12 July 1943

0   5 km

the elite armored forces of the SS Adolf Hitler and Das Reich Panzer Divisions, attempting stubbornly a breakthrough to Prokhorovka.

Steadily advancing forward, General B.S. Bakhorov, commander 18th Tank Corps, studied the local topography, placing his formation in three echelons. The corps pressed on the tank army's right flank towards the east bank of the Psel river, building up a strong strike and securing a favorable line for continued operations.

But, the situation on the tank army's left flank remained alarming. Rotmistrov believed nearly 70 German tanks had seized the villages in the neighboring 69th Army sector and developed their attack to the north. General Trufanov reported his blocking position south of Prokhorovka, but his force proved insufficient for the task. On instructions from Marshal Vasilevskii, Rotmistrov sent two brigades of the 5th Guards Mechanized Corps to General Trufanov. Simultaneously, Rotmistrov positioned a tank brigade from the 2nd Guards Tank Corps to protect the army's left flank.[80]

By midday, Rotmistrov's success in the main sector of the battle became obvious. The first echelon pushed back the Germans, inflicting heavy losses in tankers and machines. His tank army gained little territory but accomplished its main goal, stopping the enemy advance along the railroad towards Prokhorovka. The blunted German armored spearhead near Oboyan highway had now been broken. The 18th Tank Corps' attack advanced two kilometers east of the village Andreevka. The 29th Tank Corps, with a motorized rifle brigade, overcame the resistance of parts of the SS Death's Head and Adolf Hitler Divisions, achieving the state farm, Komsomol. Brigades of the 2nd Guards Tank Corps threw back parts of the Das Reich, attacking energetically in the direction of Vinograd and Belenikhino. The 2nd Tank Corps protecting the boundary between the 29th and 2nd Guards Tank Corps had the subsequent mission to develop their tactical success.

The tank army's right flank now faced a threatening situation. Although the Germans failed to advance in the center sector towards Prokhorovka, the 11th Panzer Division of the 48th Panzer Corps managed to encircle the 18th Tank Corps while attacking the adjacent 5th Guards Army. By 1300 hours, German tanks broke through a rifle division making it necessary to eliminate the immediate threat to the 5th Guards Tank Army right flank and rear.

Rotmistrov sent a tank brigade to the Voroshilov state farm, joining the right flank forces of the 18th Tank Corps and rifle units of the

5th Guards Army. Additionally, he dispatched a mechanized brigade to the northeast of Prokhorovka blocking the German advance to the northeast. The two brigades' swift march to the action and determined counterattacks against the penetrating German tank units stabilized the situation on the boundary between the 5th Guards Tank and 5th Guards Armies.

By nightfall 12 July, German and Soviet tank units were spent. They held their positions and prepared to repel any attacks. Rotmistrov had his corps refuel their machines, replenish ammunition, and feed the crews in the darkness. He wanted his tankers ready by dawn to resume the offensive. The wounded needed attention; the dead, picked up and buried; and the incapacitated tanks towed into rear echelon for repairs – all necessary activities in a modern armored fighting force.

With the cessation in fighting along the entire front, Rotmistrov left his dug-out for a stroll to shake off fatigue. He seldom counted personal cost in time and energy to complete an operation that would significantly alter the situation. He listened to the noises on the battlefield, subdued voices, clinking metal against metal, and humming truck engines. The night workers of war were on the job: engineers making their way to the frontline to lay mines where enemy tanks were expected to attack, medical personnel taking away the wounded, and logistical troops bringing up ammunition, food, fuel and lubricants. He thought about the day's events and knew the Germans were clearly prepared to resume the attack. The dawn was not far off; Rotmistrov needed rest. Without taking off his clothes, he fell asleep for a few hours, but was awakened by heavy bomb blasts. He contacted his corps commanders; all were at their posts and ready for action. Rotmistrov advised them to make better use of antitank guns, especially on the flanks.

By morning, Rotmistrov was already forward in the 29th Tank Corps command post when the Germans after a brief artillery preparation attacked the 18th Tank Corps. More than 50 tanks followed. A whole day of fighting continued into the night. It was dark before both sides, battle-weary, went over to the defensive.

The 18th Tank Corps covering the withdrawal of the 5th Guards Army left flank struck towards Andreevka, and after a short battle entered the town. Parts of the 29th Tank Corps fought strong tank engagements in the area of Komsomol state farm against the elite SS Death's Head Division. The Soviet tank corps stopped the German SS division's advance.

The 2nd Guards Tank Corps, minus one brigade sent to 69th Army, advanced after regrouping. Its attack overcame strong resistance, and by 1200 hours occupied the western bank of the Loga river. However, by mid-afternoon, the SS Das Reich Panzer Division attacked on the boundary between the 2nd Guards and 2nd Tank Corps, capturing the village of Storozhevoe and the northern edge of Vinograd. The panzer division posed a serious threat to the rear of the two corps. The commander of the 2nd Guards Tank Corps responded by placing the 25th Guards Tank Brigade in a blocking position and counterattacked the panzer division's flank with the 4th Guards Tank and 4th Guards Motorized Rifle Brigades. While the two brigades were unsuccessful in defeating the panzer division, the action checked the German advance.

During two days of fighting, the 29th Tank Corps lost totally, or temporarily, 60 per cent of its tanks; 18th Tank Corps, 30 per cent. Fifth Mechanized Corps losses were slight.[81]

For the next two days, tenacious fighting continued on the tank army's flanks, where the Germans tried to breakthrough to the rear. On the left flank, the German 3rd Panzer Corps jointly with the SS Das Reich Panzer Division attacked along the Northern Donets river, pushing back the 2nd Guards Tank Corps. The Guards tank corps, however, let German tanks through their positions, then attacked them, cutting off lines of retreat. On the flanks, the Germans resumed their attacks against the 18th and 29th Tank Corps which had assumed the defensive on Rotmistrov's orders. However, by nightfall on 15 July, the fighting calmed down along the front. The Germans were exhausted.

General Vatutin summoned Rotmistrov to the Front command post. The Front commander briefed the overall situation not only for the Front, but also actions on the Central, Western and Bryansk Fronts. He told Rotmistrov there was no time for rest and his tank army would have to fight one more time before it could be drawn out of the line for refitting.

On the morning of 17 July, the 5th Guards Tank Army went into the attack against the withdrawing panzer forces. Their advance slowed as strong German rearguard actions held them back. The tank army with too few tanks lacked the punch to pierce the holding actions. That evening General Vatutin informed Rotmistrov that his unit would be withdrawn into the Front reserve. General Vatutin looking at the map lying on the table drew a circle on it and instructed, "Hand over your sector to Zhadov (commander 5th Guards Army) along with the 2nd Guards and 2nd Tank Corps. As soon as you reach this area begin reorganizing your army."[82]

Rotmistrov was not satisfied with his army's overall performance in not fully destroying the German forces. He believed his time for preparation for the counterstrike was insufficient and his second echelon and reserve were siphoned off to protect threatened flanks of the army. Rotmistrov noted the lack of artillery in the tank army and thought greater air support should have been available.[83]

A fortnight of battles sapped the army's strength. Although casualties were relatively fewthe condition of the tank force concerned Rotmistrov. During the first two days of battles at Prokhorovka, the tank army lost more than 400 tanks, not counting those which were damaged beyond repair.[84] By working around the clock, the mechanics repaired and returned to action 112 vehicles. With a scarcity of spare parts, many parts were removed from wrecked tanks or from those requiring major repairs. But, the lack of machine tools, welding equipment, machinery and cranes to haul heavy tank turrets and engines delayed tank repairs, despite the mechanics' ingenuity. The ability to repair was one of the areas that German commanders acknowledged Soviet innovativeness. On 19 July, the tank army still had as many as 180 tanks requiring repairs. Many of the tanks remaining in action had worn out engines and needed their gears overhauled. Rotmistrov collated the figures on the army's requirements and went to General Vatutin.

General Vatutin listened attentively and ordered tank engines and spares from the Front's logistical base for the army. Priority went to the reconstitution of the 5th Guards Tank Army while General Katukov's lst Tank Army was told to make do. The need to rebuild the armored punch of both the Voronezh and Steppe Fronts delayed the counteroffensive towards Belgorod and Kharkov. The steady maintenance and supply effort restored Rotmistrov's army. By 30 July, the tank army had 503 tanks and 40 self-propelled artillery guns.

Once receiving provisional orders for the preparation of the impending offensive, Rotmistrov began planning for the second phase of the Battle of Kursk, the counteroffensive at Belgorod and Kharkov. Operation "Rumyantsev," named after Petr Aleksandrovich Rumyantsev, the famous 18th century Russian military leader and hero of the Russian-Turkish War, was designed to reduce the German Belgorod-Kharkov salient held by the 4th Panzer Army and Operational Group Kempf.

In late July, Rotmistrov's army received specific instructions from the Voronezh Front commander for Operation Rumyantsev. The 5th Guards and 1st Guards Tank Armies were to operate as the Front's mobile group for exploitation of the rifle army's breakthrough of the tactical defense. The tank armies were to breakthrough in the 5th Guards Army sector, operating on the main axis and cut off Kharkov from the west while encircling major defending German units.

The tank army's chief of staff, General V.N. Baskakov, called a meeting with the chief of operations, Lieutenant Colonel F.M. Belorzerov, and chief of intelligence, Major F. Ya. Mitin, to brief the army commander. First, they listened to the intelligence information on the enemy collected by the army and passed down by the Front. Based on an analysis of the situation, the forces and character of the German defense, Rotmistrov decided to commit the army to the breakthrough in two echelons, having in the first echelon the 18th and 29th Tank Corps; in the second, 5th Guards Mechanized Corps.

On 31 July, General Vatutin with Marshal Zhukov held a meeting to finalize the plans for the operation. After the Front mission had been briefed, Rotmistrov gave a five minute report on his decision, and the corps commanders were granted two to three minutes each. Studying the plan closely on a map, General Vatutin approved the army and corps decisions, and he directed detailed attention to coordinated actions with infantry and air support.[85] When Marshal Zhukov and General Vatutin left, Rotmistrov contacted the commanders, General Zhadov, 5th Guards Army and General Katukov, 1st Tank Army, and arranged a meeting with them at the 5th Guards Army command post. Together with their chief of staffs and heads of the army operations sections, the army commanders coordinated every phase of the operation, and most importantly plotted lines of advance for the tank corps in the offensive sector of the 5th Guards Army.

On the afternoon of 2 August, Rotmistrov's command post moved forward. By evening, the 18th and 29th Tank Corps deployed into attack positions. The tank army coiled to strike. By the time of the artillery preparation at 0500 hours the next morning, Rotmistrov was in General Zhadov's command post. Marshal Zhukov, as Stalin's representative, was also there to observe the attack. "It was the first time that I had witnessed such a devastating artillery preparation," Rotmistrov later wrote.[86]

The Front commander decided the 5th Guards Tank Army should be committed after the German's main line of defense had been penetrated by the infantry assault. Only in an emergency were the tank armies to be used in the actual breakthrough. After the attack began, Rotmistrov ordered the tank corps commanders to keep their lead brigades close behind the infantry. In the first few hours, the rifle units managed to advance only four kilometers. When the infantry advance slowed, Marshal Zhukov asked Rotmistrov if it was not time to use the tanks. Rotmistrov agreed and immediately left to expedite the order.

Calling the tank corps commanders to the tank army command post, Rotmistrov explained the rifle divisions' difficult situation, and stated only the tank corps through decisive and bold action could successfully complete the breakthrough. He ordered the attack to begin with the objective to help the infantry complete the breakthrough of the tactical zone and then strike into the operational depth according to the plan.[87]

At 1300 hours, the forward tank companies deployed in combat formation, and the uncoiling tank army of 550 tanks attacked from the march.[88] By early afternoon the tank army's first echelon moved through the German's main defensive line, overtaking the Red Army rifle units. The lst and 5th Guards Tank Armies broke through the Germans second line of defense by nightfall, advancing 25-30 kilometers. As the night fighting tapered off, the tank armies cut the important Tomarovka-Belgorod railroad, severing the link between the enemy's Tomarovka and Belgorod pockets of resistance.

At 0500 hours the next morning, the 5th Guards Tank Army resumed the offensive, seeking to change tactical into operational success. Heavy German resistance north of Belgorod prompted General Konev, commanding the Steppe Front, to ask General Vatutin for the use of the 5th Guards Tank Army. General Vatutin agreed to take the second echelon corps, the 5th Guards Mechanized Corps, turning it toward the village of Krasnoye in the rear of the German forces in the Belgorod area. Rotmistrov's lead tank corps struck the 3rd Panzer Division. With the diversion of the 5th Guards Mechanized Corps, the 5th Guards Tank Army lost some of its offensive punch.

By 6 August, Rotmistrov's tank army moving further into the depths of the German disposition maneuvered around the 6th Panzer Division, overrunning large pockets of resistance towards the key communication center of Zolochev on the main road to Kharkov. The swift advance by the Soviet tankers allowed a surprise capture of Zolochev and split the German defense in two. A 55 kilometer wedge was driven between the 4th Panzer Army and Operational Group Kempf. After reaching Zolochev, the 5th Guards Mechanized Corps rejoined the tank army.

On 10 August, Rotmistrov's full army launched a smashing attack along the railroads into Kharkov and met stiff resistance. The tank army slid west to find easier going, but was thwarted in its attempts to thrust south of Zolochev. The littered battlefield resembled a scene from the battle of Prokhorovka. "Both the enemy and our tanks were on fire, wrecked antitank guns, armored personnel carriers, trucks and motorcycles all about, farm buildings and haystacks were on fire and bluish black smoke was enveloping everything around," recalled Rotmistrov.[89]

On 15 August 1943, parts of the German SS Das Reich Division penetrated the 13th Guards Rifle Division defense on the left flank of the 5th Guards Tank Army, and struck towards Bogodukhov. Rotmistrov at 1000 hours the next day ordered his reserve, the 53rd Tank Regiment and artillery antitank reserve, to move forward from Bogodukhov to the south. By mid-afternoon the reserve assumed the defense in the designated area, stopping the German advance.

The 5th Guards Tank Army was committed in support of the 1st Tank Army, beginning four days of intensive fighting south of Bogodukhov. These battles eroded the tank strength of the two tank armies. German counterattacks in the vicinity of Akhtyrka kept Rotmistrov's army involved in major fighting, expending tanks like bullet cartridges.

Through arduous engagements, Soviet forces rolled back the German defenders, and by 17 August, the Steppe Front penetrated the German's outer defenses for Kharkov, creating favorable conditions for the encirclement of the historic city. The Soviet High command having dealt with the German threat at Akhtyrka, switched Rotmistrov's tank army from General Vatutin's Voronezh Front to the Steppe Front. General Konev was directed to use the tank army in a concentrated attack west of Kharkov to complete the encirclement of the city. On 19 August, the 5th Guards Tank Army with a diminished strength of 130 from its original 540 tanks moved eastward. The tank army approached Kharkov from the southwest.

Assembling north of the Udy river on the night of 21 August,

Rotmistrov's tank army attacked the next day east of Lyubotin. The army's low tank strength made the fighting more dramatic against German units which had moved into the area to hold open a narrow escape route from Kharkov. While Rotmistrov's army was unable to close the circle on the city, General Konev's forces made a final assault with rifle units capturing Kharkov.

The Belgorod-Kharkov operation brought Red Army operations in line with their operational intent for deep operations. The Soviets had a workable tank army structure. The tank army commanders quickly acquired skills to conduct sustained operations. The Belgorod-Kharkov operation to a great measure surpassed previous Soviet tank force operations, foreshadowing the complete rise of the Red armored Phoenix. Rotmistrov received the Order of Kutuzov lst Degree.

On 27 August, with no time for respite, General Konev assigned the 5th Guards Tank Army together with the 5th Guards Army the mission to drive the enemy southwest from Kharkov. The following pursuit operation began the great race between the German and Soviet armies for the Dnepr river. At the time, 5th Guards Tank Army possessed 66 operable tanks, representing 12 per cent of its original strength. The corps staffs were at 30-35 percent strength. Large losses were in signal equipment – in one corps they reached about 75 percent. Nearly 85 percent of company and battalion commanders were out of action.[90]

Under these conditions, Rotmistrov decided to reorganize the remaining tanks and personnel into one brigade for each corps, reinforcing them with artillery and uniting them as a special army detachment under the command of the 5th Guards Mechanized Corps commander. The mechanized corps had the highest percentage of its staff and signal equipment intact.[91] In addition, the corps received two high-powered radios and three medium powered ones from the 18th and 29th Tank Corps. The operations and intelligence sections were reinforced by officers from the appropriate sections of the army staff. The staff positions of the composite brigades were created by consolidating several brigade staffs which had lost a significant portion of their men and equipment. For example, the commander of the 25th Guards Tank Brigade headed the composite brigade of the 29th Tank Corps. Its staff had been formed from the staff officers of two other brigades. The operations and intelligence sections had been transferred from the staff of the 29th Tank Corps to the staff of the composite detachment. Engineer support was directed by the chief of engineer troops from this corps.[92]

The tank army staff set to work carrying out the plan. It sent officers to the areas where the detachments were to be organized, and they provided help, directing and inspecting the created formations for their combat readiness. These army staff officers temporarily headed the staffs of the composite detachments. A portion of the army field headquarters at the same time solved the tasks of receiving the replacements and organizing the return of damaged equipment to detachments.

These measures allowed Rotmistrov to successfully continue the offensive with a strong unit forward and two phantom corps for deception, while simultaneously stopping parts of the army for restoration. This brilliant risk and improvisation belies the conventional notion that Soviet advances came as a result of a massive superiority in personnel and equipment rather than with true military prowess.

On 29 August, the 5th Guards Tank Army and 53rd Army seized Lyubotin, opening a wide road to Poltava. Fighting German rearguards, the Red Army raced the German army to the Dnepr river. By 20 September, Rotmistrov's army could contribute little to the fight and was committed to the Stavka reserve for reconstitution of personnel and equipment.

In the first half of October 1943, the 5th Guards Tank Army was assigned back to the Steppe Front and deployed in the area of Poltava. By mid-month, the tank army moved at night 200 kilometers from Poltava to the Dnepr river area. The Soviet command sought to secretly slip the tank army on the west side of the Dnepr river. General Konev prohibited showing river crossing equipment of any kind in Rotmistrov's proposed crossing site. The tank army would cross at night. General Konev ordered the 7th Guards Army commander to keep his floating bridges on the river during the day and move all his reinforcements into the bridgehead. The 7th Army crossings attracted German bombers, alerting the German command to a buildup of Soviet forces in the southern sector. But, the Steppe Front's main effort with the 5th Guards Tank Army struck in a northern direction towards Pyatkikhatki.

In the early morning hours, 15 October, the 7th Mechanized Corps, included in Rotmistrov's army for this operation, and two brigades of the 18th tank Corps, only 105 tanks crossed the Dnepr river. The 7th and 5th Guards Armies launched their attack. The Germans immediately threw in their reserves. On the following night, two tank and one motorized rifle brigades of the 29th Tank Corps, about 109 tanks, crossed. The tank army had not managed to complete its regrouping in the established time.

On the morning of 15 October, after a powerful artillery preparation, the Steppe Front's 5th Guards and 37th Armies attacked. General Konev increased the strength of the assault by ordering Rotmistrov's corps into the fight. Timing a short 15 minute artillery strike during the Germans' evening mess hours, Rotmistrov's lead corps smashed into the German's defense.[93] However, Rotmistrov's tankers entered the battle under difficult conditions, insufficient roads and a small bridgehead constrained the tank army's full force, limiting the strike. The brigades followed along a single march route, committing the 7th Mechanized Corps by mid-afternoon in the 37th Army sector and the 18th Tank Corps two hours later in the 5th Guards Army sector. Despite the addition of armor in the attack, the Germans resisted strongly allowing only a 2-3 kilometer advance.

The following day the Germans withdrew since their initial defensive positions had been penetrated. Between the 7th Mechanized and 18th Tank Corps, Rotmistrov committed the 29th Tank Corps to maintain pressure and shatter the defense. The tank corps advanced on a sector two kilometers wide, and quickly moved 2-3 kilometers forward. Meanwhile, the 18th Tank Corps repelled German tank and infantry counterattacks from the west, and fought with the leading rifle corps. The most success came with the 7th Mechanized Corps' advance of 15-17 kilometers to the southwest edge of Likhovki, 100 kilometers northwest of Krivoi Rog, solidly carving the tank army's hold on the west side of the Dnepr river.

By 19 October, the tank army with neighboring rifle units advanced 25 kilometers capturing the large railroad center at Pyatikhatki. Moving to the western edge of the town, the 29th Tank Corps brigades fought all day repelling German counterattacks. The 7th Mechanized Corps ran into increasingly stiff resistance from the German 16th Panzer Grenadier Division. The 18th Tank Corps succeeded in capturing the towns of Zheltoe and Zelenoe. Advancing 60 kilometers from the Dnepr, the situation for the Front became favorable for developing the offensive.

The 5th Guards Tank Army supported by an air corps struck towards Krivoi Rog, but faltered in developing the attack. A shortage of ammunition and fuel became a debilitating problem for Rotmistrov's tanks. Rotmistrov spent much of his time working re-supply issues. On the morning of 19 October, he reported gathering 1000 vehicles with fuel and ammunition for his units.[94]

Since the 18th Tank Corps had not managed to take Aleksandriyu, Rotmistrov ordered an attack towards Krivoi Rog. Continuing the offensive, the 18th Tank Corps on the morning of 21 October crossed the Ingulets river in the area of Petrovo, while the 29th Tank Corps seized Annovku. Towards evening the Front's rifle armies advanced to the Ingulets river.

The next day, the 5th Guards Tank Army, regaining momentum, approached Krivoi Rog. The Front commander arrived in Rotmistrov's observation post on 23 October and watched the 18th and 29th Tank Corps fighting for the outskirts of Krivoi Rog, how-ever, the tank corps failed to penetrate the German's city defense. General Konev decided to commit other forces to the fight.

On the morning of 24 October, the 18th Tank Corps with rein-forcing infantry riding on tanks fought along streets into Krivoi Rog. The following day, the 29th Tank Corps penetrated the northern edge of the city, but since the corps lacked infantry support, withdrew. Four days later, Rotmistrov swung his units around the resisting city, hitting it from the west with three corps. But, the Germans held against the heavy blow. Rotmistrov's command of the situation deteriorated the next two days as the Germans counterattacked from the south forcing the tank army into a hasty defense. General Konev's drive was momentarily checked.

General Malinovskii's 3rd Ukrainian Front began broadening its bridgehead at Dnepropetrovsk south of General Konev's Front. The two Fronts combined their efforts to drive on Krivoi Rog, how-ever, the First Panzer Army refused to budge. The stalled attack al-lowed the German panzer army to temporarily escape the trap. On 14 November, General Konev resumed a direct attack on Krivoi Rog, but mud bogged the advance. Not until December, with heavy frost to freeze the mud, could Rotmistrov move his tanks. However, the capture of Krivoi Rog was left to rifle armies which secured the town in February 1944.

On 9 December, in a redirection of the 5th Guards Tank Army, Rotmistrov took Znamenka, 35 kilometers north of Kirovograd. The tank army prepared to strike for Kirovograd. In the Kirovograd op-eration, 5-15 January 1944, the Red Army sought to extend its holdings on the western side of the Dnepr river deeper into the Ukraine. The 5th Guards Tank Army operating as the mobile group for the 2nd Ukrainian Front attacked through the 7th Guards Army's sector, since the rifle army received no supporting tanks. Rotmistrov's mission was to attack in the direction of Pokrovskoe, cross the Ingul river south of Pokrovskoe, and by the end of the first day arrived in the area of Bezvodnaya, Fedorovka, Yurevka. With the 7th Mechanized Corps, he intended to encircle and capture Kirovograd from the south and southwest, creating a position from which to destroy any advancing German reserve.[95]

In accordance with General Konev's plan, at 0810 hours, 5 January, 1944, a powerful 50 minute artillery preparation began followed by the rifle armies. While the 5th Guards and 53rd Armies successfully penetrated the German defense, the 7th Guards Army encountered an unyielding defense. With an insufficient number of artillery guns for a breakthrough sector, the rifle army made slow progress. The Front commander in his typical early use of tank armies, decided to commit Rotmistrov's tanks after two hours of fighting. General Konev sent the tank army into a sector in which the Germans were waiting for the attack. With a poor artillery preparation and no air support, Rotmistrov's units wedged into the tactical defenses 4-5 kilometers by the end of the day.

General Konev decided to take advantage of a greater success in the 5th Guards Army sector. At 2100 hours, he instructed Rotmistrov to give the 8th Mechanized Corps in the area of Kazarna to the commander of the 5th Guards Army by 0800 hours the next morning.[96] The 5th Guards Army with the 7th and 8th Mechanized Corps was to seize Kirovograd in coordination with the 5th Guards Tank Army.

The next day General Konev's forces penetrated the German defenses, but not without cost. The tank corps weakened from the first day's fighting had lost 139 tanks and self-propelled assault guns, nearly 60% of the combat strength that sharply reduced their potential for action in the operational depth.[97] The tank army persevered attacking in the general direction of Plavni, going around Kirovograd to the southwest. By 1400 hours, 6 January, the tank army overcame the German's second line of defense along the Adzhamke river.

During the course of the fighting on 6 January, Marshal Zhukov arrived in the 5th Guards Tank Army observation post while Rotmistrov was away in the 29th Tank Corps. Upon Rotmistrov's return to the observation post, Marshal Zhukov asked how things were going. Rotmistrov reported German resistance and his tank army was still working through the tactical defense. Marshal Zhukov acknowledged the report and noted the 8th Mechanized Corps of the 5th Guards Army was having success on the west side of Kirovograd. He wanted that success reinforced.[98] But, General Konev had other plans for the tank army. With rifle forces drawing up for the assault on Kirovograd, the 18th Tank Crops cut off the withdrawal routes of the Germans. The 5th Guards Tank Army received the mission to develop the offensive in the direction of Novo-Ukrainku, further west.

Kirovograd was liberated on 8 January. The Kirovograd operation had thrown German forces back a 100 kilometers, and by mid-January, the 2nd Ukrainian Front had captured a large bridgehead west and northwest of Dnepropetrovsk in conjunction with 3rd Ukrainian Front. The Germans held tenaciously to good defensible terrain and offered serious resistance on the boundary between the 1st and 2nd Ukrainian Fronts. In the following Korsun-Shevchenkovskii operation, the two Fronts planned to reduce the stubborn salient quickly. From the end of January to mid-February, weather and terrain conditions for the operation were unfavorable with rain, sleet, and snow. Only five days during the period were without some form of precipitation and temperatures averaged between minus 5 degrees to plus 5 degrees. Weather hampered maneuver, and maneuver was necessary.

The 5th Guards and 6th Tank Armies of the 2nd and 1st Ukrainian Fronts, respectively, would execute a double envelopment. The operation began with staggered attack dates: 1st Ukrainian Front began on 26 January; the 2nd Ukrainian, 25 January.

On 16 January, Rotmistrov returned from his reconnaissance and ordered the army's regrouping from north of Kirovograd to the east of Balandino. Troops and equipment moved only at night in brigade-size formations to within 20-30 kilometers of the front line, in order to hide its movement from German intelligence.

Rotmistrov typically sought to deceive the Germans and protect his force before the operation. He directed preparation of false assembly areas near the actual ones. Engineers quickly built 126 wooden dummy tanks and 36 wooden gun models. The 31st Tank Brigade imitated the arrival of new forces in the tank army's assembly areas near Kirovograd while false radio transmissions continued to disguise the tank army's departure. Artillery fires covered tank engine noises during the actual movement. The false assembly areas drew German attention and artillery fire.

Considering the poor weather and bad roads, Rotmistrov ordered his engineers to construct lateral roads connecting the assembly areas. Over the next four days, the army engineers laid 135 kilometers of hard surfaced roads. This gave the army its necessary mobility to operate in adverse conditions.

While the tank army regrouped, Rotmistrov with his operational group reconnoitered the breakthrough sector. During the reconnaissance, he determined where to conduct his main and secondary efforts, the final attack positions, and he looked over German defensive positions. Rotmistrov concluded that the best sector for the main effort was south of Balandino in spite of the strongly entrenched German positions. German defensive preparations covered the front of their first trenchline with mines, barbed wire and other antitank obstacles. Rotmistrov, well aware of standard German tactics by this stage of the war, reasoned that the strongly fortified area meant there were fewer troops in the area and that his main blow should fall there.

As a final, comprehensive measure of preparation for the impending operation, Rotmistrov required his officers to study the Stalingrad offensive's lessons learned. As a successful encirclement operation in which Rotmistrov had participated, he wanted his officers familiar with the character of encirclement fighting and potential problem areas for armored forces.

The 5th Guards Tank Army greatly understrength from previous operations, fielded 218 tanks and 18 self-propelled assault guns for its planned commitment in the 53rd Army's sector. The tank army's objective for the second day was a penetration at Shoply, seizing Zvenigorod. The objective linked with forces of the lst Ukrainian Front, forming the outer perimeter of a large encirclement.

The operation began with a short powerful artillery strike. Forward battalions mixed with the artillery preparation achieved surprise and quickly moved to a depth of 2-6 kilometers. At 1400 hours, the attacking forward Soviet rifle divisions verged on collapse against stubborn German resistance. Rotmistrov considered the risk of losing a large number of tanks completing the breakthrough with a possible failed operation. He decided to commit, requested permission; General Konev concurred. By mid-afternoon, Rotmistrov's tank army advanced 18-20 kilometers, breaking away from the rifle formations.

During the evening briefing at the main command post, the tank army's intelligence officer reported the German's second line of defense held two seriously depleted infantry divisions and the German's 3rd and 14th Panzer Divisions were rapidly approaching the villages of Kapitanovka and Tishkovka. Conferring with General Baskakov, the chief of staff, Rotmistrov decided not to wait for the rifle units left behind earlier in the day. Early the next morning, he would strike out with only his tank forces to exploit the tactical gains and reach Lebedin in the direction of Shoply before the German reserves. General Konev agreed, the tanks should not stop.

With the morning of 26 January, the tank corps continued the attack towards Shoply. Rotmistrov spent the early morning hours at the 20th Tank Corps command post, overseeing a successful start to the attack. By noon the lead brigades pushed German defenders from Kapitanovka and reached Tishkova. Rotmistrov pleased with the progress encouraged the corps commander to reach Lebedin by nightfall.

General I.G. Lazarev's 20th Tank Corps, which started the operation with only 51 tanks, captured Lebedin by 2300 hours that night and continued toward Shoply. Meanwhile, the reports from the 29th Tank Corps were not good. The corps advance had been slowed. Rotmistrov moved to the corps command post to closely review the situation. While the corps made a slight advance of 5-6 kilometers and captured Turya, German counterattacks made further advance impossible. Reports of additional German panzer forces en route and General I. F. Kirichenko's 29th Tank Corps requesting to transition to defense posed a dilemma for Rotmistrov. But, his ability to keenly assess the situation and his willingness to change his mind led him to a correct decision. Since the 29th Tank Corps without infantry support was in no shape to fight a meeting engagement with the arriving German tank forces, Rotmistrov agreed to a hasty defense. By temporarily defending in the sector, Rotmistrov's deep advance with the 20th Tank Corps faced less risk of being cut off. Rotmistrov held his third tank corps, the 18th, in the second echelon, giving him flexibility to continue exploiting the situation.

In the evening briefing, General Baskakov informed Rotmistrov that the tank army could expect strong German counterattacks. Rotmistrov agreed that German command knew the direction of his attack and its implications for the entire German force. Again,

Rotmistrov faced the decision to turn temporarily to the defense and await the arrival of the rifle units or continue forward with the tank units. After discussion with the tank army's military council, Rotmistrov decided to continue just as he had done as a corps commander during the campaigning around Rostov. He ordered the 20th and 29th Tank Corps to advance on Shoply and Zvenigorod where it was to link with lead units of the 6th Tank Army, 1st Ukrainian Front. The 29th Tank Corps was to guard the left flank of the 20th Tank Corps.

The 20th Tank Corps, in a successful night attack, captured Shoply to maintain the momentum of the tank army's advance. And, by 1000 hours, 27 January, the town was completely in Soviet hands. At the same time, the Germans launched a sweeping counterattack retaking Tishkovka and part of Kapitanovka, attacking from the south and cutting off the 5th Guards Tank Army's lines of communications. The 20th Tank Corps command post became cut off, isolated from its brigades. Groups of German tanks moved up and down the supply routes destroying ammunition and fuel trucks destined for Rotmistrov's forward tank units.

With his lead two corps isolated from the 2nd Ukrainian Front and the tank army's rear support, Rotmistrov acted decisively. He directed the 20th Tank Corps to continue its attack towards Zvenigorod, securing the left flank in vicinity of Vodyanoye-Lipanka while Rotmistrov committed his second echelon, 18th Tank Corps, to stop and throw back the counterattacking German divisions. Only by continuing the attack to link with the 1st Ukrainian Front and fending off the counterattack would the Soviet operation be successful. Rotmistrov made the difficult decision while his tank units were low in combat strength.

General Konev impressed with Rotmistrov's performance praised his "great self-control" and "combat experience."[99] Konev recalled when he was in Rotmistrov's command post, during the operation with artillery and machinegun fire all around. And, in this alarming situation, Rotmistrov "clearly led the actions of his subordinate corps and brigades, sensibly assessing the situation and taking well-grounded decisions."[100]

Rotmistrov knew the 18th Tank Corps had only 50 operational tanks at the beginning of the operation and might be unable to halt the German counterattack. He asked for reinforcements from General Konev who immediately ordered antitank artillery brigades transferred from other Front sectors. General Konev committed rifle division from the second echelon 4th Guards Army. From the Front reserve, Konev committed the 5th Guards Cavalry Corps to work in conjunction with Rotmistrov's tank army. The additional forces enabled the Front to create an inner circle to prevent the withdrawal of German forces to the south.

Rotmistrov's boldness in continuing the attack instead of waiting for the infantry to catch up and rest his tankers saved the operation for the Front. On 28 January, the 20th Guards Tank Corps, 5th Guards Tank Army reached the town of Zvenigorod where they met the penetrating lead elements of General A. G. Kravchenko's 6th Tank Army, 1st Ukrainian Front. Rotmistrov reported the meeting to General Konev but advised him the encirclement was thin in spots where the Germans could attempt a break out or break in. In four days, the tank armies of the 1st and 2nd Ukrainian Fronts cut off all the Germans withdrawal routes from Korsun. Rotmistrov's tank army pushed the outer perimeter 15 to 25 kilometers from the inner perimeter and transitioned to defense. Rotmistrov's mission was to hold out German relief forces while the encircled pocket was annihilated. Despite relief attempts, the 5th Guards Tank Army held and the German pocket was gruesomely eliminated by 17 February. The German loss, in the words of a senior German officer, was a "miniature Stalingrad."[101]

Rotmistrov's tenacious pursuit of the tank army's objective, his exploitation of the situation, the quick and bold maneuver of his tank forces solidified his reputation for brilliance in armored warfare. The operation earned him promotion to Marshal of Armored Forces and the awarding of the Order of Suvorov, 1st degree.

While liquidating the Korsun pocket, the Red Army gained a strategic position to recapture lost Soviet territory to its frontier borders. The 2nd Ukrainian Front's role in the major offensive was to strike from Zvenigorod to Uman.

For the Uman-Botoshansk operation which began two weeks after the completion of the Korsun-Shevchenkovskii operation, all the Red Army tank armies had significant shortages, including the 5th Guards Tank Army with 221 tanks and self-propelled assault guns.[102] Nonetheless, in the operation, the 5th Guards Tank Army received the mission on the first day of the operation to advance in the 4th Guards Army's penetration and develop the attack in the general direction of Uman, and by the end of the first day force the Gornyi Tikich river.

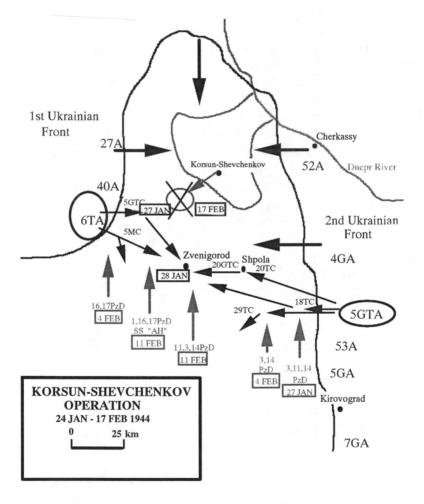

1st Ukrainian
Front

27A

Korsun-Shevchenkov

Cherkassy

52A

Dnepr River

40A

5GTC

27 JAN   17 FEB

6TA

5MC

2nd Ukrainian
Front

4GA

Zvenigorod

20GTC   Shpola

20TC

28 JAN

16,17PzD

4 FEB

1,16,17PzD
SS "AH"

11 FEB

11,3,14PzD

11 FEB

29TC

18TC

5GTA

53A

3,14
PzD

4 FEB

3,11,14
PzD

27 JAN

5GA

Kirovograd

7GA

**KORSUN-SHEVCHENKOV
OPERATION
24 JAN - 17 FEB 1944**

0   25 km

Battling for Uman, Ryblnitsy and Dubossary, March-April 1944, Rotmistrov created composite groupings from the 29th Tank Corps, an assault gun artillery regiment, and other artillery and air defense battalions. The mission of the group was to attack to Chernoye and Dubossary. The designated deputy commander for the group recalled Rotmistrov's assigning of the mission:

"The mission is not for the weak.... Tomorrow you will coordinate your actions with the rifle divisions. With it you will attack." Marshal Rotmistrov thought for a minute, as though weighing all the "pros" and "cons" then continued, "You, of course, are to liberate Chernoye. But, Dubossary will not be taken easily with the first attacks. But you try to get hold of the edge of town. And the rest of the affair will be for the infantry."[103] The ad hoc group took both towns in a few days.

At the end of March, the 5th Guards Tank Army turned south with the mission to coordinate with 3rd Ukrainian Front in destroying enemy forces along the Southern Bug river. The tank army moved to a depth of 250-300 kilometers in the Uman-Botoshansk operation.

By mid-April 1944, the 2nd Ukrainian Front consolidated on the northeastern border of Rumania, preparing for new operations. Rotmistrov's army withdrawn to the Stavka reserve in the first part of June, secretly regrouped in the area of Smolensk, where it was to be resubordinated to the 3rd Belorussian Front. Interestingly, when the 5th Guards Tank Army prepared to move to Smolensk, the Red Army General Staff discovered the 2nd Ukrainian Front, to which Rotmistrov's army had been attached, intended to keep some of its tanks and regiments of self-propelled artillery. The Front's retention of them would weaken the tank army, rendering it unfit for the impending operation by the Red Army General Staff's calculations. The following direction was promptly sent to the 2nd Ukrainian Front: "The 5th Guards Tank Army is to be sent off with Vovchenko's corps and Kirichenko's corps at full strength in men and material. The two corps must have not less than 300 tanks altogether."[104]

The Red Army during the spring of 1944 conducted a series of operations to recapture the Ukraine to the Rumanian border, but by late April and May, the momentum had dwindled to a crawl. The Soviet High Command shifted their attention to the large salient formed in Belorussia, called the "Belorussian Balcony." In a strategic offensive, the Soviets sought to recapture Belorussian and destroy the German Army Group Center.

The Belorussian operation involved four Fronts. On the northern right flank, the 1st Baltic and 3rd Belorussian Fronts would attack the German 3rd Panzer Army around Vitebsk. The 1st Baltic Front attacked on the north of Vitebsk while the 3rd Belorussian Front attacked on the south. The 3rd Belorussian Front, under the command of General Ivan Danilovich Chernyakovskii, consisted of four rifle armies, the 39th, 5th, 11th Guards and 31st Armies, and Rotmistrov's tank army. The success of the two fronts was to be exploited by the 5th Guards Tank Army. The original plan committed the 5th Guards Tank Army through the 11th Guards Army on the axis through Borisov to Minsk, but subsequent events forced the Soviets to deviate from the plan.

The 5th Guards Tank Army initially concentrated outside of Smolensk. On 16 June, the tank army was assigned to the 3rd Belorussian Front. Rotmistrov's tank army had only two tank corps, the 29th Tank Corps under the command of Major General E.I. Fominykh and General I.A. Vovchenko's 3rd Guards Tank Corps. Rotmistrov decided to move from the area of concentration to an assembly area 40-50 kilometers west of Smolensk and approximately a day's march from the front line. The move forward took five days, 17-22 June, since the army marched along one route.

Rotmistrov with only two tank corps could not create a strong second echelon and allocating a large reserve would be at the expense of the first echelon and "extremely undesirable." He decided to commit the army in a single echelon with the 29th Tank Corps on the right flank and 3rd Guards Tank Corps on the left. In reserve was the 1st Separate Guards Motorcycle Regiment, a Katyusha rocket regiment, an artillery battalion and self-propelled assault gun regiment.

On 22 June 1944, three years after the German invasion, the Soviet Belorussian operation began with a large reconnaissance-in-force effort by the 1st Baltic, 3rd Belorussian and 2nd Belorussian Fronts. The advances were so promising that the Soviet command used the momentum to begin the offensive, and by the end of the first full day of operations on 23 June, significant penetration of the German defenses were made in the 1st Baltic and 3rd Belorussian sectors, particularly around Vitebsk. While the 3rd Belorussian Front's 39th and 5th Armies made progress to the west, the 11th Guards Army sector north of Orsha proved a hard defense. General Galitskii's two left flank rifle corps encountered strongly fortified and well placed defensive fires and were unable to penetrate. His right flank rifle corps had some success through swampy terrain to the north. The lack of progress in the 11th Guards Army sector concerned General Chernyakovskii and Marshal Vasilevskii and they considered redirecting the 5th Guards Tank Army.

In a Front planning meeting to which Rotmistrov sent a subordinate to attend, the tank army commander's representative raised Rotmistrov's concern for too little time left to prepare routes and assault positions in the direction of the 5th Army sector. General Chernyakovskii indicated the Front could support the tank army in necessary routes. Then the point was raised, that it was unclear how the Germans intended to use their operational reserves in the 5th Army sector. Chernyakovskii apparently humored this point away claiming that only the German commander knew that and "You shouldn't expect that everything will be made to order for you. You yourself should foresee and unriddle the enemy design."[105]

Fortunately, the 5th Guards Tank Army could quickly advance into the fight in the 11th Guards sector or in the 5th Army sector.[106] At midday 23 June, the Front commander ordered the tank army in the early morning hours of 24 June to move to the attack position with both tank corps behind the first echelon of the 11th Guards Army. "I asked the Front commander, General I. D. Chernyakovskii not to do this, assuring him, that if we enjoyed success in this direction that the 5th Guards Tank Army will in good time commit to the fight. However, my suggestion was refused," Rotmistrov remarked.[107] Rotmistrov believed the tank army located at a road junction could operate from the depth in two directions. "However, orders are orders, and it was fulfilled," Rotmistrov wrote after the war.[108]

To exploit the success of the 5th Army, at 2000 hours, 24 June, the 5th Guards Tank Army was ordered to regroup in the 5th Army sector at Liozno by the morning of 25 June.[109] Marshal Vasilevskii recalled, "Rotmistrov was not exactly enthusiastic" at the decision.[110]

Changing the direction for the commitment created problems for the tank army. Due to a lack of lateral roads, the tank corps had to reverse their direction and conduct a 60 kilometer road march. The tank army's approach to the line of commitment was accomplished under very difficult conditions along the front line. Each tank corps moved along the march route which cut across the rear to front movement of the forward rifle armies. The movement was further complicated in that the 11th Guards and 5th Armies had not fully cleared the march routes along which moved Rotmistrov's tank army. Two or three units marched simultaneously along the routes. On 25 June in the area of Verkhne-Aleksandrov, the tank army's main forces stood six hours waiting for the march routes to free up. All this did not allow the tank on 25 June to pass the rifle corps and only on the following morning it passed the 65th Rifle Corps, 5th Army on the line Goryuchko, Khodosy, advancing into the operational depth.[111] The tank army used up precious fuel.

At 0400 hours, 26 June, Rotmistrov's army moved into a "chistyi proryv", a clean breakthrough. The 29th Tank Corps moved to the Bobr river, then Obchugev, and the 3rd Guards Tank Corps advanced on the Moscow-Minsk highway. By afternoon, forward units seized Tolochin. By 1900 hours, the tank army advanced nearly 75 kilometers with the 29th Tank Corps at Yanov and the 3rd Guards Tank Corps at Slaveny. The tank army's pace slowed the following three days, the 3rd Guards Tank Corps encountered the German reserve, 5th Panzer Division, while the 29th Tank Corps ran into wooded swamp with few roads on which the Germans placed obstacles and mines.

The tank army's performance prompted Marshal Vasilevskii to remark, "the 5th Guards Tank Army which had always distinguished itself in battle, functioned worse than usual."[112] The tank army lost too many tanks in the advance. The delay in the tank army's commitment allowed the Germans to bring up the 5th Panzer Division from the reserve which took up defensive positions across wooded-swamp land making Rotmistrov's advance extremely difficult and costly. To do this, the German commander of Army Group Center regrouped the 5th Panzer Division (130 tanks) by rail from the area of Kovel to Borisov, tasked with advancing to the Bobr river and having taken up a defense, delay the advance of the 3rd Guards Tank Corps that operated in the Krupki, Borisov direction.

But since the 3rd Guards Tank Corps crossed the Bobr river on the move late in the day on 28 June, and prevented the Germans from reaching the river, the 5th Panzer Division was forced to join in a meeting engagement under unfavorable conditions. Its tank battalions immediately after unloading at the Borisov rail station began moving towards Krupki.

Having received reconnaissance information about the 5th Panzer Division's movement at 1700 hours, General Vovchenko assessed the situation and decided receive the German tank attack while at the halt. Then, the forces of the 18th Tank Brigade would pin down the Germans in the Krupki area while the 3rd Guards Tank and 2nd Guards Motorized Rifle Brigades delivered a flank attack. By the start of the engagement, the tank corps had over 200 tanks and self-propelled assault guns.

Meanwhile, the German 5th Panzer Division having deployed into battle formation attacked, delivering the main strike on the Panskoe axis and a supporting attack at Gaponovichi.

From the right, the 29th Tank Corps having defeated the enemy's 14th Infantry Division, engaged units of the 11th Infantry Division and by 1730 hours came out at the line Zaprude-Starye Shavry.

The 3rd Guards Tank Corps repelled the German attack from stationary fire, at 1800 hours, after ground attack strikes and a brief artillery firing the corps brigades went o the offensive. By 2000 hours, the 3rd Guards Tank Brigade, after a surprise assault into the Panzer Division's flank near Gaponovichi, broke out at the northeastern outskirts of Malya Sloboda and ensured the rapid capture of Kamenka by the 25th Brigade, 29th Tank Corps. The corps reconnaissance by that time had arrived at the German rear, and suddenly came upon the location of the 5th Panzer Division headquarters, which was in the forest west of Krupki. The surprise attack by the corps reconnaissance patrol was crowned with success. The headquarters was routed, and the division commander taken prisoner.

The corps commander found out that the Germans were preparing a new counterattack with a heavy tank force. At approximately 2030 hours he decided to commit the 19th Guards Tank Brigade to the engagement from the line Bol'shaya Sloboda and western outskirts of Krupki, and, in cooperation with the 3rd and 18th Guards Tank Brigades, complete the defeat of the 5th Panzer Division, seize Krupki station, pressing home the attack to Borisov. The 2nd Guards Motorized Rifle Brigade was moved to the second echelon.

At 0700 hours the 3rd Guards Tank Corps took the important rail station at Krupki and resumed the drive on Borisov. But, the Stakva was displeased. On 28 June, Stalin wrote in a directive to Marshal Vasilevskii and General Chernyakovskii, "The Stavka demands swift and decisive action from the 5th Guards Tank Army as called for by the situation at the front."[113]

While the 3rd Guards Tank Corps was rapidly gaining ground,

the 29th Tank Corps was slowly forging ahead, sustaining casualties. The Front commander, General Ivan Danilovich Chernyakovskii, telephoned Marshal Rotmistrov to find out the reason.

"Ivan Danilovich, we are using the same offensive tactics we employed in the Battle of Kursk, on the Don, and in the Korsun area," replied Rotmistrov.

"Praise and glory to your past achievements! But let me remind you that the tactics which proved a success in the steppes near Kursk and in the Ukraine may hardly be effective in a land of hills, forests and swamps."

General Chernyakovskii was well aware of the splendid record of the 5th Guards Tank Army, but as a tanker, himself, he realized that the great casualties and the slow pace of the advance were the consequence of some tactical error. He appointed a special commission to investigate the situation on the spot.

The commission went to the battle sites and noted where the Soviet tanks had been knocked out and found the firing positions of the German tanks. The Germans had allowed the Soviet tanks to approach within 400 meters then fired for a killing effect and were able to then leave the area unscathed. General Lyudnikov, commander of the 39th Army, who had taken part in the investigation concluded, "in certain sectors the Germans followed the ambush tactics."[114] Having analyzed the commission's findings, General Chernyakovskii demanded that Rotmistrov immediately revise his army's tactics in armored combat on defiladed and semi-defiladed terrain.[115]

The tank army's forward detachments approached the Berezin river by afternoon on 29 June. By evening the 5th Guards Tank Army had three bridgeheads over the river. Fighting continued all night. The next day, the tank army crossed over the river on pontoons. Rotmistrov had the mission to seize Minsk by the end of 2 July.

By 1 July, Rotmistrov's tank losses reached 60.[116] Only forward detachments had reached the approaches to Minsk, one of the Soviet Union's largest economic and cultural centers.

At dawn 3 July, the forward detachments of the 3rd Guards Tank Corps with the 2nd Guards Tank Corps entered Minsk and by 0900 hours had cleared major German resistance from the city. Minsk lay in ruins. Its urban area had been razed with less than a dozen tall buildings standing along the main street. Meanwhile, the remainder of the 5th Guards Tank Army maneuvered to the northwest and by afternoon was out of the fight for the city, striking to the north-west. For the liberation of Minsk and his personal bravery, Rotmistrov was awarded the Second Order of Lenin.

On 4 July, Rotmistrov's army received the mission to coordinate with the 3rd Guards Mechanized Corps and liberate Vilnius. Lacking sufficient engineer assets to cross the Berezina river, Rotmistrov sent the 29th Tank Corps on to Oshmyany, avoiding the river. The 3rd Guards Tank Corps captured Volozhin and forced the Berezina river to the west. On the west side, General Vovchenko reported encountering counterattacks from two German divisions but continued the advance while battling the German forces.

The Soviet offensive continued to roll westward. In pursuing the retreating Germans, the 5th Guards Tank Army came up to Vilnius, an important city covering the approaches to East Prussia. The German command created an all-round defense and bolstered the city's garrison with a parachute landing force of 600 soldiers.

When the tank armies encountered in their offensive path a major enemy strongpoint or built-up area, they were not to engage them, but bypass these points, rushing deeply to the west. When it was not possible to do this, the tempo of their attacks decreased sharply, which adversely affected the course of the entire offensive operation. "A vivid example in this regard," a post war study noted, "is the combat actions of the troops of the 5th Guards Tank Army for the city of Vilnius, the Lithuanian capital, in the summer of 1944."[117] Lead elements of the 29th Tank Corps were at the southeastern edge of the city on 7 July. The 3rd Guards Mechanized Corps approaching from the east could not take the city from the march. The 3rd Guards Tank Corps was holding the German 7th Panzer Division in check south of the city. On 7-13 July, the 29th Tank Corps became involved in the fight to capture Vilnius. Germans dropped the 6th Parachute Regiment into the city. However, many of the jumpers landed in Rotmistrov's tank units and were captured. The objection, by Soviet military analysts, to the 5th Guards Tank Army actions at Vilnius is pointed out in the observation that an aggressive tank army, tank and mechanized corps actions are sharply lowered when they enter in battles for large population centers and centers of resistance met in the depth of the enemy defense.[118] Pursuit and destruction of the enemy's force was lost. Rotmistrov's partial commitment of tank forces in the battle for Vilnius resulted in another clash with General Chernyakovskii, the Front commander.

At the end of July to mid-August, the tank army actively participated in offensive operations in the direction of Kaunus and Shyaulya. Kaunus protected the shortest routes to East Prussia. By holding that area, the Germans hoped to prevent the war being carried into German territory. However, on 8 August 1944, Rotmistrov relinquished command of the 5th Guards Tank Army to Lieutenant General Mikhail Dimitrievich Solomatin, who ten days later left command of the tank army.

None of the tank army's succeeding commanders achieved the intensity or success of Rotmistrov's operations. Whether the clashes with the Front commander were momentary personality conflicts or Rotmistrov had truly lost his battlefield touch has never been acknowledged or developed in Soviet writings. In either case, Marshal Federenko was glad to finally get Rotmistrov as the Deputy Commander Of Red Army Armored and Mechanized Forces.

At the beginning of November 1944, Marshal Rotmistrov, as Deputy Commander of Red Army Armored and Mechanized Forces, conducted a conference on the Lvov-Samdomierz Operation. Participants in the conference were the tank army commanders, Katukov, Rybalko and Lelyushenko and all their corps commanders and chiefs of staffs. The 1st Ukrainian Front's wide scope and maneuver in the offensive operation involved three tank armies and two cavalry-mechanized groups. Rotmsitrov's conference sought to develop useful conclusions for continued theoretical use of large tank formation by the Red Army. Rotmistrov conducted similar conferences after major operations until the end of the war.

In 1945, Rotmistrov, a strong exponent of tank warfare, worked issues on the massed employment of tanks and the coordination of self-propelled assault guns with tanks and infantry. Many of the doctrinal issues Rotmistrov worked in the final years of the war, propelled him into the limelight in the post-war years with an international recognition of his expertise in Soviet tank warfare and an authoritative military figure on warfare in general through numerous publications in important military journals.

Rotmistrov possessed an uncanny ability to quickly assess a situation and devise a creative approach for decisions. Decisions came easily to Rotmistrov, in a word, he was a builder. As an authoritative theorist and practitioner, he took an active part in the reorganizing and structure of the Soviet tank army. His ways differed greatly in variety and uniqueness of methods. This, at times, put him at odds with senior commanders – especially when he believed that he had a much better idea. Rotmistrov was conscious of the credentials of his critics and was not impressed by rank or title. He was the supreme pragmatist.

Rotmistrov's fighting style of a hard, direct, and swift blow upset the enemy. Using in full measure the tank unit's agility, he broke up the enemy's main forces, encircled them, and destroyed them in detail. His rapid rise was a combination of his demonstrated erudition and his bold, decisive initiative on the battlefield. In its struggle for survival, the Red Army tolerated such an eccentric nature in its top armored guards theoretician and architect.

NOTES

1. P.A. Rotmistrov, *Stal'naya gvardiya*, Moscow: Voenizdat, 1984, p. 11.

2. Ibid., p. 39.

3. Ibid., p. 44.

4. Ibid., p. 45.

5. See P. A. Romistrov's Krasnaya Zvezda articles: "Tanki pri proryve ukreplennoi polosy," 20 August 1940, p. 3; "Deistviya tankov v gorakh," 10 September 1940, p. 2; "Deistviya tankov v predpol'ye," 29 November 1940, p. 2; "Deistviya tankov v zimnikh usloviyakh," 17 December 1940, p. 3.

6. Rotmistrov, pp. 56-7.

7. Ibid., p. 58.

8. M.V. Zakharov, *Proval gitlerovskogo nastupleniya na Moskvu*, Moscow: Nauka, 1966, p. 162.

9. Ibid., p. 165.

10. Rotmistrov, p. 61.

11. Raymond L. Garthoff, *Soviet Military Doctrine*, Glencoe, Illinois: The Free Press, 1953, p. 269.

12. Rotmistrov, p. 62.

13. Ibid., p. 64.

14. Ibid., p. 65.

15. Ibid., p. 67.

16. Ibid., pp. 73-4.

17. A. Egorov, "Tankovyi polk v boyakh pod kalininom i klinom," *Voenno-istoricheskii zhurnal* (hereafter *Vizh*), vol. 4-1971, pp. 59-61.

18. Phillip Longsworth, *The Art of Victory*, New York: 1965, p. 36.

19. P.A. Rotmistrov, *Vremya i tanki*, Moscow: Voenizdat, 1972, p. 99.

20. Rotmistrov, *Stalnaya*, p. 79.

21. Ibid.

22. Ibid., p. 80.

23. Ibid., p. 83.

24. Ibid., p. 84.

25. Ibid., pp. 86-7.

26. Ibid., p. 90.

27. D.Z. Muriev, *Proval Operatsii 'Taifun'*, Moscow: Voenizdat, 1966, p. 99.

28. Rotmistrov, *Stalnaya*, p. 97.

29. Ibid., p. 100.

30. Zakharov, p. 164.

31. Rotmistrov, *Stalnaya*, p. 111.

32. Ibid., p. 112.

33. Ibid.

34. Ibid., pp. 114-5.

35. Ibid., p. 115.

36. Ibid., p. 116.

37. Ibid., pp. 116-7.

38. Ibid., p. 118.

39. Ibid., p. 123.

40. K.S. Moskalenko, *Na yugo-zapadnom napravlenii*, Moscow: Nauka, 1973, Book l, p. 325.

41. Ibid.

42. Rotmistrov, *Stalnaya*, p. 128.

43. Ibid., p. 131.

44. Ibid.

45. Ibid., p. 132.

46. Ibid., pp. 135-6.

47. Ibid., p. 138.

48. Ibid.

49. P. Kurochkin, "Glavnyi marshal bronetankovykh voisk P.A. Rotmistrov," *Vizh*, vol. 6-1981, pp. 90-91.

50. Ibid.

51. Rotmistrov, *Stalnaya*, p. 139.

52. M.V. Zakharov, *Stalingradskaya Epopeya*, Moscow: Nauka, 1968, p. 612.

53. Ibid.

54. A.V. Egorov, *V Donskikh Stepyakh*, Moscow: DOSAAF, 1988, p. 16.

55. M. Popov, "Yuzhnee Stalingrada," *Vizh*, vol. 2-1961, p. 97.

56. Erich von Manstein, *Lost Victories*, Novato, California: Presidio, 1982, p.329.

57. Egorov, *Stepyakh*, pp. 47-8.

58. Rotmistrov, *Stalnaya*, p. 148.

59. Ibid., p. 150.

60. Ibid.

61. Ibid., p. 158.

62. Ibid., p. 158-9.

63. Egorov, *Stepyakh*, p. 93.

64. Ibid.

65. Rotmistrov, *Stalnaya*, p. 164.

66. Ibid., p. 164.

67. Ibid., p. 165.

68. Ibid., p. 166.

69. Ibid., p. 167.

70. Ibid., p. 168.

71. Ibid., p. 175.

72. Ibid.

73. Ibid., pp. 175-6.

74. Ibid., p. 176.

75. Ibid., pp. 179-80.

76. Ibid., p. 186.

77. Ibid.

78. Ibid.

79. Charles W. Sydnor, *Soldiers of Destruction*, New Jersey: Princeton University Press, 1977, p. 289.

80. Rotmistrov, *Stalnaya*, p. 188.

81. Ibid., p. 198.

82. Ibid., p. 202.

83. "Glavnyi marshal bronetankovykh voisk P. A. Rotmistrov," *Vizh*, vol. 7-1963, p. 97.

84. Rotmistrov, *Stalnaya*, p. 203.

85. A. Egorov, "Yuzhnee Kurska," *Vizh*, vol. 7-1968, p. 60.

86. Rtomistrov, Stalnaya, p. 211.

87. Egorov, Kurska, p. 62.

88. A.I. Radzievskii, *Tankovyi Udar*, Moscow: Voenizdat, 1977, p. 212.

89. Rotmistrov, *Stalnaya*, p. 222.

90. Radzievskii, p. 212.

91. Ibid., pp. 212, 215-6.

92. P.P. Tovstukha, R.M. *Portugal'skii, Upravlenie voiskami v nastuplenii*, Moscow: Voenizdat, 1981, p. 166.

93. Rotmistrov, *Vremya*, p. 166.

94. N. Shekhovtsov, "Nastuplenie voisk Stepnogo fronta na krivoroahskom napravlenii v oktyabre 1943 goda," *Vizh*, vol 10-1968, p. 38.

95. I. Konev, "Kirovogradskaya operatsiya," *Vizh*, vol. 5-1969, p. 68.

96. Ibid., p. 69.

97. Radzievskii, p. 116.

98. Rotmistov, Vremya, pp. 169-70.

99. I.S. Konev, *Zapiski komanduyushchego frontom*, Moscow: Voenizdat, 1981, p. 100.

100. Ibid.

101. F.W. von Mellenthin, *Panzer Battles*, New York: Ballantine, 1980, p. 328.

102. "Otvety na pis'ma chitatelei," *Vizh*, vol. 9-1973, p. 123.

103. I.S. Lykov, *V groznyi chas*, Moscow: Voenizdat, 1986, pp. 216-7.

104. S.M. Shtemenko, *The Soviet General Staff At War*, Moscow: Progress, 1975, p. 236.

105. A. Sharipov, *General Chernyakhovsky*, Moscow: Progress, 1980, p. 334.

106. P. Rotmistrov, "Tempy nastupleniya tankovoi armii," *Vizh*, vol. 6-1964, p. 27.

107. Ibid., p. 28.

108. Rotmistrov, *Vremya*, p. 191.

109. N. Kobrin, "Iz opyta vydvizheniya tankovykh armii iz rainov sosredotocheniya dlya vvoda v srazhenie," *Vizh*, vol. 9-1976, p. 76.

110. A.M. Vasilevsky, *A Lifelong Cause*, Moscow: Progress, 1981, p. 377.

111. Kobrin, p. 76.

112. Vasilevsky, p. 377.

113. Ibid.

114. Sharipov, p. 368.

115. Ibid.

116. Lykov, p. 237.

117. O.A. Losik, *Stroitel'stvo i boevoe primenenie sovetskikh tankovykh voisk v gody velikoi otechestvennoi voiny*, Moscow: Voenizdat, 1979, p. 139.

118. N. Kireev, "Presledovanie protivnika soedineniyami i ob'edineniyami bronetankovykh i mekhanizirovannykh voisk," *Vizh* 6-1977, p. 87.

CHAPTER VI

KRAVCHENKO

S tanding on ground where his father fought the Japanese in 1905, the tall, broad shouldered tank army commander scanned the Pacific Ocean. A quiet, steadfast, ever-dependable commander, General Andrei Grigorevich Kravchenko finished the Second World War with his tank army standing at Port Arthur in the Far East after defeating the Japanese Kwantung Army in Manchuria, in August 1945. Twice a Hero of the Soviet Union, the brave, tenacious tank commander fought both German and Japanese forces during the war.

At the beginning of 1916, Kravchenko's brother received a call to service in the Tsar's army and died three months later at the front fighting Germans. His brother's death impressed the young Andrei Grigorevich's thoughts about the Tsarist regime and service in the military. In April 1916, as a 17 year old lad, he traveled to Kiev to work in a factory. Then, he joined the revolutionary movement, fighting with a partisan group at the beginning of the Russian Civil War. A year later, he became part of the new Red Army in the 1st Regiment, 44th Rifle Division, rising to command an infantry regiment. In April 1921, he was sent to the Poltava Infantry School.

As a student, Kravchenko proved confident, competent and sociable. He befriended a more senior student, Nikolai Vatutin, who would command Kravchenko is some of his most demanding operations during the Second World War. Kravchenko was heavy-set in build for his height, but physically agile. As a biographer described, he had a "simple Russian face" with clear attentive eyes that "looked into one's soul."[1] Like many complex and quiet per-

Andrei Grigorevich Kravchenko, commander of the 5th Guards Tanks Corps, at Lyutezh bridgehead, October 1943.

sonalities, he could exhibit an impetuously, quick energy, but with an outward calmness.

After graduation from the infantry school in August 1923, he was assigned to Tiblis where he married. Two years later, he returned from field assignment for advanced military schooling at the Frunze Academy, and the same year, Kravchenko became a Communist party member.

From the Frunze Academy, Kravchenko assumed the position of Chief of Staff for the 21st Rifle Regiment, 7th Division. While serving in this position, he received a call from the Leningrad Armored Tank Course. The course created by the dynamic, forward-thinking Marshal Mikhail Nikolaevich Tukhachevskii, the famed youthful commander of the Leningrad Military District, was looking for literate commanders who could play a future role in developing a modern, mechanized Red Army. The challenge appealed to the young infantry officer.

In the tank course, Kravchenko studied hard, becoming familiar with the army's early armored vehicles, such as, BA 26 and MS 1, and he earnestly studied the writings of the Red Army military theorists, such as, Vladimir Triandafillov's Character of Contemporary Army Operations which enunciated an ambitious "deep battle" doctrine for a mechanized army. Marshal Tukhachevskii routinely lectured in the course, instilling a concept for future mobile armored warfare. A fellow student recalled Kravchenko as a "student of military affairs, erudite, good soul, with uncompromising character...."[2] Later during the Second World War, the same fellow student saw Kravchenko at the front and remarked, "Kravchenko showed his readings and writings and courage in commanding units; he was strict and thoughtful."[3]

In February 1935, Kravchenko transferred to the armored tank school at Saratov. In May 1939, he received posting to Kuibyshev to serve on the staff of the Privolzhsk Military District, and later moved to Penze as chief of staff for the 61st Rifle Division.

With the Russo-Finnish War, Colonel Kravchenko, still at Penze, formed the 173rd Motorized Rifle Division which departed to the Karelian isthmus to participate in the Red Army's grueling offensive for Vyborg. For the period of 6-12 March 1940, Kravchenko, for personal bravery, received his first distinguished military award, the Order of the Red Banner. With the end of the war in March 1940, his division returned to its original garrison for resumption of peacetime training when a month later Kravchenko received reassignment orders.

From April 1940 to February 1941, Kravchenko served as Chief of Staff in the 16th Tank Division, 2nd Mechanized Corps at Kotovsk, Odessa Military District. In March, Kravchenko rose to Chief of Staff of the newly formed 18th Mechanized Corps. The mechanized corps were authorized 1031 tanks, but like most of the newly formed units by the summer of 1941, the 18th Mechanized Corps fell well short in authorized tanks though the corps consisted of the 44th, 47th Tank and 218th Motorized Divisions.

With the German invasion in June 1941, Kravchenko sent his family east to Saratov, securing them in the country's interior. He turned his attention to moving and fighting the 18th Mechanized Corps. German forces in a major effort struck across the Dnestr river at Mogilev-Podolsky in the direction of Zhmerinka, creating a serious threat to the southern flank of the Southwestern Front. Kravchenko received orders to concentrate the corps on the line Vapnyarka-Zhmerinka, 30 kilometers south of Vinnitsu. With the mission to cover withdrawing rifle units, the 18th Mechanized Corps made its first contact with the invading German army.

Under the relentlessly, hot July days, Kravchenko, as a chief of staff, was unusually forward in the corps' observation post where he coordinated the corps' counter to German attempts at bypassing on the flanks. While successfully holding in its cohesion during the first large battle, corps units suffered heavy losses. Colonel Kravchenko experiencing his first battle with Germans began intensive and indepth self-study of German fighting techniques. He personally interrogated the first German prisoners.[4]

In September, Kravchenko received command of the 31st Tank Brigade, a new, T-34 equipped unit, and he built his brigade in the Southwestern Front near Akhtyrka. A month later, the brigade relocated to Vladimir, west of Moscow. As with other successful tank commanders, command of a tank brigade in the early months of the war became an excellent school and trial by fire for the future corps and army commanders in the armored forces. This fighting experience as Kravchenko observed, "forced one to learn in continuous battle on the snowy approaches to Moscow."[5]

After formation, organization, and minimal training, by 4 November, Kravchenko's 31st Tank Brigade was ordered to concentrate on the outskirts of Moscow, in Krasnoi Polyanoi, in preparation for an unusual event for an army in war – a parade. Upon arrival in the Soviet capital, the 31st Tank Brigade consisted of 4 KV's, 9 BT-7's, 10 T-26's with a total of 707 men.[6] On 7 November 1941, Kravchenko's unit participated in Moscow's traditional Red Army troop parade in commemoration of the 24th Anniversary of the October Revolution. Kravchenko expected anything, a new assignment or special mission, but not this. Stalin and other party leaders made speeches and held the Red Square parade as a sign of confidence in the Red Army's ability to defend and hold the nation's capital against the German Army 70-100 kilometers away. With the passage of the tanks in Red Square, the parade was over, and Kravchenko's unit moved straight for the fighting front.

From 12 through 14 November, having made a 150 kilometer road march under its own power, as part of the 2nd Guards Cavalry Corps, Kravchenko's brigade participated in fighting with the 5th Cavalry Division, encircling German units on the night of 16 November in Ekaterinovka effectively destroying a regiment in garrison.[7] On 21 November, the tank brigade relocated to the area of Klin where it became part of the 20th Army in the Western Front. The situation on the approaches to Moscow remained serious and close to disaster for the Red Army.

The German Army Group Center, in the second week of November, stood poised to drive on Moscow. Its 3rd Panzer Group, under Generaloberst Hans Reinhardt, was to attack across the Lama river, thirty kilometers west of Klin, and once south of the Volga Reservoir move towards the Moscow-Volga Canal. But it did not have enough troops and tanks to fight beyond the canal. The panzer group's original order remained in effect, and it was expected to attack east with an unclear mission. The panzer group jumped off for the attack on 16 November, pushing aside easily Soviet forces. With the ground frozen hard and a light, dry snow covering, the German armored forces made rapid progress.

By 20 November the German forces continued advancing deeply into the Red Army's defenses around Klin on the boundary between the 30th and 16th Armies. The Soviet 31st and 108th Tank Brigades with two rifle divisions fought strong defensive battles on the line Bolokhovka, Kurakino. However, by the end of the day, they withdrew behind the Shat' river. The following day German forces managed to penetrate their defensive line, requiring the Soviets to reorganize their forces.

A few days later, Kravchenko's tank brigade was assigned to General Konstantin Konstantinovich Rokossovskii's 16th Army. Kravchenko received an attack mission to drive back the Germans. After a series of counterattacks over a three day period, the Red Army units were unsuccessful in preventing the Germans from entering Klin from the north. Again, the 31st Tank Brigade under pressure from German units withdrew eastward.

The 3rd Panzer Group taking Klin on the 23rd continued heading east, and the Soviets retreated steadily. Leaving Kravchenko's force as a covering detachment, his brigade withdrew after a difficult delaying action along the Volokalamsk highway. Kravchenko endured the failure, but, he learned a practical lesson. In a candid discussion with Kravchenko the Army Commander, General Rokossovskii, acknowledged that perhaps the order to attack was premature and the conditions for its commitment were unfavorable. However, General Rokosovskii's lesson was a military leader's iron, uncompromising will without fail must be with tact towards the subordinate, and the commander's skill must be based on his wit and initiative.[8] Fortunately, Kravchenko's unit preserved its fighting vehicles in the withdrawing action.

By necessity, the Red Army High Command endeavored to move the precious few tank brigades to important sectors. At November's end, Kravchenko's brigade was reassigned to the reforming 20th Army of the Western Front. Early the next month, Kravchenko received the mission to dislodge the Germans from the villages of Kochergino and Dubinino. The operation sought to hold key villages to unhinge the German advance on Moscow. Attacking with an armored covering force of 13 tanks, the Germans tanks allowed a large distance between them and the following infantry. Kravchenko mustering only six powerful T-34 tanks waited in ambush, directing his tank battalion to strike the German's flank. The brigade's tanks lurched from their cover rushing the German formation. Through his binoculars, Kravchenko counted in a short time seven burning German tanks, and the remainder withdrew. For his bravery and boldness in the successful action, Kravchenko received his first award of the war, the Order of the Red Banner.

In later tactical movement, the 31st Tank Brigade, moving along the highway like a crawling armored caterpillar, became vulnerable to marauding German warplanes. A formation of German "Junkers," bombers, appeared overhead. The Red Army's recommended drill in such a situation instructed personnel to dismount, run from the vehicles and lie down. But, the "Junkers" appeared suddenly from the skies, and in less than a minute, they swooped over the column. As an immediate defensive reaction the drivers could move the vehicles off the roads. However, the observant Kravchenko had been at the front long enough to consider actions necessary for surviving German airstrikes. He figured in the 30-60 seconds that his vehicles would not be concealed any better by moving off the roads, and decided to disperse the vehicles within the column and without stopping move forward at top speed. In this encounter, he lost only one vehicle and continued into battle attacking from the march.

During the month of December, the temperature averaged at 20 degrees below zero. Battling through the frozen landscape and terrible killing cold often caused for the soldiers more difficulties and presented a greater threat than the enemy. In December with subzero temperatures required a greater expenditure of fuel for warming up the vehicles and made sluggish the workings of armored mechanisms. Organizing and conducting repairs under such difficult weather conditions reduced operations to small gains by tactical units.

Despite harsh elements, on 8 December, the 31st Tank Brigade with the 35th Rifle Brigade captured a small village pursuing withdrawing Germans. Developing the battle the next day, the 20th Army's forces cut off highways north and south of Solnechnogorsk, and the following day battled to the town's outskirts. Possession of a town or village on Russian winter nights proved a significant incentive for soldiers seeking shelter from the harsh cold. By 1500 hours, 11 December, Kravchenko's tankers, first to enter the town, attacked from the south. A street to street battle ensued with the tank brigade recapturing the town the following day. Kravchenko's tank brigade continued attacking in the Germans' rear area against reserve forces. A long fight on the short winter's day continued into hours of darkness. These long engagements were not easy for tankers. Kravchenko had spent hours not getting out of his command vehicle and knew his crews suffered worse, especially the tank drivers. In actuality, tankers do most everything, fight, sleep, eat, in their steel fortresses.

In March 1942, Kravchenko received a summons to Moscow for assignment as the Deputy Commander for Armored Forces in the 61st Army. However, after pleading with Lieutenant General Yakov Nikolaevich Federenko for a more active position, Kravchenko succeeded in becoming the Chief of Staff for the forming lst Tank Corps under the command of General Mikhail Efimovich Katukov.

With the lst Tank Corps in Lipetske, Kravchenko sat in long conversations with General Katukov and held private conferences with staff officers discussing possible variations for new armored operations. The operational level of warfare with tank corps presented greater implications for command techniques and staff actions. Both the commander and the chief of staff studied a new level of armored command, and they worked out operational and tactical methods. A complete reorganization of logistical support and how to support on the move became a greater concern for both Kravchenko and Katukov. Armored formations were difficult units to command effectively and efficiently. While the corps consolidated and prepared itself for combat, it remained in the Stavka reserve. But, the lst Tank Corps was soon required in the war and was sent to the Bryansk Front.

In June the lst Tank Corps completed its relocation in the Bryansk Front sector. General Katukov's corps along with the 16th Tank Corps was to make a counterstrike into the northern flank of the German advance on Voronezh. By 3 July, German armored formations crossed the Kshen river, rapidly moving eastward. Conflicting reconnaissance reports on the changing situation complicated setting the direction for the lst Tank Corps' attack. General Katukov moving forward to the combat action recalled, "I set Colonel Kravchenko as quickly as possible to finish shifting the brigades and leading the tankers in the area of Terbuny."[9]

As the tank corps' reconnaissance and forward detachments deployed, Kravchenko had his hands full. The Front staff asked every 50 minutes, "Report the situation...Don't miss the enemy."[10]

The Germans forces sliced easily through the Bryansk Front and threatened to breakthrough to the north, alarming the Soviet High Command who worried that the Germans could take Moscow from the south. The lst Tank Corps with other units managed to stop the German advance north, but the tank corps fought defensively and used its last reserves against infantry attacks. The corps managed to fight off being encircled. The Soviet High Command displeased with the Bryansk Front commander's use of the tank corps sent Colonel General A.M. Vasilevskii to admonish the Front commander and staff for using tanks like infantry.[11]

Before the tank corps completed its assigned operation, Kravchenko received designation as commander of the 2nd Tank Corps in the Bryansk Front. Like other rising tank commanders, such as, Katukov, Bogdanov, Rotmistrov, he moved from brigade to corps commander in the most thorough and unforgiving school for armored warfare – actual combat. The dramatically changing situation on the eastern front forced the Red Army to rapidly shift units, personnel, and commanders to trouble spots. The reliable commanders received assignment on the critical sectors.

The situation on the Bryansk Front stabilized, and the 2nd Tank Corps became the Front's reserve. In a short time, rumors, as in all armies, filtered down that the corps was to be sent to another sector. "Where? No one knew," recalled an officer in the tank corps. "We waited for orders. And, then it leaked through the 'soldiers' telegraph,' Stalingrad."[12]

The tank corps became part of the lst Tank Army being formed under the command of General Kirill Semenovich Moskalenko. Kravchenko's corps off-loaded from the trains and concentrated near the Log rail station.

After midnight on 24 August, Kravchenko received orders to conduct a dawn attack with his corps in the general direction of Erzovka, north of Stalingrad and destroy penetrating German units.

With little time to prepare, Kravchenko gave his orders to his brigades, and set the attack time at 0500 hours. His tank brigades received their orders between 0400 to 0430 hours which left little planning time for the corps and no time for thorough preparation by the brigades. Consequently, the units actually attacked two to four hours later.

The brigades rushed towards their assigned objectives, but the situation was unclear. "Where is your reconnaissance, Ivanovskii?!" Kravchenko asked his intelligence officer in the operational group. "Why are they late with the reports? Can it be they are sitting snug in some secluded place?"[13] Very early in the war the Red Army tank commanders learned the value and necessity for a continuous, accurate flow of information if they were to be successful in armored warfare. Kravchenko, having served as General Katukov's chief of staff, had already learned the importance of intelligence in armored warfare.

Kravchenko, as usual, positioned his observation post well forward. Although his lead units had just repulsed a German attack, a new German assault accompanied by artillery and air strikes began. Kravchenko could see advancing Germans tanks with infantry. Security for his observation post consisted of four combat vehicles and 40 submachine gunners.

A staff officer reported to the corps commander, "Comrade General, enemy tanks with infantry are attacking within 200 meters."

Kravchenko sullenly nodded. The officer tried again, "Comrade general, it is necessary for the command post to withdraw."

"No!" Kravchenko responded decisively. "There is no where better to go from here."[14]

Through a melon field Soviet tanks under Kravchenko's watchful eyes maneuvered and fired while Germans shells burst around the command post. Ripping up fragments, the shelter leaked smashed watermelon juice while the tanks continued their deadly work. By the end of the tank battle, the Germans failed in advancing further, relaxing tension in the command post.

A short time later, the intelligence officer reported to Kravchenko, "Comrade general, the Germans conducted an attack south of Sukhoi. They can breakthrough."

General Kravchenko, the chief of staff and the operations officer shoulder to shoulder in the dugout crowded over the map.

"How did they appear there, your Germans?!" the operations officer stared accusingly at the intelligence officer.

"Not mine, theirs." the annoyed intelligence officer replied.

"Is their location fixed exactly?" the chief of staff asked.

"They are already here, comrade colonel. They are attacking with infantry and tanks."

Someone swore on the side, "You are wrong with your reconnaissance information!" But, the corps' command group began considering immediate measures. After a quick deliberation, Kravchenko approved a course of action, and the corps staff gave instructions for the tank brigades to assume a defense around Sukhoi. The German's surprise attack demanded an active response, bringing to mind, the old Russian saying, "Don't yawn before God."[15]

German units probed persistently along Kravchenko's defenses for a weak point which they found and hastily brought up their forces for penetration. In the close, desperate fighting around Stalingrad even a shallow penetration turned the situation around. In the corps' weak point, German armor tried to drive a steel wedge with supporting air attacks. Although the German panzer units fought relentlessly to complete the penetration, Kravchenko's units held. And, by evening, the heavy fighting calmed down in sector.

In the difficult and rapidly changing situation around Stalingrad, the Soviet High Command maneuvered Red Army forces for advantage. The repositioning of forces not only included the divisions and corps, but also at times, their subordinate units. A regiment could be taken from the line, transferred to another critical sector, or to a weakened spot, in which the Germans were penetrating. Regrouping units with operational objectives became easier and simpler. However, shuffling smaller units presented problems and concerns for commanders, particularly within armored units. For example, in the beginning of September, Kravchenko's 2nd Motorized Rifle Brigade was transferred to the 23rd Tank Corps, and the 2nd Tank Corps received the 99th Tank Brigade. The 99th Tank Brigade had been formed from two tank battalions that had been in battle against the Germans on the northern side of Stalingrad.

Kravchenko directed his staff, "The 99th Tank Brigade takes the defense on the northeast edge of the town. It is now ours." Kravchenko showed the place on the map, and his staff made notes on their map cases. "We, as you know, have not seen it nor know it. In today's fighting strong bombing raids resulted in the loss of a few tanks, and the brigade commander was killed."[16]

The corps commander was gloomily silent, noted a staff officer.

Then, Kravchenko announced, "The unit must not remain commanderless in order that the personnel do not feel so."[17] He assigned his intelligence officer as temporary commander. Three days later a designated commander took over.

In September, Major General Kravchenko found himself on the road towards Stalingrad, as the commander of the 4th Tank Corps located north of Stalingrad in the vicinity of Samofalovka station. The 4th Tank Corps consisted of the 45th, 69th, 102nd Tank Brigades and the 4th Motorized Rifle Brigade. His new tank corps operated as the mobile group for the 1st Guards Army. The Red Army had tried three times previously to form the 1st Guards Army, but before completing the formation the unit was thrown into defensive combat on the Stalingrad approaches. German troops had taken up defensive positions in a majority of the sectors, particularly on the flank. Only in Stalingrad itself did the Germans continue to attack with forces of the 6th and 4th Panzer Armies. The defensive positions on the flank of the main German thrust were assumed by Romanian and Italian troops.

On 18 September, the day Kravchenko assumed command of the tank corps, the 1st Guards Army launched an attack to cut off German units on the northern approach to Stalingrad. At 1400 hours, the 1st Guards Army commander, General Kirill Semenovich Moskalenko, decided to commit his second echelon, Kravchenko's tank corps, into the penetration.[18] General Moskalenko's army had insufficient forces for the task and had received less than its full complement of personnel. Kravchenko's corps also lacked personnel, and the majority of his tanks were the light T-60's and T-70's with small guns and thin armor. The German defense quickly stopped the attack, forcing the Soviets to withdraw, stalemating the sector for weeks.

On 3 November, Kravchenko, having his corps transferred to the 21st Army, Southwestern Front in the vicinity of Orlovskii, received a summons to an army staff conference. General Georgi Zhukov, as the Stavka's overseeing representative, announced the impending counteroffenisve operation for the encirclement of the Germans forces around Stalingrad. By mid-November 1942, Soviet troops in the Stalingrad area had been merged into three Fronts: the Southwestern commanded by General N.F. Vatutin, Don commanded by General K.K. Rokosovskii, and the Stalingrad Front commanded by General A.I. Eremenko. The situation and balance of forces had improved enough for the Red Army to conduct a winter campaign opened with a counteroffensive. All subsequent operations depended on the success of the counteroffensive. Code-name "Uranus," the operation planned to breach German defenses from Serafimovich-Kletskii with a rapid advance to Kalach-Sovetskii, while the Stalingrad Front drove north from the Sarpin Lakes. The convergent attacks would cut-off the German forces between the Don and the Volga rivers. In preparation for the operation, Kravchenko moved his corps command post on 7 November to the west bank of the Don river near Kletskii. Kravchenko and his staff studied the new Peoples Defense Commissariat Order Number 325 on the employment of tank and mechanized corps.

Order 325 generalized the experiences of tank and mechanized forces fighting the first period of the war. It specified tank and mechanized corps, as a resource for the Front and army, were intended for operations on the main axis serving as the exploitation echelon. Splitting corps into brigades was prohibited. The order detailed procedures for coordinating tank actions with infantry, artillery, and aviation and established procedures for commitment of the tank corps to battle. An important provision of the order was the requirement to conduct tank attacks at maximum speed, firing on the move. The order further specified tank formation to execute broad maneuvers on the battlefield, directing firepower into the enemy's flanks and rear. Frontal tank attacks were forbidden. The order became the Red Army's important step in the establishment of operating procedures necessary to conduct offensive operations with large armored formations. Kravchenko and his staff studied the order earnestly.

But, Red Army tank forces, their commanders and staffs still had much to learn. In a Red Army General Staff study on war experiences noted lessons from early successful armor operations that remained valid for the rest of the war. The study observed "in selecting the site for a jump-off area, special attention should be paid to the time element. Various parts of the corps must spend as little time as possible there, but since in practice this would be very difficult to arrange, it would be a more expedient situation permitting the corps to proceed with the commitment to the breakthrough directly from the stand by area."[19]

Kravchenko found himself guilty of this common early error. On 8 November 1942, the 4th Tank Corps moved into attack positions 1.5 to 2 kilometers from the main line of contact. This forward assembly was 11 days before the start of the operation. German reconnaissance spotted the corps location, and, from 8 to 19 November, German artillery subjected the tank corps daily to methodical artillery and mortar fires accompanied by airstrikes. As a result, Kravchenko's corps lost about 250 men killed and wounded and the element of surprise since the enemy was fully aware of the tank corps presence in this area. As the study concluded, the enemy "... had all the warning he needed about the impending offensive and the direction of the main thrust."[20]

Plans for the Soviet Operation "Uranus" rested on the premise that Red Army units tied down the German's main forces at Stalingrad while launching counterstrikes on their flanks in the direction of Kalach. The Soviet operation would penetrate the operational rear, encircle the enemy grouping and destroy it. The Southwestern Front was to rout the Romanian 3rd Army and in concert with the Stalingrad Front meet with armored forces in the Kalach area. The main attack was to be implemented by the 5th Tank and 21st Rifle Armies.

According to the counteroffensive plans, the 4th Tank Corps' forward tank units coordinated their actions with the 5th Tank Army and 3rd Guards Cavalry Corps in destroying German reserves, staffs and rear elements. Additionally, they were to cut off German withdrawal routes to the west and southwest and prevent the approach of enemy reserves. The 4th Tank Corps had to be linked up with Stalingrad Front units, by 23 November, in the area of Sovetskii, completing the encirclement of the German's 6th Army at Stalingrad.

General Kravchenko understood the importance of his corps' role for the upcoming operation. Preparing for the action, he ordered extensive reconnaissance to define more precisely the forward edge of the German defense and study of their defensive system of fires.

At dawn on 19 November, a thick fog hung over the Don river. After a sleepless night, Kravchenko received the order to begin the operation. He was visibly concerned.[21] The mastery of techniques and details for employing the tank corps were still trial and error, and his command had no experience operating under the provisions of the new NKO Order 325.

From his observation post, Kravchenko watched the Russian God of War, artillery, methodically work German defensive positions. After a half hour, the infantry assaulted the German positions in the vicinity of Kletskii. The 21st Rifle Army under the command of General Ivan Mikhailovich Chistyakov penetrated the German defense from the bridgehead at Kletskii. Into this penetration, General Chistyakov committed Kravchenko's 4th Tank and the 3rd Guards Cavalry Corps. As German defensive fires weakened, colored rocket flares launched skyward signaled time for the tank corps' commitment. Kravchenko gave the codeword, "Rodina" (Motherland) over the radio to his waiting tank commanders. The 69th Tank Brigade lunged forward in the lead. At 1300 hours, Kravchenko's corps began rumbling along the road in an allotted breakthrough sector, 6-7 kilometers wide.[22] The 3rd Guards Cavalry Corps, under the command of General Issa Aleksandrovich Pliev, galloped into the breach three hours later with a subsequent mission to strike strongpoints left by Kravchenko's penetrating tank corps.

After a short advance into the German defense, the corps forward detachment drove into a strong whithering artillery fire stopping the lead tanks.

"What's going on? Why are you not moving?" Kravchenko queried the tank brigade commander over the radio. Impatient to be through the German's tactical defense, he ordered the brigade commander no matter what the situation, not to slow the attack.[23] However, in the first day's fighting despite claims of large kills and capture of German combat vehicles, the tank corps lost 20 tanks – high casualties for the tactical fight. Ignoring the heavy resistance, the 45th and 69th Tank Brigades advanced nearly 40 kilometers. The left column consisting of the 102nd Tank and 4th Motorized Brigades gained 10-12 kilometers. A 20 kilometer gap opened between the two advancing columns, but across the next few days the tank corps moved rapidly southwards. By the evening of the second day, Kravchenko's corps hammered out 10 kilometers west of the Don river outside the state farm, "Krasnyi skotovod."

In his command post, Kravchenko called the commander of the 45th Tank Brigade, Lieutenant Colonel P.K. Zhidkov. Unfolding his operational map, he asked for the present location of his 'match boxes". The brigade commander showed him the tank locations. Kravchenko directed the commander to move his tanks from the indicated location, and told him to assume the forward detachment mission. Kravchenko wanted to slip by a key bridge moving deeper into the German defense. However, the brigade commander informed Kravchenko that slipping by the bridge could not be done by his tanks because of thin ice. Pressuring the commander to find a way, Kravchenko emphasized the need for surprise, speed, and a charge.[24]

During the night, the brigade commander accomplished his orders by sending his reconnaissance across a bridge captured by the neighboring 26th Tank Corps. By morning all the brigade had crossed the Don river, capturing from the march the village of Kamyshi. After the corps' forward detachments crossed, Kravchenko moved to the west bank with his small operational group staying abreast of the lead brigade. Kravchenko's corps mission at this point was to develop the offensive from the northwest in the general direction of Sovetskii, where it was to meet with forces of the Stalingrad Front. His corps exploited its penetration of the German defense. The tank crews steered by compass across the white void of the icy steppe for the target town.

The forward detachment quickly stretched forward probing the vulnerable depths of the German rear area. When he judged the time right, Kravchenko directed lead elements to fire star clusters in the air as recognition signals between his forces and lead forces of the Stalingrad Front. At 1600 hours 23 November 1942, Kravchenko's tankers in the 45th Tank Brigade met soldiers from the 36th Mechanized Brigade, 4th Mechanized Corps. And, later that evening the two corps completed the fateful encirclement of the German 6th Army at Stalingrad.[25]

General Vasilii Timofeevich Volskii, commander of the 4th Mechanized Corps, led his corps from the southeast to link with Kravchenko's tank corps. Kravchenko and his staff were on the western edge of the settlement. The two commanders could not see each other. They did not have time. "We drove along our forces. But the staffs kept continuous communications and coordinated the exchange of information," General Volskii recalled.[26]

General Volskii confirmed by telephone that Kravchenko had returned from his observation post to his command post located nearby and with his staff moved across the settlement to the western edge. He described Kravchenko's appearance, "The commander met us – the broad shoulder, tall and well built, tired, but radiant Kravchenko. He still had not taken off his felt boots and was dressed in fur waistcoat over his field shirt."[27]

When Kravchenko called in his report, he was excited. He invited Volskii to celebrate the meeting of the two Fronts with glasses of captured champagne. They toasted the Stalingrad Front.

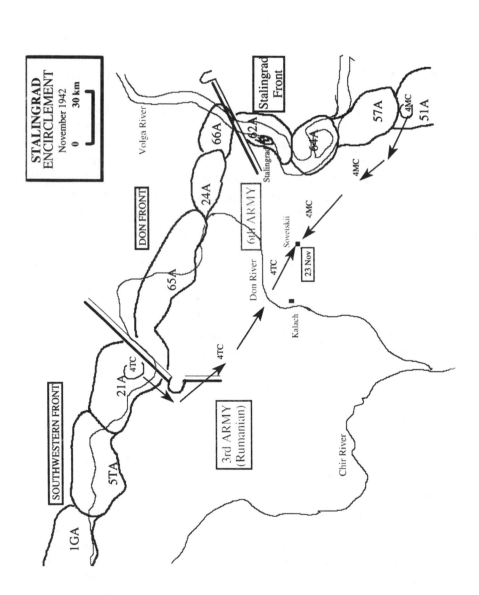

STALINGRAD ENCIRCLEMENT
November 1942
0   30 km

Kravchenko pleased with the operation recalled, "I worked out for the first time in practice the methods of coordination and technical commitment a tank corps in a breakthrough. I received practice in organizing a meeting engagement and pursuit in difficult, changing situations and fulfilling the mission of a deep raid within the enemy rear. From the moment of commitment of the corps to the penetration there was no going back. Every soldier and commander merged in strong unified combat unit, unquestioningly fulfilling the will of the senior leader."[28]

Despite the rough tactical moments, the corps operation covered a depth of 130 kilometers. While the Front staff plans considered a rate of advance of 45 kilometers per day, the corps actually achieved 25 kilometers, taking two days longer.[29] Nonetheless, the results of the operation sealed a significantly large German force in Stalingrad. The action won Kravchenko's corps its "guards" designation, becoming the 5th Guards Tank Corps on 12 February 1942.

In January 1943, the 4th Tank Corps transferred to the Voronezh Front for a major offensive aimed at destroying the Hungarian 2nd Army and 8th Italian Army at Ostrogezhsk and Rossosh. The Front operation broke through the enemy defenses, slamming into the Hungarian 2nd Army south of Voronezh and advancing to the west 140 kilometers. In 15 days, Front forces encircled and destroyed large enemy forces defending along the Don river from Voronezh to Kantemirovskii. This successful advance seemingly created favorable conditions for conducting further offensive operations. Although the more powerful Red Army with larger mechanized and armor fighting units was emerging, the Soviet high command had to learn the limits of its abilities to support and sustain deep, continuous operations. Soviet operational level commanders would learn bitter lessons about overextending their units.

On 10 January, Kravchenko's corps thrown hastily into combat operations had little time to reconstitute from the extensive operations in late 1942. The tank corps off-loaded from rail cars in the small village of Solontsy, southwest of Voronezh. The severe winter of 1943 produced deep snow blocking many roads. Riding exposed on armored vehicles, tankers risked frost bite on faces, hands and other exposed limbs. But, despite severe temperatures, Kravchenko's tankers continued moving forward in adverse conditions. Kravchenko's mission was to reinforce the 40th Army in a deep penetration and to begin a battle of encirclement against the area of

Kastornoe. The Front commander decided to strike from the north and south on the flanks of the 2nd German Army, which was beside the Hungarian 2nd Army, in the general direction of Kastornoe encircling and destroying its main forces, creating favorable conditions for developing the offensive towards Kursk.[30]

At 1300 hours 24 January, the operation began after a 30 minute artillery preparation. The 4th Tank Corps attacked in the first echelon beside rifle divisions of the 40th Army. In two hours, the corps advanced 6-8 kilometers seizing a small town, but suffered substantial losses in vehicles and failed to penetrate deeper on the first day. Such experiences led Red Army leadership to conclude that larger tank units were needed for exploitation of success in depth. The armored formations could not create the penetration and still have sufficient power for deeper operations. Casualties were too high. Large snowdrifts forced Kravchenko to select the shortest route to his objective.

By the end of the day, Kravchenko's tank corps pushed deep into the enemy defense, achieving 16 kilometers. Based on his combat experience around Stalingrad, Kravchenko avoided spending forces on small tank battles along the front line. He executed a bold maneuver, bypassing small islands of resistance and moving deeply around the enemy rear. Slipping through the German defense, his reconnaissance battalion spotted and reported by radio Germans forces withdrawing from the Don river.

Taking advantage of the reported German withdrawal, the corps penetrated to the rail station, Gorshechnoe, in the German rear area. Kravchenko moved forward to the lead brigade. At Gorshechnoe, the tank column slowed as the lead tanks came under heavy German antitank fire.

Kravchenko, calm and collected, raised the hatch of his tank and surveyed the battlefield. After assessing the situation, he quickly slammed shut the turret hatch. His tank boldly maneuvering at high speed rushed the German antitank battery, drawing fires from all the enemy guns. Seeing their commander's tank dashing forward, the other tankers also charged the guns. In a few minutes, the whole antitank battery lay smoking wrecks on blackened snow.

Later, in a tactical conference with the corps officers, one brigade commander asked whether a higher commander should take exceptional risks in battle or not show off. The officer clearly hinted at the episode near Gorshechnoe. Kravchenko, understanding the brigade commander, smiled and acknowledged that a commander was asking for trouble by thrusting himself into such a situation. Kravchenko conceded such an action could often be foolish and bad. However, he also believed that there are those rare moments when it is important to show a personal example.[31] Kravchenko's personal bravery was reminiscent of Napoleon's fearless Marshal Ney who served an inspirational example at necessary times in rearguard actions for the French Army retreat from Moscow.

After the action at Gorshechnoe, Kravchenko decided to always designate one or two aggressive, self-starting crews prepared for similar antitank encounters. These tank crews would overcome the known "hesitation" in front of antitank fire, moving rapidly forward.

On the following day, the tank corps advanced 10-18 kilometers, but lack of fuel stopped Kravchenko's tanks short of capturing Kastornoe.[32] The deep snow along the roadways complicated resupply. Each resupply train consisted of nearly 100 transports or sleigh carts. The push forward of supplies and the evacuation of wounded to the rear tied up the roads. Ammunition shortages became acute. Tank commanders reported only ten rounds per tank, and a few tanks were without a shell. Finally, the situation improved from the air; Soviet biplanes airlifted diesel and gasoline for the combat vehicles. The aerial resupply alleviated some of the problems.

At the end of January 1943, the 40th Army with the 4th Tank Corps continued liquidating encircled enemy grouping. Trapped enemy units could offer costly resistance and unforeseen difficulties that detracted attacking units from their original mission. From 2 to 8 February, Kravchenko's tank corps became caught up fighting groups of German soldiers escaping west from encirclement. These marauding groups stumbled upon Kravchenko's assembled brigades while preparing for movement in the Belgorod direction. The tank corps tied down in small battles was unable to support the 40th Army's offensive success until 8 February, after the rifle army captured the city of Belgorod.

On 12 February 1943, the 4th Tank Corps became the 5th Guards, and it entered battle, advancing rapidly on the near approaches to Kharkov. Kravchenko's tank corps and 40th Army led the Front offensive forcing German withdrawal. With Red Army forces converging on Kharkov, German plans for the defense of the city became confused. Despite Hitler's order to hold Kharkov at all costs, General Paul Hausser, commander of the occupying SS Panzer Corps, independently ordered withdrawal from the city. By 16 February, Kravchenko's tankers met Rybalko's tankers in the Kharkov city square.

On 25 February, the Front commander, General Golikov, gave new missions to the 40th Army and 5th Guards Tank Corps. He wanted to send Kravchenko's corps to the Oposhnya area, creating a favorable position for capturing Poltava from the north and north-west. Before the 40th Army or the 5th Guards Tank Corps reached Poltava, German resistance increased significantly in front of the Voronezh Front. Additionally, the Southwestern Front to the south was rapidly collapsing from Field Marshal von Manstein's counterstrike.

The Soviet High Command began shifting forces from the Voronezh to the Southwestern Front, attempting to staunch the German attack. On 1 March, General Golikov finally ordered the 40th Army to go on the defensive. The failure of Soviet action to blunt the German assault forced the Voronezh Front to withdraw. By 13 March, the situation turned worse as the German "Grossdeutschland" Division attacked the junction between the 40th and 69th Armies. Two rifle divisions and Kravchenko's tank corps fought in vain to halt the German advance and began to withdraw. Before Tomarovka, a rifle division of the 40th Army became cut off by the Grossdeutschland Division, and General Moskalenko ordered the 3rd and 5th Guards Tank Corps to open a route, helping free the encircled division. On the night of 18 March, the encircled division with tireless assistance from Kravchenko's corps fought its way east.

As the front stalled, Krachenko's adjutant remembered his commander's frustrations, "I never saw our General dispirited with such a sinking morale." By 21 March, the Soviet High Command poured enough reinforcements into the Belgorod-Karkhov area to halt the Germans. For his corps' exceptional offensive actions in late winter, Kravchenko received the Order of Suvorov. For the next few months, the front stabilized with German and Soviet armies preparing for resumed operations in the spring.

On the eve of the gigantic summer struggle at Kursk, Kravchenko rigorously trained his soldiers. The tank corps conducted tactical field exercises and fired weapons and tanks on ranges. Kravchenko personally oversaw the training and worked out the plan for the impending combat operation.

In mid-May Stalin decided the Red Army would assume a deliberate defense along the Kursk salient, allowing the German's impending offensive to break itself on dug-in Soviet units. On the northern face of the salient the Germans faced off against the Central Front; the Voronezh Front defended the southern face. To meet attacking German units from the vicinity of Belgorod, the Voronezh Front commander, General Nikolai Vatutin, believed their main attack would be toward Oboyan. The Front's left wing was held by the veteran 6th and 7th Guards Armies which had seen action at Stalingrad. The right wing was defended by the 38th and 40th Armies. In the second echelon behind the 6th and 7th Guards Armies were the 69th Rifle and lst Tank Armies and the 2nd and 5th Guards Tank Corps.

At 0530 hours, 5 July 1943, the German army began its offensive against the northern and southern faces of the Kursk salient. Located on the southern frontline, Kravchenko well forward watched intently from the observation post of the 52nd Guards Rifle Division, 6th Guards Army the first assaults by the advancing German tanks. As with the invading German units in the summer of 1941, he studied the German tank tactics. Then, he drove quickly to his corps command post at the "Kalinin" state farm to prepare his tank corps for combat. His staff maintained close communications with Katukov's tank army on their right flank.

General Vatutin gave Kravchenko the battle order: 5th Guards Tank Corps move quickly from the front reserve, and together with a tank corps of the lst Tank Army take up a second line of defense along the Belgorod-Oboyan highway. After receiving the instructions at 2400 hours 5 July, the corps moved to assume their defensive lines. Together with other Front forces, Kravchenko's corps covered the German's most likely approach on the Oboyan axis.

For Kravchenko, "6 July was the most terrible day of the whole war."[33] The day began ominously. German tanks failed to appear by 0800 hours. Kravchenko worried the Germans had managed to bypass his positions. Initially, the Germans had struck Katukov's army, and, only by afternoon directed their force to the northeast, in the direction of Luchki, against Kravchenko's corps. Kravchenko's units suffered relentless air attacks before the ground assault. The boundary between the lst Tank Army and 5th Guards Tank Corps became the focus of the German drive north into the salient.

Peering through binoculars, Kravchenko watched his tanks engage advancing German tanks. His tankers' shells bounced off the German Tiger tanks frontal armor leaving only dents. In tank against tank fight, the Soviet tankers had to compensate tactically for the superior German armor. Soviet tankers to get the necessary aimed shots for knocking out Germans tanks let them close to within 300-400 meters. The tank battle raged in large fields of tall standing rye creating a hellish fire, blackening the skies. By midday, fire and smoke blotted the sun over the battlefield. In the open field areas between burning sections Soviet tanks with gashed armor traded shell for shell with the Germans tanks.

In the midst of the swirling armor battle, Kravchenko stopped his tank to watch a tank that was not firing. It was not knocked out. Turning to his adjutant, "What are they doing?" Kravchenko asked in an agitated voice. "Immediately towards the crew." As they approached, the crew appeared from the bowels of the tank, and the adjutant asked about the Tigers. The crew leader responded "Beasts, such beasts. Pass on dear fellows, there are the living and the dead, but the Tiger overcomes all."[34] The formidable new German tanks undeniably earned the respect of Red Army tankers.

Kravchenko situated his observation post in a canvas covered trench on a hillock hiding his tank in a row of bushes. Over the field telephone, Kravchenko heard a brigade commander reporting the repulse of the German tank attack. Like all commanders of large armored formations, Kravchenko followed the battle through the reports over the radio, sensing the intensity and location of the fight from transmissions.

Red Army commanders passed an anxious night. The German SS panzer divisions, "Adolf Hitler" and "Das Reich," managed to penetrate east of Rakovlev along the boundary between the 2nd and 5th Guards Tank Corps. The Germans regrouped their forces in the Luchki direction not breaking off their violent attack with nightfall. Reconnaissance reported German units moving around the corps' right flank towards Greater Mayachki. Kravchenko ordered the brigade commander to hold and not back off his killing ground. All night the tank crews repelled German attacks and withdrew from encirclement.

The 6th Guards Rifle and 1st Tank Armies bore the brunt of the German attack on 7 July. Towards evening a strong German tank force sought to gain a penetration in the 1st Tank Army sector. General Vatutin pulled units from the 38th and 30th Armies to reinforce the defense. By the end of the fighting on 7 July, the Germans fought increasingly with exposed flanks. With the next day, German panzer units resumed their drive towards Oboyan.

Kravchenko's corps weakened from the preceding battles had serious losses. General Vatutin attempting to reinforce Kravchenko's depleted corps sent the 100th Tank Brigade, 31st Tank Corps for use against the penetration. Kravchenko received with the brigade the order to counterattack the Germans. At 1600 hours, the tank corps struck against the German flank, and, again, the fighting was within several hundred meters with Soviet tanks pulling from behind cover and firing at vulnerable spots on German tanks. But, the 5th Guards Tank Corps was forced to withdraw after meeting strong counterattacks by German air and tanks.

Kravchenko spent days in his tank moving about the battlefield. His action raised the question from his deputy after the battle of where should the commander be on the battlefield.

Kravchenko smiled, "The place is prompted by the situation. I would say the commander's place is there where he is convenient and has the best control of the forces." Kravchenko made the analogy that some men for the detail of the trees don't see the forest. Other men, on the other hand, for the forest cannot see the trees.[35] Kravchenko uniquely possessed the prized military skill and quality of mind to simultaneously see one or the other.

On 10 July, the 5th Guards Tank Corps reinforcing General Katukov's 1st Tank Army concentrated for the climatic battle against the German assault on the southern face of the Kursk salient. The 1st Tank Army and Kravchenko's corps' launched an attack as part of the Voronezh Front's counterstrike with General Rotmistrov's 5th Guards Tank Army, depriving the German 2nd SS, 3rd, and 48th Panzer Corps the potential freedom of maneuver and inflicting heavy damage on the German panzer forces.

At 1000 hours 12 July, the 5th Guards and 10th Tank Corps together with a rifle division of the 6th Guards Army overcame initially strong German resistance. Kravchenko attempting to organize tank movement in the depth of the German defense worked without success. A wall of fire barred the way for his combat vehicles. "We can't move," reported Kravchenko over the radio to Katukov. "The Germans have strong artillery and mortar fires covering the ground everywhere ahead. We are under continuous bombardment."[36]

General Katukov told him not to advance any further, but hold the ground already gained. The German division, "Großdeutschland," attacked relentlessly in 5th Guards and 10th Tank

Corps sectors. Kravchenko's corps held for two days. On the night of 16 July, the tank corps passed its sectors to the 6th Guards Army.

The German's most powerful grouping had struck against the Voronezh Front. It breached the defense line to a depth of 30-35 kilometers, but subsequent advances were halted, and the German offensive was over after eight days of operations. In a few weeks, Kravchenko had to reconstitute quickly his corps for the impending Belgorod-Kharkov counteroffensive, called Operation "Rumyantsev." For the counteroffensive, Kravchenko's corps reinforced the 1st Tank Army attacking on the right toward Tomarovka, west of Belgorod.

On the morning of 3 August, after the German forward defense had been softened with artillery and air preparations, the Voronezh and Steppe Fronts began the counteroffensive. The sudden, devastating artillery blow propelled the armored forces quickly into the depths of the German defense. Kravchenko's corps along with the 31st Tank Corps surrounded the 19th Panzer Division in Tomarovka, fully mauling it. The 5th Guards Tank Corps drove behind the German panzer division sealing its fate. The German commander, General Schmidt, was killed in the action. A number of the panzer division's officers and soldiers were captured along with combat ready Tiger tanks.

By evening 6 August, 5th Guards Tank Corps's main forces battled for towns southwest of Tomarovka. The following day, the corps received the mission to continue the advance and to seize Kupevakhoi, cutting the western approaches to Kharkov. Kravchenko aggressively maneuvered his corps pushing into the operational depth and undermining the German defense. For his corps' fight and his personal performance at Kursk, Kravchenko received the Order of Kutuzov 2nd Degree.

As a result of heavy casualties and battle losses, the 5th Guards Tank Corps was withdrawn for a short time to the reserves for refitting and reinforcements in a village south of the town of Lebedin. During the months of August and September, Kravchenko's corps advanced west over 250 kilometers liberating small villages and towns in the Red Army's drive for the Dnepr river.

On 3 October Kravchenko received a summons to the 1st Ukrainian Front headquarters. Immediately upon arrival he reported to the Front commander General Nikolai Vatutin. A short, squat man, General Vatutin was a no-nonsense, hard-driving fighter; these were necessary traits to obtain and hold a Front-level command. Kravchenko had been assigned to General Vatutin's Front since early 1943, and fought on the southern face of the Kursk salient as the Voronezh Front's armored reserve.

At General Vatutin's side sat his earthy, but astute, political officer, Nikita Khrushchev, a future premier of the Soviet Union. On this occasion, General Vatutin had good news to share with Kravchenko. Vatutin, who had an amazing ability to accurately describe the situation and foresee developing events, told Kravchenko how lead elements of the 38th Army fought to the banks of the Dnepr river and crossed north of Kiev. They forced the river with makeshift means. Using rafts from hastily felled trees, empty gas cans, and small fishing boats, they snatched a hold on the west bank of the wide river in the area of the small village of Lyutezh. Some 15 kilometers north of the prized city, Kiev, the Red Army now breached a potentially difficult German defensive line. It was not an ideal bridgehead, but nonetheless, it was large enough to move more Soviet infantry and tanks to the west bank.

"These units," said Nikita Khrushchev, sobering the momentary euphoria, "are bearing great losses and resisting continuous German counterattacks. It's unlikely that they will be successful in securing the captured bridgehead on the west bank if they are not supported by our tanks."[37]

"On the way to the Dnepr," the Front commander continued, "is a serious obstacle, the Desna River. To build a bridge across it to cover our weight requirements would take no less than eight to 10 days. That wait will preclude any timely support to the 38th Army's forward units, and it will be a difficult battle to support the bridgehead across the Dnepr."[38]

The Dnepr, the second largest Russian river, had concerned the Soviet General Staff planners since early 1943. Anticipating success in the Kursk battle during the summer, the Red Army leadership saw the Dnepr as the retreating Germans' next likely line of defensive positions, and a difficult one to breach. The river was wide, with a west bank 100 feet higher than the east. Dubbed the "eastern rampart," it offered a very defensible barrier against a continuation of the Red Army's westward advance.

Hoping to preempt a strong defensive line, advancing Soviet units on the left wing of Vatutin's Front raced the Germans to the river in early September. Advanced elements of General Rybalko's

3rd Guards Tank Army approached the Dnepr while German forces were still located on the eastern bank. The Soviets attempted to cross the river south of Kiev in the area of the Great Bukrin, a large bend in the Dnepr. In a poorly coordinated effort, the Soviet High Command attempted to assist the Voronezh Front with a hastily planned airborne operation using a full airborne corps. But, in dropping paratroopers into the Bukrin bend, everything went wrong. The airborne drop scattered jumpers on both sides of the river, some landing in the river itself. The assault was a complete disaster. The Germans slipped away to the western bank and rushed reinforcements to seal the area.

The Voronezh Front's first chance to breach the river had failed, but given the 38th Army's small bridgehead, General Vatutin's Front had another chance to achieve success. Showing his typical relentless style, General Vatutin refused to let this opportunity slip. German commanders had learned to always count on Vatutin to do the unexpected. Now, he raced against time. General Vatutin would have preferred to use the more powerful 3rd Guards Tank Army, but it was too far south in the Bukrin bend, and was engaged with strong German forces containing its bridgehead. General Kravchenko's 5th Guards Tank Corps could move faster, and appear unexpectedly in the new bridgehead – if Kravchenko could get his tanks across the Desna.

With his knack for inspiring confidence in his subordinates, General Vatutin directed Kravchenko, "You must look for a possible ford to get over the Desna."[39]

Receiving his mission with full awareness of his commander's urgency, General Kravchenko immediately left for his tank corps' assembly area, in the woods northwest of Brovary near the Desna River. There, his unit was refitting and reequipping after recent combat, and it still suffered from major personnel and equipment shortages. Of an authorized tank strength of 210, the unit had approximately 90 tanks in good repair. Interestingly, some 15 of these tanks were British Lend-Lease Churchills, a heavy, slow tank – difficult to manage compared to the faster T-34's.

In his usual quiet, muffled voice, Kravchenko directed his staff to organize an immediate reconnaissance of the Desna. A tank platoon leader was about to earn his extra pay and rations as a "Guards" lieutenant. He received the task to measure depths and find the most shallow point for a crossing. Tankers from the 20th Guards Tank

Brigade, designated for the reconnaissance, searched with local fishermen to find a possible ford.

The tankers dived several times in the cold October river waters to determine the character of the river bottom. They looked for an area with solid river bed and no large rocks, tree trunks, or other obstacles which might stop their tanks as they drove across the river bottom. It was a long, cold, arduous task.

At the same time, Kravchenko had his tank brigade commanders begin preparing their tanks for the crossing. He reported his actions to the Front commander and received from the Front staff the mission to attack in the direction of Lyutezh, to force the Desna and Dnepr rivers, and to render help to the forward units of the 38th Army in widening and securing the Lyutezh bridgehead.

The search for a river crossing finally succeeded. The tankers found a potential ford in the vicinity of the village, Letki. The width of the Desna in the crossing area was 290 meters, the depth averaged one meter and up to two meters deep in the center. The two meters was twice the fording depth of the T-34 tanks. The river bed of packed sandy soil was also a potential problem since it could easily wash out. After a few tanks crossed, it could quickly become deeper. In addition, the march route to the fording site twisted like a snake through swampy terrain. It was not the best crossing site, but Kravchenko had to risk it.

The tank crews carried out necessary river crossing preparations, displaying great inventiveness. All cracks, openings, hatches, engine louvres, and the turret race were caulked with oakum soaked in grease or tar. Any other potential openings were sealed with tarpaulins, oiled and battened-down. These were held tight by blocks and wedges. Air could reach the engines through the open turret hatch, but exhaust fumes had to be fed through exhaust pipes made from tarpaulin sleeves, which carried the gases to the water surface.

Tankers of the 22nd Guards Tank Brigade made special protective covers for their main guns, and in a few of the battalions, soldiers crafted air intakes from corrugated hoses. For all the various methods, it took 6 to 8 hours to prepare a tank for traveling underwater.

Engineers from the 38th Army assisted the tank corps and prepared the banks for the descending approach into the river. In the swampy areas, sappers laid a corduroy road made from brush wood. General Kravchenko listened attentively to his subordinates' progress reports. Later, he would attribute the success of the operation, in large measure, to hard, continuous work and precise coordination and planning by his corps chief of staff, and rigorous execution by the tank corps' engineers.

The tanks, personally led by their corps commander, began crossing the river on 4 October, less than 24 hours after receiving the mission. Across the top of the water, two rows of spar buoys marked the ford. The tanks moved along this designated path in first gear at no more than 7-8 miles per hour. The drivers drove blindly, carrying out changes in steering directions called from their tank commanders, who sat on the turret tops just out of the water. It took one tank an average of 8 minutes to cross the deep ford.[40] Exiting on the opposite bank, the tank continued moving towards the Dnepr river.

In the middle of the Desna crossing operation, General Nikandr Evlampievich Chibisov, commander of the 38th Army, arrived from his headquarters at Letki. While anxious for the tankers' arrival in his bridgehead, he was impressed by everyone's sacrifices.

"Andrei Grigorevich, what people your tankers are! For my many years of service," he observed, "I have never seen more courageous soldiers than I see at this time. The people are hours in the cold water without getting out. And such a risk the drivers take driving to the opposite bank."[41]

Tankers had to spend time in the icy cold waters, fastening chains to tanks that bogged down in the river bottom. The sandy soil was beginning to give way with the passage of so many tanks. Three such tanks had to be towed to the opposite bank. The engine compartments had leaked and flooded, causing the engines to die. In many tanks that made the crossing, the drivers did it blindly, sitting in a foot of frigid water. Upon exit on the opposite shore, tanks were quickly cleared of water and prepared for combat. By 0800 hours 5 October, in a period of 8 hours, fifty T-34's and 15 Churchill's crossed the ford.[42]

A pleased General Kravchenko, in a fur waistcoat over his field shirt, stood on the opposite bank with a broad smile. He presented awards on the spot for heroic personal efforts in the unique crossing. For the first time, a Red Army armor unit had crossed a river underwater – a first time for any army without specially designed underwater equipment. The Party and the Motherland were grateful, but none more than the waiting Front commander.

After crossing the Desna, the 5th Guards Tank Corps rushed

onwards to the Dnepr river. Time was precious. The Germans had long since learned to react quickly and strongly to Red Army bridge-heads. No matter how small the bridgehead, the Soviets would in-crease its size rapidly – a small battalion would grow overnight to a division or more, making it impossible for the Germans to reduce the bridgehead. The Russians, on the other hand, knew that every day, even every hour, increased the German's potential to cordon off the fragile bridgehead with additional forces, mines, and sys-tematic fires, as they had done at the Bukrin bend.

General Kravchenko began to think of the fight ahead. He con-tacted the commanders of the forward rifle divisions at Lyutezh. They reported that there were currently two German infantry and one tank divisions in the area. The Germans' defensive line con-sisted of three positions, each of which had trenches, prepared ma-chine gun and mortar emplacements, and earth and timber field obstacles. Forward of their positions were antipersonnel and anti-tank mines. Crossing such a defense to expand the bridgehead would be no small task for Kravchenko's corps. But, first, the 5th Guards Tank Corps had to cross the Dnepr river in the Red Army's drive for possession of the river.

The Dnepr river at this point was 650 to 750 meters wide and between 2.5 and 9 meters deep. As the corps' advanced on the water obstacle, reconnaissance was again dispatched, and, with the help of local inhabitants, they found two partially-damaged barges which the Germans had sunk while withdrawing. Once raised, the barges were repaired. Each barge could carry three tanks across the Dnepr. In addition to the restored barges, the corps prepared two tank fer-ries from pontoon bridging sections. Through the night of 5 Octo-ber, these improvised methods resulted in approximately ten trips, and by dawn, Kravchenko had 60 of his tanks in the bridgehead.

German Field Marshal Erich von Manstein's Army Group South was an old opponent of General Vatutin's Voronezh Front. The Army Group's Fourth Panzer Army had General Hauffe's XII Corps in the area of the bridgehead. The sector was defended by the Hessian 88th and Brandenburg 208th Infantry divisions along the steep river bank. In order to secure the crossing over the Dnepr, Kravchenko ordered preliminary artillery fire on German observation posts on the oppo-site bank. He also directed powerful suppressive artillery fires, sup-ported by a large number of the famed Katyusha rocket launchers, to neutralize German machine gunners and artillery positions.

The first man to cross was the 20th Guards Tank Brigade commander, Colonel Shutov, a seasoned professional who had served in the Red Army since 1918. Before the war, he had been stationed in the ancient capital of Mother Russia, Kiev, and he knew the city well. His wife and two sons had remained in Kiev since the beginning of the war. He anxiously sought battle for the relief of his family and Kiev.

The arrival of Kravchenko's tank corps was the key to the Red Army defense in the bridgehead. The morale of the forward infantry men in the rifle corps was bolstered and the reinforced German counterattacks were successfully repelled. Within 24 hours of the 5th Guards Tank Corps' appearance, the bridgehead began to expand. With the additions of the tankers, the depth of the Red Army's hold across the Dnepr expanded to a width of 8-10 kilometers and a depth of 5-6 kilometers from a previously shrinking area only 2-3 kilometers wide and 1-1.5 kilometers deep. Colonel Shutov's tank brigade had figured significantly in the fierce fighting, and Kravchenko's tankers widened and secured the bridgehead. General Hauffe's soldiers could not drive the Russians back into the river. They fought fiercely to contain the burgeoning bridgehead.

The unusual crossing method made it possible to achieve not just tactical, but operation surprise. The enemy situation map in the 4th Panzer Army intelligence section did not depict the 5th Guards Tank Corps in the Lyutezh bridgehead until 12 October.[43] Kravchenko's arrival at the bridgehead prevented the Germans from pushing it in.

Even as the corps' rear element waited to cross the Dnepr, General Kravchenko received a new order from the tireless and aggressive Front commander. The 5th Guards Tank Corps was ordered to conduct a deep raid outside the bridgehead. Its objective was to cut off the highway between Zhitomir and Kiev, in the area of Makarov, and then halt the approach of German reserves from Zhitomir to Kiev.

Kravchenko's raid to Makarov began as aggressively as the crossing of the Desna toward the Dnepr. The corps tank brigades successfully passed their tanks through the kind of difficult and marshy terrain that normally inhibited the maneuver of tank formations. The tank units churned through the swamp-lined Irpen river to the southwest of the bridgehead, moving as rapidly as possible through a large tract of forest. After overcoming light resistance from a small group of German infantry, the tank corps, upon reaching good high ground, began to maneuver in the German rear area. With specially attached airborne infantry, which rode on the tanks, Kravchenko's tankers rapidly advanced toward their assigned objectives. As usual, Kravchenko was well forward in his observation post. He always located himself at the most difficult situation, or most critical spot, sternly gazing on the action. His whole manner projected to his fighting tankers his strong-willed character. For four days, the tank corps fought toward Kiev, and the highway to the west that was the Nazi lifeline.

As the tank corps moved out for the raid, the situation in the Lyutezh bridgehead turned worse. The 38th Army was under strong German counterattacks from the areas of Vyslhgorod and Pushcha-Voditsa on the southern perimeter. The German command understood the danger of Kravchenko's tank corps maneuvering against the critical line of communications in their rear area. Strong forces of infantry and tanks struck from Kiev to the north along the Dnepr River's west bank, attempting to cut off Kravchenko's tank corps and liquidate the menacing bridgehead. It was a desperate effort to stem the Red Army's advance and breach of the Germans major defensive obstacle the Dnepr River.

Kravchenko was ordered to return his corps to the bridgehead and strike in the direction of the counterattacking German forces. This recall troubled Kravchenko. These instructions were in error, he thought. The corps' attack to Makarov was progressing successfully and bearing results.

Believing the attack should continue, he called the Front staff to question the order. He hoped to change minds, but General Vatutin himself reaffirmed his order to immediately return to the Lyutezh bridgehead. Kravchenko's tankers were still necessary for the Red Army's hold on the west bank.

"With an ache in our hearts," wrote Kravchenko after the war, "we abandoned our gains, rushed back towards the River Irpen."[44] None of his command regretted the withdrawal more than Colonel Shutov.

With the tank corps' arrival back in the bridgehead, and in coordination with the 38th Army rifle units, they repelled all the German counterattacking forces, and, again, expanded the bridgehead. Meanwhile, General Vatutin worked to rush other forces to fully exploit the Dnepr crossing.

German aircraft dropped leaflets throughout the bridgehead area. In an attempt to demoralize the tankers and dash the hopes of the infantrymen, the leaflets read, "General Kravchenko lost all his 240 tanks and now sits entrapped." Reading one of the leaflets brought to him Kravchenko remarked, "If I had had 240 tanks, I would have driven those Fascists all the way to Berlin."[45]

With the arrival of additional forces – primarily General Rybalko's 3rd Guards Tank Army – in the bridgehead, General Vatutin, on 30 October, held a war council with his army and corps commanders. The conference was conducted in the cellar of a bombed-out school house in Novo-Petrovtsy in the Lyutezh bridgehead, within the range of German artillery. General Vatutin clearly and laconically stated the operational plan, and personally assigned the army, corps, and division missions. Generally, the plan was to capture Kiev from the north and, moving in a southwest direction, destroy elements of the Fourth Panzer Army and seize important population centers to the west of the Dnepr. "The Supreme Commander (Stalin) has ordered us to launch the offensive on 3 November," he said in conclusion. "The Ukrainian capital is to be liberated not later than 6 November."[46]

Kravcehnko stood quietly in the back, against the wall. He made no comments. His tank corps, in coordinated tank and infantry tactics, would fight as a mobile group for the 38th Army. Attacking in the first echelon, his corps would again cross the Irpen River. He knew what was expected of him and he would get it done.

While in the assembly area, 5th Guards Tank Corps became the target of marauding German Stuka aircraft. Kravchenko quickly decided deception would be necessary for his unit's third crossing of the Irpen. He had his engineers build false crossing sites over the river and fabricate mock tanks from plywood in the assembly areas. The dummy tanks drew the German bombing strikes.

At 0600, 3 November, the 1st Ukrainian Front (the Voronezh Front was redesignated on 20 October), began a classic large-scale Red Army artillery preparation along the entire front south of Lyutezh. A powerful strike from a full Artillery Breakthrough Corps at the disposal of the 38th Army initiated the offensive in the direction of the main attack.

During the evening of 5 November, Kravchenko met with his staff on the outskirts of Kiev. Leaning over a map, Kravchenko indicated the march routes of the tank columns and the coordination requirements of the brigades. He marked on the map the portion of the city they would attack. He ordered the concentration of units and preparations for the advance to the final attack positions. And, then Kravchenko added a surprising requirement, "The tanks must drive in the night at high speeds with headlights on."[47]

His staff and commanders exchanged glances in disbelief. Noting the puzzled stares, Kravchenko confirmed his instructions. "Yes, all vehicles – tanks, self-propelled guns, transports – will move at a high speed with headlights on and sirens blaring."[48]

At 2000 hours, 5 November, General Vatutin gave the order to begin the final assault on Kiev. The tanks' rapid night advance, with headlights on and firing their main guns on the move, stunned the German defenders and created confusion and panic. Breaking the resistance of Germans units, Kravchenko tank corps decisively attacked into Kiev. His 20th Tank Brigade seized the state farm "Arsenal" and 22nd Tank Brigade the territorial factory "Bolshevik'. Crews of Kravchenko's tankers penetrated Kiev from the north and west.[49] Fearing encirclement, the Germans began withdrawing from the city, and , by 0400 hours, 6 November, the German resistance in Kiev ceased. Announcing the capture of the city, General Vatutin phoned Stalin, who ordered salutes in Moscow and all Russia to celebrate the victory.

In the month's fighting, Kravchenko led his tank corps in crossing the Desna, Dnepr, and – three times – the Irpen rivers, and his unit was the first to pierce to the center of Kiev. Krachenko's tireless, aggressive performance earned him his country's highest decoration, the star of the Hero of the Soviet Union. He became marked for advancement in command.

Attacking from 6 to 11 November, Kravchenko's tank corps which consisted of three tank and one motorized rifle brigades, a heavy tank regiment and a Katyusha rocket regiment struck in the direction of Vasilkov, Grebenki, Belaya Tserkov and ran into superior German forces near Germankovka, Krasnoe Slivonki. His reports back to the Front were not comforting.

General Vatutin and his new political officer, Konstantin Vasilevich Krainyukov, drove out to see Kravchenko. The weather was foggy. By nightfall they reached Kravchenko's headquarters in the village of Kodaki. In the hut a strong, grey-white tobacco smoke clouded the light from an oil lamp. Kravchenko raised from behind the table and reported that the assigned mission before the corps until now had not been accomplished. The enemy committed new forces and their attacks grew.

"Many of our people have died in the past battle," Kravchenko pronounced sadly shaking his head. Picking up later, "Yes, great losses, terrible. Especially in the 21st Guards Tank Brigade, it took the main strike of the superior enemy force."[50]

Krainyukov looking attentively at Kravchenko noted his tiredness. His face turned black from sleeplessness, eyes became sunken. In the war Kravchenko did not spare himself.[51] As one tank commander characterized him, "Decisive, strong-willed commander, with a personal example to inspire subordinates."[52]

On 22 November 1943, the 5th Guards Tank Corps was ordered to establish a protective shield around Kiev preventing German forces from cutting off the Zhitomir highway. Kravchenko immediately took to organizing the defense and placing his units, but the 1st Ukrainian Front quickly resumed the offensive to secure its hold in western Ukraine. The 5th Guards Tank Corps supported the offensive westward in the 60th Army sector, fighting through mid-December. In late December, General Vatutin wanting to create a decisive break in the German lines to the south reinforced the 40th Army with the 5th Guards Tank Corps. The tank corps forced marched from the Front's right wing to the town of Skvira and then in the direction of Zvenigorod.

The year, 1944, began badly for the German Army. Kravchenko's tank corps cut behind a large German force holding a last grip on the Dnepr river. Soviet armored pincers were crawling closer. "We could feel the pressure of the horde," a Walloonian SS officer recalled.[53] Red Army operations on the west side of the Dnepr river set up the conditions for the elimination of the German Korsun-Shevchenkovskii bulge.

On 2 January 1944, General Vatutin decided to continue the Front offensive without pause. In the period from 2 to 5 January, Front forces continued moving forward in heavy fighting. On the left wing the 40th Army with the 27th Army captured the town of Belaya Tserkov. The 5th Guards Tank Corps reinforcing the 40th Army continued to develop the attack towards Stavishche.

By 10 January, the German command concentrated a sizable force southeast of Vinnitsy for a counterstrike against Kravchenko's corps and part of the 40th Army near Khristinovki.

In January 1944, Kravchenko received the honor of the Hero of the Soviet Union for his role in the battle for Kiev. A few days later he was called to the Front headquarters where General Vatutin informed him that he had been designated for a new command. The Stavka decided to combine the 5th Guards Tank Corps and 5th Mechanized Corps to form the 6th Tank Army with Kravchenko as the commander. His chief of staff was General Major Dmitrii Ivanovich Zaev.

Kravchenko met General Mikhail Vasilevich Volkov, commander of the 5th Mechanized Corps, who formed the other half of the tank army. In his first meeting with Kravchenko, Volkov remembered a man whose stern face and a firm handshake projected a demeanor of strong will. But the hard look melted when Kravchenko bared a row of white teeth through a warm smile.[54]

In a typical direct manner, Kravchenko settled right to business. He informed General Volkov of the Stavka decision to form the new tank army and his designation as commander. "I drove here to become familiar with your corps," Kravchenko informed the corps commander.[55] Kravchenko then attentively listened as his new subordinate corps commander reported the status of his corps.

On 20 January, the 6th Tank Army came into existence and five days later, the tank army's corps and brigades concentrated in the area of Tynovka, Krasilovka. The tank army possessed 160 tanks and 50 self-propelled assault guns. The tank corps had 54 tanks and 4 assault guns; the mechanized corps, 106 tanks and 46 assault guns. The personnel in the mechanized corps were close to authorized strengths, however, in the tank corps a significant number of motorized infantry and artillery personnel were missing. Other positions were filled with inexperienced soldiers.[56] To assist the army chief of staff, General Zaev, a group of 20 staff officers arrived from the Front staff. There was no time to create an army staff, so control of the army's forces was executed through the 5th Guards Tank Corps staff. "Our main mission," General Zaev advised his staff, "is to prepare forces in a very short time for a major action and in time during the course of the operation create an army staff."[57] The 6th Tank Army was on paper only a hint of the other tank armies at the time. But, the ad hoc organization facilitated a centralized control of armored assets as a mobile group for Front operations.

The Stavka Supreme High Command worked out a plan for encircling and destroying a large German force from Army Group South with the 1st and 2nd Ukrainian Fronts in the Korsun-Shevchenkovskii operation. In the first stage of the operation, the two Fronts' tank armies were to encircle the enemy, and in the second stage, to repel enemy counterattacks from the outer perimeter of the encirclement. The operation uniquely had two tank armies (5th Guards and 6th) moving to meet each other with the objective of sealing the encirclement. Execution of the plan was not simple. An unexpected thaw in a normally frozen January complicated the task, miring cars, cannons and transports in a heavy viscous mud. Black, slippery Russian mud sucked boots off feet and buried vehicles above their axles. In addition to the wetness of snowstorms, the cold, raw wind drove the windchill factor to a minus 20 degrees. "The Russian winter was pitiless," recalled a German Army veteran at Korsun. "A serious wound to any limb meant a dead limb."[58]

Across two busy days, General Nikolai Vatutin, commander of the lst Ukrainian Front, issued the new tank army's mission. In the Front's plan, the 6th Tank Army followed the penetrating 104th Rifle Corps, 40th Army, developing the offensive to Zvenigorodka. In breaking through the German defenses, Kravchenko's tank army was to move as part of a concentric strike with Rotmistrov's 5th Guards Tank Army, 2nd Ukrainian Front at the base of the Korsun-Shevchenkovskii salient. Both tank armies directed their efforts against the approaching German reserves and kept the reserves from breaking through to the surrounded German group until destroyed by the rifle armies.

Kravchenko gathered his commanders and officers to discuss the situation and plan of action. His meeting familiarized the commanders with necessary operational details for the impending attack. The mental preparation allowed his tank commanders to act independently, yet concentrically, in the absence of orders. Together with the chief of staff and a dozen officers of the Front staff, Kravchenko worked out the army's plan of action in the operation, preparing combat orders and plans for the coordination with the 40th Rifle and 2nd Air Armies.

By late 25 January, General Kravchenko reported to the lst Ukrainian Front commander the tank army's combat preparations. General Vatutin characterized Kravchenko as a decisive and energetic military leader, who was able to fulfill great and difficult missions. A brave battle organizer and master of deep maneuver, he was "one of those tank commanders who encircled the German army around Stalingrad."[59] Kravchenko's reputation as a tank corps commander and respect of his Front commander secured his appointment as a tank army commander.

The 2nd Ukrainian Front's mobile group, the 5th Guards Tank Army, advanced in the attack on 25 January. The next morning the lst Ukrainian Front attacked, following a powerful cannonade in the area of Vinograd. From the volleys of guns and mortars, "one could not hear a conversation over the telephone or radio set," General Zaev recalled.[60] The 6th Tank Army in the first echelon advanced followed by the infantry.

Towards midday it became clear that the 104th Rifle Division, 40th Army needed assistance in penetrating the German defenses. Kravchenko decided to commit the 5th Guards Tank Corps and drove to the tank corps' headquarters checking its preparation for combat. With the corps ready, Kravchenko launched it in an aggressive attack. Towards evening Kravchenko received a called from General Zaev, the army Chief of Staff, who reported a loss of 30 tanks in the first day of the offensive.[61] Like a scythe hitting a resisting rock, the corps paid a price for their bold and energetic operation. While pressing the enemy along their assigned axis of advance, the depleted corps' could not complete its task because of their reduced numbers.

Kravchenko listened stone faced, not interrupting. He sorted through the events, mentally suspending facts to make the necessary decision. In dynamic and difficult situations, time is important and a wasted moment must not pass – when to commit the reserve seemed the key factor. If late, Kravchenko would not succeed in influencing the course of the battle.

His face brightened up as he sought additional information to confirm a course of action. "How many vehicles do we have in reserve? Fifty tanks and assault guns. And that, if turned into a strike group, or into a forward detachment? I am driving to the 233rd Tank Brigade, I am assigning it a mission."[62]

At 2200 hours, the army commander reported to the lst Ukrainian Front commander his plan for continuing the attack. The Front commander and the Stavka representative, Marshal Zhukov, confirmed the proposal. As the detachment prepared for departure, Kravchenko arrived with his last parting words. He seemed to discuss everything and reminded them, especially the forward detachment commander, that without an extraordinary reason he was not to get committed in battle against strongpoints or a strong enemy counterattack, but bypass. If a collision was unavoidable he did not want the detachment to take it head-on. Kravchenko recommended a deep, spreading maneuver against the flanks or rear of the enemy, and only when the commander could attain a surprise action. This was Kravchenko's formula for success.[63]

The forward detachment swiftly maneuvered for a surprise night strike on the Germans. The next morning, Kravchenko committed his reserve, the reinforced 233rd Tank Brigade from the 5th Mechanized Corps, to battle. As the army's forward detachment, its direction of advance crossed a series of small villages to Zvenigorodka.

With the tank army's forward detachment maneuvering north of Vinograd and slipping into the German rear area, the 5th Guards Tank Corps attacked after the 233rd Tank Brigade. The 5th Mechanized Corps continued attacking towards Vinograd and Zvenigorodka.[64] The 5th Guards Tank Corps driving east followed by the 5th Mechanized Corps which seized Vinograd. At the same time, Rotmistrov's 20th and 29th Tank Corps were advancing west towards the 5th Guards Tank Corps.

The tank army's main forces continued attacking. Kravchenko pressed his corps and brigade commanders to act more decisively, boldly in attacking between German strongpoints, and where possible go around them, aggressively penetrating deeply into their sectors. But, the 6th Tank Army encountered tenacious, organized resistance.

A difficult situation developed in the area of Pavlovki where the 45th Mechanized Brigade was to breakthrough the German defense. Reconnaissance reports identified a powerful German concentration of artillery and antitank forces. Kravchenko, with a shrewd, intuitive capacity to know where to be on the battlefield, arrived in the 45th Mechanized Brigade command post. He directed the brigade commander to identify precisely the forward edge of the German defense and spot the carefully concealed German firing points.

That night, a raid by three platoons in three directions led with reconnaissance scouts went forward to uncover the enemy firing positions. By drawing fires, the army's artillery commander brought down powerful strikes eliminating the strongpoints. The 5th Mechanized Corps in coordination with 40th Army units advanced seizing Vinograd and continued the offensive.[65]

Assessing the situation on 28 January, Kravchenko decided to send the 5th Guards Tank Corps after the forward detachment that night. He gave the corps the mission to widen the penetration and form an outer defensive front for the encirclement. On the morning of 28 January, Kravchenko received a radio report that the 233rd Forward Detachment took the northern part of Zvenigorodka. The capture impressed Marshal Zhukov who noted the commander and the forward detachment's actions in his memoirs, writing, "The group was commanded by M.I. Savelyev, a gallant and able general,...ably maneuvering [his] force boldly broke through the enemy units in the area of Lisyanka; on January 28 it joined up with the 20th Tank Corps in the town of Zvenigorodka, cutting off the major rearward communication lines of the enemy's Korsun-Shevchenkovskii group."[66] The fields crossed by the armored guards in battle near Zvenigorodka claimed many lives. There lay, as a Soviet poet wrote, "seven of every ten dead." "I had to cross these fields twice," a Red Army veteran recalled.[67]

Kravchenko's forward detachment with the lead brigades of the 20th Tank Corps, 5th Guards Tank Army in Zvenigorodka sealed a German force of nine infantry, one panzer division and the Walloonian SS Brigade.

After completing the encirclement, the tank armies moved to create an the outer perimeter defense, sustaining significant losses. The 6th Tank Army could muster only 100 tanks and approximately 20 assault guns, while the 5th Guards Tank Army possessed less than 250 tanks and assault guns.[68] The difficulty of rain and wet snow slowed the supply transports. The Front organized a resupply of fuel and ammunition with bi-planes, flying into a nearby airfield. The newly formed 6th Tank Army did not have a mature rear services organization to supply itself. Nonetheless, the offensive continued for the 1st and 2nd Ukrainian Fronts, with the 6th and 5th Guards Tank Armies and the 40th and 53rd Rifle Armies, by completing the outer perimeter of the encirclement on 3 February.

February, 1944, was a wet month. Rain and wet snow created hazards for wheeled and tracked vehicles which became stuck axle deep in mud. Even tanks required towing. Fuel and ammunition had to be flown in by small biplanes which could never satisfy the supply appetite.

On the night of 12 February, Marshal Zhukov sent the following report to the Stavka: "Opposing Kravchenko is an enemy force of up to 160 tanks, along with motorized infantry which is waging an offensive along the front.... Kravchenko possessed sufficient men and materiel to repulse enemy attacks, but during a breach of our first line defense, he lost control over some army units. Have ordered Nikolayev (codename for Vatutin) to urgently deploy 27th Army command element in Jurzhentsy and to subordinate Kravchenko to Trofimenko (commander 27th Army) in operations."[69]

Marshal Zhukov's harsh criticism about Kravchenko's loss of control was serious. Even a successful tank army commander had no protection against error or failure. Fighting for the Red Army was demanding, particularly under the unforgiving, Marshal Zhukov. But, there were mitigating circumstances for Kravchenko.

The 6th Tank Army had been created during the course of the operation and possessed an immature command and control. Control of tactical forces through various staffs and command posts relies on standard operating procedures that are developed over a period of time and tend to be unique to the unit. Command and control in armored forces was particularly difficult because of pace and dynamic actions. Subordinate units operated in different directions in three groupings, each had separate missions. The tank army's rear support remained in the vicinity where it was formed. Little experience at the operational level, the commander and newly collected staff had many things to learn. Kravchenko's transition from the tactical command of brigades and corps to the operational command of army was a big step. The indices of scale, scope, duration, and tempo of operations and actions, all drastically change between the observable, direct tactical level and the remote, subtle operational level. The change from the calculable, known ranges and capabilities of weapons systems and equipment to the artful, intangible application and understanding of resources and forces is learned with experience over time. And, again the question of where the commander should be on the battlefield becomes more difficult. In the end the commander must have a sense of timing. Timing is different at each ascending level of command, and the commander must understand what should be reported when and where. Staffs reports facts; commanders report judgment, instincts and feelings. And, the commander must bring these dimensions together in decision. Radio traffic volume and urgency at the tactical level is less reliable at the operational level.

After Marshal Zhukov's report on the night of 12 February, the situation grew worse. In the captured bridgehead at Dashukovke, the Germans struck directly at the tank army and 5th Guards Tank

Corps command posts which were located on the northwest and southern parts of the town. When the army chief of staff, General Zaev reported the threat, Kravchenko attentively listened with blood shot eyes from sleepless nights and ordered a tank brigade to clear up the situation.

The 20th Tank Brigade, commanded by Colonel S. F. Shutov who Kravchenko especially trusted, responded and became involved in particularly heavy fighting. While the 20th Tank Brigade and other units of the 5th Guards Tank Corps defended Dashukovku, Kravchenko called General Vatutin. He asked for three heavy tank regiments with the new IS-2, Joseph Stalin, heavy tanks. The next evening, Kravchenko received General Vatutin's decision to reinforce his army with heavy tank regiments. General Bogdanov, commander 2nd Tank Army, coordinated the passage of the new heavy tank regiments as reinforcements to the 6th Tank Army.

The 1st and 2nd Ukrainian Fronts' grip around the Germans held tightly, resulting in "a miniature Stalingrad."[70] In a pocket of 50,000 German troops, Field Marshal von Manstein's efforts helped a large number escape. Artillery guns had to be abandoned in the mud. Officially, the 6th Tank Army was credited with the capture and destruction of 379 tanks and self-propelled guns, 207 artillery guns, 62 armored carriers, and defeating two tank and one infantry divisions.[71]

After the Korsun-Shevchenkovskii operation on orders from the Stavka Supreme High Command, the 6th Tank Army was assigned to the 2nd Ukrainian Front, under the command of General of the Army Rodian Ya. Malinovskii. The Front's impending operations required the tank army to cross the rivers, Gornyi Tikich, Southern Bug, Dnestr, and finally the Prut from the march.

In the afternoon on 2 March, Kravchenko met with the commanders and officers of the 5th Mechanized Corps. The corps commander with maps and schematics briefed the brigade and corps combat operations. After the corps commander's briefing, Kravchenko in his quiet, soft voice stated the main points of the order to attack.

"The affair ahead is great and difficult," he addressed those in attendance. "The attack during the thawing season is serious and responsible step, requiring careful preparations. But our time for preparation is one day. Tomorrow evening we move to the attack position."[72]

The brigade and unit commanders exchanged glances. They knew campaigning in the muddy season would bring a whole host of tactical movement and maneuver problems. After Kravchenko, the corps commander gave the specific combat orders to their commanders.

In early August 1944, Andrei Grigorevich Kravchenko received a letter from the 2nd Ukrainian Front Political Directorate notifying him that his son, Vilya Andreevich, had been killed in battle on the river Pripyat near Skrigalovo on 28 June 1944. His son was only fourteen years old when Kravchenko moved his family to the interior for protection from the invading Germans. The drawn out war and its demand on Soviet manpower took Kravchenko's eighteen year old son in sacrifice. The war for Kravchenko, like Rybalko, exacted a tragic personal toll. One day after returning from the grave of his son in Belorussia, Kravchenko received a visit from the Front commander, General Malinovskii. Malinovskii, noting Kravchenko's depression, expressed his condolences and shifted the topic of conversation.

"The army will develop the operation. But, how will you deal with the situation if it turns out earlier than the planned time?" Malinovskii asked.

"Everything perhaps, comrade Front commander, especially if the enemy defense doesn't stand the first strike."

"Prepare the army so at any minute it can move on signal, and whatever you take as a precombat disposition, bury the tanks and camouflage them," Malinovskii ordered.

"It will be fulfilled, comrade General of the Army," Kravchenko assured.[73]

Kravchenko day and night rode his Willy jeep visiting all his units and positions. He appeared in the brigades, regiments and battalions, talking with the tank crews. Many years of experience taught Kravchenko that the successful leader must command great detail on every aspect of the operation and check everything. The commander must receive reports, briefings and personally become familiar with the situation, personally contact people, studying matters in each regiment, in each battalion. Kravchenko, always before an operation, drove to the army units.

In the tank battalions' training, Kravchenko would remind the platoon and company leaders, "our army attacks. Therefore in the combat preparation of the personnel focus on the conduct of the attack and especially at night."[74] Kravchenko worked all aspects of training from the individual soldier through his senior commanders and staff.

Before beginning an offensive, Kravchenko wargamed with the corps commanders different variations of their units' combat operations in a terrain sandbox. On a map, the operational scale of exercise included the operational depth, 100 to 120 kilometers. He considered the various enemy courses of action for the impending operation with its implications for coordination of the corps and their service supports until all aspects were clear. Kravchenko was coming to grips with the indices of combat at the operational level.

As a result of the successful Red Army offensive in Western Ukraine, the 2nd Ukrainian Front under the command of Marshal Ivan Konev, who two months later, on 22 May 1944, was appointed commander of the 1st Ukrainian Front, and General Rodian Malinovskii, the 2nd Ukrainian Front, reached the Soviet-Romanian border. Continuing the offensive between the Prut and Dnestr rivers, they approached Yassy and assumed the defensive on 6 May. At the same time, the 3rd Ukrainian Front under the command of General Fedor Ivanovich Tolbukhin, reached the Dnestr, seizing a number of bridgeheads on the western bank. The Red Army was in a position to attack the German Army Group Southern Ukraine and cross Romania into the Balkans.

With the Belorussian operation in mid-June, Soviet strategic deception intended to convince German intelligence that the Red Army forces on the southern wing of the Soviet-German front would remain defensive. In support of the 2nd Ukrainian Front deceptive aims, Kravchenko's army was instructed to make a hundred and fifty dummy tanks and leave them in their assembly area when the tank army moved forward.

In the first part of August 1944, the 5th Mechanized and 5th Guards Tank Corps completed replenishment with personnel, combat equipment and supplies. Receiving the order to assume positions north of Yassy, Kravchenko directed his corps commanders to aggressively develop the offensive, capturing the enemy defensive line in depth and nearly all bridges and airfields.

"You will be prepared to be committed into the penetration early with immediate speed," Kravchenko told his corps commanders. "You must forestall the advance of the enemy reserve towards the Mare mountain range."[75]

On 20 August, Kravchenko and his operational group collocated with the 5th Mechanized Corps observation post which was on the same hill as the command post for the 104th Rifle Corps, the unit making the initial penetration of the enemy defense. The Front commander, General Malinovskii, was at the same vantage point. Kravchenko, together with other generals and officers from the operational group, began to climb up along the communications trench to the hill top. Both Malinovskii and Kravchenko stood by the entrance to the bunker in their simple field overalls. The overalls disguised the high ranking officers on the front line from snipers and enemy observation.

A devastating artillery barrage signaled the beginning of the Yassy-Kishinev offensive. The 2nd and 3rd Ukrainian Fronts' attacks converged in the general direction of Husi. By noon, the powerful blow struck by the infantry in the 27th Army cut through the enemy's tactical defense to a depth of 16 kilometers and crossed the Bahlui River. As early as 1000 hours, the lead elements of the 6th Tank Army received the signal to move. Although the tank army had not planned to move until the second day of the operation, hundreds of tanks immediately advanced in the attack. With the tank army's main strike on its right flank, Kravchenko committed the 5th Guards Tank Corps into the penetration on two march routes. On the left flank, reinforced with artillery and mortars, the 5th Mechanized Corps advanced along two routes, entering the breach at 1400 hours.

In the Yassy-Kishinev operation, the 6th Tank Army, as the 2nd Ukrainian Front's mobile group, was committed ahead of schedule to the battle after the second defense zone was breached. Against the German's third defensive line which ran along the wooded Mare Ridge at a depth of 25-40 kilometers, the tank army ran into strong resistance and was unable to breakthrough without delaying the operations. By the next morning, the 6th Tank Army still attempted in vain to pierce the enemy positions. The enemy had organized counterattacks on the approaches to the defense. Throughout the day, the 27th Army and 6th Tank Army fought difficult battles against enemy reserves to secure passes through the Mare ridge.

Located in an observation post by the river Prut, Kravchenko became absorbed in the brigades' reported losses in combat equipment. He received the report that the 20th Tank Brigade fighting fearlessly had not managed to make its way across the Mare ridge. Kravchenko over the radio questioned the brigade commander, Colonel Shutov, about further brigade actions. The commanders worked out a plan to go around the strongly fortified heights from the east and west, going to the enemy's flank and cutting their withdrawal routes to the south. The tank brigade attacked capturing the height but took heavy casualties. Kravchenko worried that the brigade movement was too slow. General Malinovskii demanded more decisive, quicker movement by the tank army to assigned lines of advance. At midnight, Kravchenko called his corps commanders and gave instructions for specific routes and objectives that moved them more quickly through the enemy defense.[76]

Guards Colonel I.T. Ignatenko, deputy chief of the army's operations section recalled, " I was in the operational group from the beginning to the end of the operation. Our mission observing from the battlefield, led directly the course of the combat operations. The Army commander liked to be in the forward observation post. Where difficult and critical situations come to a head, Kravchenko was always there. He drove in a Willy jeep or a tank. Stopping beside a trench, bunker or simply in the field. Spread his cossack cloak, lay out a map and talk with us officers in the operational group: "Give to the brigades, regiments: Kravchenko is here."[77]

During the night of 21 August, 6th Tank Army penetrated the enemy's third defensive line gaining maneuver space. In the next 36 hours, Kravchenko's army advanced 70 kilometers cutting off enemy avenues of retreat from the advancing rifle units. Once Kravchenko's units overcame defenses on the Mare Ridge, the tank army passed through the rear areas of the Kishinev enemy grouping. The tank army's advance was so concentrated in armor that tanks and other combat vehicles drove with headlights on to see through the dust. Kravchenko's unstoppable advance destroyed the rear services of General Hans Friessner's, commander Army Group Southern Ukraine, operations group, and established an active, mobile outer perimeter of envelopment around the large enemy grouping.

On 22 August, the tank army received a new chief of staff, General Major Albert Ivanovich Stromberg who possessed a Doctorate in military science and had a reputation for his deep professional studies. Kravchenko, the operator, impressed the academician. As General Stromberg noted, "There was never a time when I observed the army commander in a moment of extreme danger that his self-control, calm philosophy towards death was not surprising. He like to repeat, 'A coward dies a thousand times, but a hero lives after death."[78]

On 24 August, Kravchenko instructed the 5th Mechanized Corps

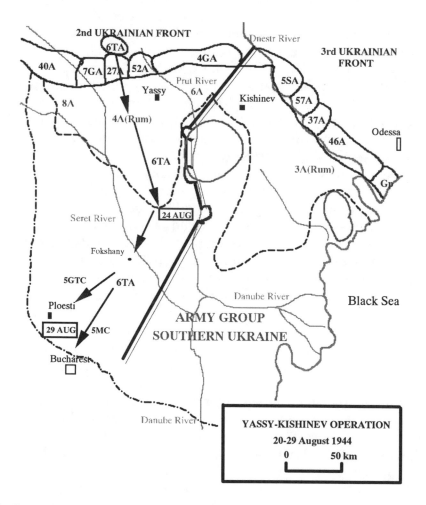

2nd UKRAINIAN FRONT

6TA

Dnestr River

3rd UKRAINIAN
FRONT

40A

7GA 27A 52A

4GA

Prut River

5SA

Yassy

6A

Kishinev

57A

8A

37A

4A(Rum)

Odessa

46A

6TA

3A(Rum)

Gp

Seret River

24 AUG

Fokshany

5GTC

6TA

Danube River

Black Sea

Ploesti

29 AUG

5MC

ARMY GROUP
SOUTHERN UKRAINE

Bucharest

Danube River

YASSY-KISHINEV OPERATION

20-29 August 1944

0   50 km

to move in two columns and quickly advance to the river Prut, then towards the towns Kagul and Galats. After the capture of Tecuci on 25 August 1944, the 5th Guards Tank Corps sent out a forward detachment with the mission to seize a bridge across the Siret river. Upon arrival at the river, the detachment identified a double-decked railroad and highway bridge being defended by the enemy. Crossing a motorized rifle company and rushing the bridge with a tank brigade, Kravchenko's tankers captured the bridge allowing the tank corps to rapidly cross. By the morning of 27 August, the 5th Mechanized Corps reached crossings over the Siret, but the crossing had been demolished, and the corps did not possess bridging equipment. Kravchenko directed the corps to move northward and cross on the 5th Guards Tank Corps captured bridge. The corps joined forces of the 3rd Ukrainian Front, sealing the encirclement of the German Southern Ukraine Group. Two days later, the tank army corps together with rifle units stormed and seized the important towns of Focsani and Buzzu. The 6th Tank Army pushed the outer belt of encirclement 120 kilometers away from the inner belt.

The following afternoon, General Malinovskii ordered Kravchenko to enter Bucharest and Ploiesti. Kravchenko decided to send one corps towards Ploiesti and two towards Bucharest, executing a swift thrust in two directions. General Kravchenko with his operational group located with the 5th Guards Tank Corps directed a powerfully fast sweep with the tank corps and 3rd Airborne Division in the Ploiesti area, capturing the Ploiesti oilfields intact. "The successful action of the 6th Tank Army," one Soviet military historian noted, "also made it possible to forestall enemy from reaching the Focsani Gate, which subsequently gave the 2nd Ukrainian Front freedom of action deep in Romania avoiding the Carpathians."[79] Having captured Ploiesti, Kravchenko's army cut off avenues of retreat to Transylvania for the enemy forces north of Bucharest. The Red Army tankers captured important areas, such as, Foscani Gate and Ploiesti, the center of Romania's oil production and rumbled through Romanian towns reaching approaches to Bucharest by the end of August.[80]

In Bucharest the fighting took a different turn. On the evening of 27 August, Kravchenko's tank corps poised in march columns were ready to rush the Romanian capital. However, the Romanian leadership declared its willingness to surrender.

The forces on the left flank of General Malinovskii's Front turned northwards, on Stavka orders. General Kravchenko's tank army with 262 tanks and 82 self-propelled guns, moved into the center of these forces. On 14 September, as it approached the Turda area, the tank army came under a strong panzer and infantry counterstrike, intending to prevent a successful development of the Front operation. General Freissner, who had been ordered by Hitler to fight to the end, drew the 6th Tank Army into a prolonged battle yielding no immediate results.

Meanwhile, the 6th Tank Army's previous accomplishments were recognized by the Soviet High Command. A People's Defense Order pronounced that "in the battle for our Soviet Motherland against German invaders the 6th Tank Army showed brave mastery, discipline and organization...." The 6th Tank Army won its "Guards" designation. Kravchenko personally received the Order of Suvorov lst Degree and promotion to the the rank of Colonel General.

The 2nd Ukrainian Front in September and October 1944, developed offensive actions with the main strike from the area south of Oradea-Mare in the general direction of Debrecen, Hungary. The Front objective was destruction of the Transylvanian enemy grouping and liberation of the Carpathian area in conjunction with the 4th Ukrainian Front.

The resumption of offensive operations by the 2nd Ukrainian Front in the first half of October 1944, placed in the 6th Guards Tank Army sector the 4th Infantry, 12th Light Infantry Hungarian Divisions and part of the 23rd German Panzer Division. Despite an enemy defensive zone 8 kilometers deep with three lines of trenches, Kravchenko's armored guards attacked in the first echelon with an assigned sector 33 kilometers wide and 10 kilometer wide breakthrough sector. For the operation, the tank army consisted of the 5th Guards Tank Corps, 9th Guards Mechanized Corps, 33rd Rifle Corps, 49th Guards Heavy Tank Regiment and other supporting units, totaling a relatively small 188 tanks.[81]

The tank army operations for Oradea-Mare began on the morning of 2 October 1944, with a 15 minute artillery strike followed by the advancing tank corps. At the end of first day's operation, Kravchenko's tank army advancing only 5-10 kilometers failed to achieve its immediate mission, penetrating the tactical zone and capturing Oradea-Mare.

Fighting the next day resulted in heavy casualties for both sides. The Stavka ordered the 6th Guards Tank Army to be used with General Issa Aleksandrovich Pliev's cavalry-mechanized group, attacking north around the west side of Debrecen. The tank army units regrouped on 4 October while reconnaissance moved along the direction of the impending operation. The following morning, lead tank units forced their way through defending Germans, and, after four days of hard attacking, penetrated the tactical defense. The slow tempo of the operation resulted from insufficient force in the initial assaults.

On 6 October the offensive operation for Debrecen began with the Front's main strike group including the 6th Guards Tank Army reinforced by the 33rd Rifle Corps. They met strong resistance the first day achieving little success, with only part of the force crossing the Keresh canal. For the next three days, Kravchenko's tank army battled strong counterattacks by German infantry and tanks, but managed to widen the bridgehead to the northern bank of the Keresh canal, south of Komadi. In these battles, the army operated unsuccessfully, losing a significant number of tanks to the counterattacking German divisions that cut off the leading corps. On the flat Hungarian plain, the tank forces chased each other in a confusing melee. General Malinovskii ordered General Pliev to assist the tank army. On 11 October, General Pliev in coordination with 33rd Rifle Corps, as well as, the broke the back of the enemy resistance capturing Oradea-Mare. From the 13th, Pliev's group, 6th Guards Tank army and 33rd Rifle Corps, 7th Guards Army mopped up enemy in the territory between the Bereto and Keresh canals. By 15 October, their mission was completed. The 5th Guards Tank Corps continued attacking in the direction of Debrecen, entering Sharand on 18 October.

By 20 October, Kravchenko's army with parts of General Pliev's force took Debrecen. Toward the conclusion of the fighting from 22-25 October, Kravchenko received orders to transfer to another sector. But, two days later, after 53 days of continuous combat operations, the tank army became the Front reserve for a well deserved respite.

In the course of the operation, Kravchenko's army advanced to a depth of more than 250 kilometers for an average rate of advance of 10-12 kilometers, forcing on a wide front the Tissu and created favorable conditions for developing the offensive towards Budapest. Kravchenko, as usual, was well forward with his operational group, no more than 5 kilometers from the front. The tank army was in the first echelon without operational pause. The army had shortages: it possessed less than 50 percent in personnel, 39 percent tanks and less than 8 percent assault guns.[82] The depletion of its combat power slowed the rate of advance through the tactical zone to four days. Tank armies were successful in the first echelon if they were employed against a weak unprepared defense. A well organized and prepared defense inflicted high casualties in men and combat vehicles on tank armies.

On 29 October 1944, the Budapest operation began with 2nd Ukrainian Front forces penetrating the enemy defense between Tisoi and Dunaem and arriving at the outer defenses of the Hungarian capital, Budapest. The 6th Guards Tank Army and General Pliev's cavalry-mechanized group were committed in the main effort. Kravchenko's tank army and Pliev's cavalry-mechanized group became a good combination in the difficult terrain. The unique nature of the cavalry-mechanized group perplexed the German command. With its cavalry corps, the group could cross terrain that blocked armored vehicles, and the mechanized corps added firepower and protection to the cavalry arm. Additionally, German commanders knew they were in for a "wild and woolly time" when Pliev appeared in their sector. He usually had a surprise for them.

By 2 November, Marshal Malinovskii's spearhead was 12 kilometers south of Budapest. The Hungarian 3rd Army vanished from the battlefield, but Germans manned the defensive ring around the Hungarian capital. The German Army Group South concentrated all its strength in panzer units to cut off the Soviets. German and Soviet tanks battled in the suburbs of Budapest on 4 and 5 November, draining Soviet units of ammunition. Marshal Malinovskii decided to take the city through a series of enveloping maneuvers. Meanwhile, Kravchenko's tank army fought on the northern right flank attempting to capture Mikolc and bring about a meeting with 4th Ukrainian Front forces when they cut through the Carpathian mountains at the Dukla pass.

The final offensive for Budapest was designated for 3 December. Working out the details of the operations, the 6th Guards Tank Army had 325 tanks and assault guns. On a gloomy morning 5 December, Kravchenko's tanks and assault guns rolled forward while he was located in the observation post of the commander of the 7th Guards Army. In the observation post he coordinated directly with Lieutenant General I. A Pliev, commander of the Cavalry-Mechanized Group, who appeared in a fur overcoat over which he wore his Cossack felt cape. General Pliev's unit, consisting of the 4th

Guards Mechanized Corps and the 4th and 6th Guards Cavalry Corps, would be committed northeast of Budapest after the 6th Guards Tank Army. The strength of this armored force was nearly 500 tanks and self-propelled assault guns. Marshal Malinovskii decided not to commit the 6th Guards Tank Army on the main axis. Instead, he sent it toward Levice where the terrain better suited tank operations, and Kravchenko's tank formations could separately penetrate the enemy defense, enveloping a large grouping. The tank army's attack would prevent enemy counterattacks against the 7th Guards Army's flank north of Budapest. Both armies did not cross the Danube river, but headed northward into the Boerzsenyi Mountains toward Sahy, the northern gateway to the western Hungarian plain.

In the Budapest operation, Kravchenko, noting the tank army placement in the Front's first echelon again, created an army artillery group consisting of artillery brigades and a guards mortar (katyusha rocket) regiment. Additionally, he took engineer and pontoon battalions from the reserve and created a mobile obstacle detachment consisting of an engineer-sapper battalion with a supply of 300-400 antitank mines in vehicles. The corps also created mobile obstacle detachments with engineer companies for use on the most probable enemy counterattack routes and on the flanks of the main army group.[83] Kravchenko paid particular attention to the allocation of engineer assets for this operation because the terrain was a major operational consideration.

The Soviet attack penetrated cleanly through the German defense, allowing Kravchenko to commit his corps for exploitation by evening. The following day, the 6th Guards Tank Army thrust northwest towards Vacs against little resistance. By 8 December, Kravchenko's 5th Guards Tank Corps fought for the eastern outskirts of Vacs while the 9th Guards Mechanized Corps moved northward toward the key town of Sahy on the Ipel river. Kravchenko poised his army to swing the 5th Guards Tank Corps south behind Budapest or continue driving northwest. Although with the deep advance, the tank army met increasingly stiff resistance, achieving little decisive action.

The 9th Guards Mechanized Corps ran into tough German obstacles in the narrow defile east of Sahy, where the Ipel river cuts through high ground. On 9 December, Marshal Malinovskii realized that the 5th Guards Tank Corps could not break through the

German defense north of Budapest and ordered the tank corps to turn northwest joining the 9th Guards Mechanized Corps to force the defile, seize Sahy, then turn the German flank north of Budapest.

Two days later, the 9th Guards Mechanized Corps battled for control of the defile while waiting the arrival of the 5th Guards Tank Corps. The fight for the defile produced an interesting enemy force. The key avenue was held by the German 357th Infantry Division and the SS Brigade "Dirlewanger," under SS Standartenfuehrer (Colonel) Oscar Dirlewanger, a unit of dubious reputation comprised of ex-communist and common criminals. The brigade was infamous for its brutality. After a fierce fight on 13 December, Kravchenko's corps forced the defile and drove for Sahy.

A stubborn battle for Sahy began the next day. The bridge across the Ipel river was blown up. That night units of the 31st Guards Mechanized Brigade maneuvering around the city forced the river to the west. With a coordinated attack from the east and west, Kravchenko's tanks captured the city, an important communications center for roads and railroads. Sahy became the target for savage German counterattacks from the north and northwest.

Kravchenko located in the command post of the 30th Guards Mechanized Brigade when a German counterattack penetrated to the command post. He charged the brigade chief of staff, a captain, with organizing the repulse of the counterattack while Kravchenko continued leading the larger battle.

"We found ourselves encircled," recalled the army's deputy chief of operations, Guards Colonel I.T. Ignatenko. "Telephone communications between the command and the auxiliary army command posts were broken."[84] Kravchenko, at this time, was located in the auxiliary command post. As Colonel Ignatenko showed the army commander on a map where the Germans cut the road, Kravchenko could hear the enemy tank engines. But, Kravchenko in a calm voice gave instructions to mine the bridge across the Gron river, limiting German armored forces to the battlefield. In the swirling tank battles that raged for the next two days, Guards Colonel M.V. Shutov, commander of the 30th Guards Mechanized Brigade, was seriously wounded. Although the war was in its final year, it continued to take its toll in lives and casualties, to include proven combat leaders. Regardless of valor or skill, the war dispensed indiscriminate death. For a bloody price, the road to Sahy was cleared and held by the tank army.

On 15 December, the 6th Guards Tank Army continued its breakout west of Sahy into the Gron river valley. At this point in the Soviet operation, the 2nd and 3rd Ukrainian Front commanders, on direction from the Stavka High Command, began planning a new phase for offensive operations aimed at encircling Budapest. While Kravchenko's tank army, Pliev's cavalry mechanized group, and the 7th Guards Army continued their advance north of Budapest, the 2nd Ukrainian forces between 14 and 20 December, carried out a regrouping of units for the new offensive. Marshal Malinovskii, however, began to see greater potentials by employing the 6th Guards Tank Army along the Danube river. By 19 December, the final assault on Budapest was set. Kravchenko's army emerged from the Gron river valley and Pliev's cavalry mechanized group moved to replace the tank army northwest of Sahy, releasing the entire tank army for an attack towards Levice on the east side of the Danube river.

Marshal Malinovskii assigned Kravchenko a separate attack sector, 12 kilometers wide, in which his army was to penetrate the defense developing the offensive in depth.[85] The immediate mission of the tank army was the seizure of an important road junction at Santov. The tank army was reinforced and received direct support from the 5th Air Army. The coordination between the air and tank army was worked out by the commanders and their staffs. For a close, responsive control of air support, air army liaison officers were placed in Kravchenko's and the corps' command posts.

Kravchenko planned to concentrate his force in the direction of Santov, using the 5th Guards Tank Corps, under the command of General M.I. Savelya, the former forward detachment commander who captured Zvenigorodka during the Korsun operation, to lead the attack. Concentrating his forces in the 5th Guards Tank Corps, Kravchenko put his army in a single echelon. In reserve, he kept primarily artillery and engineer units. At the beginning of the operation the tank army had 220 operable tanks.

The attack began 20 December with only a 10 minute artillery preparation in the main sector to weaken the defense. However, the preparation proved enough to allow the tank army to pierce the defense. Advancing 20-25 kilometers on the first day, lead tanks captured the Levice road junction and reached the Ipel river valley. The good progress occurred despite thaws and rain making cross-country travel virtually impossible. The Front's first echelon strike group, including the 6th Guards Tank Army, was compelled to use a single passable road, which formed a continuous bottleneck dozens of kilometers long. The average rate of advance of the tank army dropped to 17 kilometers per day.[86]

The following day Kravchenko ordered each corps to dispatch one brigade southward as a forward detachment. These detachments encountered a significantly large German tank force of the 3rd and 6th Panzer Divisions poised for an attack towards Sahy. The tank army's slow speed raised tactical problems by allowing enemy reserves to be brought up. The German panzer divisions' objective was to cut off the 6th Guards Tank Army from the rear, striking in the 7th Guards Army's flank. An armored meeting engagement ensued for three days with German and Soviet tank units attacking and counterattacking in the area of the Gron valley southwest of Sahy.

Using three brigades to screen against the German assault, Kravchenko decided to maneuver in a new direction. The forces of the 5th Guards Tank Corps attacked in a southern direction behind the panzer divisions, threatening encirclement. Two brigades of the 9th Guards Mechanized Corps swung into the flank of the German counterattack group. The 3rd and 6th Panzer Divisions halted their attack on Sahy, turning to deal with the 6th Guards Tank Army threat to their rear.

On 23 December, Kravchenko received reinforcements in the 4th Guards Mechanized Corps from Pliev's Cavalry-Mechanized Group, and, on the following day assumed a defense, successfully repelling a second German counterstrike from the north. This success set the stage for Kravchenko's ultimate objective.

The 5th Guards Tank and 9th Guards Mechanized Corps in the course of the 24 through early 26 December, fought an intense struggle with the counterstriking Germans. Speeding up its drive to the south, the 6th Guards Tank Army linked up with other Soviet forces and with the 7th Guards Army captured Esztergom and Dunai river. There the two armies joined troops from Marshal Fedor Ivanovich Tolbukhin's 3rd Ukrainian Front, completing the encirclement of Budapest.

On 31 December, the 6th Guards Tank Army, after the long, heavy fighting northwest of Budapest, withdrew to assembly areas near Sahy for refitting and reconstitution. The Soviet offensive had relied heavily on Kravchenko's armored force to achieve operational success. Budapest was not a town easily enveloped and bypassed.

As the tank army rearmed and refueled as the Front reserve, the German command at the same time prepared a major counterstrike from the area of Komarno. The German 4th SS Panzer Corps, with SS Panzer Divisions "Viking" and "Death's Head," began arriving in the Budapest area on 31 December.

At 2230 hours, 1 January 1945, the 4th SS Panzer Corps attacked through the hilly region northwest of Budapest against the overextended Soviet 4th Guards Army. Marshal Malinovskii reacted quickly, slightly adjusting forces to reinforce the 4th Guards Army sector. On 3 January, as the German attack gained momentum major shifts by the Soviets began to take place. The Stavka instructed the 2nd Ukrainian Front to use the 6th Guards Tank Army for a strike at the base of the German thrust from the area south of Estergom along the Dunai river to Komarno. In accordance with the Stavka instructions, Marshal Malinovskii on 4 January assigned Kravchenko the mission to strike in the general direction of Komarno and complete cutting off the German relief force by 7 January. The German's relief attempt for Budapest forced an early commitment of the 6th Guards Tank Army.

In the short respite, Kravchenko's tank army managed to increase its tank strength from 150 to 180 tanks. The tank army was in position along the Gron river by 5 January. Kravchenko's corps commanders planned to attack on a narrow sector with an intense strike that would propel the corps quickly into the depth toward Komarno. The tank army attack began at 0300 hours, 6 January without an artillery preparation. The 5th Guards Tank Corps advanced west to secure Komarno, the important railroad center through which most German reinforcements to Budapest area passed. The 9th Guards Mechanized Corps moved westward, north of the 5th Guards Tank Corps, supporting the tank corps' attack on Komarno. Using gaps in the defense, forward detachments moved quickly forward. The night attack surprised the Germans, resulting in weak resistance initially. But, the lack of strength in Kravchenko's recovering tank army worked against the success of the attack.

By 7 January, lead units of the 6th Guards Tank Army reached the outskirts of Komarno, but could not take the city. Experiencing a basic problem in the rapid advance of armored forces, the 5th Guards Tank Corps had greatly outdistanced accompanying infantry necessary for the city fight. The Red Army throughout the war never had enough trucks or combat vehicles to move its infantry. The 9th

Guards Mechanized Corps turned north in the direction of Nove-Zamky where the German 20th Panzer Division was completing its assembly for an attack.

Marshal Malinovskii decided to reinforce again Kravchenko's army with the 4th Guards Mechanized Corps, which was only partially ready for combat with about 50 tanks. The 4th Guards Mechanized Corps moved into the new salient formed by the attacking tank army, as the 5th Guards Tank Corps units seized crossings over the Dunai river near Komarno. The same day war winds shifted against the Soviets as lead units of the German 20th Panzer Division struck Kravchenko's 9th Guards Mechanized Corps on the northern flank. The German counterattack sapped the Soviet offensive, forcing Malinovskii to draw off more forces from Budapest.

Kravchenko's tank army was spread too thin, and its dwindling tank strength was scattered among the tank brigades. He could not take Komarno.

The 20th Panzer Division continued to cut deep into the northern flank threatening the tank army's vital supply lines. As a measure to conserve fighting power in the beleaguered 9th Guards Mechanized Corps, Kravchenko directed the corps to fire on advancing German tanks with artillery guns in direct fire.[87] Artillery gun crews positioned themselves in defense in accordance with the army commander's instructions. The panzer division's attack ultimately forced Kravchenko to withdraw, but only after the Germans suffered heavy losses. Additionally, the German 8th Panzer Division and a Hungarian division attacked out of Komarno attempting to link up with the 20th Panzer Division. In the end, German efforts could not break into Budapest, however, their inroads forced Kravchenko to slowly withdraw eastward.

By 11 January, Soviet rifle units assumed the 6th Guards Tank Army sector, while the tank army's brigades were used to reinforce the rifle units. As the action on the front shifted to southwest of Budapest with a major attack by the 4th SS Panzer Corps, Kravchenko's army worked feverishly to restore itself.

On 26 January, Marshal Malinovskii withdrew the 6th Guards Tank Army to the east of Budapest for a future operation. Kravchenko's army would not be used until March 1945. The battle for Buda and Pest became a long drawn out house to house, street to street fight taking nearly 23 days for Pest and another 23 days for Buda to force the German surrender. The Hungarian knot, Budapest, would not be totally cleared of Germans until 13 February 1945.

On the night of 20 February, Kravchenko received notification to concentrate the tank army 120 kilometers to the north in the vicinity of Sahy. The tank army had built its strength to 224 tanks and self-propelled assault guns.[88] Kravchenko used the restoration period to train the new tank crews. In training he emphasized "a crew is as one family." He required crew members to become familiar with the other crew members' tasks. He liked to say, "as long as a gun fires, a tank can be put out of action. As long as one crew member lives, a tank is in the formation."[89]

Marshal Malinovskii and his staff planned a major offensive to commence on 15 March 1945, aimed at smashing German defenses west of Budapest between Lake Balaton and the Danube river. On 11 March, Kravchenko moved his army from Sahy south to an assembly area near Vacs in anticipation of commitment. His tank army now approached 500 tanks in strength. German intelligence failed to pick up his army's movement into the assembly area. Kravchenko was still applying his lessons learned from Stalingrad, avoiding early detection by German intelligence. Two days later, the 6th Guards Tank Army was fully assembled west of Budapest. Behind the 9th Guards Army, Kravchenko waited for the Soviet rifle units to gnaw a hole in the German defense. The wait behind the slow, unsuccessful rifle army allowed German intelligence to identity the tank army in the sector.

The Red Army was set for the next major offensive operation, the capture of Vienna. On 16 March, the 6th Guards Tank Army became assigned to Marshal Fedor Ivanovich Tolbukhin's 3rd Ukrainian Front. Marshal Tolbukhin decided to commit the 6th Guards Tank Army in the 9th Guards Army sector on 19 March with the mission to advance toward the northern shores of Lake Balaton cutting off the withdrawal routes of the German 6th SS Panzer Army for destruction.

Moving into forward positions in the dark early morning hours, Kravchenko tankers prepared for a dawn attack. A thick morning fog prevented Soviet air force support. The 9th Guards Army failed to clear the German defenses, so with the commitment of Kravchenko's tank units they met a stiff defense with coordinated fires and obstacles. The 9th Guards Mechanized Corps met a wall of steel, stopping in its tracks. The 5th Guards Tank Corps encountering organized resistance advanced only 8-10 kilometers. That night

Kravchenko's intelligence officer reported the withdrawal of 6th SS Panzer Army from the trap. Kravchenko ordered active reconnaissance throughout the night and a high level of alertness maintained on the tank army's roads. The hilly terrain required tactical changes by the tank units. Kravchenko directed the corps commanders to wage combat in small battle groups with few tanks, fight from ambush, maneuver boldly. "Use of such tactics," he emphasized, "we inflict tangible losses and at the same time preserve our forces."[90] With the next morning, after a short artillery fire, Kravchenko resumed the attack in pursuit of his original mission. Marshal Tolbukhin wanted more decisive, dynamic action from the tank army. But, the tank army's methodical probing of the enemy's defense became locked in a continuous, tenacious combat with the German tank army for the next two days.

By late 21 March, the advance of Kravchenko's corps squeezed the 6th SS Panzer Army against the northern and northeastern edge of Lake Balaton. However, the complete encirclement and destruction of the panzer army could not be managed. While the panzer army suffered heavy losses, it found a small corridor, slipping west from Kravchenko's grasp.

From Lake Balaton, the 6th Guards Tank Army made a swift strike with air support in the general direction of Vienna. The tank army's attack to the west developed more quickly than in the previous days with both corps advancing 40-60 kilometers by 27 March. At the Austro-Hungarian border, Kravchenko with a slight pause regrouped his corps moving the 5th Guards Tank Corps to the army's right flank while the 9th Guards Mechanized Corps continued to attack, demonstrating a operational agility in maneuvering his army during a high speed operation that kept the Germans off balance. In the first days of April the tank army approached Vienna from the south, bypassing on the west. Then, the army struck simultaneously in an easterly direction in order to create an inner perimeter of envelopment and in a northwesterly direction to form an outer perimeter of envelopment of the German's Vienna grouping.[91] The difficult maneuver was conducted through wooded, mountainous countryside which favored German rearguard actions and defense. But, Kravchenko's corps successfully forged forward.

The advance of the 6th Guards Tank Army during this period was impressive. General Zaev, the tank army's chief of staff who had been with Kravchenko since Korsun-Shevchenkovskii, described

Kravchenko's ability to discern a clear action in the chaotic situation. Like a chess master playing blindfolded, all the locations of the pieces, movement of black and white were in his head. "Here is the talent possessed by our army commander. He can in advance imagine the arrangement of his units, anticipate the possible enemy courses of action, and secure victories with little blood."[92] Kravchenko seldom made errors of fact, weighing the practical effects of a decision.

Although the defense of Vienna was by the reconstituted 6th SS Panzer Army, the approaches to the city contained a system of antitank obstacles, and the streets and squares were barricaded. On 4-5 April, the 5th Guards Tank Corps attacked Vienna from the south. Kravchenko moving forward in his Willy jeep behind the attacking tank columns noted the strength of the defense on the southern outskirts. He avoided, when possible, protracted street battles, preferring to rapidly encircle a city with a pincer movement, leaving only a single escape route to the enemy. He often cautioned, "The neck of the bottle must remain uncorked."[93] An uncorked bottle allowed city defenders to withdraw, avoiding the costly house to house fight. Kravchenko decided on a deep maneuver around the city through the Viennese woods and struck the Austrian capital from the west and northwest.

By this stage of the operation, Kravchenko's brigades had very few tanks. The lead brigade for the strike from the west possessed only 13 tanks. On 6 April, the tank brigade penetrated the western outskirts without encountering German units. However, attempts to reach the center of the city met serious resistance, engaging two brigades for two days. Supply routes to the brigades were cut off.

Kravchenko received the 18th Tank Corps to protect the tank army's flank as it maneuvered to the west and northwest cutting off the German forces in Vienna. The battle for the city continued until 13 April. All soldiers in the army were awarded the medal "For Taking Vienna."

The same day, Marshal Malinovskii with his staff began organizing the offensive to Brno, the capital of Moravia, opening the way to Prague. For this objective, he again received the 6th Guards Tank Army from the Stavka. After three days into the attack, Marshal Malinovskii became convinced the terrain did not support massed tanks and a high rate of advance. He decided to transfer the tank army. On 21 April, the tank army withdrew from battle and moved in the course of two nights to the Front's other flank for a decisive strike against Brno. Kravchenko received the mission to capture Brno from the southwest. In maneuvering around the city, Kravchenko assigned the 2nd Guards Mechanized Corps the mission to seize the northern and northeastern edges of Brno and to continue the attack eastward. The 2nd Ukrainian Front assaulted Brno, capturing the city by 26 April, completing the destruction of the German forces in the western Carpathian area.

As Germany's armies were driven back to the homeland, a large force occupied Czechoslovakia. The Red Army's Prague offensive operation from 6-15 May 1945, involved the forces of the 1st, 2nd, and 3rd Ukrainian Fronts. The brutal pace of the war on the eve of the Prague operation left Kravchenko's army with only 151 tanks and self-propelled assault guns.[94]

The 2nd Ukrainain Front concentrated 200 tanks in its main effort, committing the 6th Guards Tank Army to the fight in the sector of the 7th Guards Army with the mission to develop success in the direction of Prague. The 6th Guards Tank Army had to complete a road march of nearly 90 kilometers before the Prague operation. On 5 May, the 2nd Ukrainian forces advanced in their assigned direction. Kravchenko decided for the operation to inflict the main strike on the right flank of the army with the 5th Guards Tank Corps. The 2nd Guards Mechanized Corps moved in the second echelon after the 9th Guards Mechanized Corps, prepared to support the left flank of the army.

On the morning of 8 May, the 6th Guards Tank Army passed through the 7th Guards Army's sector, advancing 80 kilometers on the first day. Kravchenko's tank army attacked swiftly in a northwesterly direction from Strakhotin, enveloping the right flank of Army Group Center. Advancing over 200 kilometers in two days, lead tanks by early afternoon on 9 May entered Prague, linking up with the troops of Lelyushenko's and Rybalko's tank armies. The Germans would not lay down their arms and surrender, but fought a withdrawal so they could surrender to the British or the Americans. Even as late as 10 May in the area of Caslav, Kravchenko's 2nd Guards Mechanized Corps encountered severe resistance from the enemy before the corps could continue on to Prague.

Despite the end to fighting in Europe in May, the war was not over for the Red Army, nor Kravchenko. Marshal Malinovskii's Front was transferred to the Far East for a campaign against the Japanese

Kwantung Army in Manchuria. In the first part of July, Kravchenko met his staff in a special train at the Far Eastern rail station, Chita.[95] The Soviet forces in the Far East were reinforced by the transfer of Red Army forces that were freed after the defeat of the German Army. The choice of the staffs and armies was by design. They were all seasoned in battles similar in terrain and types of operations that were expected in the Far Eastern Theater. Many of the senior commanders had served tours of duty in the impending areas of operation earlier in their careers.

Marshal Malinovskii, as commander of the 2nd Ukrainian Front, had conducted crossings of major rivers, encircled and wiped out large enemy forces, and conducted fast-paced operations over open steppes and in mountainous and forested areas. He was to command the Transbaikal Front which had to cross mountains and desert in the impending operation.

In the Red Army's Manchurian strategic offensive in August 1945, the Transbaikal Front played a key role in the destruction of the Japanese Kwantung army. Within the Front was Kravchenko's 6th Guards Tank Army. In accordance with the general concept of the operation the Transbaikal Front was to strike in the direction of Mukden and Chanchun to meet forces of the 1st Far East Front with the objective of dividing and destroying the main forces of the Japanese Kwantung Army occupying Manchuria.

The personnel for the tank army moved to the Manchurian border by railroad. Their tanks and assault guns were given to units remaining in Czechoslovakia while they received their new equipment at the city of Choibalsan and marched 300-350 kilometers to Tamtsak Bulak. After a few weeks in an assembly area, the tank army moved another 70-80 kilometers to its jumping-off positions for the offensive. Each unit created a special unit for water supply.

In order to execute the operation quickly, the Front commander, placed the armored forces in the first echelon. The use of the 6th Guards Tank Army in the Front's first echelon conformed to the Stavka's directive: "The operation is to be based on a sudden attack and the use of mobile forces, above all the 6th Guards Tank Army, for a swift advance."[96] The 6th Guards Tank Army with two mechanized and one tank corps, and, in addition, two motorized rifle divisions, two self-propelled artillery brigades and four separate tank battalions totaled nearly 1019 tanks and assault guns, 188 armored vehicles, 995 field guns, and 43 Katyusha rocket launchers.[97] This

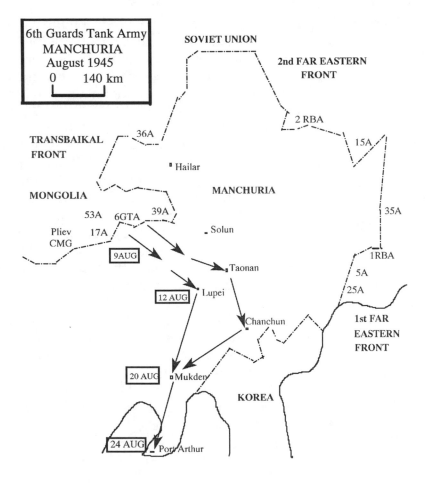

6th Guards Tank Army
MANCHURIA
August 1945
0   140 km

was an army much larger than Kravchenko had commanded in the west.

The 6th Guards Tank Army, as the main strike group for the Transbaikal Front, received the mission to aggressively strike across the Greater Khingan mountains. The tank army's advance was intended to hamper the deployment of Japanese troops and create conditions for the Front's main forces to rapidly cross the mountain and engage the Kwantung Army in the central region of Manchuria. The Front's timetable specified that the tank army not later than five days from the beginning of the operation, overcome the Greater Khingan mountains and seize the line Lupei, Tutsyuan. Further, the tank army was to develop the offensive to Mukden, Chanchun and then to seize the ports of Dalnii and Port Arthur.

In preparing for combat, Kravchenko balanced the tank army's organization and formation for combat in order to achieve a high speed maneuver while continuously supporting the army in case of contact with a large enemy grouping. Because of the anticipated high rate of advance, he placed special attention in creating forward detachments which would determine to a significant degree the success in the rapid tempo of the attack. Forward detachments were created in all the corps, even the second echelon in case it moved to the first echelon during the operation.

Combat operations for the Transbaikal Front began on 9 August. The attack began without an artillery and air preparation. Kravchenko decided the forward detachments must begin the offensive four hours earlier than the main forces. On the first day the 6th Guards Tank Army advanced 120 to 150 kilometers.[98] Kravchenko's army crossed into Manchuria through an area assessed by the Japanese as untrafficable by large armored forces. The Red armored guards' attack achieved surprise.

The 9th and 7th Mechanized Corps in the first echelon moved on about 6-8 parallel march routes each with a width of 15-20 kilometers. Approximately 100 kilometers separated the lead corps. The 5th Guards Tank Corps followed in the second echelon. The general direction of the advance was supported by airplanes. Forward at a distance of 70-80 kilometers were the reconnaissance forces, and at a distance of 30-40 kilometers operated the forward detachments. At times, the 14th Separate Motorcycle Battalion for the 9th Guards Mechanized Corps operated 200 kilometers ahead of the corps. Kravchenko's tank army encountered only slight opposition, and by the midday on the second day of the operation the forward detachments achieved the Khingan mountain range.

With his forward detachments at the foothills of the Greater Khingan, Kravchenko planned for the capture of the mountain passes and made the necessary arrangements to traverse the difficult mountain passages. On 10 August because of the good, fast cross-country mobility of the 5th Guards Tank Corps, Kravchenko moved them into the first echelon. The 9th Guards Mechanized corps was experiencing a number of difficulties in maintaining the pace. The corps was equipped with American Sherman tanks, whose mobility was slower than the T-34 and whose fuel consumption was much higher.

Crossing the Greater Khingan was done on two primary axes. In the north, 7th Guards Mechanized Corps crossed near Mokotan using two trail-like roads. In the south the 5th Guards Tank Corps with 9th Mechanized Corps in second echelon passed east of Yukoto on one road. The 5th Guard Tank Corps began probing through the mountain late on the afternoon of 10 August. Seventh Guards Mechanized Corps began crossing the next morning.

At 2300 hours, 10 August, 5th Guards Tank Corps reached the highest point of passage through the Khingan. The Greater Khingan mountains were uniquely rugged. The western wind swept slopes were a gradual ascent. At the mountain ridgeline, the eastern slopes became precipitous drops. Reconnaissance units reported the difficult and dangerous climbs for the tanks. Kravchenko forward in the tactical command posts intervened against the pessimistic tone, challenging corps and brigade commanders with sarcasm, "you're afraid of these little mountains."[99] He advised the corps commanders to select the company commanders with the unit's most experienced drivers to find ways to overcome the mountain ridges and eastern slopes. The units improvised by linking three to four vehicles with ropes and chains to ease vehicles down the steep descents. In darkness and rain, Kravchenko's Red Army tankers struggled with the weather and the terrain to move the tank units through generally formidable country to armored vehicles.

The height of the mountains significantly reduced the communications capabilities and the staff of the 6th Guards Tank Army used aircraft to help maintain communications.[100] Commanders had to meet each other for instructions. On one occasion, Kravchenko surrounded by M.V. Volkov, Mikhail Dmitrievich Solomatin, Stromberg his chief of staff, conferred over a map of the Greater Khingan Mountains on the hood of an American Lend-Lease jeep. Kravchenko now very heavy with weight, foot up on the bumper noted with the other officers the difficulties and complexities of moving through the harsh mountain range. The advance used fuel as tanks tracked up dead end ravines and had to back out of the narrow draws, doubling consumption of fuel.

In the Greater Khingan mountains, the 5th Guards Tank Corps covered a mountain section of 40 kilometers in seven hours at 5-6 kilometers per hour. No wheeled vehicles. The 7th Mechanized Corps was significantly slower.[101] This corps did not complete passage of the mountains until 11 August.[102]

On 11 August, the 7th Mechanized Corps' combat journal noted, "corps completed the most difficult movement in its history." A remark evoked in spite of the fact that units of the 7th Guards Mechanized Corps had earlier operated in mountain forest regions in Romanian, Hungary, and Czechoslovakia. Kravchenko in an after action report observed the operation in mountain and deserts allowed the "acquiring of great practice in orienteering in terrain and moving columns."[103]

Weather conditions made already poor roads worthless. In difficult sections tanks were lowered using cables. Two joined by a cable moved together so that the rear tank was breaking the downward movement of the first. Motor vehicles joined in groups of several vehicles. The mountains were crossed at night in pouring rainstorm.[104]

Much to the surprise of the Japanese Command, Kravchenko's tank army had crossed the Greater Khingan, obtaining operational space in the Central Manchurian Plain with access to key Manchurian cities. The tank army was followed by the 53rd Rifle Army from the second echelon. Overcoming the Greater Khingen mountains the 6th Guards Tank Army continued the offensive in the direction of the city of Chanchun and Mukden.

By the end of 11 August the forward detachments of the 5th Guards Tank Corps took the town of Lupei where the main forces of the corps concentrated by 13 August. A day later the 7th Mechanized Corps took Tuchuan. Kravchenko's tank army was a day ahead of their planned advance for the operation. Both corps met no significant resistance. The speed of the tank army's advanced had preempted any meaningful response and opposition by Japanese forces. In four days of operations, the tank army had covered some 350 kilometers.

Although Kravchenko accomplished a remarkable advance over formidable terrain, he was experiencing problems. Due to the tank army's rapid advance its main supply bases were up to 450 kilometers behind. Transport vehicles lagged unable to match the pace of the armored forces which expended higher than normal rates of fuel because of the speed of the advance. After the 7th Guards Mechanized Corps had secured Tuchuan and the 5th Guards Tank Corps had taken Lupei, both units incurred severe fuel shortages. The 7th had only half of its fuel supply while the 5th had only four-tenths of its fuel supply. The 9th Mechanized Corps had no fuel when it reached Lupei and stopped. Kravchenko was forced to halt the tank army for two days, 12-13 August. The Front used aircraft and motor transports to supply the 6th Guards Tank Army. On 12 August, the Front dispatched "by airplane: 35 tons of gasoline, 32 tons of diesel fuel, 10 tons of lubricants; by motor transport: 158 tons of gasoline, 102 tons of diesel fuel, 107 tons of lubricants...."[105]

Beginning with the 13-14 August, the lead corps pooled their fuel for their forward detachments to maintain the momentum of the advance. Weather conditions and the terrain presented problems. The forward elements of the 5th Guards Tank Corps encountered an impassable swampy stretch of some 120 kilometers. It traversed the difficult terrain by driving tanks over a railroad line and crossed a swollen river on a railroad bridge to keep the pace of the rapid advance.

At nightfall on 14 August, the forward detachment of the 7th Guards Mechanized Corps occupied Toanan, while the 9th Mechanized Corps continued to drive to the east toward Tungliao and Kaitung.

Kravchenko's tank army continued to march on 15 August along two major axes opposed only by disintegrating Japanese infantry divisions. The 7th Guards Mechanized Corps moved east toward Chanchun while the 9th Guards Mechanized Corps moved southeast toward Mukden. The gap between the two units widened to more than 100 kilometers. Motorcycle reconnaissance and aircraft watched the area between the units.

The command posts during the operation had to be altered from past procedures because of the terrain conditions. The operations group assumed basic leadership of the troops in units trailing the first echelon of the 6th Guards Tank Army. In the landing force at Mukden, the 7th Mechanized Corps' operations group set up and used a group of aircraft with radios to relay signals. For the purpose of increasing the mobility of the command posts and communications centers virtually all the radios were transferred to motor vehicles which possessed better cross-country capability.[106]

The cooperation between the 6th Guards Tank Army and the supporting 12th Air Army planned the location of the 12th Air Army Deputy Commander with his operational group to be located in Kravchenko's command post. The air division commanders located their operational groups in the command posts of the corps.

Towards 16 August, forward detachments of 5th Guards Tank and 7th Mechanized corps took the towns of Tungliao and Kaitung. The 5th Guards Tank Corps captured the airfield and bridge at Tungliao. The main forces receiving fuel followed on 18-19 August concentrating in these town.

On 18 August the Front ordered Kravchenko to take Mukden and Chanchun. The following day, an air landing party from the 6th Guards Tank Army consisting of units from the 30th Guards Mechanized Brigade seized the town of Chanchun. Forward detachments of 5th Guards Tank Corps on 20 August took Mukden and 7th Mechanized Corps took Chanchun on 21 August, capturing the strategic center of the Kwantung Army. Because of the fuel shortages further movement of the 6th Guards Tank Army to Port Arthur and Dalny was by rail. A reinforced brigade forced march towards Port Arthur reaching the port on 25 August.

On 29 August, tank army forces advanced on Port Arthur and Dairen. On 30 August the Front commander ordered Kravchenko to cease further movement of the 5th Guards Tank and 9th Mechanized Corps. The operation earned Kravchenko his second Gold Star, Hero of the Soviet Union, putting him in the ranks of very select few who were twice winners of the country's highest decoration.

By 24 August the 6th Guards Tank Army had achieved a depth of 1100 kilometers at an average rate of 70 kilometers per day. Kravchenko's army move 5-10 days ahead of the rifle armies, forming a unique spearhead for the Transbaikal Front. Use of the tank army in this way ensured the element of surprise, deep penetration to operational depths, and precluded the deployment of Japanese main forces. All of these aspects contributed to the rapid advance by all forces of the Front.

With a worn Cossack cape draped over his shoulders, Kravchenko stood looking over the Pacific Ocean. Like the Cossack cape he wore, Kravchenko performed his duties without flourish or fan-fare. He wore the cape not for attention, but because it was practical and durable. With little dash, he would get the job done. His superiors could count on his knowing the mission and performing to their standards. Quiet and serious, the tall commander was direct, efficient in his meetings, exacting in work.

The heroic feats of Kravchenko's units throughout the war were accomplished with greatly improvised methods. Improvisation does not come without initiative, he was extraordinarily persevering and a master of conserving resources. Kravchenko proved to be a remarkable tank commander with unsurpassed bravery and operated forward away from his command post. Not once was he wounded. The 6th Guards Tank Army conducted offensive actions chiefly in hilly terrain and wooded mountains during the capture of Romania, Hungary, Austria, Czechoslovakia and in Manchuria, forcing more decentralized and unnoticed operations. Kravchenko achieved a good balance in his leadership style between commanders and his staff with a strong sense of control and demand for detail. Duty was a word Kravchenko understood. The brave and respected armored guard commander epitomized the old Russian warrior code: "He who comes to us with a sword shall perish by the sword."

NOTES

1. Anna Stroeva, *Komandarm Kravchenko*, Kiev: Izdatel'stvo politicheskoi literatury ukrainy, 1984, p. 7.

2. E.F. Ivanovich, *Ataku nachinali tankisty*, Moscow: Voenizdat, 1984, pp. 67-68.

3. Ibid., p. 68.

4. Stroeva, p. 18.

5. Ibid., p. 19.

6. V. V. Tarnov, "Parad, izumivshii mir," *Voenno-istoricheskii zhurnal* (hereafter *Vizh*), vol. 1-1989, p. 71.

7. P.A. Belov, *Za nami Moskva*, Moscow: Voenizdat, 1963, p. 60.

8. Stroeva, p. 25.

9. M. E. Katukov, *Na ostrie glavnogo udara*, Moscow: Voenizdat, 1976, p. 155.

10. Ibid., p. 157.

11. Ibid., p. 160.

12. Ivanovskii, p. 68.

13. Ibid., p. 76.

14. Ibid., p. 79.

15. Ibid., p. 81.

16. Ibid., p. 84.

17. Ibid.

18. K.S. Moskalenko, *Na yugo-zapadnom napravlenii*, Book l, Moscow: Nauka, 1973, p. 339.

19. *Sbornik materialov po izucheniyu opyta voiny*, No. 8, Avgust-Oktyabr' 1943 g., General'nogo shtaba krasnoi armii, Moscow: Voenizdat, 1943, p. 70.

20. Ibid.

21. Stroeva, p. 35.

22. *Sbornik* No. 8, p. 66.

23. Stroeva, p. 37.

24. Ibid., p. 38.

25. Ibid., p. 39.

26. M.V. Zakharov, *Stalingradskaya epopeya*, Moscow: Nauka, 1968, p. 659.

27. Ibid.

28. Stroeva, p. 40.

29. *Sbornik* No. 8, p. 66.

30. Stroeva, p. 42.

31. Ibid., p. 43.

32. A.I. Radzievskii, *Proryv*, Moscow: Voenizdat, 1979, pp. 48-49.

33. Stroeva, p. 50.

34. Ibid., p. 51.

35. Ibid., pp. 53, 54.

36. Katukov, p. 237.

37. A. Kravchenko, "Tankisty forsiruyut reki," *Vizh* 9-1963, p. 63.

38. Ibid.

39. Ibid.

40. M. Ashik, "Iz opyta perepravy tankov pod vodoi," *Vizh* 3-1984, p. 69.

41. Stroeva, pp. 63-64.

42. A.I. Radzievskii, *Taktika v boevykh primerakh* (diviziya), Moscow: Voenizdat, 1976, p. 119.

43. Germany, Army, Fourth Panzer Army, Intelligence records, Situation maps, microfilm series T-313, roll 384, frame 8672901, National Archives and Records Administration, Washington, DC.

44. Stroeva, p. 70.

45. Ibid.

46. David Dragunsky, *A Soldier's Memoirs*, Moscow: Progress, 1983, p. 111.

47. Stroeva, p. 68.

48. Ibid.

49. K.V. Krainyukov, *Oruzhie osobogo roda*, Moscow: Voenizdat, 1977, p. 69.

50. Ibid., p. 79.

51. Ibid.

52. Ibid., pp. 79-80.

53. Leon Degrelle, *Campaign in Russia: The Waffen SS on the Eastern Front*, Torrance, California: Institute for Historical Review, 1985, p. 151.

54. G.T. Zavizion, P.A. Kornyushin, *I na Tikhom okeane...*, Moscow: Voenizdat, 1967, p. 8.

55. Ibid.

56. Ibid., pp. 15-16.

57. Ibid., p. 13.

58. Degrelle, p. 160.

59. Krainyukov, p. 126.

60. D.I. Zaev, "Tanki vstreptiis' v zvenigorodke," *Korsun-Shevchenkovskaya bitva*, Kiev: Polizdat Ukrainy, 1989, p. 115.

61. Stroeva, p. 82.

62. Ibid., p. 83.

63. Ibid., p. 84.

64. Ibid., p. 83.

65. Ibid., p. 85.

66. G. Zhukov, *Reminiscences and Reflections*, Vol. 2, Moscow: Progress, 1985, p. 240.

67. P. Repin, "Na Korsunskaye polye," *Krasnaya Zvezda*, 25 January 1989, p. 2.

68. A.I. Radzievskii, *Tankovyi udar*, Moscow: Voenizdat, 1977, pp. 167-168.

69. G. Zhukov, p. 246.

70. F.W. von Mellenthin, *Panzer Battles*, New York: Ballantine, 1980, p. 328.

71. Zavizion, p. 29.

72. Ibid., p. 31.

73. V.S. Golubovich, *Marshal R. Ya. Malinovskii*, Moscow: Voenizdat, 1984, p. 139.

74. Stroeva, p. 99.

75. Ibid., p. 101.

76. Ibid., p. 103.

77. Ibid., p. 104.

78. Stroeva, p. 105.

79. I.M. Ananev, *Tankovye armii v nastuplenii*, Moscow: Voenizdat, 1988, p. 103.

80. M.M. Kir'yan, *Vnezapnost' v nastupatel'nykh operatsiya Velikoi Otechestvennoi Voiny*, Moscow: Nauka, 1986, p. 170.

81. P. Varakin, "6-ya gvardeiskaya tankovaya armiya v Debretsenskoi operatsii," *Vizh* 11-1975, p. 71.

82. Ibid., p. 75.

83. Radzievskii, Udar, p. 69.

84. Stroeva, p. 124.

85. P. Varakin, "Nekotorye voprosy boevogo primeneniya 6-i gvardeiskoi tankovoi armii v budapeshtskoi operatsii," *Vizh* 12-1973, p. 65.

86. Ananev, p. 385.

87. Zavizion, p. 150.

88. Ibid., p. 151.

89. Stroeva, p. 131.

90. Ibid., p. 138.

91. Ananev, p. 106.

92. Stroeva, p. 142.

93. Ibid.

94. Zavizion, p. 186.

95. Ibid., p. 200.

96. S.M. Shtemenko, *The Last Six Months*, New York: Doubleday & Company, Inc., 1977, p. 86.

97. I. Krupchenko, "6-ya gvardeiskaya tankovaya armiya v Khingano-Mukdenskoi operatsii," *Vizh* 12-1962, p. 16.

98. I. Garkusha, "Osobennosti boevykh deistvii bronetankovykh i mekhanizirovannykh voisk," *Vizh* 9-1975, p. 26.

99. Stroeva, p. 153.

100. Krupchenko, p. 23.

101. Radzievskii, *Taktika* (diviziya), p. 129.

102. Krupchenko, p. 23.

103. Stroeva, p. 146.

104. Radzievskii, *Taktika* (diviziya), p. 129.

105. Golubovich, p. 180.

106. P.P. Tovstukha, *Upravlenie voiskami v nastuplenie*, Moscow: Voenizdat, 1981, p. 180.

CONCLUSION

The selection of six tank army commanders provides an exemplary collection of skillful and notable Red Army generals. As the Deputy Chief of Staff for the Red Army General Staff during the Second World War, General Sergei Shtemenko wrote, "only the most gifted, daring and resolute generals, who were ready to take full responsibility for their actions without looking back for support, were selected as commanders of the tank armies." Five tank army commanders were twice Heroes of the Soviet Union attesting to their bravery and fighting contributions. These commanders provided backbone experience and expertise for the Red Army's emerging large-scale armored operations. Their war performances illustrate clearly that the heirs of Soviet armored warfare were not handed an unthinking, automaton style of leadership to emulate, but offered a diverse, quick-witted ability in battlefield command. The tank army commanders were intelligent, knowledgeable, experienced men of strong character who would have made outstanding military leaders in any army, on any battlefield, in any period.

The armored guards commanders handled tasks that only tank armies were capable of carrying out. The uniqueness of armored force missions dictated the character of tank army operations as well as the quality of the commander himself. For tank army commanders the area of operation and scope of concern were much greater than for rifle army commanders. Tank armies operating as the Front's mobile group in wide sectors were not assigned a zone of action, but given a direction of advance in order not to hamper the army's maneuverability and stifle the tank army commander's initiative in decisions. The depth of tank army missions coincided with those of the Fronts. Fronts possessing armored formations had offensive depths 2-2.5 times greater and rates of advance 2-2.5 times faster than Fronts without armored units. The tank army's high rate of advance required commanders to decide and organize quickly combat actions. As tank commanders matured and gained experience, the depth of offensive operations increased: in 1943, 120-200 kilometers; 1944, 200-400 kilometers; and 1945, 500 or more kilometers.[1] German General F. W. von Mellenthin in his memoirs noted, the large Russian tank and mechanized formations in 1944 "developed into a mobile and keenly edged tool handled by daring and capable commanders."[2]

Commanding and controlling tank armies required men of extraordinary talents and temperaments. The tank commander's intellect, talent and style were uniquely expressed in the formulation and adoption of an operations plan; his manner, temperament, and will were exhibited in the fast-paced, dynamic execution of armored warfare. The six tank army commanders illustrate personal leadership styles as varied as fundamental human behavior. Each commander possessed a different temperament determining behavior, preferences, and attitudes that composed a distinct leadership style.

Their personal command styles become evident in the periods of generating and executing tank operations when commanders exercised intensive command and control. The first specific period involving command presence was the restoration of the army's strength with personnel and equipment and general preparatory combat training. While building a cohesive force at the company, battalion, and brigade levels, the commander planned combat training, monitored the execution of orders and provided practical assistance to units. Influencing subordinate units through directives, tank army commander exercised their control through different command and staff levels. Additionally, they visited training and preparation routinely making on the spot assessments and corrections. Tank army commanders demonstrated a detailed knowledge and understanding of individual tasks and skills as well as requirements for collective unit training. Rybalko drove new armored vehicles and tanks to know their capabilities and limitations firsthand. Katukov, Rotmistrov, and Kravchenko emphasized the importance of the tank driver's training. Lelyushenko often at the firing ranges was interested in tank gunnery.

The second period was characterized by the army's receipt of its mission and preparation for combat by all units and individuals. The commander directing headquarters staff work made decisions, planned the operation, passed the combat mission to all units, organized coordination, moved units to the assembly areas and attack positions. Ideally, under the Soviet command system, the commander gave his estimate of the situation and adopted a general plan for the operation on a map in the presence of the Chief of Staff, the political officer of the Military Council, artillery commander and chiefs of operations and intelligence. Each commander differed in this respect.

Katukov best exemplified the Soviet model of a commander's collective war council for a general plan. Bogdanov relied heavily on his chief of staff. Rotmistrov, as did Rybalko, valued the council of his subordinate commanders. Lelyushenko, Rybalko and Kravchenko decided more independently, using their staffs primarily for control of the execution of the plan.

The commander's relationship with his staff is a crucial aspect in command and control, revolving around personality and human nature. An introverted commander will react differently with staff officers and subordinate commanders than an extroverted one, determining a commander's accessibility and receptiveness to staff officers' information. A breakdown in the close working relationship between a commander and his chief of staff impacts significantly on command group operations. If the chief of staff fails to hold the commander's confidence, the entire staff suffers from its inability to anticipate the commander's information needs and execute control of the force in consonance with the commander's intent. Bogdanov found his first army chief of staff wanting and replaced him. Rybalko replaced his chief of staff during the Lvov operation for at least the culminating reason of losing traffic control in the "Koltov" corridor. Soviet sources are mute on such shortcomings in command and command relationships.

How a commander relates to people will shape his style of command. Three of the tank commanders, Katukov, Rybalko, and Lelyushenko, became animated in their dealings with subordinates, drawing energy from relationships with other people. Relationships determined whether commanders, like Katukov and Rotmistrov, preferred a collective decision with staff officers and subordinate commanders, or decided himself, as Bogdanov, Kravchenko and Rybalko did after the facts were presented. The commanders differed in their relationship with subordinate commanders, dictating how orders were fashioned and presented. While Bogdanov authoritatively imposed orders, Rotmistrov invited a participatory approach that sought a self-motivation by subordinates. Kravchenko led by example, inducing subordinates to action through inspiration. Lelyushenko was Socratic and tutorial in orders and instructions. Katukov often used a sarcastic barb to prod his commanders.

The commanders possessed individual characteristics that determined his ability to delegate responsibility and authority. The degree responsibilities were extended directly patterned control, simplicity and practicality of orders. Lelyushenko, always at the point of action, asked commanders for their course of action and then supported as necessary. Rybalko and Bogdanov directed subordinates, monitoring execution of the order. Rotmistrov sought continuous feedback from his commanders. Assigning responsibilities, Katukov and Kravchenko expected subordinate commanders to accomplish the task.

After summarizing his plan, the tank army commander shifted the center of gravity in his work to organizing the combat activities of the tank and mechanized corps, such as the reconnaissance in the area of operation with the corps commanders and the extremely important coordination with rifle formation commanders for the passage of tanks through rifle units. The tank commanders handled these activities in subtly dissimilar ways. Rotmistrov found it necessary to see the lay of the battlefield himself before reaching a plan of action and coordinating the actions of his subordinate commanders. Katukov and Lelyushenko personally worked coordinations to ensure control of the roads for an orderly commitment. Rybalko worked coordination and combat actions in detailed sandbox exercises or on large scale maps. Bogdanov seems to have left much of this aspect of command to his chief of staff.

The third period involved the commander's control during the course of an operation. The commander's main objective was to ensure coherence in command and control. Based on an elaborate network of command post, observation posts, and operations groups, tank army commanders focused execution and support of the plan and reaction to combat situations. The armored guards commanders required a talent for objective evaluation of operations. They had to possess perceptiveness and initiative in order to identify and then fix shortcomings in the tank force structure, fighting equipment, tactics and operational plans. Rotmistrov, as a major architect in the tank army structure, wanted an independent armored force capable of sustaining itself in engineers, artillery, and rear services. Rybalko, on the other hand, wanted his tankers "unchained" by stripping out the extraneous engineers, medical hospital and other support units, fashioning a powerful, streamlined instrument of war that was fast and lean. Katukov wanted to retain doctors specialized in the unique wounds of armored warfare, and he would add more artillery and road construction units to the tank army.

In theory, tank armies were to begin combat actions only after the rifle formations broke through the main, and sometimes the secondary defensive zone of the enemy. In practice, this concept was rarely achieved due to insufficient penetration power of rifle formations. When tank armies had to complete the breakthrough of the tactical defensive zone, they lost an average of 15-20 per cent of their personnel and equipment.[3] The commitment of the tank army to a breakthrough was a crucial moment in the operation. Although each commander had his sense of timing and techniques, all tank army commanders were forward to personally oversee this significant action in the operation.

The casualties trend through the war years lessened as tank army commanders, as well as subordinate commanders and staffs, improved with experience. An analysis of tank army casualties in 21 major operations showed the following losses in personnel: 3 operations, 10%; 11 operations, 10-15%; 1 operation, 20%; 6 operations, 20-30%. The highest losses of 20-30% were in the first year of tank army operations, 1943.[4] Rybalko eager to commit often suffered high casualties when assisting rifle units in the penetration of the forward defensive zone, as did Kravchenko's army which was often placed in the first echelon. Katukov preferred to clear the way with forward detachments and raids. Bogdanov through his chief of staff worked to coordinate artillery and air support to protect the tank army.

Sustaining the operation became a major command task at the operational level of warfare. A review of 42 major operations reveals the duration of tank army operations: 25 operations lasted 20 days; 7 operations, 30 days; and 10 operations, over 30 days.[5] Tank commanders paced their operations in the operational depth, maintaining minimal battle losses was a key indicator of success and unit viability. In the course of offensive operations, tank armies lost an average of 90% of their tanks and self-propelled assault guns. According to Soviet military analysis, irrecoverable losses in continuous operations of 15-20 days averaged 30% of the initial strength. The remaining 70% of losses required evacuation and restoration: 80% were the result of combat damage; 20%, mechanical failure.[6] In some operations, each tank and self-propelled assault gun was evacuated, restored and placed back into the fight 2-3 times.[7]

As the main strike force and concentration of the Front's tank force, tank armies were relatively self-reliant in sustaining their unit strength in tanks and self-propelled guns. Tank army commanders actively initiated measures that quickly restored damaged tanks to the battlefield. Like Katukov's "Tank Doctor," who managed the recovery and maintenance support, Chiefs of Rear Services became important and respected individuals in the eyes of commanders.

Where a commander located himself on the battlefield involved personal choices. How much action must the commander see or hear to sense the battle? Who must the commander confer with to change a plan or take an action, subordinate commanders or chief of staff? How much does the commander move about the battlefield? In offensive operations the tank army commander generally operated with his operations group located forward an average of 5-10 kilometers behind the army's first echelon. The operations group usually consisted of the tank army commander, the chiefs of the operations and intelligence sections, designated staff officers, the commanders of the branches of troops and their staff officers. Whenever army commanders traveled forward to the troops he took along a radio group and liaison officers furnished with various means of transportation. The size of the groups depended on the individual commander's preference. Rybalko, for example, had the largest operations group with half the army staff and radios exercising a more centralized command from the observation post. Lelyushenko operated forward with too small an operations group, making himself difficult to contact. When fighting became intensive, the army commander and his operations group located themselves at an observation post set up in the sector of the main strike, 3-5 kilometers from the forward edge of the defense.

The army's main command post usually moved once a day, and it was deployed an average of 30 kilometers behind the corps command posts. This spacing of command posts allowed the tank army commander to directly influence the course of combat activities and personally observe development of events in the main sector or at critical points on the battlefield. If the situation warranted, the army command could immediately provide any needed assistance and guidance to brigade and corps commanders. At the end of the day's fighting, the tank army commander left his observation post for the main command post, where he was briefed by the chief of staff and other staff officers. On the basis of the information he received he would either update the current plan or draw up a new one, depending on where and how he wanted to commit his combat power.

The commander's personal choice of location on the battlefield changed during the course of the operation by design or for survival, working against a regimented command and control system. Not all commanders fought effectively from a command post, and vice versa. The personal requisites and situational demands for command were too varied for prescriptive regulation. Constantly moving, Lelyushenko and Bogdanov had to be at the focal point of the action. Kravchenko successfully operated well forward. Katukov with his war council often waited in his main command post for radio reports. Rotmistrov, like Rybalko, liked to talk face to face with subordinate commanders by visiting forward or calling the commanders to his command post.

Tank army commanders studied the situation continually, observing the enemy's actions, quickly and precisely calculating the combat capabilities of their own personnel and equipment, determining the methods of action to be used by army corps and brigades in the future, and promptly transmitting new combat missions to them. How a commander makes his decisions and how he likes to receive his information varied. While all the commanders preferred actual facts, practical solutions with sensible approaches, they differed in their character of thought, how they conceptualized, understood and perceived information. This directly influenced their plans and solutions to tactical and operational problems. Depending on a personal capacity to hold information and suspend alternate courses of action varied among the commanders. Rybalko, Lelyushenko, Kravchenko possessed the ability to retain a myriad of details, withholding decision until the right moment. Katukov using his war council's collective wisdom derived an optimal solution by wargaming situations on the map. Rotmistrov possessing a greater sense of possibilities and potential of his force devised ingenious tactics that differed significantly from the others. Bogdanov, Rybalko, Lelyushenko moved forward to make the decision on the spot.

Two commanders, Bogdanov and Rybalko, exhibited a style of command somewhat impulsive, restless. They thrived on action that wielded the tank as an instrument of war. Their tank armies were an extension of themselves. Extremely brave, they exposed themselves to danger without hesitation, they would test their luck. Easily bored, they altered their daily patterns. Strong-willed and tenacious, they could tolerate only temporary setbacks. Enduring in actions in which others might give up, they strove to achieve "perfection in action."

Both commanders endured hardships well, persevering in difficult situations. They could build a unit *esprit de corps* nurtured by their mere physical presence.

Katukov, Lelyushenko, Kravchenko were commanders of a different style. These commanders carried the obligation and responsibilities of command with a disposition to serve. Pessimistic in outlook, they prepared for the worst case. They guarded against Murphy's law, "whatever can go wrong will." Military traditions and rituals were important to these commanders. They were demanding operational leaders, whose superiors could count on them for the accomplishment of the mission and to do their duty. They possessed a low tolerance for subordinates who failed to achieve assigned tasks, or could not do the right thing at the right time. Although they were conservative risk-takers on the battlefield, they would take risks and dare the long shot in a tight situation. They thoroughly knew the capabilities of their tankers and tanks. Lelyushenko remarkably improvised unit organization and battle plans on the move.

Rotmistrov uniquely differed in his interests for greater issues. He did not command for the power of the position, but pursued an influential power over the actions of armored forces. He demanded total competency in armored warfare and settled for nothing less, gaining a masterful proficiency in his field. More theoretical in his considerations, Rotmistrov questioned conventional wisdom and looked for the unexpected solution in combat. He enjoyed developing the model tank army as he focused on the future.

All the commanders exhibited a steadfastness to principles, objectives, standards and provided critical analysis on operations and subordinate commanders. However, they were not senseless robots, but exhibited human compassion. Lelyushenko could see the subjective aspects in tactics, the need for the fellow "soldier's shoulder," and Rybalko lamented the winter conditions his motorized riflemen endured. Katukov was sensitive to the degree of support he gave his subordinate commanders.

All the commanders enjoyed decision-making. Hard-driving, task oriented, they showed an ability to meet deadlines and an impatience to get the job done. Lelyushenko and Rybalko possessed a heightened ability to adapt as the situation unfolded. Seemingly suspended in time, they lived and fought for the moment, as if there was no tomorrow, exhibiting incredible personal bravery. Bogdanov thrived on action, often anxious to commit his tank army through the gap. Rotmistrov and Kravchenko with their tank army ready to commit stood by their senior commander for the attack signal.

Each tank army commander had his own strengths which contributed to his rise within the Red Army armored guards. Each leadership style exhibited the commander's attitude, behavior, and response on the battlefield. Commanders could be aggressive, determined, decisive, expedient; or, at times, they could be hesitant, unsure, indecisive, a conservative risk-taker. Exploring the differences in leadership styles illustrated a rich diversity of command within a perceived monolithic and colorless military leadership.

The Red Army command system is often perceived as a rigid, uniform and unthinking leadership. Commanders are presumably faceless automatons pushed forward by pistol-toting commissars. Ironically, by accepting this stereotypic view one concedes that Marxism succeeded in forming conditioned, mechanical military commanders. One is led to believe through a shaped environment, the Soviet commander could be molded to automatic responses, to predictable actions on the battlefield, and to always selecting empirically optimum solutions. However, the study indicates that those who rose to lead tank armies were not uniform in thought and actions. The commanders' basic temperaments and behaviors were unchanged; their individual insights and preferences in personal relationships strengthened through a lifetime of use were the basis of leadership style. The tank commanders exhibited universal traits antithetical to a rigidly controlled command system. Experiencing anxiety and self-doubt, they did not sleep on the eve of large battles. They argued with senior commanders for their plan of action. They improvised in the face of battle, fighting to conquer or survive. They were concerned about their personal reputations. Marshal Rokossovskii wrote in his memoirs after the war, "...an essential quality of every military leader is self-control, calmness and respect for his subordinates, especially in times of war. Believe an old soldier: there is nothing a man prizes more in combat than the realization that he is trusted, believed, and relied upon."[8]

Although the Soviet centralized command system had a defined organizational structure to implement assignments, commanders proved very different. Despite the Soviet ideal for military leadership and the west's stereotype of that leadership, the study shows a producable and recognizable individual character. It is possible to overlap individual commanders and their impact on the battlefield, improving our understanding of the fighting on the eastern front and the individuals who shaped it. On the battlefield, the tank army commanders continually had choices that demonstrated imagination and attenuated predictability, matching the leadership in any successful army.

Diversity in leadership within a structured, centralized command system is shaped more by a person's response to people, and how they receive information, handle stress and other aspects of command. The difference comes down to the fundamental difference between the Soviet and Western perception of the individual versus the collective. The role of the individual is heightened in the western mind. To the Soviet mind, the collective interest is the ultimate communist goal. A socialist realism imposed on Red Army commanders' accomplishments obscures the impact of personal leadership styles on the battlefield. If the form of command represents the procedures and structure of relationships, the art of command is personal style and individual methods. The clash of form and art, system and individual, produced ironies in Red Army leadership which puzzle Western military historians and analysts. A centralized, authoritative command and control having more flexibility at the operational level of warfare is enigmatic. The dichotomy of faceless, Soviet battlefield accomplishments achieved by strict individual commander responsibility within a theoretical constraint stressing collective versus individual effort is mystifying. But, the historical evidence suggests that diversity existed allowing necessary compensations within Red Army leadership to wage effective combat, and, in the end, emerged from the war victorious.

All Red Army tank armies formed during the Great Patriotic War received the "Guards" honorific title by the end of the war for notable contributions in major combat operations. The successful tank commanders who led the guards tank armies were equally worthy of recognition. The Red Army tank commanders who led the armored guards followed a long, arduous path to victory. They impressively adapted force structures and tactics, adopted new lessons and techniques, and conducted aggressive and imaginative warfare at the operational level. The tank army commanders who mastered modern armored warfare significantly influenced the fighting on the eastern front, and, consequently, the outcome of the Second World War. These Soviet generals put their armored guards in

Berlin – a triumphant response to the invading German army which held the Red Army leadership in contempt.

NOTES

1. A.I. Radzievskii, *Tankovyi udar*, Moscow: Voenizdat, 1977, pp. 47-48.

2. F.W. von Mellenthin, *Panzer Battles*, New York: Ballantine, 1980, p. 361.

3. I.M. Anan'ev, *Tankovye armii v nastuplenii*, Moscow: Voenizdat, 1988, p. 265.

4. A.I. Radzievskii, "Podershanie i vosstanovlenie boesposobnosti tankovykh armii v nastupatel'nykh operatsiyakh," *Voenno-istoricheskii zhurnal (Vizh)*, Vol. 3-1976, p. 15.

5. Radzievskii, *Tankovyi udar*, p. 49.

6. Radzievskii, *Vizh*, p. 16.

7. Ibid.

8. K.K. Rokossovskii, *A Soldier's Duty*, Moscow: Progress, 1985, p. 84.

BIBLIOGRAPHY

Archival Material
"Encirclement and Breakout of the First Panzer Army (March - April 1944), MS #F-143a-VII, Carlisle Barracks, PA: Military History Institute.
Germany, Army, Eighth Army, Intelligence Records, Situation maps, microfilm series T-312, roll 58, National Archives and Records Administration, Washington, D.C..
Germany, Army, Fourth Panzer Army, Intelligence Records, Situation maps, micorfilm series T-313, roll 384, National Archives and Records Administration, Washington, D.C.
Sbornik materialov po izucheniyu opyta voiny, Volumes 1-18, Moscow: Voenizdat, 1943-1946.

Articles
Alferov, S. "Peregruppirovka 3-i gvardeiskoi tankovyi armii v bitve za Dnepr," *Vizh*, Vol. 3-1980.
Ashik, M., "Iz opyta perepravy tankov pod vodoi," *Vizh*, Vol. 3-1984.
Dement'ev, A., S. Petrov, "Izmenenie obstanovki i novoe reshenie," *Vizh*, Vol. 7-1978.
Dorofeev, M., "O nekotorykh prichinakh neudachnykh deistrii mekhanizirovannykh korpusov v nachal'nom periode Velikoi Otechestvennoi Voiny," *Voenno Istoricheskii Zhurnal*, Vol. 3-1964.
Egorov, A., "Tankovyi polk v boyakh pod kalininom i klinom," *Vizh*, Vol. 4- 1971.
—, "Yuzhnee Kurska," *Vizh*, Vol. 7-1968.
Garkusha, I., "Osobennosti boevykh deistvii bronetankovykh i mekhanizirovannykh voisk," *Vizh*, Vol. 9-1975.
"Glavnyi marshal bronetankovykh voisk P.A. Rotmistrov," *Vizh*, Vol. 7-1963.
Kasatokov, V., "General Armii A.I. Radzievskii," *Vizh*, Vol. 7-1981.
Kazakov, M., "Na voronezhskom napravlenii letom 1942 goda," *Vizh*, Vol. 10- 1964.
Kireev, N., "Presledovanie protivnika soedineniyami i ob'edineniyami bronetankovykh i mekhanizirovannykh voisk," *Vizh*, Vol 6-1977.
Kobrin, N., "Iz opyta vydvizheniya tankovykh armii iz rainov sosredotocheniya dlya vvoda v srazhenie," *Vizh*, Vol. 9-1976.
Konev, I., "Kirovogradskaya operatsiya," *Vizh*, Vol. 5-1969.
Kravchenko, A., "Tankisty forsiruyut reki," *Vizh*, Vol. 9-1963.
Krupchenko, I., "Kharakternye cherty razvitiya i primeneniya tankovykh voisk," *Vizh*, Vol. 9-1979.
—, "6-ya gvardeiskaya tankovaya armiya v Khingano-Mukdenskoi operatsii," *Vizh*, Vol. 12-1962.
—, "Tankovye armii v Berlinskoi operatsii," *Vizh*, Vol. 7-1960.
Kurochkin, P., "Glavnyi marshal bronetankovykh voisk P.A. Rotmistrov," *Vizh*, Vol. 6-1981.
Luchinskii, A., "Na Berlin," *Vizh*, Vol. 5-1965.
Novikov, A., "Otvety na Pis'ma Chitatelei," *Vizh*, Vol. 9-1973.
Popov, M., "Yuzhnee Stalingrada," *Vizh*, Vol. 2-1961.

Portugal'skii, R., "Postanovka(dovedenie) zadach voiskom v nastupatel'noi operatsii obshchevoiskovoi(tankovoi) armii," *Vizh*, Vol. 12-1975.

Radzievskii, A.I., "Na puti k varshave," *Vizh*, Vol. 10-1971.

—, "Podershanie i vosstanovlenie boesposobnosti tankovykh armii v nastupatel'nykh operatsiyakh," *Vizh*, Vol. 3-1976.

—, "Stremitel'nye deistviye tankovykh armii," *Vizh*, Vol. 1- 1965.

Repin, P., "Na Korsunskaye polye," *Krasnaya Zvezda*, 25 January 1989.

Rotmistrov, P. A., "Boevoe primenenie brontankovykh i mekhanizirovannykh voisk," *Vizh*, Vol. 12-1967.

—, "Tempy nastupleniya tankovoi armii," *Vizh*, Vol. 6-1964.

Sandalov, L.M., "Bryanskii front v Orlovskii operatsii," *Vizh*, Vol. 8-1963.

—, "Oboronitel'naya operatsiya 4-i armii v nachal'nyi period voiny," *Vizh*, Vol. 7-1971.

—, "Stoyali Nasmert," *Vizh*, Vol. 11-1988.

Shekhovtsov, N., "Nastuplenie voisk Stepnogo fronta na krivoroahskom napravlenii v oktyabre 1943 goda," *Vizh*, Vol. 10-1968.

Smirnov, "Vstrechnyi boi tankovogo korpusa," *Vizh*, Vol. 8-1960.

Sukhomlin, "Sluzhebnye sobaki na voine," *Vizh*, Vol. 8-1971.

Suvenirov, O.F., "Vsearmeiskaya tragediya," *Vizh*, Vol 3-1989.

Tamonov, F., "Primenenie bronetankovykh voisk v bitve pod Moskvoi," *Vizh*. Vol. 1-1967.

Tarnov, V.V., "Parad, izumivshii mir," *Vizh*, Vol. 1-1989.

Tsynkalov, A., "Iz opyta povysheniya zhivuchesti tankov v nastupatel'nykh operatsiyakh," *Vizh*, Vol. 3-1983.

Tyulenev, I., "General armii D.D. Lelyushenko," *Vizh*, Vol. 11-1971.

Varakin, P., "6-ya gvardeiskaya tankovaya armiya v Debretsenskoi operatsii," *Vizh*, Vol. 11-1975.

—, "Nekotorye voprosy boevogo primeneniya 6-i gvardeiskoi tankovoi armii v budapeshtskoi operatsii," *Vizh*, Vol. 12-1973.

Volkogonov, Dmitrii, "Triumf i tragediya," *Pravda* excerpt 20 June 1988.

Yakubovskii, I., "Udar nebyvaloi sily," *Vizh*, Vol. 2-1970.

Books

Aleksandrov, I.G., Marshal Zhukov: *Polkovodets i chelovek*, Vol. 1, Moscow: Novosti, 1988.

Anan'ev, I.M., *Tankovye armii v nastuplenii*, Moscow: Voenizdat, 1988.

Anfilov, V.A.k, *Nachalo Velikoi Otechestvennoi Voiny*, Moscow: Voenizdat, 1962.

Arkhipov, V.S., *Vremya tankovykh atak*, Moscow: Voenizdat, 1981.

Babadzhanyan, A. Kh., *Dorogi Pobedy*, Moscow: Voenizdat, 1981.

—, *Lyuki otkryli v Berline*, Moscow: Voenizdat, 1973.

Belov, E.E., *Syny otchizny*, Moscow: Izdatel'stvo Politicheskoi Literatury, 1966.

Belov, P.A., *Za nami Moskva*, Moscow: Voenizdat, 1963.

Brownlow, Donald *Grey, Panzer Baron: The Military Exploits of General Hasso von Manteuffel*, North Quincy, Mass: Christopher, 1975.

Carell, Paul, *Hitler Moves East*, New York: Ballantine, 1971.

Chistyakov, I.M., *Sluzhim otchizne*, Moscow: Voenizdat, 1985.

Chuikov, V.I., *Ot Stalingrada do Berlino*, Moscow: Sovetskaya Rossiya, 1985.

—, *The End of the Third Reich*, Moscow: Progress, 1978.

Degrelle, Leon, *Campaign in Russia: The Waffen SS onthe Eastern Front*, Torrance, CA: Institute for Historical Review, 1985.

Department of the Army Pamphlet, "German Defense Tactics Against Russian Break throughs," No. 20-233, October 1951.

Dragunskii, D.A., *Gody v brone*, Moscow: Voenizdat, 1975.

—, *A Soldier's Memoirs*, Moscow: Progress, 1983.

Dremov, I.F., *Nastupala groznaya bronya*, Kiev: Politicheskoi Literatury, 1981.

Egorov, A.V., *V Donskikh Stepyakh*, Moscow: DOSAAF, 1988.

Eremenko, A., *The Arduous Beginning*, Moscow: Progress, 1966.

Fomichev, M.G., *Put' nachinalya s urala*, Moscow: Voenizdat, 1976.

Garthoff, Raymond L., *Soviet Military Doctrine*, Glencoe, Illinois, 1953.

Getman, A.L., *Tanki idut na Berlin*, Moscow: Nauka, 1973.

Glantz, David, *Soviet Military Deception in the Second World War*, London, Frank Cass, 1989.

—, "The Kiev Operation, an Overview," in 1985 Art of War Symposium – From the Dnepr to the Vistula: Soviet Offensive Operations, November 1943 -August 1944, Transcript of Proceedings 29 April - 3 May 1985, edited by Colonel David M. Glantz (Carlisle Barracks, PA, August 1985)

Golubovich, V.S., *Marshal R. Ya. Malinovskii*, Moscow: Voenizdat, 1984.

Guderian, Heinz, *Panzer Leader*, London: Futura, 1974.

Halder, Franz, *The Halder Diaries: The Private War Journals of Colonel General Franz Halder*, Boulder, Colorado: Westview, 1976.

Hart, B.H. Liddell, *The Other Side of the Hill*, London: Cassell, 1973.

Ivanov, D.A., V.P. Sabel'ev, P.V. Shemanskii, *Osnovy upravleniya voiskami v boyu*, Moscow: Voenizdat, 1977.

Ivanovich, E.F., *Ataku nachinali tankisty*, Moscow: Voenizdat, 1984.

Ivanovskii, E.F., *Ataku nachinali tankisty*, Moscow: Voenizdat, 1984.

Katukov, M.E., *Na ostrie glavnogo udara*, Moscow: Voenizdat, 1976.

Kazakov, M.I., *Nad Kartoi bylykh srazhenii*, Moscow: Voenizdat, 1971.

Kazakov, P.D., *Glubokii sled*, Moscow: Voenizdat, 1982.

Kir'yan, M.M., *Vnezapnost' v nastuplatel'nykh operatsiya Velikoi Otechstvennoi Voiny*, Moscow: Nauka, 1986.

Koltunov, G.A., B.G. Soloviev, *Kurskaya bitva*, Moscow: Voenizdat, 1970.

Konev, I.S., *Year of Victory*, Moscow: Progress, 1969.

—, *Zapiski Komanduyuskchego frontom*, Moscow: Voenizdat, 1981.

Krainyukov, K.V., *Oruzhie osobogo roda*, Moscow: Voenizdat, 1977.

Kravchenko, I.M., V.V. Burkov, *Desyatyi tankovyi Dneprovskii*, Moscow: Voenizdat, 1986.

Krupchenko, I.E., et al, *Sovietskie tankovye voiska, 1941-1945*, Moscow: Voenizdat, 1973.

Lelyushenko, D.D., *Moskva-Stalingrad-Berlin-Praga*, Moscow: Nauka, 1973.

Litvyak, M.M., *Porodnennye bronei*, Moscow: Voenizdat, 1985.

Longsworth, Phillip, *The Art of Victory*, New York, 1965.

Losik, O.A., *Stroitel'stvo i boevoe primenemie sovetskikh tankovykh voisk v gody velikoi otechesvennoi voiny*, Moscow: Voenizdat, 1979.

Lykov, I.S., *V groznyi chas*, Mosocw: Voenizdat, 1986.

Mackintosh, Malcom, *Juggernaut*, New York: MacMillan, 1967.

Malygin, K.A., *V tsentre boevogo poradka*, Moscow: Voenizdat, 1986.

Manstein, Erich von, *Lost Victories*, Novato, CA: Presidio Press, 1982.

Matsulenko, V.A., *Operativnaya maskirovka voisk*, Moscow: Voenizdat, 1975.

Mellenthin, F.W. von, *Panzer Battles*, New York: Ballantine, 1980.

Melnikov, S.I., *Marshal Rybalko*, Kiev: Izdatel'stvo Politicheskoi Literatury Ukrainy, 1980.

Moskalenko, K.S., *Na yugo-zapadnom napravlenii*, Moscow: Voenizdat, 1973.

Muriev, D.Z., *Proval Operatsii "Taifun,"* Moscow: Voenizdat, 1966.

Nersesyan, N.G., *Kievsko-Berlinskii*, Moscow: Voenizdat, 1974.

Popel, N.K., *Tank povernuli na zapad*, Moscow: Voenizdat, 1960.

—, *V peredi Berlin!*, Moscow: DOSAAF, 1970.

—, *V tryazhkuyu poru*, Moscow: Voenizdat, 1959.

Portugal'skii, R.M., P.P. Tovstukha, *Upravlenie voiskami v nastuplenii*, Moscow: Voenizdat, 1981.

Radzievskii, A.I., *Proryv*, Moscow: Voenizdat, 1979.

—, *Taktika v boevykhh primerakh (diviziya)*, Moscow: Voenizdat, 1976.

—, *Tankovye udar*, Moscow: Voenizdat, 1977.

Raftopullo, A., *V atake "tridtsat'chtverki,"* Saratov: Privolzhskoe Knizhnoe Izdatel'stvo, 1973.

Rokossovskii, K.K., *A Soldier's Duty*, Moscow: Progress, 1985.

Rotmistrov, P.A., *Stal'naya gvardiya*, Moscow: Voenizdat, 1984.

—, *Vremya i tanki*, Moscow: Voenizdat, 1972.

Ryan, Cornelius, *The Last Battle*, New York: Simon and Shuster, 1966.

Ryanzanskii, A.P., *V ogne tankovykh srazhenii*, Moscow: Nauka, 1975.

Rybalko, P., *"Udar s yuga,"* Shturm Berlina, Moscow: Voenizdat, 1948.

Sandalov, L.M., *Na Moskovskom napravlenii*, Moscow: Nauka, 1970.

—, *Perezhite*, Moscow: Voenizdat, 1966.

Semenov, G.G., *Nastupaet Udarnaya*, Moscow: Voenizdat, 1970.

Sharipov, A., *General Chernyakhovsky*, Moscow: Progress, 1980.

Shtemenko, S.M., *The Last Six Months*, New York: Doubleday & Company, Inc., 1977.

—, *The Soviet General Staff at War*, Book 1 & 2, Moscow: Progress, 1985.

Slyusarenko, Z.K., *Poslednii vystrel*, Moscow: Voenizdat, 1974.

Stroeva, Anna, *Komandarm Kravchenko*, Kiev: Izdatel'stvo politicheskoi literatury ukrainy, 1984.

Sverdlov, F.D., *Peredovye otryada v boyu*, Moscow: Voenizdat, 1986.

Sydnor, Charles W., *Soldiers of Destruction*, New Jersey: Princeton University Press, 1977.

Vasilevsky, A.M., *A Lifelong Cause*, Moscow: Progress.

Vetrov, A.A., *Tak i bylo*, Moscow: Voenizdat, 1982.

Volkogonov, Dmitrii, *Triumf i tragediya*, Moscow: Novosti, 1989.

Vysotskii, F.I., et al, *Gvardeiskaya Tankovaya*, Moscow: Voenizdat, 1963.

Yakubovskii, I.I., *Zemlya v ogne*, Moscow: Voenizdat, 1975.

Zaev, D.I., *"Tanki vstreptiis' v zvenigorodke,"* Korsun' Shevchenkovskaya bitva, Kiev: Polizdat Ukrainy, 1989.

Zakharov, M.V., editor, *Proval: Gitlerovskogo nastupleniya na Moskvu*, Moscow: Nauka, 1966.

—, *Stalingradskaya Epopeya*, Msocow: Nauka, 1968.

Zavizion, G.T., P.A. Kornyushin, *I na Tikhom okeane...*, Moscow: Voenizdat, 1967.

Zhadov, A.S., *Chetyre goda voiny*, Moscow: Voenizdat, 1978.

Zhukov, G., *The Memoirs of Marshal Zhukov*, New York: Delacorte, 1971.

_, *Reminiscences and Reflections*, Msocow: Progress, 1985.

Zhukov, Yuri, *"The Birth of the Tank Guards," Moscow-Stalingrad: Recollections, Stories, Reports*, Moscow: Progress, 1974.

Zvartsev, A.M., *3-ya gvardeiskaya tankovaya*, Msocow: Voenizdat, 1982.

INDEX

Also from the publisher

GERMAN BATTLE TACTICS ON THE RUSSIAN FRONT 1941-1945

STEVEN H. NEWTON

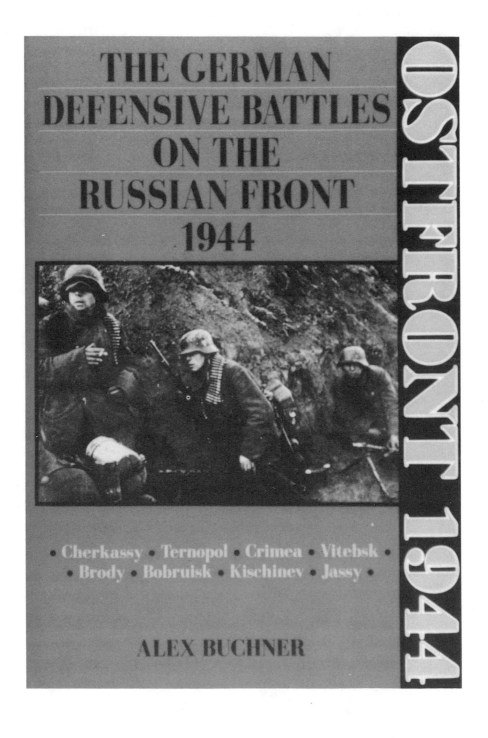

THE GERMAN DEFENSIVE BATTLES ON THE RUSSIAN FRONT 1944

• Cherkassy • Ternopol • Crimea • Vitebsk •
• Brody • Bobruisk • Kischinev • Jassy •

ALEX BUCHNER

OSTFRONT 1944

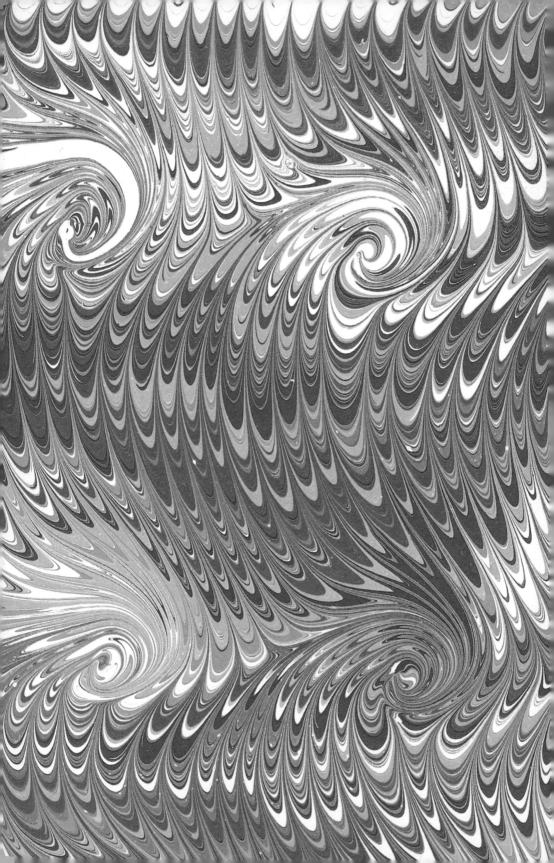